Dissecting DOS

Michael Podanoffsky

Addison-Wesley Publishing Company

Reading, Massachusetts • Menlo Park, California • New York
Don Mills, Ontario • Wokingham, England • Amsterdam
Bonn • Sydney • Singapore • Tokyo • Madrid • San Juan
Paris • Seoul • Milan • Mexico City • Taipei

Many of the designations used by manufacturers and sellers to distinguish their products are claimed as trademarks. Where those designations appear in this book, and Addison-Wesley was aware of a trademark claim, the designations have been printed in initial capital letters or all capital letters.

The authors and publishers have taken care in preparation of this book, but make no expressed or implied warranty of any kind and assume no responsibility for errors or omissions. No liability is assumed for incidental or consequential damages in connection with or arising out of the use of the information or programs contained herein.

Library of Congress Cataloging-in-Publication Data

Podanoffsky, Michael
    Dissecting DOS / Michael Podanoffsky.
        p.   cm.
    Includes Index.
    ISBN 0-201-62687-X
    1. MS-DOS (Computer file) 2. PC-DOS (Computer file) I. Title
    QA76.76.063P63 1995
    005.4'469—dc20   93-42508
                                                  CIP

Sponsoring Editor: Philip Sutherland
Project Manager: Eleanor McCarthy
Production Coordinator: Lora L. Ryan

Addison-Wesley books are available for bulk purchases by corporations, institutions, and other organizations. For more information please contact the Corporate, Government and Special Sales Department at (800) 238-9682.

To my wife, Louise, and my children, Amy and James,

whose encouragement and patience

helped make this book possible

ACKNOWLEDGMENTS

I want to extend a special thanks to Jim Kyle and Andrew Schulman for editing this book. Their contributions, comments, and critiques helped shape the book's emphasis and presentation. I'd also like to extend a special thanks to all of the fine people at Addison-Wesley for their extensive work. In particular I want to thank Phil Sutherland for supporting this project and for his suggestions and advice on writing. I found them invaluable.

CONTENTS

C H A P T E R   1

The Structure of DOS

Go-Anywhere, Do-Anything DOS—The Components of DOS—The Structure of DOS—DOS Function Calls—MS-DOS Function Handler—RxDOS Function Handler—How to Read the Source Code

DOS has served us well over the 12 or so years since its original release. It is in use by millions of people and newer and more capable versions are still being developed. Critical applications such as Novell NetWare and Windows are built on DOS, and its continued acceptability drives the fortunes of many companies still making tools and software that run on DOS.

DOS has always been an operating system that did not make major programming demands. The interface is both simple and familiar, and this in turn led in the early days to the easy and rapid development of lots of tools and applications. This drove, and was accelerated by, the hundreds of vendors who licensed DOS for their machines. Today, DOS remains the core of truly major developments such as Windows.

That DOS has made it this far and is central to so much software—despite inefficiencies and limitations that should have been addressed long ago—is surprising. For example, DOS should be able to run in protected mode, have access to all the memory available in a system, and have a reentrant, shareable file system. It could do this without sacrificing compatibility with existing DOS applications, which could choose to migrate over to a new more capable environment or be launched in virtual machine modes, much as Windows launches DOS compatibility boxes today.

So why a book on DOS? DOS is still today the basis for continued operating system development. This book reveals the elegant and sometimes less-than-elegant design of DOS by walking through the source code. It discusses its internal structure and its inefficiencies. It does so by examining RxDOS, a product internally structured in much the same way as MS-DOS. I designed RxDOS as a real-time multitasking operating system, meaning that multiple tasks (programs) could run concurrently within a single computer system and a single copy of DOS. Rx is sort of a standard designation in computer acronyms usually reserved for a real-time executive (in the operating system sense). It also plays on the idea that it "fixes" what some users consider one of the more glaring deficiencies in DOS—that it just won't handle multiple tasks.

So how different is RxDOS from MS-DOS? Well, line by line, the two source codes are radically different. After all, they are different products written at different times by different people to solve different problems. MS-DOS, like RxDOS, is a copyrighted product, and reproducing MS-DOS here in any way would be unfair if not downright illegal. RxDOS was made to behave as much as possible like MS-DOS. Anyone reading the RxDOS source code and this book will understand the mechanics, algorithms, design, and structure of MS-DOS.

It's pretty easy to determine the architectural layout of a product like DOS or Windows from its data structures. Once you understand that files are supported by a Current Directory Structure (CDS) and System File Tables (SFTs), and that device redirection is part of the file system requirements, the flow of information is largely established between the layers. My goal was different. It was to establish a reasonable DOS workalike that could also more cleverly be able to evolve into a real-time operating system.

This led to the addition of some changes. Whereas DOS utilizes data areas in the data segment for interim or internal state information, RxDOS relies heavily on creating temporary variables on the stack. You'll observe these differences in the code as RxDOS is revealed in the book.

Go-Anywhere, Do-Anything DOS

The original design goals and philosophy behind DOS may not have been much different than to create an improved version of an earlier operating system on a new processor. Essentially, that's what DOS version 1 provided. It borrowed from the concepts in CP/M liberally. Both operating systems used FCBs (file control blocks), and neither supported subdirectories. It made for easy transition of programs to the new operating system.

DOS, however, had one significant improvement. It utilized a FAT table to map file allocations. This table was vastly superior to the way in which CP/M mapped file allocations. Whereas, MS-DOS version 1 maintained the FAT table in memory, leading to high performance, particularly with large files, CP/M maintained file allocation maps in directory entries, which were limited to 16 1K allocation entries. For larger files, CP/M created other directory entries, which led to losing directory space and paying a disk search penalty with large files.

MS-DOS version 2.0 was a radically different animal when it came out approximately two years later. It was somewhat more like the DOS we know today with file handles, redirection, and subdirectories. It was at this time that several of the concepts and data structures that still serve DOS well today were introduced.

Although the application development community embraced the newer, faster, and by far easier file system provided by DOS, they spurned screen and printer services and directly addressed the hardware itself. In part, this was because the only value-added benefit provided by DOS for the screen or printer was device redirection.

Microsoft and IBM were as much to blame for lack of interest in these services since almost all official documentation recommended the use of BIOS functions for devices such as the keyboard, screen, printer, and data communications. Eventually though, the BIOS was bypassed altogether in favor of addressing the hardware directly to gain the greatest amount of performance.

This led to a go-anywhere, do-anything approach to software developed for DOS, which in turn led to confusion as well as opportunity. Novell took this opportunity to build NetWare, a local area network operating system that was able to neatly superimpose itself over DOS by intercepting file system calls and determining which functionality to support at the network layer and which should be handled locally.

Every installed DOS system has a few lines in a `config` or `autoexec` file that load a special little program or driver here and there, such as a better memory manager or a handy TSR. This is true for every mass-appeal operating system, from mainframes to Unix to DOS to the Macintosh. The success of an operating system rests on its ability to solve a problem, to add value to a solution. It, therefore, isn't only a matter of what an operating system does best, but of how well it is able to accommodate change, evolution, and additional capabilities.

The Components of DOS

Two files, `msdos.sys` and `io.sys`, make up the core of the DOS operating system. These two files contain everything that applications view as DOS, which is to say, they incorporate device drivers, the FAT management, directory searching, date and time services, critical error handling, disk buffer caching, the int 21h function handler, memory management services, and program launching. Combine with this the command shell, `command.com`, to make the essential files required to run DOS.

In the IBM version of DOS, `ibmdos.com` and `ibmbio.com` replace `msdos.sys` and `io.sys`, respectively, but the nature and organization of the operating system remain the same. These files have different names as well in RxDOS (see Figure 1-1).

The core DOS files are usually stamped as hidden or as system files, which would make them invisible to the casual user. You can change the attributes of these files using the DOS-supplied `attrib` program or a really good disk viewer like `Xtree` or Norton's `diskedit`.

Figure 1-1. DOS component filenames

Microsoft's MS-DOS	IBM's PC-DOS	RxDOS
io.sys	ibmbio.com	rxdosbio.com
msdos.sys	ibmdos.com	rxdos.com
command.com	command.com	rxdoscmd.com

The first module loaded at boot time is the `io.sys` (or in RxDOS, `rxdosbio.com`), which is responsible for interfacing DOS to the hardware layer through resident device drivers and for system initialization and configuration. Resident device drivers exist for the console, printer, communications, clock, and at least one block device capable of accessing the floppy disk drives and a standard interface hard disk. This module can be customized by an OEM, typically the hardware manufacturer, but this need has greatly diminished in light of the increased standardization of both the ROM BIOS and hardware interfaces.

One of the very first tasks performed by the `io.sys` code is to configure and initialize the DOS environment and data areas. This is performed by the SYSINIT, a replaceable component of `io.sys` that loads `msdos.sys`, initializing resident drivers, determining the amount of memory, processing the `config.sys` file, and then loading the command shell. The init process may cause the loading of installable DOS drivers, a concept introduced to DOS with version 2.0. We more fully discuss SYSINIT later in this chapter.

The `msdos.sys` is always viewed as being the bulk of DOS because it supports the FAT file system, all int 21h services, device redirection, memory management, disk cache buffering, and program launching and termination.

The roles of the different layers of DOS are roughly shown in Figure 1-2. A similar division of labor makes up RxDOS. The code is built from the following source modules:

rxdosbio.com

`rxdosbio.asm`	Contains all drivers that are supplied standard with DOS: disk drivers, line printer, communications, keyboard, and screen drivers

rxdos.com

`rxdos.asm`	Contains all the int 21 functions even though some of them are just shells to functions handled in other modules
`rxdosccb.asm`	Supports the disk cache buffer management
`rxdosdev.asm`	Contains device interface code, such as locating devices in the rxdosbio module
`rxdosexe.asm`	Launches .com and .exe programs
`rxdosfat.asm`	Provides all the logic for FAT management, such as allocating, searching, and clearing FAT entries
`rxdosfcb.asm`	File control block support
`rxdosfil.asm`	File support, navigation, subdirectory management, including searching, creating and removing subdirectories, and file services that search, open, create, read/write, close, delete, and position (lseek)
`rxdosini.asm`	DOS initialize
`rxdosmem.asm`	Memory management, allocation, and free with compaction
`rxdossft.asm`	System file table support; part of the file system support
`rxdosstr.asm`	String management, such as upper/lower case, compare, and append
`rxdosstk.asm`	Stack management

rxdoscmd.com

`rxdoscmd.asm`	Main body of command module, including command parsing, batch file starter, and file redirection
`rxdoscpy.asm`	Copy command
`rxdosdir.asm`	Dir command
`rxdosfor.asm`	Supports batch file for command
`rxdosprm.asm`	Prompt command
`rxdosren.asm`	Rename command
`rxdoscsk.asm`	Command module stack

For convenience, all DOS int 21h functions begin in the `rxdos.asm` source file. It also contains the function dispatcher, sometimes referred to as the function handler. Within RxDOS, functions are logically grouped together by subsystem. Memory support functions appear in `rxdos-mem.asm` whereas the int 21 functions 49h, 4Ah, and 4Bh (allocate, free, and resize) start in the `erxdos.asm` module, as do all int 21h functions. System file support functions appear in the `rxdossft.asm` module, but file functions such as create and open begin in `rxdos.asm`.

Figure 1-2. The roles of each DOS layer

COMMAND.COM
>   copy, ren, del, ...
>   mkdir, cd, rd, ...
>   batch programs

MSDOS.SYS

FAT Filesystem	Memory Management
FAT allocation	Memory allocation
Subdirectories	Program loading
Redirection	TSR management

IO.SYS
>   Logical sector filesystem
>   Device drivers
>   System initialization

BIOS (not part of DOS)
>   Head, sector, track disk I/O

The Structure of DOS

The overall basic organization of RxDOS in memory follows closely the organization of MS-DOS and is shown in Figure 1-3. On the left side of the figure, the entire DOS kernel is shown, beginning with the `rxdosbio.com` module. This code is always loaded first by the startup code and traditionally begins at location `70:0`. That module loads `rxdos.com` after which the stack space is allocated. The memory from the top of the stack space to the end of available memory becomes the memory allocatable through DOS.

The `rxdos.com` module begins with a data section area, followed by the function handler table, followed in turn by each DOS function and related routines. Part of the DOS data area is an area called the DOS swap area. The content of this space is considered so critical that it is sometimes saved by being swapped out and then restored. The swap area concept is a sort of poor man's multitasking, where two processes can have different contexts, like different Disk Transfer Addresses. Applications manage swapping data back and forth between their contexts.

Figure 1-3. The basic organization of RxDOS in memory

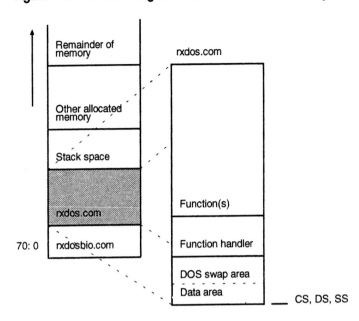

It shouldn't be overlooked that the DOS swap area is the DOS data itself and that format of the information in the DOS swap area is important to understanding DOS whether the data area is swapped out or not.

The DOS data area actually begins before the swap area. The data area begins with a list of pointers to various DOS data structures, most of which are dynamically allocated based on configuration parameters. This area is called the SYSVAR area because it is initially populated by the startup code responsible for allocating and setting the system variable areas. This section has also been referred to as the List of Lists area. The SYSVAR area contains pointers to the start of the device chain, to the system file tables, to the allocatable memory chain, to the drive parameter table, and to other data structures that we describe in greater detail later.

The start of the DOS area appears in `rxdos.asm` as shown in Figure 1-4.

Figure 1-4. The SYSVAR section from rxdos.asm

```
        ;///////////////////////////////////////////////////////////////;
        ;  DOS Data                                                      ;
        ;...............................................................;

RxDOS_start:            jmp RxDOS_initialize
_RxDOS_data             db 23 dup (0)           ; uninitialized

_RxDOS_ShareRetry       dw 0                    ; sharing retry count
```

```
_RxDOS_ShareDelay         dw 0                         ; sharing retry delay
_RxDOS_pDTA               dd 0                         ; ptr to disk transfer area
                          dw 0                         ; ptr to unread CON input
_RxDOS_pStartMemBlock     dw 0                         ; seg ptr to start of memory alloc

_RxDOS_pDPB               dd 0                         ; ptr to Drive Parameter Block (DPB)
_RxDOS_pFT                dd 0                         ; ptr to File Tables (FT)
_RxDOS_pCLOCKdriver       dd 0                         ; ptr to CLOCK$ device driver
_RxDOS_pCONdriver         dd 0                         ; ptr to CON device driver
_RxDOS_wMaxBlock          dw 0                         ; max bytes per block for any/all devices
_RxDOS_BufferList         dd 0                         ; pointer to CCB buffer list
_RxDOS_pCDS               dd 0                         ; ptr to curr directory struct
_RxDOS_pFCBs              dd 0                         ; ptr to FCB table
_RxDOS_nProtFCBs          dw 0                         ; number of protected fcbs
_RxDOS_bNumBlockDev       db 0                         ; number of block devices
_RxDOS_bLastDrive         db 0                         ; lastdrive from config.sys

        ;'''''''''''''''''''''''''''''''''''''''''''''''''''''''''''''';
        ;   NULL Device Driver                                        ;
        ;.............................................................;

_RxDOS_NULLDev            dd -1                   ; link to other device
                         dw ( DEV_CHAR + DEV_NULL + DEV_FASTCHARIO )
                         dw null_strategy
                         dw null_interrupt
                         db 'NUL    '

        ;'''''''''''''''''''''''''''''''''''''''''''''''''''''''''''''';
        ;   Installable File System Parameters                        ;
        ;.............................................................;

_RxDOS_bNumJoinDev        db 0                         ; number of JOIN'ed drives
_RxDOS_wSpecialNames      dw 0                         ; pointer to list of special names
                          dd 0                         ; pointer to IFS
                          dd 0                         ; pointer to IFS drivers
_RxDOS_Buffers            dw 0                         ; FCB BUFFERS x
                          dw 0                         ; FCB BUFFERS y
_RxDOS_BootDrive          db 0                         ; Boot Drive
                          db 0                         ; reserved
_RxDOS_ExtendedMem        dw 0                         ; extended memory size

_RxDOS_CurrentDrive       db 0                         ; current drive ( a=0, ... )

        ;'''''''''''''''''''''''''''''''''''''''''''''''''''''''''''''';
        ;   DOS Swap Data Area (Order Not compatible with DOS 6.0)    ;
        ;.............................................................;

_RxDOS_INDOSFlag          dw 0                         ; InDOS flag.

_RxDOS_Verify             dw 0                         ; NonZero if Verify.
_RxDOS_AllocStrategy      dw 0                         ; Allocation strategy.
_RxDOS_bCtrlBreakCheck    db 0                         ; Ctrl Break Flag.
_RxDOS_bSwitchChar        db '/'                       ; Switch Char.
_RxDOS_MaxMemory          dw 0                         ; max memory
```

```
        ;////////////////////////////////////////////////////////;
        ;  Error Handling                                         ;
        ;........................................................;

_RxDOS_ErrorCode          dw 0                ; Error code.

_RxDOS_CritErrorFlag      dw 0
_RxDOS_CritErrorDrive     dw 0
_RxDOS_LocusLasterror     dw 0
_RxDOS_ExtErrorcode       dw 0
_RxDOS_SuggestedAction    dw 0
_RxDOS_ClassOfError       dw 0
_RxDOS_pLastError         dd 0

        ;////////////////////////////////////////////////////////;
        ;  Current PSP                                            ;
        ;........................................................;

_RxDOS_CurrentPSP         dw 0                ; Seg Pointer to current PSP
_RxDOS_CurrentInstance    dw 0                ; Base address of current stack
_RxDOS_EnvironmentSize    dw 0                ; Environment size in Para
_RxDOS_ChildReturnCode    dw 0                ; Child return code.

_RxDOS_CurrentStackTop    dw RxDOS_StackTop   ; Reserved Stack Top ...
_RxDOS_CurrentStackBot    dw RxDOS_StackTop   ;         ... and Bottom.

        ;////////////////////////////////////////////////////////;
        ;  Shell                                                  ;
        ;........................................................;

                  even
_RxDOS_CommandShell       db 'rxdoscmd.com', 0
                          db (128 - ($-_RxDOS_CommandShell)) dup (?)

        ;////////////////////////////////////////////////////////;
        ;  Buffer                                                 ;
        ;........................................................;

                  even
_RxDOS_SharedBuffer       db 128 dup (?)      ; shared buffer.
_RxDOS_enddata            dd 0

        ;////////////////////////////////////////////////////////;
        ;  Real Time Dos Product Identification                   ;
        ;........................................................;

_RxDOS_DOSVersion:        db 6, 00            ; Dos Versions.
_RxDOS_DOSProgramName:    db 'RxDOS6.0'       ; Product Name.

        ;////////////////////////////////////////////////////////;
        ;  Invalid Characters in Filename                         ;
        ;........................................................;

_invalidFnCharacters:     db '[]<>|",;=+:', 0
sizeInvFnChars            equ ($ - _invalidFnCharacters)
```

```
;''''''''''''''''''''''''''''''''''''''''''''''''''''''''''''''';
;  Device Assign Table                                           ;
;................................................................;

stdDeviceAssignTable:    StdRedirec  < 'AUX       ', -1, sftIsDevice >
                         StdRedirec  < 'CON       ', -1, sftIsDevice + sftIsstdout
                                                                    + sftIsstdin >
                         StdRedirec  < 'PRN       ', -1, sftIsDevice >
                         dw -1
```

Access to the SYSVAR area and the DOS swap area by an application is important because of the wealth of information it references. So important has this list become to third-party software developers that it is impossible to write some software without decoding the contents of this list. Of course, the list is not documented officially by Microsoft anywhere and can change, as it did from version 2.0 to version 3.1, and as it may change again.

For example, Quarterdeck, makers of QEMM and other memory-related utilities, wanted to relocate DOS BUFFERS and FILES areas to unused upper memory blocks—that memory above 640K—long before DOS version 5 made it possible to take advantage of upper memory blocks. This would have both released some critical memory in the lower 640K and enhanced performance by permitting greater buffers and files allocation. As an undocumented list, Quarterdeck had to take a chance that the list would not change between different versions of DOS! What a mess for the poor user.

Application programs can locate the DOS data segment address that contains the SYSVAR area by using DOS function 52h, Get DPB Address. The ES register will contain the segment address. The BX register will point to a double word address that points to the space allocated for DPBs.

The DOS swap area is further up in the data segment, and the address to the start of the area and size is accessible through DOS function 5Dh, subfunction 06h, Get Address of DOS Swappable Area, an undocumented call.

```
mov ax, 5D06h
int 21h                                 ; get address Swappable Data
```

The DS:SI will point to the start of the swappable area, the DX register will contain the minimum area that must be swapped, that is, critical areas, and the CX register will contain the size of the entire DOS Swappable Area, which in DOS includes the DOS stacks. The presumption is that if you swap out the stacks, you can interrupt MS-DOS while already inside a DOS call. Things aren't so simple. Interleaving two file system calls that change the FAT tables can have disastrous effects, particularly if both calls believe that a specific FAT entry is available. DOS was not designed to be multitasked, and the only convention for avoiding a collision between two function calls is to check the InDOS flag.

Although swapping the stacks out during a function call may keep the original stack structure from being corrupted, it doesn't really solve the more fundamental problem that there are other critical sections inside DOS. Some common structures, such as System File Tables (SFTs) or the Current Directory Structure (CDS), both of which we discuss in complete detail in Chapter 2, require sharing rather than swapping. The FAT table allocation code requires very careful handling that just can't be interleaved with other function calls.

DOS Function Calls

DOS provides its services, such as memory allocation and file access, through function calls. These functions are all neatly accessible through a software interrupt instruction. Applications load specific registers and issue an int 21h instruction with the AH register containing a function code. A typical function call like File Open would appear as

```
mov dx, offset filename
mov al, fileopen_modes
mov ah, 3Dh              ; file open function code
int 21h                  ; call dos
jnc _noerror             ; if no errors ->
```

The int 21h instruction is used to access DOS, which then dispatches to a specific routine to handle the function request. The instruction causes a jump through the interrupt table located in low memory, at address 0000:0084, which normally contains the address of the DOS Function Handler. It is not uncommon to have this address changed by either applications or TSRs to intercept DOS function calls. DOS remains unaware of any of this, and expects to see on the stack the flag registers and a return address. The flag register values saved on the stack are changed to clear or set the carry bit.

Figure 1-5. The role of the DOS function handler

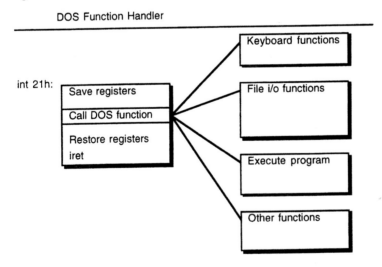

Inside DOS is a section of code called the DOS function handler. Its role is explained in Figure 1-5, which shows the function handler dispatching to various DOS functions based on the function code. A more detailed outline of the specific steps of the function handler is shown in Figure 1-6, but the actual listing of the function handler is shown in Figure 1-7.

Figure 1-6. Flow inside Int 21h handler

```
_Interrupt_21:
    Save all registers on user's stack
    Change to an RxDOS stack
    Save Pointer to caller's stack on RxDOS stack
    Save critical parameters and set the INDOS flag
    Use AH and BX to index the DOS function table
    Call the DOS function referenced in table
    If error in function, save error code
    Change back to caller's stack
    Restore registers
    Return to application
```

The function handler first insulates the application by changing to an internal DOS stack. The application should not have to nor could anticipate the stack requirements that DOS function calls will require. MS-DOS uses a different stack-switching scheme than does RxDOS. MS-DOS switches to one of three internal stacks, depending on the nature and circumstances of the function call. It does this because at times some DOS functions must be called when already inside DOS, such as displaying an error message during a critical error. The three MS-DOS stacks prevent DOS from clobbering itself.

RxDOS naturally permits DOS function calls while already inside DOS. It can do this because it always creates a new stack dynamically out of internal heap space regardless of the circumstances of the function call. The scheme is essential to making RxDOS fully reentrant.

Figure 1-7. The DOS function handler code

```
;////////////////////////////////////////////////////////////;
;   Interrupt 21                                              ;
;- - - - - - - - - - - - - - - - - - - - - - - - - - - - - - -;
;                                                             ;
;   ah    contains function request                           ;
;.............................................................;

_Interrupt_21    proc far
         push es
         push ds
         push bp
         push di
         push si
         push dx
         push cx
         push bx
         push ax
```

```
        mov bp, sp
        add bp, sizeStackFrame
        and word ptr [ _Flags ][ bp ], 0fffeh           ; clear carry bit.

;- - - - - - - - - - - - - - - - - - - - - - - - - - - - - - - -
;  switch to internal stack
;- - - - - - - - - - - - - - - - - - - - - - - - - - - - - - - -
        cli
        setES ss                                       ; old stack
        mov bx, bp                                      ; old stack to es: bx

        mov ds, word ptr cs:[ _RxDOS_CurrentSeg ]       ; Current Segment.
        mov ss, word ptr cs:[ _RxDOS_CurrentSeg ]       ; Current Segment.
        mov sp, word ptr cs:[ _RxDOS_CurrentStackTop ]  ; point to current stack.

        push bx                                         ; old stack reference
        push es

;- - - - - - - - - - - - - - - - - - - - - - - - - - - - - - - -
;  current stack parameters
;- - - - - - - - - - - - - - - - - - - - - - - - - - - - - - - -
        Entry                                          ; set [ bp ]
        def  _FctAddress

        push word ptr [ _RxDOS_CurrentStackTop ]
        sub word ptr [ _RxDOS_CurrentStackTop ], 256    ; reserve stack

        push word ptr [ _RxDOS_CurrentInstance ]        ; base address of current stack
        mov word ptr [ _RxDOS_CurrentInstance ], bp     ; base address of current stack

        push word ptr [ _RxDOS_INDOSFlag ]
        inc word ptr [ _RxDOS_INDOSFlag ]               ; INDOS

;- - - - - - - - - - - - - - - - - - - - - - - - - - - - - - - -
;  save PSP values
;- - - - - - - - - - - - - - - - - - - - - - - - - - - - - - - -
        mov ds, word ptr [ _RxDOS_CurrentPSP ]
        push word ptr ds:[ pspUserStack. _segment ]
        push word ptr ds:[ pspUserStack. _pointer ]
        push ds                                        ; old PSP
        mov dx, ds                                     ; see if PSP was ever set
        or dx, dx                                      ; was PSP zero ?
        jz _Interrupt_21_12                            ; if no valid PSP ->

        mov word ptr ds:[ pspUserStack. _segment ], es
        mov word ptr ds:[ pspUserStack. _pointer ], bx

;- - - - - - - - - - - - - - - - - - - - - - - - - - - - - - - -
;  determine function address
;- - - - - - - - - - - - - - - - - - - - - - - - - - - - - - - -
_Interrupt_21_12:
        sti
        cld
        currSegment ds                                 ; point to current segment
```

```
        mov word ptr [ _RxDOS_FunctionCall ], ax       ; AX on call
        cmp ah, _RxDOS_maxFunctionCode                 ; max function code ?
        jnc _Interrupt_21_26                           ; if out of range -->

;- - - - - - - - - - - - - - - - - - - - - - - - - - - - - - - - -
; [ds] from user call is passed in [es]
; [dx] from user call is passed in [di]
; [ds] is changed to current segment
; [ss] == [ds] is assumed
;- - - - - - - - - - - - - - - - - - - - - - - - - - - - - - - - -
        push bx
        xor bh, bh
        mov bl, ah                                     ; offset into functions table
        add bx, bx
        push word ptr [ _RxDOS_functions ][ bx ]
        pop word ptr [ _FctAddress ][ bp ]             ; save in stack
        pop bx

        mov dx, word ptr es:[ _DX      ][ bx ]         ; restore DX
        mov di, dx
        push word ptr es:[ _DataSegment][ bx ]         ; ds on call
        push word ptr es:[ _BX      ][ bx ]            ; bx on call
        pop bx
        pop es                                         ; no longer pointing to user stack

        clc
        call word ptr [ _FctAddress ][ bp ]
        jnc _Interrupt_21_24

        RetCallersStackFrame es, bx
        or  word ptr es:[ _Flags ][ bx ], 1            ; set carry bit
        mov word ptr es:[ _AX     ][ bx ], ax          ; save last error code.
        mov word ptr cs:[ _RxDOS_ErrorCode ], ax       ; save last error code.

_Interrupt_21_24:
        setDS ss
        call invalidateRemoteCCBBuffers                ; don't keep remote buffers

;- - - - - - - - - - - - - - - - - - - - - - - - - - - - - - - - -
; return registers
;- - - - - - - - - - - - - - - - - - - - - - - - - - - - - - - - -
_Interrupt_21_26:
        cli
        pop dx                                         ; restore PSP address
        pop bx
        pop cx                                         ; old user stack values
        or dx, dx                                      ; no psp address ?
        jz _Interrupt_21_32                            ; if none -->

        mov ds, dx
        mov word ptr ds:[ pspUserStack. _pointer ], bx ; restore old stack pointer
        mov word ptr ds:[ pspUserStack. _segment ], cx
```

```
_Interrupt_21_32:
        pop word ptr cs:[ _RxDOS_INDOSFlag          ]      ; restore INDOS
        pop word ptr cs:[ _RxDOS_CurrentInstance ]         ; _Instance
        pop word ptr cs:[ _RxDOS_CurrentStackTop ]

        pop bx                                             ; fct address
        pop bx                                             ; argument left on stack
        pop ss                                             ; caller's stack
        sub bx, sizeStackFrame                             ; adjusted stack pointer
        mov sp, bx

        pop ax                                             ; restore registers
        pop bx
        pop cx
        pop dx

        pop si
        pop di
        pop bp

        pop ds
        pop es
        iret
_Interrupt_21    endp
```

MS-DOS Function Handler

MS-DOS itself uses a function handler that works somewhat differently than the equivalent RxDOS function handler. The differences are more than just cosmetic. Somewhat interestingly, before the MS-DOS function handler does anything at all, it determines if the call is somehow either a special function code or called under special circumstances.

MS-DOS checks for some interesting function codes. It handles as special cases function codes for control break check, get and set PSP addresses, and the undocumented DOS function code 64h, Set Driver Lookahead Flag. This last function code is used only by print.com to call the printer driver. It saves the driver time to somehow find the printer driver directly. Why these? Why not function 34h, Get InDOS Flag Address? There is good reason the get and set PSP address functions are in this critical section, and whether we know the reason for the inclusion of the other codes or not, they too may turn out to have some reason for being treated in a special way. These function codes are fully reentrant in MS-DOS since they are not executed as part of the normal DOS flow.

The MS-DOS function handler then proceeds to save all the registers on the caller's stack and then sets the InDOS flag. The InDOS flag operates like a traffic cop, telling interrupt routines and other applications that DOS is currently running. Calling DOS while already in DOS is a sure-fire way of totally confusing if not crashing DOS.

The only way to find out if DOS is running is to first get the address of the InDOS Flag inside DOS. The flag can then be tested from outside DOS. The address avoids the inevitable collision that could result if, from inside DOS, you are asking if DOS is running. Obviously, the Get InDOS Address is not special cased because it is expected that the address was already fetched.

MS-DOS then begins the process of switching to an internal stack. The current stack pointer, that is, the caller's stack pointer, is first saved in the calling application's PSP, or Program Segment Prefix. In actuality, the PSP points only to the last application started by MS-DOS, which DOS refers to as the current application. The DOS call could have come from any application or interrupt and not strictly from the current application. That's one reason getting and setting the PSP address functions are treated specially at the start of the MS-DOS function call. Some special applications set the PSP address to trick MS-DOS into believing a different application is "currently" running.

Figure 1-8. MS-DOS stack selection logic

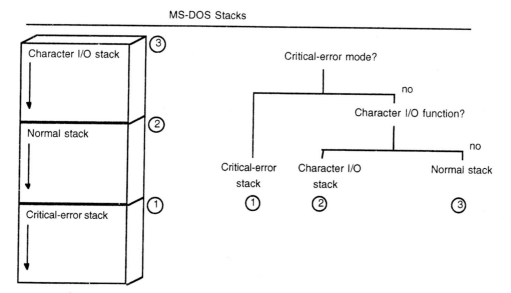

MS-DOS has three internal stacks, which it uses at different times. MS-DOS switches immediately after being called to its critical-error stack. When a critical-error is encountered, DOS is in a sort of strange mode where it has not fully completed the original function call but must permit some DOS functions to be executed. It absolutely cannot use its main stack since that stack is busy with the progress of the previous DOS function call.

If DOS is not in a critical-error mode, it switches to either a character i/o stack or its main stack, depending on the function code. Character i/o function codes 01h through 0Bh utilize a special stack. These character i/o functions, specifically those waiting on keyboard input, periodically issue int 28h interrupts, the so-called Safe-Dos interrupt. It is safe for an application to add a process to the int 28h chain that will be periodically called by DOS during keyboard wait loops. Applications called by the int 28h interrupt may issue any DOS call except for character i/o functions, which would then use the alternative main stack. Figure 1-8 shows how the MS-DOS decision on which stack to use is made.

MS-DOS then finally restores the value of the function call itself, originally passed in the AH register, into an index register like the BX register, and fetches the value stored at the word offset indexed by the index register. It uses this value to perform a NEAR call to the function.

When the DOS internal function returns, it returns to the MS-DOS function handler, which then restores all the registers from the caller's stack and performs an IRET back to the caller.

It isn't just a different stack that makes or prevents different parts of MS-DOS from being reentrant. For example, recalling into DOS while it is allocating a FAT table entry with another disk operation would be catastrophic, not because stacks couldn't be manipulated or because the address in the PSP couldn't somehow be switched, but because lots of places within MS-DOS just aren't reentrant. Memory locations are written with the expectation that no process will change their value.

Inside MS-DOS, there are certain critical sections, identified by int 2Ah calls, as shown in Figure 1-9. Interestingly, Windows patches these locations directly wherever MS-DOS is loaded with a far call to code inside Windows.

Figure 1-9. Begin critical section in MS-DOS

```
push ax
mov  ah, 82h
int  2Ah
pop  ax
```

RxDOS Function Handler

The RxDOS function handler, and with it the remainder of RxDOS itself, is designed to be fully reentrant. All the special cases where MS-DOS had to choose between one of several stacks are gone. Instead, RxDOS creates a temporary stack as it needs it from stack memory that it has allocated at boot time. Stacks so created can grow in size and begin at a minimum of 256 words. This stack is referred to as an instance.

When a call is made to RxDOS while already running inside RxDOS, a second instance is created. The second instance must complete before the first instance can continue. Figure 1-10 shows how each instance affects the RxDOS stack.

Figure 1-10. Instances are created whenever a call is made to RxDOS.

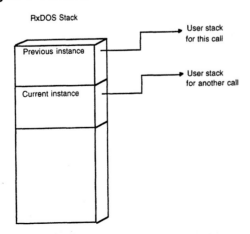

When a DOS call is made, the RxDOS function handler first saves all the registers in the caller's stack; it then creates an RxDOS stack reference or instance for this call. The saved registers in the caller's stack creates a table that is used by RxDOS both to reference the register values passed by the call and to change these values when returning results to the caller. A pointer is saved in the RxDOS stack reference back to the caller's stack. Figure 1-11 shows the relationship between the caller's stack and the RxDOS stack reference.

Figure 1-11. RxDOS creates an instance inside a temporary stack, shown on the right, that completely references the caller's stack and PSP.

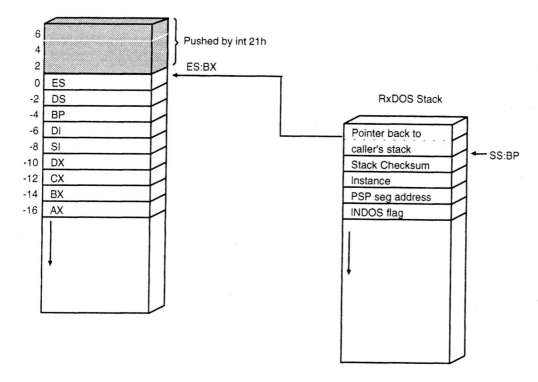

What happens inside the RxDOS function handler is best understood in terms of walking through the code itself. The function handler begins by saving all the registers on the caller's stack, then switching to an internal stack. Because there is no guarantee that interrupts are disabled, the function handler disables interrupts temporarily.

```
;///////////////////////////////////////////////////////////////;
;  Interrupt 21                                                  ;
;- - - - - - - - - - - - - - - - - - - - - - - - - - - - - - - -;
;                                                                ;
;  ah   contains function request                               ;
;................................................................;

_Interrupt_21    proc far
        push es
        push ds
        push bp
        push di
        push si
        push dx
        push cx
        push bx
        push ax

        mov bp, sp
        add bp, sizeStackFrame
        and word ptr [ _Flags ][ bp ], 0fffeh         ; clear carry bit.

;- - - - - - - - - - - - - - - - - - - - - - - - - - - - - - - -
;  switch to internal stack
;- - - - - - - - - - - - - - - - - - - - - - - - - - - - - - - -
        cli
        setES ss                                    ; old stack
        mov bx, bp                                  ; old stack to es: bx

        mov ds, word ptr cs:[ _RxDOS_CurrentSeg ]   ; Current Segment.
        mov ss, word ptr [ _RxDOS_CurrentSeg ]      ; Current Segment.
        mov sp, word ptr [ _RxDOS_CurrentStackTop ] ; point to current stack.

        push bx                                     ; old stack reference
        push es
```

One side effect of this code is shown in the last line, where the carry bit is cleared in the saved registers. Many, if not most, DOS functions return an error to the user by setting the carry bit. By clearing the flag, the function handler will have to set it only when an error occurs.

The code remembers a pointer to the registers saved in the caller's stack in the ES:BX registers and saves it in the new stack created within RxDOS. Figure 1-11 shows what is saved in the RxDOS stack on the right, and on the far left, at the caller's stack, it shows offsets from the ES:BX pointer to each of the registers. Fortunately, you don't have to reference these registers by a numerical offset because named offsets were created, which can be found in the RxDOS definitions file, rxdosdef.asm. You will see references to these registers throughout the RxDOS listing.

```
;///////////////////////////////////////////////////////////////;
;  Caller's Stack Frame                                          ;
;................................................................;

_Flags                          equ    6
_CS                             equ    4
_IP                             equ    2
```

```
_ExtraSegment                   equ    0
_DataSegment                    equ   -2
_BP                             equ   -4
_DI                             equ   -6
_SI                             equ   -8
_DX                             equ  -10
_CX                             equ  -12
_BX                             equ  -14
_AX                             equ  -16
sizeStackFrame                  equ   16
```

RxDOS maintains an area that it has allocated at boot time for the call or instance stack. The stack is at least large enough to hold three concurrent embedded calls. Each call into RxDOS reserves part of the stack to itself. A variable known as the stack top variable references the top of the next available stack. The instance variable references the start of the current stack.

```
_RxDOS_CurrentInstance  dw 0                     ; Base address of current stack
_RxDOS_CurrentStackTop  dw RxDOS_StackTop        ; Reserved Stack Top ...
```

To reserve stack space, the function handler moves the stack top pointer down by a predefined number of words. This guarantees that the space above the stack top pointer is reserved for the current call. Next, the function handler saves in the reserved stack arguments that cannot be overwritten by a subsequent DOS call. These arguments include the previous instance address, the value of the InDOS flag, and the current PSP address.

```
;- - - - - - - - - - - - - - - - - - - - - - - - - - - - - - - - - - - - - -
; current stack parameters
;- - - - - - - - - - - - - - - - - - - - - - - - - - - - - - - - - - - - - -
        Entry                                      ; set [ bp ]
        def  _FctAddress

        push word ptr [ _RxDOS_CurrentStackTop ]
        sub word ptr [ _RxDOS_CurrentStackTop ], 256   ; reserve stack

        push word ptr [ _RxDOS_CurrentInstance ]       ; base address of current stack
        mov word ptr [ _RxDOS_CurrentInstance ], bp    ; base address of current stack

        push word ptr [ _RxDOS_INDOSFlag ]
        inc word ptr [ _RxDOS_INDOSFlag  ]             ; InDOS

;- - - - - - - - - - - - - - - - - - - - - - - - - - - - - - - - - - - - - -
; save PSP values
;- - - - - - - - - - - - - - - - - - - - - - - - - - - - - - - - - - - - - -
        mov ds, word ptr [ _RxDOS_CurrentPSP ]
        push word ptr ds:[ pspUserStack. _segment ]
        push word ptr ds:[ pspUserStack. _pointer ]
        push ds                                    ; old PSP
        mov dx, ds                                 ; see if PSP was ever set
        or dx, dx                                  ; was PSP zero ?
        jz _Interrupt_21_12                        ; if no valid PSP ->

        mov word ptr ds:[ pspUserStack. _segment ], es
        mov word ptr ds:[ pspUserStack. _pointer ], bx
```

The Entry and def macros, which we describe in greater detail in the section "How to Read the Source Code," essentially set the BP to the top of the current stack and define a location at the top of the stack that can be referenced by the _FctAddress label.

The function handler then saves the caller's stack in the current PSP, but not before having saved the previous contents of the PSP's stack value. This permits multiple calls into DOS, each one saving the previously saved pointer to the caller's stack. RxDOS does this only for compatibility with MS-DOS. RxDOS actually has a separate copy to the caller's stack pointer in its own stack.

Finally, we increment the InDOS flag after having already saved the previous contents on the stack. This signals that the code, if interrupted, was actually running inside DOS. Since RxDOS is reentrant, it is no longer necessary to test this flag before making a DOS call. Stated another way, it does create the catastrophic results that calling DOS within DOS would.

The function handler is finally ready to reenable interrupts and look at the function code itself.

```
;- - - - - - - - - - - - - - - - - - - - - - - - - - - - - - - -
;  determine function address
;- -.- - - - - - - - - - - - - - - - - - - - - - - - - - - - - -

_Interrupt_21_12:
        sti
        cld
        currSegment ds                          ; point to current segment

        cmp ah, _RxDOS_maxFunctionCode          ; max function code ?
        jnc _Interrupt_21_26                    ; if out of range ->

;- - - - - - - - - - - - - - - - - - - - - - - - - - - - - - - -
;
; [ds] from user call is passed in [es]
; [dx] from user call is passed in [di]
; [ds] is changed to current segment
; [ss] == [ds] is assumed
;
;- - - - - - - - - - - - - - - - - - - - - - - - - - - - - - - -

        push bx
        xor bh, bh
        mov bl, ah                              ; offset into functions table
        add bx, bx
        push word ptr [ _RxDOS_functions ][ bx ]
        pop word ptr [ _FctAddress ][ bp ]      ; save in stack
        pop bx

        mov dx, word ptr es:[ _DX      ][ bx ]  ; restore DX
        mov di, word ptr es:[ _DX      ][ bx ]  ; restore DX
        push word ptr es:[ _DataSegment][ bx ]  ; ds on call
        push word ptr es:[ _BX     ][ bx ]      ; bx on call
        pop bx                                  ; no longer pointing
        pop es                                  ;  ...to user stack

        clc
        call word ptr [ _FctAddress ][ bp ]
```

After all that setup, we finally come to the part where the function code passed in the AH register is used to determine to which function the handler will dispatch. When RxDOS dispatches to a function, it specifically has reassigned some of the register arguments passed by the caller. The value passed in the DS:DX register pair is now passed to DOS functions in the ES:DI registers. The SS:BP register pair points to the current stack frame within RxDOS. The value in the DS register points to the RxDOS data segment. Although in its present release DS and SS are equal, this may change in future releases of RxDOS. All the other registers are passed unchanged to the function.

The function code in AH is used as a word index into the function table. The argument is copied to the BL register and doubled. The pointer to which this index into the RxDOS function table points is saved temporarily on the stack at the _FctAddress label. Next, the registers clobbered by the function handler are restored. Finally, though the ES:BX had until now pointed to the caller's stack, these are now replaced by call arguments. This section of code did not need to be interrupt disabled because it was not really in a critical section, so interrupts were enabled at the start of the section. The call at the very bottom actually jumps to the function handler.

What follows is what happens after the DOS function executes.

```
        jnc _Interrupt_21_24

        RetCallersStackFrame es, bx
        or  word ptr es:[ _Flags ][ bx ], 1           ; carry bit
        mov word ptr es:[ _AX    ][ bx ], ax          ; save last error code.
        mov word ptr cs:[ _RxDOS_ErrorCode ], ax      ; save last error code.

_Interrupt_21_24:
        setDS ss
        call invalidateRemoteCCBBuffers               ; don't keep remote buffers

;- - - - - - - - - - - - - - - - - - - - - - - - - - - - - - - - -
;  return registers
;- - - - - - - - - - - - - - - - - - - - - - - - - - - - - - - - -

_Interrupt_21_26:
        cli
        pop dx                                        ; restore PSP address
        pop bx
        pop cx                                        ; old user stack values
        or dx, dx                                     ; no psp address ?
        jz _Interrupt_21_32                           ; if none —>

        mov ds, dx
        mov word ptr ds:[ pspUserStack. _pointer ], bx  ; restore old stack pointer
        mov word ptr ds:[ pspUserStack. _segment ], cx

_Interrupt_21_32:
        pop word ptr cs:[ _RxDOS_INDOSFlag       ]    ; restore InDOS
        pop word ptr cs:[ _RxDOS_CurrentInstance ]    ; _Instance
        pop word ptr cs:[ _RxDOS_CurrentStackTop ]

        pop bx                                        ; fct address
```

```
        pop bx                              ; argument left on stack
        pop ss                              ; caller's stack
        sub bx, sizeStackFrame              ; adjusted stack pointer
        mov sp, bx

        pop ax                              ; restore registers
        pop bx
        pop cx
        pop dx

        pop si
        pop di
        pop bp

        pop ds
        pop es
        iret
_Interrupt_21   endp
```

All functions exit by setting up return register values and performing a return because all functions were called by a call instruction. When registers are being returned to the caller, these values were set by the function by directly altering the values saved in the caller's stack. Error return codes are handled a little differently. Any function may return with the carry set and an error code in the AX register.

Part of the reasoning in setting this as the return protocol is that it's easier on the function code itself. All functions must ensure that the carry bit is clear if there are no errors but may also set an error code and the carry bit when errors do occur.

The function handler code must handle the return to the caller logic. It records the error code if the carry is set and sets the carry in the return flag word. It's important to understand that the code does not rely on any registers being valid, except that the SS:BP pointer must point to the stack frame. Further, the code shows an example of how the caller's stack address can at anytime be retrieved from the stack frame.

```
        RetCallersStackFrame es, bx
        or  word ptr es:[ _Flags ][ bx ], 1     ; carry bit
        mov word ptr es:[ _AX    ][ bx ], ax    ; save last error code.
```

The return callers stack frame macro returns the caller's stack address, in the ES:BX register pair in this case. Other registers could be used with the macro. The macro serves as a convenient coding tool for calling a function that actually loads the register values.

The remainder of the function handler simply restores all the registers saved on the stack. We pop back the stack value in the PSP address, the InDOS flag, and undo the stack reservation by restoring the stack top address. Note that part of the registers restored includes the pointer to the caller's stack that was placed in the stack frame. At this point, we have managed a switch back to the caller's stack, from which we continue by restoring all the registers saved on the caller's stack.

The last statement is the iret instruction, which returns control to the caller.

```
;''''''''''''''''''''''''''''''''''''''''''''''''''''''''''''';
;  Real Time Dos                                              ;
;- - - - - - - - - - - - - - - - - - - - - - - - - - - - - -;
;                                                            ;
;                                                            ;
;  Items marked by (*) are Undocumented DOS Functions.       ;
;............................................................;

_RxDOS_functions:
        dw  _TerminateProcess_00          ; 00 -  Program terminate
        dw  _KeyboardInput                ; 01 -  Keyboard input
        dw  _DisplayOutput                ; 02 -  Display output
        dw  _AuxInput                     ; 03 -  Aux input
        dw  _AuxOutput                    ; 04 -  Aux output
        dw  _PrinterOutput                ; 05 -  Printer output
        dw  _DirectConsole                ; 06 -  Direct console
        dw  _DirectConsoleInputNoEcho     ; 07 -  Direct console input noecho
        dw  _ConsoleInputNoEcho           ; 08 -  Console input noecho
        dw  _DisplayString                ; 09 -  Display string
        dw  _BufferedKeyboardInput        ; 0A -  Buffered keyboard input
        dw  _CheckKeyboardInput           ; 0B -  Check keyboard input
        dw  _ClearBufferedKeyboardInput   ; 0C -  Clear buffered keyboard input
        dw  _DiskReset                    ; 0D -  Disk reset
        dw  _SelectDisk                   ; 0E -  Select disk
        dw  _OpenFileFCB                  ; 0F -  Open file FCB
        dw  _CloseFileFCB                 ; 10 -  Close file FCB
        dw  _SearchFirstFileFCB           ; 11 -  Search first file FCB
        dw  _SearchNextFileFCB            ; 12 -  Search next file FCB
        dw  _DeleteFileFCB                ; 13 -  Delete file FCB
        dw  _SeqReadFileFCB               ; 14 -  Seq read file FCB
        dw  _SeqWriteFileFCB              ; 15 -  Seq write file FCB
        dw  _CreateFileFCB                ; 16 -  Create file FCB
        dw  _RenameFileFCB                ; 17 -  Rename file FCB
        dw  _UnusedReturnInst             ; 18 -  Unused
        dw  _CurrentDisk                  ; 19 -  Current disk
        dw  _SetDiskTransferAddress       ; 1A -  Set disk transfer address
        dw  _GetDefaultDriveData          ; 1B -  Get default drive data
        dw  _GetDriveData                 ; 1C -  Get drive data
        dw  _UnusedReturnInst             ; 1D -  Unused
        dw  _UnusedReturnInst             ; 1E -  Unused
        dw  _GetDefaultDriveParameterBlock ; 1F -  Get default drive parameter block
        dw  _UnusedReturnInst             ; 20 -  Unused
        dw  _ReadFileFCB                  ; 21 -  Read file FCB
        dw  _WriteFileFCB                 ; 22 -  Write file FCB
        dw  _FileSizeFCB                  ; 23 -  File size FCB
        dw  _SetRelativeRecordFCB         ; 24 -  Set relative record FCB
        dw  _SetInterruptVector           ; 25 -  Set interrupt vector
        dw  _CreateNewProgramSeg          ; 26 -  Create new program seg
        dw  _RandomBlockReadFCB           ; 27 -  Random block read FCB
        dw  _RandomBlockWriteFCB          ; 28 -  Random block write FCB
        dw  _ParseFilenameFCB             ; 29 -  Parse filename FCB
        dw  _GetDate                      ; 2A -  Get date
        dw  _SetDate                      ; 2B -  Set date
```

```
dw _GetTime                       ; 2C -  Get time
dw _SetTime                       ; 2D -  Set time
dw _SetVerifySwitch               ; 2E -  Set verify switch
dw _GetDiskTransferAddress        ; 2F -  Get disk transfer address
dw _GetDOSVersion                 ; 30 -  Get DOS version
dw _TerminateStayResident         ; 31 -  Terminate stay resident
dw _GetDriveParameterBlock        ; 32 -  Get drive parameter block
dw _CtrlBreakCheck                ; 33 -  Ctrl break check
dw _GetInDOSFlagAddress           ; 34 -  Get INDOS flag address
dw _GetInterruptVector            ; 35 -  Get interrupt vector
dw _GetFreeDiskSpace              ; 36 -  Get free disk space
dw _GetSetSwitchChar              ; 37 -  Get/set switch char
dw _CountryDependentInfo          ; 38 -  Country dependent info
dw _CreateSubdirectory            ; 39 -  Create subdirectory
dw _RemoveSubdirectory            ; 3A -  Remove subdirectory
dw _ChangeSubdirectory            ; 3B -  Change subdirectory
dw _CreateFile                    ; 3C -  Create file
dw _OpenFile                      ; 3D -  Open file
dw _CloseFile                     ; 3E -  Close file
dw _ReadFile                      ; 3F -  Read file
dw _WriteFile                     ; 40 -  Write file
dw _DeleteFile                    ; 41 -  Delete file
dw _MoveFilePointer               ; 42 -  Move file pointer
dw _ChangeFileMode                ; 43 -  Change file mode
dw _IoControl                     ; 44 -* Io Control
dw _DuplicateFileHandle           ; 45 -  Duplicate file handle
dw _ForceFileHandle               ; 46 -  Force file handle
dw _GetCurrentDirectory           ; 47 -  Get current directory
dw _AllocateMemory                ; 48 -  Allocate memory
dw _FreeAllocatedMemory           ; 49 -  Free allocated memory
dw _ModifyAllocatedMemory         ; 4A -  Modify allocated memory
dw _ExecuteProgram                ; 4B -  ExecuteProgram
dw _TerminateProcess              ; 4C -  Terminate process
dw _GetReturnCode                 ; 4D -  Get return code
dw _FindFirstFile                 ; 4E -  Find first file
dw _FindNextFile                  ; 4F -  Find next file
dw _SetPSPAddress                 ; 50 -  Set PSP Address
dw _GetPSPAddress                 ; 51 -  Get PSP Address
dw _GetDosDataTablePtr            ; 52*- (Get DOS Data Table)
dw _TranslateBIOSParameterBlock   ; 53*- (Translate BIOS Parameter Block)
dw _GetVerify                     ; 54 -  Get verify
dw _DuplicatePSP                  ; 55*- (Duplicate PSP block)
dw _RenameFile                    ; 56 -  Rename file
dw _SetFileDateTime               ; 57 -  Set file date time
dw _GetAllocationStrategy         ; 58 -  Get allocation strategy
dw _GetExtendedError              ; 59 -  Get extended error
dw _CreateUniqueFile              ; 5A -  Create unique file
dw _CreateNewFile                 ; 5B -  Create new file
dw _LockFileAccess                ; 5C -  Lock file access
dw _InternalFunctions             ; 5D*- Internal Functions
dw _GetMachineName                ; 5E -  Get machine name
dw _GetRedirectionList            ; 5F -  Get redirection list
dw _GetActualFileName             ; 60*- (Get Actual FileName )
```

```
        dw _Unused                             ; 61 -  Unused
        dw _GetPSPAddress                      ; 62 -  Get PSP Address
        dw _Unused                             ; 63 -  Unused
        dw _Unused                             ; 64 -  Unused
        dw _CapitalizeFunctions                ; 65*-  (Country Dep Capitz )
        dw _Unused                             ; 66 -  Unused
        dw _SetHandlesCount                    ; 67 -  Set Handles Count
        dw _CommitFile                         ; 68 -  Commit File
        dw _GetDiskSerialNumber                ; 69*-  (Get disk serial number)
        dw _CommitFile                         ; 6A*-  Commit File (same as 68)
        dw _Unused                             ; 6B -  Unused
        dw _ExtendedOpenCreate                 ; 6C -  Extended Open/ Create
        dw _Unused                             ; 6D -  DOS in ROM Functions
        dw _Unused                             ; 6E -  DOS in ROM Functions
        dw _Unused                             ; 6F -  DOS in ROM Functions
        dw _Unused                             ; 70 -  Unused or unknown
        dw _Unused                             ; 71 -  Chicago long filenames
        dw _Unused                             ; 72 -  Chicago long filenames

_RxDOS_functionsLast:
        dw _Unused                             ; *-  items: Undocumented DOS Functions

_RxDOS_maxFunctionCode = (_RxDOS_functionsLast - _RxDOS_functions)/2
```

GetPSPAddress, An Example of a DOS Function

If the job of the function handler is to dispatch to a DOS function, it is imperative that we begin looking at how DOS functions actually perform their work, starting from the simpler DOS functions to eventually the more complex. Among the simplest is function 62h (also 51h) returning the value of the current PSP.

The PSP, or Program Segment Prefix, is a header placed at the beginning of all programs initiated by DOS. A diagram of a PSP is shown in Figure 1-11. Function code 62h is the Get Current PSP Segment function. The segment address is returned to the caller in the BX register.

```
;'''''''''''''''''''''''''''''''''''''''''''''''''''''''''''''''';
;   51h Get PSP Address                                          ;
;- - - - - - - - - - - - - - - - - - - - - - - - - - - - - - - -;
;                                                                ;
;   bx        contains PSP address to use                        ;
;................................................................;

_GetPSPAddress:
        mov bx, word ptr [ _RxDOS_CurrentPSP ]     ; Segment pointer
                                                   ;  ...of current PSP

        RetCallersStackFrame es, si
        mov word ptr es:[ _BX ][ si ], bx
        ret
```

The function is simple and straightforward. It must first get the current PSP address stored in the SYSVAR area and then return it to the user. However, to return it to the user, it must update the saved registers in the caller's stack frame.

RxDOS functions, even MS-DOS functions, can't simply return values directly in registers. The reason is the caller's registers have been saved in the caller's stack and will be restored when the DOS call exits. Instead, any value that needs to be returned to the caller must replace the value of the register saved in the caller's stack. Since this is required frequently enough, there is a function designed to return the base address of the saved registers in the caller's stack. That's what RetCallersStackFrame macro does. It returns the stack base address in a register pair. In this case, the stack pointer is returned in the ES:SI registers. To return the value in the BX register, all that is necessary is to store the value in the _BX argument. This represents the return value for the BX register.

Functions That Return Errors

Error reporting to the caller by RxDOS functions could have been handled in the same way that any other register value is handled; that is, the error code and the carry flag both could have been set by the function by directly changing the caller's stack frame. For various reasons, the error handling is handled at the function handler rather than at each function itself. When a function returns to the function handler, it must have the carry flag set clear. Otherwise, when the carry flag is set, the function handler interprets the AX register as containing an error code. It saves the error code internally for future reference, and then both returns the value as the AX register to the caller and sets the carry flag.

```
;///////////////////////////////////////////////////////////;
;  45h Duplicate File Handle                                 ;
;- - - - - - - - - - - - - - - - - - - - - - - - - - - - - -;
;                                                            ;
;  Input:                                                    ;
;    bx      existing (old) handle                           ;
;                                                            ;
;  Output:                                                   ;
;    ax      new handle                                      ;
;............................................................;

_DuplicateFileHandle:
        mov es, word ptr [ _RxDOS_CurrentPSP ]
        mov cx, word ptr es:[ pspFileHandleCount ]
        mov dx, cx                                  ; save original count
        mov al, -1
        les di, dword ptr es:[ pspFileHandlePtr ]
        repnz scasb                                 ; scan for empty slot

    ; set error flag (carry) and error code
        stc
        mov ax, errNoHandlesAvailable               ; assume error
        jnz _duplFileHandle_Return                  ; if error ->
```

```
          ...

;- - - - - - - - - - - - - - - - - - - - - - - - - - - - - - - - -
;  if error, exit with error code.
;- - - - - - - - - - - - - - - - - - - - - - - - - - - - - - - - -
_duplFileHandle_Return:
          ret
```

How to Read the Source Code

The DOS source code provided in this book makes use of some powerful macros intended to make both programming and debugging easier. Some macros were designed to make the task of programming in a reentrant system easier to handle. A good general understanding of what the macros accomplish for the code is important to understanding and reading the code.

The macros listed here are defined in the `rxdosmac.asm` file, which lists macros that may appear in the source code that are not described in detail here. We define their role as we encounter them in the source code.

Passing Arguments Between Subroutines

I designed several macros specifically to handle parameter passing between routines. Unlike its counterpart, RxDOS must be reentrant throughout. It cannot afford to pass arguments or save temporary values in local memory. Instead, RxDOS must utilize the stack for both of these storage requirements.

Accessing parameters and arguments on the stack can appear extremely unreadable. However, as you will observe, in the macros provided here, efficient stack use can be made without sacrificing readability or programming efficiency. But first we present a tutorial on our subroutine call model. This model does not differ substantially from the model used by C or Pascal functions.

When a subroutine expects arguments on the stack, the call appears as

```
          push 0005
          mov bx, offset buffer
          push bx
          push es
          call Subroutine
          .
          .
          .

Subroutine:
          push bp
          mov bp, sp
          les bx, [bp+ 4]               ; the unreadable version
          .

          .
          mov sp, bp
          pop bp
          ret 6                         ; pop 6 byte arguments on stack
```

Pascal and Windows function calls use a very similar calling convention. The rules are that the number of arguments is considered fixed, the arguments are pushed on the stack by the caller, and the called routine pops the saved arguments off the stack on a return.

Figure 1-12. Stack after entry to subroutine. The preceding subroutine example shows how to access parameters passed on the stack.

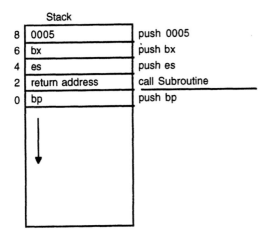

After a call to the subroutine, the stack appears as shown in Figure 1-12. The arguments and the call return address are pushed on the stack. The subroutine can push registers, but the arguments are still accessible on the stack. Although a specific offset can be used to reference these arguments, the code would be difficult to read, and complications would be created when changes are made during the development cycle.

Instead of numeric offsets, macros are used to create references to arguments, as in

```
Subroutine:
    Entry  3                      ; expecting 3 words on stack
    arg   _number                 ; points to number argument
    darg  _argpointer             ; points to es:bx

    les bx, [ _argpointer ][ bp ] ; get argument

    ...

    Return
```

The Entry macro accepts as an argument the number of words that are passed on the stack. The arg macro defines an offset to a word argument, whereas the darg macro defines the base address of a double argument. The pointer passed on the stack is considered a single double-word argument since both parts of the address, the segment and offset, are pushed on the stack. Finally, the Return macro not only performs a return but also pops the number of arguments passed on the stack.

The text shows the code generated by each macro.

```
Subroutine:
        Entry  3                              ; expecting 3 words on stack
               push bp
               mov bp, sp

        arg    _number                        ; points to number argument
        darg   _argpointer                    ; points to es:bx
               _number      equ  +0010        ; expecting 3 words + ret + push bp
               _argpointer  equ  +0006

        les bx, [ _argpointer ][ bp ]         ; get argument
               les bx, [ 0006 ][ bp ]
                  .
                  .
                  .


        Return
               mov sp, bp
               pop bp
               ret ( 2 * _numberargs )
```

There's more. RxDOS routines, like routines in virtually any programming project, need to be able to create temporary variables. These variables can be created dynamically on the stack. These temporary variables can be used like any other memory location. What makes them even handier to use is that macros are available that define temporary storage on the stack. There is no need to use numeric offsets where named references can be used instead. The relationship between arguments and temporary variables on the stack is shown in Figure 1-13.

Figure 1-13. How the stack is used with temporary variables

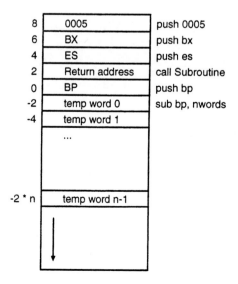

8	0005	push 0005
6	BX	push bx
4	ES	push es
2	Return address	call Subroutine
0	BP	push bp
-2	temp word 0	sub bp, nwords
-4	temp word 1	
	...	
-2 * n	temp word n-1	

```
Subroutine:
        push bp
        mov bp, sp
        sub sp, n_words

        les bx, [bp + 6]              ; the unreadable version
        mov ax, es:[bx]
        mov [bp - 2], ax             ; the unreadable version
        .
        .
        mov sp, bp
        pop bp
        ret 6                        ; pop 6 bytes
```

The example subroutine is expanded to allocate temporary variables. Not only can temporary arguments be created on the stack, but the arguments can be initialized automatically every time the routine is called.

```
Subroutine:
        Entry  3                     ; expecting 3 words on stack
        arg    _number               ; points to number argument
        darg   _argpointer           ; points to es:bx

        def    _aWord                ; not initialized
        ddef   _aDword, es, bx       ; initialized to es:bx
        def    _aCount, 0000         ; initialized
        def    _axWord, AX           ; init to AX value

        defbytes _aBuffer, 128       ; 128 byte buffer
        defwords _aWordBuffer, 128   ; 256 byte buffer

    ; other pushes and pops is still possible

        push ds
        push es

        les bx, [ _argpointer ][ bp ]    ; get argument
        mov [ _aWord ][ bp ], bx         ; using temp arguments
        ...

        pop es
        pop ds

        Return
```

Making the Code Even More Readable

Whether variables were passed or defined on the stack, they need to be accessed as offsets from the current value of the bp register. There are macros that make the access and use of temporary variables or arguments easier to code and read. Instead of accessing the arguments as

```
        mov  ax, _Xargument [ bp ]
        mov  es, _Yargument + 2 [ bp ]        ; segment
        mov  bx, _Yargument [ bp ]            ; offset
        lds  si, _Zargument [ bp ]


        ...
        mov  _Xargument [ bp ], ax
        mov  _Yargument + 2 [ bp ], es        ; segment
        mov  _Yargument [ bp ], bx            ; offset
```

the same code can be coded as

```
        getarg  ax, _Xargument
        getdarg es, bx, _Yargument           ; generates an les bx, ...
        getdarg ds, si, _Yargument           ; generates an lds si, ...


        ...
        storarg  _Xargument, ax
        stordarg _Yargument, es, bx
```

Calling FAR Routines

All these examples assumed near function calls. Near function calls push a single word on the stack containing the address relative to the current segment. Far function calls push a two-word return address on the stack representing the full code segment and offset address. To permit the routine to properly adjust for the extra segment address, the Entry macro should be replaced by a call to the FarEntry macro. All the offsets will then work properly. The code appears as

```
        Subroutine proc far
                FarEntry 4
                darg  _argpointer            ; arguments passed
                arg   _count
                arg   _anotherarg

        ; return macro
                Return                       ; generates retf 8 (4 words )

        Subroutine endp
```

Error Reporting

Traditionally within RxDOS, the carry flag is used to signify an error during a subroutine return. There are some convenient macros for setting error conditions and returning error values. The SetError macro sets the carry flag, loads an error code value into the AX register, and performs an unconditional jump to a label, presumably an error handler or exit label. The macro does only the following:

```
SetError errcode, opt_jumpto

        stc
        mov ax, errcode
        jmp opt_jumpto                    ; instruction optionally generated
```

The jump to address label is optional. If no `opt_jumpto` label is given, the jump instruction is not generated.

Another convenient macro is the `iferror` macro. This macro tests whether an error was set. It really tests only for the carry flag, which may not mean that an error was set. The macro is used only in the code when an error flag in the form of the carry flag is expected. The macro not only handles some jumps in case of errors but also provides context and readability.

```
iferror errcode, opt_jumpto

        jnc _around_this                  ; label generated automatically

        mov ax, errcode
        jmp opt_jumpto                    ; instruction optionally generated

_around_this:
```

Other Long Jump Macros

A limitation of the Intel instruction set is the conditional branch instructions that jump only a maximum of 128 bytes on either side of the current instruction. Therefore, sometimes you'll see somewhat unreadable assembly language code that looks like this.

```
        ; ...
        jnc _foo_1
        jmp _overthere_oncarry

_foo_1:

        ; ...
        jnz _foo_2
        jmp _overthere_onzero

_foo_2:
```

Four macros simplify the reading of the code: `ifc`, `ifnc`, `ifz`, and `ifnz`. These macros jump anywhere beyond the 128 byte limit.

```
; ...
ifc _overthere_oncarry

; ...
ifz _overthere_onzero
```

Another useful macro is the conditional `Goto` macro. This macro is convenient for comparing values against the AX register (or AL if the value is less than 256) and branching to a label. The branch must be local, that is, to within 128 bytes on either side of the conditional jump instruction.

```
Goto GetControlC,        __getControlC
Goto SetControlC,        __setControlC
```

Saving Registers

Because saving and restoring registers are necessary but both time consuming to type and difficult to read, several macros are part of the code that save and restore different combinations of registers. There are convenient macros that save all the registers or just the important segment registers. The register save macros work as

```
saveAllRegisters/ restoreAllRegisters

    saveAllRegisters                     ; all except flag register
    ...
    restoreAllRegisters

saveRegisters/ restoreRegisters

    saveRegisters  bx, cx, dx
    saveRegisters  es, ds
    ...
    restoreRegisters  ds, es             ; order is reverse from save
    restoreRegisters  dx, cx, bx         ; order is reverse from save

saveSegments/ restoreSegments

    saveSegments                         ; saves ds, es
    saveSegments bx, cx                  ; saves ds, es, bx, cx
    ...
    restoreSegments cx, bx               ; restores cx, bx, es, ds
    restoreSegments                      ; restores es, ds

saveStandard/ restoreStandard

    saveStandard                         ; saves ds, es, si, di
    saveStandard ax, bx                  ; same as above plus ax, bx
    ...
    restoreStandard bx, ax               ; restores bx, ax, di, si, es, ds
    restoreStandard                      ; restores di, si, es, ds
```

Looking at Macro Usage in the Program

We look at the macro usage in just one fragment of code: the `CopyBlock` routine in `rxdosstr.asm`. The routine expects two addresses, including segment and offset, passed on the stack, one representing the source address and the other the destination address, with the number of bytes to be copied passed in the CX register. This calling convention, purists would argue, should either all have been passed in registers or all on the stack. Even though I wrote the code myself, I can't make a reasoned case here. The address arguments are passed on the stack because it's more flexible than register passing.

At any rate, the routine looks like this.

```
;''''''''''''''''''''''''''''''''''''''''''''''''''''''''''''';
;  Copy Block                                                 ;
;- - - - - - - - - - - - - - - - - - - - - - - - - - - - - -;
;                                                            ;
;  Usage:                                                    ;
;   stack  source string address                             ;
;   stack  dest string address                               ;
;   cx     length                                            ;
;............................................................;

CopyBlock:
        Entry 4
        darg _src                       ; source pushed first
        darg _dest                      ; dest pushed next

        saveSegments di, si             ; we'll use ds:si and es:di

        getdarg ds, si, _src            ; load ds:si with source
        getdarg es, di, _dest           ; load es:di with destination
        shr cx, 1                       ; we'll copy words first
        rep movsw                       ; copy words first
        adc cx, cx
        rep movsb                       ; copy odd byte

        restoreSegments si, di          ; restore all of these
        Return                          ; clean up stack on exit
```

The `Entry`/`Return` pair surrounds the routine. Four words are expected to be passed as arguments. Each `darg` macro defines the argument order. That is, first the source address is pushed on the stack, followed by the destination argument. Next, the routine saves the segment registers and the `SI` and `DI` registers, which will be used in the copy. The routine then uses the `getdarg` macro, which generates `lds` and `les` instructions, to load the source and destination addresses from the stack. The routine performs a block move, followed by a restore of the saved registers. Notice that the order of the registers in the list is reversed between the save macro call and the restore macro call. Finally, the `Return` macro will automatically remove from the stack the number of arguments described in the `Entry` macro. In the preceding example, the `Entry` macro expected four words. The `Return` will automatically perform a `ret 8` to remove the eight bytes taken up by the passed arguments.

CHAPTER 2

How DOS Starts Up

Overview of the Boot Process—Cold Start, Warm Start, and Loading the Boot
Sector—Booting Io.sys—The SYSINIT Code—Processing Config.sys

DOS startup became much more complex with versions 5 and 6. Prior to that, the DOS boot process
was fairly straightforward because it did not have to enable loading DOS into the High Memory
Area. Not only does DOS have to relocate itself into these special memory locations, but it can do
so only after it has processed the config.sys file and loaded the required memory management
device drivers.

The High Memory Area, or HMA, is a 64K byte area available just above the end of the first
megabyte of memory and is accessible by enabling the A20 hardware line. This requires a device
driver such as hihem.sys (or equivalent). Otherwise, the highest address in real mode is limited
to FFFF:000F, exactly 1 MB of memory. Any address formed beyond this limit will wrap back to
low memory. This address limitation is due to the way the segmented Intel architecture forms
addresses in real mode. It utilizes 20 address lines, referred to as A0 through A19.

Enabling the A20 line prevents the address from wrapping around and extends the addressable
space in real mode by an additional 64K bytes. This space is physically the first 64K of protected
memory. The space is sufficient to load DOS, some drivers, and the cache buffers.

So why stop at the first 64K bytes? Why not address all protected memory directly? This is
tougher and more complex. The way the addresses are formed, any direct addressing beyond the
HMA would require protected mode. An entire book could be written on the uses and accessibility
of protected mode memory. Generally, though, DOS itself and most applications could not run
unchanged in protected mode. Some operations that are perfectly legal in real mode would cause
access violations in protected mode. An example of one of these would be to set the segment registers to an illegal value.

Back to how DOS loads Figure 2-1 contrasts how different memory configurations load into
memory. In versions prior to DOS 5, the modules that compose DOS, io.sys, and msdos.sys
were loaded into low memory and were followed by DOS data structures, including SFTs (System
File Tables), buffers, and the CDS (Current Directory Structure). Device drivers were loaded after
these structures.

For clarity, the data structures are separate from the data segments of either io.sys and
msdos.sys. DOS allocates space to manage logical disks, files, and disk cache buffers. These
structures are known as the CDS, SFTs, and CCBs (Cache Control Buffers), respectively. These
structures will be reallocated to their proper sizes after the config.sys file is processed.

Figure 2-1. Memory boot configurations

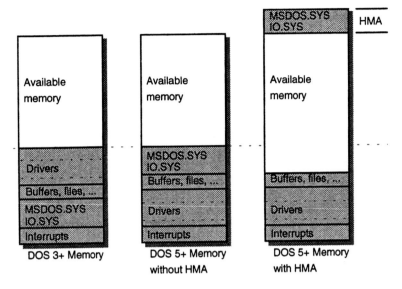

Access to the HMA depends on the status of the A20 line. This line may be unexpectedly turned off, usually the result of some action by application software. When a DOS function is called, the HMA is reenabled if required. DOS data areas, including the much used SYSVAR area, remain in accessible memory at all times. They are never located in the HMA.

Overview of the Boot Process

In MS-DOS versions 5 and 6, the final destinations of the kernel or internal device drivers are not determined until after the config.sys file has been processed. DOS needs to process this file first to determine the user's intent, as in dos=high. Since DOS itself does not have any HMA switching capability of its own, but rather relies on an HMA driver to have been loaded, DOD is not relocated until after all device drivers have been loaded.

Similarly, DOS cannot determine what space within the UMB (Upper Memory Blocks) it can utilize without the aid of a driver. Although the UMB is directly addressable from real mode, the entire area is not completely available. Unlimited access within the UMB has the potential for problems. The driver must detect and distinguish memory reserved for video display, EMS pages, and ROM that shares this space. Some of the memory must be excluded since it may interfere with installed hardware. (Some hardware maps into this space, and reading and writing in its reserved addresses will drive the hardware.)

Access to the HMA requires himem.sys or an equivalent driver, whereas access to the UMB requires emm386.sys or an equivalent driver such as Quarterdeck's qemm386.sys. The HMA driver must be loaded first.

None of this speaks to why this code was not actually made a part of the main DOS kernel. Why should code critical to the management of memory reside in loadable device drivers? The reason is not to permit alternative memory managers. In fact, except for the size a driver occupies in memory, there is very little benefit between drivers. Instead, the relegation of this task to drivers permits users to customize their systems. A surprising number of users have an investment in software that works just fine without any tweaks in memory configuration. Upgrading means taking an unwarranted risk with an otherwise working system.

When DOS loads from the hard disk, the io.sys and msdos.sys modules are temporarily loaded as high as possible within the lower 640K of memory. It reserves a 16K area at the top of low memory in the event that a link to upper memory blocks needs to be established. The io.sys and msdos.sys data segments are copied to their permanent location in low memory regardless of any future configuration choices, and a minimal set of DOS data structures are allocated low in memory to handle files, disk cache buffers, and logical drives. This creates a working version of DOS capable of processing the config.sys file.

To prevent the accidental overwrite of DOS while it is high in low memory, the total amount of system memory is artificially set to below the address of DOS in high memory. This is accomplished by setting the BIOS reported memory size value, located at 0040:0013.

Figure 2-2. Events in boot sequence

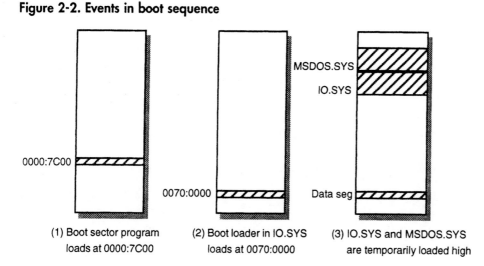

(1) Boot sector program loads at 0000:7C00

(2) Boot loader in IO.SYS loads at 0070:0000

(3) IO.SYS and MSDOS.SYS are temporarily loaded high

The boot sequence that initially loads DOS into memory is shown in Figure 2-2. It begins with the boot sector loader (explained in the next section) and follows with the io.sys loader, which loads the DOS files.

From this temporary location high in memory, DOS processes the config file. It runs through the menu options and builds an internal process table. This table contains each statement in the config file and is held there until the entire file is read. Statements in the config file are processed in the following sequence: dos, country, device, devicehigh, drivparam, multitrack, and switches. It then sets the buffers, files, fcbs, lastdrive, shell, and stacks. Three device-related files are opened for the CON, AUX, and PRN. The CON file is copied twice, meaning that its reserved count is incremented by two. The install commands are not processed until after DOS is relocated and the command shell has been loaded.

DOS initializes low memory so that it can be allocated to device drivers. The dos statement is processed, and the bit flags produced by options like umb and hma are saved. DOS loads all device drivers, and then attempts to enable the HMA and to allocate and initialize upper memory blocks if the DOS flag bits are enabled. Config file processing then continues by loading the devicehigh drivers. This enables DOS to take advantage of the space created by any memory manager drivers that have been loaded.

Allocation to the space in the UMB is made on a first-come, first-served basis, but the order provides preferential treatment to the larger allocation areas first. Buffers are allocated before files, which are allocated before the CDS.

One strategy used by RxDOS that MS-DOS should use is to break up the memory required by SFTs. SFTs, which are allocated to the number specified by the files= statement, are contained in extensible File Tables. File Tables can be subdivided into several parts so that portions might be made to fit into separate parts of the UMB as well as lower memory.

After loading device drivers and allocating the data structures, DOS can be relocated to its final position, either in the HMA or in low memory. The space occupied by DOS at its temporary location is freed, and the BIOS area memory is restored to its original value. At this point, DOS becomes a fully configured, fully installed system. DOS transfers control to the command shell, which is loaded like any other program (using DOS function 4Bh, the DOS EXEC function), which in turn runs autoexec.bat.

Throughout the remainder of these sections on booting and startup, we refer to two files, io.sys and msdos.sys. This reference is meant to be more-or-less generic. It should be understood that in the IBM version of DOS these files are known as ibmbio.com and ibmdos.com and that in the RxDOS version these are known as rxdosbio.com and rxdos.com, respectively. All the information provided herein is generally about io.sys and msdos.sys and specifically about the code in RxDOS.

Given this introduction and overview, the process of booting DOS begins at the cold or warm boot start.

Cold Start, Warm Start, and Loading the Boot Sector

When the PC starts from a cold boot, the processor resets itself to real mode, disables the A20 line and all interrupts, and begins execution at a specific memory address. On IBM personal computers and compatibles, the startup address is FFFF:0000. A far jump is located at this address to the POST (power-on self-test) routines that perform hardware checks, including the memory self-test. These tests identify the available memory and hardware configuration.

A warm boot is executed by jumping to the same cold boot start address with the code 1234 in hex at location 0040:0072. The code prevents the hardware startup check, but it otherwise continues to perform the exact same boot process. reboot.com, a program on the disk that accompanies this book, performs a warm boot. That program contains the following code (entered with debug):

```
mov ax, 40h
mov ds, ax
mov bx, 72h
mov word[ bx ], 1234h
jmp FFFF:0000
```

When the BIOS begins, it performs hardware checks and determines its configuration by detecting the number of disk drives, serial and parallel ports, and the amount of total memory. It then jumps to an internal BOOT_STRAP routine that scans available disk units, beginning with unit 0 (known in DOS as A:) and proceeding through each successive drive until a reset/read sequence can be successfully accomplished. The sector read is the boot sector of a disk drive. As a side note, some systems contain BIOS code that skips scanning diskette drives, usually as a result of a setable or configurable option.

The boot sector code is always loaded to memory address 0000:7C00, or 1K below a minimum 32K system. The BIOS doesn't really care whether it's booting DOS, RxDOS, or Unix. In fact, its only purpose is to get out of the ROM. The boot sector, physically located at sector 1 of track 0, head 0 on a disk, must contain a boot program if it is to be run or used on a PC. The contents of the boot sector are loaded and executed without any safeguard checking. There are no established conventions to ensure that the contents read are a valid boot sector program (or any other type of valid program). The BIOS loads the contents of the boot sector and jumps to it, which may cause the system to crash if the boot sector contains garbage. A simple scheme such as a checking the signature or a checksum would have been a reasonable protection against booting a corrupted or unformatted disk.

One implication of all this is that all disks, including floppy disks, must have a program at the boot sector even if they are nonsystem disks! A user who inadvertently tries to boot from a nonsystem disk receives the following message:

```
Non-System disk or disk error
Replace and press any key when ready
```

This message is not in the BIOS; instead, it's part of the boot sector program placed on every disk formatted by the DOS FORMAT program (or equivalent). The boot program for a nonsystem disk must display a message that says, "Sorry, I don't boot!"

For hard disks, the program at the boot sector of the disk is not the boot program directly but rather contains the Master Boot Record (also known as the MBR) routine. To understand its purpose, it is necessary to understand that a hard disk can be partitioned into up to four separate areas. Each partition may support a different operating system, so it is possible for a hard disk to be divided into Unix and DOS partitions. As a historical note, partitioning was also necessary because pre-DOS 5 versions were limited to addressing disks no larger than 32MB. A 50MB hard disk had to be partitioned into partitions of no larger than 32MB.

At any rate, the MBR is a small boot program that copies the partition table to a fixed location in memory (it was already loaded when the sector was loaded), determines the default startup partition, and jumps to the starting sector in the partition. This starting sector contains the DOS boot program. The partition table layout is known as the PARTITION data structure, as shown here.

```
;'''''''''''''''''''''''''''''''''''''''''''''''''''''''''''''''';
;  Partition Table Record                                         ;
;................................................................;


        PARTITION struc
_ptBootable             db ?            ; 80h = bootable, 00h = nonbootable
_ptBeginHead            db ?            ; begin head address
_ptBeginSector          db ?            ; begin sector address
_ptBeginCylinder        db ?            ; begin cylinder address
_ptFileSystemName       db ?            ; file system identifier (see below)
_ptEndHead              db ?            ; end head address
_ptEndSector            db ?            ; end sector address
_ptEndCylinder          db ?            ; end cylinder address
_ptStartSector          dd ?            ; start sector (relative to beg of disk)
_ptSectors              dd ?            ; number of sectors in partition
        PARTITION ends

;- - - - - - - - - - - - - - - - - - - - - - - - - - - - - - - -
; File System ID Codes
;- - - - - - - - - - - - - - - - - - - - - - - - - - - - - - - -
FILESYSID_12FAT         equ 01h         ; 12-bit FAT (max 10 MBytes)
FILESYSID_16FAT         equ 04h         ; 16-bit FAT (max 32 MBytes)
FILESYSID_EXTENDED      equ 05h         ; Extended DOS partition
FILESYSID_LARGE16FAT    equ 06h         ; 16-bit FAT (greater than 32 MBytes)

FILESYSID_XENIX         equ 02h         ; reserved for XENIX
FILESYSID_XENIX_OTHER   equ 03h         ; reserved for XENIX
FILESYSID_HPFS          equ 07h         ; reserved for HPFS
FILESYSID_NOVELL        equ 64h         ; reserved for Novell
FILESYSID_PCIX          equ 75h         ; reserved for PC/IX
FILESYSID_CPM           equ DBh         ; reserved for CP/M
```

The boot sector always contains a boot program and a disk format record known as the BOOTRECORD. The program shares this space within the limited sector size, typically 512 bytes. The BOOTRECORD identifies both the physical and logical layout of a disk and contains information like the number of sectors on disk, the size of each sector, the number of disk heads, and the location of disk areas like the FAT and root directory. Because each disk carries information about its layout, both physical and logical, disk exchange between systems and different versions of DOS is robust and reliable even between several hundred or thousands of different vendors.

Some disks are partitioned in order to support multiple operating systems or several logical drives. Each partition may not always contain a DOS-supported file system. DOS partitions within a single disk drive will eventually be accessible as a DOS logical drive.

The boot sector program is shown in Figure 2-3. The start of the boot sector program begins the BOOTRECORD, which itself begins with three bytes reserved for a jump instruction around the boot record. The boot program expects the drive, expressed as a hardware unit code, in the DL register. It also expects that the BIOS has copied a pointer to the correct Disk Parameter Table into the int 1Eh address. The Drive Parameter Table address, stored at int 1Eh, is a convention established between the BIOS and int 13h, the disk access function. Typical parameters define hardware-specific values such as the size of the gap between sectors.

The boot program is distributed in the disk that comes with this book, but it should never be run directly from the command line. It is meant to be called only by the BIOS. It will clobber low-memory variables and potentially disable your system. To emphasize this point, the normal ASM file extension has been replaced with a TXT extension. In addition, a deliberate syntax error has been placed in the file that will prevent it from assembling correctly.

The boot program begins by initializing the stack pointer to just below the loader where it can temporarily save some critical variables. The drive unit code and the BIOS disk parameter table are copied into this space. Once this is accomplished, the boot disk is reset. This verifies that the disk is indeed a legitimate disk.

The program then computes the location of the root directory, beginning at label RxDOSLOAD_08. It takes the number of copies of the FAT multiplied by the size in sectors of a FAT table and adds the number of hidden and reserved sectors. The root directory is read into a buffer area, which by convention is established at address 0050:0000.

How does the boot program know to load the io.sys program? Conventional wisdom would seem to dictate that it arbitrarily loads the first program that it finds on the directory or that at least it checks the SYSTEM and possibly the HIDDEN attributes. Neither is true. Whether it may have done so at one time is beyond speculation, but it does not do so today. The boot program physically compares the filenames and extensions of the first two directory entries in the root directory to MS-DOS-supplied filenames. The boot program specifically checks for the files with the names io.sys and msdos.sys.

Because of the way the boot program works, an MS-DOS version of DOS cannot be replaced with a competitive version, say one from IBM or Novell, without changing the boot program, a function normally performed only by the FORMAT utility (when used with the /s switch). That is, to install a competitive DOS product, the boot program on the hard disk must be changed. Competitive versions must be able to change the boot program and ideally restore it if at some later date the installation must be undone.

The choice made by the MS-DOS boot program to compare specific filenames instead of checking attributes could be more readily justified if the program searched the entire root directory. This would permit the placement of these files anywhere in the root directory and lead to greater flexibility when installing new versions. Unfortunately, the program checks only the first two directory entries, the exact names must match, and files must be in the correct order.

If the first two entries don't compare, the routine jumps or falls into the error message routine, displays the error, and waits for keyboard action. It then issues the reboot interrupt, int 19h. It does not expect the int instruction to return.

If these files are located where expected, the cluster address of the first directory entry is taken and converted to a sector address. Clusters are always an index reference from the root directory, so the sector address of a file is its cluster address minus two (adjusting for the two clusters taken up by the root directory) multiplied by the number of sectors per cluster. This offset is added to the root directory address, forming the actual address of the file.

The boot sector loader does not actually load the entire io.sys file (or in RxDOS, the rxdosbio.sys file). It loads only the first three sectors of the file beginning at 0070:0000. To load more sectors would mean being capable of understanding the FAT data structure, something that the limited-space boot sector program is not capable of doing.

The boot sector program actually loads a more sophisticated loader for the remainder of DOS, a FAT-aware loader that we discuss in the next section.

Figure 2-3. RxDOS boot sector program

```
;///////////////////////////////////////////////////////////;
;  Disk Parameter Block                                      ;
;...........................................................;


        DISKPARAM struc
_dptControlTimers       dw ?            ; see below for definition
_dptMotorOffDelay       db ?            ; clock ticks
_dptBytesPerSector      db ?            ; 00 = 128, 01 = 256, ...
_dptSectorsPerTrack     db ?            ;
_dptGapLength           db ?            ; gap between sectors
                                        ;  2Ah = 5.25"
                                        ;  1Bh = 3.5"
_dptDataLength          db ?            ;
_dptFormatGapLength     db ?            ; gap length when formatting
_dptFormatFillerByte    db ?            ; default F6h.
_dptHeadSettleTime      db ?            ; in milliseconds.
_dptMotorStartTime      db ?            ; in 1/8 seconds.
        DISKPARAM ends


;- - - - - - - - - - - - - - - - - - - - - - - - - - - - - -
; Control Timers
;- - - - - - - - - - - - - - - - - - - - - - - - - - - - - -

DPT_STEPRATEMASK        equ 0F000h      ; bits 15-12
DPT_HEADUNLOADTIME      equ 00F00h      ; bits 11-08 (0fh = 240 ms)

DPT_HEADLOADTIME        equ 00FEh       ; bits 07-01 (01h = 4 ms)
DPT_NONDMA_MODE         equ 0001h       ; bit 0 (always 0)


;- - - - - - - - - - - - - - - - - - - - - - - - - - - - - -
; reserved on stack
;- - - - - - - - - - - - - - - - - - - - - - - - - - - - - -
_stackReserved          equ +40
_readHead               equ 22
_readSector             equ 20
_readTrack              equ 18
_readDrive              equ 16
_rootDirectory          equ 12
_diskParameterTable     equ 0

ROMBIOS_DISKTABLE       equ ( 1Eh * 4 )


;- - - - - - - - - - - - - - - - - - - - - - - - - - - - - -
; buffers start elsewhere
;- - - - - - - - - - - - - - - - - - - - - - - - - - - - - -
                        org 500h                ; 0050:0000
RXDOS_READBUFFER:
                        org 700h                ; 0070:0000
RXDOS_DOSLOADBUFFER:


;- - - - - - - - - - - - - - - - - - - - - - - - - - - - - -
; assume starts at 0000:7C00
;- - - - - - - - - - - - - - - - - - - - - - - - - - - - - -
```

```
                        org 7C00h                 ; 07C0:0000
RxDOS_START:            jmp RxDOS_LOAD

; this information is standard for every boot sector

__bsOemName             db 8 dup(?)               ; 'RxDOS' if formatted by us
__bsBytesPerSector      dw ?                      ; 512 is default
__bsSectorsPerCluster   db ?
__bsResSectors          dw ?
__bsNumCopiesFAT        db ?
__bsMaxAllocRootDir     dw ?
__bsMaxSectors          dw ?                      ; if zero, see huge sectors
__bsMediaDescriptor     db ?
__bsSectorsPerFat       dw ?
__bsSectorsPerTrack     dw ?
__bsHeads               dw ?
__bsHiddenSectors       dd ?
__bsHugeSectors         dd ?


__bsDriveNumber         db ?
                        db ?
__bsBootSignature       db ?                      ; 29h if extended boot sector
__bsVolumeId            db 11 dup(?)              ; not same as DOS Volume Id
__bsFileSystemType      db 8 dup(?)

;- - - - - - - - - - - - - - - - - - - - - - - - - - - - - -
; the RxDOS boot process begins here
;- - - - - - - - - - - - - - - - - - - - - - - - - - - - - -
RxDOS_LOAD:
        cli                                       ; no interrupts
        cld                                       ; all that we need to init
        xor ax, ax
        mov ss, ax                                ; set stack
        mov sp, 7C00h - _stackReserved

        mov bp, sp
        mov byte ptr [ _readDrive ][ bp ], dl

        mov ds, ax
        mov es, ax
        mov bx, offset ROMBIOS_DISKTABLE
        lds si, es:[ bx ]
        lea di, offset [ _diskParameterTable ][ bp ]
        mov word ptr es:[ _pointer ][ bx ], di
        mov word ptr es:[ _segment ][ bx ], ax
        mov cx, size DISKPARAM
        rep movsb

        mov byte ptr [ _diskParameterTable._dptHeadSettleTime ][ bp ], 15
        mov cx, word ptr [ __bsSectorsPerTrack ]
        mov byte ptr [ _diskParameterTable._dptSectorsPerTrack ][ bp ], cl

        sti
        int 13h                                   ; reset disk drive (ax = 0)
        jc RxDOSLOAD_Error                        ; if error ->
```

```
;- - - - - - - - - - - - - - - - - - - - - - - - - - - - - -
; if no huge sectors, fix up huge sectors
;- - - - - - - - - - - - - - - - - - - - - - - - - - - - - -
        mov ds, ax
        mov ax, word ptr [ __bsMaxSectors ]
        or ax, ax                             ; not a huge address disk ?
        jz RxDOSLOAD_08                       ; yes ->

        mov word ptr [ __bsHugeSectors ], ax

;- - - - - - - - - - - - - - - - - - - - - - - - - - - - - -
; compute logical sector address of Root Directory
;- - - - - - - - - - - - - - - - - - - - - - - - - - - - - -
RxDOSLOAD_08:
        mov bp, sp                            ; restore stack frame.
        mov al, byte ptr [ __bsNumCopiesFAT ]
        mul word ptr [ __bsSectorsPerFat ]
        add ax, word ptr [ __bsHiddenSectors. _low ]
        adc dx, word ptr [ __bsHiddenSectors. _high ]

        add ax, [ __bsResSectors ]
        adc dx, 0000

        mov word ptr [ _rootDirectory. _low ][ bp ], ax
        mov word ptr [ _rootDirectory. _high ][ bp ], dx

    ; read first sector of Root Directory

        mov bx, offset RXDOS_READBUFFER
        call RxDOSPerformRead
        jc RxDOSLOAD_Error                    ; if error ->

        mov di, offset RXDOS_READBUFFER
        mov si, offset RxDOS_RXDOSBIOSYS
        mov cx, sizeFILENAME
        rep cmpsb                             ; compare first name
        jnz RxDOSLOAD_Error                   ; if not equal ->

        mov di, offset (RXDOS_READBUFFER. sizeDIRENTRY)
      ; mov si, offset RxDOS_RXDOSSYS         ; (si already set properly)
        mov cx, sizeFILENAME
        rep cmpsb                             ; compare second name
        jz RxDOSLOAD_LoadDOS                  ; if equal ->

;- - - - - - - - - - - - - - - - - - - - - - - - - - - - - -
; can't load
;- - - - - - - - - - - - - - - - - - - - - - - - - - - - - -
RxDOSLOAD_Error:
        mov si, offset RxDOS_NOTASYSTEMDISK
        call RxDOSLOAD_DisplayMsg
        xor ax, ax
        int 16h                               ; wait on any key
        int 19h                               ; will restart load
        jmp RxDOSLOAD_Error
```

```
;- - - - - - - - - - - - - - - - - - - - - - - - - - - - - -
; load DOS
;- - - - - - - - - - - - - - - - - - - - - - - - - - - - - -
RxDOSLOAD_LoadDOS:
        mov ax, word ptr [ RXDOS_READBUFFER. deStartCluster ]
        dec ax
        dec ax                                  ; subtract 2

        mov cl, [ __bsSectorsPerCluster ]
        xor ch, ch
        mul cx

        add ax, word ptr [ _rootDirectory. _low  ][ bp ]
        adc dx, word ptr [ _rootDirectory. _high ][ bp ]
        mov bx, offset RXDOS_DOSLOADBUFFER       ; where to load
        mov cx, 3                                ; read three sectors
      ; mov cl, byte ptr [ __bsSectorsPerCluster ]; (why not entire cluster)

RxDOSLOAD_LoadDOS_08:
        call RxDOSPerformRead
        jc RxDOSLOAD_Error                       ; if error ->

        add bx, [ __bsBytesPerSector ]
        add ax, 0001
        adc dx, 0000
        loop RxDOSLOAD_LoadDOS_08

        mov ch, byte ptr [ __bsMediaDescriptor ]
        mov dl, byte ptr [ _readDrive ][ bp ]
        mov bx, word ptr [ _rootDirectory. _high ][ bp ]
        mov ax, word ptr [ _rootDirectory. _low  ][ bp ]
        jmp RXDOS_DOSLOADBUFFER                  ; jump into DOS ->

;- - - - - - - - - - - - - - - - - - - - - - - - - - - - - -
; Display Message, wait for ANY key
;- - - - - - - - - - - - - - - - - - - - - - - - - - - - - -
RxDOSLOAD_DisplayMsg:
        lodsb                                    ; get character (ds:si)
        or al, al                                ; null terminator ?
        jz RxDOSLOAD_Return                       ; done ->

        mov ah, 0Eh
        mov bx, 0007h
        int 10h
        jmp RxDOSLOAD_DisplayMsg

RxDOSLOAD_Return:
        ret


;- - - - - - - - - - - - - - - - - - - - - - - - - - - - - -
; perform disk read
;   ------------------------
;   dx:ax logical sector to read
;   es:bx read buffer address
;- - - - - - - - - - - - - - - - - - - - - - - - - - - - - -
```

```
RxDOSPerformRead:
        push bp
        push dx
        push ax
        push cx

        div word ptr [ __bsSectorsPerTrack ]
        inc dl
        mov byte ptr [ _readSector ][ bp ], dl

        xor dx, dx
        div word ptr [ __bsHeads ]
      ; mov [ _readHead ][ bp ], ax              ; don't need to save heads
      ; mov [ _readTrack ][ bp ], dl             ; dont need to save track
        mov dh, dl                               ; track

        clc
        mov cl, 6
        shl ah, cl                               ; move read head up
        or ah, [ _readSector ][ bp ]             ; unused portion of sector
        mov cx, ax
        xchg ch, cl

        mov dl, byte ptr [ _readDrive ][ bp ]
        mov ax, 0201h                            ; read one sector.
        int 13h

        pop cx
        pop ax
        pop dx
        pop bp
        ret

RxDOSLOAD_ErrReturn:
        stc
        ret

;- - - - - - - - - - - - - - - - - - - - - - - - - - - - - - -
; match entries
;- - - - - - - - - - - - - - - - - - - - - - - - - - - - - - -
RxDOS_RXDOSBIOSYS:    db 'RXDOSBIOSYS'
RxDOS_RXDOSSYS:       db 'RXDOS   SYS'

RxDOS_NOTASYSTEMDISK:db 'Non-System disk or disk error', 0Dh, 0Ah
                     db 'Press any key to continue', 00h


;- - - - - - - - - - - - - - - - - - - - - - - - - - - - - - -
; partition table
;- - - - - - - - - - - - - - - - - - - - - - - - - - - - - - -

                    org RxDOS_START+200h-2
RxDOS_BootSignature: db 0AAh, 055h
```

Booting io.sys

The boot sector loader loads only a small portion of io.sys (or the file equivalent in IBM, Novell, or RxDOS versions). These first three sectors contain a FAT-aware loader that loads any COM style program, commencing with the remainder of io.sys, and eventually will load msdos.sys.

In pre-DOS 5 versions, the io.sys loader relocated itself high so that it could load the remainder of io.sys back at address 0070:0000. However, the process of loading DOS changed with DOS 5 and 6. It doesn't know exactly the final load address of io.sys until much later in the boot process, not until after it has processed config.sys. Therefore, with DOS 5 and 6, the io.sys loader loads at 0070:0000. It then determines the size of memory and adjusts memory downward by a computed constant (the expected size of io.sys and msdos.sys). The remainder of io.sys is loaded beginning at this address.

The MS-DOS version of io.sys checks the existing hardware configuration, determining the manufacturer type and jettisoning drivers that come prepackaged with DOS that may not be required by a specific build or hardware. RxDOS is distributed with a minimum set of drivers that it intends to keep. For virtually all standard hardware, the effect is largely the same, except that some manufacturers may have specialized software or hardware that provides additional support or better performance.

MS-DOS is distributed to manufacturers and licensees in the form of an adaptation kit, known as OAK, or the OEM Adaptation Kit. The adaptation kit provides the contents of msdos.sys in object file format, whereas the boot and io.sys components are largely distributed in source form (as ASM files). The final result of the io.sys module depends on specific customized changes made by the manufacturer or distributor.

Determining which drivers to retain is part of a larger process within the io.sys startup that assesses what devices are available in a specific system configuration, primarily the number of supportable block devices. Block devices is a term used in DOS to refer to random access hard disks. Devices that are sequentially processed but that may require block transfers cannot be treated as block devices in DOS and must be handled as character devices. The device driver would be required to handle whatever blocking was required. These types of devices would be nonstandard from DOS's point of view and would require device drivers loaded from the config file.

Inside DOS, a block device is a device that is assigned a drive letter. These devices are handled by device drivers, some of which may have to be supported by independently loaded drivers much like the nonstandard devices. The remaining block devices supportable by DOS are drivers that are either specifically packaged by an OEM or identified as standard by the BIOS. DOS recognizes two forms of standard devices: removable and fixed.

The point of all this is to distinguish between different types of block devices and to affix where and how the recognition of devices is accomplished. Unless provided for in a special case, such as when the OEM packages additional drivers, the standard behavior of io.sys is to only recognized devices, block or character, that have been identified by the BIOS.

BIOS has a recognition scheme for block devices. If a hardware device fits into this scheme, it may then be accessed by the int 13h (disk i/o) function. It is these devices that in turn are recognized as standard block device drivers in io.sys. Other block device drivers may attach themselves seamlessly through installable device drivers when they are listed in the `config.sys` file. This permits `VDISK` and networked drives to act as if they were just another block device.

The major point of this is that `io.sys` recognizes only the devices that the BIOS recognizes. The total number of block devices supported by the default driver in `io.sys` is taken from values saved by the BIOS. This number is saved at the lead byte of the device name in the default block driver's header.

The number of nonremovable disk drives is taken from the BIOS communications area at `0040:0075`. The number of removable block devices, that is, the number of floppy disk drives, is taken from the installed hardware status word provided by int 11h. For systems that contain only a single floppy drive, `io.sys` essentially manufactures a `B:` drive. `io.sys` reports that it supports a `B:` drive even when one doesn't exist. In general, most users of a single drive system are fairly happy with the low-level support provided by `io.sys` when two drives share the same physical drive unit.

For reasons that I have never understood, there can be no missing unit drive numbers within `io.sys`. As we describe in Chapter 5, block devices do not have names like character device counterparts. Instead, the lead byte of the name field contains the number of block devices that it will support. This is a workable but somewhat strange design. As block device drivers are added to the device driver chain, each new device describes how many block device units it will support and not which specific driver codes. Unit codes are not tied to specific drivers or specific devices. If it supports a single drive, it places a `01` in the block device name and not the unit code that it recognizes, such as `F:` or a physical hardware unit code. We discuss how unit codes are resolved into supported drives in Chapter 2, but one implication is that at the `io.sys` level there cannot be any missing drives.

Having completed the evaluation of device drivers, `msdos.sys` is loaded and control is transferred to its SYSINIT code. Within `io.sys`, the code detects the hardware reported to by the BIOS. It first determines the amount of memory by fetching the value returned by int 12h. This value is represented in kilobytes and must be converted to a paragraph address. It is multiplied by 64 since there are 64 paragraphs per Kilobyte.

The number of floppy drives is determined by checking the hardware configuration flags by using the int 11h function. If no floppy drives are reported, the Read Drive Parameters subfunction of int 13h is used to access the disk subsystem of the BIOS directly. This function reports, among other information, the number of floppy and hard drives detected by the BIOS. Useful as this is, it is insufficient to actually determine the number of DOS drives. A physical drive may have been partitioned so as to represent more than a single DOS logical drive.

Detecting the actual number of DOS drives is the function or service provided by `io.sys`. It presumes that each floppy drive is not partitionable. Further, if it detects more than two floppy drives, it assigns the first two floppy drives (actually referred to as removable media drives in DOS parlance) to logical units 0 and 1, representing drives `A:` and `B:`. Any additional removable drives will be assigned to drives above the drive codes assigned to fixed disks. The first fixed disk drive, typically a hard disk, is always assigned to the `C:` drive. `io.sys` checks the partition table of each fixed drive detected by the BIOS and assigns a drive letter to each DOS partition detected. All primary partitions in all drives are assigned first, and then all secondary partitions in all drives are assigned as they are encountered.

```
(from rxdosbio.asm)
        jmp RxDOSBIOS_EvaluateHardware
        ...


        ;'''''''''''''''''''''''''''''''''''''''''''''''''''''''''''';
        ;  Hardware Evaluation and Startup                           ;
        ;- - - - - - - - - - - - - - - - - - - - - - - - - - - - - -;
        ;                                                            ;
        ;  The small IO.SYS loader transfers control to here with the ;
        ;  following arguments:                                       ;
        ;                                                            ;
        ;  DL   unit address of startup drive                        ;
        ;                                                            ;
        ;                                                            ;
        ;............................................................;

RxDOSBIOS_EvaluateHardware:
        cli
        cld
        mov ax, cs
        mov ds, ax
        mov es, ax
        mov ss, ax
        mov sp, offset RxDOSBIOS_TemporaryStack      ; stack is below this module
        sti

;- - - - - - - - - - - - - - - - - - - - - - - - - - - - - - - - - -
;  initialize arguments on stack
;- - - - - - - - - - - - - - - - - - - - - - - - - - - - - - - - - -
        Entry
        def      _fixedDrives                    ; number of fixed drives
        def      _floppyDrives                   ; number of floppy disks

        mov byte ptr cs:[ RxDOSBIOS_INITBLOCK. initBootDrive ], dl
        mov word ptr cs:[ RxDOSBIOS_INITBLOCK. initLowMemSegment ], es

        mov word ptr cs:[ RxDOSBIOS_INITBLOCK. initDeviceChain. _segment ], cs
        mov word ptr cs:[ RxDOSBIOS_INITBLOCK. initDeviceChain. _pointer ], offset CON

;- - - - - - - - - - - - - - - - - - - - - - - - - - - - - - - - - -
;  Determine the amount of actual memory
;- - - - - - - - - - - - - - - - - - - - - - - - - - - - - - - - - -
        int 12h                                 ; get memory size
        mov word ptr cs:[ RxDOSBIOS_INITBLOCK. initMemParagraphs ], ax

;- - - - - - - - - - - - - - - - - - - - - - - - - - - - - - - - - -
;  Determine number of floppy drives
;- - - - - - - - - - - - - - - - - - - - - - - - - - - - - - - - - -
        int 11h                                 ; read hardware configuration
        mov word ptr [ _floppyDrives ][ bp ], 0000   ; number of floppy disks

        test ax, 1                              ; floppy disks listed ?
        jz RxDOSBIOS_EvalHardware_08            ; if no ->
```

```
        shr ax, 1                                   ; floppy bit
        shr ax, 1                                   ; math coprocessor
        shr ax, 1                                   ; memory (xt only)
        shr ax, 1                                   ;
        shr ax, 1                                   ; video mode bits
        shr ax, 1                                   ;
        and ax, 0003h
        inc ax
        jmp short RxDOSBIOS_EvalHardware_12

RxDOSBIOS_EvalHardware_08:
        push bp
        mov ah, 8                                   ; read parameters
        mov dl, 0                                   ; unit 0
        int 13h

        mov al, dl                                  ; number of drives (if any )
        mov ah, 0                                   ; restore stack reference
        pop bp                                      ; if drives reported ->
        jnc RxDOSBIOS_EvalHardware_12
        xor ax, ax

RxDOSBIOS_EvalHardware_12:
        mov word ptr [ _floppyDrives ][ bp ], ax    ; number of floppy disks

;- - - - - - - - - - - - - - - - - - - - - - - - - - - - - - - -
;  Determine number of hard disk drives
;- - - - - - - - - - - - - - - - - - - - - - - - - - - - - - - -
        xor bx, bx
        mov ax, 40h
        mov es, ax
        mov al, byte ptr es:[ _BIOS_NumFixedDrives ][ bx ]
        mov word ptr [ _fixedDrives ][ bp ], ax     ; number of fixed drives

;- - - - - - - - - - - - - - - - - - - - - - - - - - - - - - - -
;  determine (manufacture) floppy drives
;- - - - - - - - - - - - - - - - - - - - - - - - - - - - - - - -
        or ax, ax                                   ; if no hard disk, total is fine
        jnz RxDOSBIOS_EvalHardware_20               ; add 2 floppy drives ->

        cmp word ptr [ _floppyDrives ][ bp ], 0000  ; number of floppy disks
        jz RxDOSBIOS_EvalHardware_22               ; if diskless system ->

RxDOSBIOS_EvalHardware_20:
        mov word ptr [ _floppyDrives ][ bp ], 2     ; if hard disk or one floppy

RxDOSBIOS_EvalHardware_22:
        mov ax, word ptr [ _floppyDrives ][ bp ]    ; total drives is
        add ax, word ptr [ _fixedDrives ][ bp ]     ;  total of both.
        mov byte ptr cs:[ RxDOSBIOS_INITBLOCK. initTotalDrives ], al
        mov byte ptr cs:[ block. devname ], al      ; block device header

;- - - - - - - - - - - - - - - - - - - - - - - - - - - - - - - -
;  Setup remainder of INIT Block
;- - - - - - - - - - - - - - - - - - - - - - - - - - - - - - - -
```

```
        mov word ptr cs:[ initRelocHighBegAddress. _segment ], cs
        mov word ptr cs:[ initRelocHighBegAddress. _pointer ],
                            offset RxDOSBIOS_Start
        mov word ptr cs:[ initRelocHighSize          ],
                            RxDOSBIOS_LastAddress - RxDOSBIOS_Start
        mov word ptr cs:[ initRelocHighNotify        ], -1

        mov word ptr cs:[ initRelocLowBegAddress . _segment ], 0000
        mov word ptr cs:[ initRelocLowBegAddress . _pointer ], 0000
        mov word ptr cs:[ initRelocLowSize          ], 0000
        mov word ptr cs:[ initRelocHighNotify        ], -1

;- - - - - - - - - - - - - - - - - - - - - - - - - - - - - - - - - -
; Jump to Loader with Cluster and Load Address
;- - - - - - - - - - - - - - - - - - - - - - - - - - - - - - - - - -
        setES cs
        mov bx, offset RxDOSBIOS_LastAddress
        add bx, (PARAGRAPH - 1)
        and bx, NOT (PARAGRAPH - 1)                 ; round up to next para

        jmp Loader

        ;'''''''''''''''''''''''''''''''''''''''''''''''''''''''''''';
        ; Init Load Block                                           ;
        ;...........................................................;

RxDOSBIOS_INITBLOCK             db sizeSYSINIT dup(0)
```

The SYSINIT Code

SYSINIT is a discardable section of code loaded with `msdos.sys`. It is responsible for initializing DOS. It begins by initializing a fully functioning DOS with a minimal number of buffers and SFTs. After all, at this early stage it has no concept of the number of additional drives or buffers that will be required, nor of their eventual location in memory. SYSINIT processes the `config.sys` file, reallocates the required DOS data structures at their permanent location, relocates `io.sys` and `msdos.sys`, and finally transfers control to the command shell program. The SYSINIT code in RxDOS is contained within the `rxdosini.asm` module. It is called by a jump from the `io.sys` loader.

The initialization code of MS-DOS is slightly different in RxDOS. In MS-DOS, the `io.sys` code loads the `msdos.sys` file and makes a far call to the 0000h address of the newly loaded file. It passes to `msdos.sys` two arguments.

```
DX      low memory size in paragraphs
DS:SI   start address of device driver chain
```

`msdos.sys` initializes and processes the `config.sys` file and returns to the `io.sys` initialize routine the following parameters:

```
AX       bytes to relocate when dos=high, or zero
CX       bytes to relocate when dos=low
DX       call-back to MSDOS.SYS with relocation segment
ES:DI    pointer to array of addresses containing:
         00h  address to start of SYSVARS (MSDOS.SYS data segment)
         04h  address of kernel's country code
```

This arrangement is specifically designed to minimize the information that the two files need to know about each other, but it does pass to io.sys the responsibility of relocating both files. io.sys has this responsibility because the action it takes is different depending on whether it is relocated high or low.

When io.sys is to be relocated high, it creates hooks for interrupts it services in lower memory. These low-memory hooks are necessary because access to the HMA cannot always be assured. The HMA may have been disabled by some software. The low-memory interrupt hook checks on the availability of the HMA, enables it if disabled, and then continues processing the interrupt. These hooks are not necessary when io.sys is loaded low and are removed from the final DOS load.

Within RxDOS, the initialize code in the msdos.sys equivalent, that is, in rxdos.com, is passed a pointer to a sysinit structure of information that contains the number of drives, the boot disk, the size of lower memory, the address, size, and relocation notification function to the code in io.sys that is to be relocated high and an identical set of parameters for the code that is to be relocated low. This information is passed in a SYSINITRECORD. The address of the record, shown here, is passed to the module in the ES:DI register pair.

```
;,,,,,,,,,,,,,,,,,,,,,,,,,,,,,,,,,,,,,,,,,,,,,,,,,,,,,,,,,,,,,,,,,,,;
;                                                                   ;
;   SYSINIT Parameters                                              ;
;- - - - - - - - - - - - - - - - - - - - - - - - - - - - - - - - - -;
;                                                                   ;
;   These parameters are passed between rxdosbio.com and rxdos      ;
;   at startup.                                                     ;
;                                                                   ;
;...................................................................;


        SYSINIT struc
initBootDrive             db ?          ; unit code
initTotalDrives           db ?          ; detected by IO.SYS
initLowMemSegment         dw ?          ; low memory segment
initMemParagraphs         dw ?          ; memory size
initDeviceChain           dd ?

initRelocHighBegAddress dd ?
initRelocHighSize         dw ?          ; bytes to relocate
initRelocHighNotify       dw ?          ; call back function address

initRelocLowBegAddress  dd ?          ; only used if IO.SYS reloc to HMA
initRelocLowSize          dw ?          ; bytes to relocate
initRelocLowNotify        dw ?          ; call back function address
        SYSINIT ends
```

Except for the notify call back routines, the io.sys equivalent in RxDOS does not expect to participate any further in the startup process. RxDOS chose this difference in the relationship between the two files because it seems easier to discard the rxdosbio.com init routine as soon as it completes loading the rxdos.com module. A single discardable initialize routine remains.

The notification call back routines provide the relocated module a chance to modify any far addresses that it may have, for example, far jumps between the low and high components of rxdosbio.com.

The SYSINIT code begins by setting a local stack and copying some critical parameters from the INIT data structure. There are five critical parameters: the boot drive, the total number of disk drives, the memory size, the lowest allocatable memory address, and a pointer to the device chain in the io.sys equivalent. Device drivers are linked to each other, a convenient mechanism that permits adding new drivers at any time. The start of the device chain is a parameter in the SYS-VARS area of the msdos.sys module. It must be chained to the io.sys driver list in order to complete the chain of all the drivers available so far. Once this process is completed, the data segment for the msdos.sys module is relocated as low as possible in memory.

Relocating the data segment has some ramifications for DOS. How does DOS remember where its data segment is when it is called by an application? Part of the data segment relocated low contains the int 21h service routine, which transfers control to the actual code segment for DOS. When DOS is called, it is called in its data segment. DOS changes stacks to a stack contained in the data segment. It is crucial for DOS that its stack segment points to its low-memory data segment.

In order to process the config.sys file, a critical step in initialization, it must become a fully functioning, though minimal, system. All the normal DOS functionality, such as reading files and loading drivers, should be enabled although the range of accessible drives depends on where and how drivers are loaded. Networked drives, for example, can be utilized as soon as the device driver is loaded.

DOS becomes fully functioning when the SYSINIT code, shown next, runs. The code begins by initializing the underlying available memory. The size of the lower portion of memory is taken from the BIOS reported memory size located at 0040:0013. Upper memory blocks are allocated after processing the config.sys file.

Other functions allocate and initialize space for the Drive Parameter Block, the Current Directory Structure, the File Tables, and finally the disk cache buffers. Later in this section we discuss how each specific function goes about initializing its components. The initialize code, up to the time that it calls the config file parsing, looks like this.

```
(from rxdos.asm)
        jmp RxDOS_initialize                    ; go initialize ->
        ...

(from rxdosini.asm)
        ;''''''''''''''''''''''''''''''''''''''''''''''''''''''''''''''''';
        ;  Initialize                                                    ;
        ;- - - - - - - - - - - - - - - - - - - - - - - - - - - - - - - -;
        ;                                                                ;
        ;  Expects from rxdosbio.sys:                                    ;
        ;                                                                ;
        ;  DL         unit code of startup disk                         ;
        ;  ES:DI      points to SYSINIT block                           ;
        ;................................................................;
```

```
RxDOS_initialize:
        cli                                               ; disable interrupts
        cld                                               ; set direction
        mov ax, cs
        mov ds, ax
        mov ss, ax
        mov sp, offset RxDOS_StackTop
        mov word ptr [ _RxDOS_CurrentSeg ], ss            ; Current Segment.

        sti

;- - - - - - - - - - - - - - - - - - - - - - - - - - - - - - - -
;  initialize data segment
;- - - - - - - - - - - - - - - - - - - - - - - - - - - - - - - -
        Entry
        def  _files, DEFAULT_FILES
        def  _buffers, DEFAULT_BUFFERS
        ddef _InitBlockPtr, es, di
        defbytes _execBlock, sizeEXEC

        mov dl, byte ptr es:[ initBootDrive ][ di ]
        mov byte ptr [ _RxDOS_BootDrive ], dl             ; boot drive

        mov cl, byte ptr es:[ initTotalDrives ][ di ]     ; number of block devices
        mov byte ptr [ _RxDOS_bNumBlockDev ], cl          ; number of block devices

        mov cx, word ptr es:[ initLowMemSegment ][ di ]   ; low memory segment
        mov word ptr ss:[ _RxDOS_pStartMemBlock ], cx     ; until relocation

        mov cx, word ptr es:[ initMemParagraphs ][ di ]   ; available memory size
        mov word ptr [ _RxDOS_MaxMemory ], ax             ; memory available

        mov ax, word ptr es:[ initDeviceChain. _pointer ][ di ]
        mov dx, word ptr es:[ initDeviceChain. _segment ][ di ]
        mov word ptr [ _RxDOS_NULLDev. _pointer ], ax
        mov word ptr [ _RxDOS_NULLDev. _segment ], dx

;- - - - - - - - - - - - - - - - - - - - - - - - - - - - - - - -
;  initialized Environment Size
;- - - - - - - - - - - - - - - - - - - - - - - - - - - - - - - -
        mov ax, offset _RxDOS_SharedBuffer
        mov word ptr [ _RxDOS_pDTA. _pointer ], ax
        mov word ptr [ _RxDOS_pDTA. _segment ], ds

        mov word ptr [ _RxDOS_EnvironmentSize ], (DEFAULT_MINENVIRONMENT / PARAGRAPH)
        mov word ptr [ _RxDOS_CurrentPSP      ], 0000

;- - - - - - - - - - - - - - - - - - - - - - - - - - - - - - - -
;  relocate data segment low
;- - - - - - - - - - - - - - - - - - - - - - - - - - - - - - - -
        mov dx, word ptr ds:[ _RxDOS_pStartMemBlock ]     ; where to relocate ds
        call relocateDataSegmentLow

;- - - - - - - - - - - - - - - - - - - - - - - - - - - - - - - -
;  initialize memory and other buffers
;- - - - - - - - - - - - - - - - - - - - - - - - - - - - - - - -
```

```
        call RxDOSini_MemorySubSystem
        call RxDOSini_DPBSubSystem
        call RxDOSini_CDSSubSystem

        getarg ax, _files
        call RxDOSini_SFTSubSystem

        getarg ax, _buffers
        call RxDOSini_CCBSubSystem
        call RxDOSini_Drivers                        ; link drivers

;- - - - - - - - - - - - - - - - - - - - - - - - - - - - - - - - -
; parse CONFIG.SYS file
;- - - - - - - - - - - - - - - - - - - - - - - - - - - - - - - - -

        xor di, di
        mov ax, word ptr [ _RxDOS_MaxMemory ]        ; available memory
        sub ax, 64 * ( 1024 / 16 )                   ; segments
        mov es, ax

        call configProcessing
        call RxDOSini_Drivers
```

What comes out of the config processing code are reallocated data structures and a set of loaded device drivers. If the config file enabled access to the UMB, this area is also initialized. In fact, there is the very real likelihood that device drivers have already been loaded into this space. At this point, the memory layout appears as shown in Figure 2-4, where everything is in position except for the code portion of DOS.

Figure 2-4. Memory after drivers are loaded

The remainder of the DOS initialize code does the following: DOS searches for the header address of both the CON and CLOCK device drivers. It then opens three files, one each for devices AUX, CON, and PRN. It then relocates the code segment to its final location. The entire code segment is copied except for the init code currently running.

The memory size is fixed up to ensure that it points to a full system. The memory size was held low to protect the DOS code loaded high in low memory. The remainder of the init code performs a DOS function call to load and execute the command shell. The command shell should not return by performing a terminate since the calling code will no longer exist.

The remaining code appears as follows:

```
;- - - - - - - - - - - - - - - - - - - - - - - - - - - - - - -
;  locate special drivers
;- - - - - - - - - - - - - - - - - - - - - - - - - - - - - - -
RxDOS_DRIVERinit_04:
        mov ax, ( DEV_STDINPUT + DEV_STDOUTPUT )
        call checkforDeviceType
        jc RxDOS_DRIVERinit_10

        mov word ptr [ _RxDOS_pCONdriver. _pointer ], bx
        mov word ptr [ _RxDOS_pCONdriver. _segment ], es

RxDOS_DRIVERinit_10:
        mov ax, ( DEV_CLOCK )
        call checkforDeviceType
        jc RxDOS_DRIVERinit_12

        mov word ptr [ _RxDOS_pCLOCKdriver. _pointer ], bx
        mov word ptr [ _RxDOS_pCLOCKdriver. _segment ], es


;- - - - - - - - - - - - - - - - - - - - - - - - - - - - - - -
;  allocate STDIN, STDOUT, STDERR, STDAUX, STDPRN
;- - - - - - - - - - - - - - - - - - - - - - - - - - - - - - -
RxDOS_DRIVERinit_12:
        currSegment ds
        mov di, offset stdDeviceAssignTable

RxDOS_DRIVERinit_14:
        setES ds
        call checkforDeviceName                 ; locate device
        jc RxDOS_DRIVERinit_22                   ; if can't be located ->

        push bx                                  ; save pointer to driver
        push es                                  ; alloc SFT entry (es:bx)
        call FindAvailableSFTHandle
        mov word ptr [ stdIOHandle ][ di ], ax   ; save handle assigned

        pop word ptr es:[ sftDCB. _segment ][ bx ]
        pop word ptr es:[ sftDCB. _pointer ][ bx ]

        mov ax, word ptr [ stdDevInfo ][ di ]
        mov word ptr es:[ sftDevInfo ][ bx ], ax

RxDOS_DRIVERinit_22:
        add di, sizeStdRedirec
        cmp word ptr [ di ], -1                  ; at end of table ?
        jnz RxDOS_DRIVERinit_14                  ; not yet ->
```

```
;- - - - - - - - - - - - - - - - - - - - - - - - - - - - - - - - - -
; load Command.Com and transfer control
;- - - - - - - - - - - - - - - - - - - - - - - - - - - - - - - - - -
RxDOS_DRIVERinit_26:
        xor bx, bx
        mov ds, bx
        mov bx, ( 21h * 4 )                              ; int 21h
        mov word ptr __pointer [ bx ], offset _Interrupt_21
        mov word ptr __segment [ bx ], ss

        currSegment ds
        currSegment es
        lea di, offset _execBlock [ bp ]
        clearMemory sizeEXEC                             ; clear load exec block

        mov dx, offset _RxDOS_CommandShell
        Int21 ExecuteProgram, 00
        jmp RxDOS_DRIVERinit_26                          ; return not expected
```

Processing Config.sys

A major part of the work performed by the DOS init code is in the processing of the config.sys file. The config file is read, partially parsed, and saved in memory. Config statements are processed by type instead of the order in which they are encountered. This is necessary in part to avoid possible statement conflicts. For example, DOS cannot be loaded high unless a driver has already been loaded that has enabled access to the HMA. As important, statements are given priority in the order of their likely effect. The buffers statement is likely to require more space than files, so it is processed ahead of the rest of the space-allocating statements.

Although MS-DOS and RxDOS differ in the exact structures used in processing the config file, the two operating systems process the config files in similar ways. For example, both read, identify, and save the config file statements in a memory area before they are actually processed.

During the first pass, each statement read from the config file is identified by type and stored in a config lines buffer. The statement is not executed until pass two or three. Each statement saved in the lines buffer is preceded by a small header, a CONFIGLINE structure, consisting of the line number in the original file, the length of the statement, the type of statement, and a flags word. Type is identified from the first word in the config statement. Typical statement types are shown here. Each statement is null terminated.

```
(RxDOS assignments)
CONFIGTYPE_DOS              equ 0001h        ; dos = umb, high
CONFIGTYPE_NUMLOCK         equ 0002h        ; numlock = on | off
CONFIGTYPE_BREAK           equ 0003h        ; break = on | off
CONFIGTYPE_SET             equ 0004h        ; set var = arg

CONFIGTYPE_COUNTRY         equ 0005h        ; country = xxx [, ...]
CONFIGTYPE_DEVICE          equ 0006h        ; device devname [ parameters ]
CONFIGTYPE_DEVICEHIGH      equ 0007h        ; devicehigh devname [ parameters ]
```

The CONFIGLINE structure appears as follows:

```
;''''''''''''''''''''''''''''''''''''''''''''''''''''''''''''''';
; CONFIGLINE Structure (RxDOS)                                   ;
;...............................................................;

        CONFIGLINE struc
configType              dw ?                ; config statement type
configLength            dw ?                ; config line length
configFlags             dw ?                ; config statement line number
configLineNumber        dw ?                ; config statement line number
configServiceRtne       dw ?                ; config service routine
configStatement         db ?                ; statement starts here
        CONFIGLINE ends
```

For each statement type there exists a statement service handler function. The service routine executes the config line statement, which could involve reading the parameters in the statement or loading a device driver. Some service routines are fairly simple, for example, the handler shown for the buffers= statement. The number in the statement specifies the number of buffers to allocate. It is fetched from the remainder of the config file statement and used as a parameter to initialize routine. The get number routine checks to ensure that the value is within bounds. The default value is used if any errors occur in processing the statement.

```
;''''''''''''''''''''''''''''''''''''''''''''''''''''''''''''''';
; Buffers                                                        ;
;...............................................................;

_Config_Buffers:
        mov cx, DEFAULT_BUFFERS
        mov dx, CONFIGMAX_BUFFERS
        lea bx, offset _buffers [ bp ]
        call _getNumber

        call RxDOSini_CCBSubSystem
        ret
```

Beginning with DOS 6, the introduction of menus, a welcomed improvement to handle multiple configurations, means that not all the statements in the config file will be processed. Some config file statements will belong to menus that just won't be selected. When menus are used, the config file is divided into menu blocks. RxDOS marks all menus in [common] sections as enabled. Then, as the menu processing code selects blocks, it sets the enable status flag at the first statement of the block. All statements in the block are then considered enabled.

When menu processing completes, RxDOS scans through the entire config file checking through the menu blocks. If a menu block is not enabled, all the statements in the menu block are removed, ensuring that they will not be processed. Instead of physically removing strings, the statement types are changed to a remark type that will cause them to be subsequently ignored.

Internally, the end of menu processing and the removal of the unused config statements are considered the end of pass one even though one could argue that there were several passes through the statements. For purists, this is considered the end of logical pass one.

It is during pass two that the system is actually configured. A portion of the code that reconfigures the system is shown next. The `config` file is scanned for specific commands, beginning with the `dos` statement, followed by the `break`, `country`, `device`, and `devicehigh` statements. The other `config` file statements are handled later.

Immediately after loading low-memory devices, DOS attempts to link the upper memory blocks and then processes all device high statements. The upper memory link may have failed for one of several reasons ranging from a failure to load a UMB driver to the unavailability of space in the upper memory area. The device high load routine adjusts automatically for the unavailability of space in the UMB, acting as a low-memory device loader when required. Thus, no special action is required when the upper memory link fails.

```
;- - - - - - - - - - - - - - - - - - - - - - - - - - - - - - - - - -
;  reconfigure system
;- - - - - - - - - - - - - - - - - - - - - - - - - - - - - - - - - -

        getdarg es, di, _configStatements
        call processDOS                         ; dos =
        storarg _dosFlags, ax                   ; save flags

        call processBreak                       ; break = on | off
        call processCountry                     ; country =
        call processDevice                      ; device devname [ opts ]

        getarg ax, _dosFlags                    ; option flags
        call RxDOSini_LinkUpperMemory           ; attempt link upper memory

        getdarg es, di, _configStatements
        call processDeviceHigh                  ; devicehigh devname [ opts ]
```

Although lower memory is essentially mediated only by DOS, the upper memory blocks must be requested of an XMS driver like `himem.sys`. Function 10h acts substantially like DOS function 48h, where a block size in paragraphs is requested. If the block is too large, the largest available block size is returned. Because there isn't a single large pool of space in the UMB, several requests can be made for space until there is no longer any available space.

The function that links the upper memory blocks is show here.

```
(insert listing here)
        RxDOSini_LinkUpperMemory                ; attempt link upper memory
```

Device loading, whether to an upper memory block or not, is performed by using DOS function 4B03h, the load overlay function. This brings up an interesting question: Are we in DOS when reconfiguring its memory? Obviously not. The question of being in DOS revolves around whether a DOS function is currently executing. Since the reconfiguration code is not servicing a DOS function call, it cannot be in DOS. The code is technically no different from another application.

Function 4B03h serves the needs of device driver loading so well that it may have been designed specifically for driver loading. The function was designed to be loaded at a segment, which is consistent with DOS memory allocation strategy and is specifically designed to support loading of a separate program. That program can be loosely bound to the main program, as drivers are to DOS. In contrast, program overlays are usually much more tightly bound to the root or calling program, with complete address resolution for variable references.

Whatever the actual intent in the creation of the function, it provides two major benefits to device driver loading: DOS does not create a PSP for the overlay, and the loaded program is not automatically executed after it is loaded. The `config` manager takes on the responsibility of linking the driver into the driver chain and calling the driver's initialize code.

The code for loading device drivers follows. Surprisingly, the only change made in order to load devices high is to set the memory allocation strategy to access the upper memory blocks first. Memory allocation functions determine which memory block to allocate based on the setting of strategy flags. The search upper memory first flag is set using DOS function 5801h. The device high `config` statement mandates only that an available block in upper memory should be searched first.

One serious problem with function 4B03h, the load overlay function, is that it expects to receive the load segment address. This would presume that the code knew the size of the overlay or driver and that it has allocated the space necessary for the driver. RxDOS has extended the function to not require a preallocated block of memory. If the address of the overlay block is zero, the function will predetermine the program size based on its type, that is, whether it is a COM or EXE file. MS-DOS may use a variation of the function or an alternative mode of function 4Bh.

The code to load a device begins at `processDevice`. It loads the type of `config` statement and transfers control to a common load device routine. Device high statement processing begins at `processDeviceHigh`. It first saves the current allocation strategy and then changes it to first fit upper memory blocks. It next sets the `config` statement type and calls the common process function. When it returns, the original memory allocation strategy is reset. This does not release or alter the link or allocation already made to upper memory blocks.

The common processing routine extracts the device driver name from the remainder of the `config` line. It then utilizes the modified function 4B03 to allocate and load the device driver file. The device driver is linked to the head of the device driver chain and is then initialized. The common processing routine repeats this process for all device statements in the `config` file.

```
;,/////////////////////////////////////////////////////////////////';
;                                                                    ;
;   Process Device Statement(s)                                      ;
;- - - - - - - - - - - - - - - - - - - - - - - - - - - - - - - - - -;
;                                                                    ;
;   es:di  start of statements in saved config buffer                ;
;....................................................................;

processDevice:
        mov ax, CONFIGTYPE_DEVICE
        jmp processAnyDevice

;,/////////////////////////////////////////////////////////////////';
;                                                                    ;
;   Process DeviceHigh Statement(s)                                  ;
;- - - - - - - - - - - - - - - - - - - - - - - - - - - - - - - - - -;
;                                                                    ;
;   es:di  start of statements in saved config buffer                ;
;....................................................................;

processDeviceHigh:
        Entry
```

```
        ddef _ConfigStatements, es, di
        def  _memorystrategy

        Int21 GetAllocationStrategy                ; get current allocation scheme
        storarg _memorystrategy, ax

        mov bx, _MEM_FIRSTFIT_HIGH
        Int21 SetAllocationStrategy

        mov ax, CONFIGTYPE_DEVICEHIGH
        getdarg es, di, _ConfigStatements
        call processAnyDevice

        getarg bx, _memorystrategy
        Int21 SetAllocationStrategy
        Return

        ;'''''''''''''''''''''''''''''''''''''''''''''''''''''''''''';
        ;  Common Device Load                                       ;
        ;- - - - - - - - - - - - - - - - - - - - - - - - - - - - - -;
        ;                                                           ;
        ;  ax      type of statement to search                      ;
        ;  es:di   start of statements in saved config buffer       ;
        ;...........................................................;

processAnyDevice:
        Entry
        ddef _ConfigStatements, es, di
        def  _type, ax
        defbytes _devname, 128

processAnyDevice_08:
        getarg ax, _type
        call _findStatementType                    ; find statement type
        jc processAnyDevice_24                      ; if no more —>

        push es
        push di
        lea di, offset [ configStatement ][ di ]
        call ConfigPrompt                          ; check for ?= or F8 case
        jc processAnyDevice_12                      ; if ignore —>

    ; isolate device name

    ; load overlay

    ; link into device list

    ; initialize driver

      int 3
        Int21 ExecuteProgram, 03h                  ; load overlay

processAnyDevice_12:
```

```
         pop di
         pop es
         add di, word ptr es:[ configLength ][ di ]
         jmp processAnyDevice_08

;- - - - - - - - - - - - - - - - - - - - - - - - - - - - - -
; return
;- - - - - - - - - - - - - - - - - - - - - - - - - - - - - -
processAnyDevice_24:
         getdarg es, di, _ConfigStatements          ; return
         Return
```

So now that we have explained the mechanics of some of the more interesting pieces of config processing, the code can be examined in its proper and larger perspective. The config file processing code is listed next. It is passed the address of a block allocated to hold the interim states of the file in the ES:DI registers although in both MS-DOS and RxDOS the block begins at a segment boundary.

The code uses the scanDirectory function to locate the config file, which it expects to find in the root directory. The directory cluster address is passed in the DX register. The root directory is always cluster 0000 in RxDOS. In MS-DOS, the config.sys file is actually opened using DOS function 3Dh, File Open. Both are legitimate, and the MS-DOS option is better suited if eventually the file is moved from the root directory. Once the file is located, a DISKACCESS block is initialized. This block is used by lower-level file access functions to read the file and navigate through the FAT and is discussed at some length in Chapter 2.

As each line is read from the config file, all comments are removed and leading spaces are skipped. The line is scanned, and a null character is placed where comments, if any, are found, effectively ending the line. If the line contains all spaces and comments, it is dropped from further processing.

The comment character is by default the semicolon character (;), but it can be altered by the comment statement. Lines that begin with a colon (:) are also interpreted as remark lines. The general concept of the comment statement is being slowly added to config file processing. Versions prior to DOS 5 had no comment capability at all, and the end-user documentation for DOS 5 and 6, including the on-line help facility, fails to mention this command. The feature was always a programmer's feature in order to make the config file comment lines appear as familiar as possible to a power or knowledgeable user. Blocks of comment lines beginning with either the REM statement or a colon are more than sufficient and perhaps even more readable.

The only other special character handling is for block sections. Sections are created in the config file to handle and support menus. Section names are surrounded by square brackets, as in [sectionname]. The parser detects section names and special-handles the statement. When the left bracket is detected, the single-word name for the section is isolated as follows: The bracket and all spaces before the name are skipped; then the line is terminated at the first noncharacter, including all characters not considered to be delimiters. A section name can consist of letters and numbers and a few special characters.

If the config statement is not filtered by any of these checks, the first word of the statement is checked against a table of values using the _findCommand function. If the function detects a match, it returns the type id for the matched keyword together with the pointer to the first nonspace character immediately after the config line keyword. A CONFIGLINE record is built, and the statement is stored. Processing continues with the next line until the end of the config file is reached.

If an error was detected by the find command function, an error message is displayed, and processing continues with the next line.

```
;''''''''''''''''''''''''''''''''''''''''''''''''''''''''''''''';
;  Config File Processing                                        ;
;- - - - - - - - - - - - - - - - - - - - - - - - - - - - - - - -;
;                                                                ;
;  This module reads the entire  Config.sys  file from  a par-   ;
;  tially initialized system.  It expects  minimally  buffers,   ;
;  CDS, and other  DOS  data  structures.  Config  processing    ;
;  happens in two phases:  pass one gathers facts and pass two    ;
;  reconfigures data structures and loads drivers.               ;
;                                                                ;
;  Returns:                                                      ;
;  ds/es   both will point to ss                                 ;
;  ax      current drive                                         ;
;................................................................;

configProcessing:
        Entry
        ddef  _configStatements, es, di
        ddef  _configNextLine, es, di

        def   _comment    , ';'                     ; default comment character
        def   _charsread
        def   _linenumber , 0000
        def   _dosFlags,   0000

        defbytes _diskAccess, sizeDISKACCESS
        defbytes _linebuffer, 255

;- - - - - - - - - - - - - - - - - - - - - - - - - - - - - - - -
;  find/ open config.sys
;- - - - - - - - - - - - - - - - - - - - - - - - - - - - - - - -
        currSegment ds, es

        xor dx, dx
        mov al, byte ptr [ _RxDOS_CurrentDrive ]    ; startup drive
        mov di, offset _RxDOS_ConfigFile            ; search config file
        call scanDirectory                          ; open config.sys
        ifc configProcessing_Return                 ; if none found ->

;- - - - - - - - - - - - - - - - - - - - - - - - - - - - - - - -
;  find/ open config.sys
;- - - - - - - - - - - - - - - - - - - - - - - - - - - - - - - -
        push word ptr es:[ deFileSize. _low  ][ si ]
        push word ptr es:[ deFileSize. _high ][ si ]
        setES ss
        lea bx, _diskAccess [ bp ]                  ; build access control block
        call initdiskAccess                         ; [ax] is drive, [dx] is cluster
```

```
        pop word ptr ss:[ diskAcFileSize. _high ][ bx ]
        pop word ptr ss:[ diskAcFileSize. _low  ][ bx ]

configProcessing_12:
        getdarg es, di, _configNextLine
        mov word ptr es:[ configType   ][ di ], CONFIGTYPE_ENDOFARGS
        mov word ptr es:[ configLength ][ di ], 0000

        setES ss
        mov cx, 254
        lea di, offset _linebuffer [ bp ]
        lea bx, _diskAccess [ bp ]                       ; build access control block
        call readLine                                   ; read a line
        ifz configProcessing_36                         ; at end, reconfigure system ->

        inc word ptr [ _linenumber ][ bp ]              ; lines read
        lea di, offset _linebuffer [ bp ]

        getarg ax, _comment                             ; parse out comments
        call configRemoveComments                       ; remove comments
        jz configProcessing_12                          ; if nothing left on line ->
        mov word ptr [ _charsread ][ bp ], cx           ; characters read

        cmp byte ptr ss:[ di ], ':'                     ; comment line ?
        jz configProcessing_12                          ; yes, ignore ->
        cmp byte ptr ss:[ di ], '['                     ; block item specifier ?
        jz configProcessing_16                          ; yes ->

        mov si, offset _RxDOS_ConfigKeywords
        call _findCommand
        jnc configProcessing_20

        typeout msgUnknownCommandinConfig
        jmp configProcessing_12

;- - - - - - - - - - - - - - - - - - - - - - - - - - - - - - - - - -
;  [ blockitem_name ]
;- - - - - - - - - - - - - - - - - - - - - - - - - - - - - - - - - -
configProcessing_16:
        inc di
        call _skipSpaces                                ; skip any leading spaces

        push di
        call _scanToEndofName                           ; find terminating space
        mov byte ptr ss:[ di ], 0                       ; set a terminator

        pop di
        mov dx, CONFIGTYPE_MENUBLOCK                    ; menu block

;- - - - - - - - - - - - - - - - - - - - - - - - - - - - - - - - - -
;  go save statement
;- - - - - - - - - - - - - - - - - - - - - - - - - - - - - - - - - -
configProcessing_20:
        cmp dx, CONFIGTYPE_REM                          ; remark statement ?
        jz configProcessing_12                          ; ignore ->
```

```
        cmp dx, CONFIGTYPE_COMMENTS                        ; if comment, go process
        jz configProcessing_26                             ; process comment line ->

        lea si, offset _linebuffer [ bp ]
        getarg cx, _charsread
        sub cx, di
        add cx, si                                         ; length difference to remember
        mov si, di                                         ; source pointer

        getdarg es, di, _configNextLine
        mov word ptr es:[ configType    ][ di ], dx        ; save type

        mov ax, word ptr [ _linenumber ][ bp ]            ; get line number
        mov word ptr es:[ configLineNumber ][ di ], ax

        mov word ptr es:[ configLength ][ di ], cx
        add word ptr es:[ configLength ][ di ], (size CONFIGLINE)

    ; copy statement

        lea di, offset [ configStatement    ][ di ]        ; offset to statement
        rep movsb

        xor ax, ax
        stosb                                              ; null terminate

        mov di, word ptr [ _configNextLine ][ bp ]
        add di, word ptr es:[ configLength ][ di ]         ; advance beyond type
        mov word ptr [ _configNextLine ][ bp ], di
        jmp configProcessing_12

;- - - - - - - - - - - - - - - - - - - - - - - - - - - - - - - - - -
; process comment line
;- - - - - - - - - - - - - - - - - - - - - - - - - - - - - - - - - -
configProcessing_26:
        call _skipSpaces                                   ; skip any leading spaces

        mov ax, word ptr es:[ di ]                         ; get comment character
        cmp ah, ' ' + 1                                    ; space or other control ?
        jnc configProcessing_28                            ; no ->
        mov ah, 0

configProcessing_28:
        storarg _comment, ax                               ; save comment character(s)
        jmp configProcessing_12                            ; continue

;- - - - - - - - - - - - - - - - - - - - - - - - - - - - - - - - - -
; process menu
;- - - - - - - - - - - - - - - - - - - - - - - - - - - - - - - - - -
configProcessing_36:
        getdarg es, di, _configStatements
        call configMenu

        getdarg es, di, _configStatements
```

```
        call removeUnusedBlocks

;- - - - - - - - - - - - - - - - - - - - - - - - - - - - - - - - - - -
;  reconfigure system
;- - - - - - - - - - - - - - - - - - - - - - - - - - - - - - - - - - -
        getdarg es, di, _configStatements

        call processSwitchChar                     ; SwitchChar =
        call processNumLock                        ; NumLock = on | off
        call processDOS                            ; dos =
        storarg _dosFlags, ax                      ; save flags
        call RxDOSini_MemorySubSystem              ; re-initialize memory subsystem

        call processBreak                          ; break = on | off
        call processCountry                        ; country =

        getdarg es, di, _configStatements
        call processDevice                         ; device devicename [ options ]

        getarg ax, _dosFlags                       ; option flags
        call RxDOSini_LinkUpperMemory              ; attempt link upper memory

        getdarg es, di, _configStatements
        call processDeviceHigh                      ; device devicename [ options ]

        call processDrivParam                      ; drivparam =
        call processMultiTrack                     ; multitrack =
        call processSwitches                       ; switches =

        call processBuffers                        ; buffers =
        call processFCBS                           ; fcbs =
        call processFiles                          ; files =
        call processLastDrive                      ; lastdrive =
        call processShell                          ; shell =
        call processStack                          ; stacks =

;- - - - - - - - - - - - - - - - - - - - - - - - - - - - - - - - - - -
;  Return
;- - - - - - - - - - - - - - - - - - - - - - - - - - - - - - - - - - -
configProcessing_Return:
        Return
```

Menu processing begins once all the config file statements have been read and saved. The menu processor locates the first menu block and displays it on screen. It selects submenus according to selections made by the user. Menu processing largely comprises locating MENUITEM statements within a block and displaying their contents. DOS saves a pointer to these entries in a table. When a specific menu choice is made, the corresponding menu entry address is recovered, and the text reference is searched. Depending on its contents, a submenu may be displayed. Response time is rapid since the entire file is already preloaded in memory.

Each menu block selected by the user during the startup process is marked as ENABLED. After menu processing completes, the remaining unused menu blocks are removed by converting them to remark statements.

Once the menus have been processed, each of the `config` statements is processed. The statements are executed by type, with a specific sequence already described earlier in this section. Each processing routine is responsible for parsing its own statement variables. For example, the `files=` statement processor shown here expects a numeric value consisting of the number of SFTs to create. If you remove all the necessary control code that locates the `files` statement, the essential code that fetches the number of files is simply

```
mov cx, 1
mov dx, CONFIGMAX_FILES
call _getNumber
jc processFiles_12                      ; if beyond range ->
storarg _files, ax                      ; else ok to save
```

The code fetches a number and checks it against the minimum range value of one (1) in the CX register and the maximum value of CONFIGMAX_FILES in the DX register.

DOS can be made to prompt whether to include a `config` file statement. This can happen as a result of one of two possible user actions. If the F8 key is pressed during the menu startup process, a flag is set that forces each statement to be verified prior to being processed. The user may also have added a question mark just before the equal sign in a statement to force confirming the statement's inclusion in the boot sequence.

These cases are handled by the following code. The function detects whether a question mark exists just prior to the equal sign. If it does, or if the F8 flag is set, the `config` file statement is displayed on the screen followed by the options `[y,n]?`. If the user chooses to not include the statement, the carry flag is set, and the prompt function returns.

```
lea di, offset [ configStatement ][ di ]
call ConfigPrompt                       ; check for ?= or F8 case
jc processFiles_12                      ; if ignore ->
```

However, the statement is no longer available in its original source code form. The keywords and comments from any statement have been removed, so the prompt display code recreates the statement. The statement type is fetched from a table and displayed, followed by the retained portion of the original statement. This portion has no comments.

The files processing code appears as follows:

```
;''''''''''''''''''''''''''''''''''''''''''''''''''''''''''''';
;  Process Files Statement(s)                                 ;
;- - - - - - - - - - - - - - - - - - - - - - - - - - - - - - -;
;                                                             ;
;  es:di  start of statements in saved config buffer          ;
;.............................................................;

processFiles:

        Entry
        ddef _ConfigStatements, es, di
        def _files, DEFAULT_FILES
        def _fcbs, ax
```

```
processFiles_08:
        mov ax, CONFIGTYPE_FILES
        call _findStatementType              ; find statement type
        jc processFiles_24                   ; if no more ->

        push es
        push di
        lea di, offset [ configStatement ][ di ]
        call ConfigPrompt                    ; check for ?= or F8 case
        jc processFiles_12                   ; if ignore ->

        mov cx, 1
        mov dx, CONFIGMAX_FILES
        call _getNumber
        jc processFiles_12                   ; if beyond range ->
        storarg _files, ax                   ; else ok to save

processFiles_12:
        pop di
        pop es
        or word ptr es:[ configFlags ][ di ], CONFIGFLAG_PROCESSED
        add di, word ptr es:[ configLength ][ di ]
        jmp processFiles_08

;- - - - - - - - - - - - - - - - - - - - - - - - - - - - - - - - -
; return
;- - - - - - - - - - - - - - - - - - - - - - - - - - - - - - - - -
processFiles_24:
        getarg ax, _files                    ; return files
        add ax, word ptr [ _fcbs ][ bp ]
        call RxDOSini_SFTSubSystem           ; init SFTs

        getdarg es, di, _ConfigStatements
        Return
```

Having established how DOS boots itself up, we can continue by discussing how it processes the file system function calls.

C H A P T E R 3

The DOS File Functions

Overview—Software Layers—The Structure of a DOS Disk— File Handles—File
Control Blocks—Open File and Create—Directory Searching—The FAT
Structure—Logical Sector Numbers and Clusters

The DOS file system is the FAT-based file system. The FAT, or File Allocation Table, has been a part of DOS since its earliest inception and was one of its major innovations. It represented a vast improvement over the file allocation scheme used by CP/M and other microprocessor operating systems at the time. The FAT maps file allocations and provides a fast, efficient means by which to dynamically allocate disk space. It was particularly fast because in DOS 1.0 the entire FAT remained in memory. This was possible because of the small size of disks at the time. This was eventually replaced by a buffered file system, where only parts of the FAT remained in memory.

Beginning with DOS 3.1, support was added for alternative non-FAT file systems. These "other" file systems are supported by the Installable File System (IFS) interface, sometimes also referred to as the Network Redirector interface (a poor choice of a name since it leads one to think that it has something to do with device redirection, a completely different feature). The IFS permits DOS seamless access files on many different file systems. There is no question that originally Microsoft envisioned the interface as a mechanism for supporting networks, primarily its own LAN Manager product. The IFS is a general interface for non-FAT file systems. The MSCDEX driver for CD-ROM is an example of an IFS driver. So in fact, IFS is not just for networks.

Although the IFS interface is an advancement for DOS, it remains in sort of a twilight zone. It isn't officially documented or sanctioned, nor is there any real support for the IFS, leading to the possibility that it will change or be replaced. If the IFS interface changes at all, the affected clients will be the competitors of DOS, network operating system developers like Novell, Artisoft, and Banyan, some device driver developers, and probably IBM's OS/2, whose High Performance File System implements as an IFS to DOS. So though whether the IFS interface stays remains a plausible question, the IFS does provide DOS with an excellent ability to remain open and extensible. We return to the IFS several times in this chapter.

Overview

The DOS file system was designed for dynamic disk allocation. It allocates disk space from wherever it is available, even if it results in a file being fragmented on disk. The order of the different parts of the file are not lost; they are maintained in an allocation chain in the FAT. The disk space is not allocated or fragmented on a sector-by-sector basis. That would be woefully inefficient. Instead, the FAT maps allocation units known as clusters that represent one or more disk sectors. The number of sectors in a cluster is referred to as the cluster size.

Efficiency of access is not what drives the cluster size. Instead, the cluster size is determined by the limitation of the addressing space of the FAT. Early in its history, each FAT entry was an unusual 12 bits, designed to permit a more compact FAT table. These entries were limited to addressing no more than roughly 4K clusters. If a cluster represented 16 sectors, this would enable the addressing of a 32MB hard disk. Each disk allocation would take up 8K of disk space, even if only a few bytes were used. To be more effective, the 16-bit FAT was introduced, effective for addressing disks up to 512MB to 1GB (gigabyte). The days of the 1GB hard disk are here already.

Originally, the FAT table was to remain in memory with the 12-bit FAT table taking no more than around 2.7K of memory. The 16-bit FAT table could take as much as a whopping 128K of memory! Still, the 16-bit FAT is practical and remains on disks, with some entries cached in memory. The performance hit of accessing the FAT is relatively small and largely unnoticeable.

So how does the FAT map a file's allocation? Clusters form an allocation chain. Each cluster entry contains the value of the next cluster allocated to the file. This goes on until the last cluster, which contains an end-of-file mark. This is contrast with free or available clusters that contain a zero. The allocation chain is shown in Figure 3-1. DOS only needs to know the starting cluster address, which it keeps with the file's directory entry. The FAT makes disk space very dynamic where clusters may be added or removed from the file to allocate or free space on demand.

Figure 3-1. The FAT chain

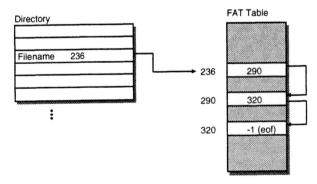

Reading a file is a matter of sequentially walking through the FAT chain. When reading reaches the end of a cluster, it goes to the FAT table entry for the current cluster and reads the next cluster in the chain. What some users may find surprising is that the only way to actually perform random access on a FAT-mapped file is to sequentially walk through the FAT chain. This practically seems like a contradiction in terms. The file pointer set by the move file pointer function, DOS function 42h, is just a reference. To locate the cluster where that reference is physically located on disk, the FAT chain for the file has to be walked. What appears to be random positioning is really executed as a sequential walk through the chain. The FAT consists of only forward-pointing cluster references, so to position at a cluster somewhere before the current cluster requires walking the FAT chain from the beginning of the file, even if the position request is just a few bytes away in a previous cluster. Fortunately, sequentially walking through the cluster chain is much faster than sequentially walking through the file itself.

Despite this, DOS delivers what has always been known as reasonably satisfactory performance. Several factors contribute to this performance. It is highly probable that the FAT that contains the next cluster reference is already cached in memory. FAT allocations are made in the current sector whenever possible so that referencing the FAT does not always require a disk access. This is the reason defragmenting your disk works. Cluster allocations for a file will be contiguous, more cluster references for the file will be within a FAT sector, and the FAT sector will be cached in memory.

Performance is also accelerated by a larger cluster size. When the cluster size is one, or one sector per cluster, the FAT must be referenced every 512 bytes read or written to disk, and a single FAT sector can contain only the allocation map of 64K of disk space. When the cluster size is a more reasonable eight sectors per cluster, the FAT need be consulted only every 4K bytes, and a FAT sector contains the allocation map of 1MB of disk space. The larger cluster size dramatically improves system performance.

Software Layers

The DOS file system is built in layers. The layered architecture is shown in Figure 3-2, which shows not only the relationship between the layers but also the source modules that contain the code. At the top layer of the architecture is the SFT layer. SFTs, or System File Tables, are internal data structures utilized by DOS that maintain state information when processing files. They are used for all file processing even if the file resides on foreign non-FAT file systems. An SFT is assigned to any file handled by the system, even FCB-processed files. Among the many services provided by the SFT layer, device redirection is handled at this layer.

The IFS layer provides a mechanism for DOS to interface and support other presumably non-FAT file systems. It is called by the SFT layer for all file functions ranging from expanding the filename to searching directories to reading and writing files. The functionality supported by the IFS depends on how well and how extensively other file systems are implemented. An IFS driver installs itself after system boot time and filters call for its file system.

Essentially, the IFS driver for the DOS FAT-based file system is the FIL layer. This layer of functions provides the actual services expected by the IFS. When the FIL layer expects to read or write a file, it utilizes FAT layer services that will navigate, allocate, and release space from the FAT. Finally, physical disk i/o is performed by a blocked device driver, which *may* perform disk i/o through the ROM BIOS.

The SFT layer is utterly unconcerned with the requirements of the FAT. It treats files as a continuous addressable array of bytes, in essence, as a flat file. The FAT layer, on the other hand, has to determine where within the FAT chain specific reads and writes take place.

Figure 3-2. Software layers

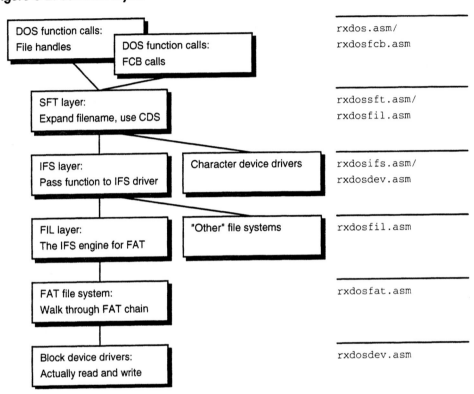

Although these layers exist within MS-DOS, most literature on its internals doesn't expose or explain the underlying code to the detail provided in this book; it is provided here to help understand the code.

The Structure of a DOS Disk

The FAT is just one of the permanent data structures on a DOS disk. Figure 3-3 shows the layout. The disk begins with a boot sector. This sector data is required on all DOS disks and contains the layout information of the remainder of the disk. The important information is the starting address and size of the FAT, the number of FAT tables, and the start of the root directory. All other space beyond the fixed-size root directory is allocatable to files and subdirectories. These permanent components are placed there by FORMAT or a similar utility.

Figure 3-3. The layout of a DOS logical disk

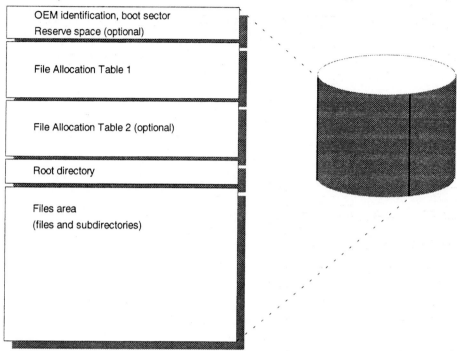

DOS File System Drive

OEM identification, boot sector
Reserve space (optional)

File Allocation Table 1

File Allocation Table 2 (optional)

Root directory

Files area
(files and subdirectories)

Every DOS disk begins with a boot record whether or not the disk is considered a bootable disk. The boot record consists of a data area that describes the layout of the remainder of the disk and a boot program. Bootable system disks are distinguished from nonbootable disks by the program they contain in the boot sector. This requirement is imposed on DOS-formatted disks because of the nature of the hardware that typically runs DOS and is discussed in Chapter 1 together with a detailed description of the entire boot process. Although a bootable system disk contains a program that searches the root directory for the operating system files, the nonbootable disk contains a program that displays the following message:

```
Non-System disk or disk error
Replace and press any key.
```

Every DOS-formatted disk contains some boot program, even if the program doesn't do much. This should obscure the fact that the format and layout of each disk are also contained as part of the all-important boot sector. The sector begins with a BOOTRECORD structure containing the following information:

```
;''''''''''''''''''''''''''''''''''''''''''''''''''''''''''''''''';
;   Boot Sector Parameter Block                                   ;
;.................................................................;
```

```
            BOOTSECTOR struc

_bsJump                  db 3 dup(?)
_bsOemName               db 8 dup(?)
_bsBytesPerSector        dw ?                    ; (start of BPB)
_bsSectorsPerCluster     db ?
_bsResSectors            dw ?
_bsNumCopiesFAT          db ?
_bsMaxAllocRootDir       dw ?
_bsMaxSectors            dw ?                    ; if zero, see huge sectors
_bsMediaDescriptor       db ?
_bsSectorsPerFat         dw ?
_bsSectorsPerTrack       dw ?
_bsHeads                 dw ?
_bsHiddenSectors         dd ?
_bsHugeSectors           dd ?                    ; (end of BPB)

_bsDriveNumber           db ?
                         db ?
_bsBootSignature         db ?                    ; 29h if extended boot sector
_bsVolumeId              db 11 dup(?)
_bsFileSystemType        db 8 dup(?)

            BOOTSECTOR ends
```

When DOS first reads a disk, whether it boots from it or not, it reads the disk format information into an internal data structure known as the DPB, or Disk Parameter Block. The boot record is always at the first sector of a disk. Specifically, it is at the first sector of a logical disk, which on partitioned hard disks may not be at the start of the physical disk. Partitioned disks exist for a variety of reasons, primarily to subdivide space between operating systems. It would be possible, for example, to have a hard disk divided between Unix and DOS partitions.

A comparison between the boot record and the DPB reveals that many of the fields are the same, after all, the boot record is the source, but that the order of the fields is different. Some of the fields in the DPB, such as the first data sector, are based on computing the size of the FAT and root directories. The DPB is therefore a distilled copy of the boot record.

```
;''''''''''''''''''''''''''''''''''''''''''''''''''''''''''''';
;  Drive Parameter Block                                      ;
;.............................................................;

            DPB struc
_dpbDrive                db ?
_dpbUnit                 db ?
_dpbBytesPerSector       dw ?
_dpbClusterSizeMask      db ?
_dpbClusterSizeShift     db ?
_dpbFirstFAT             dw ?
_dpbNumCopiesFAT         db ?
_dpbMaxAllocRootDir      dw ?
_dpbFirstDataSector      dw ?
_dpbMaxClusterNumber     dw ?
```

```
_dpbSectorsPerFat        dw  ?            ; in DOS ver 5 this became a word
_dpbFirstDirSector       dw  ?
_dpbptrDeviceDriver      dd  ?
_dpbMediaDescriptor      db  ?
_dpbAccessFlag           db  ?            ; -1 if must be rebuilt
_dpbNextDPB              dd  ?
_dpbNextFree             dw  ?            ; cluster where to search for next free
_dpbFreeCount            dw  ?            ; number of free clusters remaining
        DPB ends
```

Low-level DOS routines periodically need information about the disk layout and look to the DPB. A routine, getDPB, returns a pointer to a DPB structure in the ES:BX registers for any drive. Inside DOS, all drive codes are zero based, so a zero always refers to the A: drive, a one to the B: drive, and so on. If the drive has not been read since the last boot, the get DPB function detects an uninitialized DPB and forces a low-level disk driver call. The driver reads the boot sector, and the data is eventually formatted into a DPB. If the DPB had been initialized, there is no guarantee that the current copy of the DPB contains valid data. After all, for a removable disk, the data becomes obsolete when the disk is changed. A low-level driver call again detects changed media. The driver call sets in motion the necessary code to reload the DPB. This is just a brief description of the reliance on device drivers placed by DOS. We discuss device drivers more fully in Chapter 4.

The original DOS 1.0 has only one directory. That directory, carried over to today as the root directory, is of fixed size. Only the space on disk beyond the root directory is allocatable. All the space before the end of the root directory is preallocated. In fact, the first allocatable cluster on disk really refers to the space just beyond the root directory. Subdirectories and files all share the allocatable space. In fact, subdirectories are just files that are identified and treated as special when searching for a filename. Like files, subdirectories can be extended in size, may wind up being fragmented on disk, and must be referenced using the FAT.

Directories are made up of entries. Each entry consists of a filename, limited historically to the eight-character name and three-character extension; file attributes; file size in bytes; date and time of last update; and the starting cluster address. The attributes are used to further qualify the type of information contained in the directory entry. Attributes exist to identify system, hidden, changed, and read-only files; the volume label; and whether an entry is a subdirectory reference. The layout of a directory entry is shown in Figure 3-4. The relationship between directories and subdirectories is shown in Figure 3-5.

Chicago, Microsoft's long-promised next release of DOS and Windows 4.0, will finally offer long names. The long name will occupy several directory entries, but users and application programs will finally be able to save meaningful filenames. For every long entry, there is a matching eight-character short name for compatibility reasons.

Figure 3-4. Directory entry layout

```
;//////////////////////////////////////////////////////////;
;  Directory Entries                                        ;
;..........................................................;


        DIRENTRY struc
deName                  db '????????'
deExtension             db '???'
deAttributes            db ?
deReserved              db 10 dup (?)
deTime                  dw ?             ; Time Format
                                         ;   0 - 4 Two second intervals
                                         ;   5 -10 Minutes (0 - 59)
                                         ;  11 -15 Hours (0 - 23)


deDate                  dw ?             ; Date Format
                                         ;   0 - 4 Day (1 - 31)
                                         ;   5 - 8 Month (1 - 12)
                                         ;   9 -15 Year since 1980


deStartCluster          dw ?
deFileSize              dd ?
        DIRENTRY ends


;- - - - - - - - - - - - - - - - - - - - - - - - - - - - - -
;  Attribute bits
;- - - - - - - - - - - - - - - - - - - - - - - - - - - - - -
ATTR_NORMAL             equ 00h
ATTR_READONLY           equ 01h
ATTR_HIDDEN             equ 02h
ATTR_SYSTEM             equ 04h
ATTR_VOLUME             equ 08h
ATTR_DIRECTORY          equ 10h
ATTR_ARCHIVE            equ 20h
ATTR_MASK               equ 1Fh


;- - - - - - - - - - - - - - - - - - - - - - - - - - - - - -
;  Special Characters
;- - - - - - - - - - - - - - - - - - - - - - - - - - - - - -
DIRENTRY_NEVERUSED      equ 00h
SPECIAL_CHAR            equ 05h
DIRENTRY_DELETED        equ 0E5h
```

Figure 3-5. Subdirectories are files from a parent directory.

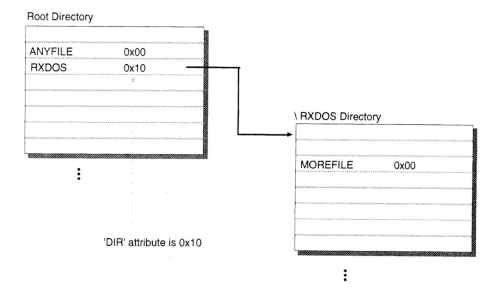

File Handles

The DOS file handle functions provide the greatest flexibility for applications. They permit pathnames to be part of the filename, reading and writing can be from virtually anywhere in memory, and they require very little overhead from the application writer. For every open or created file, DOS utilizes an SFT, or System File Table, entry. SFTs contain state information required when processing a file. Unfortunately, the number of SFTs is limited to the FILES= parameter in config.sys. DOS defaults to a paltry eight entries, a throwback to the days when unnecessary memory utilization was expensive and most applications dealt with only a few files.

SFTs contain information necessary to process a file, such as the drive, starting cluster address, file size, file attributes, access mode, date and time stamp, current file position, and a reference to the directory entry for this file in the form of a sector and offset within the sector. The SFT data structure is listed in Figure 3-6. We discuss the fields in the context of their usage throughout the chapter.

Figure 3-6. The System File Table (SFT)

```
;,///////////////////////////////////////////////////////////,
;  System File Tables                                         ;
;............................................................;

SFT struc
```

```
sftRefCount            dw ?
sftMode                dw ?
sftFileAttrib          db ?
sftDevInfo             dw ?                  ; device info
sftDCB                 dd ?                  ; file DCB address or driver address
sftBegCluster          dw ?
sftTime                dw ?
sftDate                dw ?
sftFileSize            dd ?
sftFilePosition        dd ?
sftRelCluster          dw ?
sftCurCluster          dw ?                  ; 0000 if never read/ written
sftDirSector           dd ?                  ; dir sector containing entry
sftDirIndex            db ?                  ; used in search next
sftFileName            db '????????'
sftFileExtension       db '???'
sftShareSftPointer     dd ?                  ; points to other shared file
sftOwnerMachine        dw ?                  ; virtual machine id #
sftOwnerPSP            dw ?                  ; owner process
sftShareRecordPtr      dw ?                  ; share record pointer
        SFT ends

;- - - - - - - - - - - - - - - - - - - - - - - - - - - - - - - -
; Modes
;- - - - - - - - - - - - - - - - - - - - - - - - - - - - - - - -

sftENTRY_ISFCB         equ 8000h             ; RxDOS specific
sftDENY_NONE           equ 0040h
sftDENY_READ           equ 0030h
sftDENY_WRITE          equ 0020h
sftEXCLUSIVE           equ 0010h
sftNET_FCB             equ 0070h
sftWRITE               equ 0001h
sftREAD                equ 0000h

;- - - - - - - - - - - - - - - - - - - - - - - - - - - - - - - -
; sftDevInfo
;- - - - - - - - - - - - - - - - - - - - - - - - - - - - - - - -

sftShared              equ 8000h
sftDateset             equ 4000h
sftIoctl               equ 4000h
sftIsDevice            equ 0080h
sftEof                 equ 0040h
sftBinary              equ 0020h
sftSpecial             equ 0010h
sftIsclock             equ 0008h
sftIsnul               equ 0004h
sftIsstdout            equ 0002h
sftIsstdin             equ 0001h
sftWritten             equ 0040h
sftDrivemask           equ 003fh
```

The number of SFT entries can be extended on the fly, a capability not openly exploited by DOS. SFTs are contained within File Table structures. These container structures are linked to each

other and form a chain with the start address of the chain located in the SYSVARS variable
_RxDOS_pFT. The relationship is illustrated in Figure 3-7. The only reason File Tables exist is so
that additional SFTs can be allocated at any time.

This is exactly what Windows does when it needs additional files! It allocated more File Tables
in conventional memory, that is, memory located in the first 640K that it uses for additional SFTs.
If Windows can allocate this memory, DOS should be providing this service to all applications. The
skeptical reader might wonder how to verify that Windows allocates this additional space. All it
takes is running a program that snoops inside our DOS and prints the addresses of the FT chain
before and while Windows is running. Windows always seems to add 10 SFT entries beyond what
was allocated at startup, and it guarantees at least 40 SFTs. The skeptical reader should set the
FILES= statement to something like 20 entries and then reboot the system.

SFTS is the program in the distribution diskette that displays the FT chain. Running the program *after* Windows on a system with FILES=20 is loaded provided the following output:

```
c> sfts
0116:00CC    5 sft entries
0361:0000   15 sft entries
0FD6:0000   10 sft entries
108C:0004   10 sft entries
```

But running the same program *before* Windows was loaded or *after* quitting Windows provided the
following original allocation of FTs:

```
c> sfts
0116:00CC    5 sft entries
0361:0000   15 sft entries
```

Figure 3-7. SFTs storage in file tables

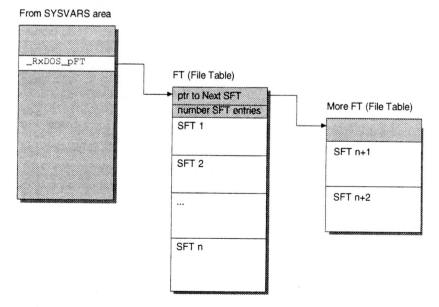

The point is that the number of SFT entries can be extended. However, merely adding additional SFTs won't provide an application with greater access to open files unless another data structure, the Job Handle Table (JHT), is also changed. The JHT is the file handle structure located in the PSP of every DOS program and is by default limited to 20 entries. The limit on the JHT, and even why it exists at all, is one of the often misunderstood concepts related to file handling.

There are other misconceptions as well. Because of the relationship between a file handle and an SFT entry, some programmers mistakenly believe that the handle returned to the application is an SFT handle. Another misconception is that the handle is an index reference to a lookup table. Finally, there exists the misconception, sometimes even mistakenly supported by Microsoft itself, that there is a 20 open file limit for DOS applications. All these statements are at some level fundamentally incorrect.

Microsoft's own documentation sometimes fuels the misconception: "The limit on the number of files and/or devices opened for a single process using handles is 20 or the number of entries in the allocated data structure, whichever is less. " (From *The MS-DOS Encyclopedia: Versions 1.0 through 3.2,* edited by Ray Duncan, 1988, p. 801.) This is a misprint. DOS corrected this limit with the release of DOS 3.2, but without a clear explanation of the difference between file handles and number of available FILES=, the misconceptions continued. As you'll come to understand, the number of file handles available to a process is *not* 20. File handles and the number of SFTs are two different variables representing entries available in two different data structures.

The file handle returned to an application from an open or create is an offset into the JHT. A default JHT, limited to 20 entries, is created for each program and by default is located at offset 18h of the process's PSP, or Program Segment Prefix. Applications can allocate a new JHT using DOS function 67h, Set File Handles. This function is imperfect at best. It attempts to allocate memory from DOS, but the call can fail since applications are usually assigned all the available memory at startup. The alternative is to relocate the table by changing the JHT pointer and file count in the PSP directly.

The JHT exists to support device redirection. When a file is opened or created, the pointer to the SFT is expressed as an internal system handle, sometimes referred to as an SFT handle, which is stored in the JHT. The handle that the application receives from the DOS function call is *not* the SFT handle. Instead, the application is returned the offset within the JHT as the file handle. This indirect relationship between the SFT and JHT handles is demonstrated in Figure 3-8.

Because a file handle is really an offset into a process's JHT, separate processes resident in memory, say an application and a TSR, can have the same file handle even when they each open two different files. That shouldn't come as a surprise. It is merely coincidental that the offsets into the separate JHTs are the same. The JHT entries will contain different SFT handles.

Figure 3-8. File handle table in PSP

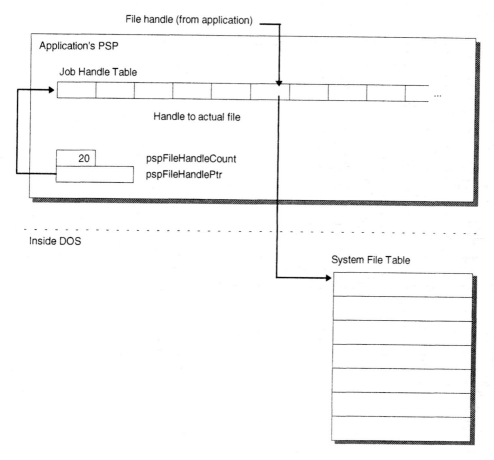

So how many files can a program open at once? No matter how large the JHT, the maximum number of different files that may be opened is limited by the number of available SFTs. Unfortunately, applications have no practical way of determining this number other than snooping through DOS data structures. This is impractical since changes are made between DOS releases. Not only should DOS have provided a function that returned the number of SFTs available, but more impressively, it should have automatically created a JHT at least large enough to accommodate the number of SFTs available as part of the process startup code, much like the environment block is now created, saving everyone else the trouble.

To understand how and why the JHT is designed to support device redirection, it is necessary to understand deeper the relationship and role between files, SFTs, and devices. The first five entries of the Job Handle Table are automatically reserved to the standard devices: stdin, stdout, stderr, stdaux, and stdprn, respectively. Although called standard devices, they are, in fact, standard device handles. As handles, they are offsets into the JHT. One should therefore expect to be able to write to the STDOUT handle, handle number 1, to output to the screen. That is, the following two DOS functions should behave identically:

```
        mov ah, 09h                              ; display string
        mov dx, offset display_message
        int 21h

        mov ah, 40h                              ; write file
        mov bx, 0001                             ; stdout
        mov cx, enddisplay_message - display_message - 1
        mov dx, offset display_message
        int 21h
        ...

display_message:
        db 'you will get this message twice. get the picture ?', 0dh, 0ah
        db 'try this with xstdout > filename', 0dh, 0ah, 0dh, 0ah, "$"

enddisplay_message:
```

The first function displays a message on screen using DOS function 09h. The second function writes to file handle 0001, which also results in displaying a message to the screen. Not only do these function calls result in the same behavior, but internally they are treated identically! The code inside DOS for the display string function writes to the stdout file handle, as do all other screen character output functions, DOS functions 02h, 06h, and 09h.

This is best seen in the RxDOS code shown for function 09h, Display String. The function maps the stdout file handle to an internal SFT handle using the JHT. It then maps the SFT handle to an SFT pointer. The function determines the length of the output string by scanning for the end $ terminator and then passes the pointer to the display message, its length, and the address of the SFT to an internal write routine, _SFTWriteFile.

```
(in rxdos.asm)
        ;,,,,,,,,,,,,,,,,,,,,,,,,,,,,,,,,,,,,,,,,,,,,,,,,,,,,,,,,,,,,,,,,;
        ;   09h Display String                                          ;
        ;- - - - - - - - - - - - - - - - - - - - - - - - - - - - - - - -;
        ;                                                               ;
        ;   Usage:                                                      ;
        ;      ds:dx  pointer to display string                         ;
        ;...............................................................;

_DisplayString:
        Entry
        ddef _sftPointer
        ddef _buffer, es, dx

        mov ax, STDOUT                           ; handle
        call MapAppToSFTHandle                   ; map to internal handle info
        call FindSFTbyHandle                     ; get corresponding SFT (es: di )
        jc _displayOutput_22                     ; if sft NOT located ->
        stordarg _sftPointer, es, di             ; save sft buffer pointer
```

```
;- - - - - - - - - - - - - - - - - - - - - - - - - - - - - - - - - - - - - -
; display to redirected file
;- - - - - - - - - - - - - - - - - - - - - - - - - - - - - - - - - - - - - -
        mov al, '$'
        mov cx, -1
        les di, dword ptr [ _buffer ][ bp ]
        repnz scasb                              ; compute length of string
        jnz _displayOutput_22                    ; strange, but exit if none -->

        neg cx
        sub cx, 2                                ; remove $ from output
        push word ptr [ _buffer. _segment ][ bp ]
        push word ptr [ _buffer. _pointer ][ bp ]

        getdarg es, di, _sftPointer              ; get sft buffer pointer
        call _SFTWriteFile                       ; write using sft (at es:di )

;- - - - - - - - - - - - - - - - - - - - - - - - - - - - - - - - - - - - - -
; exit
;- - - - - - - - - - - - - - - - - - - - - - - - - - - - - - - - - - - - - -
_displayOutput_22:
        Return
```

The code for display string looks remarkably like the following code for _WriteFile. It maps the application's handle to an SFT handle, which is then converted to an SFT pointer. The buffer pointer, buffer length, and SFT address are then passed to the internal write routine, _SFTWriteFile.

```
(in rxdos.asm)
        ;///////////////////////////////////////////////////////////;
        ;   40h Write File                                          ;
        ;- - - - - - - - - - - - - - - - - - - - - - - - - - - - - -;
        ;                                                           ;
        ;  bx    handle                                             ;
        ;  cx    bytes to write                                     ;
        ;  ds:dx buffer address                                     ;
        ;...........................................................;

_WriteFile:
        Entry
        def _handle, bx
        def _writeCount, cx
        ddef _sftPointer
        ddef _bufPtr, es, dx                     ; save buffer pointer

        call CtrlC_Check

        mov ax, bx                               ; handle
        call MapAppToSFTHandle                    ; map to internal handle info
        call FindSFTbyHandle                      ; get corresponding SFT (es: di )
        stordarg _sftPointer, es, di             ; save sft buffer pointer
        jc _WriteFile_error                       ; if could not find -->
```

```
        push word ptr [ _bufPtr. _segment ][ bp ]
        push word ptr [ _bufPtr. _pointer ][ bp ]
        getarg cx, _writeCount                          ; bytes to write
        call _SFTWriteFile                              ; write using sft (at es:di )

_WriteFile_error:
        RetCallersStackFrame ds, bx
        mov word ptr [ _AX ][ bx ], ax
        Return
```

Inside _SFTWriteFile, the SFT is tested to determine whether it is assigned to a character device or a file. If it is assigned to a character device, it sends the display buffer address and character count to the device driver. Otherwise, the function proceeds as if it were a normal file write. Users and programmers normally think of redirection to disk as the special case though one could argue that writing to a device driver really is the special case in this code.

The code inside _SFTWriteFile is shown next. The code begins by marking the SFT as changed and then tests whether the SFT is assigned to a device. If it is, the code continues with a call to device character write; otherwise, it branches to file write code. An SFT is marked as pointing to a device during open or create, which we discuss later in this section.

```
(in rxdossft.asm)
        ;,,,,,,,,,,,,,,,,,,,,,,,,,,,,,,,,,,,,,,,,,,,,,,,,,,,,,,,,,,,,,,,,;
        ;  Write To SFT                                                 ;
        ;- - - - - - - - - - - - - - - - - - - - - - - - - - - - - - - -;
        ;                                                               ;
        ;  Input:                                                       ;
        ;    es:di   sft pointer                                        ;
        ;    cx      bytes to write                                     ;
        ;    stack   buffer address                                     ;
        ;                                                               ;
        ;  Output:                                                      ;
        ;    cx      bytes actually written                             ;
        ;    cy      end of available disk space reached               ;
        ;...............................................................;

_SFTWriteFile:
        Entry 2
        darg _bufPtr
     ; ...


;- - - - - - - - - - - - - - - - - - - - - - - - - - - - - - - - - - - -
;  is file redirected to a device ?
;- - - - - - - - - - - - - - - - - - - - - - - - - - - - - - - - - - - -
        or word ptr es:[ sftDevInfo ][ di ], sftWritten  ; say file is DIRTY
        test word ptr es:[ sftDevInfo ][ di ], sftIsDevice
        jz _SFTWriteFile_16

        or cx, cx
        jz _SFTWriteFile_06                             ; if nothing to write ->

        push word ptr es:[ sftDCB. _segment ][ di ]
        push word ptr es:[ sftDCB. _pointer ][ di ]
```

```
      mov cx, word ptr [ _writeCount ][ bp ]
      getdarg es, di, _bufPtr
      call devCharWrite                          ; go to device driver ->

_SFTWriteFile_06:
      jmp _SFTWriteFile_56

    ; ...
      (remainder of routine not shown here, see section on file write)
```

To effect file redirection, DOS changes the SFT handle for the stdout entry in the Job Handle Table to point to a different device or file. You can see this in action when you dump out the PSP using debug.com. A nonredirected output of debug would look a lot like the following:

```
c> debug
-d 18, 2B
17B5:0010                    01 01 01 00 02 FF FF FF        ........
17B5:0020  FF FF FF FF FF FF FF FF-FF FF FF FF            ............
-q
```

The default JHT is located in the 20 bytes between offsets 18h and 2Bh in the PSP. The first three entries in the JHT contain the assigned values for the STDIN, STDOUT, and STDERR file handles. They are all preassigned to SFT handle 01, which points to the CON device. The next JHT entry is the STDAUX entry and is assigned to SFT handle 00, which points to the AUX device, or serial communications. Finally, the fifth entry is the STDPRN entry, and it is assigned to SFT handle 02, or the PRN device. All the other entries are free and have an FFh value.

When any of these devices is redirected, the SFT handle for the redirection file replaces the value in the standard handle. For example, when STDOUT is redirected to a file, the JHT entry is changed to the SFT handle for the redirected file, as in

```
c> debug > textdump
c> type textdump

-d 18, 2B
17B5:0010                    01 06 01 00 02 FF FF FF        ........
17B5:0020  FF FF FF FF FF FF FF FF-FF FF FF FF            ............
-q
```

The same holds for character device input, as in the next example. A console input is no different than reading from the STDIN file handle. These two functions behave the same and expect one character from the input stream.

```
      mov ah, 07h                          ; direct console input
      int 21h

      mov ah, 3Eh                          ; read file
      mov bx, 0000                         ; stdin
      mov cx, 0001                         ; one character
      int 21h
```

What is the purpose of all this, anyway? Device independence and redirection removes the distinction at the application level between a file and a character device. This makes it possible to write to a character device only to have it captured and redirected to another device or file, or to write to a file, but have it redirected to device. Because of the interchangeability between character drivers and files, it is possible to redirect output to another device, as in

```
c> type textdump > prn
```

There is a commonly held belief that the introduction of device drivers made all this transparent to DOS. It didn't. The redirection is handled by the SFT-processing routines, not by device drivers. The device driver layer is too far down to make this type of distinction. Block device drivers expect sector addresses and complete fixed-length sectors, whereas character device drivers handle a variable number of characters.

So now that we have established that *all* i/o goes through an SFT just so that it can be redirected—a feature that by the way I like and that I think has been well implemented in DOS—the next question is how did the SFT get the device and driver information? The device type is set there during open or create when the SFT is first initialized. The specific details are provided in the section on "File Open and Create" later in this chapter.

File Control Blocks

File Control Blocks were introduced as part of the original DOS 1.0 and were copied from the 8-bit CP/M operating system. It enabled an easy migration path to DOS. Although there is no indication that DOS intended to support file handles at the start, the concept of paths and subdirectories evolved soon after the initial DOS release and were incorporated as a major new feature in DOS 2.0. Most programs find it easier to use the file handle functions because FCBs provide no support for paths and require data be transferred through a Disk Transfer Area, a buffer created for FCB file i/o. File transfers are typically in fixed-length records.

An FCB is a data structure that an application program creates. It begins with a drive code, a filename, and an extension. The FCB layout is as follows:

```
;///////////////////////////////////////////////////////////////;
;   File Control Blocks                                          ;
;...............................................................;


        FCB struc
fcbDrive          db  ?
fcbName           db  '????????'
fcbExtension      db  '???'
fcbCurrBlockNo    dw  ?
fcbRecordSize     dw  ?
fcbFileSize       dd  ?
fcbDate           dw  ?
fcbTime           dw  ?
fcbSFN            db  ?              ; handle to sft system
fcbFlags          db  ?             ; modified flags
```

```
fcbDHD                      dd ?                    ; device header/DCB
fcbBegClusterNo             dw ?                    ; start of file cluster number
fcbCurrRecNo                db ?
fcbRandomRecNo              dd ?
        FCB ends
```

The read/write position can be set in one of two ways. DOS functions 14h and 15h, FCB read and write, use the old-style record position pointers separated into two fields: the current block number and the current record number. A block in FCB terminology is 128 records. This means that the record number field increments only to 127 before wrapping around. This unusual convention is copied from CP/M. To set the record number, it had to be divided by 128 and stored in two separate parts. Later, extended FCB functions 21h and 22h, random FCB read and write, introduced the Random record number field. This permitted using the more direct 32-bit record number as a random access index into a file. Record numbers point to the start of records rather than to individual bytes. This is impractical for reading text, images, or spreadsheets.

Some programmers believe that to this day some of the original FCB handling code still lurks in the inner shadows of DOS. Actually, FCBs utilize SFT entries and the file handle code. To underscore this point, recall the relationship between the file handle functions and the FCB functions in Figure 3-2.

This is a smart move. Not only is it economical in terms of the code required, but two separate sets of file i/o code would eventually and inevitably lead to incompatibilities. The FCB file open (DOS function 0Fh), which follows, utilizes the SFT file open function, _SFTOpenFile, to perform the open. It converts the FCB filename into a null terminated string, performs the file open, and then copies pertinent information like the file size, the SFT handle, the file's date and time, and the file's starting cluster address to the FCB.

```
;''''''''''''''''''''''''''''''''''''''''''''''''''''''''''';
;  0Fh Open File with FCB                                    ;
;- - - - - - - - - - - - - - - - - - - - - - - - - - - - - -;
;                                                           ;
;  ds:dx pointer to FCB                                     ;
;                                                           ;
;  Return:                                                  ;
;    al = ff, if cannot locate any matching entry           ;
;         00, if match located                              ;
;..........................................................;

_OpenFileFCB:
        Entry
        def _openMode
        ddef _fcbPointer, es, dx
        defbytes _expandedName, 128              ; expanded file name (128 bytes )


;- - - - - - - - - - - - - - - - - - - - - - - - - - - - - - - -
; convert FCB name to name usable by SFT Open
;- - - - - - - - - - - - - - - - - - - - - - - - - - - - - - - -
        mov si, dx                               ; source FCB address
        lea di, offset _expandedName [ bp ]      ; expand name
        call convFCBNametoASCIZ                  ; build asciz name
```

```
;- - - - - - - - - - - - - - - - - - - - - - - - - - - - - - - - -
;  try SFT Open
;- - - - - - - - - - - - - - - - - - - - - - - - - - - - - - - - -
        setES ss                                    ; es:
        lea dx, offset _expandedName [ bp ]         ; es: dx filename
        mov al, DEFAULT_FCBOPENMODE                 ; mode is default open mode
        call _SFTOpenFile                           ; build an SFT
        jc _OpenFileFCB_26                          ; if error ->

        getdarg ds, si, _fcbPointer                 ; fcb address
        call initFCBfromSFT                         ; [ax] handle, [es:di] ptr to sft
        or ax, ax

;- - - - - - - - - - - - - - - - - - - - - - - - - - - - - - - - -
;  return
;- - - - - - - - - - - - - - - - - - - - - - - - - - - - - - - - -
_OpenFileFCB_26:
        Return
```

So how can FCBs, which can be virtually limitless, and file handles, which are definitely limited, coexist? Every open or created FCB is assigned an SFT-like entry. In MS-DOS, FCBs are assigned SFT entries from a separate System FCB chain. This is a chain of SFTs created for the sole purpose of supporting FCBs. The number of available System FCB entries is set by the FCBS= parameter in config.sys. DOS defaults to four entries.

Since FCBs can essentially be unlimited, that is, one could create literally hundreds or thousands of FCBs within an application (and I'd like to see that application, too!), DOS is forced to play a sort of shell game with FCB entries. When a new entry is required from the System FCB chain and all the entries are already allocated to FCBs, an old entry is discarded. The file that occupied the System FCB entry is not closed, nor is any file data lost. The System FCB can be discarded because DOS records some critical file information, such as the file's starting cluster address, in the FCB. This prevents having to reopen the file later.

Because discarding a System FCB can have a negative performance impact on FCB file access, particularly for sequential file processing over large files, a complicated scheme had been developed that utilized protected FCBs. The FCBS= statement permitted both the total number of System FCBs optionally followed by the number of protected FCBs. This meant that the first few FCBs that were opened were protected from the discarding scheme. With DOS 5, this has since been dropped, and RxDOS doesn't support protected FCBs.

MS-DOS keeps SFTs and System FCBs in two different chains, but RxDOS merges both tables to form a single chain. It adds the number of FCBS= and FILES= entries to create a larger pool of available System File Tables. An FCB status bit distinguishes FCB-assigned entries in the SFT. This represents a sort of dynamic allocation of SFT entries on an "as needed" basis. In MS-DOS, System FCB entries remain unused most of the time. Few software packages use them. This represents a wasted and underutilized resource. In contrast, RxDOS assigns SFT entries as needed, even if it means assigning the entire SFT chain to FCBs. File-handle-based i/o is never constrained by this because a file handle request forces the discarding of FCB entries.

How does an FCB know that its SFT has been discarded? Unfortunately, the original FCB cannot be informed. The FCB is located in the application's memory space, which may have been located in an overlay or swappable data segment that may not be in memory at the time. The responsibility falls on DOS to detect if the FCB is still assigned to the SFT entry. For SFTs that point to files, two variables uniquely identify the file: the drive code and the starting cluster address. It is impossible for two different files to begin at the same cluster address in the same drive. DOS compares the FCB and SFT values to ensure that the SFT (or in MS-DOS, the System FCB entry) still refers to the same file. For SFT entries that point to devices, the device header address stored in the FCB and SFT are compared. The entries will not be the same if they don't point to the same device.

During the next few sections, we present the code for DOS functions like create, open, close, read, and write. Since FCB-based functions utilize large portions of the file handle code, all that we discuss applies to FCB-based functions. But the code for each FCB function call is presented separately later in this chapter. This brings clarity and definition to the code.

File Open and Create

The DOS file open and file create functions return a handle to the application after locating or initializing a directory entry. The purpose of open and create is to establish a connection to a file on disk and populate an SFT that can then be used for further file processing, typically reading and writing. The principal functionality of the open and create functions rests with locating the file on disk. For files in the DOS file system, the filename is expanded to a fully qualified pathname. As you'll see in the next few paragraphs, the file open and create functions also play an important role in establishing file redirection.

The code for file open and file create begins at `_OpenFile` and `_CreateFile`, respectively, both located in `rxdos.asm`. The steps required to complete the open or create are summarized in Figure 3-9. The functions begin with determining if an SFT is available and then expanding the filename to its fully qualified name. The expanded filename is searched on disk. If the item is found but the function is to create a file, the original file's contents are deleted. For create, an available directory entry is initialized. An SFT is then assigned to the file and initialized from the contents of the directory entry. Finally, the SFT handle is recorded in the Job Handle Table.

Figure 3-9. Layout of the CDS (Current Directory Structure)

Open or create steps.

1. Ensure that there is available SFT and JHT entries.
2. Expand the name to a fully qualified name using ExpandFileName (in rxdosfil.asm).
3. Search file on disk using LocateFile (in rxdosfil.asm).
4. If Create and item found, delete file using ReleaseClusterChain (in rxdosfat.asm).
5. Find a free directory entry using LocateFreeDirSlot (in rxdosfil.asm).
6. Initialize dir entry if create (at _createSFTEntry_24, in rxdossft.asm).
7. Initialize SFT using initSFTfromDirEntry (in rxdossft.asm).
8. Update JHT if file handle function.

Some programmers believe that a directory search is optimized by the use of the . and ..
entries in the pathname. That is, they believe that the directory search for a filename such as
`..\anyname.txt` begins at the current directory, locates the .. entry in the directory, which
points to the parent directory, and then continues searching within the parent directory. That belief
is incorrect. Both MS-DOS and RxDOS search the current directory or begin searching at the top
of the directory tree, which for most drives is likely to be the root directory.

A simple experiment can be undertaken to check the veracity of this observation. If DOS utilized the .. entry in a directory, then changing it to point to another directory or changing its name
would cause DOS commands such as

```
c:\foo>dir ..
c:\foo>type ..\anyfile.txt
```

to either not work, display the wrong directories, or not find the requested file. If indeed DOS used
these entries, then the observed change in behavior should be logically traceable to the changes
made. For example, the directory produced would be of the newly addressed directory. Actually,
nothing unusual happens, leading to the obvious conclusion that DOS just doesn't use the . and ..
entries although to be fair the same experiment had to be made with both entries. DOS just doesn't
use or need these entries. The concept of keeping these entries in the directory was borrowed from
Unix, which may use these entries for directory navigation, just as DOS may at one time have as
well.

What is really going on is that DOS expands the pathname to a fully qualified path before any
disk searching begins. DOS can do this because it knows the current default directory for all drives.
It maintains this information in the Current Directory Structure, or CDS. There is a CDS entry for
each logical drive in the system, where the number of logical drives is set by the LASTDRIVE=
statement. The CDS is shown in Figure 3-10. The algorithm utilized by DOS to convert a filename
to its fully expanded filename is fairly obvious and essentially begins with the current directory and
appends the unqualified name passed. It then canonically builds the actual path name by removing
. and .. entries as appropriate.

Primarily, the CDS exists to identify the default directory for each drive. DOS expands the filename before any search begins for several reasons. The name expansion is necessary to support the
somewhat infrequently used SUBST and JOIN commands. SUBST maps a drive letter to the subdirectory of a disk. This capability is useful, for example, in mapping floppy disk drives to subdirectories on the hard disk. JOIN maps a subdirectory from one disk to another drive. Essentially,
you see the JOINed drive as a subdirectory.

One subtle effect of expanding the filename is that the drive may change. The SUBST command shown here maps the \lotus directory to the e: drive. Any reference to the e: drive actually is mapped back to its actual drive under c:\lotus.

```
c>SUBST e: c:\lotus
c>dir e:
    (directory of c:\lotus contents)
```

One final side benefit of the early name mapping has actually nothing to do with mapping or
name expansion. If the name passed contains no subdirectory references whatsoever, that is, it uti-

lizes the current directory, the starting cluster address just happens to be known in the CDS, and the search throughout the disk is avoided altogether. The required directory is known.

Figure 3-10. Layout of the CDS

```
;////////////////////////////////////////////////////////////;
; Current Directory Entries                                  ;
;............................................................;

        CDS struc

_cdsActualDirectory     db 67 dup (?)           ; asciz name
_cdsFlags               dw ?
_cdsPtrToDPB            dd ?
_cdsStartClusterDir     dw ?                    ;
                        dw ?                    ; padding for network record
_cdsNetwParameter       dw ?                    ; padding for network record
_cdsNonSubstOffset      dw ?

                        db ?                    ; compatability byte
_cdsPtrtoIFSDriver      dd ?
                        dw ?                    ; compatability word

        CDS ends

;- - - - - - - - - - - - - - - - - - - - - - - - - - - - - - - -
; Redirection for IFS
;- - - - - - - - - - - - - - - - - - - - - - - - - - - - - - - -

_cdsRedirectIFSPtr      equ _cdsStartClusterDir

;- - - - - - - - - - - - - - - - - - - - - - - - - - - - - - - -
; Flags
;- - - - - - - - - - - - - - - - - - - - - - - - - - - - - - - -

_CDS_NETWORKEDDRIVE     equ 8000h
_CDS_PHYSICALDRIVE      equ 4000h
_CDS_JOINEDDRIVE        equ 2000h
_CDS_SUBSTDRIVE         equ 1000h
```

We continue with the behavior expected during the open and create functions. What is supposed to happen when a file named CON is opened and read? Of course, the filename is not to just any file; it references the console device. Both the open and create functions will work successfully when a device name is passed. The returned file handle can be used to read from the "file." Each read will transfer the requested number of characters from the device. That is, reading from a file opened with the CON device name is somewhat similar to calling the DOS function 0Ah, the buffered keyboard input function.

The same behavior applies to files opened using the FCB file functions. FCB file function read and writes exhibit the same device redirection that file handle functions do when a device name is used during the open or create.

This is even true of when an open or create is performed with a name that contains drive and path information but references a device name. The following open function will also succeed so long as both the drive and pathname are valid:

```
        mov ax, 3D02h                    ; open function
        mov dx, _notjust_anyname         ; points to CON
        int 21h
        ...

_notjust_anyname:
        db "c:\rxbook\CON", 0
```

This is consistent with the expectations of device redirection. Devices can be read and written as files. This should not come as much of a surprise. In fact, the standard device assignments in DOS, such as stdin and stdout are nothing more than file handles created by opening the CON device.

When DOS functions try to perform an open or create, each component of the name supplied is checked, including the drive, path, and filename. Drives are checked in the Current Directory Structure where there exists one entry for each existing drive. Each directory name in a path is checked by searching through the disk for a valid matching directory entry. Finally, a filename is checked against installed device drivers before it is searched on disk.

An open is successful when it passes all the preceding tests. An SFT is assigned to the opened file. If the file references a device, the SFT is identified by the sftIsDevice flag, and the device's header address is stored in the SFT. This flag is checked everytime the file is to be read or written. If the flag is set, the read or write request is made from the associated device. Otherwise, the routine presumes that the SFT references a file on disk and proceeds with the normal file read or write.

The SFT read function makes the device or file distinction as follows:

```
_SFTReadFile:
        Entry 2
        darg _bufPtr
        ...

;- - - - - - - - - - - - - - - - - - - - - - - - - - - - - - - - - -
;  is file redirected to a device
;- - - - - - - - - - - - - - - - - - - - - - - - - - - - - - - - - -
        test word ptr es:[ sftDevInfo ][ di ], sftIsDevice
        jz _SFTReadFile_06

        push word ptr es:[ sftDCB. _segment ][ di ]
        push word ptr es:[ sftDCB. _pointer ][ di ]
        mov cx, word ptr [ _readCount ][ bp ]
        getdarg es, di, _bufPtr
        call devCharReadLine                              ; read til cr or eof.
        jmp _SFTReadFile_36


;- - - - - - - - - - - - - - - - - - - - - - - - - - - - - - - - - -
;  initialize disk access block
;- - - - - - - - - - - - - - - - - - - - - - - - - - - - - - - - - -
```

```
_SFTReadFile_06:
        or cx, cx                          ; reading any ?
        jz _SFTReadFile_36                 ; if length is zero ->
        ...
```

This code segment tests the SFT to determine if it is assigned to a device or a file. If it is assigned to a device, it pushes the address of the device header, referred to here as the DCB or Device Control Block, to the stack and calls character read line. The read is performed by the character device.

Establishing that MS-DOS Doesn't Use . and . . Entries—the Proof

I have made a great point in the text of saying that MS-DOS doesn't use the . and . . directory entries. To eliminate any debate, such a statement requires proof, which is provided here. This test was performed under both DOS 6.0 and 3.2 versions.

The proof that DOS doesn't use these entries involves, unfortunately, changing directory entries on disk. This cannot be performed with anything less than a disk editor such as Norton's diskedit. If DOS uses either of the . and . . entries, either because of their position in the directory or because of their names, then changing them in some way should affect the observed behavior of DOS commands in predictable ways.

For the first part of the proof, the directory cluster addresses in the . and . . entries are changed to point to other directories. Because they nevertheless point to valid directories, all DOS commands will still work fine. If we presume that the . . entry is changed to point to the \windows directory, then the command dir . . should display the contents of the \windows directory. However, that would be true only if DOS actually used the . . entry.

In fact, DOS does not use the . . entry, but the directory command will always still be able to display the parent directory. DOS never actually looks at the . . entry. It just follows the path from the root directory. This isn't just limited to the directory command. More in-depth tests prove that DOS uses the same basic strategy for finding files regardless of the DOS command or file function.

I don't expect acceptance of this fact to be taken at face value so what follows is the sequence of events that proofs the point. Two directories are created called \dirtest and subdir. In these directories, a file is created in each directory. These files are AAAA and BBBB, respectively. Norton's disk editor is called, which permits altering the cluster address of the . . directory entry. As noted before, the cluster address was changed to point to the \windows directory. the result of the test is shown here.

```
c> md \dirtest
c> cd \dirtest
c> rem Make file AAAA
c> echo this is the parent directory > AAAA

c> md subdir
c> cd subdir
c> rem Make file BBBB
c> echo this is a file in the subdirectory > BBBB

c> rem THIS IS WHERE WE CHANGE THE . . DIRECTORY ENTRY to \windows
c> diskedit
```

At this point, the current directory is in the changed `\dirtest\subdir`. A directory display of the current directory reveals that it contains the BBBB entry. What should display when the `dir ..` command is issued? If DOS really used the `..` entry, the directory displayed would be the `\windows` directory (because of the changed address value). In fact, DOS correctly continues to display the parent directory, that is, the `\dirtest` directory, proof enough that `..` entry is never used by DOS.

```
c> cd
C:\DIRTEST\SUBDIR

c> dir

 Volume in drive C is MIKEPAPI
 Volume Serial Number is 1ACE-73BC
 Directory of C:\DIRTEST\SUBDIR

 .              <DIR>      06-06-94   9:15p
 . .            <DIR>      06-06-94   9:15p
 BBBB                  37 06-06-94   9:15p
         3 file(s)           37 bytes
                       36020224 bytes free

c> dir . .

 Volume in drive C is MIKEPAPI
 Volume Serial Number is 1ACE-73BC
 Directory of C:\DIRTEST

 .              <DIR>      06-06-94   9:15p
 . .            <DIR>      06-06-94   9:15p
 AAAA                  31 06-06-94   9:15p
 SUBDIR         <DIR>      06-06-95   9:15p
         4 file(s)           31 bytes
                       36020224 bytes free
```

Why, or better yet, how was DOS able to find the parent directory? Regardless of the path used in any DOS function or command, the pathname is canonically expanded. It knows that the current directory was `\dirtest\subdir`. To this it appends the `..` entry, and then it removes extra unnecessary terms. The `.` and `..` entries fall out. The resulting directory name is simply `\dirtest`. The parent directory is located without ever searching the disk!

This isn't simply limited to locating the parent directory. Regardless of how complex the pathname becomes, any `.` and `..` terms simply fall out during the text evaluation without ever searching the disk.

It simply does not matter what happens to the `.` and `..` entries on disk. They can be set to point to invalid disk cluster addresses, or the entries can be deleted or even renamed. DOS functions are not affected. The only visible effect is that CHKDSK will complain that the edited directory is no longer a valid directory. The problem goes away when the subdirectory is removed or the entries corrected.

It is because of this redirection capability that the DOS `copy` command works the way it does. When a command like

```
c> copy con file.bat
...^Z
```

is executed, both arguments in the command are treated as files. The command processor performs an open function on the first filename and a create function on the second filename without checking or caring whether the name references a device or file. It then performs reads and writes to transfer the data. It is only because of the redirection capability of DOS that the command reads from the keyboard and writes to a file. Without redirection, this command would have to be handled in a much different way.

As a historical note, the FCBs used in DOS 1.0 were tagged as devices or files much as SFTs are today. The copy command still worked, but because FCB handling functions performed the device redirection.

It may appear somewhat backward for DOS to check pathnames when the filename is a device name. After all, the disk check would seem to be a waste of time. However, the search scheme adopted by DOS provides a way to check whether a drive and pathname exist. It is possible to determine whether a drive or path exists by appending a device name, such as the NUL device, and performing an open, as follows:

```
mov ax, 3D00h          ; open function
mov dx, _check_dirname ; points to directory
int 21h                ; does dir exist ?
jnc _yup_direxists     ; yes it does —>
...

_check_dirname:
     db "c:\rxbook\NUL", 0
```

The function call will fail if the drive or path is invalid. This is a *hidden feature* of DOS although an argument exists on whether it was a deliberate feature. Unfortunately, if your purpose was only to check the validity of a file path, the file handle returned by the open must be closed. MS-DOS should have provided an extra bit flag in the mode, such as -1, to simply check the path without actually performing an open. The function would not have a need for a device name.

Many readers know about the hidden DOS TRUENAME command supported by DOS function 60h. The purpose of the function, listed later in this chapter, is to return the expanded canonical filename. This is different from qualifying the filename as recommended using the open function. The TRUENAME command is followed by a filename. The filename is expanded and displayed to the stdout device. For example,

```
c:\>cd \foo
c:\foo>truename aaa
C:\FOO\AAA

c:\foo>truename ..\aaa
C:\AAA
```

```
c:\foo>truename c:\aaa\aaa\aaa\*.*
C:\AAA\AAA\AAA\????????.???

c:\foo>
```

In all these examples, the files and directories named AAA did not exist. The command, which utilizes DOS function 60h, converts the name to a proper form removing any . and .. arguments but does not check the arguments to determine if they exist on disk.

So what does the code for file open or create really look like?

File Open with Handle

	On Entry	On Return
AX	AH = 3Dh; AL= access code	AX = handle, or error if carry
BX		
CX		
DS:DX	pointer to ASCIZ filename	
Flags		CY = set if error

Related Functions:
   3Ch Create File; 3Eh Close File; 3Fh Read File; 40h Write File.

The code for the file open function begins at _OpenFile, located in rxdos.asm. Open determines if there is both an available SFT and a place in the JHT to record the SFT handle. The filename is expanded to a fully qualified name and then searched on disk. If the file is found, an available SFT is assigned and populated with directory information, such as the file size, starting cluster address, date and time stamp, and the location of the entry in the directory.

To trace how the functions work and what code is utilized during open, an outline of the code executed is shown in Figure 3-11. Open is really performed by the _SFTOpenFile function, located in rxdossft.asm. This function is shared by both file handle and FCB opens. Both require an SFT.

_OpenFile, listed here, handles only the mapping of the handle back to the JHT, which is not required by the FCB open function. It begins by checking whether a Control-C or Control Break has interrupted the program and verifies that an SFT is available. The function should obviously not continue if eventually it will not be able to assign an SFT. It then restores argument pointers to the filename and open mode and attempts an open using _SFTOpenFile, also listed. The returned SFT handle, if successful, is then recorded into the program's Job Handle Table.

Figure 3-11. File Open flow outline

_OpenFile (in rxdos.asm)
   CtrlC_Check (in rxdos.asm)
   verifyAvailableHandle (in rxdossft.asm)
   _SFTOpenFile (in rxdossft.asm)
      LocateFile (in rxdosfil.asm)
         ConvFCBNametoASCIZ (in rxdosfil.asm)
         ExpandFileName (in rxdosfil.asm)
         scanDirectory (in rxdosfil.asm)
            this is the routine that "walks" through the directory tree
            _FATReadRandom (in rxdosfat.asm)
               getDPB
               getNextCluster
               computeLogSectorNumber
               ReadBuffer
            compareDirEntries

      FindAvailableFileHandle (in rxdossft.asm)
      InitSFTEntry (in rxdossft.asm)
      convFilenametoFCBString (in rxdosstr.asm)
      initSFTfromDirEntry (in rxdossft.asm)
         locateCCBPHeader (in rxdosccb.asm)

   MapSFTToAppHandle (in rxdossft.asm)

```
(in rxdos.asm)
        ;''''''''''''''''''''''''''''''''''''''''''''''''''''''''''''''';
        ;  3dh Open File                                                ;
        ;- - - - - - - - - - - - - - - - - - - - - - - - - - - - - - - -;
        ;                                                               ;
        ;  al    open mode                                              ;
        ;  ds:dx pointer to filename( path included )                   ;
        ;...............................................................;

_OpenFile:
        Entry
        def _mode, ax

        call CtrlC_Check
        call VerifyAvailableHandle               ; see if handle available
        jc _OpenFile_42                          ; exit if none ->

        RetCallersStackFrame es, si
        mov dx, word ptr es:[ _DX           ][ si ]
        mov es, word ptr es:[ _DataSegment  ][ si ]
        mov ax, word ptr [ _mode ][ bp ]
        call _SFTOpenFile                        ; build an SFT
        jc _OpenFile_42                          ; exit if error ->
```

```
        call MapSFTToAppHandle                          ; record SFT handle into JHT
_OpenFile_42:
        RetCallersStackFrame ds, si
        mov word ptr [ _AX ][ si ], ax                  ; return handle or error code
        Return

(in rxdossft.asm)
        ;'''''''''''''''''''''''''''''''''''''''''''''''''''''''''''';
        ;  Open SFT                                                 ;
        ;- - - - - - - - - - - - - - - - - - - - - - - - - - - - - -;
        ;                                                           ;
        ;  Input:                                                   ;
        ;  es:dx   unexpanded filename                              ;
        ;  ax      open mode                                        ;
        ;                                                           ;
        ;  Output:                                                  ;
        ;  es:di   sft pointer                                      ;
        ;  zr      means end of file or wrong address              ;
        ;...........................................................;

_SFTOpenFile:
        Entry
        def   _handle, -1
        def   _openMode, ax
        ddef  _filename, es, dx                          ; arg passed internally as es:dx
        ddef  _sftPointer                                ; sft reserved pointer
        defbytes _dirAccess, sizeDIRACCESS

;- - - - - - - - - - - - - - - - - - - - - - - - - - - - - - - -
;  does file exist ?
;- - - - - - - - - - - - - - - - - - - - - - - - - - - - - - - -
        mov ax, (FILE_ORDEVICE + FILECANNOT_BEDIRECTORY)
        mov si, dx                                       ; name from caller (es: si )
        lea di, offset _dirAccess [ bp ]                 ; work dir access block
        call LocateFile                                  ; locate file on disk
        ifc _SFTOpenFile_50                              ; error code already set

;- - - - - - - - - - - - - - - - - - - - - - - - - - - - - - - -
;  name is valid. populate sft.
;- - - - - - - - - - - - - - - - - - - - - - - - - - - - - - - -
        call FindAvailableFileHandle                     ; find an available file handle
        ifc _SFTOpenFile_50                              ; if none available ->

        mov word ptr [ _handle ][ bp ], ax
        stordarg _sftPointer, es, bx                     ; sft reserved pointer
        call InitSFTEntry                                ; clear entry

;- - - - - - - - - - - - - - - - - - - - - - - - - - - - - - - -
;  if file opened is a device
;- - - - - - - - - - - - - - - - - - - - - - - - - - - - - - - -
        getdarg dx, ax, _dirAccess.fileAcDevicePtr
        or dx, dx                                        ; _segment
        jz _SFTOpenFile_22                               ; if not a device ->
```

```
        or word ptr es:[ sftDevInfo ][ bx ], sftIsDevice
        mov word ptr es:[ sftDCB. _segment ][ bx ], dx
        mov word ptr es:[ sftDCB. _pointer ][ bx ], ax

        push ds
        setDS ss
        mov si, word ptr [ _dirAccess.fileAcNameOffset ][ bp ]
        les di, dword ptr [ _sftPointer ][ bp ]            ; get sft pointer
        lea di, offset sftFileName [ di ]
        call convFilenametoFCBString                       ; convert to a match template
        pop ds
        jmp short _SFTOpenFile_26

;- - - - - - - - - - - - - - - - - - - - - - - - - - - - - - - - - - - - - -
;  if open is to file
;- - - - - - - - - - - - - - - - - - - - - - - - - - - - - - - - - - - - - -
_SFTOpenFile_22:
        push word ptr [ _dirAccess.fileAcBufferPtr. _segment ][ bp ]
        mov ax, word ptr [ _dirAccess.fileAcBufferPtr. _pointer ][ bp ]
        add ax, word ptr [ _dirAccess.fileAcDirOffset ][ bp ]
        push ax

        push word ptr [ _sftPointer. _segment ][ bp ]
        push word ptr [ _sftPointer. _pointer ][ bp ]

        call initSFTfromDirEntry

        mov al, byte ptr [ _openMode ][ bp ]
        mov byte ptr es:[ sftMode. _AL ][ di ], al       ; set mode.

;- - - - - - - - - - - - - - - - - - - - - - - - - - - - - - - - - - - - - -
;  return
;- - - - - - - - - - - - - - - - - - - - - - - - - - - - - - - - - - - - - -
_SFTOpenFile_26:
        mov ax, word ptr [ _handle ][ bp ]
        clc

;- - - - - - - - - - - - - - - - - - - - - - - - - - - - - - - - - - - - - -
;  if error, release locked sft
;- - - - - - - - - - - - - - - - - - - - - - - - - - - - - - - - - - - - - -
_SFTOpenFile_50:
        getdarg es, di, _sftPointer                      ; sft reserved pointer
        Return
```

_SFTOpenFile expands the filename and determines whether it exists on disk using LocateFile. Clearly, functions like open, create, delete, and rename rely heavily on directory search services. Among those services is LocateFile, a function located in rxdosfil.asm. The function accepts an unexpanded filename pointer in the ES:SI registers, search options in the AX register, and a DIRACCESS block pointer in the SS:DI registers. The function locates a file, if available, and fills the directory access block. The search options available tailor the response expected from the function. For example, one option is that the file being searched may not exist. This prevents the function from returning an error if the file is not found. A more comprehensive look at the internal workings of the locate function is provided in the "Directory Searching" section of this chapter.

The LocateFile function returns a filled DIRACCESS block, shown in Figure 3-12. The access block contains the drive and cluster where the located file exists, the sector where the directory entry can be located, a pointer to the cache block that contains the current directory entry, a device pointer if the located file is a device, the expanded qualified pathname of the file, and an offset to the name portion in the expanded name. The pointer to the current entry in the cache block is a reference to the other information contained in a directory entry for a file, such as file attributes like date and size.

Figure 3-12. The DIRACCESS block

```
;'''''''''''''''''''''''''''''''''''''''''''''''''''''''''''''';
;   Directory Access Block                                     ;
;..............................................................;


        DIRACCESS struc
fileAcDrive             dw ?                ; which drive file is located
fileAcCluster           dw ?                ; which cluster file is located
fileAcDirCluster        dw ?                ; which dir cluster
fileAcDirSector         dd ?                ; which dir sector
fileAcDirOffset         dw ?                ; offset in directory sector
fileAcBufferPtr         dd ?                ; pointer to directory buffer
fileAcDevicePtr         dd ?                ; if device, device driver address
fileAcNameOffset        dw ?                ; offset in Expanded Name
fileAcExpandedName      db 128 dup (?)
        DIRACCESS ends
```

The _SFTOpenFile function begins by determining if the file exists. According to the search options, the file can be a file or device, and the filename cannot be that of a directory; in other words, it must terminate in a file. LocateFile performs the search and returns an error if the file cannot be found. Otherwise, it returns a filled directory access block. The function then finds an available file handle by searching the system file handles. Although there is an error branch, the chances of an error are unlikely because the open function first determined that there was an available SFT handle. The SFT is initialized, and then depending on whether the file to be opened is a file or a device, the initialization of the SFT is a little different. The address to the SFT is maintained in the ES:BX registers. If this is a file, the SFT needs to be initialized from the contents of the directory entry. The function terminates by returning the system file handle in the AX register and the SFT pointer in the ES:DI register pair.

A number of system file handle functions are utilized within open. _OpenFile determines early that an SFT handle is available and later converts a system file handle to an application handle. _SFTOpenFile finds an available SFT. These functions are listed later in this section. One SFT support function, however, is used only with open, initSFTfromDirEntry, which is listed later.

When the file is located on disk, its directory entry is located somewhere inside a read cache buffer. The directory entry layout was shown in Figure 3-4. One of the parameters returned in the

DIRACCESS block was a pointer to the directory entry in the cache buffer. Initializing the SFT from the directory entry is partly a matter of copying arguments from the directory entry and partly a matter of saving parameters such as the directory entry's sector address and offset to be used later in file close and commit to update the directory entry.

The SFT is first cleared to zeros except for the reference count word. When an SFT entry is assigned to a file, its reference count is incremented by one, indicating that at least one process is using this SFT. The reference count was set earlier for this SFT when the FindAvailableFileHandle function assigned this SFT to the file. Every time that handle to this SFT is duplicated, it is again incremented by one. Handles are duplicated when applications request file handle duplication, DOS functions 45h or 46h, or when a child process is spawned.

Next, the following items are copied from the directory entry to the SFT: The filename and extension are copied first, followed by the file attributes, time, date, starting cluster address, and file size. The current process's PSP address is set in the SFT though it is never used.

The start address of the cache buffer is computed using a cache support function. The function determines the cache header address of a buffer pointer. The directory sector is copied to the SFT, followed by the current drive (the file resides on the same drive as the cache buffer although it could have utilized the drive returned in the DIRACCESS block), followed by an index reference into the sector. Up to 16 directory entries can be within a sector. This index is a reference to 1 of these 16 entries.

While the file remains open, and this applies to created files as well, the directory entry cannot move. For example, the directory should not be sorted or removed while DOS maintains an active link to a directory entry. Eventually, during close or commit, DOS may need to update the directory entry, and if it has inadvertently moved, the results will be unpredictable. It may change another directory entry altogether!

```
(in rxdossft.asm)
        ;''''''''''''''''''''''''''''''''''''''''''''''''''''''''''''''''';
        ;  Build Directory /SFT Entries                                   ;
        ;- - - - - - - - - - - - - - - - - - - - - - - - - - - - - - - - -;
        ;                                                                 ;
        ;  Input:                                                         ;
        ;   stack  pointer to directory entry                            ;
        ;   stack  sft pointer                                           ;
        ;                                                                 ;
        ;  Input:                                                         ;
        ;   es:di  sft pointer                                           ;
        ;.................................................................;

initSFTfromDirEntry:
        Entry 4
        darg _dirAddress
        darg _sftPointer                                ; sft pointer


;- - - - - - - - - - - - - - - - - - - - - - - - - - - - - - - - - -
;  zero SFT
;- - - - - - - - - - - - - - - - - - - - - - - - - - - - - - - - - -
        push ds
        xor ax, ax
```

```
        getdarg es, di, _sftPointer                      ; sft pointer
        add di, 2                                        ; skip Count entry
        mov cx, (sizeSFT - sftRefCount - 2)/ 2           ; effective count
        rep stosw                                        ; must have pointer at es: di

;- - - - - - - - - - - - - - - - - - - - - - - - - - - - - - - - - -
;  copy filename
;- - - - - - - - - - - - - - - - - - - - - - - - - - - - - - - - - -
        getdarg ds, si, _dirAddress                      ; directory
        getdarg es, di, _sftPointer                      ; sft pointer
        lea di, offset sftFileName [ di ]                ; offset to filename
        mov cx, sizeFILENAME                             ; length of name/ ext
        rep movsb                                        ; copy name


;- - - - - - - - - - - - - - - - - - - - - - - - - - - - - - - - - -
;  populate sft
;- - - - - - - - - - - - - - - - - - - - - - - - - - - - - - - - - -
        getdarg ds, si, _dirAddress                      ; directory
        getdarg es, di, _sftPointer                      ; sft pointer

        push word ptr [ deAttributes ][ si ]             ; attribute byte
        push word ptr [ deTime ][ si ]                   ; time last updated
        push word ptr [ deDate ][ si ]                   ; date last updated
        push word ptr [ deStartCluster ][ si ]           ; beginning cluster
        push word ptr [ deFilesize. _low  ][ si ]        ; file size
        push word ptr [ deFilesize. _high ][ si ]        ; file size

        pop word ptr es:[ sftFileSize. _high ][ di ]
        pop word ptr es:[ sftFileSize. _low  ][ di ]
        pop word ptr es:[ sftBegCluster      ][ di ]
        pop word ptr es:[ sftDate ][ di ]
        pop word ptr es:[ sftTime ][ di ]
        pop ax
        mov byte ptr es:[ sftFileAttrib ][ di ], al

    ; set owner PSP

        mov ax, word ptr cs:[ _RxDOS_CurrentPSP ]        ; get owner PSP
        mov word ptr es:[ sftOwnerPSP ][ di ], ax

    ; set where in directory

        push es
        push di                                          ; pointer to sft
        setES ds                                         ; point dir buffer as [es][si]
        call locateCCBPHeader                            ; get ccb header into es:di
        mov si, di                                       ; ccb Header at [ds:si]

        pop di
        pop es                                           ; pointer to sft
        mov ax, word ptr [ ccbLBN. _low    ][ si ]
        mov dx, word ptr [ ccbLBN. _high   ][ si ]
        mov word ptr es:[ sftDirSector. _low  ][ di ], ax
        mov word ptr es:[ sftDirSector. _high ][ di ], dx
```

```
        mov cl, byte ptr [ ccbDrive ][ si ]              ; get drive
        and cx, sftDrivemask
        or word ptr es:[ sftDevInfo ][ di ], cx          ; include drive

        mov ax, word ptr [ _dirAddress ][ bp ]
        sub ax, si                                       ; dist from beg of ccb header
        sub ax, ccbData                                  ; dist from beg of dir sector
        mov cl, sizeDIRENTRY                             ; bytes per entry
        div cl                                           ; remainder should be zero

        mov byte ptr es:[ sftDirIndex ][ di ], al

;- - - - - - - - - - - - - - - - - - - - - - - - - - - - - - - - - - -
;  return
;- - - - - - - - - - - - - - - - - - - - - - - - - - - - - - - - - - -
        pop ds
        Return
```

FindAvailableFileHandle. The function scans through all SFTs searching for an available entry. SFTs reside inside File Table (FT) containers. Each FT is searched. SFTs are reserved by a count incremented by a file open or create and decremented by a fil close. An SFT whose count is zero is available and is reserved by incrementing its count.

```
        ;'''''''''''''''''''''''''''''''''''''''''''''''''''''''''''''''';
        ;  Find Available (SFT) File Handle                            ;
        ;- - - - - - - - - - - - - - - - - - - - - - - - - - - - - - - -;
        ;                                                              ;
        ; Returns:                                                     ;
        ; ax    handle id #                                            ;
        ; es:bx pointer to available SFT entry                         ;
        ;                                                              ;
        ; SFT    entry is automatically reserved and must be cleared   ;
        ;        if it wont be used.                                   ;
        ;..............................................................;

FindAvailableFileHandle:
        Entry
        ddef _currentFT
        def  _entries
        def  _handle, 0000

        les bx, dword ptr cs:[ _RxDOS_pFT ]

;- - - - - - - - - - - - - - - - - - - - - - - - - - - - - - - - - - -
;  look for available handle
;- - - - - - - - - - - - - - - - - - - - - - - - - - - - - - - - - - -
findFileHandle_08:
        stordarg _currentFT, es, bx

        mov cx, word ptr es:[ numberSFTEntries ][ bx ]   ; get # files at this sft
        mov word ptr [ _entries ][ bp ], cx

        lea bx, offset sizeFT [ bx ]
        or cx, cx
        jle findFileHandle_22
```

```
;- - - - - - - - - - - - - - - - - - - - -- - - - - - - - - - - - - - - -
;  is handle available ?
;- - - - - - - - - - - - - - - - - - - - - - - - - - - - - - - - - - - - -
findFileHandle_12:
        cli
        cmp word ptr es:[ sftRefCount ][ bx ], 0      ; entry available ?
        jnz findFileHandle_14                         ; no -->
        inc word ptr es:[ sftRefCount ][ bx ]         ; reserve entry
        mov ax, word ptr [ _handle ][ bp ]            ; count handles
        jmp short findFileHandle_30                   ; exit -->

findFileHandle_14:
        sti
        inc word ptr [ _handle ][ bp ]
        add bx, sizeSFT                               ; next SFT entry
        loop findFileHandle_12                        ; if more -->

        les bx, dword ptr [ _currentFT ][ bp ]
        les bx, dword ptr es:[ nextFTPointer ][ bx ]
        mov ax, es
        or ax, bx
        jnz findFileHandle_08                         ; go to next FT -->

;- - - - - - - - - - - - - - - - - - - - - - - - - - - - - - - - - - - - -
;  if out of handles system wide
;- - - - - - - - - - - - - - - - - - - - - - - - - - - - - - - - - - - - -
findFileHandle_22:
        stc
        mov ax, errNoHandlesAvailable

;- - - - - - - - - - - - - - - - - - - - - - - - - - - - - - - - - - - - -
;  return
;- - - - - - - - - - - - - - - - - - - - - - - - - - - - - - - - - - - - -
findFileHandle_30:
        sti
        Return
```

MapSFTToAppHandle. SFT handles are saved in an application's JHT, or Job Handle Table. The SFT handle, a short identifier to a unique SFT, is stored into the JHT by this function. The JHT is scanned for an available entry, one containing a -1, and the SFT handle is stored in the entry. The offset to the JHT is returned as the application's handle.

```
;,,,,,,,,,,,,,,,,,,,,,,,,,,,,,,,,,,,,,,,,,,,,,,,,,,,,,,,,,,,,,,;
;  Map handle found to App handle                             ;
;- - - - - - - - - - - - - - - - - - - - - - - - - - - - - - -;
;                                                             ;
;  Returns:                                                   ;
;  ax   handle id #                                           ;
;.............................................................;

MapSFTToAppHandle:
        cmp word ptr cs:[ _RxDOS_CurrentPSP ], 0000
        jz MapSFTToAppHandle_16                       ; if no app -->
```

```
        push es
        push si
        push cx

        mov es, word ptr cs:[ _RxDOS_CurrentPSP ]        ; get PSP
        mov cx, word ptr es:[ pspFileHandleCount ]       ; get max count
        les si, dword ptr es:[ pspFileHandlePtr  ]       ; get JHT pointer

MapSFTToAppHandle_04:
        cmp byte ptr es:[ si ], -1                        ; empty slot ?
        jz MapSFTToAppHandle_08                           ; yes, allocate ->

        inc si                                           ; next
        loop MapSFTToAppHandle_04                         ; continue looping

        stc
        mov ax, errNoHandlesAvailable                    ; problem, no app handles left
        jmp short MapSFTToAppHandle_12                    ; exit ->

;- - - - - - - - - - - - - - - - - - - - - - - - - - - - - - -
; allocate App Handle
;- - - - - - - - - - - - - - - - - - - - - - - - - - - - - - -
MapSFTToAppHandle_08:
        mov byte ptr es:[ si ], al                       ; replace sys handle into app
        mov ax, si                                       ; app handle offset
        sub ax, word ptr es:[ pspFileHandlePtr. _pointer ]

;- - - - - - - - - - - - - - - - - - - - - - - - - - - - - - -
; return
;- - - - - - - - - - - - - - - - - - - - - - - - - - - - - - -
MapSFTToAppHandle_12:
        pop cx
        pop si
        pop es

MapSFTToAppHandle_16:
        ret
```

File Create with Handle

	On Entry	On Return
AX	AH = 3Ch	AX = handle, or error if carry
BX		
CX	file attributes	
DS:DX	pointer to ASCIZ filename	
Flags		CY = set if error

Related Functions:
    3Dh Open File; 3Eh Close File; 3Fh Read File; 40h Write File;
    5Ah Create Unique File; 5Bh Create New File; 6Ch Extended Open/Create.

The DOS file create function creates a new file or replaces the contents of an existing file. Two related functions have been added to DOS to prevent the inadvertent replacement of files. Create New, DOS function 5Bh, creates a file only if it doesn't already exist. Create Unique, DOS function 5Ah, creates a file with a unique filename. Finally, Extended Open/Create, DOS function 6Ch, tailors whether or not to replace the file if it already exists depending on its action code.

A flow outline of the create code is shown in Figure 3-13. The code for the file create function begins at _CreateFile. Like with open, create code is handled by an SFT layer function, _SFTCreateFile. This architecture is necessary because file create and FCB create share the same code. Create is not substantially different from open, and many parallels exist. Create determines if a file handle is available and then searches for an existing file on disk. If the file is located, it is deleted. A free directory entry is then initialized with the filename. The SFT for this entry is initialized, and the handle is placed in the application's JHT.

Figure 3-13. File Create flow outline.

```
_CreateFile (in rxdos.asm)
    CtrlC_Check (in rxdos.asm)
    verifyAvailableHandle (in rxdossft.asm)
    _SFTCreateFile (in rxdossft.asm)
        LocateFile (in rxdosfil.asm)
            ExpandFileName (in rxdosfil.asm)
            ConvFCBNametoASCIZ (in rxdosfil.asm)
            scanDirectory (in rxdosfil.asm)
                this is the routine that "walks" through the directory tree
                _FATReadRandom (in rxdosfat.asm)
                    getDPB
                    getNextCluster
                    computeLogSectorNumber
                    ReadBuffer
                compareDirEntries

        createSFTEntry (in rxdossft.asm)
            FindAvialableFileHandle
            ReleaseClusterChain (in rxdosfat.asm)
            LocateFreeDirSlot (in rxdosfil.asm)
            convFilenametoFCBString (in rxdosstr.asm)
            getSysDateinDirFormat
            locateCCBPHeader (in rxdosccb.asm)
            CCBChanged (in rxdosccb.asm)

        initSFTfromDirEntry (in rxdossft.asm)
        MapSFTToAppHandle (in rxdossft.asm)
```

All the DOS functions that perform create, such as create, create new, and create unique, utilize one common create directory entry function, createSFTEntry. This function handles assigning an SFT entry, locating a free directory entry, and initializing both the directory entry and the SFT. The function actually handles the file create.

The code for create function begins earlier in _CreateFile, where the code checks for a Control Break and to ensure that a file handle exists. It then calls _SFTCreateFile. If the create succeeds, the SFT handle returned is mapped to the application's JHT. The mapping functions are described in the File Read with Handle section of the next chapter.

Inside the SFT create function, the unexpanded filename is expanded and qualified using LocateFile, which we describe in greater detail later in this chapter under "Directory Searching." The function will return an error if the filename contains illegal characters, wild characters, or an illegal drive or invalid path, not if the filename could not be located because the FILE-MAY_EXIST search option was set. It also returns a filled DIRACCESS block. The block, shown in Figure 3-12, contains the expanded filename even if the file was not found. Whether the file was located or not, the DIRACCESS block is passed to the createSFTEntry, which will complete the create function.

The code for _CreateFile and _SFTCreateFile are shown here.

```
(in rxdos.asm)
        ;''''''''''''''''''''''''''''''''''''''''''''''''''''''''''''''';
        ;   3Ch Create File                                            ;
        ;- - - - - - - - - - - - - - - - - - - - - - - - - - - - - - -;
        ;                                                              ;
        ;   cx     attributes                                          ;
        ;   ds:dx pointer to filename( path included )                 ;
        ;..............................................................;

_CreateFile:
        call CtrlC_Check
        call VerifyAvailableHandle              ; see if handle available
        jc _CreateFile_42                       ; exit if none ->

        RetCallersStackFrame es, si
        mov cx, word ptr es:[ _CX ][ si ]       ; attributes
        mov dx, word ptr es:[ _DX ][ si ]
        mov es, word ptr es:[ _DataSegment ][ si ]
        call _SFTCreateFile
        jc _CreateFile_42                       ; exit if error ->

        call MapSFTToAppHandle                  ; if no space, create error

_CreateFile_42:
        RetCallersStackFrame ds, si
        mov word ptr [ _AX ][ si ], ax          ; return handle or error code
        ret

(in rxdossft.asm)
        ;''''''''''''''''''''''''''''''''''''''''''''''''''''''''''''''';
        ;   Create SFT File                                            ;
        ;- - - - - - - - - - - - - - - - - - - - - - - - - - - - - - -;
        ;                                                              ;
        ;   Input:                                                     ;
        ;     es:dx  unexpanded filename                               ;
        ;     cx     attributes                                        ;
        ;     ax     open mode                                         ;
```

```
;                                                                      ;
;  Output:                                                             ;
;    es:di   sft pointer                                               ;
;    zr      means end of file or wrong address                       ;
;.....................................................................;

_SFTCreateFile:
        Entry
        def _attributes, cx                         ; attributes
        defbytes _dirAccess, sizeDIRACCESS

;- - - - - - - - - - - - - - - - - - - - - - - - - - - - - - - -
;  see if path is valid
;- - - - - - - - - - - - - - - - - - - - - - - - - - - - - - - -
        mov ax, (FILE_NODEVICENAME + FILEMAY_EXIST + FILECANNOT_BEDIRECTORY)
        mov si, dx                                  ; name from caller
        lea di, offset _dirAccess [ bp ]            ; work dir access block
        call LocateFile
        jc _SFTCreateFile_42                         ; if path invalid ->

        lea di, offset _dirAccess [ bp ]            ; work dir access block
        mov cx, word ptr [ _attributes ][ bp ]      ; get attributes
        call createSFTEntry                         ; create/init SFT entry
        or ax, ax

;- - - - - - - - - - - - - - - - - - - - - - - - - - - - - - - -
;  return
;- - - - - - - - - - - - - - - - - - - - - - - - - - - - - - - -
_SFTCreateFile_42:
        Return
```

When `createSFTEntry` is called, all it requires is a pointer to a filled DIRACCESS block, the result of calling `LocateFile`, and the create file attributes. The directory access block may have been only partially filled if the file was not located on disk. `LocateFile` sets the high-order bit of the drive word in the access block to notify any subsequent users of the block that the contents are only partially filled.

`createSFTEntry` first assigns to itself an SFT. Since the create function determined ahead of time that an SFT is available, the function can be expected to succeed. Next, the DIRACCESS block's high-order bit is tested to determine if the file described in the block exists. If it does, the file must be deleted. Within DOS, to delete a file means releasing its FAT allocation chain. Files within DOS are assigned space on disk from the FAT table. The allocation is represented as a chain in the FAT. To release the allocated space, the assigned space allocated in the FAT is zeroed, making it reallocatable.

If the file has not been found, the high-order bit of the drive word is cleared, and a free directory entry is searched for using `LocateFreeDirSlot`. We discuss that function in greater detail later in this section. The empty directory slot point references a location in a cached directory buffer, just like the pointer returned by the locate file function.

Since the directory slot is empty, it must be initialized. The filename in the DIRACCESS block is converted to the directory style name. That layout is identical to the FCB style name, with the eight-character filename and the three-character extension in uppercase and no period separator between them. The name is updated directly into an empty entry in the directory sector stored in the cached buffers.

To create the new directory entry, the filename, attributes, and date and time are set into the directory entry. The remaining fields in the directory entry are zeroed. The file has no allocated cluster or file size. Since all we have done is updated the cached block, the address of the cache header is computed, and the block is marked as changed, meaning that it will be updated to disk. Once the directory entry has been created, the SFT can be initialized.

The only major problem that the routine can encounter is not being able to create a directory entry. There may not be any additional free disk space available to allocate new blocks to the directory, or the directory may not be extensible, such as the root directory. If the entry cannot be created, the function must exit and pass along the error code back to the caller. However, since it has reserved an SFT that it will no longer utilize, the SFT must be freed by decrementing its use count.

The `createSFTEntry` function is listed here.

```
;'''''''''''''''''''''''''''''''''''''''''''''''''''''''''''''''''';
;   Build Directory /SFT Entries                                   ;
;- - - - - - - - - - - - - - - - - - - - - - - - - - - - - - - - -;
;                                                                  ;
;   Input:                                                         ;
;     es:di   pointer to diraccess                                 ;
;     cx      attributes                                           ;
;                                                                  ;
;   Output:                                                        ;
;     ax      handle to an SFT                                     ;
;..................................................................;

createSFTEntry:
        Entry
        def _handle, -1
        def _attributes, cx
        ddef _dirAccess, ss, di
        ddef _dirAddress                    ; address of empty loc found
        ddef _sftPointer                    ; sft pointer

;- - - - - - - - - - - - - - - - - - - - - - - - - - - - - - - - - -
;  find an available SFT
;- - - - - - - - - - - - - - - - - - - - - - - - - - - - - - - - - -
        call FindAvailableFileHandle        ; find an available file handle
        ifc _createSFTEntry_42              ; if none available ->

        mov word ptr [ _handle ][ bp ], ax  ; handle
        stordarg _sftPointer, es, bx        ; sft pointer

;- - - - - - - - - - - - - - - - - - - - - - - - - - - - - - - - - -
;  if file exists, delete file by releasing its clusters
;- - - - - - - - - - - - - - - - - - - - - - - - - - - - - - - - - -
        mov si, word ptr [ _dirAccess. _pointer ][ bp ]

        mov ax, word ptr ss:[ fileAcDrive ][ si ]
        test ax, 8000h                      ; does not exist flag ?
        jnz _createSFTEntry_20              ; if no file ->
```

```
        mov si, word ptr [ _dirAccess. _pointer ][ bp ]
        les di, dword ptr ss:[ fileAcBufferPtr ][ si ]
        add di, word ptr ss:[ fileAcDirOffset ][ si ]    ; offset to entry in dir
        stordarg _dirAddress, es, di                      ; address of empty loc found

        mov dx, word ptr ss:[ fileAcCluster ][ si ]
        mov word ptr ss:[ fileAcCluster ][ si ], 0000
        call ReleaseClusterChain
        jmp short _createSFTEntry_24

;- - - - - - - - - - - - - - - - - - - - - - - - - - - - - - - - -
; if no file, locate empty slot and populate
;- - - - - - - - - - - - - - - - - - - - - - - - - - - - - - - - -
_createSFTEntry_20:
        and ax, 7FFFh
        mov word ptr ss:[ fileAcDrive      ][ si ], ax
        mov dx, word ptr ss:[ fileAcDirCluster ][ si ]
        call LocateFreeDirSlot                            ; can we find an empty entry ?
        jc _createSFTEntry_40                             ; no ->

        stordarg _dirAddress, es, si                      ; address of empty loc found

        mov di, si                                        ; convert name to dir style
        mov si, word ptr [ _dirAccess. _pointer ][ bp ]
        mov si, word ptr ss:[ fileAcNameOffset ][ si ]
        call convFilenametoFCBString                      ; dir style name [si]->[di]

;- - - - - - - - - - - - - - - - - - - - - - - - - - - - - - - - -
; update latest entry
;- - - - - - - - - - - - - - - - - - - - - - - - - - - - - - - - -
_createSFTEntry_24:
        xor ax, ax
        mov cx, sizeDIRENTRY - sizeFILENAME               ; remainder of dir entry
        getdarg es, di, _dirAddress                       ; restore di pointer
        lea di, deAttributes [ di ]                       ; starting at attribs
        rep stosb                                         ; clear rest of entry

        mov si, word ptr [ _dirAddress. _pointer ][ bp ]
        mov cx, word ptr [ _attributes ][ bp ]            ; get attributes
        mov byte ptr es:[ deAttributes ][ si ], cl        ; attribute byte

        call getSysDateinDirFormat
        mov word ptr es:[ deTime ][ si ], ax              ; time created
        mov word ptr es:[ deDate ][ si ], dx              ; date created

        mov word ptr es:[ deStartCluster   ][ si ], 0000
        mov word ptr es:[ deFileSize. _low ][ si ], 0000
        mov word ptr es:[ deFileSize. _high ][ si ], 0000

        call locateCCBPHeader                             ; get ccb header into es:di
        call CCBChanged                                   ; mark changes made

;- - - - - - - - - - - - - - - - - - - - - - - - - - - - - - - - -
; fix-up SFT
;- - - - - - - - - - - - - - - - - - - - - - - - - - - - - - - - -
```

```
        push word ptr [ _dirAddress. _segment ][ bp ]
        push word ptr [ _dirAddress. _pointer ][ bp ]     ; dir entry
        push word ptr [ _sftPointer. _segment ][ bp ]
        push word ptr [ _sftPointer. _pointer ][ bp ]     ; sft pointer
        call initSFTfromDirEntry

;- - - - - - - - - - - - - - - - - - - - - - - - - - - - - - - - - -
;  return
;- - - - - - - - - - - - - - - - - - - - - - - - - - - - - - - - - -
        clc
        jmp short _createSFTEntry_42


;- - - - - - - - - - - - - - - - - - - - - - - - - - - - - - - - - -
;  if error, release locked sft
;- - - - - - - - - - - - - - - - - - - - - - - - - - - - - - - - - -
_createSFTEntry_40:
        les bx, dword ptr [ _sftPointer ][ bp ]           ; get sft pointer
        dec word ptr es:[ sftRefCount ][ bx ]             ; release completely
        stc


;- - - - - - - - - - - - - - - - - - - - - - - - - - - - - - - - - -
;  return
;- - - - - - - - - - - - - - - - - - - - - - - - - - - - - - - - - -
_createSFTEntry_42:
        getarg ax, _handle
        Return
```

LocateFreeDirSlot. The purpose of the locate free slot function is to locate an empty slot in the directory. A directory, like any file, may have been allocated several clusters. The directory is read using a DISKACCESS block, which is initialized to point to the beginning of the directory. The code sets the position pointer to zero in the file and then utilizes _FATReadRandom to return a pointer within a sector to the byte offset in the directory. If the entry is not free, the function continues advancing the pointer until either an empty, deleted, or never-used entry is located, or until the end of the allocated space in the directory is encountered.

When the end of the directory is encountered, a new cluster is allocated to the directory unless of course this is the root directory. The new cluster is initialized and appended to the end of the cluster chain.

```
;'''''''''''''''''''''''''''''''''''''''''''''''''''''''''''''''';
;  Locate Empty Slot in Directory                                 ;
;- - - - - - - - - - - - - - - - - - - - - - - - - - - - - - - - -;
;  Note:                                                          ;
;    This will allocate space to any  subdirectory  except  the   ;
;    root directory itself  in  order  to  create  additional     ;
;    directory entries.                                           ;
;- - - - - - - - - - - - - - - - - - - - - - - - - - - - - - - - -;
;                                                                 ;
;  Input:                                                         ;
;    ax    drive                                                  ;
;    dx    cluster of dir to search                               ;
;                                                                 ;
;  Output:                                                        ;
```

```
        ;   ax      drive                                           ;
        ;   es:si   pointer to located directory entry              ;
        ;   cy      if item not found                               ;
        ;....................................................................;

LocateFreeDirSlot:
        Entry
        defbytes _diskAccess, sizeDISKACCESS

;- - - - - - - - - - - - - - - - - - - - - - - - - - - - - - - - -
;  init access
;- - - - - - - - - - - - - - - - - - - - - - - - - - - - - - - - -
        setES ds
        lea bx, offset _diskAccess [ bp ]                ; pointer to access block
        call initdiskAccess                              ; [ax] is drive, [dx] is cluster


;- - - - - - - - - - - - - - - - - - - - - - - - - - - - - - - - -
;  search for empty entry
;- - - - - - - - - - - - - - - - - - - - - - - - - - - - - - - - -
        mov word ptr [ _diskAccess. diskAcPosition. _low ][ bp ], -sizeDIRENTRY
        mov word ptr [ _diskAccess. diskAcPosition. _high ][ bp ], -1
        mov word ptr [ _diskAccess. diskAcOptions        ][ bp ], (ccb_isDIR)

locateFreeDirSlot_12:
        add word ptr [ _diskAccess. diskAcPosition. _low  ][ bp ], sizeDIRENTRY
        adc word ptr [ _diskAccess. diskAcPosition. _high ][ bp ], 0000
        lea bx, offset _diskAccess [ bp ]                ; pointer to access block
        call _FATReadRandom                              ; read into buffer
        stc                                              ; just in case error,
        jz  locateFreeDirSlot_18                         ; if no more data ->

        cmp byte ptr es:[ deName ][ bx ], DIRENTRY_NEVERUSED
        jz locateFreeDirSlot_16
        cmp byte ptr es:[ deName ][ bx ], DIRENTRY_DELETED
        jnz locateFreeDirSlot_12                         ; if item not found ->

;- - - - - - - - - - - - - - - - - - - - - - - - - - - - - - - - -
;  item found
;- - - - - - - - - - - - - - - - - - - - - - - - - - - - - - - - -
locateFreeDirSlot_16:
        mov si, bx                                       ; dir entry to si
        or si, si                                        ; no carry
        Return


;- - - - - - - - - - - - - - - - - - - - - - - - - - - - - - - - -
;  if not root directory, append a cluster
;- - - - - - - - - - - - - - - - - - - - - - - - - - - - - - - - -
locateFreeDirSlot_18:
        cmp word ptr [ _diskAccess. diskAcBegCluster ][ bp ], 0000
        stc                                              ; just in case error,
        jz locateFreeDirSlot_28                          ; if root dir, can't extend ->

        mov ax, word ptr [ _diskAccess. diskAcDrive      ][ bp ]
        mov dx, word ptr [ _diskAccess. diskAcCurCluster ][ bp ]
```

```
        call AllocateInitCluster                       ; init a cluster
        jc locateFreeDirSlot_28                        ; if can't append ->

        mov cx, dx                                     ; cluster address to update
        mov ax, word ptr [ _diskAccess. diskAcDrive      ][ bp ]
        mov dx, word ptr [ _diskAccess. diskAcCurCluster ][ bp ]
        call updateClusterValue
        mov si, di                                     ; dir address to di
        or si, si                                      ; no carry

;- - - - - - - - - - - - - - - - - - - - - - - - - - - - - - - - - - - - -
; return
;- - - - - - - - - - - - - - - - - - - - - - - - - - - - - - - - - - - - -
locateFreeDirSlot_28:
        Return
```

Create Unique File

	On Entry	On Return
AX	AH = 5Ah	AX = handle, or error if carry
BX		
CX	file attributes	
DS:DX	pointer to ASCIZ filename	
Flags		CY = set if error

Related Functions:
   3Ch Create File; 3Dh Open File; 3Eh Close File; 3Fh Read File; 40h Write File;
   5Bh Create New File; 6Ch Extended Open/Create.

Create Unique, sometimes referred to as the create temporary filename, generates a name that is guaranteed to be unique. Because the name is probably meaningless to a user, it is used mostly to create temporary files that contain intermediate data, such as the temporary output of a compiler or word processor. Although there are other algorithms for generating a unique filename, the name produced by this function begins by taking the current time of day and converting its hexadecimal representation into ASCII. The eight-character filename is separated into four two-character fields, representing the hours, minutes, seconds, and hundredths of seconds in hex form.

Up to DOS 3.3, the unique filename generated contained numbers and was created by taking the ASCII value of each digit. For example, 1pm would produce 0D000000 since 1pm is 13 hours, or 0Dh. Commencing with DOS 5.0, the unique filename algorithm changed. Each digit is added to the letter A to produce a letter. A hex digit of 0 produces the letter A, a hex digit of 1, the letter B, and so on until the hex digit of F, which produces the letter P (hex 50h). Thus at 1:30 pm, the filename produced would be ANBOAAAA, where AN represents the hour derived from taking 0Dh, for 13 hours, and adding the letter A to each digit. The letters BO are derived from the minutes, which is 1E in hex, and adding the letter A to each digit. The remainder of the letters are zeros with the letter A added.

There is, of course, the possibility that the names generated in this way will collide, especially among networked drives. For that to happen, two clocks on different machines would have to be fully synchronized and interrupt at the same time and rate. A more likely possibility may be that the name already exists from create on a previous day.

To ensure that cannot happen, the file is searched for on disk, and if it already exists, the name is incremented. The last column of the name is incremented and tested until it reaches the letter Z, at which point the immediately preceding character is incremented. This process continues recursively until an unused entry is found. It would be highly unusual for there to be a significant number of collisions in the name space.

The function is called with the file attributes to assign to the file eventually created in the CX register and a pointer to a partially initialized 128-byte buffer in the DS:DX registers. The path can contain anything from an optional drive letter, encoded as the drive letter and a colon, and may or may not be followed by a path. Obviously, the path must exist for the function to be successful.

The function begins by checking both for a Control Break and that an SFT will be available. After all, this function is in all other respects still a file create function. Next, the string length in the path argument is computed so that the string can be copied to an internal string buffer. It is copied to an internal buffer so that the expanded filename can be placed in the output buffer. For example, the user may supply a legitimate relative path that consists of . and .. characters. The path is expanded and qualified and returned to the user. The path argument cannot exceed 128 bytes.

The current time of day is fetched and returned in the CH:CL and DH:DL registers, representing the hours, minutes, seconds, and hundredths of seconds, respectively. The ASCII store function converts the two nibbles in each register and adds the letter A. This produces a name based on the time of day. The function then searches the disk to determine if the name exists. If it does, it scans the name from back to front, incrementing the last letter until it reaches the letter Z, and then loops through the entire sequence of possible letters.

Eventually, the routine will encounter a unique name combination. An SFT must be assigned and initialized. The function calls the common file create function, createSFTEntry. The SFT handle that is returned is then mapped to the JHT. Finally, the function copies the expanded buffer back to the caller's supplied buffer and returns the file's handle.

```
(from rxdos.asm)
        ;,,,,,,,,,,,,,,,,,,,,,,,,,,,,,,,,,,,,,,,,,,,,,,,,,,,,,,,,,,,,,,,,,,;
        ;   5Ah Create Unique File Name                                    ;
        ;- - - - - - - - - - - - - - - - - - - - - - - - - - - - - - - - -;
        ;                                                                  ;
        ;   cx        attributes                                           ;
        ;   ds:dx     pointer to asciz containing path                     ;
        ;..................................................................;

_CreateUniqueFile:
        Entry
        def     _handle, -1
        def     _tempnamePointer
        def     _bytecount
        def     _attributes, cx                        ; attributes
        ddef    _returnnamePointer, es, dx
        defbytes _dirAccess, sizeDIRACCESS
        defbytes _tempname, 128
```

```
;- - - - - - - - - - - - - - - - - - - - - - - - - - - - - - - - -
;  file handle available ?
;- - - - - - - - - - - - - - - - - - - - - - - - - - - - - - - - -
        call CtrlC_Check
        call VerifyAvailableHandle                ; see if handle available
        ifc _CreateUniqueFile_40                  ; exit if none ->

;- - - - - - - - - - - - - - - - - - - - - - - - - - - - - - - - -
;  copy buffer
;- - - - - - - - - - - - - - - - - - - - - - - - - - - - - - - - -
        push word ptr [ _returnnamePointer. _segment ][ bp ]
        push word ptr [ _returnnamePointer. _pointer ][ bp ]
        mov cx, 128
        call condStringLength
        jz _CreateUniqueFile_08
        SetError errIllegalName, _CreateUniqueFile_40

_CreateUniqueFile_08:
        storarg _bytecount, cx                    ; save byte count
        push ax                                   ; character just before null

        push word ptr [ _returnnamePointer. _segment ][ bp ]
        push word ptr [ _returnnamePointer. _pointer ][ bp ]
        push ss
        lea di, offset _tempname [ bp ]
        push di
        call CopyString

        pop ax
        cmp al, '\'                               ; ended with \ ?
        jz _CreateUniqueFile_12                   ; yes ->

        mov al, '\'
        stosb                                     ; we'll make one.

_CreateUniqueFile_12:
        storarg _tempnamePointer, di

;- - - - - - - - - - - - - - - - - - - - - - - - - - - - - - - - -
;  create a unique filename
;- - - - - - - - - - - - - - - - - - - - - - - - - - - - - - - - -
        call getExpandedDateTime                  ; expand time ch:cl dh:dl

        getarg di, _tempnamePointer
        mov al, ch                                ; hours
        call __ascii_stosb

        mov al, cl                                ; minutes
        call __ascii_stosb

        mov al, dh                                ; seconds
        call __ascii_stosb

        mov al, dl                                ; hundreths of second
        call __ascii_stosb
```

```
        xor al, al
        stosb                                           ; null term


;- - - - - - - - - - - - - - - - - - - - - - - - - - - - -
; make sure file does not exist
;- - - - - - - - - - - - - - - - - - - - - - - - - - - - -
_CreateUniqueFile_16:
        mov ax, (FILE_NODEVICENAME + FILECANNOT_BEDEFINED + FILECANNOT_BEDIRECTORY)
        lea si, offset _tempname [ bp ]
        lea di, offset _dirAccess [ bp ]        ; work dir access block
        call LocateFile                         ; check file path
        jnc _CreateUniqueFile_36                ; if path invalid ->

        getarg di, _tempnamePointer
        mov cx, (sizefnName - 1)
        add di, cx

_CreateUniqueFile_18:
        cmp byte ptr ss:[ di ], 'Z'             ; already at end of alphabet ?
        jnz _CreateUniqueFile_32                ; no ->
        mov byte ptr ss:[ di ], 'A'             ; cycle to prev column
        dec di                                  ; adj address
        loop _CreateUniqueFile_18               ; and loop ->
        stc                                     ; just in case
        jmp short _CreateUniqueFile_40          ; we'll have an error exit ->

_CreateUniqueFile_32:
        inc byte ptr ss:[ di ]
        jmp _CreateUniqueFile_16


;- - - - - - - - - - - - - - - - - - - - - - - - - - - - -
; it doesn't, so we'll make one.
;- - - - - - - - - - - - - - - - - - - - - - - - - - - - -
_CreateUniqueFile_36:
        lea di, offset _dirAccess [ bp ]        ; work dir access block
        mov cx, word ptr [ _attributes ][ bp ]  ; get attributes
        and cx, not ( ATTR_VOLUME + ATTR_DIRECTORY )
        call createSFTEntry                     ; create SFT entry
        jc _CreateUniqueFile_40                 ; if error ->

        call MapSFTToAppHandle                  ; if no space, create error

        push ax
        push ss
        push word ptr [ _tempnamePointer ][ bp ]
        getdarg es, di, _returnnamePointer
        add di, word ptr [ _bytecount ][ bp ]   ; point to null terminator

        push es
        push di
        call CopyString                         ; copy name back to user

        pop ax
        clc
```

```
;- - - - - - - - - - - - - - - - - - - - - - - - - - - - - - - - - - - -
;  return
;- - - - - - - - - - - - - - - - - - - - - - - - - - - - - - - - - - - -
_CreateUniqueFile_40:
        RetCallersStackFrame ds, bx
        mov word ptr [ _AX ][ bx ], ax
        Return

(from rxdosstr.asm)
        ;''''''''''''''''''''''''''''''''''''''''''''''''''''''''''''''';
        ;  Convert al byte to es:[di]                                   ;
        ;- - - - - - - - - - - - - - - - - - - - - - - - - - - - - - - -;
        ;                                                               ;
        ;  Input:                                                       ;
        ;   al      byte                                                ;
        ;                                                               ;
        ;  Output:                                                      ;
        ;   [di]   two byte ascii contents of [al]                      ;
        ;...............................................................;

        push ax
        mov ah, al
        shr al, 1
        shr al, 1
        shr al, 1
        shr al, 1
        and ax, 0f0fh                   ; mask off extra bits
        add ax, 'AA'                    ; convert to ascii
        stosw                           ; save
        pop ax                          ; restore ax
        ret
```

Create New File

	On Entry	On Return
AX	AH = 5Bh	AX = handle, or error if carry
BX		
CX	file attributes	
DS:DX	pointer to ASCIZ filename	
Flags		CY = set if error

Related Functions:
   3Ch Create File; 3Dh Open File; 3Eh Close File; 3Fh Read File; 40h Write File;
   5Ah Create Unique File; 6Ch Extended Open/Create.

Create New creates a file only if it doesn't already exist. This is unlike File Create (DOS function 3Ch), where the create will delete the contents of an existing file by the same name. Because of the similarities between these two create functions, the only perceivable difference is the checking that Create New must perform to ensure that the file does not already exist before calling the low-level create function, createSFTEntry.

The function calls `LocateFile` to determine whether the file already exists. The call specifically uses the "cannot exist" flag to generate an error if the file is found. Except for this call, the function is identical to File Create. It begins by checking for a Control Break and an available SFT and terminates by taking the SFT handle and mapping it to the JHT.

```
        ;/ / / / / / / / / / / / / / / / / / / / / / / / / / / / / / / / / / / / / / / / / / / / / / / /';
        ;  5Bh Create New File                                            ;
        ;- - - - - - - - - - - - - - - - - - - - - - - - - - - - - - - -;
        ;                                                                 ;
        ;  cx       attributes                                            ;
        ;  ds:dx    pointer to filename( path included )                  ;
        ;.................................................................;

_CreateNewFile:
        Entry
        def _handle, -1
        def _attributes, cx                         ; attributes
        defbytes _dirAccess, sizeDIRACCESS

;- - - - - - - - - - - - - - - - - - - - - - - - - - - - - - - -
;  file handle available ?
;- - - - - - - - - - - - - - - - - - - - - - - - - - - - - - - -
        call CtrlC_Check
        call VerifyAvailableHandle                  ; see if handle available
        jc _CreateNewFile_40                         ; exit if none ->

;- - - - - - - - - - - - - - - - - - - - - - - - - - - - - - - -
;  make sure file does not exist
;- - - - - - - - - - - - - - - - - - - - - - - - - - - - - - - -
        RetCallersStackFrame es, bx
        mov si, word ptr es:[ _DX ][ bx ]
        mov es, word ptr es:[ _DataSegment ][ bx ]

        mov ax, (FILE_NODEVICENAME + FILECANNOT_BEDEFINED + FILECANNOT_BEDIRECTORY)
        lea di, offset _dirAccess [ bp ]            ; work dir access block
        call LocateFile                             ; check file path
        jc _CreateNewFile_40                         ; if path invalid ->

        RetCallersStackFrame es, bx
        mov cx, word ptr es:[ _CX ][ bx ]
        mov dx, word ptr es:[ _DX ][ bx ]
        mov es, word ptr es:[ _DataSegment ][ bx ]

        lea di, offset _dirAccess [ bp ]            ; work dir access block
        mov cx, word ptr [ _attributes ][ bp ]      ; get attributes
        call createSFTEntry                         ; create SFT entry
        jc _CreateNewFile_40                         ; exit if none ->

        call MapSFTToAppHandle                       ; if no space, create error

;- - - - - - - - - - - - - - - - - - - - - - - - - - - - - - - -
;  return
;- - - - - - - - - - - - - - - - - - - - - - - - - - - - - - - -
```

```
_CreateNewFile_40:
        RetCallersStackFrame ds, bx
        mov word ptr [ _AX ][ bx ], ax
        Return
```

Extended Open/Create File

	On Entry	On Return
AX	AH =6Ch	AX = handle, or error if carry
BX	open mode (see fct 3Ch)	
CX	file attributes (see fct 3Ch)	
DX	action code	
DS:SI	pointer to ASCIZ filename	
Flags		CY = set if error

Related Functions:
    3Ch Create File; 3Dh Open File; 3Eh Close File; 3Fh Read File; 40h Write File;
    5Ah Create Unique File; 5Bh Create New.

The Extended Open and Create function is the last of the open and create functions supported by DOS. The function's behavior depends on the action code that defines whether an open or a create will be performed. It would largely appear that the function does not provide any additional functionality not already provided by the other DOS functions. However, there is a case where the extended open and create function does provide a service. To understand this, it is necessary to review how the action code behaves.

The action code is a set of flags that when used in combinations defines the expected behavior of the function. Since some flags are tested before others, preference and priority are given in some cases. The flags available are known as the create, open, and truncate flags, defined as follows:

```
EXTENDEDACTION_CREATE           equ 0001h               ; fail if exists
EXTENDEDACTION_OPEN             equ 0010h
EXTENDEDACTION_TRUNCATE         equ 0020h
```

Setting just the create flag will cause the function to behave like the Create New function, DOS function 5Bh, and setting both the create and truncate flags will force the function to behave like Create, DOS function 3Ch.

Setting both the create and open flags would seem like a conflict, but in fact, looking at the code reveals how the function will perform. The function first performs a check to determine if the file exists. If it doesn't, it creates the file if the create flag is set. If the file exists, the function determines whether it can be opened. This is different from the services all other DOS functions provide. Before this function became available, it was possible to truncate an existing file, or to open an existing file, but not to open or create a file. The other bit combinations don't make any sense, but for completeness the following chart should help. The chart identifies the behavior taken by the function as different flags are selected.

Equivalent DOS Functions	Open	Create	Truncate
3Ch - File Create		✔	✔
3Dh - File Open	✔		
5Bh - File Create New		✔	
Open or Create	✔	✔	
3Ch - File Create	✔	✔	✔
3Ch - File Create			✔
Open or Create	✔		✔

We have already described the behavior of the function; however, the following should explain how the flags are checked. The function determines first if the file exists or not. If it does exist, it checks the open flag first and, if set, performs the file open function. If the open flag is not set, the truncate flag is checked. The file may be truncated using create if the flag is set. Otherwise, the function fails, which makes its behavior like Create New.

If the file could not be located on disk, the function tests either the create or truncate flags. Either of these will cause the file to be created. Otherwise, the function fails in open. Why call open at this point? The file may not have been found because it was either a pathname or a device name, either of which will be caught by the open call.

```
        ;///////////////////////////////////////////////////////;
        ;   6Ch Extended Open/Create                             ;
        ;- - - - - - - - - - - - - - - - - - - - - - - - - - - -;
        ;                                                        ;
        ;  bx      mode                                          ;
        ;  cx      attributes                                    ;
        ;  dx      action to take                                ;
        ;  ds:si pointer to filename                             ;
        ;........................................................;


_ExtendedOpenCreate:
        Entry
        def   _mode, bx
        def   _attributes, cx
        def   _action, dx
        ddef _filename, es, si
        defbytes _dirAccess, sizeDIRACCESS

        call CtrlC_Check
        call VerifyAvailableHandle               ; see if handle available
        jc _ExtendedOpenCreate_42                ; if error ->


;- - - - - - - - - - - - - - - - - - - - - - - - - - - - - - -
;  determine if file exists
;- - - - - - - - - - - - - - - - - - - - - - - - - - - - - - -
        RetCallersStackFrame es, bx
        mov si, word ptr es:[ _DX ][ bx ]
        mov es, word ptr es:[ _DataSegment ][ bx ]

        mov ax, (FILE_NODEVICENAME + FILECANNOT_BEDEFINED + FILECANNOT_BEDIRECTORY)
```

```
        lea di, offset _dirAccess [ bp ]                 ; work dir access block
        call LocateFile                                  ; check file path
        jnc _ExtendedOpenCreate_FileFound                ; if file, see if replace ->

        test word ptr [ _action ][ bp ], EXTENDEDACTION_CREATE
        jnz _ExtendedOpenCreate_Create                   ; ok to create ->
        test word ptr [ _action ][ bp ], EXTENDEDACTION_TRUNCATE
        jnz _ExtendedOpenCreate_Create                   ; ok to create ->

;- - - - - - - - - - - - - - - - - - - - - - - - - - - - - - - - -
;  open file
;- - - - - - - - - - - - - - - - - - - - - - - - - - - - - - - - -
_ExtendedOpenCreate_Open:
        RetCallersStackFrame es, si
        mov dx, word ptr es:[ _SI          ][ si ]
        mov es, word ptr es:[ _DataSegment ][ si ]
        mov ax, word ptr [ _mode ][ bp ]
        call _SFTOpenFile                                ; build an SFT
        jc _ExtendedOpenCreate_42                        ; if error ->

        call MapSFTToAppHandle                           ; record SFT handle into JHT
        jmp _ExtendedOpenCreate_42

;- - - - - - - - - - - - - - - - - - - - - - - - - - - - - - - - -
;  create file
;- - - - - - - - - - - - - - - - - - - - - - - - - - - - - - - - -
_ExtendedOpenCreate_Create:
        RetCallersStackFrame es, si
        mov cx, word ptr es:[ _CX          ][ si ]       ; attributes
        mov dx, word ptr es:[ _SI          ][ si ]       ; filename in ds:si
        mov es, word ptr es:[ _DataSegment ][ si ]
        call _SFTCreateFile
        jc _ExtendedOpenCreate_42                        ; if error ->

        call MapSFTToAppHandle                           ; record SFT handle into JHT
        jmp _ExtendedOpenCreate_42

;- - - - - - - - - - - - - - - - - - - - - - - - - - - - - - - - -
;  if file found, determine if truncate
;- - - - - - - - - - - - - - - - - - - - - - - - - - - - - - - - -
_ExtendedOpenCreate_FileFound:
        test word ptr [ _action ][ bp ], EXTENDEDACTION_OPEN
        jnz _ExtendedOpenCreate_Open                     ; ok to open ->
        test word ptr [ _action ][ bp ], EXTENDEDACTION_TRUNCATE
        jnz _ExtendedOpenCreate_Open                     ; ok to open ->

        stc
        mov ax, errAccessDenied

;- - - - - - - - - - - - - - - - - - - - - - - - - - - - - - - - -
;  return
;- - - - - - - - - - - - - - - - - - - - - - - - - - - - - - - - -
_ExtendedOpenCreate_42:
        RetCallersStackFrame es, bx
        mov word ptr es:[ _AX ][ bx ], AX
        Return
```

Directory Searching

Directory searching is performed internally within RxDOS by `LocateFile`, listed further later. The routine accepts an unexpanded filename and returns a filled `DIRACCESS` block, which in part contains the expanded name and the cluster address where the file exists. Much of the information returned in the block will be placed in an SFT, such as the starting cluster address of the file, the directory cluster, and the offset into the directory where the file resides.

The function is used exhaustively by virtually all DOS functions ranging from file handle open to remove directory to FCB open and create. The FCB name is converted into canonical form. An options parameter tailors the search. For example, the function can be used to just locate a subdirectory, as required by Remove Directory, or to find a filename or device name, as required by Open. The options available are shown in Figure 3-14.

Figure 3-14. Options used in Locate File

Function	Filename May exist	Filename Must exist	Device name Allowed	Subdirectories
Open	✔	n	✔	n
Create	n	✔	✔	n
Delete	✔	n	n	n
Rename (fn1)	✔	n	n	n
Rename (fn2)	n	n	n	n
Change Attrib	✔	n	n	✔
Change Dir	n	n	n	✔
Make Dir	n	n	n	n
Remove Dir	n	n	n	✔

An example of the options parameter, which follows, is taken from the Make Directory function. The options selected are: a device name cannot be located, the pathname cannot contain a filename, and the name searched cannot be defined or does not exist. These options are loaded into the AX register as follows:

```
      mov ax, (FILE_NODEVICENAME + FILEHAS_NOFILENAME + FILECANNOT_BEDEFINED)
      mov si, dx                              ; name from caller
      lea di, offset _dirAccess [ bp ]        ; work dir access block
      call LocateFile                         ; check file path
```

If much of the `DIRACCESS` block contents is copied to an SFT, why not use an SFT instead? Not all DOS functions use or have an SFT available, such as file delete, rename, or change directory. The `DIRACCESS` block is a low-level interim data structure, originally shown in Figure 3-12. Not only does the block contain some information about where the file is located on disk, but it also points to the directory entry contents itself. A pointer to the directory entry in a cache buffer is saved in the `DIRACCESS` block so that its contents are available after a successful search.

At any rate, it rests on `LocateFile`, whose logic is outlined in Figure 3-15. It is the function of this routine to search and navigate through directories. The filename is expanded, removing `.` and `..` terms, and is then searched on disk. An optimization checks whether the search begins at the root directory or can proceed within the current directory although I believe that a relative path search would be faster overall.

Figure 3-15. Outline of LocateFile

---

1. If FCB passed, convert name to ASCIZ string.

2. Expand filename, using ExpandFileName (in rxdosfil.asm). The current directory for a drive is located in the CDS. A failure can occur if the name contains illegal characters or a bad drive letter. This routine determines whether the filename contains path information or not, an optimization that permits LocateFile to speed up the search for the file.

3. Get parameters for current drive letter.

4. If just a filename, skip expanded name and search current directory; otherwise, extract the first path argument.

5. If the argument extracted is a filename, that is, it is not followed by a backslash, search the device driver list. Return error if driver names are not allowed.

6. Use scanDirectory to locate argument name in directory, and return its file attribute and cluster address.

7. If found, see if we need to walk down another directory level and scan for next argument in pathname. Then repeat items 5–7.

The `SUBST` and `JOIN` commands may cause the drive letter specified or implied in a filename to be substituted. If the `F:` drive is really substituted to point to `C:\RxDOS`, then the expanded name will change, as follows:

```
f:foobar.txt  -> c:\rxdos\foobar.txt
```

To optimize the search, `ExpandFileName` returns the cluster address of the current directory if the filename did not contain any path information whatsoever. That address is taken from the CDS. This even works for substituted drives. However, if the filename contains any path information at all, even `./filename`, the cluster address at the top of the directory tree is returned, typically of the root directory. However, whether or not the current cluster address can be optimized, `ExpandFileName` always fully expands the filename. The following examples might provide some useful insight:

```
Current Drive:     C:
Current Directory: \BOOK\RXDOS
                                                          Current
name used in open             name expanded by ExpandFileName  Cluster

anyfile.exe                   C:\BOOK\RXDOS\ANYFILE.EXE          Yes
./anyfile.exe                 C:\BOOK\RXDOS\ANYFILE.EXE          No
..\anyfile.exe                C:\BOOK\ANYFILE.EXE                No
..\sub\..\foo\anyfile.exe     C:\BOOK\FOO\ANYFILE.EXE            No

*.bat                         C:\BOOK\RXDOS\????????.BAT         Yes
..\rx*.bat                    C:\BOOK\RX??????.BAT               No
c:\anysub\anyfile.exe         C:\ANYSUB\ANYFILE.EXE              No

if e: is a SUBST'd drive, as in SUBST e: c:\windows

e:foo.bmp                     C:\WINDOWS\FOO.BMP                 Yes
```

Each `Yes` in the chart means that the current cluster is known. Notice that `ExpandFileName` converts the asterisk wild character to a series of question marks. Subsequent pattern-matching routines will use the question mark character as a wild character.

Programmers at all familiar with Unix know that Unix's pattern-matching capabilities are more sophisticated than those provided by DOS. Under Unix, it is possible to search filenames that have specific endings, such as `*JULY.WK4`. One of the reasons DOS doesn't support this capability is that the search pattern is expanded before the search begins. Asterisks are expanded to question marks, the DOS wild character symbol. The pattern `*JULY.WK4` expands to `????????.WK4`, which of course, matches every spreadsheet file. The letters `JULY` get dropped, as would any extra characters in the filename beyond the maximum eight characters.

`LocateFile` begins by creating a work area on the stack and saving its call parameters. These parameters are the options, the filename to search, and a pointer to a `DIRACCESS` block, which the routine clears to all zeros using the `clearMemory` macro. Next, if an FCB is passed, identified by one of the option flags, the routine converts the FCB name into an `ASCIZ` style string, followed by calling the expand filename routine. `ExpandFileName` expects a work area address to where to return the expanded name, which is located in the `DIRACCESS` block, and returns the starting search cluster address in the DX register. This address is the address either of the root directory or of the current directory.

```
;'''''''''''''''''''''''''''''''''''''''''''''''''''''''''''''';
;  Locate/Validate File                                        ;
;- - - - - - - - - - - - - - - - - - - - - - - - - - - - - - -;
;                                                              ;
;  This function takes a FCB pointer or ASCIZ path name and    ;
;  determines whether the name and path are valid, and whether ;
;  the file exists.  It returns a pointer to the file entry    ;
;  in a directory buffer.                                      ;
;                                                              ;
;  Input:                                                      ;
;   es:si  pointer to input filename or fcb.                   ;
```

```
        ;   ss:di  pointer to directory work area.                        ;
        ;   ax     options, as follows:                                   ;
        ;                                                                  ;
        ;   FILEIS_FCB                 name is an FCB                      ;
        ;   FILE_NODEVICENAME          no device name allowed             ;
        ;   FILEHAS_WILDCHARS          allowed in name                     ;
        ;   FILEHAS_NOFILENAME         no filename expected                ;
        ;   FILECANNOT_BEDEFINED       filename must not exist             ;
        ;   FILECANNOT_BEDIRECTORY     filename cannot be directory        ;
        ;   FILEMAY_EXIST              file may exist (cluster not -1 )     ;
        ;   FILE_ORDEVICE              file or device must exist           ;
        ;                                                                  ;
        ;   Output:                                                        ;
        ;   ss:di  pointer to directory work area.                        ;
        ;   dx     cluster address of located file                        ;
        ;   cx     cluster address of dir in which located file found     ;
        ;   ax     drive                                                   ;
        ;   cy     means path/filename is not valid.                      ;
        ;                                                                  ;
        ;   Assumes ss == ds                                               ;
        ;...............................................................;

LocateFile:
        Entry
        def  _drive
        def  _cluster, 0000
        def  _dirCluster, 0000
        def  _terminatingChar
        def  _begfilenamePointer
        ddef _endfilenamePointer

        def  _options, ax
        ddef _filename, es, si
        ddef _dirLocate, ss, di
        defbytes _tempFileName, sizeTempFILENAME

;- - - - - - - - - - - - - - - - - - - - - - - - - - - - - - - - -
;   clear/ init dir access block
;- - - - - - - - - - - - - - - - - - - - - - - - - - - - - - - - -
        push es
        push ds

        push es
        setES ss
        clearMemory sizeDIRACCESS
        pop es                                    ; restore source segment

;- - - - - - - - - - - - - - - - - - - - - - - - - - - - - - - - -
;   expand name to a usable form
;- - - - - - - - - - - - - - - - - - - - - - - - - - - - - - - - -
        setDS ss
        mov di, word ptr [ _dirLocate._pointer ][ bp ]
        lea di, offset fileAcExpandedName [ di ]        ; expand name to store
        test word ptr _options [ bp ], FILEIS_FCB
```

```
        jz locateFile_12                              ; if not fcb ->
        call convFCBNametoASCIZ                       ; build asciz name

locateFile_12:
        push es
        push si                                       ; filename passed
        push ss
        push di                                       ; expected expanded filename
        call ExpandFileName                           ; expanded filename
        mov word ptr [ _cluster ][ bp ], dx           ; where to start search
        jnc locateFile_16                             ; if path valid ->

        SetError errPathNotFound, locateFile_PathNotFound  ; if path invalid ->
```

At this point, the only field in the DIRACCESS block with valid data is the expanded filename. The routine extracts the drive letter from the expanded filename, which is returned in the AX register. The drive value is 0 for the A: drive, 1 for the B: drive, and so on. Almost as important, the text pointer into the expanded filename is positioned past the starting drive letter. This text pointer, referred to in the routine as the end filename pointer, is sort of a moving cursor through the expanded filename. The drive letter is checked to ensure that it references a legitimate drive by using the init drive parameters routine. It will return an error if the drive does not exist.

```
;- - - - - - - - - - - - - - - - - - - - - - - - - - - - -
;  get disk parameters
;- - - - - - - - - - - - - - - - - - - - - - - - - - - - -
locateFile_16:
        les si, dword ptr [ _dirLocate ][ bp ]        ; point to expanded filename
        lea si, offset fileAcExpandedName [ si ]      ; expanded name store
        call getDrive                                 ; extract drive name (es:si)
        mov word ptr [ _drive ][ bp ], ax             ; get drive.
        stordarg _endfilenamePointer, es, si          ; save ptr to working dir
        ifc locateFile_PathNotFound                   ; if illegal drive ->

        call initDriveParameters                      ; get drive parameters
        ifc locateFile_PathNotFound                   ; if illegal drive ->
```

LocateFile now determines whether it should begin the disk search at the root directory or from the current directory. Although the expanded filename function always returns a fully expanded name, the function has also determined whether the named reference contained any directory references. If it has, the search begins at the root directory. Otherwise, it optimizes by searching from the current directory. The search never backs up through the directories. The full path need not be searched when the current directory address is known.

At Locate_20, the code begins a loop where each term from the expanded filename is extracted and searched. The pointer has already been advanced forward if the full path isn't being searched. A term, that is, a subdirectory or filename taken from the fully expanded name, is extracted and converted to an FCB style pattern match so that it can be more readily compared to the directory entries.

```
;- - - - - - - - - - - - - - - - - - - - - - - - - - - - -
;  if search only current directory, skip to name
;- - - - - - - - - - - - - - - - - - - - - - - - - - - - -
```

```
        cmp word ptr [ _cluster ][ bp ], 0000        ; if NOT search in subdir
        jz locateFile_20                             ; ok as name is -->

        les si, dword ptr [ _endfilenamePointer ][ bp ]
        call skipToLast                              ; skip to starting name
        stordarg _endfilenamePointer, es, si

;- - - - - - - - - - - - - - - - - - - - - - - - - - - - - - - - - - -
;  get next name
;- - - - - - - - - - - - - - - - - - - - - - - - - - - - - - - - - - -
locateFile_20:
        setES ss
        lea di, offset _tempFileName [ bp ]          ; pointer to temp name
        lds si, dword ptr [ _endfilenamePointer ][ bp ]
        call skipToNextName                          ; skip to starting name
        storarg _begfilenamePointer, si              ; save starting pointer
        call convFilenametoFCBString                 ; convert to a match template
        jnz locateFile_24                            ; if name is not blank -->

        test word ptr _options [ bp ], FILECANNOT_BEDIRECTORY
        ifnz locateFile_FileNotFound                 ; if cannot be a directory -->
        jmp locateFile_56                            ; else ret what's found -->
```

The character that follows the extracted term in the expanded path is important to the remainder of the logic and is saved. The terminating character is either a backslash or a null byte and represents whether another subdirectory term is available. For example, it is used in part to determine whether within the search a subdirectory name is expected.

Next, the name is checked for wild characters which, in this case, means searching for the question mark since asterisks have already been processed out. Wild characters are not allowed if the terminating character for this term is a backslash. This only makes common sense since DOS provides no functions that permit an argument like c:\win*\sys* although perhaps it should. Why should users have to type every character where a unique portion will match?

Wild characters are also not allowed if the function call does not permit their use, such as for file open or file create.

```
;- - - - - - - - - - - - - - - - - - - - - - - - - - - - - - - - - - -
;  scan for wild characters
;- - - - - - - - - - - - - - - - - - - - - - - - - - - - - - - - - - -
locateFile_24:
        stordarg _endfilenamePointer, ds, si
        mov word ptr [ _terminatingChar ][ bp ], ax

        setES ss
        lea di, offset _tempFileName [ bp ]          ; pointer to temp name
        mov cx, sizeTempFILENAME - 1                 ; count
        mov al, '?'
        repnz scasb                                  ; scan for wild characters
        jnz locateFile_26                            ; if no wild chars found -->

        cmp byte ptr [ _terminatingChar ][ bp ], '\'
        ifz locateFile_PathNotFound                  ; inside path def, error -->
        test word ptr _options [ bp ], FILEHAS_WILDCHARS
        ifz locateFile_FileNotFound                  ; if wild chars NOT allowed -->
```

A term name is compared first to device names. Recall from our earlier discussion of device redirection that a device name passed as a filename should open the device and not a file. The device name is checked here because device names are also not allowed in the path. For example, it is impossible to have a pathname that contains the terms `c:\lpt1\con\filename`.

If the term is a device name, the terminating character is checked. If the term was in the middle of a path specification, that is, it was not a filename reference, the routine returns with a path-not-found error. The options flags are checked to determine whether device names are allowed, and if not, the routine exits with a filename-not-found error. Otherwise, the address of the device header is saved in the DIRACCESS block.

```
;- - - - - - - - - - - - - - - - - - - - - - - - - - - - - - - - - - -
;   see if entry is a device name
;- - - - - - - - - - - - - - - - - - - - - - - - - - - - - - - - - - -
locateFile_26:
        currSegment ds, es                              ; set to seg address
        lea si, offset _tempFileName [ bp ]             ; search es: si
        call getDevice                                  ; determine if it's a device name
        ifc locateFile_32                               ; if not a device name ->

        cmp byte ptr [ _terminatingChar ][ bp ], '\'    ; was name part of path ?
        ifz locateFile_PathNotFound                     ; inside path def, error ->
        test word ptr _options [ bp ], FILE_NODEVICENAME; are device names allowed ?
        ifnz locateFile_FileNotFound                    ; if no ->

        clc                                             ; if NO error
        mov si, word ptr [ _dirLocate._pointer ][ bp ]
        mov word ptr ss:[ fileAcDevicePtr._segment ][ si ], es
        mov word ptr ss:[ fileAcDevicePtr._pointer ][ si ], bx
        jmp locateFile_60
```

Finally, at `locateFile_32`, the extracted search term is searched using `scanDirectory`, a routine that walks sequentially through a single directory until either a match is found or the last used directory entry is located. The routine expects a drive code, the cluster address of the directory to search, and an FCB style filename to pattern match. The name can contain wild characters.

Each time a term is located on disk, the cluster address allocated to the found entry is saved. If the entry is a subdirectory, the cluster address is used in the search for the next entry, ensuring that the search tree is followed. Stated another way, the cluster address of the found entry is used as the search subdirectory address for each subsequent term in the expanded pathname.

```
;- - - - - - - - - - - - - - - - - - - - - - - - - - - - - - - - - - -
;   scan for path in directory
;- - - - - - - - - - - - - - - - - - - - - - - - - - - - - - - - - - -
locateFile_32:
        currSegment ds, es
        lea di, offset _tempFileName [ bp ]             ; search es: di

        mov ax, word ptr [ _drive   ][ bp ]             ; get drive
        mov dx, word ptr [ _cluster ][ bp ]             ; cluster to search next
        mov word ptr [ _dirCluster ][ bp ], dx          ; start cluster of directory
```

```
        call scanDirectory                      ; scan for name in directory
        jnc locateFile_48                       ; if an item was found -->

        or word ptr [ _drive ][ bp ], 8000h     ; not found.
        cmp byte ptr [ _terminatingChar ][ bp ], '\'
        jz locateFile_PathNotFound              ; inside path def, error -->

        test word ptr _options [ bp ], (FILECANNOT_BEDEFINED + FILEMAY_EXIST)
        jnz locateFile_56                       ; if not defined is ok -->
        jmp locateFile_FileNotFound
```

If the entry was *not* found, a check is first made to determine whether the failure occurred in the path name. A check is made to determine if additional path characters were expected, and if so, a path-not-found error message is returned. A check is made to determine if the file cannot be defined. If so, the routine is successful and exits with a clear carry flag. Otherwise, a file-not-found error message is returned.

If the entry is found, its cluster address is saved and a test is made for the type of entry found by checking its file attributes. If the entry is not a subdirectory, a check is made to ensure that none was expected by checking the terminating term character. The options are tested to ensure that it can be a filename and that it can exist. This is to be sure that the item located on disk is a file and that a file was expected.

```
;- - - - - - - - - - - - - - - - - - - - - - - - - - - - - - - - - - - -
;  is FOUND entry a filename ?
;- - - - - - - - - - - - - - - - - - - - - - - - - - - - - - - - - - - -
locateFile_48:
        mov word ptr [ _cluster ][ bp ], dx     ; cluster to search next

        test bx, (ATTR_VOLUME + ATTR_DIRECTORY) ; is entry a directory ?
        jnz locateFile_50                       ; if not a file -->

        cmp byte ptr [ _terminatingChar ][ bp ], '\'
        jz locateFile_PathNotFound              ; if path expected, error -->

        test word ptr _options [ bp ], (FILECANNOT_BEDEFINED + FILEHAS_NOFILENAME)
        jnz locateFile_PathNotFound             ; if path expected, error -->
        jmp short locateFile_Return
```

The item found is checked to determine if it is a directory entry, and the terminating character of the search name is checked for a backslash. If both of these match, then the directory term was expected, and the code loops back to LocateFile_20 to continue to search through the next term in the path. Otherwise, the search options flag is checked to determine if the search name cannot be a directory, and an error may result.

```
;- - - - - - - - - - - - - - - - - - - - - - - - - - - - - - - - - - - -
;  is FOUND entry a directory ?
;- - - - - - - - - - - - - - - - - - - - - - - - - - - - - - - - - - - -
locateFile_50:
        test bx, ATTR_DIRECTORY                 ; is item a directory ?
        jz locateFile_FileNotFound              ; if not, its an error -->
        cmp byte ptr [ _terminatingChar ][ bp ], '\'
        ifz locateFile_20                       ; if path expected, get next -->
```

```
        test word ptr _options [ bp ], FILECANNOT_BEDIRECTORY
        jnz locateFile_FileNotFound                    ; if cannot be a directory ->
        test word ptr _options [ bp ], FILECANNOT_BEDEFINED
        jz locateFile_Return                           ; if everything is ok ->
```

The remainder of the routine is just cleanup. The routine fills the DIRACCESS block and exits.

```
;- - - - - - - - - - - - - - - - - - - - - - - - - - - - - - - - -
;  in case of error
;- - - - - - - - - - - - - - - - - - - - - - - - - - - - - - - - -
locateFile_FileNotFound:
        SetError errFileNotFound, locateFile_60


locateFile_PathNotFound:
        SetError errPathNotFound, locateFile_60


;- - - - - - - - - - - - - - - - - - - - - - - - - - - - - - - - -
;  return
;- - - - - - - - - - - - - - - - - - - - - - - - - - - - - - - - -
locateFile_Return:
        call locateCCBPHeader                          ; si dir pointer/ di ccb

        mov bx, word ptr [ _dirLocate. _pointer ][ bp ]
        mov word ptr [ fileAcBufferPtr. _segment ][ bx ], es
        mov word ptr [ fileAcBufferPtr. _pointer ][ bx ], di
        mov word ptr [ fileAcDirOffset ][ bx ], cx      ; offset in dir sector

        mov ax, word ptr es:[ ccbLBN. _low  ][ di ]
        mov dx, word ptr es:[ ccbLBN. _high ][ di ]
        mov word ptr [ fileAcDirSector. _low  ][ bx ], ax; which dir sector
        mov word ptr [ fileAcDirSector. _high ][ bx ], dx

locateFile_56:
        mov bx, word ptr [ _dirLocate. _pointer ][ bp ] ; restore bx
        mov ax, word ptr [ _drive ][ bp ]               ; drive
        mov dx, word ptr [ _cluster ][ bp ]             ; cluster
        mov word ptr [ fileAcDrive   ][ bx ], ax
        mov word ptr [ fileAcCluster ][ bx ], dx

        mov cx, word ptr [ _dirCluster ][ bp ]          ; start cluster of directory
        mov word ptr [ fileAcDirCluster ][ bx ], cx
        clc


;- - - - - - - - - - - - - - - - - - - - - - - - - - - - - - - - -
;  exit
;- - - - - - - - - - - - - - - - - - - - - - - - - - - - - - - - -
locateFile_60:
        currSegment ds
        mov bx, word ptr [ _dirLocate. _pointer ][ bp ]
        push word ptr [ _begfilenamePointer ][ bp ]
        pop word ptr [ fileAcNameOffset ][ bx ]

        pop ds
        pop es
        Return
```

Get Actual Filename

	On Entry	On Return
AX	AH = 60h	AL = last character of name
BX		
CX		
DX		
DS:SI	pointer to ASCIZ filename	
ES:DI	128-byte result buffer	
Flags		CY = set if error

Related Functions:
    3Ch Create File; 3Eh Close File; 3Fh Read File; 40h Write File.

In the previous section, we separated locating a file from expanding the filename. The function that expanded the filename is concerned with the canonical expansion of the file already explained in some detail in the preceding sections. That function is accessible through an undocumented DOS function call, DOS function 60h, Get Actual File Name. Although the name is expanded, it is not qualified. The name may contain subdirectory and filename references that do not actually exist.

The reason this function exists is to make it easier to write the command processor, command.com. Functions such as directory listing are able to take the somewhat complex string passed in as an argument and display the directory name only because of DOS function 60h, such as

```
Directory of c:\rxdos
```

The function is just a call interface directly to the expand filename routine. The original registers from the caller are pushed on the stack, and the expand function is called. The destination buffer is updated.

```
;''''''''''''''''''''''''''''''''''''''''''''''''''''''''''''''''';
;   60h Get Actual (Expanded) File Name                           ;
;- - - - - - - - - - - - - - - - - - - - - - - - - - - - - - - - -;
;                                                                 ;
;   Input:                                                        ;
;    ds:si pointer to filename( path included )                   ;
;    es:di pointer to expanded filename                           ;
;                                                                 ;
;   Output:                                                       ;
;    ax  0000  if name is local.                                  ;
;    ax  005c  if name is networked.                              ;
;                                                                 ;
;   -- DOS Undocumented Feature ─────────────── ;                 ;
;.................................................................;

_GetActualFileName:
        RetCallersStackFrame es, bx
        push word ptr es:[ _DataSegment ][ bx ]       ; non-canonical name
        push word ptr es:[ _SI ][ bx ]
```

```
    push word ptr es:[ _ExtraSegment ][ bx ]        ; expanded filename
    push word ptr es:[ _DI ][ bx ]
    call ExpandFileName
    ret
```

ExpandFileName

ExpandFileName is used to lexically convert a filename, which may include . and .. symbols, to a fully expanded filename. The emphasis is on lexical expansion because it makes no attempt to verify that the pathnames actually exist on disk. The function is used by LocateFile, which does physically check to make sure the terms in the pathname exist, and is the basis for undocumented DOS function 60h, Get Actual File Name, which returns an expanded filename. In fact, all a call to that function does is to call the expand filename routine. To understand how ExpandFileName works, you can use the undocumented DOS command, TRUENAME, which returns the lexical expansion of a path based on this function.

An example of what ExpandFileName does in converting a string can be seen in the following example. It may not seem like much, but we reference this example later.

```
input:  ..\foobar
output: c:\foobar
```

The job of expand filename is basically to

1. Prepend the current directory to a filename, if any is required.
2. Resolve . and .. terms in the name.
3. Check for invalid characters.
4. Return a flag when the input string used backslash characters
   (in order to optimize search).

ExpandFileName expects two ASCIZ string pointers passed on the stack. The first is a pointer to the unexpanded source text, the second a pointer to the expanded text. RxDOS usually passes 32-bit pointers between functions so that the arguments have the flexibility on being anywhere.

A brief look at the mechanics of the routine will help you understand how the routine works. For a simple expression containing just a filename or a drive and filename, the expansion requires only the insertion of the drive letter and current directory, as in

```
input: justname.ext
output: c:\currdir\justname.ext

input: e:justname.ext
output: e:\currdir\justname.ext
```

For a somewhat more complex expression, the current directory is inserted if the expression does not begin with a backslash, and then all . and .. terms are eliminated, as in

```
input:              ..\path1\path2\..\path3\anyfile.ext
output parsing:

  begins with:    c:\currdir\..\path1\path2\..\path3\anyfile.ext
  1st .. removed: c:\path1\path2\..\path3\anyfile.ext
  2nd .. removed: c:\path1\path3\anyfile.ext
```

The expand filename routine begins by defining the arguments it expects on the stack through the `darg` macro references. The two arguments are the string pointers to the original and output strings. It then initializes some temporary variables on the stack, such as the drive, cluster address, and network drive flag. The routine then attempts to extract the drive letter from the unexpanded original string using the `getDrive` routine, listed at the end of the expand filename routine. The routine always returns a drive code. If the drive is not available, the current drive is returned. Otherwise, the function checks to ensure that the drive letter is valid; for example, it cannot exceed the maximum drive letters defined by `LASTDRIVE=`. The original string is then checked for illegal characters.

A point should be made about the use of the drive field. Some software, like Novell's NetWare, assign drive codes that exceed the `LASTDRIVE=` value. If the low-level DOS code was ever asked to access drives with these values, it would have to fail the request since it would not understand how to expand the filename. Additional low-level problems would exist that are too numerous and too tangential to our discussion. Novell's NetWare works because it intercepts calls to its drives before DOS is required to act on them.

```
;'''''''''''''''''''''''''''''''''''''''''''''''''''''''''''';
;  Expand File Name                                          ;
;- - - - - - - - - - - - - - - - - - - - - - - - - - - - - -;
;                                                            ;
;  Input:                                                    ;
;   arg    ptr to filename passed                            ;
;   arg    ptr to expanded filename                          ;
;                                                            ;
;  Output:                                                   ;
;   es:di  ptr to expanded filename                          ;
;   dx     current cluster, if search to begin here          ;
;   ax     drive, or error                                   ;
;   cy     if error detected                                 ;
;............................................................;

ExpandFileName:
        Entry 4
        darg _UnexpandedFileName
        darg _ExpandBuffer

        xor ax, ax
        def _drive, ax                          ; initialize to 0's
        def _currCluster, ax
        def _cds_SubstOffset, ax
        def _NetworkPathName, ax                ; False
        def _startPointer
```

```
;- - - - - - - - - - - - - - - - - - - - - - - - - - - - - - - - - -
; skip through any leading spaces
;- - - - - - - - - - - - - - - - - - - - - - - - - - - - - - - - - -
        push ds
        currSegment ds                          ; point to default segment
        les si, dword ptr [ _UnexpandedFileName ][ bp ]
        call getDrive
        storarg _drive, ax                      ; save argument
        ifc expandFileName_Error                ; invalid drive ->

        call scanInvalidFilenameChars           ; make sure filename is ok
        ifc expandFileName_Error                ; if error ->

        mov word ptr [ _UnexpandedFileName._pointer ][ bp ], si
```

Part of the initialization continues by using the drive returned by getDrive to look up the
current path in the CDS, or Current Directory Structure, shown in Figure 3-16. Recall that there is
a CDS entry for each available drive letter. The current directory is copied into the expanded filename output, and the cluster address of the current directory, taken from the CDS, is saved by the
routine for future reference.

Figure 3-16. Layout of the CDS

```
;/ / / / / / / / / / / / / / / / / / / / / / / / / / / / / / / / / / / / / / / / / / / / / / / ';
; Current Directory Entries                                            ;
;............................................................;

        CDS struc
_cdsActualDirectory      db 67 dup (?)          ; asciz name
_cdsFlags                dw ?
_cdsPtrToDPB             dd ?
_cdsStartClusterDir      dw ?
                         dw ?                   ;
                         dw ?                   ; padding for network record
_cdsNetwParameter        dw ?                   ; padding for network record
_cdsNonSubstOffset       dw ?

                         db ?                   ; compatability byte
_cdsPtrtoIFSDriver       dd ?
                         dw ?                   ; compatability word
        CDS ends


;- - - - - - - - - - - - - - - - - - - - - - - - - - - - - - - - - -
; Redirection for IFS
;- - - - - - - - - - - - - - - - - - - - - - - - - - - - - - - - - -
_cdsRedirectIFSPtr       equ _cdsStartClusterDir


;- - - - - - - - - - - - - - - - - - - - - - - - - - - - - - - - - -
; Flags
;- - - - - - - - - - - - - - - - - - - - - - - - - - - - - - - - - -
_CDS_NETWORKEDDRIVE      equ 8000h
_CDS_PHYSICALDRIVE       equ 4000h
_CDS_JOINEDDRIVE         equ 2000h
_CDS_SUBSTDRIVE          equ 1000h
```

A subtle transformation may actually occur here that could easily be missed unless you were extremely familiar with the contents of the CDS. The expanded filename always contains a drive letter, as shown in the example provided at the start of this section. Looking at the code, there is seemingly no place where the drive letter is actually stored to the output string. That's because the drive letter is actually copied from the string in the CDS. Recall that the printout produced by printCDS showed each drive with its drive letter. Moreover, for a SUBST'd drive, the drive letter fetched from the CDS is the destination drive, which may be better seen in an example. Assuming that the E: drive is SUBST'd, then observe the drive change in the output expanded string.

```
c> subst e: c:\rxdos
c> truename e:foobar
   C:\RXDOS\FOOBAR

c> truename e:..\foobar
   Path not found - E:..\FOOBAR
```

The last entry in this example is designed to show what happens when you try to back up over a substituted directory. In reality, E: just points to C:\RXDOS, so why can't the command back up over the subdirectory when referenced from the E: drive? The CDS entry for the E: drive contains the number of characters that are nonsubstitutable. The entry completely protects the substitute path, which prevents the . . entry from backing up a directory level.

Within the routine, the CDS string is copied and made to terminate with a backslash if one is not already provided.

```
;- - - - - - - - - - - - - - - - - - - - - - - - - - - - - - - - -
;  get selected drive current directory
;- - - - - - - - - - - - - - - - - - - - - - - - - - - - - - - - -
        getarg ax, _drive
        mov cl, sizeCDS
        mul cl                          ; ax contains offset to current drive

        lds si, dword ptr cs:[ _RxDOS_pCDS ]    ; actual address in CDS
        add si, ax                      ; from
        add si, _cdsActualDirectory     ; proper offset

        xor cx, cx
        mov cl, byte ptr [ _cdsNonSubstOffset ][ si ]
        mov word ptr [ _cds_SubstOffset ][ bp ], cx

        mov dx, word ptr [ _cdsStartClusterDir ][ si ]
        mov word ptr [ _currCluster ][ bp ], dx ; current starting cluster

        push ds
        push si
        call StringLength               ; length of source string

        getdarg es, di, _ExpandBuffer   ; address of expanded buffer
        rep movsb                       ; copy buffer
```

```
;- - - - - - - - - - - - - - - - - - - - - - - - - - - - - - - -
; does path end with a \ ?
;- - - - - - - - - - - - - - - - - - - - - - - - - - - - - - - -
        mov  al, '\'
        cmp  byte ptr es:[ di - 1 ], al      ; ends with trailing \ ?
        jz   expandFileName_18               ; yes, else add -->
        stosb                                ; add trailing \
```

The routine then determines whether the unexpanded filename begins with a directory delimiter, that is, a slash or backslash. If the routine does begin with a directory delimiter, everything in the current directory string is removed except for the protected nonsubstitutable path. Since the routine recognized the use of a path symbol in the name, the current directory cluster address is invalidated, and the cluster address is changed to zero. The cluster address is zeroed if a directory delimiter is located later in the string as well.

```
;- - - - - - - - - - - - - - - - - - - - - - - - - - - - - - - -
; does path start with root reference ?
;- - - - - - - - - - - - - - - - - - - - - - - - - - - - - - - -
expandFileName_18:
        lds  si, dword ptr [ _UnexpandedFileName ][ bp ]
        cmp  byte ptr [ si ], '\'
        jz   expandFileName_20
        cmp  byte ptr [ si ], '/'
        jnz  expandFileName_30

expandFileName_20:
        mov  di, word ptr [ _ExpandBuffer. _pointer ][ bp ]
        add  di, word ptr [ _cds_SubstOffset ][ bp ]
        inc  si
        mov  word ptr [ _currCluster ][ bp ], 0000 ; path name info supplied
```

The routine now scans each name, uppercasing and copying each name to the expanded output string. If the term copied is a .. term, the routine backs up a subdirectory term. The string \AAA\BBB\.., after the backup, returns simply to \AAA\. The remainder of the routine just makes sure that the string is null terminated.

```
;- - - - - - - - - - - - - - - - - - - - - - - - - - - - - - - -
; scan for only valid characters
;- - - - - - - - - - - - - - - - - - - - - - - - - - - - - - - -
expandFileName_30:
        cmp  byte ptr [ si ], ' '+1
        ifc  expandFileName_Error            ; null strings not parsed -->
        storarg _startPointer, si

expandFileName_32:
        lodsb

        call upperCase
        stosb                                ; save at es:di
        cmp  al, ' '+1                       ; end of string ?
        jc   expandFileName_36               ; yes -->
```

```
        call ifPathSeparator                  ; path separator ?
        jnz expandFileName_32                  ; not yet ->
        mov byte ptr es:[ di - 1 ], al         ; make sure separator is \
        mov word ptr [ _currCluster ][ bp ], 0000 ; path name info supplied

;- - - - - - - - - - - - - - - - - - - - - - - - - - - - - - - - - -
;  validate path separator
;- - - - - - - - - - - - - - - - - - - - - - - - - - - - - - - - - -
expandFileName_36:
        mov byte ptr es:[ di ], 0              ; null terminate

        mov cx, si
        sub cx, word ptr [ _startPointer ][ bp ]; length of string
        dec cx                                 ; excluding last \ ...
        jg expandFileName_38                   ; if more than one character ->
        cmp al, '\'                            ; terminates with a \ ?
        jz expandFileName_Error                ; \\ combination not permitted ->

expandFileName_38:
        cmp cx, 2                              ;
        jg expandFileName_48                   ; if not . or .., go get next ->

        cmp word ptr es:[ di - 3 ], '..'       ; back subdirectory
        jz expandFileName_42                   ; go backup to previous ->
        cmp word ptr es:[ di - 3 ], '.\'       ; current subdirectory
        jnz expandFileName_48                  ; all set ->

        sub di, cx                             ;
        dec di                                 ; fix current
        jmp short expandFileName_48            ; go process next ->

;- - - - - - - - - - - - - - - - - - - - - - - - - - - - - - - - - -
;  backup to previous directory
;- - - - - - - - - - - - - - - - - - - - - - - - - - - - - - - - - -
expandFileName_42:
        sub di, cx                             ;
        dec di                                 ; fix to current,

        mov cx, di
        sub cx, word ptr [ _ExpandBuffer. _pointer ][ bp ]
        sub cx, word ptr [ _cds_SubstOffset ][ bp ]
        jle expandFileName_48

expandFileName_44:
        dec di
        cmp byte ptr es:[ di - 1 ], '\'
        jz expandFileName_48
        loop expandFileName_44

;- - - - - - - - - - - - - - - - - - - - - - - - - - - - - - - - - -
;  more to go ?
;- - - - - - - - - - - - - - - - - - - - - - - - - - - - - - - - - -
expandFileName_48:
        mov cx, di
```

```
        sub cx, word ptr [ _ExpandBuffer. _pointer ][ bp ]
        cmp cx, word ptr [ _cds_SubstOffset ][ bp ]
        jge expandFileName_50

        mov di, word ptr [ _cds_SubstOffset ][ bp ]
        add di, word ptr [ _ExpandBuffer. _pointer ][ bp ]

expandFileName_50:
        cmp byte ptr [ si - 1 ], ' '+1        ; was null ?
        jnc expandFileName_30                 ; no, go get next ->

;- - - - - - - - - - - - - - - - - - - - - - - - - - - - - - - -
;  clean up string at end
;- - - - - - - - - - - - - - - - - - - - - - - - - - - - - - - -
        xor ax, ax
        mov byte ptr es:[ di ], al            ; add terminator

        mov di, word ptr [ _ExpandBuffer. _pointer ][ bp ]
        mov cx, 128
        repnz scasb                           ; scan for null terminator

        dec di
        mov cx, di
        sub cx, word ptr [ _ExpandBuffer. _pointer ][ bp ]
        cmp cx, word ptr [ _cds_SubstOffset ][ bp ]
        jle expandFileName_56                 ; if minimal string ->

        cmp byte ptr es:[ di - 1 ], '\'       ; string ends with \ ?
        jnz expandFileName_56                 ; no, ignore fix up ->
        mov byte ptr es:[ di - 1 ], 0         ; kill any terminating (needless \)

expandFileName_56:
        getarg ax, _drive
        or ax, ax                             ; return drive.
        jmp short expandFileName_72

;- - - - - - - - - - - - - - - - - - - - - - - - - - - - - - - -
;  if error
;- - - - - - - - - - - - - - - - - - - - - - - - - - - - - - - -
expandFileName_Error:
        stc
        mov ax, errIllegalName

;- - - - - - - - - - - - - - - - - - - - - - - - - - - - - - - -
;  return
;- - - - - - - - - - - - - - - - - - - - - - - - - - - - - - - -
expandFileName_72:
        les di, dword ptr [ _ExpandBuffer ][ bp ] ; set return pointer.
        mov dx, word ptr [ _cluster ][ bp ]        ; where to start search.
        pop ds
        Return
```

```
;'''''''''''''''''''''''''''''''''''''''''''''''''''''''''''''';
; Get Drive from String                                         ;
;- - - - - - - - - - - - - - - - - - - - - - - - - - - - - - -;
;                                                               ;
; Input:                                                        ;
;   es:si  input string                                         ;
;                                                               ;
; Output:                                                       ;
;   es:si  past ':', is any.                                    ;
;   ax     current drive or drive named.                        ;
;   cy     error, invalid drive.                                ;
;...............................................................;

getDrive:
        mov ax, word ptr es:[ si ]              ; save drive info available
        cmp ah, ':'                             ; drive break in string ?
        jnz getDrive_14                         ; no, return current ->

        xor ah, ah                              ; clear carry
        call upperCase                          ; convert drive to upper case
        sub al, 'A'                             ; convert to a range
        jc getDrive_12                          ; if invalid, ret valid drive ->

        cmp al, byte ptr cs:[ _RxDOS_bLastDrive ]   ; within valid range ?
        jge getDrive_12                         ; yes ->

        add si, 2                               ; skip drive letter / colon

;- - - - - - - - - - - - - - - - - - - - - - - - - - - - - - - -
; return valid drive.
;- - - - - - - - - - - - - - - - - - - - - - - - - - - - - - - -
        cbw                                     ; valid drive
        or ax, ax
        ret


;- - - - - - - - - - - - - - - - - - - - - - - - - - - - - - - -
; return valid drive.
;- - - - - - - - - - - - - - - - - - - - - - - - - - - - - - - -
getDrive_12:
        stc
        mov al, byte ptr cs:[ _RxDOS_CurrentDrive ]
        ret


;- - - - - - - - - - - - - - - - - - - - - - - - - - - - - - - -
; return default drive.
;- - - - - - - - - - - - - - - - - - - - - - - - - - - - - - - -
getDrive_14:
        xor ax, ax                              ;clear carry
        mov al, byte ptr cs:[ _RxDOS_CurrentDrive ]
        ret
```

scanDirectory

scanDirectory performs an exact match search for a directory entry. It expects a name in directory format, that is, two blank-filled fields, one of eight characters followed by a three-character extension. The routine searches a subdirectory and stops at the first entry that matches the name. The subdirectory to search is identified by the drive code and cluster address. The root directory is not normally a file. RxDOS treats cluster 0000 as a root directory selector. This permits the root directory to be treated transparently as a file by most of the functions in RxDOS.

When the entry is found, the routine returns the attributes, file size, and cluster address of the located item.

Reading a subdirectory is no different from reading any other file. Subdirectories, like files, are allocated space from the FAT chain. At the end of this chapter, we describe the specifics of the structure of the FAT and how it can be traversed in order to sequentially read allocated clusters. A function, _FATReadRandom, exists within RxDOS that accepts a file offset and returns the correct disk sector, taking care of navigating through the low-level FAT structure. The function name is meant to imply that it is a FAT layer function, that it navigates the FAT, and that it can read anywhere at random in the file. It requires a DISKACCESS work area buffer to properly work.

Directories in DOS consist of fixed-size entries. Directory entries that are in use usually reference either a file or a subdirectory. Unused entries have never been used, or they represent deleted entries. An entry that has never been used is identified by a zero byte at the start of the name, whereas a deleted entry is identified by an E5h value in the same byte location. One benefit of the never-used entry is that it also represents the logical end of a directory, that is, there are no entries beyond a never-used directory entry. Directory searching can stop when it encounters a never-used directory entry.

scanDirectory initializes a DISKACCESS work area then enters a loop where it reads directory entries one at a time. The data read remains in the cache buffer area, and the ES:BX register pair points to that location. The entry is compared to the search entry. If the entries don't match, the routine continues looping by incrementing the offset value within the DISKACCESS work area. This offset is automatically used for navigating to the correct cluster and sector within a file.

The compareDirEntries function is used to compare directory entries and behaves much like a rep cmpsb instruction. It takes arguments in the DS:SI and ES:DI register pairs. The routine, listed next, first checks to make sure that the entry is not deleted or has never been used. It then compares the two fixed-length strings.

When a directory entry is finally located, the directory entry's address in a cached buffer is returned to the caller in the ES:BX registers, together with the cluster address of the file, its size, and attributes in other registers.

```
;,,,,,,,,,,,,,,,,,,,,,,,,,,,,,,,,,,,,,,,,,,,,,,,,,,,,,,,,,,,,,,,,,;
;   Scan Directory (Exact Search)                                ;
;- - - - - - - - - - - - - - - - - - - - - - - - - - - - - - - -;
;                                                                ;
;   Note:                                                        ;
;     Subdirectories are implemented as files.  That means that  ;
```

```
        ;   after each sector we must search for the next FAT table    ;
        ;   entry to get the next cluster.                             ;
        ;                                                              ;
        ;- - - - - - - - - - - - - - - - - - - - - - - - - - - - - -;
        ;                                                              ;
        ;  Input:                                                      ;
        ;   ax     drive                                               ;
        ;   dx     cluster of dir to search                            ;
        ;   es:di  filename to search                                  ;
        ;                                                              ;
        ;  Output:                                                     ;
        ;   if item found:                                             ;
        ;   ax     drive                                               ;
        ;   bx     attributes                                          ;
        ;   cx     file size                                           ;
        ;   dx     cluster                                             ;
        ;   es:si  pointer to located directory entry                  ;
        ;                                                              ;
        ;   if item NOT found:                                         ;
        ;   cy     if item not found                                   ;
        ;..............................................................;

scanDirectory:
        Entry
        ddef _filenamePtr, es, di
        defbytes _diskAccess, sizeDISKACCESS


;- - - - - - - - - - - - - - - - - - - - - - - - - - - - - - - - - - - -
; init access
;- - - - - - - - - - - - - - - - - - - - - - - - - - - - - - - - - - - -
        setES ds
        lea bx, offset _diskAccess [ bp ]            ; pointer to access block
        call initdiskAccess                          ; [ax] is drive, [dx] is cluster


;- - - - - - - - - - - - - - - - - - - - - - - - - - - - - - - - - - - -
; lookup entry
;- - - - - - - - - - - - - - - - - - - - - - - - - - - - - - - - - - - -
        mov word ptr [ _diskAccess. diskAcPosition. _low  ][ bp ], -sizeDIRENTRY
        mov word ptr [ _diskAccess. diskAcPosition. _high ][ bp ], -1

scanDir_36:
        add word ptr [ _diskAccess. diskAcPosition. _low  ][ bp ], sizeDIRENTRY
        adc word ptr [ _diskAccess. diskAcPosition. _high ][ bp ], 0000
        lea bx, offset _diskAccess [ bp ]            ; pointer to access block
        call _FATReadRandom                          ; read into buffer
        stc                                          ; just in case error,
        jz  scanDir_56                               ; if no more data ->

        lea di, offset deName[ bx ]                  ; get pointer to name
        cmp byte ptr es:[ di ], DIRENTRY_NEVERUSED
        stc                                          ; just in case error,
        jz  scanDir_56                               ; if no more data ->

        lds si, dword ptr [ _filenamePtr ][ bp ]     ; pointer to search file name
        call compareDirEntries
        jnz scanDir_36                               ; if item not found ->
```

```
;- - - - - - - - - - - - - - - - - - - - - - - - - - - - - - - - - - - -
;  item found
;- - - - - - - - - - - - - - - - - - - - - - - - - - - - - - - - - - - -
        mov si, bx                                         ; dir entry to si
        mov dx, word ptr es:[ deStartCluster ][ si ]       ; cluster
        mov cx, word ptr es:[ deFileSize      ][ si ]       ; file size
        mov bl, byte ptr es:[ deAttributes    ][ si ]       ; attributes
        xor bh, bh                                         ; zero, nc

        mov ax, word ptr [ _diskAccess. diskAcDrive ][ bp ]

scanDir_56:
        Return

        ;''''''''''''''''''''''''''''''''''''''''''''''''''''''''''''''';
        ;  Compare Entries                                              ;
        ;- - - - - - - - - - - - - - - - - - - - - - - - - - - - - - - -;
        ;                                                               ;
        ;  Compare two directory entries.  If the Lead character of     ;
        ;  source string is E5, it is converted to 05 to help search.   ;
        ;                                                               ;
        ;  Input:                                                       ;
        ;   ds:si  source string (may contain ? character )             ;
        ;   es:di  match string (may not contain wild character )       ;
        ;                                                               ;
        ;  Output:                                                      ;
        ;   zr     entry located                                        ;
        ;...............................................................;

compareDirEntries:
        cmp byte ptr [ si ], DIRENTRY_DELETED              ; E5 ?
        jnz compareDirEntries_04
        mov byte ptr [ si ], SPECIAL_CHAR

compareDirEntries_04:
        cmp byte ptr es:[ di ], DIRENTRY_NEVERUSED
        jz compareDirEntries_08
        cmp byte ptr es:[ di ], DIRENTRY_DELETED
        jnz compareDirEntries_12

compareDirEntries_08:
        mov al, byte ptr es:[ di ]
        cmp al, '.'                                        ; force non zero
        ret

compareDirEntries_12:
        push di
        push si
        mov cx, sizeFILENAME
        call CompareString                                 ; source / dest compare
        pop si
        pop di                                             ; restore pointers
        ret
```

The FAT Structure

The FAT management code is encapsulated into a few functions that walk the FAT chain, release the FAT chain, or append a FAT entry to an existing end of file. Support functions also exist to scan the FAT for free entries, to count the number of free FAT entries, and to initialize an allocated cluster.

The entire disk is subdivided into clusters with each cluster having an entry in the FAT. A cluster, as noted earlier, comprises one or more disk sectors. When a file needs additional space, it allocates the space from the FAT. It updates the contents of the previous end-of-file cluster with the value of the newly allocated cluster, and it marks the current cluster as allocated. The FAT not only identifies allocation, but the entries for a file form a chain that specifies the reading or allocation order. The first allocated cluster points to each subsequent allocated cluster for the file until the end of the allocation chain. The FAT chain was shown in Figure 3-1.

There is the 12-bit or 16-bit FAT. The 12-bit FAT entries can address only a maximum of 4,095 entries. The 12-bit FAT has the advantage that it can pack more FAT entries per sector, minimizing the time required to access other FAT sectors. Although sufficient to address a 32MB disk, it's clear that the FAT would have to be expanded if larger disks would be supported. This led to the development of the 16-bit FAT format, which could comfortably address disks up to 512MB and larger.

To access a 32MB hard disk using a 12-bit FAT, the cluster size, that is, the number of sectors per cluster, must be set to 16. That is determined as follows: 32MB divided by the 512 bytes per sector yields 65,536 sectors. Dividing the number of sectors by 4,096, the maximum addressable cluster address, yields 16 sectors per cluster. At a cluster size of 16, every allocation on this disk takes up 8K of disk space. A 2GB hard disk would require a cluster size of 64, using a 16-bit FAT, where each allocation would be given 32K of disk space.

Each entry in a 16-bit FAT occupies 4 nibbles, which fits conveniently within a 512-byte sector. Each 12-bit FAT entry requires 3 nibbles, allowing for 340 entries, plus 1 nibble. Some FAT entries must straddle two sectors when they appear at a sector boundary. This is a somewhat inefficient design since two FAT sectors must be altered when a cluster crosses a sector boundary. It is a remnant of a DOS 1.0 design decision where the FAT remained in memory and cross-sector boundaries were never a problem.

Cross-sector boundaries are more of a problem because no two sectors have the same crossover problem, as shown in Figure 3-17. The first sector has an extra nibble, which contains the start of the next cluster. The entries in the second sector are now all shifted by one nibble, and two nibbles of the FAT can be stored in the last entry. And so on it goes.

Figure 3-17. 12-bit FAT entries straddle sector boundaries. Depending on whether it's an odd or even sector offset from the beginning of the FAT, a cluster will straddle two sectors with one or two nibbles in each sector. This is a throwback to an earlier DOS architecture where the FAT was always resident in memory.

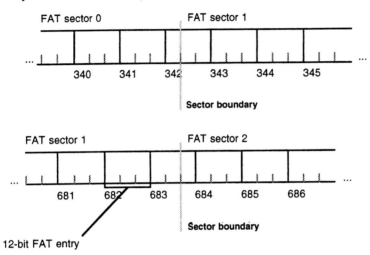

The discussion of the cluster support routines continues with fetching cluster values from the FAT. Throughout, the FAT routines presume that it can contain the differences between the 12- and 16-bit FAT entries to fetch and update routines.

GetNextCluster

getNextCluster reads the contents of the FAT. It expects the drive and a cluster address, and it returns the contents or value at the FAT entry. This value is typically the next allocated cluster address in the chain, hence the function's name.

The routine reads the maximum cluster number in the DPB for the current drive. If that number is greater than 4,095, the 16-bit FAT format is assumed. The original developers of DOS did not envision disks that might contain formats other than the 12-bit FAT and made no provisions to identify the FAT type used on disk. DOS was designed at a time when 10MB hard disks were expensive. It was probably viewed that anything beyond 32MB was unlikely.

To get the cluster's value, the cluster address must be converted into a FAT sector and offset within sector addresses. For the 16-bit FAT, the cluster number is divided by the number of entries per sector. The remainder is the byte offset into the sector. For the 12-bit FAT, the problem is a bit more complex because of the sector straddling problem. It is handled by a special get 12-bit value routine, which then reads either one or two FAT sectors that contain the cluster reference.

The sector that contains the 12-bit FAT entry can be determined by computing the nibble address of the entry. The cluster address is multiplied by 3, then divided by the number of nibbles in a sector. This provides both the sector address and the nibble offset within the sector where the entry begins. If the byte offset to the entry is exactly the last byte in the sector, the next sector is read. When a 12-bit FAT entry is read, the word at the computed offset is read and then is shifted down 4 bits if the original cluster address is odd. Odd-addressed entries will always be offset by a nibble.

Whether the FAT is 12 or 16 bits, the values returned for the FAT are always converted to 16-bit format. End-of-file entries in 12 bits are FFFh, whereas for 16 bits, they are FFFFh. The routine always returns the value to FFFFh regardless of the size of the FAT entry. Moreover, it is possible for some FAT entries to contain values in the range of FF6–FFFh. Some of these are error codes, but since they break the FAT chain, they are treated as end-of-file codes. The routine returns FFFFh for these entries as well. This makes it easier for any routine to understand the value received without further processing.

```
(in rxdosfat.asm)
        ;'''''''''''''''''''''''''''''''''''''''''''''''''''''''''''''';
        ;  Get Next Cluster                                           ;
        ;- - - - - - - - - - - - - - - - - - - - - - - - - - - - - - -;
        ;                                                             ;
        ;  Input:                                                     ;
        ;   ax       drive                                            ;
        ;   dx       current cluster                                  ;
        ;                                                             ;
        ;  Output:                                                    ;
        ;   dx       next cluster                                     ;
        ;   zr       if end of cluster chain.                         ;
        ;.............................................................;

getNextCluster:
        Entry
        def _drive, ax
        def _cluster, dx

        saveRegisters es, di, si, cx, bx, ax
        call getDPB                                 ; (es:bx) Device Parameter Block

;- - - - - - - - - - - - - - - - - - - - - - - - - - - - - - - - - - -
;  determine whether its 12 or 16 bit FAT entries
;- - - - - - - - - - - - - - - - - - - - - - - - - - - - - - - - - - -
        mov dx, -1                                  ; presume end if error
        mov ax, word ptr [ _cluster ][ bp ]         ; get cluster #
        or ax, ax                                   ; invalid number
        jz getNextCluster_04                        ; exit ->
        cmp ax, word ptr es:[ _dpbMaxClusterNumber ][ bx ]
        jc getNextCluster_08                        ; if valid cluster # ->

getNextCluster_04:
        jmp short getNextCluster_Return

getNextCluster_08:
        xor dx, dx
        test word ptr es:[ _dpbMaxClusterNumber ][ bx ], 0F000h
        jnz getNextCluster_16Bits                   ; if 16 ->
```

```
;- - - - - - - - - - - - - - - - - - - - - - - - - - - - -
;  12 bit FAT entries
;- - - - - - - - - - - - - - - - - - - - - - - - - - - - -
getNextCluster_12Bits:
        mov ax, word ptr [ _drive ][ bp ]           ; get drive
        mov dx, word ptr [ _cluster ][ bp ]         ; and cluster
        call _get_12Bit_ClusterValue
        jmp short getNextCluster_Return


;- - - - - - - - - - - - - - - - - - - - - - - - - - - - -
;  16 bit FAT entries
;- - - - - - - - - - - - - - - - - - - - - - - - - - - - -
getNextCluster_16Bits:
        mov cx, word ptr es:[ _dpbBytesPerSector ][ bx ]
        shr cx, 1
        div cx                                      ; FAT sector/ Offset

    ; ax will contain FAT sector
    ; dx will contain byte offset into FAT sector

        add dx, dx                                  ; make word offset
        push dx


        xor cx, cx
        mov dx, word ptr es:[ _dpbFirstFAT ][ bx ]  ; where is first FAT table ?
        add dx, ax                                  ; add offset required
        mov ax, word ptr [ _drive ][ bp ]           ; get drive
        call readBuffer                             ; read FAT Table
        or byte ptr es:[ ccbStatus ][ di ], ( ccb_isFAT )

        pop bx                                       ; word offset into FAT table
        mov dx, word ptr es:[ ccbData ][ bx + di ]  ; get FAT word

        mov ax, dx
        and ax, 0FFF8h                              ; FAT value, 12 bit entries.
        cmp ax, 0FFF8h                              ; end of chain ?
        jnz getNextCluster_Return                   ; no ->
        mov dx, -1                                  ; if end, set end value


;- - - - - - - - - - - - - - - - - - - - - - - - - - - - -
;  return
;- - - - - - - - - - - - - - - - - - - - - - - - - - - - -
getNextCluster_Return:
        restoreRegisters ax, bx, cx, si, di, es
        cmp dx, -1                                  ; set if end of chain
        Return


        ;,,,,,,,,,,,,,,,,,,,,,,,,,,,,,,,,,,,,,,,,,,,,,,,,,,,,,,,,,,,;
        ;  Get 12Bit FAT Table Value                               ;
        ;- - - - - - - - - - - - - - - - - - - - - - - - - - - - - -;
        ;                                                          ;
        ;  Input:                                                  ;
        ;    ax      drive                                         ;
        ;    dx      current cluster                               ;
```

```
        ;                                               ;
        ; Output:                                       ;
        ;   dx      value at cluster (next cluster)      ;
        ;   zr      if end of cluster chain.             ;
        ;..............................................;

_get_12Bit_ClusterValue:
        Entry
        def  _drive, ax
        def  _cluster, dx
        def  _sectorsize
        ddef _sector
        ddef _dpb, es, bx

        mov ax, dx
        add ax, ax
        add ax, dx                                      ; nibble address

        xor dx, dx
        mov cx, word ptr es:[ _dpbBytesPerSector ][ bx ]
        mov word ptr [ _sectorsize ][ bp ], cx
        shl cx, 1                                       ; nibbles / sector
        div cx                                          ; sector to read

    ; ax will contain sector
    ; dx will contain nibble offset

        shr dx, 1                                       ; word offset
        push dx                                         ;

        xor cx, cx                                      ; 32 bit address
        mov dx, ax
        add dx, word ptr es:[ _dpbFirstFAT ][ bx ]      ; where is first FAT table ?
        stordarg _sector, cx, dx                        ; 32 bit sector address

        mov ax, word ptr [ _drive ][ bp ]               ; get drive
        call readBuffer                                 ; read FAT Table
        or byte ptr es:[ ccbStatus ][ di ], ( ccb_isFAT )

        pop bx                                          ; word offset into FAT table
        mov dx, word ptr es:[ ccbData ][ bx + di ]      ; get FAT word

        dec word ptr [ _sectorsize ][ bp ]
        cmp bx, word ptr [ _sectorsize ][ bp ]          ; at sector size -1 boundry ?
        jnz _get_12Bit_ClusterValue_12                  ; no, ok to return as is ->

        push dx                                         ; else save what we have
        getdarg cx, dx, _sector                         ; read next cluster sector
        add dx, 0001                                    ; incr by one
        adc cx, 0000

        mov ax, word ptr [ _drive ][ bp ]               ; get drive
        call readBuffer                                 ; read FAT Table
        or byte ptr es:[ ccbStatus ][ di ], ( ccb_isFAT )
```

```
            pop dx
            mov dh, byte ptr es:[ ccbData ][ di ]            ; get FAT word

_get_12Bit_ClusterValue_12:
            test word ptr [ _cluster ][ bp ], 1             ; is cluster Odd ?
            jz _get_12Bit_ClusterValue_14                   ; no, just take value ->

            mov cl, 4
            shr dx, cl

_get_12Bit_ClusterValue_14:
            and dx, 0FFFh                                   ; 12 bit mask
            mov ax, dx
            and ax, 00FF8h                                  ; FAT value, 12 bit entries.
            cmp ax, 00FF8h                                  ; end of chain ?
            jnz _get_12Bit_ClusterValue_16                  ; no ->
            mov dx, -1                                      ; if end, set end value

_get_12Bit_ClusterValue_16:
            Return
```

UpdateClusterValue

The update cluster routine not only updates the value at a cluster address, it also returns the value at that cluster prior to it being changed. The code that releases the FAT chain relies on this feature. As it frees each cluster, the function returns the address of next cluster in the chain. The major difficulty for the function is in updating clusters that lie on cross-sector boundaries.

The code begins by addressing the DPB for the current drive to determine if the disk supports the 12- or 16-bit FAT tables. Within the 12-bit FAT, the correct sector and offset are computed, and if the offset address is to the last byte of the sector, the code calls a cross-sector update routine to read and update the next sector. The routine is careful to be able to work with a single cache buffer. Instead of reading and then updating both sectors of a cross-sector cluster value, the routine reads and updates a portion of one sector and then reads and updates the subsequent sector.

Since there are typically two FAT tables, how are both or several FAT tables updated synchronously? When data is read from the FAT, it is read to a cache buffer marked as containing FAT data. This data typing is very important. When the buffer is updated, it is marked as changed. The cache buffer management routine eventually detects that the changed buffer needs to be updated to disk. Since the buffer is a FAT data type, the corresponding sector is updated in all the copies of the FAT table.

```
(in rxdosfat.asm)
        ;'''''''''''''''''''''''''''''''''''''''''''''''''''''''''''''''''''';
        ;   Update Cluster Value                                            ;
        ;- - - - - - - - - - - - - - - - - - - - - - - - - - - - - - - - - -;
        ;                                                                   ;
        ;   Updates the value given for any cluster.                        ;
        ;                                                                   ;
        ;   Input:                                                          ;
```

```
        ;   ax      drive                                       ;
        ;   dx      cluster                                     ;
        ;   cx      update value                                ;
        ;.............................................................;

updateClusterValue:
        Entry
        def _drive, ax
        def _cluster, dx
        def _value, cx
        def _origvalue
        def _sectorsize
        ddef _sector

        saveRegisters es, di, si, dx, bx, ax

;- - - - - - - - - - - - - - - - - - - - - - - - - - - - - - - - -
; determine whether its 12 or 16 bit FAT entries
;- - - - - - - - - - - - - - - - - - - - - - - - - - - - - - - - -
        or dx, dx                                   ; invalid number
        jz updateClusterValue_04                     ; exit ->

        call getDPB                                 ; (es:bx) Device Parameter Block
        mov ax, word ptr [ _cluster ][ bp ]         ; get cluster #
        cmp ax, word ptr es:[ _dpbMaxClusterNumber ][ bx ]
        jc updateClusterValue_08                     ; if valid cluster # ->

updateClusterValue_04:
        stc
        jmp updateClusterValue_Return

updateClusterValue_08:
        xor dx, dx
        test word ptr es:[ _dpbMaxClusterNumber ][ bx ], 0F000h
        jz updateClusterValue_12Bits                 ; if 12 ->
        jmp updateClusterValue_16Bits                ; if 16 ->

;- - - - - - - - - - - - - - - - - - - - - - - - - - - - - - - - -
; 12 bit FAT entries
;- - - - - - - - - - - - - - - - - - - - - - - - - - - - - - - - -
updateClusterValue_12Bits:
        mov cx, ax
        add ax, ax
        add ax, cx                                   ; nibble address

        mov cx, word ptr es:[ _dpbBytesPerSector ][ bx ]
        mov word ptr [ _sectorsize ][ bp ], cx
        dec word ptr [ _sectorsize ][ bp ]
        shl cx, 1                                    ; nibbles / sector
        div cx                                       ; sector to read

    ; ax will contain sector
    ; dx will contain nibble offset
```

```
        shr dx, 1                                    ; word offset
        push dx                                      ; word offset

        xor cx, cx                                   ; 32 bit address
        mov dx, ax
        add dx, word ptr es:[ _dpbFirstFAT ][ bx ]   ; where is first FAT table ?
        stordarg _sector, cx, dx                     ; read next cluster sector
        mov ax, word ptr [ _drive ][ bp ]            ; get drive
        call readBuffer                              ; read FAT Table
        or byte ptr es:[ ccbStatus ][ di ], ( ccb_isFAT )

        getarg cx, _cluster                          ; get cluster value
        getarg dx, _value                            ; get value to update
        and dx, 0FFFh

        pop bx                                       ; word offset into FAT table
        cmp bx, word ptr [ _sectorsize ][ bp ]       ; at sector size -1 boundry ?
        jnz updateClusterValue_16                    ; no, ok to return as is ->

        call _updateCrossSectorEntry
        jmp short updateClusterValue_Return

    ; see if odd or even cluster

updateClusterValue_16:
        shr cx, 1                                    ; even or odd cluster
        jnc updateClusterValue_20                    ; even, keep value ->

        shl dx, 1
        shl dx, 1
        shl dx, 1
        shl dx, 1                                    ; shift value

        mov cx, word ptr es:[ ccbData ][ bx + di ]   ; get current value
        and word ptr es:[ ccbData ][ bx + di ], 000Fh ; clear area.

        shr cx, 1
        shr cx, 1
        shr cx, 1
        shr cx, 1                                    ; old value shifted correctly
        jmp short updateClusterValue_22

updateClusterValue_20:
        mov cx, word ptr es:[ ccbData ][ bx + di ]   ; get current value
        and word ptr es:[ ccbData ][ bx + di ], 0F000h ; clear area.

updateClusterValue_22:
        or word ptr es:[ ccbData ][ bx + di ], dx    ; update FAT word

updateClusterValue_26:
        and cx, 0FFFh                                ; mask off unwanted bits
        mov ax,. cx
        and ax, 0FF8h                                ; FAT value, 12 bit entries.
        cmp ax, 0FF8h                                ; end of chain ?
```

```
        jnz updateClusterValue_Update                  ; no ->

        mov cx, -1                                     ; if end, set end value
        jmp short updateClusterValue_Update

;- - - - - - - - - - - - - - - - - - - - - - - - - - - - - - - - - - - -
;  16 bit FAT entries
;- - - - - - - - - - - - - - - - - - - - - - - - - - - - - - - - - - - -
updateClusterValue_16Bits:
        mov cx, word ptr es:[ _dpbBytesPerSector ][ bx ]
        shr cx, 1
        div cx                                         ; FAT sector/ Offset

    ; ax will contain FAT sector
    ; dx will contain byte offset into FAT sector

        add dx, dx                                     ; make word offset
        push dx

        xor cx, cx
        mov dx, word ptr es:[ _dpbFirstFAT ][ bx ]     ; where is first FAT table ?
        add dx, ax                                     ; add offset required
        mov ax, word ptr [ _drive ][ bp ]              ; get drive
        call readBuffer                                ; read FAT Table
        or byte ptr es:[ ccbStatus ][ di ], ( ccb_isFAT )

        pop bx                                         ; word offset into FAT table
        getarg dx, _value
        mov word ptr es:[ ccbData ][ bx + di ], dx     ; update value

;- - - - - - - - - - - - - - - - - - - - - - - - - - - - - - - - - - - -
;  update
;- - - - - - - - - - - - - - - - - - - - - - - - - - - - - - - - - - - -
updateClusterValue_Update:
        push cx
        call CCBChanged
        pop cx
        or cx, cx

;- - - - - - - - - - - - - - - - - - - - - - - - - - - - - - - - - - - -
;  return
;- - - - - - - - - - - - - - - - - - - - - - - - - - - - - - - - - - - -
updateClusterValue_Return:
        restoreRegisters ax, bx, dx, si, di, es
        Return

        ;'''''''''''''''''''''''''''''''''''''''''''''''''''''''''''''';
        ;  Update Cross Sector Entry                                  ;
        ;- - - - - - - - - - - - - - - - - - - - - - - - - - - - - - -;
        ;                                                             ;
        ;  Input:                                                     ;
        ;   es:di   points to current ccb                             ;
        ;   bx      offset into buffer                                ;
        ;   dx      value to update                                   ;
```

```
;   cx       cluster number                                    ;
;                                                              ;
;  Output:                                                     ;
;   cx       value at cluster (value before update)            ;
;.............................................................;

_updateCrossSectorEntry:
        Entry
        def  _sectorflag, cx
        def  _updatevalue, dx
        def  _returnvalue

        mov ax, word ptr es:[ ccbData ][ bx + di ]      ; get value at current sector
        storarg _returnvalue, ax

        shr cx, 1                                       ; even or odd cluster
        jnc _updateCrossSector_20                       ; even, take value —>

        shl dx, 1
        shl dx, 1
        shl dx, 1
        shl dx, 1
        and dx, 0FFF0h
        storarg _updatevalue, dx
        and byte ptr es:[ ccbData ][ bx + di ], 0Fh     ; init area
        or byte ptr es:[ ccbData ][ bx + di ], dl       ; set high nibble
        jmp short _updateCrossSector_22                 ;

_updateCrossSector_20:
        mov byte ptr es:[ ccbData ][ bx + di ], dl      ; update low order FAT word


;- - - - - - - - - - - - - - - - - - - - - - - - - - - - - -
;   update next sector
;- - - - - - - - - - - - - - - - - - - - - - - - - - - - - -
_updateCrossSector_22:
        call CCBChanged

        xor ah, ah
        mov al, byte ptr es:[ ccbDrive        ][ di ]
        mov cx, word ptr es:[ ccbLBN. _high  ][ di ]
        mov dx, word ptr es:[ ccbLBN. _low   ][ di ]
        inc dx
        adc cx, 0                                       ; 32 bit add
        call ReadBuffer                                 ; read next sector

        getarg dx, _updatevalue
        mov ax, word ptr es:[ ccbData ][ di ]           ; get value at current sector
        test word ptr [ _sectorflag ][ bp ], 1          ; even or odd cluster
        jz _updateCrossSector_30                         ; even, take value —>
        mov byte ptr es:[ ccbData ][ di ], dh           ; set low order value

        xchg ah, al
        mov al, byte ptr [ _returnvalue ][ bp ]
        shr ax, 1
```

```
        shr ax, 1
        shr ax, 1
        shr ax, 1                               ; return value in ax
        jmp short _updateCrossSector_32         ;

_updateCrossSector_30:
        and byte ptr es:[ ccbData ][ di ], 0F0h  ; clear high order
        or byte ptr es:[ ccbData ][ di ], dh     ; update high order FAT word

        xchg ah, al
        mov al, byte ptr [ _returnvalue ][ bp ]

;- - - - - - - - - - - - - - - - - - - - - - - - - - - - - - - - - - - -
;  rebuild original value
;- - - - - - - - - - - - - - - - - - - - - - - - - - - - - - - - - - - -
_updateCrossSector_32:
        push ax
        call CCBChanged

        pop cx
        and cx, 0FFFh
        Return
```

ReleaseClusterChain

The purpose of releasing a cluster chain is to free the space used by a file. Each item in the cluster is marked as free, thereby making it available for reallocation at some later time. The release cluster chain routine depends on the value returned by update cluster. As a cluster is updated, the update cluster function returns the previous value in the cluster. Since each item in a cluster chain points to the next cluster allocated to the chain, freeing the first item will return the cluster address of the next cluster in the chain. This continues until the end of the chain.

The code expects the drive code in the AX register and the starting cluster address to release in the DX register. The cluster address is checked to ensure that it is within a valid range. The update value for a free cluster is zero, which is loaded into the CX register. The value is updated, and the previous value, returned by the update function, is tested to determine if the end of the chain was reached. The update cluster function normalizes the end-of-chain value so that, whether the FAT is 12 or 16 bit, the value of -1 is returned if the end of chain was detected.

(in rxdosfat.asm)

```
        ;''''''''''''''''''''''''''''''''''''''''''''''''''''''''''''''''';
        ;  Delete Cluster Chain                                          ;
        ;- - - - - - - - - - - - - - - - - - - - - - - - - - - - - - - - -;
        ;                                                                ;
        ;  Removes cluster addressed in dx from *both* FAT tables and    ;
        ;  returns pointer to next cluster ( or FFFF).                   ;
        ;                                                                ;
        ;  Input:                                                        ;
        ;    ax      drive                                               ;
        ;    dx      cluster                                             ;
```

```
;                                                                    ;
;  Output:                                                           ;
;    dx      next cluster                                            ;
;    zr      if end of cluster chain.                                ;
;.................................................................... ;

ReleaseClusterChain:
        saveAllRegisters
        call getDPB                           ; (es:bx) Device Parameter Block

        or dx, dx                             ; cluster valid ?
        jz releaseClusterChain_12             ; no, exit —>
        cmp dx, word ptr es:[ _dpbMaxClusterNumber ][ bx ]
        jnc releaseClusterChain_12            ; no, exit —>

releaseClusterChain_08:
        xor cx, cx
        call updateClusterValue               ; release cluster at ax:dx
        jz releaseClusterChain_12             ; no more —>

        mov dx, cx                            ; next cluster
        cmp dx, -1                            ; end of chain ?
        jnz releaseClusterChain_08            ; no —>

releaseClusterChain_12:
        restoreAllRegisters
        ret
```

AmountFreeSpace

The purpose of the AmountFreeSpace routine is to count the number of free clusters. The number of free clusters, times the cluster size, times the size of each sector is the number of total bytes free. A cluster is free if it contains a zero value. The routine must begin at the first available cluster and proceed through all the clusters until it reaches the maximum clusters for a drive.

This would be simpler and somewhat faster if the routine would detect 16-bit FAT entries since it could more readily scan a buffer. However, it treats 12- and 16-bit FAT tables the same, scanning each table by a cluster address.

```
(in rxdosfat.asm)
        ;'''''''''''''''''''''''''''''''''''''''''''''''''''''''''''''''''';
        ;  Find All Free Space                                            ;
        ;- - - - - - - - - - - - - - - - - - - - - - - - - - - - - - - -  ;
        ;                                                                 ;
        ;  Input:                                                         ;
        ;    ax       drive                                               ;
        ;                                                                 ;
        ;  Output:                                                        ;
        ;    ax       drive                                               ;
        ;    cx       # free clusters                                     ;
        ;    es:bx    pointer to DPB                                      ;
        ;.................................................................;
```

```
AmountFreeSpace:
        Entry
        def  _drive, ax
        def  _freespace, 0000
        def  _maxclusters
        ddef _dpb

        call getDPB                                  ; (es:bx) Device Parameter Block
        stordarg _dpb, es, bx

        mov dx, word ptr es:[ _dpbMaxClusterNumber ][ bx ]
        mov word ptr [ _maxclusters ][ bp ], dx

;- - - - - - - - - - - - - - - - - - - - - - - - - - - - - - - - - -
;  loop through entire FAT table
;- - - - - - - - - - - - - - - - - - - - - - - - - - - - - - - - - -
        xor dx, dx                                   ; starting cluster

amountFree_12:
        push dx
        mov ax, word ptr [ _drive ][ bp ]            ; get drive
        call getNextCluster                          ; get value at cluster
        or dx, dx                                    ; cluster free ?
        jnz amountFree_18                            ; no -->
        inc word ptr [ _freespace ][ bp ]

amountFree_18:
        pop dx
        inc dx
        cmp dx, word ptr [ _maxclusters ][ bp ]
        jc amountFree_12

;- - - - - - - - - - - - - - - - - - - - - - - - - - - - - - - - - -
;  return
;- - - - - - - - - - - - - - - - - - - - - - - - - - - - - - - - - -
amountFree_Return:
        getarg ax, _drive
        getarg cx, _freespace
        getdarg es, bx, _dpb

        Return
```

AllocateCluster and AppendCluster

Allocate cluster will search through the FAT for an available cluster value. Append cluster will allocate a cluster and add it to the cluster chain for a file by updating the current end-of-file cluster. In short, it will append a cluster to an existing file. Of the two functions, append cluster is the easier to understand.

AppendCluster, listed here, first allocates a cluster from the FAT and then updates the value at the current end of file. It relies on the premise that the current end-of-file cluster address is passed in the DX register. The routine returns the carry flag if a cluster could not be allocated; otherwise, it returns the address of the allocated cluster. Append cluster is used by the write routine to add file space or to locate free directory space when additional directory space is required.

```
        ;/////////////////////////////////////////////////////////;
        ;  Append A Cluster                                       ;
        ;- - - - - - - - - - - - - - - - - - - - - - - - - - - - -;
        ;                                                         ;
        ;  Input:                                                 ;
        ;    ax      drive                                        ;
        ;    dx      cluster to append                            ;
        ;                                                         ;
        ;  Output:                                                ;
        ;    ax      drive                                        ;
        ;    dx      new cluster value                            ;
        ;.........................................................;

AppendCluster:
        Entry
        def _drive, ax
        def _cluster, dx

;- - - - - - - - - - - - - - - - - - - - - - - - - - - - - - - -
; allocate a free cluster / sector
;- - - - - - - - - - - - - - - - - - - - - - - - - - - - - - - -
        push bx
        call AllocateCluster                     ; allocate a cluster
        jc appendCluster_08

        push dx                                  ; allocated cluster
        mov cx, dx                               ; use it to link to prev cluster
        getarg dx, _cluster
        call updateClusterValue                  ; update cluster value
        pop dx                                   ; restore allocated cluster

appendCluster_08:
        pop bx
        Return
```

AllocateCluster scans the FAT table for an available cluster. Searching begins at a recommended cluster search address and proceeds to the end of the FAT. The search then loops around back to the start of the FAT and searches until the recommended cluster address. This search strategy is intended to maximize the number of clusters it allocates together, thus generally reducing read and FAT search overhead.

The code for the allocate cluster routine is in two loops. It begins by determining the maximum cluster value for the disk and the address of the cluster at the start of the sector. It then uses the get next value routine to walk through the FAT table. This routine is used to avoid the complications imposed by the cross-sector FAT entries in the 12-bit FAT format.

Once an empty cluster is located, it is updated to a -1, indicating that it is now reserved. Since all allocations to a file are always made at the end of the file, placing an end-of-file marker at an allocated cluster makes sense.

The address of the newly allocated cluster is returned to the caller.

(in rxdosfat.asm)

```
        ;'''''''''''''''''''''''''''''''''''''''''''''''''''''''''''''';
        ;   Allocate Next Free Cluster                                ;
        ;- - - - - - - - - - - - - - - - - - - - - - - - - - - - - -;
        ;                                                             ;
        ;   Input:                                                    ;
        ;    ax      drive                                            ;
        ;    dx      recommended start search address                 ;
        ;                                                             ;
        ;   Output:                                                   ;
        ;    ax      drive                                            ;
        ;    dx      allocated cluster number                         ;
        ;    cy      if end of cluster chain.                         ;
        ;.............................................................;

AllocateCluster:

        Entry
        def _drive, ax
        def _cluster, dx
        def _maxclusters
        ddef _dpb

        call getDPB                             ; (es:bx) Device Parameter Block
        stordarg _dpb, es, bx                   ; save _dpb address

        mov dx, word ptr es:[ _dpbMaxClusterNumber ][ bx ]
        mov word ptr [ _maxclusters ][ bp ], dx

;- - - - - - - - - - - - - - - - - - - - - - - - - - - - - - - - -
;  loop through entire FAT table search for free cluster
;- - - - - - - - - - - - - - - - - - - - - - - - - - - - - - - - -
        getarg dx, _cluster                     ; starting cluster

allocateCluster_12:
        push dx
        mov ax, word ptr [ _drive ][ bp ]       ; get drive
        call getNextCluster                     ; get value at cluster

        mov cx, dx                              ; cluster value
        pop dx                                  ; cluster number
        or cx, cx                               ; is cluster free ?
        jz allocateCluster_18                   ; yes ->

        inc dx
        cmp dx, word ptr [ _cluster ][ bp ]     ; back at recommended cluster ?
        jz allocateCluster_NoneFree             ; end of search ->

        cmp dx, word ptr [ _maxclusters ][ bp ]
        jc allocateCluster_12

        xor dx, dx                              ; loop back to start of disk
```

```
            jmp allocateCluster_12

;- - - - - - - - - - - - - - - - - - - - - - - - - - - - - - - -
;  if no space available on disk
;- - - - - - - - - - - - - - - - - - - - - - - - - - - - - - - -
allocateCluster_NoneFree:
            stc
            jmp short allocateCluster_Return

;- - - - - - - - - - - - - - - - - - - - - - - - - - - - - - - -
;  update allocated buffer
;- - - - - - - - - - - - - - - - - - - - - - - - - - - - - - - -
allocateCluster_18:
            push dx
            mov cx, 0FFFFh                         ; updated value
            call updateClusterValue                ; update value

            pop dx
            or dx, dx                               ; no carry

;- - - - - - - - - - - - - - - - - - - - - - - - - - - - - - - -
;  return
;- - - - - - - - - - - - - - - - - - - - - - - - - - - - - - - -
allocateCluster_Return:
            getarg ax, _drive
            getdarg es, bx, _dpb
            Return
```

AllocateInitCluster utilizes the allocate function to allocate the cluster. The cluster is completely initialized to zeros. The function is utilized by directory services when a cluster is allocated to a directory. Directories require the cluster to be fully initialized. The code allocates a cluster, and then it converts the cluster address to a logical sector address. SelBuffer returns an available cache buffer, using the sector number to determine if there already is a match. It will not read a sector from disk.

The sector buffer returned from the cache is initialized to zeros and it is repeatedly written to disk, each time incrementing the sector. The single cache buffer is reused to clear the entire cluster. Finally, the sector address at the start of the cluster is restored to the cache buffer, and the buffer pointer returned to the caller.

```
;/////////////////////////////////////////////////////////////;
;  Allocate/Init A Cluster.                                    ;
;- - - - - - - - - - - - - - - - - - - - - - - - - - - - - - -;
;  Note:                                                       ;
;    This function will allocate a cluster and completely fill ;
;    it with zeroes.  Ideal for directories which must have    ;
;    initialized entries.                                      ;
;- - - - - - - - - - - - - - - - - - - - - - - - - - - - - - -;
;                                                              ;
;  Input:                                                      ;
;    ax    drive                                               ;
;                                                              ;
;  Output:                                                     ;
```

```
        ;    ax      drive                                          ;
        ;    cx      number of writes-1 to clear out entire cluster ;
        ;    dx      cluster                                        ;
        ;    es:di   pointer to a ccb buffer                        ;
        ;................................................................;

AllocateInitCluster:
        Entry
        def _drive, ax
        def _secPerCluster
        def _cluster
        ddef _sector

;- - - - - - - - - - - - - - - - - - - - - - - - - - - - - - -
; allocate a free cluster / sector
;- - - - - - - - - - - - - - - - - - - - - - - - - - - - - - -
        saveRegisters si, bx

        call getDPB                                     ; point to dpb

        mov cx, 0001
        add cl, byte ptr es:[ _dpbClusterSizeMask ][ bx ]
        mov word ptr [ _secPerCluster ][ bp ], cx

        call AllocateCluster                            ; allocate a cluster
        mov word ptr [ _cluster ][ bp ], dx
        jc AllocateInitCluster_12

        call computeLogSectorNumber                     ; cluster -> sector number
        stordarg _sector, cx, dx                        ; save sector #

;- - - - - - - - - - - - - - - - - - - - - - - - - - - - - -
; allocate a buffer/ init
;- - - - - - - - - - - - - - - - - - - - - - - - - - - - - -
        call selBuffer                                  ; select a buffer
        push di                                         ; pointer to header
        lea di, offset ccbData [ di ]                   ; point to data buffer
        clearMemory sizeCCBData                         ; clear to zeroes
        pop di                                          ; pointer to header

AllocateInitCluster_08:
        call updateChangedCCB                           ; force write updated buffer

        add word ptr es:[ ccbLBN. _low  ][ di ], 0001
        adc word ptr es:[ ccbLBN. _high ][ di ], 0000
        dec word ptr [ _secPerCluster ][ bp ]
        jnz AllocateInitCluster_08

;- - - - - - - - - - - - - - - - - - - - - - - - - - - - - -
; return
;- - - - - - - - - - - - - - - - - - - - - - - - - - - - - -
        getdarg cx, dx, _sector
        mov word ptr es:[ ccbLBN. _low  ][ di ], dx
        mov word ptr es:[ ccbLBN. _high ][ di ], cx
        or cx, cx                                       ; no carry.
```

```
AllocateInitCluster_12:
        getarg ax, _drive
        getarg dx, _cluster

        restoreRegisters bx, si
        Return
```

Logical Sector Numbers and Clusters

Although allocations are made on a cluster basis, low-level DOS functions access sectors through a Logical Sector Number, or LSN. There can be confusion in the reader's mind between what these two terms represent and how they relate to the physical disk access. The physical disk address is a head, track, and sector address. The physical address is flattened to form the Logical Sector Number.

A physical disk may be partitioned. Partitioning divides a disk into areas, or partitions. A partition table exists at the first physical sector on disk, at head 0, track 0, sector 0. There are many reasons a disk may be partitioned. Partitions on disk may be set aside to another operating system, such as a system that runs both DOS and Unix, or they may simply represent different DOS logical drives. Whatever the case, a partition starts at an offset expressed in sectors from the physical start of the disk. Although expressed in sectors, it can represent several tracks on disk. The total number of sectors per track are added to express the address at the start of the partition. The partition address does not have to begin at the start of a track, and no advantage, other than to best utilize the available hard disk space, is to be gained by starting a partition at any special location.

Each disk partition accessible by DOS becomes a logical disk drive. All logical disk drives begin at logical sector number 0, where the boot sector exists and from which the all-important Disk Parameter Block is created. The DPB contains the logical sector number of the FAT tables, the root directory, and the start of file data. How these are used is the subject of the next few paragraphs.

An LSN is relative to the start of the partition. The LSN is passed to the device driver, which in turn adds the number of sectors to the start of the partition. This converts the LSN to a Physical Flat Sector Address. This address is then converted to the physical head, track, and sector number. The flat sector address is first divided by the number of sectors per track. The remainder is the sector number. The remaining quotient is then divided by the heads per cylinder. The remainder is the head number, and the new resulting quotient is the track number. This is easier to visualize in code.

```
; LSN is in the DX:AX register

        add ax, word ptr partition_start. _low
        adc dx, word ptr partition_start. _high

        mov cx, word ptr sector_per_track
        call div32                          ; remainder in cx
        mov word ptr [ sector ], cx

        mov cx, word ptr heads_per_cylinder
        call div32                          ; remainder in cx
        mov word ptr [ head ], cx
        mov word ptr [ track ], ax
```

The entire allocatable portion of a disk begins after the root directory. This space is subdivided into clusters, with each cluster representing one or more sectors. DOS performs all reads and writes using logical sector numbers, not clusters, but it is forced to allocate space based on clusters. Once a cluster is allocated to a file, the cluster address is converted to a logical sector address. This logical sector address is added to the start of the data address to form a logical sector number. The LSN can then be converted, as shown, to a physical disk address.

Clusters 0 and 1 are always reserved. Cluster 2 is the first allocatable cluster number, and it references the first data sector. Because of this offset by two for the cluster, converting the cluster number to a logical sector number begins by decrementing the cluster by two, as in the following code:

```
; DX contains cluster address

        mov ax, dx
        dec ax
        dec ax                          ; cluster - 2
        mul word ptr sectors_per_cluster ;

        add ax, word ptr [ _dpbFirstDataSector. _low  ][ bx ]
        adc dx, word ptr [ _dpbFirstDataSector. _high ][ bx ]

; LSN is in the DX:AX register
```

The 32-bit size of the LSN was one of the major contributions of DOS 5. In versions prior to that release, the LSN was a single word, which limited the largest addressable disk sector to 65,535. The largest supported disk could not exceed 32MB (65K sectors times 512 bytes per sector). Today, DOS disk addressing is based on 32 bits, which provides for a maximum addressable limit of 4 terabytes as the largest DOS-supported disk. Someday this will seem small although probably not any time soon!

C H A P T E R   4

Reading and Writing Disks

Reading and Writing—Disk Buffers—Cache Management

Reading and Writing

The read and write functions transfer up to 64K between disk and memory. Since the allocation of space on disk is fragmented into clusters and clusters may not only be anywhere on disk, even across track boundaries, the lower-level read or write functions cannot take advantage of multisectored data transfer functions provided by either the BIOS or disk device drivers. DOS doesn't even try. It caches sectors in memory and deals with all disk i/o on a sector-by-sector basis. However, this should not prevent hardware manufacturers from prereading and caching multiple sectors or tracks of data, since clusters usually comprise at least several sectors, or from caching write sectors freeing the computer from waiting for the completion of a disk operation.

Read and write begins at the current file pointer, a position on disk setable by DOS function 42h, Move File Pointer. When a read or write function call is made, the file pointer location is mapped to a physical sector, which usually involves walking through the FAT allocation chain. This is perhaps best illustrated by Figure 4-1. A file consists of several clusters, each of which is made up of one or more sectors. To move forward in the file allocation chain, the difference between the current position and the requested position divided by the sector size describes how many sectors to move forward. Because the FAT is a chain of forward-only pointers, moving backward in the file requires walking the FAT from the beginning of the file even if the requested position is within a few bytes of the current position but in a previous cluster.

The logic of navigating through the FAT is handled within _FATReadRandom, which we discuss in greater detail in the section "Navigating Through Clusters."

Figure 4-1. The problem of moving between clusters requires walking through the FAT.

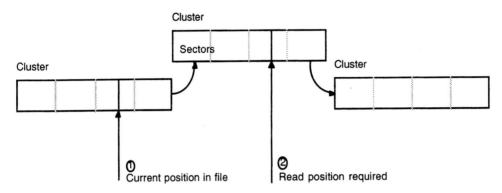

The architecture of file reading is shown in Figure 4-2. Whether the read is from the keyboard, from an FCB, or from a file handle, the read utilizes a file handle. This is to support device redirection, a subject described in some detail in the previous chapter. These functions call _SFTReadFile, which determines if the function call is to a device or a file. To read from a file, the function calls readLogicalBuffer to fill as much as possible of the read buffer supplied. Finally, the read requires positioning at the correct cluster and sector, detecting sector boundaries, and following the cluster chain as the buffer is filled. That is accomplished by _FATReadRandom.

The examination of the code begins at the file read function, DOS function 3Fh.

File Read with Handle

	On Entry	On Return
AX	AH = 3Fh	bytes actually read
BX	file handle	
CX	bytes to read	
DS:DX	pointer to read buffer	
Flags		CY = set if error

Related Functions:
   3Ch Create File; 3Dh Open File; 3Eh Close File; 40h Write File.

The File Read with Handle accepts a file handle, a buffer pointer, and a read byte count. The function can request as much as 64K minus one byte of data to be read. The code for the function begins at _ReadFile, located in the rxdos.asm module (see Figure 4-3). The main purpose of the function is to determine that handle is valid and to locate the SFT address prior to calling _SFTReadFile. A handle is valid if it is within range of the allocated JHT, whether the location

Figure 4-2. Console input, FCB file read, and file handle file read functions utilize the same common read code. For console functions, the common file handle read functions provide file redirection services.

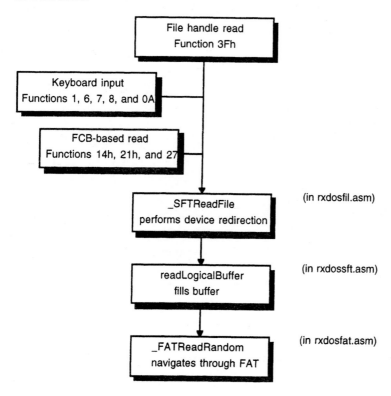

within the JHT contains an SFT handle, as opposed to a -1 entry, and if the corresponding SFT handle is opened. That is accomplished by the following code:

```
getarg  ax, _handle                 ; get file handle
call    MapAppToSFTHandle           ; map to internal handle info
call    FindSFTbyHandle             ; get corresponding SFT (es: di )
stordarg _sftPointer, es, di        ; save sft buffer pointer
jc      _ReadFile_error             ; if could not find ->
```

The map application to SFT handle function looks up the SFT handle within the JHT. It reports any errors as a -1 or as an invalid file handle. The second function finds the SFT address from the SFT handle. The code for both functions appears later in this section.

Figure 4-3. File Read flow outline

```
_ReadFile (in rxdos.asm)
    NormalizeBuffer
    CtrlC_Check (in rxdos.asm)
    MapAppToSFTHandle
    FindSFTbyHandle

    _SFTReadFile (in rxdossft.asm)
        devCharReadLine (in rxdosdev.asm)
        buildAccessRef (in rxdosfil.asm)
        readLogicalBuffer(in rxdosfil.asm)
        _FATReadRandom (in rxdosfat.asm)
            getDPB
            getNextCluster
            computeLogSectorNumber
            ReadBuffer

    _computeRelativeCluster (in rxdosfil.asm)
```

The code for the DOS File Read function is shown here. The function checks for a Control Break and then maps the file handle to an SFT pointer. It passes the buffer, buffer size, and both the SFT handle and the SFT pointer to the SFT read routine. The value returned, if it is not an error, is the count of bytes actually read, which is then returned to the caller.

```
(in rxdos.asm)
        ;,,,,,,,,,,,,,,,,,,,,,,,,,,,,,,,,,,,,,,,,,,,,,,,,,,,,,,,,,,,;
        ;                                                           ;
        ;   3fh Read File                                           ;
        ;- - - - - - - - - - - - - - - - - - - - - - - - - - - - - -;
        ;                                                           ;
        ;   bx    handle                                            ;
        ;   cx    max bytes to read                                 ;
        ;   ds:dx buffer address                                    ;
        ;...........................................................;


_ReadFile:
        Entry
        def _handle, bx
        def _readCount, cx
        ddef _sftPointer
        ddef _bufPtr, es, dx                    ; save buffer pointer

        call CtrlC_Check                        ; check for Control C

        getarg ax, _handle                      ; get file handle
        call MapAppToSFTHandle                  ; map to internal handle info
        call FindSFTbyHandle                    ; get corresponding SFT (es: di )
        stordarg _sftPointer, es, di            ; save sft buffer pointer
        jc _ReadFile_error                      ; if could not find —>
```

```
        push word ptr [ _bufPtr. _segment ][ bp ]
        push word ptr [ _bufPtr. _pointer ][ bp ]
        getarg cx, _readCount                    ; bytes to read
        getarg ax, _handle                       ; if STDIN
        call _SFTReadFile                        ; read using sft (at es:di )

_ReadFile_error:
        RetCallersStackFrame ds, bx
        mov word ptr [ _AX ][ bx ], ax
        Return
```

_SFTReadFile. This function is called to perform a read anytime an SFT file handle is utilized.
It is called, as noted earlier, from keyboard input functions, FCBs, and the file read function. Just
as important is from where it is *not* called. It is not used to read directories. It is in fact a higher-
level function designed to map, by calling the correct functions, the SFT to the FAT file system.

Recall that some SFTs point not to files but to devices. This is a result of opening or creating
a file with the name of a character device and is the method by which DOS supports device redirection. The redirection is accomplished at the SFT layer and not by the clever use of a character
device. The very first instruction checks whether this SFT is redirected to a device, and if it is, it
redirects the call to read from the device. The function calls a read line routine that reads either one
or two characters or no more than a single line.

```
;- - - - - - - - - - - - - - - - - - - - - - - - - - - - - - - - - - - -
;  is file redirected to a device
;- - - - - - - - - - - - - - - - - - - - - - - - - - - - - - - - - - - -
        test word ptr es:[ sftDevInfo ][ di ], sftIsDevice
        jz _SFTReadFile_06                       ; if file ->

        push word ptr es:[ sftDCB. _segment ][ di ]
        push word ptr es:[ sftDCB. _pointer ][ di ]
        mov cx, word ptr [ _readCount ][ bp ]
        getdarg es, di, _bufPtr
        call devCharReadLine                     ; read til cr or eof.
        jmp _SFTReadFile_36
```

If the SFT is not redirected to a device, the function determines how much space is left to read
in the file and makes sure that the read request does not exceed beyond the end of the file. When a
file is allocated a cluster, the size of the cluster may exceed the actual characters written to the cluster. This prevents reading past the actual end of the file.

The read function code is shown here.

```
(in rxdossft.asm)
        ;'''''''''''''''''''''''''''''''''''''''''''''''''''''''''''''''''';
        ;  Read From SFT                                                  ;
        ;- - - - - - - - - - - - - - - - - - - - - - - - - - - - - - - - -;
        ;                                                                 ;
        ;  Input:                                                         ;
        ;    ax      00 if read from stdin                                ;
        ;    cx      bytes to read                                        ;
        ;    es:di   sft pointer                                          ;
        ;    stack   buffer address                                       ;
```

```
        ;                                                             ;
        ;  Output:                                                    ;
        ;   cx       bytes actually read                              ;
        ;   zr       means end of file or wrong address               ;
        ;..............................................................;

_SFTReadFile:
        Entry 2
        darg _bufPtr

        def _readFromStdin, ax
        def _readCount, cx
        ddef _sftpointer, es, di
        defbytes _diskAccess, sizeDISKACCESS

;- - - - - - - - - - - - - - - - - - - - - - - - - - - - - - - - - -
;  is file redirected to a device
;- - - - - - - - - - - - - - - - - - - - - - - - - - - - - - - - - -
        test word ptr es:[ sftDevInfo ][ di ], sftIsDevice
        jz _SFTReadFile_06                          ; if file ->

        push word ptr es:[ sftDCB. _segment ][ di ]
        push word ptr es:[ sftDCB. _pointer ][ di ]
        mov cx, word ptr [ _readCount ][ bp ]
        getdarg es, di, _bufPtr
        call devCharReadLine                        ; read til cr or eof.
        jmp _SFTReadFile_36

;- - - - - - - - - - - - - - - - - - - - - - - - - - - - - - - - - -
;  initialize disk access block
;- - - - - - - - - - - - - - - - - - - - - - - - - - - - - - - - - -
_SFTReadFile_06:
        or cx, cx                                   ; reading any ?
        jz _SFTReadFile_36                          ; if length is zero ->

        lea bx, _diskAccess [ bp ]                  ; build access control block
        call buildAccessRef                         ; ...from sft

        xor cx, cx                                  ; bytes read (none yet )
        mov ax, word ptr es:[ sftFileSize. _low  ][ di ]
        mov dx, word ptr es:[ sftFileSize. _high ][ di ]

        sub ax, word ptr es:[ sftFilePosition. _low  ][ di ]
        sbb dx, word ptr es:[ sftFilePosition. _high ][ di ]
        jc _SFTReadFile_36                          ; if past end of file ->

        mov cx, word ptr _readCount [ bp ]          ; count: cx
        or dx, dx                                   ; more than 65k of file left ?
        jnz _SFTReadFile_12                         ; ok to continue reading ->

        cmp ax, cx                                  ; enough space to absorb read ?
        jnc _SFTReadFile_12                         ; ok to continue reading ->

        mov cx, ax                                  ; max read just to end of file
```

```
        or cx, cx                                    ; if zero, no need to read
        jz _SFTReadFile_36

;- - - - - - - - - - - - - - - - - - - - - - - - - - - - - - - - - - -
;  if stdin, read line even if from a file
;- - - - - - - - - - - - - - - - - - - - - - - - - - - - - - - - - - -
_SFTReadFile_12:
        mov ax, word ptr es:[ sftFilePosition. _low ][ di ]
        mov dx, word ptr es:[ sftFilePosition. _high ][ di ]
        getdarg es, di, _bufPtr                      ; buffer es: di

        cmp word ptr [ _readFromStdin ][ bp ], STDIN  ; reading from STDIN ?
        jnz _SFTReadFile_16                           ; no, do file read ->
        call ReadLine                                 ; if stdin
        jmp short _SFTReadFile_22                      ;

;- - - - - - - - - - - - - - - - - - - - - - - - - - - - - - - - - - -
;  else read count
;- - - - - - - - - - - - - - - - - - - - - - - - - - - - - - - - - - -
_SFTReadFile_16:
        call readLogicalBuffer                        ; Access buffer: ds: bx

_SFTReadFile_22:
        getdarg es, di, _sftPointer                   ; restore pointer to sft buffer
        add word ptr es:[ sftFilePosition. _low ][ di ], cx
        adc word ptr es:[ sftFilePosition. _high ][ di ], 0000

        mov dx, word ptr ss:[ diskAcCurCluster ][ bx ]
        mov word ptr es:[ sftCurCluster ][ di ], dx
        call _computeRelativeCluster
        clc                                           ; no carry

_SFTReadFile_36:
        mov ax, cx                                    ; return count
        Return
```

Beginning at _SFTReadFile_06, the code first determines if the bytes to read count is zero. This is unlikely but not impossible. Next, the code builds an all-important DISKACCESS block. The details of why the disk access block is necessary will become clear later in this section. The code compares the read count against the bytes remaining in the file. Beginning at _SFTReadFile_06, the code first determines if the bytes to read count is zero. This is unlikely but not impossible. Next, the code builds an all important DISKACCESS block. The details of why the disk access block is necessary will become clear later in this section. The code then compares the read count against the bytes remaining in the file. The read count is adjusted so that it does not attempt to read past the end of the file. Otherwise, the count is compared to the remaining size and adjusted accordingly. The count of bytes to read cannot exceed the file size.

The read function then cheats. If the read is from any file handle other than stdin, the read uses the logical read buffer routine. For the stdin device, the function reads only a single line at a time. This is to make device redirection from a file behave like a keyboard buffer.

The count of bytes read is returned in the CX register which is used to advance the file position pointer in the SFT. The file position is then used to remember the relative cluster number, a seemingly unimportant variable that should not be ignored. The purpose of the relative cluster number is to remember the all-important reference to the position at the start of the current cluster. We discuss its importance in greater detail in the section "Navigating Through Clusters."

The relative cluster number is the current file position divided by the size of the cluster in bytes. When this number is expanded back out by the read logic, it will contain the file offset to the start of the cluster. The variable is important because, as we note in greater detail in the next section, file access depends on knowing when it can search forward from the start of the cluster, even if that position is several sectors before the current position.

The code for determining and storing the relative cluster number into the SFT is as follows:

```
;/////////////////////////////////////////////////////////////;
;                                                              ;
;  Set Relative Cluster Number From SFT FilePosition           ;
;- - - - - - - - - - - - - - - - - - - - - - - - - - - - - - -;
;                                                              ;
;  Input:                                                      ;
;    es:di  SFT entry                                          ;
;..............................................................;

_computeRelativeCluster:
        push cx
        push es
        push di

        mov ax, word ptr es:[ sftDevInfo    ][ di ]
        and ax, sftDrivemask
        call getDPB                                    ; es:bx

        mov ax, word ptr es:[ _dpbBytesPerSector ][ bx ]
        mov cl, byte ptr es:[ _dpbClusterSizeShift ][ bx ]
        shl ax, cl                                     ; bytes per cluster
        mov cx, ax

        pop di
        pop es
        mov ax, word ptr es:[ sftFilePosition. _low  ][ di ]
        mov dx, word ptr es:[ sftFilePosition. _high ][ di ]
        call _div32

        mov word ptr es:[ sftRelCluster ][ di ], ax
        pop cx
        ret
```

MapAppToSFTHandle. This is the kind of function that in its straightforward simplicity sometimes makes you understand what the code is really trying to accomplish. It accepts as input the file handle that the application has received from an open or create and converts it into an SFT handle. The SFT handle will eventually be converted into a pointer to the SFT.

SFT handles are stored in the Job Handle Table, a data structure maintained in the current Program Segment Prefix. If the function cannot locate a PSP, which could be the case early in start-up in DOS, the function skips the handle lookup and conversion. The function also performs a bit of data checking. If the handle passed is beyond the size of the JHT, the handle is invalid and a -1 is returned in the AL.

Otherwise, the function looks up the SFT handle in the JHT.

```
;''''''''''''''''''''''''''''''''''''''''''''''''''''''''''''''''''''';
;  Map App Handle to Sys Handle                                       ;
;- - - - - - - - - - - - - - - - - - - - - - - - - - - - - - - - - - -;
;                                                                     ;
;  Returns:                                                           ;
;  ax    SFT handle id #                                              ;
;.....................................................................;

MapAppToSFTHandle:
        push es
        push si
        cmp word ptr cs:[ _RxDOS_CurrentPSP ], 0000
        jz MapAppToSFTHandle_08                         ; if no app ->

        mov si, ax
        mov ax, 00FFh                                   ; assume can't be found

        mov es, word ptr cs:[ _RxDOS_CurrentPSP ]       ; get PSP
        cmp si, word ptr es:[ pspFileHandleCount ]      ; beyond max handles
        jnc MapAppToSFTHandle_08                         ; yes, con't convert ->
        les ax, dword ptr es:[ pspFileHandlePtr ]       ; get JHT address
        add si, ax                                      ; use file handle as offset
        mov al, byte ptr es:[ si ]                      ; get SFT handle
        mov ah, 0

MapAppToSFTHandle_08:
        pop si
        pop es
        cmp ax, 00FFh                                   ; see if its unused
        ret
```

FindSFTByHandle. SFTs are distributed in containers called File Tables, or FTs. The SFT handle does not represent a table offset. The code locates the first FT, determines if the SFT handle could reside within the FT, and if it cannot, moves on to the next FT. Eventually, it determines that there is no valid corresponding SFT, or it locates the FT container where the referenced SFT can be found. The SFT is then a table offset from the start of the File Table.

```
;''''''''''''''''''''''''''''''''''''''''''''''''''''''''''''''''''''';
;  Find SFT by Handle                                                 ;
;- - - - - - - - - - - - - - - - - - - - - - - - - - - - - - - - - - -;
;                                                                     ;
;  Input:                                                             ;
;  ax      handle id #                                                ;
;                                                                     ;
;  Output:                                                            ;
;  es:di   pointer to matching SFT entry                              ;
;.....................................................................;

FindSFTbyHandle:
        push ax
        push es
```

```
        les di, dword ptr cs:[ _RxDOS_pFT ]
        cmp ax, 00FFh                              ; if not assigned
        jnc FindSFTbyHandle_12                     ; if greater than or equal ->

FindSFTbyHandle_08:
        cmp ax, word ptr es:[ numberSFTEntries ][ di ]
        jc FindSFTbyHandle_16                      ; if within this block ->

        sub ax, word ptr es:[ numberSFTEntries ][ di ]
        cmp word ptr es:[ nextFTPointer. _pointer ][ di ], 0FFFFh
        jz FindSFTbyHandle_12
        les di, dword ptr es:[ nextFTPointer ][ di ]
        jmp FindSFTbyHandle_08

;- - - - - - - - - - - - - - - - - - - - - - - - - - - - - - - - -
;  if error
;- - - - - - - - - - - - - - - - - - - - - - - - - - - - - - - - -
FindSFTbyHandle_12:
        pop es                                     ; restore es:
        pop ax                                     ; restore ax
        stc
        ret

;- - - - - - - - - - - - - - - - - - - - - - - - - - - - - - - - -
;  if located handle space
;- - - - - - - - - - - - - - - - - - - - - - - - - - - - - - - - -
FindSFTbyHandle_16:
        push cx
        mov cx, sizeSFT
        mul cl                                     ; find offset
        add di, sizeFT                             ; point past header
        add di, ax                                 ; plus offset

        pop cx                                     ; restore cx
        pop ax                                     ; throw away es:
        pop ax                                     ; restore ax (handle)
        clc
        ret
```

Navigating Through Clusters

The low-level read and write routines don't use SFTs. For example, SFTs are not available when DOS searches through a directory. Instead, the pertinent information necessary to process through a file is contained within RxDOS in a DISKACCESS block, shown here. MS-DOS maintains basically the same information in variables contained in the Swappable Data Area to perform the same function. Both operating systems need these parameters to walk through the FAT chain and to maintain a position of where they are relative to the start of the file.

```
;''''''''''''''''''''''''''''''''''''''''''''''''''''''''''''''';
;  System Access Control Block                                  ;
;...............................................................;
```

```
        DISKACCESS struc
diskAcDrive              dw  ?              ;*
diskAcBegCluster         dw  ?              ;* (cluster #)
diskAcFileSize           dd  ?              ;* file size in bytes
diskAcPosition           dd  ?              ;* read request (access position)
diskAcCurCluster         dw  ?              ;* (cluster #)
diskAcCurSector          dd  ?              ;  (LSN  #)
diskAcOffAtBegCluster    dd  ?              ;* (file offset )
diskAcOffAtBegBuffer     dd  ?              ;  (file offset )
diskAcBufferPtr          dd  ?              ;  dynamically assigned
diskAcOptions            dw  ?              ;  optimize options
        DISKACCESS ends
```

It is unlikely that the disk access block can be understood without first understanding the details of navigating through the fragmented cluster allocation scheme utilized by DOS. Read and write begin at a requested file position. That position needs to be translated to a cluster, sector, and offset within sector. The only way to translate a file position to a cluster is to navigate through the FAT chain, which takes time. From there, determining the sector and offset within the sector is basic arithmetic. A file position is worthless unless it also provides the cluster address.

To locate the sector that is referenced by a file position, the code compares the requested position to the file offset at the start of the current cluster, which is different from the current position. If the difference is negative, the requested position is before the current cluster, and the navigation process must begin from the beginning of the file. If the difference between the requested position and the start of the current cluster is smaller than the size of the cluster in bytes, then the requested position is within the current cluster and the sector can be located. Otherwise, the code determines both the next cluster address and the file position at the next cluster and repeats this test loop until it reaches the correct cluster or the end of file.

Once the correct cluster is located, the difference remaining in bytes between the requested position and the file position at the start of the cluster can be divided by the sector size to yield both the number of sectors from the start of the cluster and the byte offset within the sector.

Since an example may well be worth several thousand words here, presume a 512-byte sector and cluster size of four sectors per cluster. Each cluster is 2K. File position 5320 is located in the third cluster from the start of the file, second sector, byte 200. The file offset at the beginning of the third cluster begins at byte 4096. The difference between the requested position and the start of the third cluster is 1224, or 5320 minus 4096. The difference divided by the sector size, or 1224 ÷ 512 yields 2 sectors and a remainder of 200 bytes.

The code for _FATReadRandom requires the DISKACCESS block to be filled with the following information: the drive, file size, beginning cluster address, the requested file position, the current cluster address, and the offset at the beginning of the current cluster. These are the items marked by an asterisk in the comment field of the preceding block definition.

From an SFT, this information is inserted into the block by the buildAccessRef code shown next. The block is initialized to all zeros with the drive and beginning cluster address. The cluster size in bytes is determined from the Device Parameter Block, or DPB, for the drive. The relative cluster number maintained in the SFT is multiplying by the byte size of each cluster to compute the file offset at the start of the cluster. The remainder of the initialization sets the current file pointer to the beginning of the cluster since the actual current position is not necessary. Only the position at the beginning of the cluster is necessary and important.

```
        ;'''''''''''''''''''''''''''''''''''''''''''''''''''''''''';
        ;  Build Access Area from SFT                               ;
        ;- - - - - - - - - - - - - - - - - - - - - - - - - - - - - -;
        ;                                                           ;
        ;  Input:                                                   ;
        ;    es:di  SFT entry                                       ;
        ;    ss:bx  access block                                    ;
        ;...........................................................;

buildAccessRef:
        Entry
        ddef _fileposAtBegCluster
        def  _clusterSize
        saveRegisters si, cx

        push es
        push di
        push bx

        mov ax, word ptr es:[ sftDevInfo    ][ di ]
        and ax, sftDrivemask
        push ax

        mov dx, word ptr es:[ sftBegCluster ][ di ]
        call initdiskAccess                         ; [ax] is drive, [dx] is cluster

        pop ax                                       ; restore drive
        call getDPB

        mov ax, word ptr es:[ _dpbBytesPerSector ][ bx ]
        mov cl, byte ptr es:[ _dpbClusterSizeShift ][ bx ]
        shl ax, cl                                   ; bytes per cluster
        storarg _clusterSize, ax

        pop bx
        pop di
        pop es

        mov cx, word ptr es:[ sftRelCluster ][ di ]
        or cx, cx                                    ; cluster zeroed out ?
        jz buildAccessRef_08                         ; can't use curr cluster ->

        xor dx, dx
        mul cx                                        ; file pos at start of cluster
        stordarg _fileposAtBegCluster, dx, ax         ; save

        mov ax, word ptr es:[ sftFilePosition. _low  ][ di ]
        mov dx, word ptr es:[ sftFilePosition. _high ][ di ]
        sub ax, word ptr [ _fileposAtBegCluster. _low  ][ bp ]
        sbb dx, word ptr [ _fileposAtBegCluster. _high ][ bp ]
        jc buildAccessRef_08                         ; can't use curr cluster ->
        or dx, dx                                    ; distance greater than 65k ?
        jnz buildAccessRef_08                        ; can't use curr cluster ->
```

```
        cmp ax, word ptr [ _clusterSize ][ bp ]          ; greater than cluster size ?
        jg buildAccessRef_08                             ; can't use curr cluster -->

        mov dx, word ptr es:[ sftCurCluster ][ di ]
        mov word ptr ss:[ diskAcCurCluster ][ bx ], dx   ; ok, within cluster

        getdarg dx, ax, _fileposAtBegCluster             ; offset at start of cluster
        mov word ptr ss:[ diskAcOffAtBegBuffer. _low  ][ bx ], ax
        mov word ptr ss:[ diskAcOffAtBegBuffer. _high ][ bx ], dx
        mov word ptr ss:[ diskAcOffAtBegCluster. _low  ][ bx ], ax
        mov word ptr ss:[ diskAcOffAtBegCluster. _high ][ bx ], dx

buildAccessRef_08:
        restoreRegisters cx, si
        Return
```

_FATReadRandom. The purpose of the routine is to read a sector from disk given a random position in the file and a filled DISKACCESS block. The function will access any position at random and will optimize its access based on the current position. This routine also accesses the root directory, which is not mapped in the FAT. The routine is listed next.

We described the algorithm in the previous few pages, but we now describe it in the context of the code. The first test performed by the function is whether the requested position is before or after the file position at start of the cluster. If positioning to some location before the current cluster, the file pointer is moved to the beginning of the file since the FAT chain cannot be accessed in the reverse direction.

Next, the DPB pointer is fetched since the cluster size needs to be computed at some point. Some other initialization is performed. For example, there is a difference between the current cluster and the cluster at the beginning of the file. The current cluster cannot be zero unless the file begins at cluster zero, so the current cluster is set to the beginning of the file if it isn't initialized already.

Only one file begins at cluster zero, the root directory, and only because of an RxDOS convention. The root directory is not FAT mapped, and there is no cluster chain. To trick the routine into never looking at the FAT chain, the cluster is artificially made to equal the size of the root directory. The function will not encounter the end of the cluster and attempt to read the FAT chain.

At _FATReadRandom_22, the code begins a loop of advancing to the next cluster where necessary. If the difference between the requested position and the start of the current cluster exceeds the bytes per cluster, it must advance to the next cluster. It calls the FAT function getNextCluster and increments the position at the beginning of the cluster by the cluster size. It then loops back to test the position again. If there are no additional clusters, the routine returns with a zero exit flag.

At _FATReadRandom_32, the routine has reached the required cluster. It converts the cluster address to a logical sector number. This is, of course, the sector address at the start of the cluster. The number of sectors offset from the start of the cluster is computed, as is the byte offset within the sector. The required sector is read, and a pointer to the cache buffer is returned in the ES:DI. The cached block data type is set. Data type can be set to a directory or data block.

Finally, the function returns the number of bytes remaining in the sector, determined by taking the difference between the position at the end of the current sector and the requested position pointer passed on call. To understand why this value is important, remember that read and write transfer data of varying lengths that do not necessarily fit exactly on sector boundaries. The bytes to the end of the sector help determine whether additional sector reads or writes will be necessary.

```
(in rxdosfat.asm)
        ;''''''''''''''''''''''''''''''''''''''''''''''''''''''''''''''''''''';
        ;    Read Random Buffer FAT File                                      ;
        ;- - - - - - - - - - - - - - - - - - - - - - - - - - - - - - - - - - -;
        ;                                                                     ;
        ;    Input:                                                           ;
        ;      ss:bx   fat short control block                                ;
        ;                                                                     ;
        ;    Output:                                                          ;
        ;      es:bx   pointer in block buffer to data                        ;
        ;      cx      remaining bytes in block                               ;
        ;      zr      means end of file or wrong address                     ;
        ;.....................................................................;

_FATReadRandom:
        Entry
        ddef _accessControl, ss, bx
        ddef _reqOffset
        def  _bytesPerCluster
        ddef _DPBPointer

        saveRegisters ds, di, si, dx, ax

;- - - - - - - - - - - - - - - - - - - - - - - - - - - - - - - - - - - - - -
; if request is before start of buffer
;- - - - - - - - - - - - - - - - - - - - - - - - - - - - - - - - - - - - - -
        setDS ss
        mov ax, word ptr [ diskAcPosition. _low  ][ bx ]
        mov dx, word ptr [ diskAcPosition. _high ][ bx ]
        stordarg _reqOffset, dx, ax

        sub ax, word ptr [ diskAcOffAtBegCluster. _low  ][ bx ]
        sbb dx, word ptr [ diskAcOffAtBegCluster. _high ][ bx ]
        jl _FATReadRandom_08
        jmp short _FATReadRandom_16

_FATReadRandom_08:
        xor ax, ax
        mov word ptr [ diskAcOffAtBegBuffer. _low  ][ bx ], ax
        mov word ptr [ diskAcOffAtBegBuffer. _high ][ bx ], ax
        mov word ptr [ diskAcOffAtBegCluster. _low  ][ bx ], ax
        mov word ptr [ diskAcOffAtBegCluster. _high ][ bx ], ax
        mov word ptr [ diskAcCurCluster ][ bx ], ax

;- - - - - - - - - - - - - - - - - - - - - - - - - - - - - - - - - - - - - -
; get DPB
;- - - - - - - - - - - - - - - - - - - - - - - - - - - - - - - - - - - - - -
_FATReadRandom_16:
        push bx
        mov ax, word ptr [ diskAcDrive ][ bx ]
```

```
        call getDPB                               ; (es:bx) Dev Param Block
        stordarg _DPBPointer, es, bx
        mov si, bx                                ; es: si
        pop bx


;- - - - - - - - - - - - - - - - - - - - - - - - - - - - - - - - - - - -
;   locate starting cluster and sector
;- - - - - - - - - - - - - - - - - - - - - - - - - - - - - - - - - - - -
        cmp word ptr [ diskAcCurCluster ][ bx ], 0000
        jnz _FATReadRandom_18
        mov ax, word ptr [ diskAcBegCluster ][ bx ]
        mov word ptr [ diskAcCurCluster ][ bx ], ax

_FATReadRandom_18:
        mov ax, word ptr es:[ _dpbBytesPerSector ][ si ]
        mov cl, byte ptr es:[ _dpbClusterSizeShift ][ si ]
        shl ax, cl                                ; bytes per cluster

;- - - - - - - - - - - - - - - - - - - - - - - - - - - - - - - - - - - -
;   compute a fake sector size if addressing cluster 0 (root dir).
;- - - - - - - - - - - - - - - - - - - - - - - - - - - - - - - - - - - -
        cmp word ptr [ diskAcBegCluster ][ bx ], 0000
        jnz _FATReadRandom_20
        mov ax, word ptr es:[ _dpbMaxAllocRootDir ][ si ]
        mov cx, sizeDIRENTRY
        mul cx

_FATReadRandom_20:
        mov word ptr [ _bytesPerCluster ][ bp ], ax

;- - - - - - - - - - - - - - - - - - - - - - - - - - - - - - - - - - - -
;   see if within current cluster
;- - - - - - - - - - - - - - - - - - - - - - - - - - - - - - - - - - - -
_FATReadRandom_22:
        mov dx, word ptr [ _reqOffset. _low ][ bp ]
        mov cx, word ptr [ _reqOffset. _high ][ bp ]
        sub dx, word ptr [ diskAcOffAtBegCluster. _low ][ bx ]
        sbb cx, word ptr [ diskAcOffAtBegCluster. _high ][ bx ]
        jnz _FATReadRandom_26                     ; must cont search forward —>
        cmp dx, word ptr [ _bytesPerCluster ][ bp ]   ; beyond cluster size ?
        jc _FATReadRandom_32                      ; no, current cluster is ok —>

_FATReadRandom_26:
        mov ax, word ptr [ diskAcDrive ][ bx ]
        mov dx, word ptr [ diskAcCurCluster ][ bx ]
        or dx, dx                                 ; zero cluster ?
        jz _FATReadRandom_28                      ; yes —>

        call getNextCluster
        jz _FATReadRandom_28                      ; if end of cluster chain —>

        mov cx, word ptr [ _bytesPerCluster ][ bp ]
        add word ptr [ diskAcOffAtBegCluster. _low ][ bx ], cx
        adc word ptr [ diskAcOffAtBegCluster. _high ][ bx ], 0000
```

```
        mov word ptr [ diskAcCurCluster        ][ bx ], dx
        jmp _FATReadRandom_22


_FATReadRandom_28:
        xor cx, cx
        jmp _FATReadRandom_Return


;- - - - - - - - - - - - - - - - - - - - - - - - - - - - - -
;  see if within current sector
;- - - - - - - - - - - - - - - - - - - - - - - - - - - - - -
_FATReadRandom_32:
        lds bx, dword ptr [ _accessControl ][ bp ]
        mov ax, word ptr [ diskAcDrive ][ bx ]
        mov dx, word ptr [ diskAcCurCluster ][ bx ]
        call computeLogSectorNumber                    ; cluster -> sector number

        push cx
        push dx                                         ; save logical sector number

        mov ax, word ptr [ _reqOffset. _low ][ bp ]
        mov dx, word ptr [ _reqOffset. _high ][ bp ]
        sub ax, word ptr [ diskAcOffAtBegCluster. _low ][ bx ]
        sbb dx, word ptr [ diskAcOffAtBegCluster. _high ][ bx ]
        div word ptr  es:[ _dpbBytesPerSector ][ si ]

        mov cx, word ptr [ _reqOffset. _low ][ bp ]
        sub cx, dx                                      ; subtract out remainder
        mov word ptr [ diskAcOffAtBegBuffer. _low ][ bx ], cx
        mov cx, word ptr [ _reqOffset. _high ][ bp ]
        mov word ptr [ diskAcOffAtBegBuffer. _high ][ bx ], cx

        pop dx
        pop cx                                          ; restore lsn
        add dx, ax                                      ; real sector offset
        adc cx, 0

;- - - - - - - - - - - - - - - - - - - - - - - - - - - - - -
; read sector
;- - - - - - - - - - - - - - - - - - - - - - - - - - - - - -
        mov ax, word ptr [ diskAcDrive ][ bx ]
        mov word ptr [ diskAcCurSector. _low ][ bx ], dx
        mov word ptr [ diskAcCurSector. _high ][ bx ], cx

        call ReadBuffer
        mov ax, word ptr [ diskAcOptions ][ bx ]
        or byte ptr es:[ ccbStatus ][ di ], al          ; type of block

        lea di, offset ccbData [ di ]                   ; point to data
        mov word ptr [ diskAcBufferPtr. _segment ][ bx ], es
        mov word ptr [ diskAcBufferPtr. _pointer ][ bx ], di


;- - - - - - - - - - - - - - - - - - - - - - - - - - - - - -
;  return pointer
;- - - - - - - - - - - - - - - - - - - - - - - - - - - - - -
```

```
        lds bx, dword ptr [ _accessControl ] [ bp ]
        les si, dword ptr [ _DPBPointer    ] [ bp ]
        mov cx, word ptr es: [ _dpbBytesPerSector ] [ si ]

        mov ax, word ptr [ _reqOffset. _low  ] [ bp ]
        mov dx, word ptr [ _reqOffset. _high ] [ bp ]
        sub ax, word ptr [ diskAcOffAtBegBuffer. _low  ] [ bx ]
        sbb dx, word ptr [ diskAcOffAtBegBuffer. _high ] [ bx ]

        les bx, dword ptr [ diskAcBufferPtr ] [ bx ]
        add bx, ax                              ; offset into buffer
        sub cx, ax                              ; bytes remaining in buffer

;- - - - - - - - - - - - - - - - - - - - - - - - - - - - - -
;  return
;- - - - - - - - - - - - - - - - - - - - - - - - - - - - - -
_FATReadRandom_Return:
        restoreRegisters ax, dx, si, di, ds
        Return
```

_FATReadRandom reads and returns a single sector. The function is used by the directory search functions and the buffered read and write functions used when a file handle or FCB function requests a read or write.

readLogicalBuffer. The function fills a buffer that may cross several sectors. It repeatedly calls _FATReadRandom to position and return the correct sector on disk. It uses the fact that the DISKACCESS block, initialized by the SFT read routine, is meant to be used to perform recursive reads. The function is listed next.

The function is called with an initialized access block, a pointer to a buffer in memory, the file position where the read will begin, and a count of the number of bytes to read. The buffer address is normalized, and _FATReadRandom is called to return a pointer to a cached disk buffer. If the function returns a zero byte count, the end of file has been reached, and the routine prepares to exit. Otherwise, the count represents the number of bytes available in the current sector. The count is compared to the remaining bytes to read and the minimum of the two is passed to the fastmove, which generates rep move instructions. The current position on disk is advanced by the bytes read, and if there are more bytes to read, the routine loops back to read to as many bytes as possible. The bytes read is returned to the caller.

```
(in rxdosfil.asm)
        ;''''''''''''''''''''''''''''''''''''''''''''''''''''''''''''';
        ;  Read To App Buffer                                       ;
        ;- - - - - - - - - - - - - - - - - - - - - - - - - - - - - -;
        ;                                                           ;
        ;  Input:                                                   ;
        ;    ss:bx  Access Control Buffer                           ;
        ;    es:di  buffer address                                  ;
        ;    dx:ax  file position to start reading                  ;
        ;    cx     bytes to read                                   ;
        ;                                                           ;
        ;  Output:                                                  ;
        ;    ss:bx  Access Control Buffer                           ;
        ;    es:di  buffer address                                  ;
```

```
        ;   cx      bytes actually read                              ;
        ;   zr      means end of file or wrong address               ;
        ;................................................................;

readLogicalBuffer:
        Entry
        ddef _accessControl, ss, bx
        ddef _readbuffer
        def  _bytestoRead, cx
        def  _bytesRead, 0000

        SaveSegments di, si, dx, bx, ax
        mov word ptr ss:[ diskAcPosition. _low  ][ bx ], ax
        mov word ptr ss:[ diskAcPosition. _high ][ bx ], dx

readLogicalBuffer_08:
        NormalizeBuffer es, di                  ; normalize buffer pointer
        stordarg _readbuffer, es, di            ; save read buffer pointer

        getarg bx, _accessControl               ; make sure we point to access block
        mov word ptr ss:[ diskAcOptions ][ bx ], (ccb_isDATA)
        call _FATReadRandom                     ; get buffer, read at position

        or cx, cx                               ; any bytes left ?
        jz readLogicalBuffer_20                 ; no -->

        cmp cx, word ptr [ _bytestoRead ][ bp ] ; compare against length needed
        jc readLogicalBuffer_12                 ; if less are available -->
        mov cx, word ptr [ _bytestoRead ][ bp ] ; minimize

readLogicalBuffer_12:
        push ds
        push cx
        setDS es
        mov si, bx                              ; where data read [ds: si]
        les di, dword ptr [ _readbuffer ][ bp ] ; to destination  [es: di]
        fastmove si, di                         ; move buffer

        pop cx
        pop ds
        getarg bx, _accessControl               ; make sure we point to access block
        add word ptr ss:[ diskAcPosition. _low  ][ bx ], cx
        adc word ptr ss:[ diskAcPosition. _high ][ bx ], 0000
        getdarg es, di, _readbuffer             ; read buffer pointer
        add di, cx                              ; position beyond buffer

        add word ptr [ _bytesRead ][ bp ], cx
        sub word ptr [ _bytestoRead ][ bp ], cx ; compare against length needed
        jc readLogicalBuffer_20                 ; if no more to read -->
        jz readLogicalBuffer_20                 ; if no more to read -->
        jmp readLogicalBuffer_08                 ; continue reading -->

readLogicalBuffer_20:
        mov cx, word ptr [ _bytesRead ][ bp ]

        RestoreSegments ax, bx, dx, si, di
        Return
```

File Write with Handle

	On Entry	On Return
AX	AH = 40h	bytes written
BX	file handle	
CX	bytes to write	
DS:DX	pointer to write buffer	
Flags		CY = set if error

Related Functions:
   3Ch Create File; 3Dh Open File; 3Eh Close File; 3Fh Read File.

File Write is a bit more complicated than File Read since space beyond the end of the file must be allocated to the file before the write can complete. A special DOS convention will set the file size for a file when a zero length buffer is written. This may cause the file to be either expanded or truncated, with the corresponding effect of either allocating or releasing file space.

   File Write transfers a buffer of up to 64K to the disk at any file position set. If the file position is past the end of the file, DOS will allocate but not initialize space for the file. Although file handle write begins in _WriteFile, in rxdos.asm, the actual write handle function is at _SFTWriteFile. This common function is used by several other DOS functions, including display output, FCB write functions, and the file handle write function. Figure 4-4 shows the relationship of functions called.

   _WriteFile checks for a Control Break and then determines if the file handle is to a valid open file. The file handle must point to a handle inside the JHT, and the entry in the JHT must point to a valid open SFT handle. The SFT handle, the SFT address, the buffer pointer, and the write count are passed to _SFTWriteFile, where the actual file write is handled. The return value from the function, which can be either an error or the count of bytes written, is returned to the caller, and the function terminates.

   The function appears as shown here.

```
;'''''''''''''''''''''''''''''''''''''''''''''''''''''''''''''''''';
;  40h Write File                                                  ;
;- - - - - - - - - - - - - - - - - - - - - - - - - - - - - - - - - -;
;                                                                  ;
;  bx    handle                                                    ;
;  cx    bytes to write                                            ;
;  ds:dx buffer address                                            ;
;..................................................................;

_WriteFile:
        Entry
        def _handle, bx
        def _writeCount, cx
        ddef _sftPointer
        ddef _bufPtr, es, dx                    ; save buffer pointer

        call CtrlC_Check

        mov ax, bx                              ; handle
```

```
        call MapAppToSFTHandle                      ; map to internal handle info
        call FindSFTbyHandle                        ; get corresponding SFT (es: di )
        stordarg _sftPointer, es, di                ; save sft buffer pointer
        jc _WriteFile_error                         ; if could not find ->

        push word ptr [ _bufPtr. _segment ][ bp ]
        push word ptr [ _bufPtr. _pointer ][ bp ]
        getarg cx, _writeCount                      ; bytes to write
        call _SFTWriteFile                          ; write using sft (at es:di )

_WriteFile_error:
        RetCallersStackFrame ds, bx
        mov word ptr [ _AX ][ bx ], ax
        Return
```

Figure 4-4. Console output, FCB file write, and file handle file write functions utilize the same common write code. For console functions, the common file handle write functions provide file redirection services.

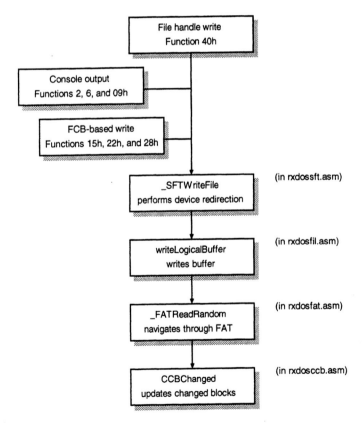

_SFTWriteFile. The function handles write to a file that has an open SFT handle. This function, as noted earlier, is used by display output, FCB write functions, and the file handle write function. The write function first checks to determine if SFT has been assigned to a character device. If so, the function initiates the character device output.

The action taken by the remainder of the routine when the SFT is assigned to a file is conditioned by whether zero bytes are being written. When a zero byte write is performed, the file is truncated to the current position pointer. However, it unfortunately is not a simple matter of testing for just a zero byte write. A zero byte write sets the file size, which may involve either a file truncation or expansion. The expansion is handled early in the routine, whereas the truncation is handled later. That's because the file size must be expanded when the position pointer, set by DOS function 42h, is set at some location past the end of the file, regardless of the size of the write.

The general flow of the routine is as follows. The routine first checks whether the file has any allocated space. If it does not, and if this is not a zero byte write, the routine allocates a cluster from the FAT to the file. It then checks to determine whether additional clusters need be allocated to the file by comparing the current file size with the requested position pointer. If the file pointer is beyond the last allocated cluster, new clusters are allocated to the file, using fillLogicalBuffer, expanding its size. The buffer address to write and its size are passed to writeLogicalBuffer, which writes the buffer to disk. It does nothing if the buffer size is zero. The buffer pointer is advanced by the number of bytes written. If only a portion of the buffer has been written, the actual number of bytes written is returned, ensuring that the updated position pointer remains accurate.

A check is then made to determine if the file is to be truncated. The original byte count is checked for zeros. To truncate the file, all the clusters beyond the current cluster are released. The truncate code begins at the end of the function, where a test is made for a zero write count. The drive and current cluster address are fetched, and a test is made to determine if the final file size will be zero. If the final size is zero, then the file should not contain any allocated clusters. The code therefore bypasses the getNextCluster function call. If the file is to contain at least a single byte, then it must retain the current cluster. The next cluster address is fetched from the allocation chain and passed to the release cluster function. All clusters allocated to the file beyond the current cluster are deleted.

Finally, the file size is adjusted to ensure that it is correct. The number of bytes written is returned to the caller. The function listing follows:

```
;'''''''''''''''''''''''''''''''''''''''''''''''''''''''''''''';
;  Write To SFT                                                 ;
;- - - - - - - - - - - - - - - - - - - - - - - - - - - - - - - -;
;                                                               ;
;  Input:                                                       ;
;    es:di   sft pointer                                        ;
;    cx      bytes to write                                     ;
;    stack   buffer address                                     ;
;                                                               ;
;  Output:                                                      ;
;    cx      bytes actually written                             ;
;    cy      end of available disk space reached                ;
;..............................................................;
```

```
_SFTWriteFile:
        Entry 2
        darg _bufPtr

        def _actuallyWritten, 0000
        def _writeCount, cx
        ddef _sftpointer, es, di
        defbytes _diskAccess, sizeDISKACCESS

;- - - - - - - - - - - - - - - - - - - - - - - - - - - - - - - - -
;  is file redirected to a device
;- - - - - - - - - - - - - - - - - - - - - - - - - - - - - - - - -
        or word ptr es:[ sftDevInfo ][ di ], sftWritten
        test word ptr es:[ sftDevInfo ][ di ], sftIsDevice
        jz _SFTWriteFile_16

        or cx, cx
        jz _SFTWriteFile_06                       ; if nothing to write ->

        push word ptr es:[ sftDCB. _segment ][ di ]
        push word ptr es:[ sftDCB. _pointer ][ di ]
        mov cx, word ptr [ _writeCount ][ bp ]
        getdarg es, di, _bufPtr
        call devCharWrite

_SFTWriteFile_06:
        jmp _SFTWriteFile_56

;- - - - - - - - - - - - - - - - - - - - - - - - - - - - - - - - -
;  initialize disk access block
;- - - - - - - - - - - - - - - - - - - - - - - - - - - - - - - - -
_SFTWriteFile_16:
        cmp word ptr es:[ sftBegCluster ][ di ], 0000  ; begin cluster allocated ?
        jnz _SFTWriteFile_24                           ; yes ->
        cmp word ptr [ _writeCount ][ bp ], 0000       ; not attempting to actually write
        jz _SFTWriteFile_24                            ; if no write ->

        mov ax, word ptr es:[ sftDevInfo    ][ di ]
        and ax, sftDrivemask
        call AllocateCluster                           ; allocate cluster
        ifc _SFTWriteFile_56                           ; if can't allocate space ->

        getdarg es, di, _sftpointer
        mov word ptr es:[ sftBegCluster ][ di ], dx    ; save beginning cluster

_SFTWriteFile_24:
        lea bx, _diskAccess [ bp ]                     ; build access control block
        call buildAccessRef                            ;  ...from sft
        mov word ptr [ _diskAccess. diskAcOptions ][ bp ], DISKAC_OPTIMIZEDWRITE

        xor cx, cx
        mov ax, word ptr es:[ sftFilePosition. _low ][ di ]
        mov dx, word ptr es:[ sftFilePosition. _high ][ di ]
```

```
        sub ax, word ptr es:[ sftFileSize. _low ][ di ]
        sbb dx, word ptr es:[ sftFileSize. _high ][ di ]
        jc _SFTWriteFile_32                 ; if not past end of file ->
        or ax, dx                           ; positive offset ?
        jz _SFTWriteFile_32                 ; if not past end of file ->

;- - - - - - - - - - - - - - - - - - - - - - - - - - - - - - - - - - - -
; file pointer past end of file.  fill to current pointer.
;- - - - - - - - - - - - - - - - - - - - - - - - - - - - - - - - - - - -
        push word ptr es:[ sftFileSize. _low ][ di ]
        push word ptr es:[ sftFileSize. _high ][ di ]
        call fillLogicalBuffer              ; Access buffer: ss: bx
        jc _SFTWriteFile_56                 ; no more room on disk ->

        getdarg es, di, _sftPointer         ; restore pointer to sft buffer
        add word ptr es:[ sftFileSize. _low ][ di ], ax
        adc word ptr es:[ sftFileSize. _high ][ di ], dx

;- - - - - - - - - - - - - - - - - - - - - - - - - - - - - - - - - - - -
; write cx bytes to file from buffer passed
;- - - - - - - - - - - - - - - - - - - - - - - - - - - - - - - - - - - -
_SFTWriteFile_32:
        getarg cx, _writeCount
        mov ax, word ptr es:[ sftFilePosition. _low ][ di ]
        mov dx, word ptr es:[ sftFilePosition. _high ][ di ]
        getdarg es, di, _bufPtr             ; buffer es: di
        call writeLogicalBuffer             ; Access buffer: ss: bx

        getdarg es, di, _sftPointer         ; restore pointer to sft buffer
        add word ptr es:[ sftFilePosition. _low ][ di ], cx
        adc word ptr es:[ sftFilePosition. _high ][ di ], 0000
        add word ptr [ _actuallyWritten ][ bp ], cx

        mov dx, word ptr ss:[ diskAcCurCluster ][ bx ]
        mov word ptr es:[ sftCurCluster ][ di ], dx
        call _computeRelativeCluster

;- - - - - - - - - - - - - - - - - - - - - - - - - - - - - - - - - - - -
; truncate size ?
;- - - - - - - - - - - - - - - - - - - - - - - - - - - - - - - - - - - -
        cmp word ptr [ _writeCount ][ bp ], 0000   ; was it truncate special case ?
        jnz _SFTWriteFile_44                        ; no, go see if eof moved ->

        mov ax, word ptr [ _diskAccess. diskAcDrive      ][ bp ]
        mov dx, word ptr [ _diskAccess. diskAcCurCluster ][ bp ]

        mov cx, word ptr es:[ sftFilePosition. _low ][ di ]
        or cx, word ptr es:[ sftFilePosition. _high ][ di ] ; at beg of file ?
        jz _SFTWriteFile_38                        ; yes ->

        call getNextCluster                        ; get next cluster, if any
        jz _SFTWriteFile_46                        ; if already at end ->

_SFTWriteFile_38:
```

```
        call ReleaseClusterChain                           ; truncate file to here
        jmp short _SFTWriteFile_46

;- - - - - - - - - - - - - - - - - - - - - - - - - - - - - - -
;  update file size
;- - - - - - - - - - - - - - - - - - - - - - - - - - - - - - -
_SFTWriteFile_44:
        mov ax, word ptr es:[ sftFilePosition. _low  ][ di ]
        mov dx, word ptr es:[ sftFilePosition. _high ][ di ]
        sub ax, word ptr es:[ sftFileSize. _low  ][ di ]
        sbb dx, word ptr es:[ sftFileSize. _high ][ di ]
        jc _SFTWriteFile_56                               ; if not past end of file ->

_SFTWriteFile_46:
        mov ax, word ptr es:[ sftFilePosition. _low  ][ di ]
        mov dx, word ptr es:[ sftFilePosition. _high ][ di ]
        mov word ptr es:[ sftFileSize. _low  ][ di ], ax
        mov word ptr es:[ sftFileSize. _high ][ di ], dx

;- - - - - - - - - - - - - - - - - - - - - - - - - - - - - - -
;  return
;- - - - - - - - - - - - - - - - - - - - - - - - - - - - - - -

_SFTWriteFile_56:
        mov cx, word ptr [ _actuallyWritten ][ bp ]
        mov ax, cx                                        ; return count
        or ax, ax
        Return
```

To accomplish the write, _SFTWriteFile utilizes several other lower-level functions which we describe further in this chapter. Figure 4-5 shows the outline of the functions called.

Figure 4-5. File Write flow outline

```
_SFTWriteFile (in rxdossft.asm)
    devCharWriteLine (in rxdosdev.asm)
    buildAccessRef (in rxdosfil.asm)
    writeLogicalBuffer(in rxdosfil.asm)
        fillLogicalBuffer(in rxdosfil.asm)
        _FATReadRandom (in rxdosfat.asm)
            getDPB
            getNextCluster
            computeLogSectorNumber
            ReadBuffer
        CCBChanged (in rxdosccb.asm)

    _computeRelativeCluster (in rxdosfil.asm)
    getNextCluster (in rxdosfat.asm)
    ReleaseClusterChain (in rxdosfat.asm)
```

writeLogicalBuffer. A write buffer may be split across several disk sectors, which is the essential purpose of the writeLogicalBuffer function. The process of write begins at the current file pointer, which can be translated into a sector by utilizing _FATReadRandom, which we already explained in detail. The FAT read routine returns a sector, and the write buffer routine updates the sector. This process continues for as long as there is buffer data to be written.

Although some writes update only a portion of a sector, it is possible to optimize writes that will update the entire sector by bypassing the read altogether. After all, it is pointless to read a buffer that will be fully destroyed. The _FATReadRandom function returns a sector, but bypasses the read if three conditions are met. The read-optimize flag is set, the amount of data remaining to update the buffer is at least the size of the sector, and the data pointer begins at the start of the sector.

The writeLogicalBuffer routine listed next works as follows: The _FATReadrandom routine is called with the file position pointer. It returns a sector address with the number of bytes available to write. This is the number of bytes remaining in the sector past the file pointer. If the byte count is zero, there is no valid sector, and an additional cluster must be appended to the file. If the append function fails, the disk is full. Otherwise, the read random function is called again to position on the sector. This process may continue for several loops because the file pointer may be past the current end of file.

Once a sector is returned, the count of bytes remaining in the sector is compared to the buffer byte count, and the minimum bytes is copied to the sector. The sector header address is computed, and the block is marked changed for subsequent output to disk. The number of bytes written and the number of bytes remaining to write are updated, as is the current position in the file. When all the characters are written, or when an error is encountered, the routine exists.

```
;''''''''''''''''''''''''''''''''''''''''''''''''''''''''''''''''''';
;  Write From App Buffer                                            ;
;- - - - - - - - - - - - - - - - - - - - - - - - - - - - - - - -  -;
;                                                                   ;
;  Note:                                                            ;
;                                                                   ;
;  Write uses FATRead to compute the  correct  logical  sector     ;
;  from cluster information.  If  a sector cannot be located,       ;
;  then we attach a new cluster to the end of the file.             ;
;                                                                   ;
;- - - - - - - - - - - - - - - - - - - - - - - - - - - - - - - -  -;
;                                                                   ;
;  Input:                                                           ;
;    ss:bx  Access Control Buffer                                   ;
;    es:di  buffer address                                          ;
;    dx:ax  file position to start writing                          ;
;    cx     bytes to write                                          ;
;                                                                   ;
;  Output:                                                          ;
;    ss:bx  Access Control Buffer                                   ;
;    es:di  buffer address                                          ;
;    cx     bytes actually written                                  ;
;    zr     means end of file or wrong address                      ;
;...................................................................;
```

```
writeLogicalBuffer:
        Entry
        ddef _accessControl, ss, bx
        ddef _appBuffer
        def  _bytestoWrite, cx
        def  _bytesWritten, 0000

        SaveSegments di, si, dx, bx, ax
        mov word ptr ss:[ diskAcPosition. _low  ][ bx ], ax
        mov word ptr ss:[ diskAcPosition. _high ][ bx ], dx

writeLogicalBuffer_08:
        NormalizeBuffer es, di                  ; normalize buffer pointer
        stordarg _appbuffer, es, di             ; save app buffer pointer

writeLogicalBuffer_10:
        getarg cx, _bytestoWrite                ; bytes to write
        getarg bx, _accessControl               ; make sure we point to access block
        call _FATReadRandom                     ; get buffer, read at position
        or cx, cx                               ; any bytes left ?
        jnz writeLogicalBuffer_14               ; yes, no need to alloc more ->

        getarg bx, _accessControl               ; make sure we point to access block
        mov ax, word ptr ss:[ diskAcDrive      ][ bx ]
        mov dx, word ptr ss:[ diskAcCurCluster ][ bx ]
        call AppendCluster                      ; else, append a cluster
        jnc writeLogicalBuffer_10               ; go try to link to it now ->
        jmp writeLogicalBuffer_20               ; go try to link to it now ->

writeLogicalBuffer_14:
        cmp cx, word ptr [ _bytestoWrite ][ bp ]; compare against length needed
        jc writeLogicalBuffer_16                 ; if less are available ->
        mov cx, word ptr [ _bytestoWrite ][ bp ]; maximize

writeLogicalBuffer_16:
        or cx, cx                               ; more to write
        jz writeLogicalBuffer_20                ; no ->

        push ds
        push cx
        mov di, bx                              ; where to write data [es: di]
        lds si, dword ptr [ _appbuffer ][ bp ]  ; data source [ds: si]
        fastmove si, di                         ; move buffer

        mov si, bx                              ; where data written
        call locateCCBPHeader                   ; find ccb header
        call CCBChanged                         ; mark block changed

        pop cx
        pop ds
        add word ptr [ _bytesWritten ][ bp ], cx
        sub word ptr [ _bytestoWrite ][ bp ], cx; compare against length needed
        jc writeLogicalBuffer_20                 ; if no more to write ->
        jz writeLogicalBuffer_20                 ; if no more to write ->
```

```
        getarg bx, _accessControl           ; make sure we point to access block
        add word ptr ss:[ diskAcPosition. _low ][ bx ], cx
        adc word ptr ss:[ diskAcPosition. _high ][ bx ], 0000
        getarg es, di, _appbuffer           ; app buffer pointer
        add di, cx                          ; position beyond buffer
        jmp writeLogicalBuffer_08           ; continue writting ->

writeLogicalBuffer_20:
        mov cx, word ptr [ _bytesWritten ][ bp ]

        RestoreSegments ax, bx, dx, si, di
        Return
```

Move File Pointer with Handle

	On Entry	On Return
AX	AH = 42h; AL = method	low order absolute position
BX	handle	
CX	high order relative offset	
DX	low order relative offset	high order absolute position
Flags		CY = set if error

Related Functions:
   3Ch Create File; 3Dh Open File; 3Eh Close File; 3Fh Read File; 40h Write File.

The function sets the file pointer file, but no actual movement is executed until a read or write. The pointer may be set anywhere inside or beyond the file. Setting the file to some value beyond the end of the actual file size may be useful if the purpose is to create or expand the file size by preallocating file space. Setting the file pointer by itself does not cause the file size to change. Only the file write function can change the file size.

The function code begins at _MoveFilePointer, located in rxdos.asm. The function is listed next. The file handle is first converted to an SFT pointer. The offset passed with the function call is then added either to the beginning of the file position, to the current position, or to the end of the file position, depending on the method passed with the call. The offset may be negative or zero.

The purpose of the routine is to set the current file position. To move to the end of the file, the function should be called with an offset of 0000, and the method should be to position relative to the end of the file. To back up over a line just read, the negative of the line size should be passed, and the method should be to position from the current file pointer. For random access in the file, the offset value passed should be set relative to the beginning of the file.

The code jumps to one of three labels based on the move method, where the offset value passed is added to either the file size or the current position. The result is set as the updated current position. The resulting value is then returned to the caller in the DX:AX register pair.

```
;////////////////////////////////////////////////////////////;
;  42h Lseek (Move) File Pointer                              ;
;- - - - - - - - - - - - - - - - - - - - - - - - - - - - - - -;
```

```
        ;                                                       ;
        ;  al      move method                                  ;
        ;  bx      handle                                       ;
        ;  cx:dx   distance to move pointer                     ;
        ;....................................................;

_MoveFilePointer:
        Entry
        def _method, ax
        def _handle, bx
        ddef _moveDistance, cx, dx
        ddef _newPosition

        mov ax, bx                              ; handle
        call MapAppToSFTHandle                  ; map to internal handle info
        call FindSFTbyHandle                    ; get corresponding SFT (es: di )
        jc _moveFilePointer_36                  ; if could not find ->

        getdarg cx, dx, _moveDistance
        mov ax, word ptr [ _method ][ bp ]      ; only AL used
        Goto SEEK_BEG,   _moveFilePointer_beg
        Goto SEEK_CUR,   _moveFilePointer_cur
        Goto SEEK_END,   _moveFilePointer_end
        SetError -1,     _moveFilePointer_36

;- - - - - - - - - - - - - - - - - - - - - - - - - - - - - - -
;  seek from end
;- - - - - - - - - - - - - - - - - - - - - - - - - - - - - - -
_moveFilePointer_end:
        add dx, word ptr es:[ sftFileSize. _low  ][ di ]
        adc cx, word ptr es:[ sftFileSize. _high ][ di ]
        jmp short _moveFilePointer_beg

;- - - - - - - - - - - - - - - - - - - - - - - - - - - - - - -
;  seek from current position
;- - - - - - - - - - - - - - - - - - - - - - - - - - - - - - -
_moveFilePointer_cur:
        add dx, word ptr es:[ sftFilePosition. _low  ][ di ]
        adc cx, word ptr es:[ sftFilePosition. _high ][ di ]
     ;  jmp short _moveFilePointer_beg

;- - - - - - - - - - - - - - - - - - - - - - - - - - - - - - -
;  seek from beginning
;- - - - - - - - - - - - - - - - - - - - - - - - - - - - - - -
_moveFilePointer_beg:
        mov word ptr es:[ sftFilePosition. _low  ][ di ], dx
        mov word ptr es:[ sftFilePosition. _high ][ di ], cx

;- - - - - - - - - - - - - - - - - - - - - - - - - - - - - - -
;  Return
;- - - - - - - - - - - - - - - - - - - - - - - - - - - - - - -

_moveFilePointer_36:
```

```
RetCallersStackFrame ds, bx
mov word ptr [ _AX ][ bx ], dx
mov word ptr [ _DX ][ bx ], cx
Return
```

Disk Buffers Cache Management

Much of the reason performance is fairly high for DOS systems is its cache buffers. Frequently accessed disk sectors remain cached in memory. Up to a limit, the greater the number of cache buffers, the greater the overall disk system performance. Too many cache buffers are unlikely to increase performance, which is achieved only when a desired sector is already buffered in memory, avoiding the costly penalty of actually reading or writing to disk. Too many buffers cache past history, but may not actually contain the disk sectors needed for future work, thus limiting their overall performance effectiveness. Your mileage will vary depending on what applications you use and the specific profile of your access needs.

A reasonable number for buffers is between 30 and 40. Each buffer occupies 532 bytes. The default number of buffers allocated by DOS depends on the system memory size, a necessary throwback to the days when systems did not come with at least 2MB to 4MB. The default for a system with a full complement of memory is 15 buffers. The remaining memory configuration defaults are as follows:

```
XT machines (under 128K of memory)          buffers=  2
AT machines (under 128K of memory)          buffers=  3
Systems with > 128K                         buffers=  5
Systems with > 256K                         buffers= 10
Systems with > 512K                         buffers= 15
```

In theory, a system is visualized as operating so balanced that the required disk sector is in the cache when required. In practice, cache buffers sometimes fill with the often unwanted contents of directory searches and other disk activity. The Least Recently Used (LRU) logic employed by DOS aggravates performance because desired sectors are sometimes pushed toward the least-used end of the cache chain during disk searches. RxDOS somewhat improves on this by limiting the number of cache buffers used during directory searches, thus avoiding the problem of filling the cache with probably unwanted directory data by reusing the same cache buffers during directory searches. However, neither MS-DOS nor RxDOS accurately anticipates a user's cache needs, and neither solution is fully perfect.

Cache buffers contain a tag that identifies the type of data it contains. Cache buffers can contain either FAT, directory, or user data. Directory and FAT read routines know the data type of the sectors they are reading and tag the cache sectors accordingly. For FAT sectors, this tagging is critical to supporting multiple copies of the FAT. When a buffer containing a FAT sector is updated to disk, all copies of the FAT are synchronized on that drive by automatically updating each copy. This is handled by the cache disk update logic.

When a sector needs to be read or written, the drive and sector number are compared to the available buffers in the cache. If the sector cannot be found, the least recently used buffer is made available. Its contents are written to disk if the buffer is dirty. The buffer is then filled with the requested sector data. From a program's point of view, the cache always appears to contain the required sector.

The highest level of throughput for a caching system would be achieved by withholding writes to disk as long as possible and then performing writes only during idle computer time. Smartdrv offered this aggressive type of caching outside the normal DOS-caching capability with disastrous consequences since users have been conditioned to pop disks out or shut power off as soon as certain operations complete. Every user expects that a copy is complete as soon as the DOS prompt appears.

DOS forces the cache to write to the disk when a file is closed or buffers are committed using DOS function 68h. Some older applications duplicate and close a file handle. The close forces a cache commit, as would the application terminating.

Networked drives provide special problems in maintaining valid caches. A sector may have been updated by another system after it has been read into the cache. This problem is far more serious than at first appears since it is almost everyone's presumption that the problem must be when files are shared. The problem truly exists when any disk space is shared and updated and can be seen just as prevalently in FAT and directory sectors. DOS handles this problem by making some disk drives noncacheable. The implication of noncacheable drives is that buffers for these drives are always marked invalid between DOS functions. The buffers must be reread before they can be reused.

This, by the way, is one area where close ties between the network and the operating system pay off in performance dividends. The network should provide special services that can verify whether the contents of a cache or sector are valid without having to retransfer the entire sector over the network.

Cache buffers are stored within a single allocated block of memory. Each buffer is linked to the other by a double-linked list consisting of a previous and next pointer. The purpose of the linked list is to be able to extract a buffer from the list at any time. When a buffer is read, it is placed at the top of the list. By repeatedly moving most used sectors to the top of the list, the least frequently used buffer moves to the end of the list. This last buffer is always the first candidate for reuse.

Cache buffers contain the header shown here. Aside from the link pointers, the header contains the drive, sector address, data type, and status byte. DOS places information about the FAT layout of the disk into every cache buffer. This information is a copy of the information maintained in the drive parameter block, or DPB. RxDOS chooses not to use this duplicate information, instead, it relies on the DPB itself. In fact, reliance on the FAT layout in the cache header can lead to dangerous consequences. If the cache buffer represents a sector on removable media, it's too late to perform a write after the disk has been changed. Worse, relying on them after the disk has been changed can lead to unwanted consequences. Instead, RxDOS checks the DPB for changed disk information. It may be that these fields are part of some earlier version of the cache buffer that have since become obsolete and are no longer used.

```
;,,,,,,,,,,,,,,,,,,,,,,,,,,,,,,,,,,,,,,,,,,,,,,,,,,,,,,,,,,,,,,,,,,,,,,,';
;  Buffers (Cache) Block                                               ;
;.....................................................................;
```

```
        CCB struc
ccbNext                 dw ?                        ; next cache control block
ccbPrev                 dw ?                        ; prev cache control block
ccbDrive                db ?                        ; drive
ccbStatus               db ?                        ; status flags
ccbLBN                  dd ?                        ; block number (sector)
ccbNumCopies            db ?                        ; number of FAT copies (*)
ccbSectorOffsets        dw ?                        ; offset between FAT sectors (*)
ccbDPB                  dd ?                        ; pointer to drive parameter block
ccbCount                dw ?                        ; count if remote
ccbSFTIdent             db ?                        ; system sft Handle
ccbData                 db 512 dup ( ? )            ; data
                                                    ; (*) unused by RxDOS
        CCB ends

;- - - - - - - - - - - - - - - - - - - - - - - - - - - - - - - - - - -
;  Flags
;- - - - - - - - - - - - - - - - - - - - - - - - - - - - - - - - - - -
ccb_isFAT               equ 02h
ccb_isDIR               equ 04h
ccb_isDATA              equ 08h
ccb_isVALID             equ 20h                     ; contains valid data
ccb_isDIRTY             equ 40h
ccb_isREMOTE            equ 80h
```

The cache-level sector read function is accomplished by readBuffer. It eventually calls a device driver. There is no cache-level write function as such. The buffer returned by the read may be marked dirty by changedCCB. The buffer may be forced to write to disk by calling updateChangedCCB. The function acts as an equivalent of the write, but often it is preferable to simply mark the block as changed. Finally, there is a function to update all changed buffers, which is listed later.

In the rest of this section, we describe how specific cache functions work.

readBuffer

The read buffer routine returns to the caller a pointer to a cache buffer containing the requested sector data. All cache routines are located in rxdosccb.asm module. The routine relies on SelBuffer, whose job it is either to locate the cache buffer for the requested drive and sector or to free up a buffer by writing out the contents of the least-used buffer. The select buffer routine returns a nonzero flag if it has valid data, meaning that it has located the buffer for the drive and sector.

If the returned flag is zero, a buffer has been made available, but it does not contain any valid data. The data must be filled from disk by using readSelBuffer, which reads to a selected buffer. The routine completes by setting the ccb_isValid flag after the buffer has been read.

It would seem that the logic for cache-optimized disk access would be defined along different lines. There should be a locate function that determined whether there is a matching cache buffer. This would then be followed by a different function that would assign a cache buffer and execute a read. That would be a read centric view of caching. The cache buffers support read and write. If writing were always to involve parts of sectors, then a read would always be part of a write function. The write would always require the sector to be in memory so that it could fill the part that needs to be written or updated. However, writing is optimized by not having to always read a buffer. A write of several thousand characters should not require several unnecessary reads. Other write-optimized cases include writing new data past the end of a file, where no data read is required. Imagine the time that it would take to create a file if every sector had first to be read. The cache logic avoids this problem by being buffer-centric; it reports whether a buffer is available or not. The routine is simple and straightforward.

```
(in rxdosccb.asm)
        ;///////////////////////////////////////////////////;
        ;  Read Buffer                                       ;
        ;- - - - - - - - - - - - - - - - - - - - - - - - - -;
        ;                                                    ;
        ;  Input:                                            ;
        ;   cx:dx   sector to read                           ;
        ;   ax      drive                                    ;
        ;   bx      attributes to claim buffer               ;
        ;                                                    ;
        ;  Output:                                           ;
        ;   es:di   pointer to selected buffer               ;
        ;....................................................;

readBuffer:
        call SelBuffer                          ; find a buffer
        jnz readBuffer_08                       ; if buffer is valid ->

        call readSelBuffer                      ; else read buffer
        or byte ptr es:[ ccbStatus ][ di ], ( ccb_isVALID )

readBuffer_08:
        ret
```

Read select buffer completes the function of read buffer after having tried to locate a matching buffer. The buffer pointer, drive, and sector information are passed to the read routine, which in turn simply determines the address to the data portion of the buffer and performs a device read. The device read routine performs the physical read.

```
(in rxdosccb.asm)
        ;///////////////////////////////////////////////////;
        ;  Read Selected Buffer                              ;
        ;- - - - - - - - - - - - - - - - - - - - - - - - - -;
        ;                                                    ;
        ;  Input:                                            ;
        ;   es:di   pointer to selected buffer               ;
        ;   cx:dx   sector to read                           ;
        ;   ax      drive                                    ;
        ;                                                    ;
        ;  Output:                                           ;
        ;   es:di   pointer to selected buffer               ;
```

```
        ;   cx:dx  sector to read                                    ;
        ;...................................................;

readSelBuffer:
        SaveAllRegisters

        mov bx, 0001
        lea di, offset ccbData [ di ]               ; buffer address
        call DevRead

        RestoreAllRegisters
        ret
```

SelBuffer

Select buffer, as already noted, returns a pointer to a cache buffer. It selects the buffer based on whether a match exists in the cache for the drive and sector requested. A nonzero status flag is returned to indicate that the data is valid. Otherwise, the buffer returned contains no valid data.

The routine scans through all cached buffers to determine if there is a match. Each buffer is first checked whether it contains valid data. If it does, its drive and sector address are also valid and can be compared to the requested drive and sector. If a match is found, most of the remainder of the routine can be skipped. The routine must move the pointer to the beginning of the cache buffer chain.

If the pointers don't match, the next buffer is checked by following the next pointer. When the end of the chain is located and there was no buffer match, the buffers are rescanned, beginning at selBuffer_16, to locate an invalidated buffer. A cache buffer may be invalid if at one time it contained data for a removable drive, a shared drive, or a shared file or if it was never used before. Invalidated buffers do not have the VALID bit set.

At selBuffer_30, the end of the buffer chain has been reached without finding an available unused buffer, so the buffer at the end of the list, the currently least-used buffer, is selected. Its contents are written to disk by updateCCB if the buffer is dirty. A buffer becomes dirty when changes are made to it by other functions in DOS. At selBuffer_32, an available disk buffer is updated with the current drive and sector information. It is preinitialized, but another routine will have to set the VALID flag before the buffer will be treated as containing any data. Finally, the DPB pointer for the selected drive is fetched and stored in the cache header.

At selBuffer_36, the selected or found cache buffer must be placed at the beginning of the cache chain. A test is made to ensure that it already isn't at the top, and if it is not, it is first unlinked from its current place in the chain and linked at the beginning of the chain. We explain link and unlink further later.

```
(in rxdosccb.asm)
        ;''''''''''''''''''''''''''''''''''''''''''''''''''''''''''';
        ;  Selected Buffer                                          ;
        ;- - - - - - - - - - - - - - - - - - - - - - - - - - - - - -;
        ;                                                           ;
        ;  Input:                                                   ;
```

```
;    ax     drive                                                     ;
;    cx:dx  sector to read                                            ;
;                                                                     ;
;   Output:                                                           ;
;    es:di  pointer to selected buffer                                ;
;    nz     buffer contains valid data                               ;
;           all registers preserved                                   ;
;..............................................................;


SelBuffer:
        SaveRegisters ax, bx, cx, dx
        les di, dword ptr cs:[ _RxDOS_BufferList ]

selBuffer_04:
        test byte ptr es:[ ccbStatus ][ di ], ( ccb_isVALID )
        jz selBuffer_08                                 ; unallocated buffer ->

        cmp byte ptr es:[ ccbDrive ][ di ], al          ; compare drives
        jnz selBuffer_08                                ; not this block, try next ->

        cmp cx, word ptr es:[ ccbLBN. _high][ di ]      ; compare logical block numbers
        jnz selBuffer_08                                ; not this block, try next ->
        cmp dx, word ptr es:[ ccbLBN. _low ][ di ]      ; compare logical block numbers
        jz selBuffer_36                                 ; buffer located ->

selBuffer_08:
        mov di, word ptr es:[ ccbNext ][ di ]
        cmp di, -1
        jnz selBuffer_04

;- - - - - - - - - - - - - - - - - - - - - - - - - - - - - - - - - -
;  if could not find a matching buffer, find an empty buffer
;- - - - - - - - - - - - - - - - - - - - - - - - - - - - - - - - - -
        les di, dword ptr cs:[ _RxDOS_BufferList ]

selBuffer_16:
        test byte ptr es:[ ccbStatus ][ di ], ( ccb_isVALID )
        jz selBuffer_32                                 ; unallocated buffer ->

        cmp word ptr es:[ ccbNext ][ di ], -1
        jz selBuffer_30                                 ; write all, use least used ->
        mov di, word ptr es:[ ccbNext ][ di ]
        jmp selBuffer_16

;- - - - - - - - - - - - - - - - - - - - - - - - - - - - - - - - - -
; prep returned buffer
;- - - - - - - - - - - - - - - - - - - - - - - - - - - - - - - - - -
selBuffer_30:
        call updateCCB                                  ; just in case update required

selBuffer_32:
        mov byte ptr es:[ ccbDrive      ][ di ], al     ; set drive
        mov word ptr es:[ ccbLBN. _high][ di ], cx      ; set logical block number
        mov word ptr es:[ ccbLBN. _low ][ di ], dx      ; set logical block number
```

```
        mov byte ptr es:[ ccbStatus    ][ di ], 00      ; clear status
        call setFlagIfDriveIsRemote                     ; sets remote flag

        push es
        push di
        call getDPB                             ; pointer to dpb
        mov dx, es                              ; pointer was in [es:bx]

        pop di
        pop es
        mov word ptr es:[ ccbDPB. _segment ][ di ], dx
        mov word ptr es:[ ccbDPB. _pointer ][ di ], bx

selBuffer_36:
        cmp di, word ptr cs:[ _RxDOS_BufferList. _pointer ]
        jz selBuffer_38                             ; if already at beginning ->

        call unlinkCCB                          ; unlink CCB buffer
        call linkBegCCB                         ; link to front of CCB chain

selBuffer_38:
        test byte ptr es:[ ccbStatus ][ di ], ( ccb_isVALID )
        RestoreRegisters dx, cx, bx, ax
        ret
```

Some drives are remote or networked drives, and caching doesn't work effectively for them. As we noted earlier, the contents of a shared drive may be updated by another system, rendering the copy maintained in the cache as useless or misleading. Buffers that point to shared devices are invalidated between DOS function calls. When a buffer is first selected for a drive, it is checked against the CDS, or Current Directory Structure, to determine if it is remote. The remote flag is set accordingly.

```
        ;'''''''''''''''''''''''''''''''''''''''''''''''''''''''''''''';
        ;  Is Drive Remote                                            ;
        ;- - - - - - - - - - - - - - - - - - - - - - - - - - - - - - -;
        ;                                                             ;
        ;  al      drive                                              ;
        ;  es:di   points to ccb buffer                               ;
        ;.............................................................;

setFlagIfDriveIsRemote:
        push es
        push di

        mov cl, sizeCDS
        mul cl                                  ; ax contains current drive
        les di, dword ptr cs:[ _RxDOS_pCDS ]    ; actual address of CDS
        add di, ax                              ; current drive
        test word ptr es:[ _cdsFlags ][ di ], _CDS_NETWORKEDDRIVE
        pop di
        pop es
        jz IfDriveIsRemote_12                   ; if not remote ->
```

```
         or byte ptr es:[ ccbStatus ][ di ], ( ccb_isREMOTE )

IfDriveIsRemote_12:
         ret
```

Link and unlink of buffers in the CCB, or cache control buffers, is accomplished by functions unlinkCCB and linkBegCCB. Both functions are listed next. Since RxDOS is reusable (see Chapter 1), some functions cannot be handled with interrupts enabled. The status word containing the interrupt flag is saved, and interrupts are disabled. The interrupts are reenabled when the status word is restored.

To unlink a buffer, both the previous and next pointers of the current buffer are copied to registers. The purpose of the routine is to change the previous buffer to point past the current buffer to the next buffer in the chain and to remove the previous pointer in the next buffer to point to the buffer that precedes the current buffer. Got that? Either pointer could be a negative one, indicating that the current buffer is at the beginning or end of the chain. If the previous pointer is a -1, there is no previous buffer. The top of the list should be made to point to the next buffer. Next, if there is no next pointer, there is no need to update its previous pointer. Finally, the previous buffer's next pointer is updated to point to the next buffer. The buffer is unlinked from the chain and, technically, lost in space until it is relinked.

Linking anywhere but at the beginning of the chain makes no sense in this cache management. The linking at the beginning means that the previous pointer of the current top buffer must be made to point to the new top buffer. The new top buffer's next pointer must point to the previous top buffer. To complete, the start of the buffer list must point to the new top buffer.

```
(in rxdosccb.asm)
        ;'''''''''''''''''''''''''''''''''''''''''''''''''''''''''''''';
        ;   Remove CCB Buffer from Linked List                         ;
        ;- - - - - - - - - - - - - - - - - - - - - - - - - - - - - - -;
        ;                                                              ;
        ;   es:di   points to ccb buffer                               ;
        ;..............................................................;

unlinkCCB:
        pushf                                   ; save current interrupt status
        push ax
        push di
        cli                                     ; disable interrupts

        mov ax, word ptr es:[ ccbPrev ][ di ]
        mov di, word ptr es:[ ccbNext ][ di ]
        cmp ax, -1                              ; no previous ?
        jnz unlinkCCB_06                        ; no ->
        mov word ptr cs:[ _RxDOS_BufferList. _pointer ], di  ; update beg of list

unlinkCCB_06:
        cmp di, -1                              ; no next pointer ?
        jz unlinkCCB_08                         ; skip removing Prev pointer ->
        mov word ptr es:[ ccbPrev ][ di ], ax   ; next's prev fixed.

unlinkCCB_08:
```

```
        cmp ax, -1                                      ; no previous ?
        jz unlinkCCB_12                                 ; no —>
        xchg di, ax
        mov word ptr es:[ ccbNext ][ di ], ax           ; prev's next fixed.

unlinkCCB_12:
        pop di
        mov word ptr es:[ ccbPrev ][ di ], -1           ; unlink current pointers
        mov word ptr es:[ ccbNext ][ di ], -1
        pop ax
        popf                                            ; restore interrupt status
        ret

        ;''''''''''''''''''''''''''''''''''''''''''''''''''''''''''''';
        ;  Link CCB Buffer to Beginning of List                      ;
        ;- - - - - - - - - - - - - - - - - - - - - - - - - - - - - -;
        ;                                                            ;
        ;  es:di   points to ccb buffer                              ;
        ;............................................................;

linkBegCCB:
        pushf                                           ; save current interrupt status
        push ax
        cli                                             ; disable interrupts

        mov ax, di
        les di, dword ptr cs:[ _RxDOS_BufferList ]
        cmp ax, di                                      ; relink ccb to beg of list ?
        jz linkBegCCB_08                                ; yes, don't do it —>

        mov word ptr es:[ ccbPrev ][ di ], ax           ; previous to orig prev

        xchg di, ax
        mov word ptr es:[ ccbNext ][ di ], ax           ; this next to old next
        mov word ptr es:[ ccbPrev ][ di ], -1           ; current no more previous

        mov word ptr cs:[ _RxDOS_BufferList. _pointer ], di

linkBegCCB_08:
        pop ax
        popf
        ret
```

Updating Changed Buffers

Four routines are used to perform output to disk of dirty cached blocks. These routines, however, cannot be discussed until we describe some of the other more general support routines. DOS routines make updates to the data in cache buffers. When they do, they are required to set the DIRTY flag. This informs the cache system to update the changes before this buffer is reused. DOS functions utilize the CCBChanged function to set the dirty bit. This insulates them from potential changes in the structure of the cache. The function that physically sets the dirty bit is very small, but it does require a pointer to the cache buffer header. Often, the DOS function has the pointer to the buffer but not to its header. The header address for any cache buffer can be returned by the located CCB header function, listed here.

```
(in rxdosccb.asm)
        ;///////////////////////////////////////////////////////////;
        ;   Mark CCB buffer changed.                                 ;
        ;- - - - - - - - - - - - - - - - - - - - - - - - - - - - - -;
        ;                                                            ;
        ;   es:di  pointer to selected buffer                        ;
        ;............................................................;

CCBChanged:
        or byte ptr es:[ ccbStatus ][ di ], ( ccb_isDIRTY )
        ret

        ;///////////////////////////////////////////////////////////;
        ;   Locate from reference actual start of CCB buffer         ;
        ;- - - - - - - - - - - - - - - - - - - - - - - - - - - - - -;
        ;                                                            ;
        ;   Input:                                                   ;
        ;     si     pointer into a CCB buffer                       ;
        ;                                                            ;
        ;   Output:                                                  ;
        ;     es:di  pointer to CCB Header                           ;
        ;     cx     offset from start of data                       ;
        ;............................................................;

locateCCBPHeader:
        les di, dword ptr cs:[ _RxDOS_BufferList ]

locateCCBPHeader_04:
        mov cx, si
        sub cx, di                          ; how far from start of buffer
        jl locateCCBPHeader_08              ; go to next ->
        cmp cx, sizeCCB                     ; within a CCB buffer ?
        jg locateCCBPHeader_08              ; go to next ->

        or cx, cx                           ; no carry (leave offset alone )
        ret

locateCCBPHeader_08:
        mov di, word ptr es:[ ccbNext ][ di ]
        cmp di, -1
        jnz locateCCBPHeader_04

        stc
        ret
```

The routine accepts a pointer into a cache buffer, passed in the SI register. It converts this pointer to an offset from the start of data, returned in the CX register, and a pointer to the header, returned in the ES:DI register pair. The routine determines if the pointer passed is within the size range of a buffer. If it is, it knows the header address and can compute the offset from the header.

updateCCB writes a cached buffer, if dirty, to disk. The write is handled by devWrite, which requires the drive, sector address, and a data pointer reference. The routine is shown here. A check is made to determine if the buffer contains the contents of a FAT table sector, and all subsequent FAT tables on that drive are updated by calling the update alternative FAT function. FAT tables are at a fixed offset from each other, and that offset is added to the sector address to update the secondary FAT table.

```
(in rxdosccb.asm)
        ;'''''''''''''''''''''''''''''''''''''''''''''''''''''''''''''';
        ;   Update CCB buffer, always.                                 ;
        ;- - - - - - - - - - - - - - - - - - - - - - - - - - - - - - -;
        ;                                                              ;
        ;   es:di   pointer to selected buffer                         ;
        ;..............................................................;

updateCCB:
        test byte ptr es:[ ccbStatus ][ di ], ( ccb_isDIRTY )
        jnz updateChangedCCB
        ret

updateChangedCCB:
        SaveAllRegisters

        push es
        push di
        mov bx, 0001
        mov dx, word ptr es:[ ccbLBN. _low  ][ di ]       ; get sector
        mov cx, word ptr es:[ ccbLBN. _high ][ di ]
        mov al, byte ptr es:[ ccbDrive ][ di ]            ; get drive number
        cbw
        lea di, offset ccbData [ di ]                     ; buffer address
        call DevWrite

        pop di
        pop es
        test byte ptr es:[ ccbStatus ][ di ], ( ccb_isFAT )
        jz updateCCB_12                                   ; not a FAT buffer ->
        call updateAlternateFATTables                     ; update FAT tables

updateCCB_12:
        RestoreAllRegisters
        and byte ptr es:[ ccbStatus ][ di ], not ( ccb_isDIRTY )
        ret

        ;'''''''''''''''''''''''''''''''''''''''''''''''''''''''''''''';
        ;   Update Alternate FAT Table                                 ;
        ;- - - - - - - - - - - - - - - - - - - - - - - - - - - - - - -;
        ;                                                              ;
        ;   Given a FAT sector address, copies the sector to the alter-;
        ;   nate FAT Table.                                            ;
        ;                                                              ;
        ;   Input:                                                     ;
        ;    es:di  pointer to a FAT CCB Buffer                        ;
        ;..............................................................;
```

```
updateAlternateFATTables:
        Entry
        ddef  _ccb, es, di
        def   _dpbNumberFat
        def   _dpbFATSectors

        test byte ptr es:[ ccbStatus ][ di ], ( ccb_isFAT )
        jz updateAlternateFATTables_22                   ; not a fat designated sector —>

        les bx, dword ptr es:[ ccbDPB  ][ di ]           ; get assigned DPB
        mov ax, word ptr es:[ _dpbSectorsPerFat ][ bx ]
        storarg _dpbFATSectors, ax
        mov ax, word ptr es:[ _dpbNumCopiesFAT  ][ bx ]
        storarg _dpbNumberFat, ax

        getdarg es, di, _ccb
        mov dx, word ptr es:[ ccbLBN. _low  ][ di ]      ; get original sector
        mov cx, word ptr es:[ ccbLBN. _high ][ di ]
        mov al, byte ptr es:[ ccbDrive ][ di ]           ; get drive number
        cbw

        lea di, offset ccbData [ di ]                    ; buffer address

updateAlternateFATTables_08:
        dec word ptr [ _dpbNumberFat ][ bp ]
        jle updateAlternateFATTables_22                  ; if not more than 1 —>

        mov bx, 0001
        add dx, word ptr [ _dpbFATSectors ][ bp ]        ; adjust for fat size
        adc cx, 0000
        SaveRegisters es, di, dx, cx, ax
        call devWrite
        RestoreRegisters ax, cx, dx, di, es
        jmp updateAlternateFATTables_08

updateAlternateFATTables_22:
        Return
```

A routine exists to update all the changed cache buffers. The routine simply walks through all buffer chains and calls updateCCB, which handles testing for a dirty flag and updating FAT sectors.

```
(in rxdosccb.asm)
        ;'''''''''''''''''''''''''''''''''''''''''''''''''''''''''''''''';
        ;  Update All Changed Buffers                                    ;
        ;................................................................;

updateAllChangedCCBBuffers:
        SaveAllRegisters
        les di, dword ptr cs:[ _RxDOS_BufferList ]

updateAllChanged_04:
        call updateCCB                                   ; write updated buffer

        mov di, word ptr es:[ ccbNext ][ di ]
```

```
cmp di, -1
jnz updateAllChanged_04

RestoreAllRegisters
ret
```

The last cache function invalidates buffers that contained data for sharable remote drives. These buffers are identified by the remote flag, which was set when the buffer was created. We discussed the role and importance of the remote flag in the section "Sel Buffer." The update function simply ensures that the data is always updated to the disk so that it can be shared. The function walks through the cache chain and updates any remote buffer. More important, it invalidates the data for that cache buffer to force a reread of the information.

(in rxdosccb.asm)

```
;///////////////////////////////////////////////////////////;
;   Invalidate Remote CCB Buffers                           ;
;- - - - - - - - - - - - - - - - - - - - - - - - - - - - - -;
;                                                           ;
;   Input:                                                  ;
;     ax      drive                                         ;
;     cx:dx   sector to read                                ;
;                                                           ;
;   Output:                                                 ;
;     es:di   pointer to selected buffer                    ;
;     nz      buffer contains valid data                    ;
;             all registers preserved                       ;
;...........................................................;

invalidateRemoteCCBBuffers:
        les di, dword ptr cs:[ _RxDOS_BufferList ]

invBuffer_04:
        test byte ptr es:[ ccbStatus ][ di ], ( ccb_isREMOTE )
        jz invBuffer_16                             ; not remote ->

        call updateCCB                              ; updated buffer
        and byte ptr es:[ ccbStatus ][ di ], NOT ( ccb_isVALID )

invBuffer_16:
        mov di, word ptr es:[ ccbNext ][ di ]
        cmp di, -1
        jnz invBuffer_04

        ret
```

File Management

File Commit

	On Entry	On Return
AX	AH = 68h	AX = error if carry
BX	file handle	
CX		
DX		
Flags		CY = set if error

Related Functions:
   3Ch Create File; 3Dh Open File; 3Eh Close File.

The commit function rolls out to disk the changes made to a file and its directory entry. It is an invaluable function to applications where files may be shared between applications in the same or different machines since a close is essentially nothing more than a commit and a release of the SFT. A commit is therefore a close without releasing the SFT.

The commit function performs two functions. It updates the directory entry for the open file handle, and it updates all changed cache buffers to disk. For performance reasons, unchanged SFTs do not get updated, and the function performs no action.

The code for commit begins in rxdos.asm, where the file handle is converted to an SFT address. The SFT address is passed to the commit function in rxdossft.asm, where checks are made to ensure that the SFT has been updated and that it isn't pointing to a device. No action is taken if the SFT points to a device. For validated SFTs, the current date and time are stamped into the SFT if it hasn't already been set by the set date/time function (DOS function 5701h), the archive bit is set, and the directory sector is reread from disk.

The offset to the directory entry for this file is remembered by the open or create functions as an index value stored in the SFT. The index value is multiplied by the size of a directory entry to compute the offset into the directory sector. The general purpose of the code at this point is to read the directory sector and update the entry for this file. The offset to the directory entry and the updateable SFT entries are saved on the stack around the file read code because the SFT pointer will be destroyed by the read sector function. The SFT pointer has been saved at entry to this routine, so there is no danger of completely loosing the pointer. It just won't be readily available.

The routine reads the directory sector. The data is kept in a cached buffer. The pointer to the buffer is returned in the ES:DI register pair. To update the directory entry, the contents of the cached buffer are updated directly, and the cache buffer is marked as changed. The offset to the directory entry is popped from the stack into the BX register. The directory entry to update can be addressed by the combination of registers ES:(DI+BX), as shown in the code.

Finally, the cached buffer is marked changed, all changed cache buffers are written to disk, and the update and date set flags are cleared in the SFT. The changes to the file and the file directory entry are all updated.

```
(in rxdos.asm)
        ;,'''''''''''''''''''''''''''''''''''''''''''''''''''''''''''''';
        ;   68h Commit File                                            ;
        ;- - - - - - - - - - - - - - - - - - - - - - - - - - - - - - -;
        ;                                                              ;
        ;   bx handle to open file                                     ;
        ;..............................................................;

_CommitFile:
        call CtrlC_Check

        mov ax, bx                      ; handle
        call MapAppToSFTHandle          ; map to internal handle info
        call FindSFTbyHandle            ; get corresponding SFT (es: di )
        jc _CommitFile_error            ; if could not find ->

        call _SFTCommitFile             ; commit SFT Entry
        or bx, bx                       ; no carry

_CommitFile_error:
        ret

(in rxdossft.asm)
        ;,'''''''''''''''''''''''''''''''''''''''''''''''''''''''''''''';
        ;   Commit SFT File                                            ;
        ;- - - - - - - - - - - - - - - - - - - - - - - - - - - - - - -;
        ;                                                              ;
        ;   Input:                                                     ;
        ;   es:di  SFT entry to close                                  ;
        ;   ax     Handle                                              ;
        ;..............................................................;

_SFTCommitFile:
        Entry
```

```
        ddef _sftPointer, es, di                      ; save sft buffer pointer

;- - - - - - - - - - - - - - - - - - - - - - - - - - - - - - - - -
; was device ever written to ?
;- - - - - - - - - - - - - - - - - - - - - - - - - - - - - - - - -
        test word ptr es:[ sftDevInfo ][ di ], sftIsDevice
        jnz _SFTCommitFile_36                          ; if device, no need to update ->

        test word ptr es:[ sftDevInfo ][ di ], sftWritten
        jz _SFTCommitFile_36                           ; if not changed, don't update->

;- - - - - - - - - - - - - - - - - - - - - - - - - - - - - - - - -
; update dir entries from sft
;- - - - - - - - - - - - - - - - - - - - - - - - - - - - - - - - -
        test word ptr es:[ sftDevInfo ][ di ], sftDateset ; date already set ?
        jnz _SFTCommitFile_16                          ; if date already set ->

        call getSysDateinDirFormat
        mov word ptr es:[ sftTime ][ di ], ax          ; time last updated
        mov word ptr es:[ sftDate ][ di ], dx          ; date last updated

_SFTCommitFile_16:
        push word ptr es:[ sftTime ][ di ]             ; time last updated
        push word ptr es:[ sftDate ][ di ]             ; date last updated

        or word ptr es:[ sftFileAttrib ][ di ], ATTR_ARCHIVE
        push word ptr es:[ sftFileAttrib ][ di ]
        push word ptr es:[ sftBegCluster ][ di ]
        push word ptr es:[ sftFileSize. _low ][ di ]
        push word ptr es:[ sftFileSize. _high ][ di ]

    ; get dir entry

        mov al, sizeDIRENTRY
        mul byte ptr es:[ sftDirIndex ][ di ]          ; get offset into directory
        and ax, maskDIRINDEX                           ; all we need is bottom bits
        push ax                                        ; save dir sector offset

        mov dx, word ptr es:[ sftDirSector. _low  ][ di ]
        mov cx, word ptr es:[ sftDirSector. _high ][ di ]
        mov ax, word ptr es:[ sftDevInfo     ][ di ]
        and ax, sftDrivemask
        call readBuffer                                ; returns es:di pointer to buffer

    ; update dir entry

        pop bx                                         ; dir offset
        pop word ptr es:[ ccbData. deFileSize. _high ][ di + bx ]
        pop word ptr es:[ ccbData. deFileSize. _low  ][ di + bx ]
        pop word ptr es:[ ccbData. deStartCluster    ][ di + bx ]

        pop ax
```

```
        mov byte ptr es:[ ccbData. deAttributes ][ di + bx ], al

        pop word ptr es:[ ccbData. deDate ][ di + bx ]  ; date created
        pop word ptr es:[ ccbData. deTime ][ di + bx ]  ; time created

        call CCBChanged
        call updateAllChangedCCBBuffers

        getdarg es, di, _sftPointer                    ; save sft buffer pointer
        and word ptr es:[ sftDevInfo ][ di ], not (sftWritten + sftDataset)

;- - - - - - - - - - - - - - - - - - - - - - - - - - - - - - - -
; release sft
;- - - - - - - - - - - - - - - - - - - - - - - - - - - - - - - -

_SFTCommitFile_36:
        Return
```

File Close with Handle

	On Entry	On Return
AX	AH = 3Eh	AX = error if carry
BX	file handle	
CX		
DX		
Flags		CY = set if error

Related Functions:
  3Ch Create File; 3Dh Open File; 3Fh Read File; 40h Write File.

The close function updates the directory entry for an open file and decrements the usage count of an SFT entry. The SFT entries may be duplicated, as described in the open file section in Chapter 3. When the usage count drops to zero, the SFT is no longer owned by any process and may be reused.

File close is essentially a file commit and an SFT count decrement. So it shouldn't come as any surprise if the SFT layer code to handle the close is exactly two lines of code.

```
_SFTCloseFile:
        call _SFTCommitFile
        call releaseSFT
        ret
```

releaseSFT, listed later in this section, decrements the SFT reserved count. The file close function predates file commit, and at one time all the logic that is now in commit was once part of a larger close function. When commit was introduced in DOS 3.1, the routines were split, resulting in the current close function.

(in rxdos.asm)

```
        ;'''''''''''''''''''''''''''''''''''''''''''''''''''''''''''''''';
        ;   3Eh Close File                                               ;
        ;- - - - - - - - - - - - - - - - - - - - - - - - - - - - - - - -;
        ;                                                                ;
        ;   bx handle to open file                                       ;
        ;................................................................;

_CloseFile:
        Entry
        def _handle, bx
        ddef _sftPointer
        defbytes _diskAccess, sizeDISKACCESS

        mov ax, bx                              ; handle
        call MapAppToSFTHandle                  ; map to internal handle info
        call FindSFTbyHandle                    ; get corresponding SFT (es: di )
        jc _CloseFile_error                     ; if could not find ->

        call _SFTCloseFile                      ; close SFT Entry

        call getHandleTable                     ; get handle table
        jz _CloseFile_error                     ; if error ->

        add bx, word ptr [ _handle ][ bp ]
        mov byte ptr es:[ bx ], -1              ; cancel handle reference in PSP

        or bx, bx                               ; no carry

_CloseFile_error:
        Return
```

(in rxdossft.asm)

```
        ;'''''''''''''''''''''''''''''''''''''''''''''''''''''''''''''''';
        ;   Close SFT File                                               ;
        ;- - - - - - - - - - - - - - - - - - - - - - - - - - - - - - - -;
        ;                                                                ;
        ;   Input:                                                       ;
        ;     es:di  SFT entry to close                                  ;
        ;                                                                ;
        ;................................................................;

_SFTCloseFile:
        call _SFTCommitFile
        call releaseSFT
        ret
```

An internal routine exists in RxDOS to close all files owned by a process. This function, _SFTCloseAllFiles, is called when a process terminates with DOS function 4Ch. DOS does not close and release SFTs for a process that terminates but stays resident. The function utilizes the same SFT close file routine already described. To locate all file handles that are still open for a process, the function first retrieves the current process PSP address where DOS maintains a pointer to a file handle table. Each entry in the table is examined to determine if it is a valid file handle and then is converted to an SFT address. The SFT address is passed to the close routine. The routine walks through all file handles.

```
(in rxdossft.asm)
        ;/////////////////////////////////////////////////////////////;
        ;  Close All Files Owned By Current PSP                        ;
        ;- - - - - - - - - - - - - - - - - - - - - - - - - - - - - -;
        ;                                                             ;
        ;.............................................................;

_SFTCloseAllFiles:
        cmp word ptr cs:[ _RxDOS_CurrentPSP ], 0000
        jz _SFTCloseAllFiles_36                      ; if no app ->

        mov es, word ptr cs:[ _RxDOS_CurrentPSP ]    ; get PSP
        mov cx, word ptr es:[ pspFileHandleCount ]
        les si, dword ptr es:[ pspFileHandlePtr  ]

_SFTCloseAllFiles_04:
        cmp byte ptr es:[ si ], -1                    ; empty slot ?
        jz _SFTCloseAllFiles_12                       ; yes, skip entry ->

        SaveRegisters es, si, cx
        mov ax, word ptr es:[ pspFileHandleCount ]
        sub ax, cx                                   ; actual handle value
        call MapAppToSFTHandle                        ; map to internal handle info
        call FindSFTbyHandle                          ; get corresponding SFT (es: di )
        call _SFTCloseFile                            ; do a normal close

        RestoreRegisters cx, si, es
        mov byte ptr es:[ si ], -1                    ; make slot empty

_SFTCloseAllFiles_12:
        inc si                                        ; next
        loop _SFTCloseAllFiles_04                     ; continue ->

_SFTCloseAllFiles_36:
        ret
```

releaseSFT. An SFT is reserved by count since it may have been duplicated. It is this count that enables SFTs to be duplicated and closed while still keeping a valid handle to a file.

```
        ;/////////////////////////////////////////////////////////////;
        ;  Release SFT                                                 ;
        ;- - - - - - - - - - - - - - - - - - - - - - - - - - - - - -;
        ;                                                             ;
        ;  Input:                                                     ;
        ;   es:di  pointer to SFT entry                               ;
        ;                                                             ;
        ;  Output:                                                    ;
        ;   es:di  pointer to matching SFT entry                      ;
        ;.............................................................;
```

```
releaseSFT:
        cmp word ptr es:[ sftRefCount ][ di ], 0000
        jz releaseSFT_08                                ; already released -->
        dec word ptr es:[ sftRefCount ][ di ]           ; clear entry count

releaseSFT_08:
        ret
```

File Get/Set Date and Time

	On Entry	On Return
AX	AH = 57h; AL= get/set flag	AX = error if carry
BX	file handle	
CX	time, in dir format	
DX	date, in dir format	
Flags		CY = set if error

Related Functions:
  3Ch Create File; 3Dh Open File; 3Eh Close File; 3Fh Read File; 40h Write File.

The get and set date and time functions read from or alter the contents of the SFT entry for an open or created file. The date and time are updated to disk when the file is closed or committed. File close or commit has other positive ramifications. These functions update other changes made to the file, such as its size and attributes, and they update all cached disk buffers. For a number of reasons, this is the behavior that has the most overall benefit. Files that are shared are most often in need of frequent updates to disk, including the date and time, and the DOS behavior ensures that all pertinent changes are made at once.

No DOS function will change a file's date and time without an open although it is possible to get the date and time from a file without an open by using the Find First or Find Next functions. The FINDENTRY record returned by these functions contains the date, time, attributes, size, and other directory information.

touch and stamp are both widely available programs that stamp a date and time on files on disk. To stamp a date or time, these programs must open the file, set the time and date using DOS function 5701h, and then close the file. The close operation actually changes the directory entry on disk when the cached buffer is updated to disk. A commit operation will actually force the cache to update.

The date and time fields are coded in a directory entry format. This format is different from the date and time formats returned by DOS Get Date and Get Time functions (DOS functions 2Ah and 2Ch, respectively). The layout for the directory date and time fields is listed in the rxdosdef.asm module, where all data structure definitions are listed, in the DIRENTRY, or directory entry section.

The directory entry date is actually the day, month, and year fields packed into a single word. The year since 1980 is stored in bits 9–15 of the date word, the month is stored in bits 5–8, beginning with a 1 for January, and the day in bits 0–4, ranging from 1–31. The seven bits for the year means that the DOS file system can handle a healthy 128 years of file date information. By that time, 100 GB disks will come in wrist watches.

For the time field, bits 11–15 encode the hour, starting with 00 for the first hour of the day. Bits 5–10 contain the minutes, ranging from 0–59. Every second cannot be coded in this format, but bits 0–4 can hold every two-second interval.

Because the functions don't actually alter anything except the SFT itself, the functionality is fairly straightforward. The function performs a control-C check and then maps the file handle to an SFT address. If the subfunction code passed in AL is 00, that is, to get the date and time, the routine jumps around the set code, gets a pointer to the caller's saved registers, and copies the date and time from the SFT, into the CX and DX registers. The routine exits by clearing the carry flag.

If the subfunction code was to set the date and time (subfunction code 01), the value in the CX and DX registers are saved in the SFT, and the sftDateset and sftWritten flags are both set. The date set flag prevents the close and commit functions from changing the date. The written flag indicates that the SFT has been updated. Close and commit functions do not update SFTs that have not been altered to save time.

The code for the function can be located in rxdos.asm.

```
(in rxdos.asm)
        ;,,,,,,,,,,,,,,,,,,,,,,,,,,,,,,,,,,,,,,,,,,,,,,,,,,,,,,,,,,,;
        ;                                                          ;
        ;  5700h Get File Date Time                                ;
        ;  5701h Set File Date Time                                ;
        ;- - - - - - - - - - - - - - - - - - - - - - - - - - - -  -;
        ;                                                          ;
        ;  al = 00, get date/time                                  ;
        ;       01, set date/time                                  ;
        ;                                                          ;
        ;  bx    file handle                                       ;
        ;  cx    time                                              ;
        ;  dx    date                                              ;
        ;                                                          ;
        ;.........................................................;


_SetFileDateTime:
        call CtrlC_Check

        push ax                             ; save mode
        mov ax, bx                          ; handle
        call MapAppToSFTHandle              ; map to internal handle info
        call FindSFTbyHandle                ; get corresponding SFT (es: di )

        pop ax                              ; restore mode
        jc _SetFileDateTime_20              ; if could not find ->

        or al, al
        jz _SetFileDateTime_08              ; if get date/ time ->


;- - - - - - - - - - - - - - - - - - - - - - - - - - - - - - - -
;  set date/ time
;- - - - - - - - - - - - - - - - - - - - - - - - - - - - - - - -
```

```
        mov word ptr es:[ sftTime ][ di ], cx              ; time
        mov word ptr es:[ sftDate ][ di ], dx              ; date
        or word ptr es:[ sftDevInfo ][ di ], sftDateset + sftWritten
        ret

;- - - - - - - - - - - - - - - - - - - - - - - - - - - - - - - - - - - -
; get date/ time
;- - - - - - - - - - - - - - - - - - - - - - - - - - - - - - - - - - - -
_SetFileDateTime_08:
        RetCallersStackFrame ds, bx
        mov cx, word ptr es:[ sftTime ][ di ]              ; time
        mov dx, word ptr es:[ sftDate ][ di ]              ; date
        mov word ptr [ _CX ][ bx ], cx
        mov word ptr [ _DX ][ bx ], dx
        or ax, ax                                          ; no carry

_SetFileDateTime_20:
        ret
```

File Get/Set Attributes

	On Entry	On Return
AX	AH = 43h; AL= get/set flag	AX = error if carry
BX		
CX	attributes	
DS:DX	pointer to ASCIZ filename	
Flags		CY = set if error

Related Functions:
  3Ch Create File; 3Fh Read File; 40h Write File.

The attribute bits in directory entries identify properties such as achievable, hidden, and system file. The attribute values of any entry can be fetched or set through a DOS function. However, some bits cannot be altered. The function permits only setting the archive, read-only, hidden, and system attributes. This means that the function cannot be used to convert a directory into a file by removing an attribute bit.

The function begins by attempting to locate the file. No restrictions are placed on the search for the entry. It could be either a file or a directory but, obviously, it cannot be a device name. If the file cannot be located, the error code reported by the search function is passed back to the caller when the function exits. Otherwise, the pointer to the sector containing the directory entry is set in the ES:DI registers, and the offset within the sector is set in the BX register. A dispatch is made to the location within the function that handles the subfunction mode. The attributes are read from the directory entry and returned to the caller in the CX register.

For set attributes, the value passed is checked to ensure that no additional or unsettable bits are requested by the caller, such as setting the Directory attribute. Otherwise, the function returns an error. All the settable bits are first cleared, then an or instruction sets the selected bits into place.

Once the sector is changed in memory, the buffer is marked as changed so that it can be written back out to disk.

One more point. It is possible to set a directory as read-only, which is pretty meaningless. All other DOS functions ignore this bit in directories, and both files and subdirectories can be created into a directory with the read-only flag. All the other attributes, like Hidden, work as documented.

```
;''''''''''''''''''''''''''''''''''''''''''''''''''''''''';
;  43h Get/Set File Attributes                             ;
;- - - - - - - - - - - - - - - - - - - - - - - - - - - - -;
;                                                          ;
;  ds:dx    file name                                      ;
;  al       get/set flag                                   ;
;  cx       attributes                                     ;
;..........................................................;

_ChangeFileMode:
        Entry
        def   _mode, ax                       ; get/set flag.
        def   _attributes, cx                 ; attributes, if change.
        ddef  _filename, es, dx               ; arg passed internally as es:dx
        ddef  _dirEntry                       ; directory entry
        defbytes _dirAccess, sizeDIRACCESS

        call CtrlC_Check

;- - - - - - - - - - - - - - - - - - - - - - - - - - - - - - - - --
;  parse file name
;- - - - - - - - - - - - - - - - - - - - - - - - - - - - - - - - -
        mov   ax, (FILE_NODEVICENAME)
        mov   si, dx                          ; name from caller
        lea   di, offset _dirAccess [ bp ]    ; work dir access block
        call  LocateFile                      ; locate file
        jc    _ChangeFileMode_18              ; if file/path valid ->

;- - - - - - - - - - - - - - - - - - - - - - - - - - - - - - - - -
;  if found, either get or set the attribute
;- - - - - - - - - - - - - - - - - - - - - - - - - - - - - - - - -
        les   di, dword ptr [ _dirAccess. fileAcBufferPtr ][ bp ]
        mov   bx, word ptr [ _dirAccess. fileAcDirOffset ][ bp ]

        mov   al, byte ptr [ _mode ][ bp ]
        Goto  00, _ChangeFileMode_GetAttrib      ; get
        Goto  01, _ChangeFileMode_SetAttrib      ; set

        SetError errInvalidFunction, _ChangeFileMode_18 ; else ->

;- - - - - - - - - - - - - - - - - - - - - - - - - - - - - - - - -
;  if get file attributes
;- - - - - - - - - - - - - - - - - - - - - - - - - - - - - - - - -
_ChangeFileMode_GetAttrib:
        RetCallersStackFrame ds, si
        xor   cx, cx
        mov   cl, byte ptr es:[ deAttributes ][ di + bx ]
        mov   word ptr [ _CX ][ si ], cx
        Return
```

```
;- - - - - - - - - - - - - - - - - - - - - - - - - - - - - -
;  if set file attributes
;- - - - - - - - - - - - - - - - - - - - - - - - - - - - - -
_ChangeFileMode_SetAttrib:
        mov cx, word ptr [ _attributes ][ bp ]
        test cx, not ATTR_SETTABLE
        jz _ChangeFileMode_12
        SetError errAccessDenied, _ChangeFileMode_18

_ChangeFileMode_12:
        and byte ptr es:[ deAttributes ][ di + bx ], ATTR_SETTABLE
        or byte ptr es:[ deAttributes ][ di + bx ], cl

        call CCBChanged                         ; update changed buffer
        clc

_ChangeFileMode_18:
        Return
```

File Delete

	On Entry	On Return
AX	AH = 41h	AX = error if carry
BX		
CX		
DS:DX	pointer to ASCIZ filename	
Flags		CY = set if error

Related Functions:
   3Ch Create File; 3Eh Open File; 3Fh Read File; 40h Write File.

The File Delete function expects an unexpanded filename in the DS:DX register pair. The file must be located on disk using LocateFile. Unlike file open and some other functions, the function cannot locate a device or a directory. When the file is found, all its allocated clusters are released, and the file entry is marked as deleted. The file delete function is listed next.

LocateFile returns a completed DIRACCESS block, which we discussed in the file open section in Chapter 3, which contains a pointer to a cached disk buffer that contains the directory entry for the located file. The entry is marked as deleted by writing an 0E5h to the first byte of the filename and marking the cache buffer as changed.

Finally, the function releases the allocated clusters for the file. We described the release function in detail in Chapter 3 under "The FAT Structure." Briefly, disk space is allocated to a file by searching for free (available) clusters in the FAT. The cluster release function walks through the chain of allocated clusters in the FAT and marks them as available, making them available for reallocation at a later date.

```
;''''''''''''''''''''''''''''''''''''''''''''''''''''''''''''';
;  41h Delete File                                            ;
;- - - - - - - - - - - - - - - - - - - - - - - - - - - - - - -;
```

```
        ;                                                        ;
        ;  ds:dx Asciz name of file to delete (no wild chars)    ;
        ;...................................................;

_DeleteFile:
        Entry
        ddef _filename, es, dx                    ; arg passed internally as es:dx
        ddef _dirEntry                            ; directory entry
        defbytes _dirAccess, sizeDIRACCESS

;- - - - - - - - - - - - - - - - - - - - - - - - - - - - - -
;  parse file name
;- - - - - - - - - - - - - - - - - - - - - - - - - - - - - -
        mov ax, (FILE_NODEVICENAME + FILECANNOT_BEDIRECTORY)
        mov si, dx                                ; name from caller
        lea di, offset _dirAccess [ bp ]          ; work dir access block
        call LocateFile
        jc _DeleteFile_18                             ; if file/path valid ->

;- - - - - - - - - - - - - - - - - - - - - - - - - - - - - -
;  mark found entry in directory as deleted
;- - - - - - - - - - - - - - - - - - - - - - - - - - - - - -

        call IFSFileDelete
        jnz _DeleteFile_18

        les di, dword ptr [ _dirAccess. fileAcBufferPtr ][ bp ]
        mov bx, word ptr [ _dirAccess. fileAcDirOffset  ][ bp ]
        mov byte ptr es:[ di + bx ], DIRENTRY_DELETED
        call CCBChanged

        mov ax, word ptr [ _dirAccess. fileAcDrive   ][ bp ]
        mov dx, word ptr [ _dirAccess. fileAcCluster ][ bp ]
        call ReleaseClusterChain
        or ax, ax                                 ; return no error

_DeleteFile_18:
        Return
```

File Rename

	On Entry	On Return
AX	AH = 56h	AX = error if carry
BX		
CX		
DS:DX	pointer to old filename	
ES:SI	pointer to new filename	
Flags		CY = set if error

Related Functions:
   3Ch Create File; 3Eh Open File; 3Fh Read File; 40h Write File.

Rename is passed two filenames, a source and a destination name. The filenames do not support wildcard characters. The MS-DOS version of command.com accomplishes renaming with wild characters by using the FCB-based DOS function 17h. The RxDOS version of the command processor utilizes a combination of Find First, Find Next, and the File Rename function. The function does not just rename the file, but it can also move them across different directories. This does not require physically moving the file. It requires only removing the entry from one directory and placing it in another directory, so long as the file remains in the same drive.

The function begins by checking that the file exists at the source name, that the destination file path is valid, and that the destination filename does not already exist, It can accomplish this by calling LocateFile. It provides different DIRACCESS blocks to expand the filename and return information about where the file was located. For the first filename, the location of the disk, directory, and filename found are expected. For the second filename, the expected parameters are the disk and directory cluster.

The parameters for the two files are checked. First, both the source and destination must be located in the same drive. It doesn't make sense to rename across different drives in DOS. Next, to determine if both source and destination are to the same directory, the function could have compared the expanded filenames. There is a more secure and shorter comparison. The cluster address for the source and destination directories will be the same if they reference the same directory.

If the rename does *not* require a cross-directory move, the destination filename is converted to a directory style name. The output will be the cache buffer containing the entry found in the source lookup. The cache control header address is computed, and the block is marked as updated.

If the rename is across directories, a free slot is located in the destination directory, the source entry is copied to the destination entry, and the new name, if any, is converted to a directory style and placed at the destination. The destination cache buffer is marked for output. The source directory entry is then marked as deleted. The file allocation remains intact.

```
        ;''''''''''''''''''''''''''''''''''''''''''''''''''''''''''''''''';
        ;  56h Rename File                                                ;
        ;- - - - - - - - - - - - - - - - - - - - - - - - - - - - - - - - -;
        ;                                                                 ;
        ;  ds:dx pointer to ASCIZ existing file/path                      ;
        ;  es:di pointer to ASCIZ rename file/path                        ;
        ;.................................................................;

_RenameFile:
        Entry
        ddef _wherePointer
        defbytes _existfileAccess, sizeDIRACCESS
        defbytes _renfileAccess, sizeDIRACCESS

        call CtrlC_Check

;- - - - - - - - - - - - - - - - - - - - - - - - - - - - - - - - - - - - -
; does existing file exist ?
;- - - - - - - - - - - - - - - - - - - - - - - - - - - - - - - - - - - - -
        mov ax, (FILE_NODEVICENAME + FILECANNOT_BEDIRECTORY)
        mov si, dx                                   ; name from caller
        lea di, offset _existfileAccess [ bp ]       ; work dir access block
```

```
        call LocateFile                                 ; check file path
        ifc _renameFile_40                              ; if file does not exist ->

        push ds
        RetCallersStackFrame ds, bx
        mov es, word ptr [ _ExtraSegment ][ bx ]
        mov si, word ptr [ _DI           ][ bx ]        ; get user's parameter
        pop ds

        mov ax, (FILE_NODEVICENAME + FILECANNOT_BEDEFINED + FILECANNOT_BEDIRECTORY)
        lea di, offset _renfileAccess [ bp ]            ; renamed file dir access block
        call LocateFile                                 ; check file path
        ifc _renameFile_40                              ; if file does not exist ->

;- - - - - - - - - - - - - - - - - - - - - - - - - - - - - - - - - -
; both files seem ok, so we'll move them
;- - - - - - - - - - - - - - - - - - - - - - - - - - - - - - - - - -
        mov al, byte ptr [ _existfileAccess. fileAcDrive ][ bp ]
        cmp al, byte ptr [ _renfileAccess. fileAcDrive ][ bp ]
        mov ax, errPathNotFound
        stc
        ifnz _renameFile_40                             ; cannot move across drives ->

        mov ax, word ptr [ _existfileAccess. fileAcDirCluster ][ bp ]
        cmp ax, word ptr [ _renfileAccess. fileAcDirCluster ][ bp ]
        jnz _renameFile_22                              ; if must move across dirs ->

        setDS ss
        mov si,  word ptr [ _renfileAccess. fileAcNameOffset  ][ bp ]
        les di, dword ptr [ _existfileAccess. fileAcBufferPtr ][ bp ]
        add di,  word ptr [ _existfileAccess. fileAcDirOffset ][ bp ]
        call convFilenametoFCBString                    ; convert name

        les si, dword ptr [ _existfileAccess. fileAcBufferPtr ][ bp ]
        call locateCCBPHeader
        call CCBChanged                                 ; update buffer
        jmp short _renameFile_38                        ; exit ->

;- - - - - - - - - - - - - - - - - - - - - - - - - - - - - - - - - -
; move entry between directories
;- - - - - - - - - - - - - - - - - - - - - - - - - - - - - - - - - -
_renameFile_22:
        and word ptr [ _renfileAccess. fileAcDrive      ][ bp ], 7FFFh
        mov ax, word ptr [ _renfileAccess. fileAcDrive      ][ bp ]
        mov dx, word ptr [ _renfileAccess. fileAcDirCluster ][ bp ]
        call LocateFreeDirSlot                          ; can we find an empty entry ?
        ifc _renameFile_40                              ; if can't find free slot ->

        stordarg _wherePointer, es, si
        mov di, si                                      ; where entry must be copied to

        lds si, dword ptr [ _existfileAccess. fileAcBufferPtr ][ bp ]
        add si,  word ptr [ _existfileAccess. fileAcDirOffset ][ bp ]
        mov cx, ( sizeDIRENTRY / 2 )
```

```
        rep movsw                                    ; copy entry from source dir

        setDS ss
        getdarg es, di, _wherePointer
        mov si, word ptr [ _renfileAccess. fileAcNameOffset ][ bp ]
        call convFilenametoFCBString                 ; rename file

        getdarg es, si, _wherePointer
        call locateCCBPHeader
        call CCBChanged                              ; update buffer

        les di, dword ptr [ _existfileAccess. fileAcBufferPtr ][ bp ]
        mov bx,  word ptr [ _existfileAccess. fileAcDirOffset ][ bp ]
        mov byte ptr es:[ di + bx ], DIRENTRY_DELETED
        call CCBChanged

;- - - - - - - - - - - - - - - - - - - - - - - - - - - - - - - - - - - -
;  return
;- - - - - - - - - - - - - - - - - - - - - - - - - - - - - - - - - - -
_renameFile_38:
        or ax, ax                                    ; no carry

_renameFile_40:
        Return
```

Find First

	On Entry	On Return
AX	AH = 4Eh	AX = error code if carry
BX		
CX	search attributes	
DS:DX	filename to search	
DTA	function uses Disk Transfer	Address
Flags		CY = set if error

Related Functions:
   4Fh Find Next; 1Ah Set Disk Transfer Address; 2Fh Get Disk Transfer Address.

Find First combined with Find Next is the service that DOS provides to enable applications to walk through a directory. Find First initializes a FINDENTRY block, which is used by Find Next in subsequent searches. Because of this find block, applications are free to perform almost any other DOS file system function with the values returned by the find function. Some programs fear that the delicate balance that is somewhat implied by the Find First and Find Next relationship will somehow be broken if other file operations are performed. Feel free to stretch DOS to the limit here.

The FINDENTRY structure begins with a 21-byte reserved block, followed by information derived from the directory. The reserved portion of the block is shown here. It begins with the search pattern, including any wild characters in the name and search attributes. Since the search routine must use _FATReadRandom, it requires the current cluster directory address. Since directories are always searched in the forward direction, the beginning cluster address to the directory is not actually needed in this structure. The current position pointer is maintained by something called the directory entry. This is not a directory offset. The offset is computed by multiplying the entry by the size of a directory entry.

```
            FINDENTRY struc
findSrchDrive           db  ?
findSrchName            db  '????????'           ; name to search
findSrchExtension       db  '???'
findSrchAttributes      db  ?
findDirEntry            dw  ?                     ; dir entry (** Not Double **)
findDirBegCluster       dw  ?                     ; dir beg cluster
findDirCurrCluster      dw  ?                     ; dir curr cluster
findCCBPointer          dw  ?                     ; ccb pointer

findFileAttribute       db  ?
findFileTime            dw  ?
findFileDate            dw  ?
findFileSize            dd  ?
findFileName            db  13 dup (?)            ; null terminated name
            FINDENTRY ends
```

Find First begins by using `LocateFile` to expand the pathname and determine that the path exists. It locates the parent directory since neither the directory nor the file option bits are set. A `FINDENTRY` is initialized at the current Disk Transfer Area to all zeros. The search name is converted into a search pattern. Other parameters such as the current cluster address are set in the block, and a search is begun using a locate by attribute function. The results of the search are returned to the caller.

Locate by attribute is a slightly different directory search routine. It matches files based on name and attributes.

```
        ;''''''''''''''''''''''''''''''''''''''''''''''''''''''''''';
        ;   4Eh Find First Matching Name                            ;
        ;- - - - - - - - - - - - - - - - - - - - - - - - - - - - - -;
        ;                                                           ;
        ;   ds:dx    file name                                      ;
        ;   cx       attributes                                     ;
        ;...........................................................;


_FindFirstFile:
        Entry
        def _attributes, cx
        ddef _filename, es, dx                    ; arg passed internally as es:dx
        defbytes _dirAccess, sizeDIRACCESS

        call CtrlC_Check


;- - - - - - - - - - - - - - - - - - - - - - - - - - - - - - - - - -
;  make sure path is ok, try to match file
;- - - - - - - - - - - - - - - - - - - - - - - - - - - - - - - - -
```

```
        mov     ax, (FILE_NODEVICENAME + FILEHAS_WILDCHARS)
        mov     si, dx                          ; name from caller (es: si )
        lea     di, offset _dirAccess [ bp ]    ; work dir access block
        call    LocateFile                      ; don't worry about finding a file
        jc      _FindFirstFile_50               ; error code already set  ->

;- - - - - - - - - - - - - - - - - - - - - - - - - - - - - - - - - - - - -
;  setup find search template
;- - - - - - - - - - - - - - - - - - - - - - - - - - - - - - - - - - - - -
        les     di, dword ptr [ _RxDOS_pDTA ]
        clearMemory sizeFINDENTRY, 0000         ; clear area to zeros

;- - - - - - - - - - - - - - - - - - - - - - - - - - - - - - - - - - - - -
;  start at beginning of directory, locate by attribute and name
;- - - - - - - - - - - - - - - - - - - - - - - - - - - - - - - - - - - - -
        mov     si, word ptr [ _dirAccess. fileAcNameOffset ][ bp ]
        mov     di, word ptr [ _RxDOS_pDTA. _pointer ]
        lea     di, offset findSrchName [ di ]
        call    convFilenametoFCBString         ; convert to a match template

;- - - - - - - - - - - - - - - - - - - - - - - - - - - - - - - - - - - - -
;  start at beginning of directory, locate by attribute and name
;- - - - - - - - - - - - - - - - - - - - - - - - - - - - - - - - - - - - -
        mov     di, word ptr [ _RxDOS_pDTA. _pointer ]
        mov     al, byte ptr [ _dirAccess. fileAcDrive ][ bp ]
        mov     byte ptr es:[ findSrchDrive ][ di ], al

        mov     cl, byte ptr [ _attributes ][ bp ]
        mov     byte ptr es:[ findSrchAttributes ][ di ], cl

        mov     ax, word ptr [ _dirAccess. fileAcDirCluster ][ bp ]
        mov     word ptr es:[ findDirBegCluster  ][ di ], ax
        mov     word ptr es:[ findDirCurrCluster ][ di ], ax
        call    LocateFileByAttribute           ; lookup by attribute

;- - - - - - - - - - - - - - - - - - - - - - - - - - - - - - - - - - - - -
;  if error, release locked sft
;- - - - - - - - - - - - - - - - - - - - - - - - - - - - - - - - - - - - -
_FindFirstFile_50:
        RetCallersStackFrame ds, bx
        mov     word ptr [ _AX ][ bx ], ax      ; return possible error code
        Return
```

LocateFileByAttribute. The function expects an initialized and perhaps already used FINDENTRY block. In the block, it expects an offset of where within the directory to begin searching, a search template with possible wild characters, and an attribute selector byte. The purpose of the routine is to not only select on filenames or their extension, but possibly on attributes as well. For example, the routine could match on subdirectory names or files marked as achievable.

After some initialization, the routine converts the entry index into a file position. The file is read, one entry at a time, skipping deleted entries. The filenames are compared, and if the entries match, including wild characters, the attributes must match. Attribute matching is not exact. If any search attributes match the entry in the directory, the search is said to match. If this search pattern fails, then the archive bit is considered inconsequential to the search, and the search determines whether any of the other attribute flags are set. The function does not match on the volume label bit.

Once a match is discovered, the FINDENTRY block is initialized with information from the directory entry, and the function returns.

```
;'''''''''''''''''''''''''''''''''''''''''''''''''''''''''''''';
;   Locate File by Attribute                                   ;
;- - - - - - - - - - - - - - - - - - - - - - - - - - - - - - -;
;                                                              ;
;   (important: starts search at offset in 'findDirEntry')     ;
;                                                              ;
;   es:di  pointer to find access block                        ;
;..............................................................;


LocateFileByAttribute:
        Entry
        def  _attributes
        ddef _findAccess, es, di
        defbytes _diskAccess, sizeDISKACCESS
        defbytes _tempname, sizeTempExpandedFCBNAME


;- - - - - - - - - - - - - - - - - - - - - - - - - - - - - - -
;  init access
;- - - - - - - - - - - - - - - - - - - - - - - - - - - - - - -
        saveSegments
        getdarg es, di, _findAccess                  ; point to find access

        xor ah, ah
        mov al, byte ptr es:[ findSrchDrive      ][ di ]
        mov dx, word ptr es:[ findDirBegCluster  ][ di ]

        mov cl, byte ptr es:[ findSrchAttributes ][ di ]
        and cl, ATTR_MASK
        mov byte ptr [ _attributes ][ bp ], cl       ; save for fast search

        setES ss
        lea bx, offset _diskAccess [ bp ]            ; pointer to access block
        call initdiskAccess                          ; [ax] is drive, [dx] is cluster


;- - - - - - - - - - - - - - - - - - - - - - - - - - - - - - -
;  lookup entry
;- - - - - - - - - - - - - - - - - - - - - - - - - - - - - - -
        getdarg es, di, _findAccess                  ; point to find access
        mov cx, sizeDIRENTRY
        mov ax, word ptr es:[ findDirEntry ][ di ]
        dec ax
        mul cx
        mov word ptr [ _diskAccess. diskAcPosition. _low  ][ bp ], ax
        mov word ptr [ _diskAccess. diskAcPosition. _high ][ bp ], dx
        mov word ptr [ _diskAccess. diskAcOptions          ][ bp ], (ccb_isDIR)


locByAttrib_18:
```

```
        setDS ss                                    ; ensure ds == ss

        lea bx, offset _diskAccess [ bp ]           ; pointer to access block
        add word ptr [ diskAcPosition. _low  ][ bx ], sizeDIRENTRY
        adc word ptr [ diskAcPosition. _high ][ bx ], 0000
        call _FATReadRandom                         ; read into buffer
        stc                                         ; just in case error,
        ifz  locByAttrib_56                         ; if no more data —>

        lea di, offset deName[ bx ]                 ; get pointer to name
        cmp byte ptr es:[ di ], DIRENTRY_NEVERUSED
        stc                                         ; just in case error,
        ifz locByAttrib_56                          ; if no more data —>
        cmp byte ptr es:[ di ], DIRENTRY_DELETED
        jz locByAttrib_18                           ; don't bother —>

        lds si, dword ptr [ _findAccess ][ bp ]     ; pointer to search file name
        lea si, offset findSrchName[ si ]           ;
        call compareDirEntries
        jnz locByAttrib_18                          ; if item not found —>

        mov cl, byte ptr [ _attributes ][ bp ]      ; template attributes
        mov ch, byte ptr es:[ deAttributes ][ bx ]
        and ch, ATTR_MASK
        test ch, cl                                 ; test for special cases
        jnz locByAttrib_42                          ; if match —>
        cmp ch, cl
        jz locByAttrib_42                           ; normal file filter —>

        and cl, not ( ATTR_HIDDEN + ATTR_SYSTEM + ATTR_DIRECTORY )
        cmp ch, cl
        jnz locByAttrib_18                          ; no match —>

;- - - - - - - - - - - - - - - - - - - - - - - - - - - - - - - - - - - -
;  item found
;- - - - - - - - - - - - - - - - - - - - - - - - - - - - - - - - - - - -
locByAttrib_42:
        push bx
        push word ptr es:[ deDate          ][ bx ]
        push word ptr es:[ deTime          ][ bx ]
        push word ptr es:[ deFileSize. _low  ][ bx ]
        push word ptr es:[ deFileSize. _high ][ bx ]
        push word ptr es:[ deAttributes    ][ bx ]

        lea si, offset deName-1 [ bx ]              ; drive here doesn't matter
        lea di, offset _tempname [ bp ]            ; expand name
        call convFCBNametoASCIZ                    ; expand name

        getdarg ds, di, _findAccess                ; point to find access
        pop ax
        mov byte ptr [ findFileAttribute   ][ di ], al
        pop word ptr [ findFileSize. _high ][ di ]
        pop word ptr [ findFileSize. _low  ][ di ]
        pop word ptr [ findFileTime        ][ di ]
```

```
        pop word ptr [ findFileDate       ][ di ]
        pop word ptr [ findCCBPointer     ][ di ]

        setDS ss
        lea si, [ _tempname + 2 ][ bp ]                ; drive doesn't matter
        getdarg es, di, _findAccess                    ; point to find access
        lea di, offset findFileName [ di ]             ; resultant filename
        mov cx, (sizeTempExpandedFCBNAME - 2)
        rep movsb                                      ; copy effectively
        clc

;- - - - - - - - - - - - - - - - - - - - - - - - - - - - - - - - - - -
; return
;- - - - - - - - - - - - - - - - - - - - - - - - - - - - - - - - - - -
locByAttrib_56:
        getdarg es, di, _findAccess                    ; point to find access

        mov ax, word ptr [ _diskAccess. diskAcPosition. _low  ][ bp ]
        mov dx, word ptr [ _diskAccess. diskAcPosition. _high ][ bp ]
        mov cx, sizeDIRENTRY
        call _div32
        mov word ptr es:[ findDirEntry ][ di ], ax

        mov ax, word ptr [ _diskAccess. diskAcBegCluster ][ bp ]
        mov dx, word ptr [ _diskAccess. diskAcCurCluster ][ bp ]
        mov word ptr es:[ findDirBegCluster ][ di ], ax
        mov word ptr es:[ findDirCurrCluster ][ di ], dx

        restoreSegments
        Return
```

Find Next

	On Entry	On Return
AX	AH = 4Fh	
DTA	function uses Disk Transfer	Address
Flags		CY = set if error

Related Functions:
    4Eh Find First; 1Ah Set Disk Transfer Address; 2Fh Get Disk Transfer Address.

Find Next expects the FINDENTRY block that was returned by the Find First function. The code ensures that the search continues from where the previous search terminated. It does this by incrementing the search find entry. The search will begin with the next entry. All Find Next has to do is call the locate by attribute function to continue the search.

If we look carefully at the code, there are only two places where the Disk Transfer Address becomes important for Find First and Find Next. One is in this function, and the other is in Find First. The question then becomes, why didn't MS-DOS require a pointer to a find block, thus freeing applications from the somewhat arbitrary selection of the Disk Transfer Address?

```
;'''''''''''''''''''''''''''''''''''''''''''''''''''''''''''''';
;   4Fh Find Next Matching Name                                 ;
;- - - - - - - - - - - - - - - - - - - - - - - - - - - - - - -;
;                                                               ;
;   no parameters. uses find record in DTA.                     ;
;..............................................................;

_FindNextFile:
        call CtrlC_Check

        les di, dword ptr [ _RxDOS_pDTA ]
        inc word ptr es:[ findDirEntry ][ di ]
        call LocateFileByAttribute                  ; lookup by attribute

        RetCallersStackFrame ds, bx
        mov word ptr [ _AX ][ bx ], ax              ; return possible error code
        ret
```

Duplicate File Handle

	On Entry	On Return
AX	AH = 45h	AX = new handle, or error if carry
BX	original handle	
CX		
DX		
Flags		CY = set if error

Related Functions:
   3Ch Create File; 3Fh Read File; 40h Write File; 46h Force Duplicate Handle.

File handles are references to SFT entries. When the file handle is duplicated, the reference to the same SFT is duplicated. Both file handles map to the same SFT entry. Because of this, moving the file pointer through one file handle moves the file pointer for both file handles. Actually, and to be more precise, moving the file pointer changes the value stored in the shared SFT. To actually be able to maintain two separate file pointers, and with it a performance boost when accessing different parts of the same file, open the file twice.

So why duplicate the file handle? Since stdin, stdout, and stderr share the same file handle, the duplicate file handle function provided the means by which to reuse SFTs. It turned out later that duplicating the file handle, and then closing the duplicate handle, performed the same function as the newer Commit File function, DOS function 68h.

Duplicate file handle begins by performing consistency checks. The current handle must be legitimate and point to an open SFT entry. Next, there must be an available entry in the current JHT, or Job Handle Table. If there isn't, a file handle cannot be returned, and an error is returned. A free entry is located by scanning the JHT for a -1 entry. The free entry is replaced by the SFT handle taken from the old (original) file handle. JHT entries contain SFT handles. The SFT handle from the original entry is stored in the new JHT entry.

Since there is now an additional copy of the SFT handle, the SFT reference count must be incremented. The SFT handle is converted to an SFT address, and the reference count is incremented.

```
;///////////////////////////////////////////////////////;
; 45h Duplicate File Handle                              ;
;- - - - - - - - - - - - - - - - - - - - - - - - - - - -;
;                                                        ;
; Input:                                                 ;
;   bx      existing (old) handle                        ;
;                                                        ;
; Output:                                                ;
;   ax      new handle                                   ;
;........................................................;

_DuplicateFileHandle:
        mov es, word ptr [ _RxDOS_CurrentPSP ]
        mov cx, word ptr es:[ pspFileHandleCount ]
        mov dx, cx                                      ; save original count
        cmp bx, word ptr es:[ pspFileHandleCount ]      ; illegal reference ?
        jc _duplFileHandle_12                           ; if valid ->

_duplFileHandle_InvHandleError:
        seterror errInvalidHandle, _duplFileHandle_Return ; if illegal ->

_duplFileHandle_12:
        les di, dword ptr es:[ pspFileHandlePtr  ]
        mov bl, byte ptr es:[ di + bx ]                 ; get SFT handle from current
        cmp bl, -1                                      ; invalid entry ?
        jz _duplFileHandle_InvHandleError               ; if error ->

    ; is there an available entry ?

        mov al, -1
        repnz scasb                                     ; scan for empty slot
        jnz _duplFileHandle_InvHandleError              ; if error ->

        sub dx, cx                                      ; get count
        dec dx
        push dx
        mov byte ptr es:[ di - 1 ], bl                  ; duplicate handle

        xor ax, ax
        mov al, bl                                      ; old handle
        call FindSFTbyHandle                            ; get corresponding SFT (es: di )
        inc word ptr es:[ sftRefCount ][ di ]           ; bump in use count

        pop ax                                          ; new handle
        or ax, ax                                       ; no carry

;- - - - - - - - - - - - - - - - - - - - - - - - - - - - - - - -
; if error, exit with error code.
;- - - - - - - - - - - - - - - - - - - - - - - - - - - - - - - -
```

```
_duplFileHandle_Return:
        RetCallersStackFrame ds, bx
        mov word ptr [ _AX ][ bx ], ax
        ret
```

Force Duplicate File Handle

	On Entry	On Return
AX	AH = 46h	AX = new handle, or error if carry
BX	original handle	
CX	new handle	
DX		
Flags		CY = set if error

Related Functions:
   3Ch Create File; 3Fh Read File; 40h Write File; 45h Duplicate Handle.

Duplicating a file handle is used by applications to commit changes to disk. The Force Duplicate File Handle function is used for a different purpose. It is typically used to redirect device output by a command shell or other program. An application creates or opens a file and then forces the duplication of its handle to the device handle, such as to stdin or stdout devices.

   The function must check first if both file handles passed are valid. Then it closes the destination device if it is still open. The SFT handle at the original handle is copied to the destination handle, and the destination handle is returned to the user in the AX register. The SFT handle is converted to an SFT address, and the reference count is incremented.

```
        ;''''''''''''''''''''''''''''''''''''''''''''''''''''''''''''';
        ;   46h Force File Handle Duplicate                           ;
        ;- - - - - - - - - - - - - - - - - - - - - - - - - - - - - - -;
        ;                                                             ;
        ;   Input:                                                    ;
        ;   bx      existing open handle                              ;
        ;   cx      duplicate handle                                  ;
        ;                                                             ;
        ;   Output:                                                   ;
        ;   ax      new handle                                        ;
        ;.............................................................;

_ForceFileHandle:
        mov es, word ptr [ _RxDOS_CurrentPSP ]
        les di, dword ptr es:[ pspFileHandlePtr ]
        cmp bx, word ptr es:[ pspFileHandleCount ]
        jnc _ForceFileHandle_InvHandleError         ; if error value ->
        cmp cx, word ptr es:[ pspFileHandleCount ]
        jnc _ForceFileHandle_InvHandleError         ; if error value ->

        push bx
        push cx
```

```
        xor ah, ah
        xchg bx, cx
        mov al, byte ptr es:[ di + bx ]       ; SFT handle for duplicate
        cmp al, -1                            ; file open ?
        jz _ForceFileHandle_12                ; no ->

        call FindSFTbyHandle                  ; get corresponding SFT (es: di )
        jc _ForceFileHandle_InvHandleError    ; if can't, error ->
        call _SFTCloseFile                    ; close SFT Entry

_ForceFileHandle_12:
        pop cx
        pop bx                                ; restore handles
        mov dl, byte ptr es:[ di + bx ]       ; SFT handle for original
        cmp dl, -1                            ; original file open ?
        jz _ForceFileHandle_InvHandleError    ; no, error ->

        xchg bx, cx
        mov byte ptr es:[ di + bx ], dl       ; duplicate handle

        RetCallersStackFrame es, bx
        mov word ptr es:[ _AX ][ bx ], cx     ; return new handle

        xor ah, ah
        mov al, dl                            ; SFT handle
        call FindSFTbyHandle                  ; get corresponding SFT (es: di )
        inc word ptr es:[ sftRefCount ][ di ] ; bump in use count
        or ax, ax                             ; no carry
        ret

_ForceFileHandle_InvHandleError:
        RetCallersStackFrame ds, bx
        mov word ptr [ _AX ][ bx ], errInvalidHandle   ; can't duplicate inv handle
        stc
        ret
```

Creating and Removing Subdirectories

The directory management code that follows parallels in many respects the code already shown for files. This should not be surprising since a subdirectory is at the FAT layer really just another file. As a file, it must be navigated through allocated clusters. The code begins with the simplest of the directory management functions, the Get Current Directory function.

Get Current Directory

	On Entry	On Return
AX	AH = 47h	AX = error if carry
BX		
CX		
DX	DL = drive number	
DS:SI	64-byte buffer to store path	
Flags		CY = set if error

Related Functions:
  39h Create Directory; 3Ah Remove Directory; 3Bh Change Directory.

DOS maintains a list of current directory assignments for each drive in the CDS, appropriately the Current Directory Structure. The CDS is used by DOS functions that perform directory search, such as file open, create, delete, and others to expand the filename. The Get Current Directory function is almost just a matter of copying the name stored in the CDS to the buffer provided by the function.

The drive code in the DL register is checked to be sure that it is within a valid range and is then converted to an internal drive code. The conversion is performed by getActualDrive, which interprets a zero drive code as a reference to the current selected drive. This converted drive code is used as an index into the CDS.

The current directory path in the CDS consists of the full pathname, such as c:\amipro, but the first three characters are nonsubstitutable for reasons that we explained in the section on expanding the filename in Chapter 3. At any rate, the nonsubstitutable portion of the current directory string is never copied back to the user, leading to the somewhat bizarre convention where the drive and leading backslash of the current directory are never returned. If the current directory for a drive is the root directory, the string returned by the function is a null string.

The code to get the current directory is simply a copy from the entry maintained in the CDS.

```
;'''''''''''''''''''''''''''''''''''''''''''''''''''''''''''';
;   47h Get Current Directory                                ;
;- - - - - - - - - - - - - - - - - - - - - - - - - - - - - -;
;                                                            ;
;   ds:si   pointer to max 64 byte user memory area          ;
;   dl      drive number                                     ;
;............................................................;

_GetCurrentDirectory:
        push dx
        call getActualDrive             ; actual drive (in ax)
        jnc getCurrDir_14               ; if no error ->

        RetCallersStackFrame ds, bx
        mov word ptr [ _AX ][ bx ], ax
        ret
```

```
getCurrDir_14:
        mov cl, sizeCDS
        mul cl                                  ; ax contains current drive

        lds si, dword ptr [ _RxDOS_pCDS ]       ; actual address in CDS
        add si, ax                              ; address drive

        mov ax, _cdsActualDirectory             ; proper offset
        add al, byte ptr [ _cdsNonSubstOffset ][ si ]
        add si, ax

        push ds
        RetCallersStackFrame ds, bx
        mov es, word ptr [ _DataSegment ][ bx ]
        mov di, word ptr [ _SI ][ bx ]
        pop ds

getCurrDir_22:
        lodsb                                   ; copy buffer
        stosb
        or al, al
        jnz getCurrDir_22

        clc
        ret                                     ; ds:si will be returned
```

The getActualDrive function accepts a drive code as an argument on the stack. The drive code can be a letter in either uppercase or lowercase or a binary number (as in the case where the argument of the form A=1, B=2, ... is passed). If the argument passed is a zero, it is replaced by the current drive code. The original argument is compared to the maximum available drive for this system, and an error code is returned if the drive is out of range.

```
;'''''''''''''''''''''''''''''''''''''''''''''''''''''''''''''';
;  Get Actual (Current Drive as a = 0, b = 1, ... )            ;
;..............................................................;

GetActualDrive:
        Entry 1
        Arg _drive

        push ds
        currSegment ds
        mov al, byte ptr [ _drive ][ bp ]
        and ax, 001fh
        dec al
        jge GetActualDrive_20
        mov al, byte ptr [ _RxDOS_CurrentDrive ]

GetActualDrive_20:
        mov dx, ax
        cmp al, byte ptr [ _RxDOS_bLastDrive ]
        jnc GetActualDrive_Error
        clc
```

```
GetActualDrive_Return:
        pop ds
        Return

GetActualDrive_Error:
        stc
        mov ax, errInvalidDrive
        jmp GetActualDrive_Return
```

Change Directory

	On Entry	**On Return**
AX	AH = 3Bh	AX = error if carry
BX		
CX		
DX	pathname	
Flags		CY = set if error

Related Functions:
  39h Create Directory; 3Ah Make Directory; 47h Get Directory.

Changing the current directory is necessary to primarily support FCB functions that have no pathname capabilities or for shell and file management programs whose behavior depends on selecting a current directory. In general, programs maintain the pathname with the filename so that files are easier to track. Changing the directory requires passing a valid pathname. That pathname may contain a drive letter. The pathname is validated, and the corresponding entry in the CDS is changed.

The function checks for a Control Break and then verifies that the path is correct. The pathname may not contain a device or filename. LocateFile returns the drive code searched, but it may be the substituted drive, and using it as an index into the CDS would change the wrong entry. A drive code is substituted when the drive is substituted or joined. Additional information is available in the section on expanding the filename (see Chapter 3).

The original drive code can be extracted from the original pathname using getDrive, a function listed in the expand filename section. It determines if a drive code was used in the string or defaults to the current selected drive. The drive code returned by this function is valid because LocateFile would have failed if it wasn't. The code is then used as an index to the correct CDS entry. The expanded pathname is copied into the CDS, as is the located cluster address, all part of the current directory optimization.

One question of technical importance is what happens to the protected nonsubstituted part of the string? It turns out that it doesn't have to be handled as a special case. When the pathname is expanded, it carries with it the nonsubstituted part. In what may appear as a complicated example, suppose that the f: drive is substituted by c:\rxdos. Changing the directory to f:\source will produce c:\rxdos\source. The nonsubstitutable text is carried along in the expanded filename and is just copied back to the CDS.

The code for the change directory function follows:

```
(in rxdos.asm)
        ;////////////////////////////////////////////////////////////;
        ;  3Bh  Change Subdirectory                                   ;
        ;- - - - - - - - - - - - - - - - - - - - - - - - - - - - - -;
        ;                                                            ;
        ;  ds:dx pointer to subdirectory                             ;
        ;............................................................;

_ChangeSubdirectory:
        Entry
        ddef _pathname, es, dx                   ; arg passed internally as es:dx
        defbytes _dirAccess, sizeDIRACCESS

        call CtrlC_Check
;- - - - - - - - - - - - - - - - - - - - - - - - - - - - - - - - -
;  parse file name
;- - - - - - - - - - - - - - - - - - - - - - - - - - - - - - - - -
        mov ax, (FILE_NODEVICENAME + FILEHAS_NOFILENAME)
        getdarg es, si, _pathname                ; arg passed internally as es:dx
        lea di, offset _dirAccess [ bp ]         ; work dir access block
        call LocateFile                          ; check file path
        jc _ChgSubDir_40                         ; if path invalid ->

;- - - - - - - - - - - - - - - - - - - - - - - - - - - - - - - - -
;  copy path to CDS table.
;- - - - - - - - - - - - - - - - - - - - - - - - - - - - - - - - -
        push ds                                  ; save current segment
        push dx                                  ; cluster address

        getdarg es, si, _pathname                ; arg passed internally as es:dx
        call getDrive

        les di, dword ptr [ _RxDOS_pCDS ]        ; actual address in CDS
        mov cl, sizeCDS
        mul cl                                   ; ax contains current drive
        add di, ax                               ; from
        push di

        setDS ss                                 ; copy from stack
        lea si, offset _dirAccess. fileAcExpandedName [ bp ]
        lea di, offset _cdsActualDirectory [ di ]

_ChgSubDir_22:
        lodsb                                    ; copy buffer
        stosb
        or al, al
        jnz _ChgSubDir_22

        pop di                                   ; restore CDS pointer
        pop word ptr es:[ _cdsStartClusterDir ][ di ]
        pop ds                                   ; restore ds
```

```
;- - - - - - - - - - - - - - - - - - - - - - - - - - - - -
;   normal exit
;- - - - - - - - - - - - - - - - - - - - - - - - - - - - -
_ChgSubDir_40:
        Return
```

Make Directory

	On Entry	On Return
AX	AH = 39h	AX = error if carry
BX		
CX		
DX	pathname	
Flags		CY = set if error

Related Functions:
   3Ah Remove Directory; 3Bh Change Directory; 47h Get Directory.

A directory is a file with the directory attribute. This informs DOS that files can be recorded and searched within the directory. One additional difference is that DOS expects the directory to be preinitialized. Empty unused entries at the end of the directory have a specific character, 00h, and although not used by DOS, directories begin with two standard entries, the . and . . entries.

   The Make Directory function verifies that the pathname does not already exist. A free directory entry is assigned and is initialized to the new subdirectory name. One feature of LocateFile is that it returns the cluster address of the last directory searched when the file cannot exist flag is set. This is ideal for performing directory services such as creating files or subdirectories.

   A cluster is allocated for the new subdirectory using AllocateInitCluster, which fills the entire cluster with zeros. A cluster is the minimum allocatable unit of disk space under DOS. The allocate cluster function returns the address of a buffer pointer it has utilized to clear the cluster. The buffer is preset with the sector address at the start of the cluster. This buffer is updated for the . and . . entries. The . entry will contain the current date and time and a pointer to the current cluster address. The . entry contains a cluster reference to the parent directory. Once these changes are made to the current buffer, the buffer is marked as updated, and the directory entry in the parent directory can be updated. The allocated cluster address for the new directory is set in place, together with the date and time. That buffer is then updated.

```
(in rxdos.asm)
        ;''''''''''''''''''''''''''''''''''''''''''''''''''''''''''''';
        ;   39h Create Subdirectory                                  ;
        ;- - - - - - - - - - - - - - - - - - - - - - - - - - - - - -;
        ;                                                            ;
        ;   ds:dx pointer to subdirectory                            ;
        ;............................................................;

_CreateSubdirectory:
        Entry
```

```
        ddef _pathname, es, dx                        ; arg passed internally as es:dx
        ddef _dirAddress                              ; dir reference
        def  _alloccluster                            ; allocated cluster
        ddef _datetime
        defbytes _dirAccess, sizeDIRACCESS

        call CtrlC_Check
```

```
;- - - - - - - - - - - - - - - - - - - - - - - - - - - - - - - -
;  does entry already exist ?
;- - - - - - - - - - - - - - - - - - - - - - - - - - - - - - - -
        mov ax, (FILE_NODEVICENAME + FILEHAS_NOFILENAME + FILECANNOT_BEDEFINED)
        getdarg es, si, _pathname                     ; arg passed internally as es:dx
        lea di, offset _dirAccess [ bp ]              ; work dir access block
        call LocateFile                               ; check file path
        ifc _MakeSubDir_40                            ; if path invalid ->
```

```
;- - - - - - - - - - - - - - - - - - - - - - - - - - - - - - - -
;  find next empty directory entry
;- - - - - - - - - - - - - - - - - - - - - - - - - - - - - - - -
        and word ptr [ _dirAccess. fileAcDrive   ][ bp ], 7FFFh

        mov ax, word ptr [ _dirAccess. fileAcDrive   ][ bp ]
        mov dx, word ptr [ _dirAccess. fileAcDirCluster ][ bp ]
        call LocateFreeDirSlot                        ; valid empty entry ?
        ifc _MakeSubDir_40                            ; if can't find free slot ->

        mov di, si                                    ; convert name to dir style
        stordarg _dirAddress, es, di                  ; address of empty loc found
        clearMemory sizeDIRENTRY                      ; init to zeros

        lea si, word ptr [ _dirAccess ][ bp ]
        mov si, word ptr [ fileAcNameOffset ][ si ]
        call convFilenametoFCBString                  ; dir style name

        call getSysDateinDirFormat
        stordarg _datetime, dx, ax                    ; make sure we get these
```

```
;- - - - - - - - - - - - - - - - - - - - - - - - - - - - - - - -
;  Allocate cluster for subdirectory
;- - - - - - - - - - - - - - - - - - - - - - - - - - - - - - - -
        mov ax, word ptr [ _dirAccess. fileAcDrive   ][ bp ]
        call AllocateInitCluster                      ; init/ allocate
        storarg _alloccluster, dx                     ; save cluster
        ifc _MakeSubDir_40                            ; if error ->
```

```
;- - - - - - - - - - - - - - - - - - - - - - - - - - - - - - - -
;  init (.) entry
;- - - - - - - - - - - - - - - - - - - - - - - - - - - - - - - -
        lea si, offset ccbData [ di ]                 ; point to data
        call blankinitDirName                         ; initialize file name
        mov byte ptr es:[ deName ][ si ], '.'         ; set dot entry

        getarg dx, _alloccluster                      ; get cluster
```

```
        mov word ptr es:[ deStartCluster ][ si ], dx

        getdarg dx, ax, _datetime                    ; get date/ time
        mov word ptr es:[ deTime ][ si ], ax         ; time created
        mov word ptr es:[ deDate ][ si ], dx         ; date created
        mov byte ptr es:[ deAttributes ][ si ], ATTR_DIRECTORY

;- - - - - - - - - - - - - - - - - - - - - - - - - - - - - - - -
;   init (..) entry
;- - - - - - - - - - - - - - - - - - - - - - - - - - - - - - - -
        lea si, offset ccbData.sizeDIRENTRY [ di ]
        call blankinitDirName                        ; initialize file name
        mov word ptr es:[ deName ][ si ], '..'       ; set double dot entry

        mov dx, word ptr [ _dirAccess. fileAcDirCluster ][ bp ]
        mov word ptr es:[ deStartCluster ][ si ], dx

        getdarg dx, ax, _datetime                    ; get date time
        mov word ptr es:[ deTime ][ si ], ax         ; time created
        mov word ptr es:[ deDate ][ si ], dx         ; date created
        mov byte ptr es:[ deAttributes ][ si ], ATTR_DIRECTORY

        call CCBChanged                              ; mark changes made

;- - - - - - - - - - - - - - - - - - - - - - - - - - - - - - - -
;   in parent directory, build entry
;- - - - - - - - - - - - - - - - - - - - - - - - - - - - - - - -
        getarg dx, _alloccluster
        getdarg es, si, _dirAddress                  ; restore si pointer
        mov word ptr es:[ deStartCluster ][ si ], dx
        mov byte ptr es:[ deAttributes   ][ si ], ATTR_DIRECTORY

        getdarg dx, ax, _datetime                    ; get date time
        mov word ptr es:[ deTime ][ si ], ax         ; time created
        mov word ptr es:[ deDate ][ si ], dx         ; date created

        call locateCCBPHeader                        ; get ccb header into es:di
        call CCBChanged                              ; mark changes made

        xor ax, ax                                   ; clear carry

;- - - - - - - - - - - - - - - - - - - - - - - - - - - - - - - -
;   normal exit
;- - - - - - - - - - - - - - - - - - - - - - - - - - - - - - - -
_MakeSubDir_40:
        Return
```

Remove Directory

	On Entry	On Return
AX	AH = 3Ah	AX = error if carry
BX		
CX		
DX	pathname	
Flags		CY = set if error

Related Functions:
   39h Create Directory; 3Bh Change Directory; 47h Get Directory.

The function accepts the name of an existing directory. If the directory is located, it is checked to be sure that it is blank before the directory is removed from its parent. Otherwise, the function returns an error. The function cannot delete the current default directory.

The directory is searched on disk. Its cluster address is returned in the DX register if found. The cluster address cannot point to the root directory. It also cannot reference the current directory. The cluster address of the current directory is maintained in the CDS, or Current Directory Structure, and can be retrieved by an internal function, getCurrDirCluster. The function accepts the drive in the AX register, locates the CDS entry for that drive, and returns the cluster address from the CDS.

To determine if the directory found by the locate function is blank, it must be read. A disk access block is created to read the directory. The disk access block is used to read through any FAT-based file. The file offset is set past the . and .. entries. Each entry is read to be sure that it was either never used or deleted.

Finally, if the directory has passed these checks, it can be deleted. Deleting a directory is virtually like deleting a file. Its allocated cluster chain is released, and the directory entry for the subdirectory is marked as deleted. Both the directory entry and the released clusters may now be reused by other DOS functions.

```
(in rxdos.asm)
        ;,,,,,,,,,,,,,,,,,,,,,,,,,,,,,,,,,,,,,,,,,,,,,,,,,,,,,,,,,,,,,,;
        ;  3Ah Remove Subdirectory                                     ;
        ;- - - - - - - - - - - - - - - - - - - - - - - - - - - - - - -;
        ;                                                              ;
        ;  ds:dx pointer to subdirectory                               ;
        ;..............................................................;

_RemoveSubdirectory:
        Entry
        ddef _pathname, es, dx                       ; arg passed internally as es:dx
        defbytes _dirAccess, sizeDIRACCESS
        defbytes _diskAccess, sizeDISKACCESS
        defbytes _tempfilename, sizeTempFILENAME

        call CtrlC_Check
```

```
;- - - - - - - - - - - - - - - - - - - - - - - - - - - - - - -
;  parse file name
;- - - - - - - - - - - - - - - - - - - - - - - - - - - - - - -
        mov ax, (FILE_NODEVICENAME + FILEHAS_NOFILENAME)
        getdarg es, si, _pathname                   ; arg passed internally as es:dx
        lea di, offset _dirAccess [ bp ]            ; work dir access block
        call LocateFile                             ; check file path
        jc _RemoveSubDir_40                         ; if path invalid ->


;- - - - - - - - - - - - - - - - - - - - - - - - - - - - - - -
;  trying to remove current directory ?
;- - - - - - - - - - - - - - - - - - - - - - - - - - - - - - -
        or dx, dx                                   ; root directory ?
        jz _RemoveSubDir_08                         ; can't rd root ->
        mov cx, dx                                  ; save returned dir cluster
        call getCurrDirCluster                      ; get cluster of curr directory

        cmp cx, dx                                  ; same directory as current ?
        jnz _RemoveSubDir_12                        ; dir is ok ->

_RemoveSubDir_08:
        SetError errCurrentDirectory, _RemoveSubDir_40


;- - - - - - - - - - - - - - - - - - - - - - - - - - - - - - -
;  see if directory is empty (contains other than . and .. )
;- - - - - - - - - - - - - - - - - - - - - - - - - - - - - - -
_RemoveSubDir_12:
        setES ds
        mov ax, word ptr [ _dirAccess. fileAcDrive   ][ bp ]
        mov dx, word ptr [ _dirAccess. fileAcCluster ][ bp ]
        lea bx, offset _diskAccess [ bp ]           ; pointer to access block
        call initdiskAccess                         ; [ax] is drive, [dx] is cluster


;- - - - - - - - - - - - - - - - - - - - - - - - - - - - - - -
;  scan directory sectors
;- - - - - - - - - - - - - - - - - - - - - - - - - - - - - - -
        mov word ptr [ _diskAccess. diskAcOptions        ][ bp ], (ccb_isDIR)
        mov word ptr [ _diskAccess. diskAcPosition. _low ][ bp ], sizeDIRENTRY

_RemoveSubDir_22:
        add word ptr [ _diskAccess. diskAcPosition. _low  ][ bp ], sizeDIRENTRY
        adc word ptr [ _diskAccess. diskAcPosition. _high ][ bp ], 0000
        lea bx, offset _diskAccess [ bp ]           ; pointer to access block
        call _FATReadRandom                         ; read into buffer
        jz _RemoveSubDir_32                         ; if no more files ->

        cmp byte ptr es:[ bx ], DIRENTRY_NEVERUSED
        jz _RemoveSubDir_32                         ; if no more files ->
        cmp byte ptr es:[ bx ], DIRENTRY_DELETED; entry deleted ?
        jz _RemoveSubDir_22                         ; yes, keep searching ->

        SetError errIllegalName, _RemoveSubDir_40
```

```
;- - - - - - - - - - - - - - - - - - - - - - - - - - - - - - - - -
;  ok to remove this entry.
;- - - - - - - - - - - - - - - - - - - - - - - - - - - - - - - - -
_RemoveSubDir_32:
        mov ax, word ptr [ _dirAccess. fileAcDrive    ][ bp ]
        mov dx, word ptr [ _dirAccess. fileAcCluster ][ bp ]
        call ReleaseClusterChain

        les di, dword ptr [ _dirAccess. fileAcBufferPtr ][ bp ]
        mov bx, word ptr [ _dirAccess. fileAcDirOffset  ][ bp ]

        mov byte ptr es:[ di + bx ], DIRENTRY_DELETED
        call CCBChanged

        or ax, ax                                ; return no error

;- - - - - - - - - - - - - - - - - - - - - - - - - - - - - - - - -
;  normal exit
;- - - - - - - - - - - - - - - - - - - - - - - - - - - - - - - - -
_RemoveSubDir_40:
        Return
```

FCB File I/O

Some readers have an interest in FCBs, or File Control Blocks, mainly because their applications, now or in the past, depended on these structures. FCBs utilize SFTs, so most of the FCB code is basically a conversion between the parameters stored in the FCB and the requirements of the SFT functions. For example, the FCB record size field is used as the length parameter in _SFTReadFile, and the Disk Transfer Address is used as the read buffer pointer.

DOS plays a shell game with FCBs. The SFT assigned to an FCB may have been reassigned between any two successive file function calls. Within MS-DOS, the only cause of the FCB reassignment is another FCB-based function. Within RxDOS, it may be any file function. Neither is more prone to happen since FCB-based applications are more likely to continue using FCBs.

Because of the reassignment possibilities, FCB-based functions must ensure that the SFT they believe to be utilizing is still assigned to their FCB. Otherwise, a new SFT will have to be assigned and initialized before the FCB function can continue. These functions call FindMatchingFCBSFT to determine if the SFT is valid, and if not, to assign a valid SFT. This function, therefore, always works because at minimum one SFT is always available to FCBs.

An SFT belongs to the FCB if the drive and cluster addresses between the two structures match. If the SFT is redirected to a device, which may be the case if the FCB opened a file with a device name, such as LPT1, then the device handler addresses must match.

```
;///////////////////////////////////////////////////////////////;
;  Find Matching FCB SFT                                         ;
;- - - - - - - - - - - - - - - - - - - - - - - - - - - - - - - -;
;                                                                ;
;  Input:                                                        ;
;    es:di  FCB address                                          ;
```

```
        ;                                                        ;
        ;  Output:                                               ;
        ;   es:di  pointer to matching SFT entry                 ;
        ;.......................................................;

findmatchingFCBSFT:
        Entry
        ddef _fcbaddress, es, di                 ; fcb pointer
        ddef _sftPointer                         ; sft pointer
        def  _sftHandle                          ; sft handle

        xor ax, ax
        mov dx, word ptr es:[ fcbBegClusterNo ][ di ]
        mov al, byte ptr es:[ fcbSFN        ][ di ]

        call FindSFTbyHandle                     ; locate matching SFT
        jc findmatchingFCBSFT_08                 ; if cannot locate SFT ->

        cmp dx, word ptr es:[ sftBegCluster ][ di ]
        ifz findmatchingFCBSFT_26                ; if entry matches ->

;- - - - - - - - - - - - - - - - - - - - - - - - - - - - - -
;  if not found, try to allocate new SFT
;- - - - - - - - - - - - - - - - - - - - - - - - - - - - - -
findmatchingFCBSFT_08:
        call FindAvailableSFTHandle
        ifc findmatchingFCBSFT_26                ; if can find an entry ->

        storarg  _sftHandle, ax                  ; sft handle
        stordarg _sftPointer, es, bx             ; sft pointer

        push ds

    ; clear SFT

        xor ax, ax
        mov di, bx                               ; pointer to SFT
        add di, 2                                ; skip Count entry
        mov cx, (sizeSFT - sftRefCount - 2)/ 2   ; effective count
        rep stosw                                ; must have pointer at es: di

        getdarg ds, si, _fcbAddress              ; fcb address
        getdarg es, di, _sftPointer              ; sft pointer
        or word ptr es:[ sftMode ][ di ], sftENTRY_ISFCB

    ; set owner PSP

        mov ax, word ptr cs:[ _RxDOS_CurrentPSP ]   ; get owner PSP
        mov word ptr es:[ sftOwnerPSP ][ di ], ax

    ; set drive

        mov cl, byte ptr [ fcbDrive ][ si ]      ; get drive
        and cx, sftDrivemask
```

```
        mov word ptr es:[ sftDevInfo ][ di ], cx        ; include drive

        push word ptr [ fcbTime ][ si ]                 ; time last updated
        push word ptr [ fcbDate ][ si ]                 ; date last updated
        push word ptr [ fcbBegClusterNo ][ si ]         ; beginning cluster
        push word ptr [ fcbFileSize. _low ][ si ]       ; file size
        push word ptr [ fcbFileSize. _high ][ si ]      ; file size
        push word ptr [ fcbDHD. _pointer ][ si ]        ; device header
        push word ptr [ fcbDHD. _segment ][ si ]        ;

        push word ptr es:[ sftDCB. _segment ][ di ]
        push word ptr es:[ sftDCB. _pointer ][ di ]
        pop word ptr es:[ sftFileSize. _high ][ di ]
        pop word ptr es:[ sftFileSize. _low ][ di ]
        pop word ptr es:[ sftBegCluster ][ di ]
        pop word ptr es:[ sftDate ][ di ]
        pop word ptr es:[ sftTime ][ di ]

        lea di, offset sftFileName [ di ]               ; offset to filename
        lea si, offset fcbName [ si ]                   ; offset to filename
        mov cx, sizeFILENAME                            ; length of name/ ext
        rep movsb                                       ; copy name

        pop ds

        getdarg es, di, _fcbAddress                     ; fcb address
        getarg  ax, _sftHandle                          ; sft handle
        mov byte ptr es:[ fcbSFN ][ di ], al

        getdarg es, di, _sftPointer                     ; sft pointer
        clc

;- - - - - - - - - - - - - - - - - - - - - - - - - - - - - - - - - -
; return
;- - - - - - - - - - - - - - - - - - - - - - - - - - - - - - - - - -
findmatchingFCBSFT_26:
        Return
```

Other points of general interest are getting and setting the Disk Transfer Address. Surprising to me is the fact that the DTA address is systemwide. Once one program changes it, it remains changed for all currently running programs. One side effect of this occurs when a program spawns a child program. The launching process changes the DTA automatically but fails to reset it when the child program terminates. The DTA address should be handled defensively. When in doubt, set it.

After a brief look at the DTA get and set functions, we examine each FCB function in greater detail. For FCB-based functions, the real issues are not how to open and create a file, which in themselves are straightforward enough, but how to handle read and write using its record-oriented architecture and what actually happens to recover the SFT when it has been discarded.

Getting/Setting the Disk Transfer Address

	On Entry	On Return
AX	AH = 1Ah	
BX		
CX		
DS:DX	new DTA address	
Flags		

Related Functions:
    14h/15h FCB Read/Write File; 21h/22h FCB Read/Write Random;
    27h/28h FCB Read/Write Block; 2Fh Get Disk Transfer Address.

The Disk Transfer Address is a location remembered by DOS used to transfer the contents of FCB read and write functions. It is also used by file handle Find First and Find Next functions. As shown, there is virtually nothing to the code. The values passed at call time are stored internally within DOS. The value can be retrieved by DOS function 2Fh, whose listing follows.

    Every programmer who's done at least some DOS function call work knows that the DTA address is passed in the DS:DX register pair. However, an internal RxDOS convention copies the caller's DS to the ES register and loads the DS register with the value of the RxDOS data segment. That is why this code saves the value of the ES register.

```
;''''''''''''''''''''''''''''''''''''''''''''''''''''''''''''''''';
;                                                                 ;
;   1Ah Set Disk Transfer Address                                 ;
;- - - - - - - - - - - - - - - - - - - - - - - - - - - - - - - - -;
;                                                                 ;
;   ds:dx    Disk Transfer Address                                ;
;                                                                 ;
;   (see related function 2F - Get Disk Transfer Address)         ;
;.................................................................;

_SetDiskTransferAddress:
        mov     word ptr [ _RxDOS_pDTA. _pointer ], dx
        mov     word ptr [ _RxDOS_pDTA. _segment ], es
        ret
```

	On Entry	On Return
AX	AH = 2Fh	
BX		
CX		
ES:BX		DTA address
Flags		

Related Functions:
    14h/15h FCB Read/Write File; 21h/22h FCB Read/Write Random;
    27h/28h FCB Read/Write Block; 1Ah Set Disk Transfer Address.

If the code for saving the DTA address was small, the code for returning the DTA address to the caller is only slightly larger because the address of the caller's register stack has to be fetched first. The function simply consists of

```
;,,,,,,,,,,,,,,,,,,,,,,,,,,,,,,,,,,,,,,,,,,,,,,,,,,,,,,,,,,,,,,';
;  2Fh Get Disk Transfer Address                               ;
;- - - - - - - - - - - - - - - - - - - - - - - - - - - - - - -;
;                                                              ;
;  Returns:                                                    ;
;    es:bx  Disk Transfer Address                              ;
;                                                              ;
;  (see related function 1A - Set Disk Transfer Address)       ;
;..............................................................;

_GetDiskTransferAddress:
        les bx, dword ptr [ _RxDOS_pDTA. _pointer ]

        RetCallersStackFrame ds, si
        mov word ptr [ _ExtraSegment ][ si ], es
        mov word ptr [ _BX           ][ si ], bx
        ret
```

FCB File Open

	On Entry	On Return
AX	AH = 0Fh	AL = 00, if success, else error code
BX		
CX		
DS:DX	FCB address	
Flags		

Related Functions:
  16h FCB File Create; 10h FCB File Close;
  3Ch Create File; 3Dh Open File; 3Eh Close File.

FCB open utilizes the file handle open function, _SFTOpenFile. The FCB is then initialized from the assigned SFT. The name passed in the FCB is converted to an ASCIZ string. The drive letter, if used, is followed by the name and extension. This name is then passed to the SFT open function. FCBs can take full advantage of the SFT services. An FCB can be redirected to a device by opening or creating a file with a character device name, such as CON, PRN, or LPT1. Characters written to the FCBs will be redirected to the corresponding output devices.

When the file is open, the assigned SFT address is returned to the FCB open function. It converts any errors it discovers to an FCB style error. The FCB is initialized by the contents of the SFT, and a linkage is established between the two data structures. The SFT handle is recorded into the FCB, as is the file's drive, the beginning cluster address, and character device handler, if appropriate.

FCB errors don't rely on the carry flag and error code combination utilized by file handle functions. Instead, an FFh is returned in the AL register if an error occurred. This applies to all functions that DOS carried over from CP/M. In the file open FCB code, the SFT error code is converted from the SFT convention.

Overall, the FCB open function is extremely straightforward.

```
(in rxdos.asm)
        ;'''''''''''''''''''''''''''''''''''''''''''''''''''''''''''';
        ;   0Fh Open File with FCB                                   ;
        ;- - - - - - - - - - - - - - - - - - - - - - - - - - - - - -;
        ;                                                           ;
        ;   ds:dx pointer to FCB                                    ;
        ;                                                           ;
        ;   Return:                                                 ;
        ;     al = ff, if cannot locate any matching entry          ;
        ;          00, if match located                             ;
        ;...........................................................;

_OpenFileFCB:
        Entry
        def   _openMode
        ddef  _fcbPointer, es, dx
        defbytes _expandedName, 128            ; expanded file name (128 bytes)

        call  CtrlC_Check
;- - - - - - - - - - - - - - - - - - - - - - - - - - - - - - - - -
;  convert FCB name to name usable by SFT Open
;- - - - - - - - - - - - - - - - - - - - - - - - - - - - - - - - -
        mov   si, dx                          ; source FCB address
        lea   di, offset _expandedName [ bp ] ; expand name
        call  convFCBNametoASCIZ              ; build asciz name


;- - - - - - - - - - - - - - - - - - - - - - - - - - - - - - - - -
;  try SFT Open
;- - - - - - - - - - - - - - - - - - - - - - - - - - - - - - - - -
        setES ss                              ; es:
        lea   dx, offset _expandedName [ bp ] ; es: dx filename
        mov   al, DEFAULT_FCBOPENMODE         ; mode is default open mode
        call  _SFTOpenFile                    ; build an SFT
        jc    _OpenFileFCB_26                 ; if error ->

        getdarg ds, si, _fcbPointer           ; fcb address
        call  initFCBfromSFT                  ; [ax] handle, [es:di] ptr to sft
        or    ax, ax

;- - - - - - - - - - - - - - - - - - - - - - - - - - - - - - - - -
;  return
;- - - - - - - - - - - - - - - - - - - - - - - - - - - - - - - - -
_OpenFileFCB_26:
        call  setFCBErrorIfCarry
        Return

(in rxdosfcb.asm)
```

```
        ;'''''''''''''''''''''''''''''''''''''''''''''''''''''''''';
        ;  Init FCB from an opened SFT                              ;
        ;- - - - - - - - - - - - - - - - - - - - - - - - - - - - - -;
        ;                                                           ;
        ;  Usage:                                                   ;
        ;   ds:si  fcb pointer                                      ;
        ;   es:di  sft pointer                                      ;
        ;   ax     handle assigned                                 ;
        ;...........................................................;

initFCBfromSFT:
        mov byte ptr [ fcbSFN          ][ si ], al
        mov word ptr [ fcbRecordSize   ][ si ], 128

        xor dx, dx
        mov word ptr [ fcbRandomRecNo. _low  ][ si ], dx
        mov word ptr [ fcbRandomRecNo. _high ][ si ], dx
        mov word ptr [ fcbCurrBlockNo     ][ si ], dx
        mov word ptr [ fcbCurrRecNo       ][ si ], dx
        mov byte ptr [ fcbFlags           ][ si ], dl

        mov dx, word ptr es:[ sftFileSize. _high ][ di ]
        mov ax, word ptr es:[ sftFileSize. _low  ][ di ]
        mov word ptr [ fcbFileSize. _high ][ si ], dx
        mov word ptr [ fcbFileSize. _low  ][ si ], ax

        mov dx, word ptr es:[ sftDate ][ di ]
        mov ax, word ptr es:[ sftTime ][ di ]
        mov word ptr [ fcbDate ][ si ], dx
        mov word ptr [ fcbTime ][ si ], ax

        mov dx, word ptr es:[ sftDCB. _high ][ di ]
        mov ax, word ptr es:[ sftDCB. _low  ][ di ]
        mov word ptr [ fcbDHD. _high ][ si ], dx
        mov word ptr [ fcbDHD. _low  ][ si ], ax

        mov ax, word ptr es:[ sftBegCluster ][ di ]
        mov word ptr [ fcbBegClusterNo ][ si ], ax
        or word ptr es:[ sftMode ][ di ], sftENTRY_ISFCB
        ret

(in rxdos.asm)
        ;'''''''''''''''''''''''''''''''''''''''''''''''''''''''''';
        ;  Set FCB Error if Carry                                  ;
        ;- - - - - - - - - - - - - - - - - - - - - - - - - - - - - -;
        ;                                                          ;
        ;   if carry, set AL to -1, else set AL to 0.             ;
        ;..........................................................;

setFCBErrorIfCarry:
        pushf
        push es
        push bx
        mov al, 0
```

```
        jnc setFCBErrorIfCarry_08

        mov al, -1

setFCBErrorIfCarry_08:
        RetCallersStackFrame es, bx
        mov byte ptr es:[ _AX._AL ][ bx ], al          ; set/clear error.
        pop bx
        pop es
        popf
        ret
```

FCB File Create

	On Entry	On Return
AX	AH = 16h	AL = 00, if success, else error code
BX		
CX		
DS:DX	FCB address	
Flags		

Related Functions:
  0Fh FCB File Create; 10h FCB File Close;
  3Ch Create File; 3Dh Open File; 3Eh Close File.

FCB file create is virtually identical to the FCB file open in concept. It relies on the SFT create function. The filename passed in the FCB for create is first converted to an ASCIZ string, and like the open function, the name can reference a character device to establish redirection. FCB create has only a single option when it encounters an existing file by the same name. The file is truncated to zero, unlike some file handle create functions where options determine the action taken.

```
(in rxdos.asm)
        ;''''''''''''''''''''''''''''''''''''''''''''''''''''''''''''''';
        ;  16h Create File with FCB                                     ;
        ;- - - - - - - - - - - - - - - - - - - - - - - - - - - - - - -;
        ;                                                              ;
        ;  ds:dx pointer to FCB                                        ;
        ;                                                              ;
        ;  Return:                                                     ;
        ;    al = ff, if cannot locate any matching entry              ;
        ;         00, if match located                                 ;
        ;..............................................................;

_CreateFileFCB:
        Entry
        ddef _fcbPointer, es, dx
        defbytes _expandedName, 128               ; expanded file name (128 bytes)
```

```
        call CtrlC_Check
;- - - - - - - - - - - - - - - - - - - - - - - - - - - - - - - - -
;  convert FCB name to name usable by SFT Open
;- - - - - - - - - - - - - - - - - - - - - - - - - - - - - - - - -
        mov si, dx                              ; source FCB address
        lea di, offset _expandedName [ bp ]     ; expand name
        call convFCBNametoASCIZ                 ; build asciz name


;- - - - - - - - - - - - - - - - - - - - - - - - - - - - - - - - -
;  try SFT Open
;- - - - - - - - - - - - - - - - - - - - - - - - - - - - - - - - -
        setES ss                                ; es:
        lea dx, offset _expandedName [ bp ]     ; es: dx filename
        mov al, DEFAULT_FCBOPENMODE             ; mode is default open mode
        xor cx, cx                              ; expected attributes
        call _SFTCreateFile                     ; build an SFT
        jc _CreateFileFCB_26                    ; if error -->

        getdarg ds, si, _fcbPointer             ; fcb address
        call initFCBfromSFT                     ; [ax] handle, [es:di] ptr to sft
        or ax, ax


;- - - - - - - - - - - - - - - - - - - - - - - - - - - - - - - - -
;  return
;- - - - - - - - - - - - - - - - - - - - - - - - - - - - - - - - -
_CreateFileFCB_26:
        call setFCBErrorIfCarry
        Return
```

FCB File Read Functions

	On Entry	**On Return**
AX	AH = 14h; 21h; or 27h	AL =0 if ok; 01 if eof; 02 DTA seg
BX		
CX		
DS:DX	pointer to FCB	
Flags		

Related Functions:
    0Fh FCB File Create; 10h FCB File Close; 15h FCB File Write Sequential;
    3Ch Create File; 3Dh Open File; 3Eh Close File; 40h Write File.

There are three FCB read functions, file functions 14h, 21h, and 27h. Except for minor variations in the services they provide, the code for these functions is similar enough to be discussed in a single section. FCB functions address records on disk rather than bytes. This forces reads to be performed in blocks, which tends to be somewhat inconvenient. Positioning within the file is a factor of the record size, and the record size could be set to a single byte, thus providing a direct byte positioning capability to these functions.

The difference between the three functions is as follows: FCB Read Sequential, DOS function 14h, uses an addressing scheme carried over from CP/M, where the record number is always module 128, and any overflow is carried over to a block number field. This addressing scheme may have been designed to prevent some problem associated with the carry bit, since CP/M was designed to operate on an 8-bit machine. A maximum of 32,767 records could be addressed.

FCB Read File and FCB Read Random, DOS functions 21h and 27h, use an extended 32-bit record address scheme, although after each operation, the record and block numbers used in the original addressing scheme are set from the extended address. DOS function 27h reads multiple blocks or records to memory.

All three functions utilize the lower level file handle functions to perform the read. Their record positions and record size are converted to a byte position. The SFT assigned to the FCB is checked to be sure that it has not been allocated to a file handle request. Otherwise a new SFT is allocated from either an available SFT or from another FCB allocated SFT.

Once the SFT read is performed, the record number is incremented by the number of records read, usually 1.

```
;'''''''''''''''''''''''''''''''''''''''''''''''''''''''''''''';
;   14h Read Sequential/ FCB                                    ;
;- - - - - - - - - - - - - - - - - - - - - - - - - - - - - - - -;
;                                                               ;
;   ds:dx pointer to FCB                                        ;
;                                                               ;
;   Return:                                                     ;
;     al = ff, if cannot locate any matching entry              ;
;          00, if match located                                 ;
;...............................................................;

_SeqReadFileFCB:
        Entry
        def _readCount
        ddef _position
        ddef _fcbPointer, es, dx

        call CtrlC_Check
;- - - - - - - - - - - - - - - - - - - - - - - - - - - - - - - -
;   ok to read if valid fcb
;- - - - - - - - - - - - - - - - - - - - - - - - - - - - - - - -
        mov di, dx
        mov cx, word ptr es:[ fcbRecordSize ][ di ]
        mov word ptr [ _readCount ][ bp ], cx        ; bytes to read to dta
        or cx, cx
        stc
        jz _SeqReadFileFCB_Return


;- - - - - - - - - - - - - - - - - - - - - - - - - - - - - - - -
;   compute byte offset from block/rec nos
;- - - - - - - - - - - - - - - - - - - - - - - - - - - - - - - -
        mov ax, 128
        mul word ptr es:[ fcbCurrBlockNo ][ di ]      ; block # times 128
```

```
        add al, byte ptr es:[ fcbCurrRecNo    ][ di ]      ; full 23-bit address
        mul cx                                             ; actual byte offset
        stordarg _position, dx, ax

;- - - - - - - - - - - - - - - - - - - - - - - - - - - - - - -
;  find corresponding sft
;- - - - - - - - - - - - - - - - - - - - - - - - - - - - - - -
        call findmatchingFCBSFT                            ; find matching SFT
        jc _SeqReadFileFCB_Return                          ; if no space ->

;- - - - - - - - - - - - - - - - - - - - - - - - - - - - - - -
;  init disk access block
;- - - - - - - - - - - - - - - - - - - - - - - - - - - - - - -
        getdarg cx, dx, _position                          ; restor position
        mov word ptr es:[ sftFilePosition. _low  ][ di ], dx
        mov word ptr es:[ sftFilePosition. _high ][ di ], cx
        mov ax, -1                                          ; ! stdin

        mov cx, word ptr [ _readCount ][ bp ]               ; bytes to read to dta
        push word ptr [ _RxDOS_pDTA. _segment ]             ; disk transfer address
        push word ptr [ _RxDOS_pDTA. _pointer ]
        call _SFTReadFile                                   ; read using sft (at es:di )

;- - - - - - - - - - - - - - - - - - - - - - - - - - - - - - -
;  compute return logical position
;- - - - - - - - - - - - - - - - - - - - - - - - - - - - - - -
        getdarg es, di, _fcbPointer
        getdarg dx, ax, _position
        add ax, word ptr es:[ fcbRecordSize  ][ di ]
        adc dx, 0000
        div word ptr es:[ fcbRecordSize  ][ di ]           ; actual byte offset

        xor dx, dx
        mov cx, 128
        div cx
        mov byte ptr es:[ fcbCurrRecNo    ][ di ], dl
        mov word ptr es:[ fcbCurrBlockNo ][ di ], ax
        or ax, ax


;- - - - - - - - - - - - - - - - - - - - - - - - - - - - - - -
;  return
;- - - - - - - - - - - - - - - - - - - - - - - - - - - - - - -
_SeqReadFileFCB_Return:
        call setFCBErrorIfCarry
        Return

        ;,,,,,,,,,,,,,,,,,,,,,,,,,,,,,,,,,,,,,,,,,,,,,,,,,,,,,,,,,,,,;
        ;  21h Read Sequential/ FCB                                 ;
        ;- - - - - - - - - - - - - - - - - - - - - - - - - - - - - -;
        ;                                                           ;
        ;  ds:dx pointer to FCB                                     ;
        ;                                                           ;
        ;  Return:                                                  ;
        ;   al = ff, if cannot locate any matching entry            ;
        ;        · 00, if match located                             ;
        ;...........................................................;
```

```
_ReadFileFCB:
        Entry
        def  _readCount
        ddef _position
        ddef _fcbPointer, es, dx

        call CtrlC_Check
;- - - - - - - - - - - - - - - - - - - - - - - - - - - - - - - - - - -
;  ok to read if valid fcb
;- - - - - - - - - - - - - - - - - - - - - - - - - - - - - - - - - - -
        mov di, dx
        mov cx, word ptr es:[ fcbRecordSize ][ di ]
        mov word ptr [ _readCount ][ bp ], cx          ; bytes to read to dta
        or cx, cx
        stc
        jz _ReadFileFCB_Return

;- - - - - - - - - - - - - - - - - - - - - - - - - - - - - - - - - - -
;  compute byte offset from block/rec nos
;- - - - - - - - - - - - - - - - - - - - - - - - - - - - - - - - - - -
        mov ax, word ptr es:[ fcbRandomRecNo. _low  ][ di ]
        mov dx, word ptr es:[ fcbRandomRecNo. _high ][ di ]
        mov cx, word ptr es:[ fcbRecordSize ][ di ]
        call _mul32
        stordarg _position, dx, ax

;- - - - - - - - - - - - - - - - - - - - - - - - - - - - - - - - - - -
;  find corresponding sft
;- - - - - - - - - - - - - - - - - - - - - - - - - - - - - - - - - - -
        call findmatchingFCBSFT                     ; find matching SFT
        jc _ReadFileFCB_Return                       ; if no space ->

;- - - - - - - - - - - - - - - - - - - - - - - - - - - - - - - - - - -
;  init disk access block
;- - - - - - - - - - - - - - - - - - - - - - - - - - - - - - - - - - -
        getdarg cx, dx, _position                   ; restore position
        mov word ptr es:[ sftFilePosition. _low  ][ di ], dx
        mov word ptr es:[ sftFilePosition. _high ][ di ], cx
        mov ax, -1                                  ; ! stdin

        mov cx, word ptr [ _readCount ][ bp ]       ; bytes to read to dta
        push word ptr [ _RxDOS_pDTA. _segment ]     ; disk transfer address
        push word ptr [ _RxDOS_pDTA. _pointer ]
        call _SFTReadFile                           ; read using sft (at es:di )

;- - - - - - - - - - - - - - - - - - - - - - - - - - - - - - - - - - -
;  compute return logical position
;- - - - - - - - - - - - - - - - - - - - - - - - - - - - - - - - - - -
        getdarg es, di, _fcbPointer          .
        mov ax, word ptr es:[ fcbRandomRecNo. _low  ][ di ]
        mov dx, word ptr es:[ fcbRandomRecNo. _high ][ di ]
        mov cx, 128
        call _div32
        mov word ptr es:[ fcbCurrBlockNo ][ di ], ax
```

```
        mov dl, byte ptr es:[ fcbRandomRecNo. _low  ][ di ]
        and dl, 127
        mov byte ptr es:[ fcbCurrRecNo    ][ di ], dl
```

```
;- - - - - - - - - - - - - - - - - - - - - - - - - - - - - - -
;  return
;- - - - - - - - - - - - - - - - - - - - - - - - - - - - - - -
_ReadFileFCB_Return:
        call setFCBErrorIfCarry
        Return
```

```
        ;,,,,,,,,,,,,,,,,,,,,,,,,,,,,,,,,,,,,,,,,,,,,,,,,,,,,,,,,,,,,,,;
        ;  27h Random Read / FCB                                      ;
        ;- - - - - - - - - - - - - - - - - - - - - - - - - - - - - -;
        ;                                                            ;
        ;  cx       number of blocks to read                         ;
        ;  ds:dx    pointer to FCB                                    ;
        ;                                                            ;
        ;  Return:                                                   ;
        ;    al = ff, if cannot locate any matching entry            ;
        ;          00, if match located                              ;
        ;..........................................................;
```

```
_RandomBlockReadFCB:
        Entry
        def  _error, 0000
        def  _readCount
        def  _numBlocks, cx
        ddef _position
        ddef _fcbPointer, es, dx
```

```
        call CtrlC_Check
;- - - - - - - - - - - - - - - - - - - - - - - - - - - - - - -
;  ok to read if valid fcb
;- - - - - - - - - - - - - - - - - - - - - - - - - - - - - - -
        mov di, dx
        mov cx, word ptr es:[ fcbRecordSize ][ di ]
        mov word ptr [ _readCount ][ bp ], cx          ; bytes to read to dta
        or cx, cx
        stc
        jz _ReadBlockFCB_Return
```

```
;- - - - - - - - - - - - - - - - - - - - - - - - - - - - - - -
;  compute byte offset from block/rec nos
;- - - - - - - - - - - - - - - - - - - - - - - - - - - - - - -
        mov ax, word ptr es:[ fcbRandomRecNo. _low  ][ di ]
        mov dx, word ptr es:[ fcbRandomRecNo. _high ][ di ]
        mov cx, word ptr es:[ fcbRecordSize ][ di ]
        call _mul32
        stordarg _position, dx, ax
```

```
;- - - - - - - - - - - - - - - - - - - - - - - - - - - - - - -
;  find corresponding sft
;- - - - - - - - - - - - - - - - - - - - - - - - - - - - - - -
```

```
        call findmatchingFCBSFT                         ; find matching SFT
        jc _ReadBlockFCB_Return                          ; if no space -->

;- - - - - - - - - - - - - - - - - - - - - - - - - - - - - - - - - - - -
;  init disk access block
;- - - - - - - - - - - - - - - - - - - - - - - - - - - - - - - - - - - -
        getdarg cx, dx, _position                       ; restor position
        mov word ptr es:[ sftFilePosition. _low  ][ di ], dx
        mov word ptr es:[ sftFilePosition. _high ][ di ], cx

        mov ax, word ptr [ _numBlocks ][ bp ]           ; number of blocks
        mul word ptr [ _readCount ][ bp ]               ; bytes to read to dta
        mov cx, ax                                      ; total bytes to read
        or dx, dx                                       ; over 64k ?
        jz _ReadBlockFCB_12                             ; if ok -->
        mov word ptr [ _error ][ bp ], errFCBSizeTooLarge ; too large
        mov cx, 0FFFFh                                   ; read as much as possible

_ReadBlockFCB_12:
        mov ax, -1                                      ; ! stdin
        push word ptr [ _RxDOS_pDTA. _segment ]         ; disk transfer address
        push word ptr [ _RxDOS_pDTA. _pointer ]
        call _SFTReadFile                               ; read using sft (at es:di )

;- - - - - - - - - - - - - - - - - - - - - - - - - - - - - - - - - - - -
;  compute return logical position
;- - - - - - - - - - - - - - - - - - - - - - - - - - - - - - - - - - - -
        getdarg es, di, _fcbPointer
        getdarg dx, ax, _position
        add ax, word ptr es:[ fcbRecordSize  ][ di ]
        adc dx, 0000
        div word ptr es:[ fcbRecordSize  ][ di ]        ; actual byte offset

        xor dx, dx
        mov cx, 128
        div cx
        mov byte ptr es:[ fcbCurrRecNo   ][ di ], dl
        mov word ptr es:[ fcbCurrBlockNo ][ di ], ax

        mov ax, word ptr [ _numBlocks ][ bp ]           ; number of blocks
        add word ptr es:[ fcbRandomRecNo. _low  ][ di ], ax
        adc word ptr es:[ fcbRandomRecNo. _high ][ di ], 0000

;- - - - - - - - - - - - - - - - - - - - - - - - - - - - - - - - - - - -
;  return
;- - - - - - - - - - - - - - - - - - - - - - - - - - - - - - - - - - - -
_ReadBlockFCB_Return:
        call setFCBErrorIfCarry
        Return
```

FCB File Write Sequential

	On Entry	On Return
AX	AH = 15h	AL = error code
BX		
CX		
DS:DX	pointer to FCB	
Flags		

Related Functions:
16h FCB Create File; 0Fh FCB Open File; 10h FCB Close File; 14h FCB Read File;
21h FCB Read Random; 22h FCB Write Random; 27h FCB Read Block; 28h FCB Write Block.

FCB file writes expect an opened FCB in the DS:DX register. The record number to write is set within the FCB as either a block/record combination or a record number. The differences between the method used to set the next record to read depend on the function. The two different methods exist because of historical reasons.

Regardless of the FCB write function, the strategy is essentially the same. The SFT assigned to the FCB must be located. If it cannot be located, a new FCB must be assigned. The read/write buffer pointer is the DTA (Disk Transfer Address), set by DOS function 1Ah. The write byte count is the record size. The file position address for the write should be a byte offset, but in an FCB, it is expressed as a record number.

For DOS function 15h, FCB Write Sequential, the record number is expressed as the older block/record addressing style. The file position is computed by first determining the actual record number. The record number is the block number times 128 plus the record number in the current block. This becomes the actual record number, which is identical to the record number provided by the other two FCB write functions. The file position as a byte offset is the actual record number multiplied by the record size.

The FCB code for all three FCB write functions follows. The actual write is handled by _SFTWriteFile, which we discuss further later.

DOS function 15h, FCB Write Sequential, begins by performing a control break test. The FCB address is passed to the DI register, and the record size is checked to be sure that it isn't zero. A zero record size forces an error exit in the file. This is a prevention against accidentally truncating the file. The actual file position for this function is computed by taking the record size times the record number. So long as the record size is zero, the file will be completely truncated no matter what the value of the record number. Since no position can be set, there should not be an inadvertent way in which to completely delete the file's contents.

Next, the old-style block/record number is converted to file read/write position. The number of blocks times 128 plus the record number gives the actual record number. This is multiplied by the nonzero record size to provide a 32-bit byte address within the file.

DOS function 15h continues by locating the FCB's assigned SFT. The SFT can be verified as assigned to the FCB if its drive/begin cluster addresses match the addresses in the FCB since these two variables ensure a unique DOS file. If the SFT is assigned to a device, the device driver's header address must match. This is all handled by findMatchingFCBSFT, which if it cannot locate the assigned SFT, will appropriate and initialize another SFT. In either case, a valid SFT address is returned.

The write request file position is set in the SFT, and the _SFTWriteFile function is called. The record size is passed as the write buffer size.

When the write completes, the terminating block/record offset is incremented. The record offset is incremented first. If it then exceeds 128, the block count is incremented, and the record number is recycled back to zero. The function then sets the error flag and exits.

```
;'''''''''''''''''''''''''''''''''''''''''''''''''''''''''''';
;   15h Write Sequential/ FCB                                 ;
;- - - - - - - - - - - - - - - - - - - - - - - - - - - - - -;
;                                                             ;
;   ds:dx pointer to FCB                                      ;
;                                                             ;
;   Return:                                                   ;
;     al = ff, if cannot locate any matching entry            ;
;          00, if match located                               ;
;.............................................................;

_SeqWriteFileFCB:
        Entry
        def _writeCount
        ddef _position
        ddef _fcbPointer, es, dx

        call CtrlC_Check
;- - - - - - - - - - - - - - - - - - - - - - - - - - - - - - -
;   ok to write if valid fcb
;- - - - - - - - - - - - - - - - - - - - - - - - - - - - - - -
        mov di, dx
        mov cx, word ptr es:[ fcbRecordSize ][ di ]
        mov word ptr [ _writeCount ][ bp ], cx     ; bytes to write from dta
        or cx, cx                                   ; if bytes are zero
        stc
        jz _SeqWriteFileFCB_Return


;- - - - - - - - - - - - - - - - - - - - - - - - - - - - - - -
;   compute byte offset from block/rec nos
;- - - - - - - - - - - - - - - - - - - - - - - - - - - - - - -
        mov ax, 128
        mul word ptr es:[ fcbCurrBlockNo ][ di ]    ; block # times 128
        add al, byte ptr es:[ fcbCurrRecNo ][ di ]  ; full 23-bit address
        mul cx                                      ; actual byte offset
        stordarg _position, dx, ax


;- - - - - - - - - - - - - - - - - - - - - - - - - - - - - - -
;   find corresponding sft
;- - - - - - - - - - - - - - - - - - - - - - - - - - - - - - -
        call findmatchingFCBSFT                      ; find matching SFT
        jc _SeqWriteFileFCB_Return                    ; if no space ->
```

```
;- - - - - - - - - - - - - - - - - - - - - - - - - - - - - - - - -
;   init disk access block
;- - - - - - - - - - - - - - - - - - - - - - - - - - - - - - - - -
        getdarg cx, dx, _position                   ; restore position
        mov word ptr es:[ sftFilePosition. _low  ][ di ], dx
        mov word ptr es:[ sftFilePosition. _high ][ di ], cx

        getarg cx, _writeCount                       ; bytes to write to dta
        push word ptr [ _RxDOS_pDTA. _segment ]      ; disk transfer address
        push word ptr [ _RxDOS_pDTA. _pointer ]
        call _SFTWriteFile                           ; write using sft (at es:di )

;- - - - - - - - - - - - - - - - - - - - - - - - - - - - - - - - -
;   compute return logical position
;- - - - - - - - - - - - - - - - - - - - - - - - - - - - - - - - -
        getdarg es, di, _fcbPointer
        inc byte ptr es:[ fcbCurrRecNo   ][ di ]
        test byte ptr es:[ fcbCurrRecNo  ][ di ], 128
        jz _SeqWriteFileFCB_22
        inc word ptr es:[ fcbCurrBlockNo ][ di ]

_SeqWriteFileFCB_22:
        and byte ptr es:[ fcbCurrRecNo   ][ di ], 127

;- - - - - - - - - - - - - - - - - - - - - - - - - - - - - - - - -
;   return
;- - - - - - - - - - - - - - - - - - - - - - - - - - - - - - - - -
_SeqWriteFileFCB_Return:
        call setFCBErrorIfCarry
        Return
```

FCB File Write Random

	On Entry	On Return
AX	AH = 22h	AL = error code
BX		
CX		
DS:DX	pointer to FCB	
Flags		

Related Functions:
    16h FCB Create File; 0Fh FCB Open File; 10h FCB Close File; 14h FCB Read File;
    15h FCB Write File; 21h FCB Read Random; 27h FCB Read Block; 28h FCB Write Block.

DOS function 22h, FCB Write Random, shares much in common with the FCB Write Sequential, with some differences. The record number addressing uses the random record number field in the FCB instead of the older block/record style. The random record number is multiplied by the record size to produce a 32-bit file offset, which is used as the write position. To maintain consistency within the FCB, the random record number is converted back to block/record numbers. The remainder of the function calls _SFTWriteFile to write the buffer.

```
;''''''''''''''''''''''''''''''''''''''''''''''''''''''''''''';
;  22h Write Sequential/ FCB                                   ;
;- - - - - - - - - - - - - - - - - - - - - - - - - - - - - - -;
;                                                              ;
;  ds:dx pointer to FCB                                        ;
;                                                              ;
;  Return:                                                     ;
;   al = ff, if cannot locate any matching entry               ;
;        00, if match located                                  ;
;..............................................................;

_WriteFileFCB:
        Entry
        def _writeCount
        ddef _position
        ddef _fcbPointer, es, dx

        call CtrlC_Check
;- - - - - - - - - - - - - - - - - - - - - - - - - - - - - - - -
;  ok to Write if valid fcb
;- - - - - - - - - - - - - - - - - - - - - - - - - - - - - - - -
        mov di, dx
        mov cx, word ptr es:[ fcbRecordSize ][ di ]
        mov word ptr [ _writeCount ][ bp ], cx           ; bytes to write to dta
        or cx, cx
        stc
        jz _WriteFileFCB_Return


;- - - - - - - - - - - - - - - - - - - - - - - - - - - - - - - -
;  compute byte offset from block/rec nos
;- - - - - - - - - - - - - - - - - - - - - - - - - - - - - - - -
        mov ax, word ptr es:[ fcbRandomRecNo. _low  ][ di ]
        mov dx, word ptr es:[ fcbRandomRecNo. _high ][ di ]
        mov cx, word ptr es:[ fcbRecordSize  ][ di ]
        call _mul32
        stordarg _position, dx, ax


;- - - - - - - - - - - - - - - - - - - - - - - - - - - - - - - -
;  compute block/ sector
;- - - - - - - - - - - - - - - - - - - - - - - - - - - - - - - -
        mov ax, word ptr es:[ fcbRandomRecNo. _low  ][ di ]
        mov dx, word ptr es:[ fcbRandomRecNo. _high ][ di ]
        mov cx, 128
        call _div32
        mov word ptr es:[ fcbCurrBlockNo ][ di ], ax

        mov dl, byte ptr es:[ fcbRandomRecNo. _low  ][ di ]
        and dl, 127
        mov byte ptr es:[ fcbCurrRecNo   ][ di ], dl


;- - - - - - - - - - - - - - - - - - - - - - - - - - - - - - - -
;  find corresponding sft
;- - - - - - - - - - - - - - - - - - - - - - - - - - - - - - - -
        call findmatchingFCBSFT                     ; find matching SFT
```

```
        jc _WriteFileFCB_Return                          ; if no space ->

;- - - - - - - - - - - - - - - - - - - - - - - - - - - - - - - - - -
;  init disk access block
;- - - - - - - - - - - - - - - - - - - - - - - - - - - - - - - - - -
        getdarg cx, dx, _position                        ; restore position
        mov word ptr es:[ sftFilePosition. _low  ][ di ], dx
        mov word ptr es:[ sftFilePosition. _high ][ di ], cx

        mov cx, word ptr [ _writeCount ][ bp ]           ; bytes to write to dta
        push word ptr [ _RxDOS_pDTA. _segment ]          ; disk transfer address
        push word ptr [ _RxDOS_pDTA. _pointer ]
        call _SFTWriteFile                               ; write using sft (at es:di )

;- - - - - - - - - - - - - - - - - - - - - - - - - - - - - - - - - -
;  return
;- - - - - - - - - - - - - - - - - - - - - - - - - - - - - - - - - -
_WriteFileFCB_Return:
        call setFCBErrorIfCarry
        Return
```

FCB File Write Random Block

	On Entry	On Return
AX	AH = 28h	AL = error code
BX		
CX	# records to write	
DS:DX	pointer to FCB	
Flags		

Related Functions:
    16h FCB Create File; 0Fh FCB Open File; 10h FCB Close File; 14h FCB Read File;
    15h FCB Write File; 21h FCB Read Random; 22h FCB Write Random; 27h FCB Read Block.

DOS function 28h, FCB Write Random Block, provides FCB functions with an opportunity to write one or more disk sectors. The term *block* used by the function name conflicts with what is meant by blocks in the FCB. The language is taken directly from Microsoft's own name for this function and is retained here for easy identification. A block in the FCB is 128 records. This function should be correctly called FCB Write Random Records because it writes multiple records. The function can be used to set the file size if the number of records to be written is set to zero.

The function first computes the file position by multiplying the random record number by the record size. This can set any legitimate file size, including extending the file size. Next, the byte count to write is computed by taking the record size and multiplying it by the number of sectors to write. Once the SFT is located, and the write is performed, the random record number and the old-style block/record number are computed. The byte position at the end of the write is divided by the record size to produce the random access record number, which is then divided by 128 to produce a block number.

```
;///////////////////////////////////////////////////////////;
;   28h Random Write / FCB                                   ;
;- - - - - - - - - - - - - - - - - - - - - - - - - - - - - -;
;                                                            ;
;   cx        number of blocks to write                      ;
;   ds:dx     pointer to FCB                                 ;
;                                                            ;
;   Return:                                                  ;
;     al = ff, if cannot locate any matching entry           ;
;          00, if match located                              ;
;............................................................;

_RandomBlockWriteFCB:

        Entry
        def  _error, 0000
        def  _writeCount
        def  _numBlocks, cx
        ddef _position
        ddef _fcbPointer, es, dx

        call CtrlC_Check

;- - - - - - - - - - - - - - - - - - - - - - - - - - - - - - -
;  compute byte offset from block/rec nos
;- - - - - - - - - - - - - - - - - - - - - - - - - - - - - - -
        mov di, dx
        mov ax, word ptr es:[ fcbRandomRecNo. _low  ][ di ]
        mov dx, word ptr es:[ fcbRandomRecNo. _high ][ di ]
        mov cx, word ptr es:[ fcbRecordSize  ][ di ]
        call _mul32
        stordarg _position, dx, ax

;- - - - - - - - - - - - - - - - - - - - - - - - - - - - - - -
;  find corresponding sft
;- - - - - - - - - - - - - - - - - - - - - - - - - - - - - - -
        call findmatchingFCBSFT                 ; find matching SFT
        jc _WriteBlockFCB_Return                ; if no space ->

;- - - - - - - - - - - - - - - - - - - - - - - - - - - - - - -
;  init disk access block
;- - - - - - - - - - - - - - - - - - - - - - - - - - - - - - -
        getdarg cx, dx, _position                   ; restor position
        mov word ptr es:[ sftFilePosition. _low  ][ di ], dx
        mov word ptr es:[ sftFilePosition. _high ][ di ], cx

        mov ax, word ptr [ _numBlocks ][ bp ]       ; number of blocks
        mul word ptr [ _writeCount ][ bp ]          ; bytes to write to dta
        mov cx, ax                                  ; total bytes to Write

        or dx, dx                                   ; over 64K ?
        jz _WriteBlockFCB_12                        ; if ok ->
        mov word ptr [ _error ][ bp ], errFCBSizeTooLarge ; too large
        mov cx, 0FFFFh                              ; read as much as possible
```

```
_WriteBlockFCB_12:
        push word ptr [ _RxDOS_pDTA. _segment ]           ; disk transfer address
        push word ptr [ _RxDOS_pDTA. _pointer ]
        call _SFTWriteFile                                ; write using sft (at es:di )

;- - - - - - - - - - - - - - - - - - - - - - - - - - - - - - - - - -
;  compute return logical position
;- - - - - - - - - - - - - - - - - - - - - - - - - - - - - - - - - -
        getdarg es, di, _fcbPointer
        getdarg dx, ax, _position
        add ax, word ptr es:[ fcbRecordSize  ][ di ]
        adc dx, 0000
        mov cx, word ptr es:[ fcbRecordSize  ][ di ]     ; record size
        call _div32

        mov word ptr es:[ fcbRandomRecNo. _low  ][ di ], ax
        mov word ptr es:[ fcbRandomRecNo. _high ][ di ], dx

        mov cx, 128
        call _div32                                       ; divide by 128
        mov word ptr es:[ fcbCurrBlockNo ][ di ], ax

        mov dx, word ptr es:[ fcbRandomRecNo. _low  ][ di ]
        and dl, 127
        mov byte ptr es:[ fcbCurrRecNo   ][ di ], dl

;- - - - - - - - - - - - - - - - - - - - - - - - - - - - - - - - - -
;  return
;- - - - - - - - - - - - - - - - - - - - - - - - - - - - - - - - - -

_WriteBlockFCB_Return:
        call setFCBErrorIfCarry
        Return



        ;/ ' ' ' ' ' ' ' ' ' ' ' ' ' ' ' ' ' ' ' ' ' ' ' ' ' ' ' ' ' ' ' ' ' ';
        ;   23h Get File Size FCB                                             ;
        ;- - - - - - - - - - - - - - - - - - - - - - - - - - - - - - - - -;
        ;                                                                     ;
        ;   ds:dx pointer to FCB                                              ;
        ;.....................................................................;

_FileSizeFCB:

        mov di, dx
        cmp word ptr es:[ fcbRecordSize      ][ di ], 0000
        stc
        jz _FileSizeFCB_12

        mov ax, word ptr es:[ fcbFileSize. _low  ][ di ]
        mov dx, word ptr es:[ fcbFileSize. _high ][ di ]
        mov cx, word ptr es:[ fcbRecordSize      ][ di ]
        call _div32                                       ; [ax:dx] / [cx]
```

```
        mov word ptr es:[ fcbRandomRecNo. _low   ][ di ], ax
        mov word ptr es:[ fcbRandomRecNo. _high  ][ di ], dx
        or ax, ax

_FileSizeFCB_12:
        call setFCBErrorIfCarry
        ret

        ;''''''''''''''''''''''''''''''''''''''''''''''''''''''''''''''';
        ;  24h Set Random Record Number FCB                             ;
        ;- - - - - - - - - - - - - - - - - - - - - - - - - - - - - - - -;
        ;                                                               ;
        ;  ds:dx pointer to FCB                                         ;
        ;...............................................................;

_SetRelativeRecordFCB:

        mov di, dx
        mov ax, 128                                 ; records/block
        mul word ptr es:[ fcbCurrBlockNo ][ di ]    ; block # times record address
        add al, byte ptr es:[ fcbCurrRecNo  ][ di ] ; full 23-bit address

        mov word ptr es:[ fcbRandomRecNo. _low   ][ di ], ax
        mov word ptr es:[ fcbRandomRecNo. _high  ][ di ], dx

        RetCallersStackFrame es, bx
        mov byte ptr es:[ _AX. _AL ][ bx ], 00      ; al always set to 00.
        clc
        ret
```

FCB File Delete

	On Entry	On Return
AX	AH = 28h	AL = error code
BX		
CX	# records to write	
DS:DX	pointer to FCB	
Flags		

Related Functions:
   16h FCB Create File; 0Fh FCB Open File; 10h FCB Close File.

The FCB delete function provides a service that file handle delete does not. It permits the use of wild characters in the filename. It isn't really clear why MS-DOS disables wild characters in the file-handle-based delete function (DOS function 41h), and it may well have to do with how early implementations of the code in MS-DOS were developed. One reason the file handle functions don't permit wild characters may have to do with its evolved vision of networks. Networking code would sit on top of DOS and must be given a chance to deny access to files locked or in use by other users. It could not monitor filenames as easily if DOS permitted wild card deletes to be performed.

The RxDOS implementation of FCB delete utilizes the same function used by Find First and Find Next functions to walk the directory. However, this function doesn't care whether the filename originally came from an FCB function or a file handle function. That means that implemented in this way, the DOS file handle delete function could have just as easily permitted wild characters.

The code for file handle delete follows the MS-DOS tradition. It does not loop through a directory, and it enforces no wild characters in the name by not permitting their use when the pathname and filename are verified using LocateFile.

The FCB file delete code works as follows. It builds the find block required by the search routine from the FCB. The find block is the block that is returned to an application after calling file handle Find First and Find Next functions. RxDOS builds this block in order to perform the search. The block contains the filename and the starting directory cluster address for the current directory for the drive specified in the FCB. The function searches the directory. If the item found is read-only, the entry is skipped and the search continues. Otherwise, the found item is marked deleted, and the cluster chain for the file is released. A deleted flag is incremented, identifying that at least one item was deleted. The function then loops to search for the next item.

When there are no longer any matching entries in the current directory, the routine jumps out of the loop and checks whether any files were deleted. If there were none, an error return is set.

```
;,,,,,,,,,,,,,,,,,,,,,,,,,,,,,,,,,,,,,,,,,,,,,,,,,,,,,,,,,,,,,,,,,;
;  13h Delete File FCB                                            ;
;- - - - - - - - - - - - - - - - - - - - - - - - - - - - - - - -;
;                                                                 ;
;  ds:dx pointer to FCB, wild cards allowed                       ;
;                                                                 ;
;  Return:                                                        ;
;    al = ff, if cannot locate any matching entry                 ;
;         00, if match located                                    ;
;.................................................................;

_DeleteFileFCB:
        Entry
        ddef _fcb, es, dx
        def  _deleted, 0000
        defbytes _findEntry, sizeFINDENTRY

        call CtrlC_Check
;- - - - - - - - - - - - - - - - - - - - - - - - - - - - - - - -
;  build find entry
;- - - - - - - - - - - - - - - - - - - - - - - - - - - - - - - -
        lea di, offset _findEntry [ bp ]
        push es
        push dx
        push ss
        push di
        xor dx, dx                              ; begin at start of dir
        call buildFindFromFCB


;- - - - - - - - - - - - - - - - - - - - - - - - - - - - - - - -
;  keep looping until all matching are deleted
;- - - - - - - - - - - - - - - - - - - - - - - - - - - - - - - -
```

```
_deleteFileFCB_08:
        setES ss
        lea di, offset _findEntry [ bp ]
        call LocateFileByAttribute                  ; locate item
        jc _deleteFileFCB_20

        mov si, word ptr [ _findEntry. findCCBPointer ][ bp ]
        call locateCCBPHeader                       ; get buffers segment

        test byte ptr es:[ deAttributes ][ si ], ATTR_READONLY
        jnz _deleteFileFCB_08

        mov al, byte ptr [ _findEntry. findSrchDrive ][ bp ]
        mov dx, word ptr es:[ deStartCluster ][ si ]
        mov byte ptr es:[ si ], DIRENTRY_DELETED
        call ReleaseClusterChain                    ; release cluster chain
        call CCBChanged                             ; release buffer at [es:di]

        inc word ptr [ _deleted ][ bp ]             ; say some items deleted
        jmp _deleteFileFCB_08

;- - - - - - - - - - - - - - - - - - - - - - - - - - - - - - - -
;  return
;- - - - - - - - - - - - - - - - - - - - - - - - - - - - - - - -
_deleteFileFCB_20:
        cmp word ptr [ _deleted ][ bp ], 0000       ; any deleted ?
        jg _deleteFileFCB_24                        ; yes —>
        stc                                         ; if none found

_deleteFileFCB_24:
        call setFCBErrorIfCarry
        Return

        ;''''''''''''''''''''''''''''''''''''''''''''''''''''''''''''';
        ;  Init Find Record from an FCB                               ;
        ;- - - - - - - - - - - - - - - - - - - - - - - - - - - - - -;
        ;                                                            ;
        ;  Usage:                                                    ;
        ;    stack  pointer to fcb                                   ;
        ;    stack  pointer to find record                           ;
        ;    dx     dir offset to insert                             ;
        ;                                                            ;
        ;  Returns:                                                  ;
        ;    es:di  points to find record                            ;
        ;.............................................................;

buildFindFromFCB:
        Entry 4
        darg _fcb
        darg _findEntry
        def _dirOffset, dx
        def _attributes, 0000

        saveRegisters ds, si, bx
```

```
;- - - - - - - - - - - - - - - - - - - - - - - - - - - - - - -
; if we have an extended FCB
;- - - - - - - - - - - - - - - - - - - - - - - - - - - - - - -
        getdarg es, bx, _fcb
        cmp byte ptr es:[ extSignature ][ bx ], -1      ; do we have an extended fcb ?
        jnz buildFindFromFCB_08                         ; no ->

        mov al, byte ptr es:[ extAttribute ][ bx ]      ; get attributes from
        mov byte ptr [ _attributes ][ bp ], al
        add bx, offset sizeExtendedFCBHdr
        mov word ptr [ _fcb._pointer ][ bp ], bx         ; adjust to fcb address


;- - - - - - - - - - - - - - - - - - - - - - - - - - - - - - -
; if we have a
;- - - - - - - - - - - - - - - - - - - - - - - - - - - - - - -
buildFindFromFCB_08:
        push ds
        setDS es
        lea si, offset fcbName [ bx ]

        getdarg es, di, _findEntry
        lea di, offset findSrchName [ di ]
        mov cx, sizeFILENAME

buildFindFromFCB_12:
        lodsb                                            ; get character
        call upperCase                                   ; uppercase
        stosb
        loop buildFindFromFCB_12

        pop ds
        getdarg es, bx, _fcb
        push word ptr es:[ fcbDrive ][ bx ]
        call getActualDrive                              ; correct drive
        call getCurrDirCluster

        getdarg es, di, _findEntry
        mov word ptr es:[ findDirBegCluster ][ di ], dx
        mov byte ptr es:[ findSrchDrive ][ di ], al      ; store drive

        mov al, byte ptr [ _attributes ][ bp ]
        mov byte ptr es:[ findSrchAttributes ][ di ], al

        mov ax, word ptr [ _dirOffset ][ bp ]
        mov word ptr es:[ findDirEntry ][ di ], ax

        restoreRegisters bx, si, ds
        Return
```

Recovering from Errors

Errors happen. For instance, if a user doesn't close the floppy drive door, the system detects this condition and displays the informative "Not ready reading drive B. Abort, Retry, Fail?" Other errors are far more cryptic, but fortunately DOS had the foresight to provide a user error handler function, int 24h. Application programs can detect errors when they happen and provide either better handling, more complete explanations, or better screen display of the error.

You would think that error handling imposed several hardships and special logic on DOS. After all, something out of the ordinary is happening. But it turns out that handling errors worked out to be surprisingly easy to handle and support. How errors are handled begins down deep in the DOS code.

In fact, two general types of errors may occur while executing a DOS function. The first class involves cases where the hardware works as expected, but the parameters passed are incorrect, such as a wrong parameter, incorrect path, or file doesn't exist. These are essentially soft errors. The other class of errors involves hard errors. These range from drives not being ready to physical hardware problems such as bad or missing disk sectors. Error handling concerns itself only with these hardware-level errors, which are reported only from physical device drivers.

Requests for data read and write are eventually passed to a device driver. There are two types of drivers, and either type may report an error. The driver types are character and blocked devices. A character device handles the transfer data of varying lengths between DOS and devices such as a keyboard, screen, printer, or serial port. Blocked devices handle essentially one or multiple blocks of fixed-length data such as disk sectors.

DOS communicates with a device driver by populating a request header or packet. Although specific contents of each request header vary with the type of request being made, some common fields exist, such as identifying the function to be handled, that is, whether this is a read or write request, and where the return status is to be placed. An example of the read request header is displayed here. The `rwrFunction` and the `rwrStatus` contain the function and return status fields, respectively.

```
;''''''''''''''''''''''''''''''''''''''''''''''''''''''''''''''';
;  Read/Write Request Header Definition                         ;
;..............................................................;


READReqHeader struc

rwrLength            db ?
rwrUnit              db ?
rwrFunction          db ?
rwrStatus            dw ?
rwrReserved          db 8 dup ( ? )

rwrMediaID           db ?                    ;
rwrBuffer            dd ?                    ;
rwrBytesReq          dw ?                    ;
rwrStartSec          dw ?                    ;
rwrVolumeID          dd ?                    ; volume identifier
rwrHugeStartSec      dd ?                    ; 32-bit sector

READReqHeader ends
```

Devices within DOS have an accessible device header that contains a set of flags describing what services the device provides, for example, whether it is a blocked or character device, and the address of two entry points. These are the strategy and interrupt entry points. The term *interrupt* here has nothing to do with hardware interrupts. If a device driver provides interrupt handling support, it links directly to the interrupt address vector in low memory. Rather, the strategy and interrupt entry points are misnamed entry points. They would more aptly be named request and execute entry points.

DOS chose a somewhat restrictive mechanism for communicating with device drivers. This mechanism requires calling the device driver twice for every function call. The first call is to the device driver's strategy entry point. The caller must pass the request header or packet's address, which the driver saves. The second call is to the driver's interrupt entry point. The driver executes the request made in the previous call.

The unfortunate and restrictive aspect of this calling sequence relates to their use in real-time applications. No application should interfere between the two function calls made to a device driver. However, there is no way to actually know that another application may be running, that a device driver request was made, or that it may be interrupting a device driver call in progress, except that the interface is restricted to being used by DOS and DOS provides an in-use flag to prevent more than one function call at a time. A somewhat better interface would have been a single request/execute call.

To support the two-call strategy and execute requirement of device drivers, RxDOS makes a single function call to an internal routine that handles the driver protocol. These functions are `CharDevRequest` and `BlockedDevRequest`, for character and blocked devices, respectively. These functions are also responsible for detecting errors reported by device drivers, the only errors for which error handling is required.

The blocked device handler code, which we explain at the end of the listing, follows:

```
;'''''''''''''''''''''''''''''''''''''''''''''''''''''''''''''''';
;  Call Blocked Device Strategy /Interrupt Routines             ;
;- - - - - - - - - - - - - - - - - - - - - - - - - - - - - - - -;
;                                                               ;
;  Input:                                                       ;
;   es:bx   request block                                       ;
;                                                               ;
;  Output:                                                      ;
;   cy      abort requested on error                            ;
;................................................................;

BlockedDevRequest:
        Entry
        def  _retries, CRITERROR_STDRETRIES          ; # retries
        ddef _strategy
        ddef _interrupt
        ddef _packet, es, bx

        saveSegments bp, bx, ax

        xor ax, ax
        mov al, byte ptr es:[ mrUnit ][ bx ]
```

```
        call getAddrDPB                              ; (es:bx) Device Parameter Block

        cmp word ptr es:[ _dpbptrDeviceDriver. _segment ][ bx ], 0000
        jz BlockedDevRequest_28                      ; no device info ->

        les bx, dword ptr es:[ _dpbptrDeviceDriver ][ bx ]
        mov ax, word ptr es:[ devStrategy  ][ bx ]
        stordarg _strategy, es, ax

        mov ax, word ptr es:[ devInterrupt ][ bx ]
        stordarg _interrupt, es, ax

BlockedDevRequest_06:
        getdarg es, bx, _packet                      ; restore packet address
        call dword ptr [ _strategy ][ bp ]           ; strategy
        call dword ptr [ _interrupt ][ bp ]          ; interrupt

        getdarg es, bx, _packet                      ; restore packet address
        cmp word ptr es:[ mrStatus ][ bx ], 0
        jz BlockedDevRequest_08
        test word ptr es:[ mrStatus ][ bx ], OP_ERROR
        jz BlockedDevRequest_32

;- - - - - - - - - - - - - - - - - - - - - - - - - - - - - - -
;     Abort, Retry, Ignore ?
;- - - - - - - - - - - - - - - - - - - - - - - - - - - - - - -
BlockedDevRequest_08:
        dec word ptr [ _retries ][ bp ]              ; # retries
        jnz BlockedDevRequest_06                     ; auto retry ->
        mov word ptr [ _retries ][ bp ], CRITERROR_STDRETRIES

        call _callCriticalError                      ; switch context stack

        Goto CRITERROR_IGNORE        , BlockedDevRequest_32
        Goto CRITERROR_RETRY         , BlockedDevRequest_06
        Goto CRITERROR_TERMINATE     , BlockedDevRequest_16
        Goto CRITERROR_FAILOPERATION, BlockedDevRequest_28
        jmp short BlockedDevRequest_28

;- - - - - - - - - - - - - - - - - - - - - - - - - - - - - - -
; terminate application
;- - - - - - - - - - - - - - - - - - - - - - - - - - - - - - -
BlockedDevRequest_16:
        int 22h

;- - - - - - - - - - - - - - - - - - - - - - - - - - - - - - -
; exit
;- - - - - - - - - - - - - - - - - - - - - - - - - - - - - - -
BlockedDevRequest_28:
        stc

BlockedDevRequest_32:
        restoreSegments ax, bx, bp
        Return
```

The function handles the mechanics of interfacing with the blocked device driver. The driver's address is determined by passing the logical drive to `getAddrDPB`, which returns the address of the corresponding DPB, or device parameter block for the drive. The device header's address is one of the fields in the data structure. From the device header, the strategy and interrupt addresses are retrieved, and the functions are called.

The device performs the requested function, usually a data transfer to or from disk. At the return from the driver, the completion flag is checked to determine if an error has occurred. If the error bit is set in the request block's status field, the critical error handler routine is called to display and handle the error. That routine, which we describe further later, will perform an int 24h, which can be trapped by an application to intercept the error.

When the critical error handler returns, it should contain one of four action values, ranging from ignoring the error, retrying the request, terminating the application, or failing the operation. Ignoring the error is the easiest to handle. The error is cleared, and the function returns as normal. Retrying the operation is equally easy. The code calls the device driver with the same request packet. The operation is then retried.

To fail a device request, the routine sets the carry flag and returns to the caller. By convention, the caller detects that the operation was failed, and it returns an error until the DOS function call exists.

The abort request causes an int 22h instruction to be executed. Unless trapped by the application program, the standard int 22h handler will terminate the current application by calling the internal terminate application function. The task is terminated. If an application has special termination requirements, such as releasing interrupt vectors that it may have taken over, it should trap the int 22h vector. This will cause an abort to be sent to the application, which could perform any necessary clean-up. The int 22h handler should use DOS function 4Ch, the terminate application function.

Even more interesting is what happens when an application traps errors using int 24h. When an error occurs, the critical error function issues an int 24h instruction. This interrupt normally calls code that displays the error message and accepts an action response like abort, retry, or ignore. The stack will be the application's stack and will contain the registers shown here. Recall that the stack grows downward.

```
flags
CS          from original int 21
IP
ES
DS
BP
DI
SI
DX
CX
BX
AX          registers saved on user's stack during function call
flags       pushed on stack by int 24
CS
IP
```

At the top of the chart are the flag and CS:IP registers, placed there by the original int 21h instruction. The register values at the time of the DOS function call follow. Finally, the flag and CS:IP registers are pushed on the stack from the int 24h instruction.

The critical error function needs to only switch back to the application's stack and issue an int 24h instruction. On return, it must then be able to recover its own stack address. The code for the critical error function, shown next, begins by saving some critical register values. It then checks to be sure that an application is running. Very early in the boot sequence it is possible that this code is run, for example, in reading the config.sys file, where an application may not be running.

If an application is running, the device header address, passed to this function in the ES:BX registers is copied to the BP:SI register pair. This convention seems somewhat unusual, but it does provide an opportunity to return the original value in the DS and ES registers to the application. Next, the code saves the current stack pointer locally in a code section variable. This would prevent this code from eventually being run in ROM though it could easily and readily be changed in some later version. However, the saved location must always be in some safe location. MS-DOS handles the same problem differently. It retains the DOS data segment address in the DS register, which it expects to receive. The RxDOS approach is somewhat more robust in that it is totally self-reliant. So long as the code returns from the int 24h, it can recover its original state.

Next, the critical error handler switches to the application's stack. In RxDOS, the instance pointer references the top of the current RxDOS stack, where the application's stack is conveniently saved. (In MS-DOS, the application's stack pointer is saved in a variable in the Swappable Data Area.) The stack pointer is moved passed the saved registers. The application's original DS and ES registers are restored, again as a protective measure. It avoids the incidental bug where data is inadvertently altered in the DOS data area by code that expected the DS to have been set within the application's data area.

After the int 24h returns, the stack is switched back to the original RxDOS stack. The returned value, that is, the ignore, retry, abort, or fail return codes are matched against allowed settings for the error. According to MS-DOS rules, when ignore or retry is not allowed by the error, the response is converted to a fail. If a fail is not allowed, it must be converted to a terminate.

The function can now return by restoring all its saved registers.

```
;''''''''''''''''''''''''''''''''''''''''''''''''''''''''''''''''''';
;  Call User's Critical Error Handler                               ;
;- - - - - - - - - - - - - - - - - - - - - - - - - - - - - - - - - -;
;                                                                   ;
;  Input:                                                           ;
;    es:di   pointer to current device header                      ;
;    ax      options available for error                           ;
;..................................................................;

_callCriticalError:
        push bx
        push bp
        push es
        push ds

        push word ptr cs:[ _callCriticalError_CurrStack. _segment ]
        push word ptr cs:[ _callCriticalError_CurrStack. _pointer ]
```

```
            push ax

            mov dl, CRITERROR_TERMINATE
            cmp word ptr ss:[ _RxDOS_CurrentPSP ], 0000
            jz _callCriticalError_08                    ; if no valid PSP ->

            cli
            mov bp, es                                  ; point to driver's header
            mov si, bx                                  ; es:bx -> bp:si

            mov word ptr cs:[ _callCriticalError_CurrStack. _segment ], ss
            mov word ptr cs:[ _callCriticalError_CurrStack. _pointer ], sp

            mov bx, word ptr ss:[ _RxDOS_CurrentInstance ]  ; base address of current stack
            les bx, dword ptr ss:[ _pointer ][ bx ]

            mov dx, es
            mov ss, dx
            mov sp, bx
            sub sp, sizeStackFrame                      ; adjust user stack ptr
            sti

            push word ptr es:[ _DataSegment ][ bx ]
            push word ptr es:[ _ExtraSegment ][ bx ]
            pop es
            pop ds

            Int intCRITICALERROR                        ; perform int 24h

            cli
            mov dl, al
            mov ss, word ptr cs:[ _callCriticalError_CurrStack. _segment ]
            mov sp, word ptr cs:[ _callCriticalError_CurrStack. _pointer ]
            sti

;  fix-up returned codes if conflict between allowed and returned

            pop ax
            push ax                                     ; get options
            cmp dl, CRITERROR_IGNORE                    ; ignore returned ?
            jnz _callCriticalError_12                   ; no ->
            test ax, CRITERROR_IGNOREALLOWED            ; ignore allowed ?
            jnz _callCriticalError_32                   ; yes ->
            mov dl, CRITERROR_FAIL                      ; otherwise default to fail

_callCriticalError_12:
            cmp dl, CRITERROR_RETRY                     ; retry returned ?
            jnz _callCriticalError_14                   ; no ->
            test ax, CRITERROR_RETRYALLOWED             ; retry allowed ?
            jnz _callCriticalError_32                   ; yes ->
            mov dl, CRITERROR_FAIL                      ; otherwise default to fail

_callCriticalError_14:
            cmp dl, CRITERROR_FAIL                      ; fail returned ?
```

```
        jnz  _callCriticalError_32            ; no ->
        test ax, CRITERROR_FAILALLOWED        ; fail allowed ?
        jnz  _callCriticalError_32            ; yes ->
        mov  dl, CRITERROR_TERMINATE          ; otherwise default to terminate

_callCriticalError_32:
        pop ax
        pop word ptr cs:[ _callCriticalError_CurrStack. _pointer ]
        pop word ptr cs:[ _callCriticalError_CurrStack. _segment ]

        pop ds
        pop es
        pop bp
        pop bx
        mov al, dl
        ret


_callCriticalError_CurrStack:    dd 0
```

Control Break

Within DOS, a mechanism was established to signal running programs when the user typed either the Control-C or Control-Break key. Programs can interpret the meaning of these keys any way they choose. When a DOS internal control-break flag is off, the Control-C (or Control-Break) key is checked only during keyboard, display, and print function calls (DOS functions 01h through 0Ch). When the internal control-break flag is on, checking is performed when servicing any DOS function. The most actively used DOS functions are frequently disk and file access functions. The internal control-break flag can be set or cleared by using DOS function 3301h, Set/Clear Control-C flag.

The Control-C check is performed at the beginning of a DOS function for a very practical reason. Although a Control C is often used to abort a program, it is also used because an error condition has developed, such as a bad disk, dropped communications line, or printer error. Checking for the Control C avoids encountering the problem yet another time.

One look at what the code has to do to check for a Control C, shown here, reveals why it seems that the Control C is not checked more often. Although quite a few additional instructions are executed, in practice, they amount to a small percentage of the total time required to perform an operation like a disk read. We explain the code at the end of the listing.

```
(in rxdos.asm)
        ;''''''''''''''''''''''''''''''''''''''''''''''''''''''''''''';
        ;  Control C Check                                           ;
        ;............................................................;

CtrlC_Check:
        cmp byte ptr ss:[ _RxDOS_bCtrlBreakCheck ], 00  ; check for control C ?
        jnz CtrlC_Check08                               ; if perform check ->
        ret

CtrlC_Check08:
```

```
            Entry
            defbytes reqBlock, sizeMaxReqHeader

            SaveAllRegisters

            mov ah, NONDESTRREAD
            lea di, offset reqBlock [ bp ]
            call initReqBlock

            mov dx, word ptr [ _RxDOS_pCONdriver. _segment ][ bp ]
            or dx, word ptr [ _RxDOS_pCONdriver. _pointer ][ bp ]
            jz CtrlC_Check48                        ; if no CON driver ->

            push word ptr [ _RxDOS_pCONdriver. _segment ][ bp ]
            push word ptr [ _RxDOS_pCONdriver. _pointer ][ bp ]
            call CharDevRequest                     ; test for character

            test word ptr [ reqBlock.ndrStatus ][ bp ], OP_DONE
            jz CtrlC_Check48                         ; if no character ->
            test word ptr [ reqBlock.ndrStatus ][ bp ], OP_BUSY
            jnz CtrlC_Check48                        ; if no character ->

;- - - - - - - - - - - - - - - - - - - - - - - - - - - - - - - - -
;  see if character is control-c
;- - - - - - - - - - - - - - - - - - - - - - - - - - - - - - - - -

            mov al, byte ptr [ reqBlock.ndrCharRead ][ bp ]
            cmp al, 03                              ; control - C ?
            jnz CtrlC_Check48                       ; if not control Break ->

            int intCONTROLC                         ; cause int 23 if Control C
            jc CtrlC_Check52                         ; if carry (terminate) ->

CtrlC_Check48:
            clc                                     ; no carry exit

CtrlC_Check52:
            RestoreAllRegisters                     ; restore all
            Return
```

The code begins by checking whether Control-Break processing is enabled. If it isn't, the code just returns. Otherwise, all the registers are saved, and a device request block is initialized. A nondestructive read is then performed of the keyboard device. The character is checked for a Control C, and if one is detected, an `int 23h` control break is performed. When the interrupt function is returned, a check is made for the carry flag. This indicates a request to terminate the process and is handled when the function returns. The return is performed by setting the carry flag as required; the registers are then restored, and the function returns.

C H A P T E R   6

Process Management

Parent–Child Relationship—Restarting the Parent Process
Spawning a Child Process—The COM File Format—The EXE File Format
Load and Execute Process—Debugger Support—Terminate Process—Terminate
and Stay Resident—Get Return Code—Duplicate PSP—Create Child PSP

There is a popular belief that DOS is a single-process operating system. This belief is reinforced by the observation that an application must run to completion before any other application can run. DOS never provided a great deal of support for multiple concurrent processes, but it would be incorrect to propagate the notion of DOS as strictly a single-process system. DOS evolved early in its development to recognize that multiple processes reside within a single system. These processes exist in the form of TSR (Terminate and Stay Resident) programs and as spawned child programs.

Within DOS, each application loaded by the Load and Execute function (DOS function 4Bh) becomes a new process. It becomes a child of the process that spawned it. Most programs become child processes of the DOS command shell since this shell is used in most cases to launch application programs.

The child process concept is significant in DOS because it provides the essential mechanism for flow between processes. When a process terminates, control returns to its parent process. The parent process did not terminate; it was suspended during the execution of the child process. In fact, execution of the parent process resumes at the instruction immediately after the spawn function call.

Child and parent processes are not the only example of multiple active processes within DOS. TSRs are by far the most common perception among users of multiple processes. TSRs respond to real-time external events such as clock ticks, keystrokes, and other interrupts, and must be capable of switching the internal context of DOS into believing that they are the currently active process. TSRs must be cognizant of the potential conflicts that may arise as they share and utilize resources. We discuss these issues later in this chapter.

The existence of multiple processes imposes on DOS some requirements. It tracks resource allocations by process ID, which are automatically released when the process terminates. This is but one of the reasons TSRs cannot always simply run as the same process as the program that it interrupts. A TSR that opens or creates files cannot have its resource allocation automatically closed when the program it interrupted terminates. A TSR's resources must remain active for the duration of the TSR's life.

Each process within DOS begins with a Program Segment Prefix, or PSP. The segment address of the PSP is utilized as a process ID (PID). The current context is switched when the current PSP address is changed, using DOS functions 50h and 51h, Get and Set the current PSP Address, respectively.

The PSP is a 256-byte area created at the beginning of the process space used for control and communications. The PSP is used by DOS for a variety of purposes, including passing commands to the process at startup, managing active file handles during processing, and restoring the system state when the process terminates.

The purpose of setting the current PSP is so that all subsequent memory and file allocations will belong to the process. The address passed to the Set PSP function must point to a valid PSP. DOS saves the PSP address passed without performing any validation or verification. The code is a very straightforward save function.

```
(in rxdos.asm)
        ;''''''''''''''''''''''''''''''''''''''''''''''''''''''''''''';
        ;  50h Set PSP Address                                        ;
        ;- - - - - - - - - - - - - - - - - - - - - - - - - - - - - -;
        ;                                                             ;
        ;  bx        contains PSP address to use                      ;
        ;.............................................................;

_SetPSPAddress:
        mov word ptr [ _RxDOS_CurrentPSP ], bx       ; Seg Pointer to current PSP
        ret
```

The Get PSP Address function is only slightly more complex. The current PSP address stored in DOS is returned in the user's BX register. The routine retrieves the pointer to the caller's stack and returns the PSP address in the saved registers.

```
(in rxdos.asm)
        ;''''''''''''''''''''''''''''''''''''''''''''''''''''''''''''';
        ;  51h Get PSP Address                                        ;
        ;- - - - - - - - - - - - - - - - - - - - - - - - - - - - - -;
        ;                                                             ;
        ;  bx        PSP value returned                               ;
        ;.............................................................;

_GetPSPAddress:
        RetCallersStackFrame es, si
        mov bx, word ptr [ _RxDOS_CurrentPSP ]       ; Seg Pointer of current PSP
        mov word ptr es:[ _BX ][ si ], bx
        ret
```

Strange as it may seem, the PSP segment address cannot always be relied on as a unique process ID since the introduction of Windows 3.0. Multiple DOS compatibility boxes are handled by Virtual Machines (VMs) under Windows. Each of these gives the appearance of multiple copies of DOS. The same PSP segment address can now point to different processes in different compatibility boxes, necessitating the creation and tracking of a Virtual Machine ID together with the process ID. Together, these two values form a unique process identifier.

To make this point very clear, only a single copy of DOS is running on a system even under Windows 3.1 (and earlier). That copy is the original real-mode copy loaded during system startup and runs in virtual 8086 mode. WINOLDAP, the Windows application that creates compatibility boxes, merely swaps selected portions of memory known as Instance Data in support of each compatibility box. This data includes the SDA (Swappable Data Area), data structures such as the CDS (Current Directory Structure), and any program loaded after the Windows loader, win.com. WINOLDAP maps data back and forth between the single copy of DOS addressable in virtual 8086 emulation mode.

Inside Windows, a small time-sliced preemptive scheduler mediates among Virtual Machines. This is different from the scheduler that mediates among Windows applications since there are two schedulers within Windows. The scheduler that allocates time among Virtual Machines, located in WIN386, is fully preemptive. The other scheduler, located in KERNEL, runs when GetMessage() has nothing to do and looks at the message queue in order to activate Windows applications.

Virtual Machines are created for applications that require a change in machine state, say between protected and emulation mode. All Windows applications run in a single Virtual Machine in part because the machine state remains unchanged in protected mode. This will change with the upcoming release of Chicago. Under Chicago (Windows 4.0), each 32-bit application will run in its own Virtual Machine and thus be able to take advantage of the preemptive time slicing.

This leads to what appears to some as a strange set of affairs. Windows applications all must compete to run inside the nonpreemptive scheduler, the famous cooperative yielding that Windows applications must do in order to permit switching among applications. Yet DOS boxes run under a preemptive scheduler that arbitrarily interrupts Windows applications and swaps among DOS boxes and machine states!

The actual process involved in switching among Virtual Machines is more complex and the details engrossing enough to takes us on a tangent. Additional details can be found in Schulman et al., *Undocumented DOS, 2nd Edition* (Addison-Wesley, 1994); and in Schulman, Maxey, and Pietrek, *Undocumented Windows* (Addison-Wesley, 1993).

The function of WINOLDAP is to swap out critical areas from the original copy of DOS into what is called Instance Data. The term *Instance* here should not be confused with the use of the same variable in RxDOS. These instances are copies of DOS data structures, such as the Current Directory Structure, and of application programs and data. Of course, the old application manager doesn't really spend all its time copying data. It simply maps the allocated data to form virtual-8086 addressable space.

From DOS's point of view, it all looks like contiguous addressable memory, but we know that there are many copies of this memory, each to form a different compatibility box. When there are several compatibility boxes, processes are highly likely to have the same process ID but run on different Virtual Machines. This is another way of saying that several processes running on different Virtual Machines are highly likely to begin at the same segment address. This only stands to reason. Windows loads a small loader, win.com, into real mode. When a program is started in a DOS compatibility box, it is loaded immediately after win.com. In fact, no matter how many compatibility boxes are started, they will all load the next application immediately after win.com but in separate DOS boxes. Nonetheless, they will all have the same starting segment address.

To support Windows, the process ID is extended by a VM identifier. Surprisingly, the only resource that really cares about a VM identifier are SFTs. That's because they persist in real mode and are not swapped out between Virtual Machines. Memory blocks are the only other resource that DOS tracks by process ID, but they are swapped out with the Instance Data and therefore remain unique across Virtual Machines.

Parent–Child Relationship

Except for the startup code loaded by the ROM-BIOS and the initialization code that processes the config.sys file, every process loaded by DOS has a parent. The parent is the process that launched or spawned the current child process, which for most programs is the command shell, typically command.com, although any process (program) can be a parent process.

This conceptually simple design between parent and child processes provides an important structure to the flow between processes in DOS. When the child process terminates, execution resumes with the parent process. In fact, one may argue that the sole purpose of the parent–child relationship between processes is so that DOS can reactivate the parent process on termination of the child process. This can be effectively seen when command.com launches a program. When the launched child program terminates, DOS reactivates the parent process, in this case, the command shell.

Since the parent cannot run until the child process terminates, how do TSRs relinquish control? After all, TSRs still run after they terminate. From DOS's point of view, the Terminate and Stay Resident function is the end of the process like any other child process. It causes the reactivation of the parent process. However, the Terminate and Stay Resident function call does not release the resources allocated to the process. Whatever memory is allocated to the process is retained, as are all the file handles.

Restarting the Parent Process

When a process is launched using the EXEC function, DOS function 4Bh, the return address and registers are saved in the caller's, that is, the parent's stack. This is a result of how DOS operates. The int instruction places both the value of the flag's register and a return address on the parent's stack. DOS pushes all the remaining registers on the parent's stack and saves the stack address at the current PSP.

The EXEC function creates the new process PSP and places the old PSP address, that is, the segment address of the parent's process, in the child's PSP. In other words, the child process contains the PSP address of the parent. DOS then loads and executes the child program. The parent process is blocked.

When the child program performs any one of the terminate function calls, that is, either the terminate process or terminate and stay resident, the parent process is restarted. The terminate function retrieves the parent's segment address from the child process's PSP, the parent's stack address is then recovered from the parent's PSP, the current PSP address is changed to that of the parent, and a normal exit from DOS is performed. The exit recovers the stack address from the PSP (now the parent's PSP), the saved registers are restored, and a return from the int instruction is made. The return is made to the instruction immediately after the int 21h that spawned the child process.

It does not matter how the spawned program terminated or whether the process terminated with a Terminate and Stay Resident function call. The specific steps involved in switching to the child process and then back to the parent process are summarized here.

1. Parent's stack: Save all registers.
2. Parent's PSP: Save stack pointer.
3. Load child program, save parent PSP address in child PSP.
4. Allow child to execute.
5. Upon child termination: Get parent's PSP address.
6. Free child resources.
7. Set parent's PSP as current.
8. Parent's stack: Restore registers and return.

Spawning a Child Process

Within DOS, a process is spawned by loading a program. There is no mechanism for spawning a process for code already loaded or for spawning a separate thread within a program. The function that spawns a new process, the DOS EXEC function, was developed to support the requirements of the program shell, specifically, the requirements of command.com and of debug programs like debug and cv (codeview). None of these require spawning a process that did not also require loading a program. Thus, within the DOS context, the terms *process* and *program* are synonymous.

The DOS EXEC function, DOS function 4Bh, always spawns a child process. The parent process is the currently running process. The function will load either a com or exe program. DOS determines the format of the program to load by checking for an EXE header at the start of the file and not by the file's extension. Additional program formats that exist today to support 16-bit and 32-bit applications for Windows, Win32s, and NT are not supported by DOS.

Later in this chapter, we discuss the specific mechanics of the DOS EXEC function. This section deals with the requirements of process creation. Each spawned process is allocated both an environment block and a PSP. The program is loaded immediately after the PSP. The spawned process inherits the parent's device redirection, its open file handles, and an environment block. All open file handles are duplicated in the child process except those opened as NO INHERIT.

File handles are duplicated by incrementing their in-use count at the SFT. Even if the child closes the file, causing an update to disk of the directory contents, the SFT will remain owned by the parent process and in use.

The Environment Block

An environment block is created for every process spawned. The block is an area of memory that contains a list of string variables and values that are passed to the spawned program. Although typically this list of parameters is a copy of the parent's environment block, it could comprise any set of parameters.

DOS maintains a master environment block, which is created the first time the command shell is loaded. It is initially blank, but each SET and PROMPT command entered either from a batch file, like autoexec.bat, or from the keyboard alters the contents of the environment block. When the command shell spawns a child process, it copies this environment block to the child process.

DOS appends the fully expanded pathname of the spawned program to the end of the environment block. However, this name is not normally visible when displayed by the command shell because it is appended to the end of the "additional strings" section. The environment block is divided into two parts. The first part contains keyword–value pairs that are familiar to DOS users. Each line or statement in this section is terminated by a NULL byte. The end of this area is identified by a NULL string. One convenient way of detecting this is to search for two consecutive NULL bytes. This is followed by a word containing the number of additional strings where the expanded filename is appended.

The additional strings term is somewhat misleading. The only portion of the environment block that is inherited between parent and child processes is the keyword–value section. The additional strings section is never inherited. This leads to a situation where every process always begins, and usually only ever carries, a single string in the additional section.

The Program Segment Prefix

The PSP is an area created to support control and communications between the operating system and the process. Other operating systems utilize a concept similar to the PSP. Under Unix, a stack frame is created to control a process. A PSP is automatically created by DOS for a process when it is spawned. It is used to pass arguments at startup and to reactivate the parent process on termination.

The PSP serves a role during the process's life. It points to the inherited environment block and contains the all-important JHT, or Job Handle Table. The command tail area serves as a default Disk Transfer Area unless explicitly changed. The PSP also contains two FCBs, or File Control Blocks. These fields played a more significant role when FCBs were in greater use, where programs relied more heavily on the command line parsing supplied by DOS. The FCBs were populated by the program names used in command lines.

The layout of the PSP is shown here.

```
;//////////////////////////////////////////////////////////////';
;  Program Segment Prefix (PSP)                                  ;
;................................................................;


           PSP struc
pspInt20                dw  ?              ; Int 20 instruction
pspNextParagraph        dw  ?              ; seg address of next paragraph
                        db  ?              ; not used
pspDispatcher           db 5 dup ( ? )     ; long call to MS-DOS
pspTerminateVect        dd  ?              ; Terminate Vector (Int 22h)
pspControlCVect         dd  ?              ; Control-C Vector (Int 23h)
pspCritErrorVect        dd  ?              ; CritError Vector (Int 24h)
pspParentId             dw  ?              ; PSP seg of parent
```

```
pspHandleTable         db 20 dup ( ? )        ; Allocated Handle Table
pspEnvironment         dw ?                   ; seg address of environment block
pspUserStack           dd ?                   ; user stack
pspFileHandleCount     dw ?                   ; handles allocated
pspFileHandlePtr       dd ?                   ; pointer to handle table
pspShareChain          dd ?                   ; Share chain pointer
                       db    4 dup ( ? )      ; unused
pspVersion             dw ?                   ; Major, Minor version (VERS)
                       db   10 dup ( ? )      ; unused
pspDTASave             dd ?                   ; RxDOS usage: save DTA address
pspDosCall             db    3 dup ( ? )      ; int 21/ retf
                       db    9 dup ( ? )      ; unused
pspFCB_1               db   16 dup ( ? )      ; FCB 1
pspFCB_2               db   16 dup ( ? )      ; FCB 2
                       db    4 dup ( ? )
pspCommandTail         db  128 dup ( ? )      ; command tail (also default DTA )
        PSP ends
```

The PSP contains several fields, too many to discuss fully in this section. It contains the restore addresses for interrupts 22h, 23h, and 24h; the segment address of the environment block; and other fields whose role has more or less already been discussed in other books and references. One field is the pspParentID. This is the segment address of the parent process and is, of course, used when the spawned child process terminates.

Offset 5 of the PSP contains a far call to DOS. The call itself is not very useful at this location because if it ever were used, the return would be to the location immediately after the call within this PSP. Since the PSP contains data and no other instructions, the call is useless. A far jump at this location would have been preferable.

The address referenced by the call appears to point to somewhere in high memory, but relied on address wraparound to point, correctly it should be noted, to location 0000:00C0, which is the int 30h address in the low-memory interrupt vector table. A jump instruction is located at this address that calls DOS. Typically, most other address vectors contain addresses as opposed to instructions. With the introduction of DOS in high memory, the jump is inserted in high memory to point to the same location as the jump at int 30h.

Some confusion has arisen about whether the address at the call instruction points to the correct location. Some texts on DOS claim that the address is actually 2 bytes off. The address value, as far as I can determine, is accurate. However, for reasons that I don't understand, the value reported by debug and other debuggers can lead to the wrong conclusion.

The most common way to view the contents of the PSP or other memory locations is to load debug. All the accessible memory is displayable, including the PSP. However, the PSP that debug leads a user to believe is the currently running PSP, because the DS register refers to it, is actually not a valid running PSP. It was probably created by DOS function 26h, create PSP.

In DOS 6, the address placed at the call instruction is exactly 2 bytes off, as reported, and references location F01D:FEEE. More interesting, DOS 3.3 contains an address that is also 2 bytes off, and contains the value F31E:CEDE, which also is 2 bytes off. Perhaps the difference in values between the versions is related to the amount of memory available on the system. Both addresses, with address wraparound, refer to location 0000:00BE, which is 2 bytes off from the target address of 0000:00C0.

However, despite appearances, the PSP that is viewed with debug is not a valid or real PSP. An entirely different story emerges when you actually run a program. The address at the call instruction with the PSP, for both DOS 3.3 and DOS 6 contains the correct address value. It contains F01D:FEF0, which correctly points, again using address wraparound, to location 0000:00C0.

In fact, you don't need to physically run another program to discover this change. You can enter a command like debug x.com, where x could be any program. When debug is to run a program, it spawns a new PSP using DOS function 4B01h, load and execute program. This function creates a valid PSP where the correct address can be seen. The spawned program can be in either com or exe formats.

The observed differences between running debug with and without a spawned program are most obviously the result of differences between two different DOS function calls, that is, between DOS function 26h and DOS function 4Bh.

Beginning with DOS 6.0, MS-DOS introduced a mechanism for setting the DOS version number on a per-applications basis. MS-DOS released setver, which maintains a list of program names and the DOS version numbers to report. setver intercepts DOS function 4Bh after the process is spawned and replaces the DOS version maintained in the PSP. To support this capability, DOS 6.0 added the pspVersion field. The version number stored in this field is the value returned by DOS function 30h, Get DOS Version. The true DOS version number is returned by DOS function 3306h.

A brief look at DOS function 30h, Get DOS Version, reveals that it actually returns considerably more information than just the version number. DOS tracks both a little-used user serial number and an OEM identification number. Each OEM is assigned a unique id value.

```
(in rxdos.asm)
        ;''''''''''''''''''''''''''''''''''''''''''''''''''''''''''''''''''';
        ;  30h Get DOS Version                                              ;
        ;- - - - - - - - - - - - - - - - - - - - - - - - - - - - - - - - -;
        ;                                                                   ;
        ;  Input:                                                           ;
        ;    al   00h return OEM version number in bh                       ;
        ;         01h return version flag in bh                             ;
        ;                                                                   ;
        ;  Returns:                                                         ;
        ;    al    major version                                            ;
        ;    ah    minor version                                            ;
        ;  bl:cx user's serial number                                       ;
        ;    bh    OEM identification number                                ;
        ;          or version flag                                          ;
        ;.................................................................;

_GetDOSVersion:
        mov cx, word ptr cs:[ _RxDOS_UserSerialNumber ]
        mov bx, word ptr cs:[ _RxDOS_UserSerialNumber + 2 ]
        mov bh, byte ptr cs:[ _RxDOS_DOSOEMVersion ]
      ; mov ax, word ptr cs:[ _RxDOS_DOSVersion ]          ; pre DOS 5 (see 3306h)

        mov es, word ptr [ _RxDOS_CurrentPSP ]             ; Seg Pointer of current PSP
        mov ax, word ptr es:[ pspVersion      ]            ; Major, Minor version (VERS)
```

```
        RetCallersStackFrame ds, si
        mov word ptr [ _AX ][ si ], ax
        mov word ptr [ _BX ][ si ], bx
        mov word ptr [ _CX ][ si ], cx
        clc
        ret
```

The actual Get DOS Version function appears as

(in rxdos.asm)

```
        ;'''''''''''''''''''''''''''''''''''''''''''''''''''''''''''''''';
        ;   3300h Get ControlC Check Flag                                ;
        ;   3301h Set ControlC Check Flag                                ;
        ;   3305h Get Startup Drive                                      ;
        ;   3306h Get DOS Version                                        ;
        ;................................................................;

_CtrlBreakCheck:
        RetCallersStackFrame es, si

        Goto GetControlC,       __getControlC
        Goto SetControlC,       __setControlC
        Goto GetStartupDrive,   __getStartupDrive
        Goto GetExtDosVersion,  __getExtDosVersion

        stc
        call setFCBErrorIfCarry
        ret

        ...

;- - - - - - - - - - - - - - - - - - - - - - - - - - - - - - - - - -
;  get startup drive
;- - - - - - - - - - - - - - - - - - - - - - - - - - - - - - - - - -
__getStartupDrive:
        mov dl, byte ptr ss:[ _RxDOS_BootDrive ]
        mov byte ptr es:[ _DX._DL ][ si ], dl
        ret

;- - - - - - - - - - - - - - - - - - - - - - - - - - - - - - - - - -
;  get extended DOS version
;- - - - - - - - - - - - - - - - - - - - - - - - - - - - - - - - - -
__getExtDosVersion:
        mov bx, word ptr ss:[ _RxDOS_DOSVersion ]
        mov word ptr es:[ _BX ][ si ], bx
        mov word ptr es:[ _DX ][ si ], 0000
        ret
```

The COM File Format

COM programs are binary memory images that can contain no relocatable references. Thus, a COM program cannot contain any far instructions or segment immediate references that require relocation. For example, it is legal to contain a segment reference to the BIOS area at 0040h since this is an absolute reference, but it would be illegal to reference a Label within the program since that would require an address relocation.

```
mov ax, 0040h
mov es, ax                      ; this is legal

mov ax, seg Label               ; these would require relocation
call 0x850:0x550                ;    "
jmp 0x850:0x550                 ;    "
```

Other restrictions apply to COM programs. They must start at offset 100h, and a stack is arbitrarily set at the top of the startup segment. The space occupied in memory for a COM program is its file size. Because the stack is arbitrarily created at the end of the first segment created for the COM program, any COM file whose size exceeds 64K will have a stack created inside its executable space.

COM programs are great for quick, small programs, but they have for the most part outlived their usefulness. Although COM programs can be created with the EXE2BIN utility, just as common is the practice of using debug to write quick-and-dirty programs whose memory image can be saved as a COM program with the w (write) command.

When a COM program is loaded, the four segment registers, CS, DS, ES, and SS, all point to the PSP segment. The instruction counter, IP, is set to 100h, and the stack pointer, SP, is set to FFFEh. Early releases of DOS used to set the stack at the end of the command tail, at address 00FEh. The stack is. constantly active servicing clock tick interrupts. The command tail becomes partly corrupted, particularly as more TSRs trap on the clock tick interrupt.

Register Assignments for COM Load

CS:IP	CS set to PSP; IP set to 100h
SS:SP	SS set to PSP; SP set to FFFEh
DS	set to PSP
ES	set to PSP
AX	0000
BX:CX	size of program loaded
DX	0000
SI	0000
DI	0000

The logic for loading a COM program is fairly straightforward. DOS allocates the largest available memory block and then creates a PSP in the first 256 bytes of the allocated space. The size of the program is determined from the file size, and the file is read into the memory space. A stack is created at 0xFFFE, even if the program is larger than 64K. This means that interrupts that occur from the timer and other devices, and that can occur at any time, will clobber whatever memory image is loaded at just below the 64K limit. The COM program layout was never intended to support larger than 64K memory images.

The EXE File Format

The EXE file layout permits larger and far more complex programs. It has none of the restrictions of COM programs. The stack and starting address can be anywhere in the file and avoids the problem of the stack being arbitrarily placed in the first segment, as with a COM program. Far addresses and immediate segment references are supported through a segment relocation table.

The EXE file format consists of a header, the relocation table, the loadable part of the EXE file, an uninitialized data allocation, and an optional attached data portion. The EXE header is located at the start of the file and contains an identifying MZ signature, which are the initials of one of the original MS-DOS developers. Like a COM file, the EXE file is largely an image of the program in memory. That is to say, the program is read into memory as is, except for the relocation table. Although the EXE program may be subdivided into different segments, the entire memory image created by the multiple segments creates a single, usually large, loadable binary.

The number of bytes loaded in the binary image is described in the file header. The bytes actually loaded may be only a portion of the EXE file. The remainder of the EXE file may be stored with overlays, resources, or other data. Microsoft and Borland, for example, use this additional space beyond the EXE file to store debug symbol and line number information. Overlay linkers, not to be confused with the overlay loading capability provided by DOS, use this space to store the overlays. Figure 6-1 shows how the space beyond the EXE file can be utilized. Windows takes advantage of this feature by adding its "New" Windows program format to the end of a standard stub EXE and simply prints "This program requires Microsoft Windows" when the program is run from DOS. DOS only loads and executes the stub.

Technically speaking, a COM program can also carry "extra" data. All that is required is to append the data to the end of the COM program, and it will automatically always be loaded into memory. This makes the COM file format impractical for handling overlays but could be used for loading resources and configuration information.

Figure 6-1. Different ways in which the EXE layout is used with attached data

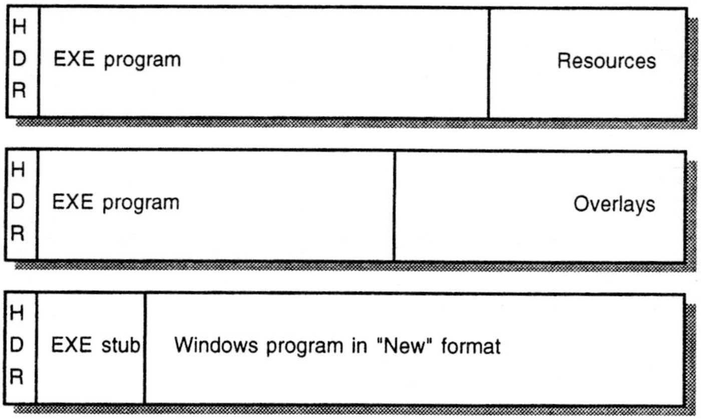

The portion of the EXE file that is loaded is described in the EXE header in terms of pages. A page is 512 bytes in the EXE layout. Even though the number of bytes used in the last page is given as part of the EXE header, an interesting and sometimes problematic aspect of the EXE file layout is that DOS loads whole pages, even if the last page is only partially filled. This happens only when there are overlays or when the physical EXE file extends beyond the last page.

The EXE file header appears as shown here.

```
;'''''''''''''''''''''''''''''''''''''''''''''''''''''''''''''''';
;  Exe File Header                                                ;
;................................................................;


        EXEHEADER struc
exeSignature            dw ?                ; .EXE file signature
exeExtraBytes           dw ?                ; number of bytes in last partial page
exePages                dw ?                ; number of whole and partial pages
exeRelocItems           dw ?                ; number of pointers in reloc table
exeHeaderSize           dw ?                ; size of header, in paragraphs
exeMinAlloc             dw ?                ; minimum allocation (parag)
exeMaxAlloc             dw ?                ; maximum allocation (parag)
exeInitSS               dw ?                ; initial ss value
exeInitSP               dw ?                ; initial sp value
exeChecksum             dw ?                ; complemented checksum
exeInitIP               dw ?                ; initial ip value
exeInitCS               dw ?                ; initial cs value
exeRelocTable           dw ?                ; byte offset to reloc table
exeOverlay              dw ?                ; overlay number
        EXEHEADER ends

EXE_SIGNATURE           equ 5A4DH           ; 'MZ'
```

When DOS loads an EXE formatted file, it allocates only the amount of memory requested to run the program. The amount is determined by the size of the program, computed from the number of pages it requires to load, plus the maximum additional allocation amount requested. That request is maintained in the exeMaxAlloc field in the EXE header. In almost every case, that figure is arbitrarily set to FFFF by the Microsoft (and other) linkers to represent essentially all memory. Since this request amount cannot normally be satisfied in real mode, DOS allocates only the maximum actual available memory.

Although the maximum allocation field is set to accommodate heap and stack space that the program might require, the minimum allocation field in the EXE file header is set to the additional memory beyond the actual EXE program that the program requires in order to run. This additional space is set aside for uninitialized memory referenced by the program.

When the maximum allocation value is set to zero, the largest memory block available is allocated to the program, and the executable binary is loaded high. The program is not loaded to an Upper Memory Block, or UMB, in the same way that DOS is loaded high; rather, it is loaded in the upper part of the allocated block.

When DOS loads a program, it presets specific register values. The program start address and the stack pointer are set by the contents of the EXE header. The segment address in DS and ES registers is set to point to the PSP.

Register Assignments for EXE Load

CS:IP	CS:IP actual start address
SS:SP	SS:SP actual stack address
DS	set to PSP
ES	set to PSP
AX	0000
BX:CX	size of program loaded
DX	0000
SI	0000
DI	0000

One question never addressed is why a relocation table exists in the EXE file format and why fix-ups are required. When far jump, far call, or segment immediate references, as shown, are made in a program, the Intel architecture requires a segment address as part of the instruction address. That segment address is not known at compile or link time. The address must be set after the program is loaded when the true destination or segment address is known. The relocation table is a set of entries that point to segment values within the loadable EXE program that must be set at load time.

Assuming the address of `farlabel` in the instruction shown here was actually two segments away from the start of the program, the instruction encoding before the fix-up, that is, after compile and link, would be (the offset value in the address is inconsequential and is listed as `xxxx`)

```
9A 0002:xxxx  call farlabel
```

To correct the segment value in the program, the load segment value is added. If the program were loaded at segment 1122, the corrected segment value would appear as

```
9A 1124:xxxx  call farlabel
```

The differences between loading EXE and COM programs are as follows:

Loading an EXE program
1. Find program on disk.
2. Allocate required memory.
3. Determine paragraphs to load.
4. Load file.
5. Relocate items.
6. Compute SS:SP and CS:IP for program

Loading a COM program
1. Find program on disk.
2. Allocate all memory.
3. Get file size.
4. Load file size bytes from file.
5. Default CS and SS to load address; IP to 100h and SP to FFFEh.

Now that we have provided a description of the program file layouts, and some of the issues regarding program loading and allocation, we are ready to discuss specific DOS function calls.

Load and Execute Process

	On Entry	On Return
AX	AH = 4Bh; AL = subfunction	
BX	ES:BX ptr to param block	
CX		
DX	DS:DX ptr to ASCIZ prog name	

Related Functions:
   31h Terminate Stay Resident; 4Ch Terminate; 4Dh Get Return Code of Child Process.

The function is used to begin a new process or to load COM or EXE programs, the only two program formats supported by DOS. The action taken by the load and execute function depends on the subfunction code passed in the AL register. The first two subfunctions supported spawn a new process, which involves suspending execution of the current process. The subfunctions supported by the function are

- 00h, load and execute program
- 01h, load program, return debug information
- 03h, load overlay
- 05h, set execution state

Except for subfunction 05, set execution state, the function loads a program. A program is a binary-formatted file, usually the output of a link process, in either COM or EXE formats.

The subfunction codes are defined in the rxdosdef.asm module and appear as

```
;''''''''''''''''''''''''''''''''''''''''''''''''''''''''''''''''''';
; Load and Exec Subfunctions                                        ;
;..................................................................;

execLoadAndExecute          equ 00h     ; load and execute
execLoadAndReturnDebug      equ 01h     ; load and return to debugger
execLoadOverlay             equ 03h     ; load overlay
execSetExecuteMode          equ 05h     ; set execution mode
```

Subfunction 00, load and execute program, creates a child process by allocating memory for both an environment block and the program. The function will fail if neither memory block can be allocated or if the program file cannot be located. The child process is given control after loading and executes. The parent process regains control only after the child terminates.

The function expects a program name pointer passed in the DS:DX register pair and an EXEC block pointer passed in the ES:BX registers. The EXEC block, shown here, contains parameters passed to the child program and includes the segment address of an environment block, the command tail beginning with a byte count and terminated with a carriage return, and two preinitialized FCBs. The environment block for the current process is passed to the child when the environment segment is 0000.

```
;''''''''''''''''''''''''''''''''''''''''''''''''''''''''''''''';
;  Load and Execute                                             ;
;...............................................................;

        EXEC struc
lexecEnvironment        dw ?
lexecCommandTail        dd ?
lexecFCB_1              dd ?
lexecFCB_2              dd ?
        EXEC ends
```

Subfunction 01, load program and return debug information, was created specifically to support debuggers. The function performs exactly the same function as subfunction 00, except that it does not automatically switch to the child process. It accepts a load program block, or LOADPROG, where it returns the stack pointer and the start execution address. This enables the debugger to stop at the start of execution of a program. Additional information about this mode is provided in the section "Debugger Support," later in this chapter.

```
;''''''''''''''''''''''''''''''''''''''''''''''''''''''''''''''';
;  Load Program                                                 ;
;...............................................................;

        LOADPROG struc
lprogEnvironment        dw ?
lprogCommandTail        dd ?
lprogFCB_1              dd ?
lprogFCB_2              dd ?
lprogCSID               dd ?        ; starting code address
lprogSSSP               dd ?        ; starting stack address
        LOADPROG ends
```

Subfunction 03, load overlay, loads a COM or EXE program at a given segment address. The function is passed a LOADOVERLAY block that contains two parameters: the load segment address and a relocation factor. The relocation factor is applied only to EXE files. In most cases, the relocation factor is zero, meaning that no additional relocation other than the starting address of the program need be applied. One of the primary uses for subfunction 03, which does not spawn a process, is to load device drivers. Not only is a program merely loaded into memory, it is not automatically executed. The application program must prepare the code and data segment registers to correspond with the address of the loaded program.

One of the problems with subfunction 03 is that the caller has the responsibility for ensuring that sufficient memory is available to fit the program. DOS has what could be considered a bug in its implementation of this subfunction. Load overlay does not perform any memory checks when it loads a program and will overwrite even DOS's own memory control blocks! Memory management is left completely to the calling program.

```
;///////////////////////////////////////////////////////////;
;  Load Overlay                                              ;
;...........................................................;

         LOADOVERLAY struc
loverSegLoadAddress      dw ?
loverRelocFactor         dw ?               ; .EXE files only
         LOADOVERLAY ends
```

Subfunction 05, set execution state, expects a pointer to an EXECSTATE structure. DOS loads the named program into memory, as it would with any other load and execute function call, and then fills the contents of the structure with the PSP address, the program's start address, and the program's allocated size. This function is limited to inheriting the current environment block.

MS-DOS's implementation of this facility has a curious implementation restriction. When this function returns, it returns to the original launching program. However, it does not permit any DOS function calls, ROM-BIOS calls, or other system interrupts. The original caller's code must perform a jump to the new program's start address as soon as possible.

This restriction exists because from DOS's point of view, the new program is running, that is, the PSP address saved in DOS is to the new program. Any files opened or memory allocated would belong to the new program. The DS, ES, and SS:SP registers all point to the new program space. These values are set to the new program so that a jump to the program start address will appear in every regard as if it was any other program launch.

```
;///////////////////////////////////////////////////////////;
;  Execution State                                           ;
;...........................................................;

         EXECSTATE struc
                         dw ?               ; Reserved
execFlags                dw ?
execProgName             dd ?
execPSP                  dw ?
execStartAddr            dd ?
execProgSize             dd ?
         EXECSTATE ends
```

All these descriptions of the functions should lead to the conclusion that DOS does not distinguish between program loading and the process spawning. They are handled by the same code.

The steps in the spawn child process are summarized as follows:

1. Determine if program exists.
2. Allocate environment block.
3. Allocate memory for program, plus PSP.
4. Load program.
5. Initialize PSP.
6. Pass control to child process.

The steps to loading a program are probably best understood by reading the code. The code for function 4Bh begins in rxdos.asm, as do all other DOS functions, but the only code there is a call to load the program function located in rxdosexe.asm.

```
;''''''''''''''''''''''''''''''''''''''''''''''''''''''''''''';
;   4Bxxh Load and Execute Program                            ;
;- - - - - - - - - - - - - - - - - - - - - - - - - - - - - - -;
;                                                             ;
;   ds:dx    program name                                     ;
;   es:bx    program arguments                                ;
;.............................................................;

_ExecuteProgram:
        call loadProgram
        ret
```

The real code for the function begins in rxdosexe.asm. The DOS EXEC function first determines if the program to load exists by calling LocateFile. This is the same function used internally by DOS to locate any other file and results in the return of a directory access control block. This control block, explained in greater detail in the "File Open with Handle" section of Chapter 3, contains the fully expanded filename, the size of the file, and the drive and starting cluster address of where the file can be located. This is then followed by a check to determine if the file header contains the EXE file signature. If it does, the code must call LoadExe_Program. Some portion of process spawning must be handled differently by COM and EXE loaders because the actual size of the module to be spawned is not known until the EXE header is examined.

Loading a COM Program

We look first at the simpler case, what it takes to load a COM file. Of course, this section is more than just about loading the file; it is about spawning a process.

```
(in rxdosexe.asm)
        ;''''''''''''''''''''''''''''''''''''''''''''''''''''''''''''';
        ;   Load Program Image (COM, SYS, etc... )                    ;
        ;- - - - - - - - - - - - - - - - - - - - - - - - - - - - - - -;
        ;                                                             ;
        ;   Input:                                                    ;
        ;   ds:dx   asciz name of program to load                     ;
        ;   es:bx   address of LOADEXEC structure                     ;
        ;   al      mode (subfunction)                                ;
        ;                                                             ;
        ;   Output:                                                   ;
        ;   dx      PSP segment address                               ;
        ;   cy      load failed                                       ;
        ;.............................................................;

loadProgram:
        Entry
```

```
        def  _Mode, ax
        def  _programPSP
        def  _StartSegment
        def  _SizePara
        ddef _filesize
        ddef _ExecBlock, es, bx
        defbytes _exeHeader, sizeEXEHEADER
        defbytes _diskAccess, sizeDISKACCESS
        defbytes _dirAccess, sizeDIRACCESS
        defbytes _relocitem, 4

        xor cx, cx
        storarg _programPSP  , cx
        storarg _StartSegment, cx

;- - - - - - - - - - - - - - - - - - - - - - - - - - - - - - - - -
; program file exist ?
;- - - - - - - - - - - - - - - - - - - - - - - - - - - - - - - - -
        cmp al, execSetExecuteMode          ; load a program ?
        jnz _loadProgram_04                 ; yes ->
        call _SetExecuteMode
        jmp _loadProgram_56

_loadProgram_04:
        mov ax, (FILE_NODEVICENAME)
        mov si, dx                          ; name from caller (es: si )
        lea di, offset _dirAccess [ bp ]    ; work dir access block
        call LocateFile                     ; try to find file
        ifc _loadProgram_56                 ; if cannot ->

;- - - - - - - - - - - - - - - - - - - - - - - - - - - - - - - - -
; initialize disk access block
;- - - - - - - - - - - - - - - - - - - - - - - - - - - - - - - - -
        setES ss
        lea bx, offset _diskAccess [ bp ]   ; build access control block
        call initdiskAccess                 ; [ax] is drive, [dx] is cluster

        call checkEXEHeader                 ; exe file ?
        jnz _loadProgram_12                 ; no, COM or SYS type ->

        getarg ax, _Mode                    ; get subfunction code
        lea di, word ptr [ _dirAccess ][ bp ]   ; dir information
        getdarg es, bx, _ExecBlock          ; original load exec
        call loadExe_Program                ; pass off control to load EXE
        ifc _loadProgram_56                 ; if cannot ->
        jmp _loadProgram_50                 ; switch stack ->

;- - - - - - - - - - - - - - - - - - - - - - - - - - - - - - - - -
; load COM or SYS
;- - - - - - - - - - - - - - - - - - - - - - - - - - - - - - - - -
_loadProgram_12:
        les di, dword ptr [ _dirAccess. fileAcBufferPtr ][ bp ]
        add di, word ptr [ _dirAccess. fileAcDirOffset ][ bp ]
        mov ax, word ptr es:[ deFileSize. _low  ][ di ]
```

```
        mov dx, word ptr es:[ deFileSize. _high ][ di ]
        stordarg _filesize, dx, ax                      ; save file size

        add ax, (PARAGRAPH - 1)
        adc dx, 0                                       ; just in case carry

        shr dx, 1
        rcr ax, 1
        shr dx, 1
        rcr ax, 1
        shr dx, 1
        rcr ax, 1
        shr dx, 1
        rcr ax, 1
        storarg _SizePara, ax                           ; save as paragraphs needed

        mov dx, 0FFFFh                                  ; max request (all of memory)
        getdarg es, bx, _ExecBlock                      ; load exec module
        call _LoaderAllocMemory                         ; alloc memory for env block/ PSP
        ifc _loadProgram_56                             ; if cannot allocate ->

        storarg _StartSegment, es                       ; where data load begins
        storarg _programPSP, ax                         ; save seg address of PSP

;- - - - - - - - - - - - - - - - - - - - - - - - - - - - - - - - - - - - -
;  load module
;- - - - - - - - - - - - - - - - - - - - - - - - - - - - - - - - - - - - -
        xor di, di                                      ; load at es:0000
        mov word ptr ss:[ diskAcPosition. _high ][ bx ], di
        mov word ptr ss:[ diskAcPosition. _low  ][ bx ], di

_loadProgram_20:
        mov cx, 60 * 1024                               ; read 60K at a time
        mov ax, word ptr [ _filesize. _low  ][ bp ]
        mov dx, word ptr [ _filesize. _high ][ bp ]
        sub ax, word ptr ss:[ diskAcPosition. _low  ][ bx ]
        sbb dx, word ptr ss:[ diskAcPosition. _high ][ bx ]
        or dx, dx                                       ; more than 60K ?
        jnz _loadProgram_22                             ; yes ->
        cmp ax, cx                                      ; more than 60K ?
        jnc _loadProgram_22                             ; yes ->
        mov cx, ax                                      ; exact bytes to read

_loadProgram_22:
        or cx, cx                                       ; more to read ?
        jz _loadProgram_24                              ; if no more to read ->

        mov dx, word ptr ss:[ diskAcPosition. _high ][ bx ]
        mov ax, word ptr ss:[ diskAcPosition. _low  ][ bx ]
        lea bx, offset _diskAccess [ bp ]               ; build access control block
        call readLogicalBuffer                          ; Access buffer: ss: bx
        or cx, cx                                       ; bytes actually read
        jz _loadProgram_24                              ; if no more to read ->
```

```
        push cx
        shr cx, 1
        shr cx, 1
        shr cx, 1
        shr cx, 1                                   ; chars read in paras
        mov ax, es
        add ax, cx
        mov es, ax
        pop cx
        and cx, (PARAGRAPH - 1)
        add di, cx
        jmp _loadProgram_20

;- - - - - - - - - - - - - - - - - - - - - - - - - - - - - -
;   switch to new process
;- - - - - - - - - - - - - - - - - - - - - - - - - - - - - -
_loadProgram_24:
        getarg es, _programPSP                      ; child process's PSP
        mov word ptr [ _RxDOS_CurrentPSP ], ax      ; change running PSP

        call _getMemBlockSize                       ; get size

        xor si, si
        cmp cx, (1024 /PARAGRAPH) * 64              ; greater than 64K ?
        jnc _loadProgram_28                         ; yes, use max value for seg
        mov si, cx
        shl si, 1
        shl si, 1
        shl si, 1                                   ; actual words

_loadProgram_28:
        sub si, 2                                   ; top value minus word
        mov word ptr es:[ pspUserStack. _pointer ], si
        mov word ptr es:[ pspUserStack. _segment ], es

        sub si, _Flags
        mov bx, word ptr cs:[ _RxDOS_CurrentInstance ]
        mov word ptr ss:[ _pointer ][ bx ], si
        mov word ptr ss:[ _segment ][ bx ], es      ; new proc startup stack

        or si, si
        pushf
        pop word ptr es:[ _Flags        ][ si ]

        mov word ptr es:[ _IP           ][ si ], 100h
        mov word ptr es:[ _CS           ][ si ], es
        mov word ptr es:[ _ExtraSegment ][ si ], es
        mov word ptr es:[ _DataSegment  ][ si ], es
        mov word ptr es:[ _BP           ][ si ], 0000
        mov word ptr es:[ _DI           ][ si ], 0000
        mov word ptr es:[ _SI           ][ si ], 0000
        mov word ptr es:[ _DX           ][ si ], 0000

        getdarg bx, cx, _filesize
```

```
          mov word ptr es:[ _CX         ][ si ], cx
          mov word ptr es:[ _BX         ][ si ], bx
          mov word ptr es:[ _AX         ][ si ], 0000

;- - - - - - - - - - - - - - - - - - - - - - - - - - - - - - - - - -
; set DTA on the way out; switch stacks.
;- - - - - - - - - - - - - - - - - - - - - - - - - - - - - - - - - -
_loadProgram_50:
          mov es, word ptr [ _RxDOS_CurrentPSP ]          ; new PSP
          mov word ptr [ _RxDOS_pDTA. _segment ], es
          mov word ptr [ _RxDOS_pDTA. _pointer ], pspCommandTail

          cli
          mov bx, word ptr cs:[ _RxDOS_CurrentInstance ]
          mov ax, word ptr es:[ pspParentId    ]          ; parent PSP address
          sti                                             ; reenable interrupts
          or ax, ax                                       ; if no current PSP
          jz _loadProgram_56                              ; none ->

          push word ptr cs:[ _segment ][ bx ]
          push word ptr cs:[ _pointer ][ bx ]
          pop word ptr es:[ pspUserStack. _pointer ]
          pop word ptr es:[ pspUserStack. _segment ]

;- - - - - - - - - - - - - - - - - - - - - - - - - - - - - - - - - -
; exit.
;- - - - - - - - - - - - - - - - - - - - - - - - - - - - - - - - - -
_loadProgram_56:
          Return
```

It may seem a little boring to look at the code for loading a COM program. After all, if the EXE file layout is more sophisticated for handling larger and more interesting programs, why bother with a COM program? It is necessary to understand this code since it lays the necessary groundwork for the loading of an EXE file, which is not that much more complex.

The steps necessary to load the program are to determine the program size to load and then to allocate space for both an environment block, the PSP, and the program itself. The function that allocates this space is the _LoaderAllocMemory, which accepts the EXEC block in order to copy the Environment block, and both the required and requested paragraphs to load the program in the AX and DX registers, respectively. The requested paragraphs for a COM file are all memory. The required paragraphs are the size of the program.

Looking at the listing of the LoadProgram function, the size of a COM program is taken from the DIRACCESS block returned by the file locate function and is converted to paragraphs. The largest theoretically loadable file is the entire 1MB available in real mode, or 65536 paragraphs. The paragraph size can be safely stored in a word.

If the memory allocation routine fails, the error code is returned in the AX register together with the carry flag set, the sort of standard error reporting convention used throughout RxDOS. If it succeeds, the PSP segment address is returned in the AX register, and the actual load segment address in the ES register. Almost always, these two addresses are within the size of the PSP apart from each other, as shown on the left in Figure 6-2. Because an EXE program can sometimes be loaded high within an allocated block, the two addresses may differ by a substantial amount.

Figure 6-2. How EXE programs are loaded high

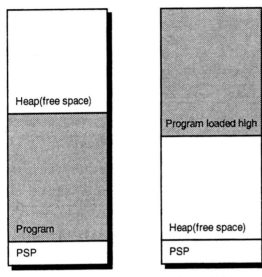

EXE loaded normally   EXE loaded high

_LoaderAllocMemory is called whether it's loading a COM or EXE program and is responsible for allocating the memory needed for the program, the PSP, and the environment block. The routine is called with both minimum and maximum memory requirements. The code tries to allocate a memory block that fits within these parameters. The memory block allocated depends on the memory subsystem allocation strategy, which is settable by DOS function 58h. The allocation strategy can be set to either First Fit, Best Fit, or Last Fit, with First Fit being the DOS default strategy. The allocations made for a program are based on the internal memory allocation functions DOS uses and are subject to the strategy established when the program is loaded. Since DOS relies on the memory strategy, it is possible to allocate and load programs in the UMBs, or Upper Memory Blocks.

```
(in rxdosexe.asm)
        ;////////////////////////////////////////////////////////////////;
        ; Allocate Loader Memory, copy Env block, init PSP               ;
        ;- - - - - - - - - - - - - - - - - - - - - - - - - - - - - - - - -;
        ;                                                                 ;
        ; Input:                                                          ;
        ;   es:bx   load execute block                                    ;
        ;   ax      paragraphs of program expected                        ;
        ;   dx      max requested paragraphs                              ;
        ;                                                                 ;
        ; Output:                                                         ;
        ;   ax      PSP segment address                                   ;
```

```
        ;   es        Data segment address                              ;
        ;   cx        size in paras of area allocated                   ;
        ;   cy        if cannot create                                  ;
        ;.................................................................;

_LoaderAllocMemory:
        Entry
        ddef  _ExecBlock, es, bx
        def   _requiredParas, ax
        def   _maxRequestedParas, dx
        def   _allocatedSize, 0000
        def   _envSeg, 0000
        def   _AllocEnv, 0000
        def   _programPSP, 0000
        def   _loadHIGH, FALSE
        def   _StartSegment
        def   _envSize
        add word ptr [ _requiredParas ][ bp ], (sizePSP / PARAGRAPH)

        or dx, dx                                  ; special 0000 request ?
        jnz _loaderAllocMemory_04                  ; no -->
        mov word ptr [ _maxRequestedParas ][ bp ], FFFFh
        mov word ptr [ _loadHIGH ][ bp ], TRUE

_loaderAllocMemory_04:
        mov ax, word ptr [ _requiredParas ][ bp ]
        cmp ax, word ptr [ _maxRequestedParas ][ bp ]
        jc _loaderAllocMemory_08
        jz _loaderAllocMemory_08
        mov word ptr [ _maxRequestedParas ][ bp ], ax

;- - - - - - - - - - - - - - - - - - - - - - - - - - - - - - - - - - -
;  determine the size of the environment block, if any.
;- - - - - - - - - - - - - - - - - - - - - - - - - - - - - - - - - - -
_loaderAllocMemory_08:
        mov ax, word ptr es:[ lexecEnvironment ][ bx ]
        or ax, ax                                  ; env block address passed ?
        jnz _loaderAllocMemory_12                  ; if segment passed -->

        mov ax, word ptr cs:[ _RxDOS_CurrentPSP ]
        or ax, ax                                  ; current PSP available ?
        jz _loaderAllocMemory_18                   ; no, go figure something -->

        mov es, ax
        mov ax, word ptr es:[ pspEnvironment ]     ; get environment block address
        or ax, ax                                  ; none available -->
        jz _loaderAllocMemory_18                   ; no, go figure something -->

_loaderAllocMemory_12:
        storarg _envSeg, ax                        ; save env segment to copy

        mov es, ax            ,                    ; memory block address
        call _getMemBlockSize                      ; get size
        storarg _envSize, cx                       ; save size in paras
```

```
        call allocateMemBlock                 ; ret seg ptr to memory
        jc _loaderAllocMemory_50              ; if insuf space to load ->
        storarg _AllocEnv, es                 ; store alloc environment

;- - - - - - - - - - - - - - - - - - - - - - - - - - - - - - - - - -
; copy environment
;- - - - - - - - - - - - - - - - - - - - - - - - - - - - - - - - - -
        push ds
        xor di, di
        xor si, si
        getarg ds, _envSeg
        getarg cx, _envSize                   ; env size in paras
        shl cx, 1                             ; convert to words !
        shl cx, 1
        shl cx, 1
        rep movsw                             ; copy env block

        pop ds

;- - - - - - - - - - - - - - - - - - - - - - - - - - - - - - - - - -
; allocate block
;- - - - - - - - - - - - - - - - - - - - - - - - - - - - - - - - - -
_loaderAllocMemory_18:
        getarg ax, _requiredParas
        getarg dx, _maxRequestedParas
        call _allocateMinMaxMemBlock          ; ret seg ptr memory
        jc _loaderAllocMemory_50              ; if insuf space to load ->
        storarg _programPSP, es               ; save PSP seg address
        storarg _allocatedSize, cx            ; allocated size

;- - - - - - - - - - - - - - - - - - - - - - - - - - - - - - - - - -
; create child PSP
;- - - - - - - - - - - - - - - - - - - - - - - - - - - - - - - - - -
        getarg cx, _AllocEnv                  ; new environment block
        getdarg dx, ax, _ExecBlock            ; load exec structure
        call createPSP                        ; build PSP
        storarg _StartSegment, es             ; PSP here

;- - - - - - - - - - - - - - - - - - - - - - - - - - - - - - - - - -
; ensure parent's handle are set for both blocks
;- - - - - - - - - - - - - - - - - - - - - - - - - - - - - - - - - -
        getarg dx, _programPSP
        mov ax, dx
        sub ax, (sizeMEMBLOCK/ PARAGRAPH)
        mov es, ax                            ; point to allocation block
        mov word ptr es:[ _memParent ], dx    ; assign parent

        getarg ax, _AllocEnv
        or ax, ax                             ; none required ?
        jz _loaderAllocMemory_56              ; no ->
        sub ax, (sizeMEMBLOCK/ PARAGRAPH)
        mov es, ax                            ; point to allocation block
        mov word ptr es:[ _memParent ], dx    ; assign parent
        jmp short _loaderAllocMemory_56       ; if everything is ok ->
```

```
;- - - - - - - - - - - - - - - - - - - - - - - - - - - - - - - -
;   free env block if error
;- - - - - - - - - - - - - - - - - - - - - - - - - - - - - - - -
_loaderAllocMemory_50:
        getarg ax, _AllocEnv
        or ax, ax                                    ; Env allocated ?
        jz _loaderAllocMemory_54                      ; no ->

        mov es, ax
        call _freeMemBlock

_loaderAllocMemory_54:
        SetError errNotEnoughMemory

;- - - - - - - - - - - - - - - - - - - - - - - - - - - - - - - -
;   return
;- - - - - - - - - - - - - - - - - - - - - - - - - - - - - - - -
_loaderAllocMemory_56:
        getarg ax, _programPSP
        getarg es, _StartSegment
        getarg cx, _allocatedSize

        Return
```

Here's how the process allocation function works. There are two allocation size limits, the requested size, which represents a sort of desirable maximum value, and the required size, which is the minimum size required for the program to load. The required size is adjusted by the size of the PSP. This now represents the actual size in paragraphs needed to load the program, and it is compared to the requested size. If the requested size is too small, it is made to equal the required size.

Having adjusted the allocation request sizes, the environment block is allocated ahead of the program space. The routine determines if an environment block address was passed in the EXEC block. If the environment block address passed is zero, the environment block of the current process is fetched. In some internal RxDOS circumstances, such as when first loading the command shell, there is neither a current PSP nor an environment block, so the routine performs internal checks to ensure that the wrong memory location is not accessed. It is also possible that some software set the PSP address to zero. This routine tries to be defensive and protective about the environment.

If there is an environment block, the size of the block is retrieved by calling _getMemBlockSize. The routine insulated the program loader from changes to the memory block architecture, however remote and unlikely. With the size of the environment block available, the memory allocation routine is called, which returns the segment address of the new environment control block area. The routine performs an error jump if the allocation routine could not allocate the memory block; otherwise, the segment address is saved, and the contents of the parent environment block are copied to the spawned environment block.

Next, a memory block must be allocated to the program. If successful, the block returned is a block that fits between the minimum and maximum blocks requested, or as stated in the program, between the required and requested blocks. The function used to allocate the block is located in rxdosmem.asm. Internal to RxDOS is a memory allocation routine that, given a size request and an allocation strategy, scans, evaluates, and possibly allocates an available memory block. The strategy for allocating a program is different. The block must meet the minimum requirement, but it must also be as large as possible without exceeding the largest request size. Although the common allocation routines have a pass/fail strategy based on a single request size, programs utilize a more flexible allocation strategy.

The memory allocation function is listed next. It first attempts to access the requested block. If this request is allocated, the function returns with the allocated block. However, this request often fails because it is either the FFFFh paragraphs set by the linker for EXE files or by the COM program loader to represent all memory. In real mode, this request would fail because all memory available is never available. The allocate routine returns the largest available memory block size. This size is compared to the minimum required size. If the block's size is at least as big as the required size, the block is reallocated for the amount of memory available.

After the program memory block is allocated, minor clean-up is required before the routine can successfully return. A PSP must be created at the start of the program's allocated block, and the owner (parent field) of each of the two allocated blocks must be set to the new spawned PSP. This commits these data structures to the new process. If the program memory block cannot be allocated, it frees the allocated environment block.

The routine terminates by returning the segment addresses of the PSP, the start segment to load the program, which is always just above the PSP itself, and the allocated size of the block.

```
(in rxdosmem.asm)
        ;'''''''''''''''''''''''''''''''''''''''''''''''''''''''''''''';
        ;                                                              ;
        ;   Allocate Min Max Memory Block                              ;
        ;- - - - - - - - - - - - - - - - - - - - - - - - - - - - - -;
        ;                                                              ;
        ;   Input:                                                     ;
        ;   ax    minimum block                                        ;
        ;   dx    maximum block                                        ;
        ;                                                              ;
        ;   Returns:                                                   ;
        ;   es    segment address of allocated memory block            ;
        ;   ax    segment address of allocated memory block header     ;
        ;   cx    size of memory available                             ;
        ;..............................................................;

_allocateMinMaxMemBlock:
        Entry
        def _minParag, ax
        def _maxParag, dx

        mov cx, dx                                  ; try for max
        call allocateMemBlock                       ; will probably fail
        jnc _allocateMinMaxMemBlock_20              ; if ok ->

        cmp cx, word ptr [ _minParag ][ bp ]        ; largest available will fit ?
        jnc _allocateMinMaxMemBlock_12             ; yes, go for max ->
        SetError errNotEnoughMemory, _allocateMinMaxMemBlock_20

_allocateMinMaxMemBlock_12:
        call allocateMemBlock                       ; allocate largest available
        mov es, ax                                  ; segment address
```

```
        sub  ax, (sizeMEMBLOCK/ PARAGRAPH)
        or   ax, ax

_allocateMinMaxMemBlock_20:
        Return
```

So far all we have covered of the COM loading is the allocation of the environment and program blocks. The allocation routine returns two segment addresses, one to the PSP in the AX register and the other to where the program should load, in the ES register. These two segment addresses almost always differ by the size of the PSP, except for the special case of EXE files that are loaded high within the allocated block.

To differentiate between the various load options, DOS can load a program in high or low space or wherever space is available in memory. This is controlled by the memory system allocation strategy, settable through DOS function 58h. When a memory block is allocated, it is at least as large as the required space. However, it may be much larger than required, depending on the requested space. Since the allocated block may be larger than the program size, the space between the top of the program and the end of the allocated block is available as the heap. However, it is possible to request that the program be relocated high within the allocated area, forcing the heap to reside below the program. It is used by some forms of Pascal. However, a COM program cannot be loaded high within an allocated block.

After the allocation of memory blocks, the next immediate task is to load the program image to memory. The readLogicalBuffer routine reads from disk to a buffer located at ES:DI. The position pointer in the file, the byte count to read, and the disk access block containing the file's disk drive, starting cluster, and file size must be provided to the read routine, which we introduced and discussed in Chapter 2. Unfortunately, the routine can read only slightly less than a 64K buffer at each call. Therefore, the code immediately on either side of the read call is to set the buffer size and the buffer pointer. Immediately before the call, the file position is subtracted from the file size to determine the buffer count. If the buffer count exceeds 64K, the buffer is arbitrarily set to 60K. To prevent memory wraparound, the program is loaded in 60K blocks. It could just as easily have been loaded in 32K or 64K minus one paragraph sized blocks. After the buffer read, the read segment address is advanced by the read count. The math is segment oriented with the count first being converted to paragraphs so that it can be added to the segment register. The unused part of the count, the remainder in the low order nibble, is added to the buffer address.

Eventually, the entire file, whatever its size, is fully read into memory. The amount read is guaranteed to be within the allocated buffer, otherwise an error exit would have been taken, so there is no need for error checking during reading.

If the program successfully loaded to memory, the final stage is to switch processes. This code begins at _LoadProgram_24. A valid PSP has been created and initialized, so it is possible to simply set the current PSP with the value of the new PSP. But what happens to the value of the old PSP? When the new PSP was created, in createPSP, the current PSP value had already been saved.

Once the program for the new process has been loaded, it should be just a matter of setting the registers for the data segments and stack and jumping to start address. This would leave DOS in a funny state. The InDOS flag would remain set, and in RxDOS, valuable internal stack space would be wasted. Instead, a call stack is created in the user's address space, DOS then internally switches context, and a normal return is performed. The normal return will return on the new process's stack to the new process's start address.

The stack address for the new process is determined. The stack is created at the highest address possible within the first segment. The allocated memory segment for the process, though it may include all the available memory, may be smaller than a full 64K segment. Therefore, the stack is not always at the top end of a segment.

The code determines the total size of the block allocated to contain the PSP. If the block exceeds 64K, a stack is arbitrarily placed at the upper limit of the segment, at 0FFFEh. If the allocated block is less than 64K, the stack is placed at the upper limit of the allocated block. The stack decision is based on the belief that the stack must be accessible from the data segment, and the data segment points to the PSP. Therefore, the stack must be within 64K of the PSP. The stack address of the new process must be recorded in the PSP, where it is used later to return to the process.

A new stack address is created, and then it is adjusted by the number of words used by DOS. A DOS call created by an int 21h will require a word for the flag registers, two words for the far return address, and one word for each of the 16-bit registers. Not coincidentally, that is, purposefully, the label _Flags is exactly the number of words used by DOS on the stack since it is the offset between the last register saved on the stack and the first register saved by the hardware when performing the int 21h call.

What about DOS function calls that do not utilize the int 21h convention? Although in this it doesn't matter since we are just emulating the int 21h call, all DOS calls perform an int 21h, even if at one time they begin as a call far instruction. DOS internally either must emulate the int 21h or actually perform the int 21h function.

At any rate, the return stack must still be built in the new process and a pointer set within DOS to point to the new stack. The code begins at label _loadProgram_28. The stack address computed earlier based on the size of the allocated segment is temporarily maintained in the ES:SI register pair. It is first adjusted down by a word so as to not overflow the segment limit. It is then adjusted downward again by the number of words used by DOS.

Whenever an int 21h is executed, DOS saves the registers passed by the user into the caller's stack. Since this is a new process, the new process's stack is made to appear as if it were populated by the saved registers. DOS can then perform a normal exit from a function call, which will cause the values stored on the new process's stack to be restored to registers. The return address saved in the new process's stack points to the starting address of the program.

The flag register is set to no carry, not zero, by the following instructions:

```
or si, si
pushf
pop word ptr es:[ _Flags        ][ si ]
```

The or instruction sets the flag bits. The resulting value is copied to the new process's stack, pointed to by the ES:SI registers.

Next, the remaining registers in the stack are initialized. The CS:IP register pair is set to the start of the program, that is, at the process's load segment beginning at address 100h. The rest of the registers are set to zero except for the BX:CX register pair, which is set to the file size.

```
        mov   word ptr es:[ _IP          ][ si ], 100h
        mov   word ptr es:[ _CS          ][ si ], es
        mov   word ptr es:[ _ExtraSegment ][ si ], es
        mov   word ptr es:[ _DataSegment ][ si ], es
        mov   word ptr es:[ _BP          ][ si ], 0000
        mov   word ptr es:[ _DI          ][ si ], 0000
        mov   word ptr es:[ _SI          ][ si ], 0000
        mov   word ptr es:[ _DX          ][ si ], 0000

        getdarg bx, cx, _filesize
        mov   word ptr es:[ _CX          ][ si ], cx
        mov   word ptr es:[ _BX          ][ si ], bx
        mov   word ptr es:[ _AX          ][ si ], 0000
```

The caller's stack is referred to by an Instance pointer in RxDOS. The reason this is called an Instance pointer is RxDOS, unlike MS-DOS, can be interrupted while already executing a DOS function. Each interruption is referred to as an Instance. Instance pointers point to the caller's stack. When a process is spawned, the stack is initialized in the new process and must be instanced within RxDOS. This enables DOS to return through the new stack.

Beginning at _loadProgram_50, both the COM and EXE program logic merge. Earlier in load routine, EXE programs were detected and loaded by an EXE loader. We describe that loader in the next few pages. Both the COM and EXE functions return and join here to perform common last-minute setup.

One of the major vestiges of DOS as a single-process operating system is exemplified by the code that follows. The DTA, or Disk Transfer Address, is set. One could argue that DOS has a serious and unadvertised bug. Although the DTA is changed to the command tail area of the new process, it is never restored when the spawned process terminates. Programs that spawn other processes like command.com must remember then restore the DTA.

Ordinarily, this bug isn't very catastrophic. Few programs shell out to DOS or to any other process. However, the fact that the DTA is changed and is left pointing to memory no longer owned by the process qualifies as a bug that should be corrected. dtabug, a program provided on the diskette included with this book, demonstrates this bug even in MS-DOS 6.0. The program reports the DTA addresses both before and after it launches a child program.

The last few lines of the COM load program function are as follows:

```
;- - - - - - - - - - - - - - - - - - - - - - - - - - - - - - - - - - -
;  set DTA on the way out; switch stacks.
;- - - - - - - - - - - - - - - - - - - - - - - - - - - - - - - - - - -
_loadProgram_50:
        mov   es, word ptr [ _RxDOS_CurrentPSP ]           ; new PSP
        mov   word ptr [ _RxDOS_pDTA._segment ], es
        mov   word ptr [ _RxDOS_pDTA._pointer ], pspCommandTail

        cli
        mov   bx, word ptr ss:[ _RxDOS_CurrentInstance ]
        mov   ax, word ptr es:[ pspParentId   ]            ; parent PSP address
        sti                                                ; reenable interrupts
        or    ax, ax                                       ; if no current PSP
        jz    _loadProgram_56                              ; none -->
```

```
        push word ptr ss:[ _segment ][ bx ]
        push word ptr ss:[ _pointer ][ bx ]
        pop word ptr es:[ pspUserStack. _pointer ]
        pop word ptr es:[ pspUserStack. _segment ]

;- - - - - - - - - - - - - - - - - - - - - - - - - - - - - - - - - -
;  exit.
;- - - - - - - - - - - - - - - - - - - - - - - - - - - - - - - - - -
_loadProgram_56:
        Return
```

The program sets the DTA address. The old value of the DTA has already been saved in the call registers for the dormant parent task. The current stack pointer must be set in the PSP for the return to be properly accomplished.

In summary, the process is created by allocating memory, loading the program to the allocated memory, placing the initial register values, including the program's starting address and data segment values, into the new process's stack, switching the Instance and current PSP variables in DOS to the new process, and then performing a normal exit from DOS.

The normal exit DOS performs from any function call will no longer exit through the parent process. Rather, because the current PSP (and internally, the current call Instance) was changed, DOS exits to the new process. The parent process (there is no old process) remains in memory in a suspended dormant state, believing it is still inside DOS executing DOS function 4Bh. It is restarted when the child process terminates using either the normal DOS terminate or the terminate and stay resident functions, that is, DOS functions 4Ch, 31h (TSR), or other terminate functions such as int 20h or int 27h.

Loading an EXE Program

There are many similarities between loading an EXE program and loading a COM program. The load EXE function is called from within the load program function when an EXE header is detected. The load program doesn't care or check the program file's extension. EXE programs contain a specific signature in the first 2 bytes.

Specifically, the program's header is read using a DISKACCESS block. The block is filled by the directory locate function. If the file exists, the block contains the file's disk drive, starting cluster, and file size. The header bytes are read and checked to ensure that the signature field contains the EXE file signature, an MZ. The EXE header is laid out as shown. The signature is the first 2 bytes of the header.

```
        ;,,,,,,,,,,,,,,,,,,,,,,,,,,,,,,,,,,,,,,,,,,,,,,,,,,,,,,,,,,,,,;
        ;  Exe File Header                                            ;
        ;............................................................;

        EXEHEADER struc
exeSignature            dw ?            ; .EXE file signature
exeExtraBytes           dw ?            ; number of bytes in last partial page
exePages                dw ?            ; number of whole and partial pages
```

```
exeRelocItems          dw ?                    ; number of pointers in reloc table
exeHeaderSize          dw ?                    ; size of header, in paragraphs
exeMinAlloc            dw ?                    ; minimum allocation (parag)
exeMaxAlloc            dw ?                    ; maximum allocation (parag)
exeInitSS             dw ?                    ; initial ss value
exeInitSP             dw ?                    ; initial sp value
exeChecksum            dw ?                    ; complemented checksum
exeInitIP             dw ?                    ; initial ip value
exeInitCS             dw ?                    ; initial cs value
exeRelocTable          dw ?                    ; byte offset to reloc table
exeOverlay             dw ?                    ; overlay number
                       dw 16 dup( ? )          ; reserved (unused)
exeNewExe             dd ?                    ; pointer to new EXE header
        EXEHEADER ends

EXE_SIGNATURE          equ 5A4DH               ; 'MZ'
```

The code that checks for the EXE signature is shown here.

```
(in rxdosexe.asm)
        ;'''''''''''''''''''''''''''''''''''''''''''''''''''''''''''''''';
        ;  Determine if file is EXE formatted                          ;
        ;- - - - - - - - - - - - - - - - - - - - - - - - - - - - - - -;
        ;                                                              ;
        ;  Input:                                                      ;
        ;   ss:bx  disk access block                                   ;
        ;                                                              ;
        ;  Output:                                                     ;
        ;   zr     file is an EXE                                      ;
        ;   nz     file is not an EXE                                  ;
        ;..............................................................;

checkEXEHeader:
        Entry
        defbytes _exeHeader, sizeEXEHEADER

        xor dx, dx
        xor ax, ax                             ; file pointer to beg of file
        mov cx, sizeEXEHEADER
        lea di, offset _exeHeader [ bp ]
        call readLogicalBuffer                 ; Access buffer: ss: bx

        cmp word ptr [ _exeHeader. exeSignature ][ bp ], EXE_SIGNATURE
        Return
```

If the file contains the EXE signature, the EXE loader function is called. The EXE loader allocates space for the EXE program, loads the program to memory performing any segment and address relocations required, and then sets the initial values for the register in the new program's stack. There is considerable overlap in the process and requirements between loading an EXE and a COM file, but the details are different.

The amount of memory to allocate for the EXE program is not taken from the file size. Rather, it is computed by taking the number of pages recorded in the EXE header. An EXE program can contain additional data beyond the program, such as debugger symbols, resources, or other data. In other words, the size of an EXE file may be larger than the size of the program itself.

The EXE load routine begins by reinitializing a DISKACCESS block. This repositions the file pointer to the beginning of the file. The EXE header is reread. Since there exists at least one disk cache block, the contents to be read are already in memory. The routine rereads the header buffer here because as an EXE load routine it aims to be independent of whatever process occurred prior to it having been called.

The listing for the load EXE function is as follows:

```
(in rxdosexe.asm)
        ;//////////////////////////////////////////////////////////;
        ;  Load Exe Program                                         ;
        ;- - - - - - - - - - - - - - - - - - - - - - - - - - - - -;
        ;                                                          ;
        ;  Input:                                                  ;
        ;   ss:di  pointer to directory block                     ;
        ;   es:bx  address of EXEC structure                      ;
        ;   ax     subfunction code                               ;
        ;                                                          ;
        ;  Output:                                                 ;
        ;   dx     PSP segment address                            ;
        ;   cy     load failed                                    ;
        ;..........................................................;

loadExe_Program:
        Entry
        def   _Mode, ax
        def   _programPSP
        def   _StartSegment
        def   _SizePara
        def   _actualSizePara
        def   _CheckSum
        ddef  _ExecBlock, es, bx
        ddef  _dirAccess, ss, di
        defbytes _exeHeader, sizeEXEHEADER
        defbytes _diskAccess, sizeDISKACCESS
        defbytes _relocitem, 4

        xor   cx, cx
        storarg _programPSP   , cx
        storarg _StartSegment, cx
        storarg _CheckSum     , cx

;- - - - - - - - - - - - - - - - - - - - - - - - - - - - - - - - -
;  initialize disk access block
;- - - - - - - - - - - - - - - - - - - - - - - - - - - - - - - - -
        mov ax, word ptr ss:[ fileAcDrive   ][ di ]
        mov dx, word ptr ss:[ fileAcCluster ][ di ]
        lea bx, offset _diskAccess [ bp ]            ; build access control block
        call initdiskAccess                          ; [ax] is drive, [dx] is cluster

        les si, dword ptr [ fileAcBufferPtr ][ di ]
```

```
        add si, word ptr [ fileAcDirOffset ][ di ]
        mov ax, word ptr es:[ deFileSize. _low  ][ si ]
        mov dx, word ptr es:[ deFileSize. _high ][ si ]
        mov word ptr [ _diskAccess. diskAcFileSize. _low  ][ bp ], ax
        mov word ptr [ _diskAccess. diskAcFileSize. _high ][ bp ], dx

        xor dx, dx
        xor ax, ax                              ; position to beg of file
        setES ss
        lea di, offset _exeHeader [ bp ]
        mov cx, sizeEXEHEADER
        call readLogicalBuffer                  ; Access buffer: ss: bx
        call computeChecksum
        mov word ptr [ _CheckSum ][ bp ], ax

;- - - - - - - - - - - - - - - - - - - - - - - - - - - - - - - - - - - -
;  compute size in pages of load module
;- - - - - - - - - - - - - - - - - - - - - - - - - - - - - - - - - - - -
        mov dx, word ptr [ _exeHeader. exeExtraBytes ][ bp ]
        add dx, (PARAGRAPH - 1)                 ; round up parags needed
        shr dx, 1
        shr dx, 1
        shr dx, 1
        shr dx, 1                               ; paragraphs at end needed

        mov ax, word ptr [ _exeHeader. exePages ][ bp ]
        dec ax                                  ; adjust for last block
        shl ax, 1                               ; conv pages to paragraphs
        shl ax, 1                               ;   4
        shl ax, 1                               ;   8
        shl ax, 1                               ;  16
        shl ax, 1                               ;  32
        sub ax, word ptr [ _exeHeader. exeHeaderSize ][ bp ]
        add ax, dx                              ; actual paragr needed
        add ax, word ptr [ _exeHeader. exeMinAlloc ][ bp ]
        storarg _SizePara, ax                   ; save as paragraphs needed
        storarg _actualSizePara, ax             ; save actual also

        mov dx, word ptr [ _exeHeader. exeMaxAlloc ][ bp ]
        getdarg es, bx, _ExecBlock              ; load exec module
        call _LoaderAllocMemory                 ; alloc memory for env block/ PSP
        ifc loadExe_Program50                   ; if cannot allocate ->

        storarg _StartSegment, es               ; where data load begins
        storarg _programPSP, ax                 ; save seg address of PSP

;- - - - - - - - - - - - - - - - - - - - - - - - - - - - - - - - - - - -
;  load module
;- - - - - - - - - - - - - - - - - - - - - - - - - - - - - - - - - - - -
        dec word ptr [ _SizePara ][ bp ]        ; all but last para

        mov ax, word ptr [ _exeHeader. exeHeaderSize ][ bp ]
        shl ax, 1                               ;   2
```

```
        shl ax, 1                                    ; 4
        shl ax, 1                                    ; 8
        shl ax, 1                                    ; 16 byte offset
        xor dx, dx

loadExe_Program08:
        push es
        push dx
        push ax                                      ; save position in file

        mov cx, word ptr [ _SizePara ][ bp ]         ; get paras to read
        test cx, 0F000h                              ; over 65K ?
        jz loadExe_Program12                         ; no, read whole file ->
        mov cx, 0FFFh                                ; read as much as possible

loadExe_Program12:
        push cx                                      ; save paras to read

        shl cx, 1
        shl cx, 1
        shl cx, 1
        shl cx, 1
        push cx                                      ; save bytes actually to read

        xor di, di                                   ; load at _StartSeg:0000
        lea bx, offset _diskAccess [ bp ]            ; build access control block
        call readLogicalBuffer                       ; Access buffer: ss: bx
        call computeChecksum
        add word ptr [ _CheckSum ][ bp ], ax

        pop cx                                        ; bytes read
        pop bx                                        ; paras read
        pop ax                                        ; previous file offset
        pop dx
        add ax, cx                                    ; incr position by bytes read
        adc dx, 0000

        pop cx                                        ; segment loaded
        add cx, bx                                    ; increment by paras read
        mov es, cx                                    ; set new read segment

        sub word ptr [ _SizePara ][ bp ], bx          ; subtract paragraphs used.
        jnz loadExe_Program08

        xor di, di                                    ; load at _StartSeg:0000
        mov cx, word ptr [ _exeHeader. exeExtraBytes ][ bp ]
        and cx, (PARAGRAPH - 1)                        ; last 15 bytes
        jz loadExe_Program20                          ; if none to read ->

        lea bx, offset _diskAccess [ bp ]             ; build access control block
        call readLogicalBuffer                        ; Access buffer: ss: bx
        call computeChecksum
        add word ptr [ _CheckSum ][ bp ], ax
```

```
;- - - - - - - - - - - - - - - - - - - - - - - - - - - - - - - - - - -
;   address relocation blocks
;- - - - - - - - - - - - - - - - - - - - - - - - - - - - - - - - - - -
loadExe_Program20:
        mov ax, word ptr [ _exeHeader. exeRelocItems ][ bp ]
        or ax, ax
        jz loadExe_Program32

loadExe_Program28:
        setES ss
        mov cx, 4
        xor dx, dx
        mov ax, word ptr [ _exeHeader. exeRelocTable ][ bp ]
        lea di, offset _relocitem [ bp ]
        lea bx, offset _diskAccess [ bp ]              ; build access control block
        call readLogicalBuffer                          ; Access buffer: ss: bx
        call computeChecksum
        add word ptr [ _CheckSum ][ bp ], ax

        getdarg dx, bx, _relocitem                      ; get reloc item
        getarg ax, _StartSegment                        ; starting segment

        add dx, ax
        mov es, dx
        add word ptr es:[ bx ], ax                      ; relocate load module

        add word ptr [ _exeHeader. exeRelocTable ][ bp ], 4
        dec word ptr [ _exeHeader. exeRelocItems ][ bp ]
        jnz loadExe_Program28

;- - - - - - - - - - - - - - - - - - - - - - - - - - - - - - - - - - -
;   execute
;- - - - - - - - - - - - - - - - - - - - - - - - - - - - - - - - - - -
loadExe_Program32:
        mov ax, word ptr [ _CheckSum ][ bp ]
        add ax, word ptr [ _exeHeader. exeChecksum  ][ bp ]

        getarg es, _programPSP                          ; child process's PSP
        mov dx, word ptr [ _exeHeader. exeInitSS  ][ bp ]
        add dx, word ptr [ _StartSegment ][ bp ]
        mov si, word ptr [ _exeHeader. exeInitSP  ][ bp ]

        sub si, 2
        mov word ptr es:[ pspUserStack. _pointer ], si
        mov word ptr es:[ pspUserStack. _segment ], dx

        setES dx                                        ; child program's stack seg
        sub si, _Flags
        mov bx, word ptr cs:[ _RxDOS_CurrentInstance ]
        mov word ptr ss:[ _pointer ][ bx ], si
        mov word ptr ss:[ _segment ][ bx ], dx          ; new process stack

        or si, si
        pushf
```

```
        pop word ptr es:[ _Flags        ][ si ]

        mov dx, word ptr [ _StartSegment ][ bp ]
        add dx, word ptr [ _exeHeader. exeInitCS    ][ bp ]
        mov ax, word ptr [ _exeHeader. exeInitIP    ][ bp ]
        mov word ptr es:[ _IP          ][ si ], ax
        mov word ptr es:[ _CS          ][ si ], dx

        getarg bx, _programPSP                          ; child process's PSP
        mov word ptr es:[ _ExtraSegment ][ si ], bx
        mov word ptr es:[ _DataSegment  ][ si ], bx
        mov word ptr es:[ _BP          ][ si ], 0000
        mov word ptr es:[ _DI          ][ si ], 0000
        mov word ptr es:[ _SI          ][ si ], 0000
        mov word ptr es:[ _DX          ][ si ], 0000

        mov ax, PARAGRAPH
        mul word ptr [ _actualSizePara ][ bp ]

        mov word ptr es:[ _CX          ][ si ], ax
        mov word ptr es:[ _BX          ][ si ], dx
        mov word ptr es:[ _AX          ][ si ], 0000

;- - - - - - - - - - - - - - - - - - - - - - - - - - - - - - - -
; copy startup command line to _PSP
;- - - - - - - - - - - - - - - - - - - - - - - - - - - - - - - -
        getarg ax, _programPSP                          ; child process's PSP
        mov word ptr [ _RxDOS_CurrentPSP ], ax          ; change running PSP
        or ax, ax

loadExe_Program50:
        Return
```

The routine examines the header to determine the memory size requirements of the program. The minimum required size is computed by taking the size of the program in pages, minus the header size and adjusting for the unused space in the last page. Each page is 512 bytes.

The MS-DOS loader presumes that the last page is always full, an assumption that causes it sometimes to load more data than necessary. One additional side effect of the MS-DOS loader is that the minimum requirements are up to 480 bytes larger. It eats space in upper memory blocks, and in really constrained memory cases, some programs cannot load. These cases are unusual, and the additional space utilized is minimal.

RxDOS converts the bytes at the last page to paragraphs, then takes the number of pages in the EXE header, subtracts one to account for the last page, and converts the number of pages to paragraphs. Finally, from the sum of the paragraphs between all the pages it subtracts the number of paragraphs taken by the header. To this the minimum number of additional paragraphs are added, creating the actual minimum required paragraphs for this program.

The maximum or requested paragraphs are taken from the EXE header. As we noted in the previous section, the requested size is often set by the linker to all memory, denoted by the convenient 0FFFFh. This large number is only a requested size. The actual size returned is the largest allocatable block of memory if it is large enough to meet the minimum or required memory size.

We discussed the memory allocation function in detail in the section "Loading a COM Program." It not only allocates the memory, but it also creates and copies the environment block and initializes the PSP.

Once memory has been allocated, the EXE program can be loaded. Both the RxDOS COM and EXE loaders are careful about the number of bytes it loads. The EXE file loader begins by positioning the file just past the EXE header. It reads chunks of the file that are 64K or less, depending on how much file space remains to be read. The 64K limit is due to a limitation of the read logical routine.

If you examine the code carefully, you'll notice that after every read, the checksum value is updated. The code appears as

```
lea bx, offset _diskAccess [ bp ]          ; build access control block
call readLogicalBuffer                      ; Access buffer: ss: bx
call computeChecksum
add word ptr [ _CheckSum ][ bp ], ax
```

Checksum support was dropped from the EXE file, if it was ever supported. The checksum field is almost always zero, and MS-DOS will accept any value in this field. Although RxDOS computes the checksum, it is never checked against the header. Checksum support was never implemented, and correctly so in my opinion, to permit an EXE file to be patched.

Once the EXE file is read, segment references, far calls, and far jumps require segment relocation. Each EXE file contains a relocation table. The relocation table is immediately after the header in EXE files. Each entry is a double-word offset into the memory image. The offset points to a word in memory that is to be relocated. The segment address of where the file was loaded is added to this word.

The size of the relocation table for some programs can be huge. Each far function call represents an entry in the relocation table. This is especially true for large model C programs.

The segment relocation begins at loadEXE_Program20. If there are any relocation items, each double-word entry is read from disk, one at a time. The word read is an offset from the beginning of the memory image of the file. The load segment address is applied to the high-order word of the relocation offset. This points to the correct word in the loaded file. The location referenced is then relocated by the file's load address.

At loadEXE_Program32, the stack reference in the EXE header is relocated by the program's load address and is stored in the new process's PSP. The RxDOS Instance, which points to the caller's stack, is made to point to the new process's stack. As with COM program loading, an area is created to simulate a DOS function call. This enables DOS to terminate through a normal exit. When it restores the user's registers, it will properly set and return to the start of the newly loaded program.

Debugger Support

A debugger needs to intercept a program before it begins execution if for no other reason than to insert breakpoints. In support of this, DOS provides function 4B01h. The function performs exactly the same function as subfunction 00, except that it does not automatically switch to the child process. It populates the load program block (LOADPROG) with the child processes stack pointer and start execution address. We showed the format of the LOADPROG block earlier in the chapter.

In order to support debuggers, DOS permits the EXEC function to spawn the new process, initialize, and switch to the new stack. It then checks to determine if this is subfunction 01, the debugger support function. If it is, the stack and return address values are fetched from the new process's stack and stored in the LOADPROG structure. The return address is fetched from the previous process and used in the current instance. In other words, EXEC's subfunction 01 is really the functionality of subfunction 00 followed by returning variables in the supplied structure and a return to the parent process.

Specifically, the steps are as follows: Once the EXEC function completes, the current PSP address points to the new process. It contains a pointer back to the old PSP and to its current stack. The return address at the top of the stack is the starting address of the new process. The address is copied from the stack to the LOADPROG data structure. The top of the stack address is also copied to the data structure. The register values for the new process stack are copied back to the old process stack, and the internal Instance variable where RxDOS maintains the current caller's stack address is restored to the parent's process. DOS performs a normal return to the parent process.

Terminate Process

	On Entry	On Return
AX	AH = 4Ch; AL= return code	
BX		
CX		
DX		

Related Functions:
  31h Terminate and Stay Resident; 4Bh Load and Execute; 4Dh Get Return Code of Child Process.

When a process terminates, all its allocated resources are released, including the space allocated to the termination program. The parent process is located and restarted. The completion code returned in the AL register is saved within DOS so that it can later be retrieved through function 4Dh, Get Return Code. No specific meanings are assigned to completion codes, and the action taken depends solely on the parent's interpretation. However, a convention generally established for batch programs is that the higher the completion code value, the higher the severity of the error. A zero value generally means no error.

The segment address of the parent's process is stored in the child's PSP under the parent ID field. The contents of this word are the segment address of the parent's PSP. The PSP address is assumed to be correct. No checks are made to ensure the validity of the data in either the child or parent PSPs. This is shown in Figure 6-3.

The values of the int 22h, 23h, and 24h interrupt vectors are restored from the child's PSP, and all the memory allocated to the child process is released, including the memory allocated to the child program. Int 22h is the terminate process address, int 23h is the control C trap address, and int 24h is critical error handler.

Prior to this, all open files were closed, and the modified cache disk buffers are written to disk. The error handling interrupt should not be removed until after all the files are closed. Moreover, files are closed from the end to the beginning of the Job Handle Table to ensure that the STDIN and STDOUT assignments for process remain active during error recovery.

Once the child process's resources are fully released, the parent process must be restarted. When the parent process originally called the DOS EXEC function, the return address and the value of all registers were saved on the caller's stack. The stack reference address was recorded in the parent's PSP. These values remain on the caller's stack while the child process was executing.

When the child process terminates, the parent's segment address is fetched from the child's PSP. The saved stack address reference in the parent's PSP is reactivated as the current instance. The current instance is an internal pointer RxDOS maintains to the caller's stack. By altering the current instance, the stack on which the return is made is altered. When DOS executes its return code, the register values saved from the parent's call are restored. A return is made from the DOS EXEC function. In this way, all the parent's original pointers, segment addresses, and stack are properly restored even though another process was run.

Figure 6-3. How the parent process is reactivated

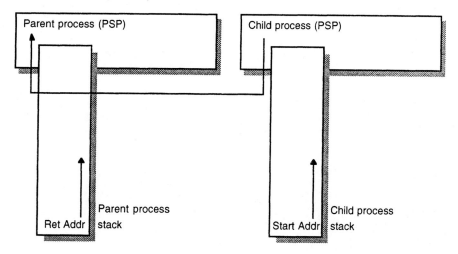

The entire process termination code follows. It manages the release of resources and the switch from one process to another. The Terminate and Stay Resident code is fairly similar to this function call and is discussed in the next section, including why this code checks for a NULL in the parent process ID field.

Early in DOS's history, int 20h was encouraged as the process terminate service. Today, int 20h simply falls into the terminate process code with a 00 exit code.

```
(in rxdosexe.asm)
        ;'''''''''''''''''''''''''''''''''''''''''''''''''''''''''''''''''';
        ;   4Ch Terminate Process                                         ;
        ;- - - - - - - - - - - - - - - - - - - - - - - - - - - - - - - - -;
```

```
        ;                                                     ;
        ;   al       return value                             ;
        ;..................................................;

_TerminateProcess_00:
        mov al, 0

_TerminateProcess:
        Entry
        def  _parentPSP, 0000

        sti
        mov ah, TERMINATE_NORMAL
        mov word ptr [ _RxDOS_ChildReturnCode ], ax      ; save return status code

;- - - - - - - - - - - - - - - - - - - - - - - - - - - - - -
; see if there is a parent process
;- - - - - - - - - - - - - - - - - - - - - - - - - - - - - -
        mov es, word ptr ss:[ _RxDOS_CurrentPSP ]
        mov dx, word ptr es:[ pspParentId ]              ; get parent PSP
        mov word ptr es:[ pspParentId ], 0000            ; kill parent for next time
        storarg _parentPSP, dx                           ; save for later
        or dx, dx                                        ; no parent ?
        jz _TerminateProcess_20                          ; can't terminate ->

;- - - - - - - - - - - - - - - - - - - - - - - - - - - - - -
; close/ commit all files
;- - - - - - - - - - - - - - - - - - - - - - - - - - - - - -
        call _SFTCloseAllFiles                           ; close/ commit all files

;- - - - - - - - - - - - - - - - - - - - - - - - - - - - - -
; restore interrupts/ return to parent PSP
;- - - - - - - - - - - - - - - - - - - - - - - - - - - - - -
        cli
        xor ax, ax
        mov ds, ax
        mov es, word ptr ss:[ _RxDOS_CurrentPSP ]

        mov bx, offset ( intTERMINATEAPP * 4 )           ; Int22 terminate vector
        mov ax, word ptr es:[ pspTerminateVect. _pointer ]
        mov dx, word ptr es:[ pspTerminateVect. _segment ]
        mov word ptr es:[ _pointer ][ bx ], ax
        mov word ptr es:[ _segment ][ bx ], dx

        mov bx, offset ( intCONTROLC * 4 )               ; Int23 control-C vector
        mov ax, word ptr es:[ pspControlCVect. _pointer ]
        mov dx, word ptr es:[ pspControlCVect. _segment ]
        mov word ptr es:[ _pointer ][ bx ], ax
        mov word ptr es:[ _segment ][ bx ], dx

        mov bx, offset ( intCRITICALERROR * 4 )          ; Int24 criterror vector
        mov ax, word ptr es:[ pspCritErrorVect. _pointer ]
        mov dx, word ptr es:[ pspCritErrorVect. _segment ]
        mov word ptr es:[ _pointer ][ bx ], ax
```

```
        mov word ptr es:[ _segment ][ bx ], dx
        sti

;- - - - - - - - - - - - - - - - - - - - - - - - - - - - - - - - - - -
;  free all allocated memory
;- - - - - - - - - - - - - - - - - - - - - - - - - - - - - - - - - - -
        call _releaseOwnerMemoryBlocks                  ; release memory
        call _collectMemoryBlocks                       ; collect free blocks

;- - - - - - - - - - - - - - - - - - - - - - - - - - - - - - - - - - -
;  return to parent process
;- - - - - - - - - - - - - - - - - - - - - - - - - - - - - - - - - - -
        getarg es, _parentPSP                           ; get PSP
        mov word ptr ss:[ _RxDOS_CurrentPSP ], es       ; restore

        mov dx, word ptr es:[ pspUserStack. _segment ]
        mov ax, word ptr es:[ pspUserStack. _pointer ]  ; parent user's stack

        mov bx, word ptr ss:[ _RxDOS_CurrentInstance ]  ; base address of current stack
        mov word ptr ss:[ _segment ][ bx ], dx
        mov word ptr ss:[ _pointer ][ bx ], ax

;- - - - - - - - - - - - - - - - - - - - - - - - - - - - - - - - - - -
;  return
;- - - - - - - - - - - - - - - - - - - - - - - - - - - - - - - - - - -
_TerminateProcess_20:
        Return
```

Terminate and Stay Resident

	On Entry	On Return
AX	AH = 31h; AL= return code	
BX		
CX		
DX	# paragraphs to save	

Related Functions:
    4Bh Load and Execute; 4Ch Terminate; 4Dh Get Return Code of Child Process.

The purpose of the Terminate and Stay Resident function is to return to the parent process but maintain some portion of the child program in memory. The number of paragraphs retained are passed to DOS as an argument value in the DX register. The presumption is that the TSR has hooked itself to monitor events of one type or another, for example, to listen to the keyboard, timer, or data communications interrupts. It is able to monitor events because it remains resident in memory.

It is important to note that a design bug exists in DOS with regard to the terminate and stay resident function. Although the memory block allocated to the program is expected to be modified, there is no way to report an error to the TSR. The TSR may believe that it has allocated to itself memory that it does not really own. The problem exists only if the requested memory size exceeds the current program size.

To avoid the problem altogether, the TSR should attempt the reallocation using DOS function 4Ah, Resize Memory. The segment address for the resize function should be the current PSP address. Once the function succeeds, the correct memory size is allocated.

The TSR function performs a normal process terminate, just like DOS function 4Ch. The parent process is reactivated and its registers restored from the parent's stack. Because the parent is no longer dormant, the TSR can terminate only once. That is, it cannot issue a terminate and stay resident function call more than once, nor can it issue any other terminate process function call, such as DOS function 4Ch or an int 20h. All terminate functions want to reactivate the dormant parent process. Once they reactivate the parent, there is no longer any dormant parent process waiting on this child process.

As a protection against multiple terminate function calls, which can be a danger if a program has terminated but remained resident, the parent ID field in the PSP is set to a NULL once the child issues the terminate. Any other terminate function no longer has a parent process address to restart.

The only substantial difference between the terminate but stay resident function (DOS function 31h) and the terminate child process function (DOS function 4Ch) is that the TSR call does not release any allocated resources. All files remain open, the cache disk buffers are not flushed to disk, and any memory allocated to the process, including the Environment block, is not released. The only memory block that may be affected is the memory block allocated to the program, which may be modified as requested. It is incumbent on the TSR program to release any unnecessary memory allocated to the process, such as the Environment block.

The code for the DOS function 31h is as follows:

```
(in rxdosexe.asm)
        ;///////////////////////////////////////////////////////;
        ;  31h Terminate But Stay Resident                       ;
        ;- - - - - - - - - - - - - - - - - - - - - - - - - - - -;
        ;                                                        ;
        ;  al      return value                                  ;
        ;  dx      keep memory size                              ;
        ;........................................................;

_TerminateStayResident:
        Entry
        def _parentPSP, 0000

        mov ah, TERMINATE_TSR
        mov word ptr [ _RxDOS_ChildReturnCode ], ax     ; save return status code

;- - - - - - - - - - - - - - - - - - - - - - - - - - - - - - -
;  fix size of current PSP block
;- - - - - - - - - - - - - - - - - - - - - - - - - - - - - - -
        mov es, word ptr [ _RxDOS_CurrentPSP ]
        mov bx, dx                                      ; keep size
        call _modifyMemBlock                            ; fix size

;- - - - - - - - - - - - - - - - - - - - - - - - - - - - - - -
;  see if there is a parent process
;- - - - - - - - - - - - - - - - - - - - - - - - - - - - - - -
        mov es, word ptr cs:[ _RxDOS_CurrentPSP ]
        mov dx, word ptr es:[ pspParentId ]             ; get parent PSP
        mov word ptr es:[ pspParentId ], 0000           ; kill parent for next time
```

```
        storarg _parentPSP, dx                          ; save for later
        or dx, dx                                       ; no parent ?
        jz _TerminateStayResident_20                    ; can't terminate ->

;- - - - - - - - - - - - - - - - - - - - - - - - - - - - - - - - - - - - - -
;  restore interrupts/ return to parent PSP
;- - - - - - - - - - - - - - - - - - - - - - - - - - - - - - - - - - - - - -
        cli
        xor ax, ax
        mov ds, ax
        mov es, word ptr ss:[ _RxDOS_CurrentPSP ]

        mov bx, offset ( intTERMINATEAPP * 4 )          ; Int22 terminate vector
        mov ax, word ptr es:[ pspTerminateVect. _pointer ]
        mov dx, word ptr es:[ pspTerminateVect. _segment ]
        mov word ptr es:[ _pointer ][ bx ], ax
        mov word ptr es:[ _segment ][ bx ], dx

        mov bx, offset ( intCONTROLC * 4 )              ; Int23 control-C vector
        mov ax, word ptr es:[ pspControlCVect. _pointer ]
        mov dx, word ptr es:[ pspControlCVect. _segment ]
        mov word ptr es:[ _pointer ][ bx ], ax
        mov word ptr es:[ _segment ][ bx ], dx

        mov bx, offset ( intCRITICALERROR * 4 )         ; Int24 criterror vector
        mov ax, word ptr es:[ pspCritErrorVect. _pointer ]
        mov dx, word ptr es:[ pspCritErrorVect. _segment ]
        mov word ptr es:[ _pointer ][ bx ], ax
        mov word ptr es:[ _segment ][ bx ], dx
        sti

;- - - - - - - - - - - - - - - - - - - - - - - - - - - - - - - - - - - - - -
;  return to parent process
;- - - - - - - - - - - - - - - - - - - - - - - - - - - - - - - - - - - - - -
        getarg es, _parentPSP                           ; get PSP
        mov word ptr ss:[ _RxDOS_CurrentPSP ], es        ; restore

        mov dx, word ptr es:[ pspUserStack. _segment ]
        mov ax, word ptr es:[ pspUserStack. _pointer ]   ; parent user's stack

        mov bx, word ptr ss:[ _RxDOS_CurrentInstance ]   ; base address of current stack
        mov word ptr ss:[ _segment ][ bx ], dx
        mov word ptr ss:[ _pointer ][ bx ], ax

;- - - - - - - - - - - - - - - - - - - - - - - - - - - - - - - - - - - - - -
;  return
;- - - - - - - - - - - - - - - - - - - - - - - - - - - - - - - - - - - - - -
_TerminateStayResident_20:
        Return
```

The terminate and stay resident function attaches a condition to the exit code and saves this for use eventually by DOS function 4Dh, Get Child Process Return Code. Next, the function uses the equivalent to DOS function 4Ah to modify the size of the memory allocated to the program, represented by the current PSP. The current PSP is the segment address of the program that is exiting.

The function does nothing if the size has already been resized by the program prior to its exit. As we noted, the TSR has no way on knowing whether the resize worked.

Next, the parent ID field is retrieved from the terminating process's PSP. If it is zero, the process termination is not allowed to continue. Since the parent's ID can never be zero, DOS is at a dilemma. It cannot switch to a parent process, so it simply returns.

Since a program can never issue a terminate and stay resident followed eventually by a terminate process (function 4Dh), how do TSRs unload? A TSR must restore any interrupts they may have hooked, and then release all memory blocks allocated, including the memory allocated for the program itself. When the TSR returns from the interrupt that called it, the remaining system will contain no traces of its allocation. For a brief time, the TSR will be running in space that has been freed, so if there is any danger at all that the space may be reclaimed before the interrupt return can take place, which could happen if a TSR is loaded that either allocates memory or time-slices between different processes, then it is necessary to engineer a more fail-safe unload process.

Get Return Code

	On Entry	**On Return**
AX	AH = 4Dh	AH = termination method; AL = code
BX		
CX		
DX		

Related Functions:
31h Terminate and Stay Resident; 4Bh Load and Execute; 4Ch Terminate Process.

The return code is a value returned by a terminating process. It is saved by DOS for future reference. The only action that the routine does is to simply read the last termination value and return it to the caller. The termination value contains an explanation code of how it terminated in the AH register. The function need only fetch the return code value, locate the caller's stack frame, and save the output in the returned registers.

In MS-DOS, the returned child code is zeroed as a result of using this function. The code here is slightly incompatible between the two operating systems.

```
(in rxdos.asm)
        ;,,,,,,,,,,,,,,,,,,,,,,,,,,,,,,,,,,,,,,,,,,,,,,,,,,,,,,,,,,,,,,,;
        ;  4Dh Get Return Code                                         ;
        ;- - - - - - - - - - - - - - - - - - - - - - - - - - - - - - -;
        ;                                                              ;
        ;..............................................................;

_GetReturnCode:
        mov ax, word ptr [ _RxDOS_ChildReturnCode ]

        RetCallersStackFrame ds, bx
        mov word ptr [ _AX ][ bx ], ax
        ret
```

Duplicate PSP

	On Entry	On Return
AX	AH = 26h	
BX		
CX		
DX	segment address for PSP	
CS	must point to current PSP	

Related Functions:
4Bh Load and Execute; 55h Create Child PSP.

The Duplicate PSP function was intended to be called only by COM programs and has been superseded by the more powerful Create Child PSP, DOS function 55h. The CS register must point to the current PSP. This condition can be successfully satisfied only by a COM program since the PSP is expected at the start of the segment. However, within RxDOS, the CS restriction has been removed. The PSP created is a copy of the current process executing. This change has had no effect on the only program in wide use that utilizes this function, debug.

This function simply creates a valid PSP, the first step toward creating a valid process, and is used to create the appearance of a process when there isn't a program to load. When debug has a program to load, it utilizes DOS function 4B01h.

The function begins in the copy current PSP routine, where the entire PSP is literally copied. The file handle table and the parent ID process must be corrected. Although the file table has been copied, the corresponding SFTs must be examined to determine if the NO INHERIT flag is set. Otherwise, the SFT in use count must be incremented. Unfortunately, there is no corresponding mechanism for decrementing the in-use counts if the debug session is terminated without actually starting a new process. The issue is largely academic since the increased counts has no effect on the user or DOS itself.

```
(in rxdos.asm)
        ;'''''''''''''''''''''''''''''''''''''''''''''''''''''''''''''';
        ;   26h Create New Program Segment Prefix                      ;
        ;- - - - - - - - - - - - - - - - - - - - - - - - - - - - - - - -;
        ;                                                              ;
        ;   dx       segment address                                  ;
        ;                                                              ;
        ;   (see related function 55 - Duplicate PSP )                ;
        ;..............................................................;

_CreateNewProgramSeg:
        mov es, dx                              ; new PSP segment address
        call copyCurrentPSP                     ; create a new PSP here
        ret

(in rxdosexe.asm)
        ;'''''''''''''''''''''''''''''''''''''''''''''''''''''''''''''';
        ;   Copy Current PSP                                           ;
        ;- - - - - - - - - - - - - - - - - - - - - - - - - - - - - - - -;
```

```
        ;                                                           ;
        ;  Usage:                                               ;
        ;  es        PSP segment address to update              ;
        ;.............................................................;

copyCurrentPSP:
        push    ds
        mov     ax, word ptr ss:[ _RxDOS_CurrentPSP ]       ; current PSP
        or      ax, ax                                      ; any current PSP ?
        jz      copyCurrentPSP_36                           ; no ->

        xor     si, si
        xor     di, di
        mov     ds, ax                                      ; current PSP
        mov     cx, ( sizePSP / 2 )
        rep     movsw

;- - - - - - - - - - - - - - - - - - - - - - - - - - - - - - - - -
; duplicate all file handles (except for no inherit)
;- - - - - - - - - - - - - - - - - - - - - - - - - - - - - - - - -
        mov     ax, word ptr ds:[ _RxDOS_CurrentPSP ]
        mov     word ptr es:[ pspParentId    ], ax          ; parent PSP address

        mov     di, es
        sub     di, ax                                      ; differences in segment sizes
        sub     word ptr es:[ pspNextParagraph ], di        ; set memory size

        xor     di, di
        mov     cx, sizePSPHandleTable
        mov     word ptr es:[ pspFileHandleCount ], cx
        mov     word ptr es:[ pspFileHandlePtr. _segment ], es
        mov     word ptr es:[ pspFileHandlePtr. _pointer ], PSPHandleTable

copyCurrentPSP_08:
        SaveSegments di
        les     bx, dword ptr ds:[ pspFileHandlePtr ]

        xor     ax, ax
        mov     al, byte ptr [ di + bx ]                    ; get old handle
        call    MapAppToSFTHandle                           ; map to internal handle info
        call    FindSFTbyHandle                             ; get corresponding SFT (es: di )
        test    word ptr es:[ sftDevInfo ][ di ], sftNoInherit
        jnz     copyCurrentPSP_12                           ; if no inherit ->

        inc     word ptr es:[ sftRefCount ][ di ]           ; bump in use count
        RestoreSegments di
        jmp     short copyCurrentPSP_14

copyCurrentPSP_12:
        RestoreSegments di
        mov     byte ptr es:[ PSPHandleTable ][ di ], -1    ; free SFT in copy of psp

copyCurrentPSP_14:
        inc     di
```

```
        cmp di, sizepspHandletable
        jl copyCurrentPSP_08

;- - - - - - - - - - - - - - - - - - - - - - - - - - - - - - - - -
; done
;- - - - - - - - - - - - - - - - - - - - - - - - - - - - - - - - -
copyCurrentPSP_36:
        pop ds
        ret
```

Create Child PSP

	On Entry	On Return
AX	AH = 55h	
BX		
CX		
DX	segment address for PSP	
SI	value to place in memory field	

Related Functions:
  4Bh Load and Execute; 26h Duplicate PSP.

The Create Child Process function builds a new PSP. It replaces the constraint imposed by DOS function 26h, Create New PSP. The function does not merely create a copy of the current PSP. Instead, it creates a child process, that is, a separate executable thread. The thread becomes the new running process.

The new process has limited functionality, so it isn't surprising that the feature is undocumented. The new process's execution continues with the instruction immediately after the int 21h return, so in some ways the function can be viewed as a crude implementation of a fork( ) function. The new process cannot be terminated using DOS function 4Ch or 31h, or int 20h. There is no waiting process on the stack, and the system will crash if one of these terminate functions is used.

The usability of this function is limited within a DOS system as presently designed.

```
(in rxdos.asm)
        ;'''''''''''''''''''''''''''''''''''''''''''''''''''''''''''''''''''';
        ; 55h Duplicate PSP                                                 ;
        ;- - - - - - - - - - - - - - - - - - - - - - - - - - - - - - - - -;
        ;                                                                   ;
        ; dx     segment where to set up new PSP                            ;
        ; si     value to place in memory size field                       ;
        ;                                                                   ;
        ; (see related function 26 - Create PSP )                          ;
        ;                                                                   ;
        ; -- DOS Undocumented Feature ——————————— ;
        ;...................................................................;
```

```
_DuplicatePSP:
        push dx                                        ; new seg
        push si                                        ; new size

        mov es, dx                                     ; new PSP segment address
        call copyCurrentPSP                            ; create a new PSP here

        pop si
        pop es                                         ; new PSP address
        mov word ptr es:[ pspNextParagraph ], si       ; set size
        ret
```

CHAPTER 7

Memory Management

Where Is All of My Memory?—Why Not Protected Mode DOS?—Using XMS (Read/Write Anywhere While in DOS)—High Memory Area—How DOS Sees Memory—Walking Through Memory—How DOS Allocation and Free Work—DOS Memory Allocation Is Not malloc()—Allocate Memory—Free Allocated Memory—Reallocate Memory—Set Allocation Strategy

By the time DOS 3.0 was released, it should have been clear that both users and applications needed and wanted better and more uniform methods for allocating and using larger and larger amounts of memory, particularly memory above the DOS magical 640K limit. However, it was not until DOS 5.0 that all the available RAM in the first megabyte of memory could be allocated. With systems with several megabytes of memory, why are we today limited to the first megabyte? The answer has to do with some very real limitations imposed by hardware.

Where Is All of My Memory?

Although Intel processors, from the 386 on up, can address up to 4GB (4,294,967,296 bytes) of memory, applications running under DOS cannot directly address beyond 1MB of memory. DOS and DOS-based applications must run these processors in one of two modes that emulate the original Intel 8086 called real mode, or virtual 8086 mode. Both impose a maximum address limit of 1MB of memory for some important hardware-related reasons.

Beginning with the Intel 286 processor, new and welcomed power was added to Intel processors that made them more powerful and better suited for the operating systems to come, such as Windows, OS/2, and Windows/NT. These new features offered each application, and the operating system, protection against data corruption and program crashes. These features necessitated the creation of protected mode.

Protected mode (as it existed since the 80386) not only provided access rights to memory, but offered hardware memory mapping so that an application could be loaded anywhere, even in pieces, and mapped to appear as if it was contiguous. Memory management could benefit greatly because a lot of small free memory blocks could be mapped to appear as a larger memory block. And, these processors support Virtual Memory, where a program may believe that there exists much more memory than is physically installed. With Virtual Memory, part of the program or its data may remain on disk and recalled when required. When a reference is made to memory that does not physically exist, the reference causes a hardware trap that is then converted to a disk access. Because of memory mapping, the memory is physically loaded anywhere, even swapping out memory used by an inactive program. Windows is an excellent memory manager, among other things, and takes advantage of all these features.

DOS-based applications have a difficult time running in protected mode unchanged. The go-anywhere do-anything style of many DOS-based applications won't work in protected mode. There are restrictions on access, and segment registers cannot be set to illegal or protected values. It is these very necessary restrictions that keep one application from inadvertently crashing the system. DOS-based applications access and change segments at will, changing interrupt tables, screen display areas, and the BIOS communications area at segment 0040h. Just writing an illegal or invalid value in a segment register causes a program fault in protected mode. Some DOS-based programs use the segment registers to hold values that would be illegal in protected mode.

The following code, valid in real mode, would cause a fault in protected mode:

```
xor ax, ax              ; 0000h
mov es, ax              ; exception 13 in protected mode
mov bx, offset 040h
```

The designers of DOS chose to continue to keep DOS real mode based, and that decision has kept DOS-based applications trapped in the 1MB limit. This limit comes from the original 8086 processor, which could not generate more than a 20-bit address value. The 20-bit maximum address came from the way the 8086 addressed memory. The value in the segment register was offset 4 bits to the left before adding the offset. Take, for example, the address 8E08:0123, which translates to a linear address of 8E1A3h

No matter how you look at Figure 7-1, the maximum address that this architecture can produce is a 20-bit sum, or a maximum address of FFFFFh bytes (1,024K). Protected mode avoids this 20-bit problem by using the segment register as a selector. The selector is an offset into Global and Local Descriptor Tables. Each descriptor provides both a 32-bit address and other access rights information. The 32-bit base address from the descriptor table is added to a 32-bit value in an index register, such as the extended EBX, ESI, or EDI registers, to form a 32-bit sum. This limits the maximum address value to a 4GB address range. How protected mode is able to address more memory than real mode is shown in Figure 7-2.

Figure 7-1. Segment register is offset to the left 4 bits when added to offset register to produce a 20-bit address.

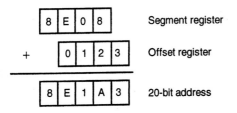

Real mode and virtual 8086 modes have been used interchangeably, and both modes behave identically in emulating the 8086 processor. Both modes limit direct memory access to 1MB. But there is an important difference between real and virtual 8086 modes. When the processor is in real mode, protected mode is completely switched off, terminating protected mode programs like Windows. Virtual 8086 mode, on the other hand, maps some portion of memory and interrupts to create 8086 processor behavior while still allowing other applications, like Windows and any Windows-compliant applications, to remain running in protected mode. One of the implications of this is that a 386 can be configured to run several virtual 8086 sessions such as multiple independent DOS sessions while still running Windows. You can see that when you run Windows. Each DOS session in a DOS compatibility box is really running in virtual 8086 mode.

Figure 7-2. How memory is addressed through Global and Local Descriptor Tables in Intel 386 and higher processors

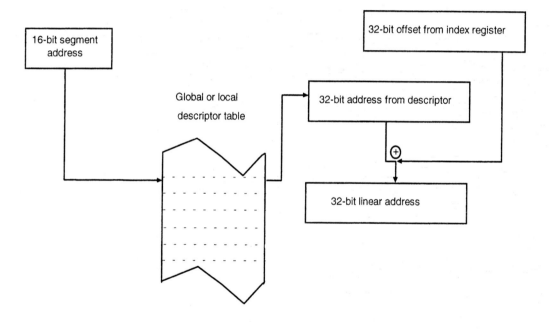

Why Not Protected Mode DOS?

Early in the history of DOS, say with version 3.1, Microsoft and leading software developers could have established the goal of releasing a DOS that would run within protected mode, or at the very least, have some applications be able to state whether they are protected mode compliant and have DOS be able to load them or treat them differently. All that would really have been required is enough lead time for practical software development, good programming practices by developers, and a set of specifications for memory and other resource allocations. All noncompliant software would then still have to run within real or virtual 8086 mode, but an evolutionary path would have been created. None exists for DOS today, although it has been promised for the upcoming DOS 7.0 version, to be released concurrently with Chicago or Microsoft Windows version 4.0.

Part of the evolutionary process that did take place is that developers can take advantage of protected mode programming by migrating their applications to Windows or OS/2. Many applications today have moved to Windows because of market potential and because development under the DOS limits became impossible. Before Windows 3.0's availability, many DOS applications such as Lotus 1-2-3 Release 3 and AutoCad took advantage of DOS extenders like Phar Lap's 386|DOS-Extender, which provided 32-bit protected mode access while still running under DOS. For applications that need to remain DOS based, this is an excellent development environment.

DOS Extenders permit applications to run in protected mode. Any DOS and BIOS calls cause the extender to either execute the call in protected mode or to switch back to real mode, execute the function, and then switch back to protected mode.

Using XMS (Read/Write Anywhere While in DOS)

But wait a minute! I have a RAM disk and a spreadsheet that utilizes all memory. Why am I limited to 1MB in DOS when I know that some of my software can access much more memory? Of course, you are right. Using a combination of either expanded or extended memory (XMS), your DOS software can utilize all memory, or at least as much as was allocated to expanded or extended memory. This memory cannot be directly addressed in the same way as conventional memory can be addressed. Directly accessible memory can be referenced with a single instruction reference. Memory accessible through EMS and XMS is not directly accessed at all. Instead, the DOS-based application requests that some portion of memory be transferred between conventional memory and extended memory. The XMS (extended memory) service switches to protected memory, copies the memory block, and then switches back to real mode. Usually an access to extended memory this way involves two copies, one to save some conventional memory followed by another to get additional data. Extended memory can be used quite effectively, but the copy process carries an overhead, so effective programming design is essential.

Except for the 286 processor, switching in and out of protected modes is a matter of initializing global and local descriptor tables that map memory and then setting or clearing the PE (Protect Enable) flag in the machine status word of 386 and up processors. For the 286 processor, the switch back is more complex and time consuming. Although the 286 processor will switch into protected mode by setting its PE flag, it provides no capability for switching back to real mode. Clearing the PE (Protect Enable) flag will not switch the processor back to real mode. Perhaps the designers of the 286 never envisioned anyone ever wanting to get out of the clearly more superior protected mode. Since all processors initially start up in real mode, a switch back to real mode could be accomplished by literally resetting the processor! In order for the processor to be switched back, special code was added to the ROM-BIOS to trap a special case reset of the processor. To switch back to real mode, a special value was set in a specific location in memory, all the registers were saved, and the processor was reset. When the processor restarted, a check was made for the special value, and execution continued at the saved register values. Talk about a little overhead! Although

I give credit for the ingenious solution, it should be realized that this limits access to several hundred switches back and forth from and into protected mode are possible per second. This issue is important only within a 286.

Within the 386 and up processors, and in particular those running in virtual 8086 mode where protected mode is already running, extended memory provides somewhat faster access to all memory since it can simply switch memory maps. It does not, however, provide direct access to protected mode, which would be even faster.

The 286 does not allow memory mapping, which has been a significant limitation to the development of protected mode operating systems. As a result of these limitations, the 286 has become effectively obsolete, as has the 8086.

HIGH Memory Area

In the search for ever more memory, it was discovered that an extra 64K of memory could be addressed directly from real or virtual 8086 modes. The extra memory was available for only the Intel 286 and up processors and only on systems that had over 1MB installed. This gave these systems 1,088K of accessible direct memory instead of the usual 1,024K (1MB). This extra space is in reality the memory immediately above the first 1MB of memory in extended memory.

On 8086 processors, the address FFFF:FFFFh is really interpreted as 0000:FFEFh. This is the address you would get when you perform segment math. Early machines with only 20 physical address lines would loose any carry produced by this addition. Figure 7-3 shows how 21-bit address arithmetic, enabled by the A20 line, increases the address space.

Figure 7-3. Segment math in 20- and 21-bit systems

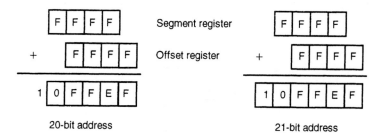

20-bit address   21-bit address

However, on systems that support 24- or 32-bit address lines (the 286 supported 24-bit address lines, all others support 32-bit addresses), the overflow bit can be preserved, which enables the extra addressing space. This allows addressing memory between FFFF0h and 10FFEFh without leaving real mode.

The extra space is not automatically available on all systems. The carry bit from the address math performed internally by the processor must be used to address the 21st address line. These processors enable this capability by providing an A20 enable flag. This memory cannot be accessed unless an extended memory driver like emm386.exe or equivalent is loaded when DOS is started, as in the following config.sys statements:

```
DEVICE=C:\DOS\emm386.exe
DOS=HIGH, UMB
```

How DOS Sees Memory

Within the 1MB available in virtual 8086 or real modes, memory is distinguished further between the lower 640K, known as conventional memory, which extends from 0000:0000h to A000:0000h, and upper memory, which extends from the 640K limit to the top of available memory or between A000:0000h and FFFF:0000h.

Whether in conventional or upper memory, available space is made allocatable by assigning memory to specific arenas. An arena is a section of memory. Conventional memory is entirely continuous and represents originally a single arena. A dummy, preallocated memory block surrounds any nonallocatable space in upper memory such as the space used to display RAM or the ROM-BIOS. Figure 7-4 shows how memory is subdivided into arenas.

When memory is allocated from an arena, the arena is subdivided into two arenas: one is allocated to the requested space, and the other remains free for a subsequent allocation request. When allocated memory is released, it is tagged free and merged with other free abutting arenas.

Figure 7-4. Memory layout in real or virtual 8086 modes

	BIOS	1024k
Available RAM		
	ROM	Upper memory blocks
Available RAM		
	Video RAM	640k
		Conventional memory
Available RAM		
	Resident DOS	2k
	Reserved BIOS	0k

Unallocatable memory   Arena headers

Each arena begins with an arena header, also known as a memory control block (MCB). The MCB contains the size and owner of the memory block (arena) that it represents. The next memory block will be exactly at the address of the current block plus the size in the memory control block, plus one for the size of the control block itself. Each memory control block starts at a paragraph boundary, and the entire memory layout takes advantage of the segmented architecture of the Intel processor. Sizes within the MCB are in paragraphs, making it easy to perform segment math. All allocations are made on the basis of numbers of paragraphs and return a segment address, and allocations are always made exactly at paragraph boundaries.

In addition to size and owner, each memory control block begins with an identifying signature byte. The signature byte of every block except for the last block contains a 4Dh (the letter M). The last memory control block contains a 5Ah (the letter Z). It probably would not be a surprise to learn that the principal architect of the DOS memory manager was Mark Zbikowski who, by the way, also was responsible for designing the EXE header.

The signature byte not only serves to identify the last memory block from the rest, but also identifies memory block corruption. The memory allocation functions return a bad block error when the memory control block referenced has been corrupted. The only check performed to determine if the block is corrupted is to check for either of the signature byte values.

Each allocated memory block also contains an owner field. The owner of a memory block is the process that requested the allocation. Although DOS is a single-tasking operating system, several processes are potentially running. Each TSR, a command shell, and an application are all individual processes that exist within DOS at any one given time. The owner or process ID of the process currently running is actually the segment address of the process's PSP, or Program Segment Prefix. We discussed PSPs in Chapter 4. When the process terminates, all the blocks allocated to that process are automatically released.

This can lead to a bit of confusion. If a TSR program chooses to allocate memory while DOS is running another process, the allocated memory would actually be given the process ID of the running application rather than of the TSR. TSRs gain control usually by interrupts to a running process and not through any knowledge that DOS may have participated or provided. TSRs operate under somewhat different conditions from other programs.

```
        ;'''''''''''''''''''''''''''''''''''''''''''''''''''''''''''''';
        ;  Memory Management Blocks                                    ;
        ;..............................................................;

        MEMBLOCK struc
_memSignature           db ?                    ; always 4D or 5A
_memParent              dw ?                    ; seg address of owner
_memAlloc               dw ?                    ; allocated size
_memReserved            db '???'
_memPgmName             db 8 dup (?)            ; program name or null
        MEMBLOCK ends

_RxDOS_MEMSIGNATURE     equ 4Dh                 ; any block
_RxDOS_ENDSIGNATURE     equ 5Ah                 ; last block
_RxDOS_DOSPARENT        equ 0008h               ; mem parent signature
_RxDOS_FREE_MEMBLOCK    equ 0000h               ; mem block is free
```

Walking Through Memory

`Memwalk` is a little program that walks through the memory control blocks allocated on any DOS system, identifying each block, its size and owner, and the total free and allocated memory. The segment address of the first memory area is located in the SYSVARS area and can be located using DOS function 52h. Within DOS 5 and 6, the pointer to the start of the allocatable memory is at offset 24h, at `_RxDOS_pStartMem Block`.

To construct a pointer to the first memory area, the address to the SYSVARS area is retrieved. The segment address, returned in the ES register, is saved. The offset address is a constant. The address is constructed by the following code:

```
r.h.ah = 0x52;                            // use undoc function 52
_intdosx( &r, &r, &s );                   // es contains seg address of DOS
FP_SEG( lpMemStartSeg ) = s.es;
FP_OFF( lpMemStartSeg ) = _RXDOS_STARTARENAS;
FP_SEG( lpMemBlock ) = *lpMemStartSeg;
```

The first four lines form an address pointer into the DOS data area. The last line fetches the segment address of the first memory block. The next arena header can then be computed by adding the size of the current arena to the address of the current arena plus 1 (for the size of arena header in paragraphs). In memwalk.c, this is expressed rather easily as

```
FP_SEG( lpMemBlock ) += lpMemBlock-> _memSize + 1;
```

The code for memwalk.c shows just how easy walking through DOS memory segments really is.

```
// memwalk.c
#include <string.h>
#include <stdio.h>
#include <dos.h>

// where DOS keeps the start of the allocation Arenas.
#define _RXDOS_STARTARENAS        0x0024
#define _RxDOS_PARENT_SIGNATURE   0x0008      /* DOS is parent */
#define _RxDOS_FREE_MEMBLOCK      0x0000      /* Block is Free */
#define _RxDOS_PSP_ENV            0x002C      /* Env Address in PSP */

// DOS Arena Header
#pragma pack(1)
typedef struct _MEMBLOCK {
    char        _memSignature;
    int         _memOwner;
    int         _memSize;
    char        _memUnused[ 3 ];
    char        _memName[ 8 ];

    } MEMBLOCK, far * LPMEMBLOCK;
#pragma pack()
```

```
//////////////////////////////////////////////////////////////
static char BlockisFree[]                  = "block is free";
static char BlockwasAllocbyDOS[]           = "block was allocated by DOS";
static char BlockisProgramPSP[]            = "block is a program PSP";
static char BlockisAnEnvControlBlock[] = "block is an env control block";
static char NoComment[] = "";

//////////////////////////////////////////////////////////////
static void CleanUpName( LPMEMBLOCK lpMemBlock, char far * Text )
{
    int n;
    char far * lpText = lpMemBlock-> _memName;

    for ( n = 0; n < 8; ++n, ++lpText )
       {
       Text[ n ] = *lpText;

       if ( *lpText < ' ' )
          Text[ n ] = ' ';

       if ( *lpText > 0x7F )
          Text[ n ] &= 0x7F;
       }
}

//////////////////////////////////////////////////////////////
main()
{
    union _REGS r;
    struct _SREGS s;

    LPMEMBLOCK lpMemBlock = NULL;
    int far *  lpMemStartSeg;
    int far *  lpData  = NULL;
    int far *  lpEnv   = NULL;
    int far *  lpOwner = NULL;

    char   _Name[ 9 ];
    char * _Comment;

    // initialize

    FP_OFF( lpEnv ) = _RxDOS_PSP_ENV;
    memset( _Name, '\0', sizeof( _Name ));

    // first, we get the start of DOS memory

    r.h.ah = 0x52;                         // use undoc function 52
    _intdosx( &r, &r, &s );                // es contains seg address of DOS

    FP_SEG( lpMemStartSeg ) = s.es;
    FP_OFF( lpMemStartSeg ) = _RXDOS_STARTARENAS;

    FP_SEG( lpMemBlock ) = *lpMemStartSeg;
```

```
printf ( " t  seg  owner  size  program name and comment\n" );
printf ( " -  — —-  —  ————————————-\n" );

// then we loop through memory
while ( 1 )
    {
    _Name[0] = '\0';
    FP_SEG( lpData ) = FP_SEG( lpMemBlock ) + 1;
    FP_SEG( lpOwner ) = lpMemBlock-> _memOwner;
    FP_SEG( lpEnv  ) = FP_SEG( lpOwner );

    if ( lpMemBlock-> _memOwner == _RxDOS_PARENT_SIGNATURE )
       _Comment = BlockwasAllocbyDOS;

    else if ( lpMemBlock-> _memOwner == _RxDOS_FREE_MEMBLOCK )
       _Comment = BlockisFree;

    else if ( lpData == lpOwner )
        {
        _Comment = BlockisProgramPSP;
        CleanUpName( lpMemBlock, _Name );
        }

    else if ( *lpEnv == FP_SEG( lpData ))
       _Comment = BlockisAnEnvControlBlock;

    else
       _Comment = NoComment;

    printf ( " %c  %4X  %4X  %4X  %-8s  %s\n",
       lpMemBlock-> _memSignature,
       FP_SEG( lpMemBlock ),
       lpMemBlock-> _memOwner,
       lpMemBlock-> _memSize,
       _Name,
       _Comment );

    if ( lpMemBlock-> _memSignature == 'M' )
       FP_SEG( lpMemBlock ) += lpMemBlock-> _memSize + 1;

    else
       break;
    }
}
```

The output of memwalk shows just how many memory blocks are allocated.

```
C:\RXBOOK>memwalk
 t  seg  owner  size  program name and comment
 -  — —-  —  ————————————————
 M   253     8  C4E           block was allocated by DOS
 M   EA2     8    4           block was allocated by DOS
 M   EA7   EA8   A4  COMMAND  block is a program PSP
 M  ·F4C   EA8    4
 M   F51   EA8   40           block is an env control block
```

```
M   F92   EA8     4
M   F97   FB0    17               block is an env control block
M   FAF   FB0    57   WIN         block is a program PSP
M  1007  1022    19               block is an env control block
M  1021  1022    DE   win386      block is a program PSP
M  1100  111A    18
M  1119  111A    A4   COMMAND     block is a program PSP
M  11BE  111A    17               block is an env control block
M  11D6  11F0    18               block is an env control block
M  11EF  11F0  1189   MEMWALK     block is a program PSP
Z  2379     0  7C85               block is free
```

Here are some general comments about the output of `memwalk`.

- Program names are valid only for PSP blocks. All other blocks contain garbage there. Unlike DOS, RxDOS will place the program name in every allocated block, except for environment blocks. Environment blocks have the name blank in RxDOS.
- This list was generated from a DOS session running in Windows because both `win` and `win386` are listed as programs, and there is a second copy of the `command` shell.
- There is only one free block in the listing, and by coincidence, it is the last block. This map shows a very stable memory allocation pattern that has not left any empty memory holes.

A memory block contains a PSP when the owner field in the memory block points to itself, as in the example shown next. The reason there is a discrepancy of 1 between the segment address and the owner value is the owner field always points to the PSP, which is in the data portion of an allocated block and not the block's header. A header is always one paragraph below the data address.

```
t  seg  owner  size  program name and comment
-  ---  -----  ----  ------------------------
M  11EF  11F0  1189  MEMWALK     block is a program PSP
```

Identifying the program's environment control block is only slightly more complicated. To test if a block is an environment control block, we look to the block's owner address, which is a PSP. Each PSP contains the segment address of the environment control block for this program. The segment address points to the environment data, not its control block, so we have to subtract 1. If the owner of the current block, its PSP, contains an environment segment address pointing back to the current memory block, then this is that program's environment block.

```
t  seg  owner  size  program name and comment
-  ---  -----  ----  ------------------------
M  11D6  11F0    18               block is an env control block
M  11EF  11F0  1189  MEMWALK      block is a program PSP
```

A block is allocated by DOS, as opposed to any other program, when the owner field contains a unique identifying DOS signature in the owner field. Unlike all other allocated blocks, the owner field for DOS-allocated blocks does not actually point to a PSP.

```
t  seg  owner  size  program name and comment
-  ---  -----  ----  ------------------------
M  253     8   C4E               block was allocated by DOS
```

How DOS Allocation and Free Work

Memory allocation requires finding a free memory block large enough to satisfy the allocation request, and then splitting that free block into two parts, the allocation part and the free remaining part. The free remaining block can subsequently be used in allocating other requests. You allocate blocks on the basis of paragraphs, as follows:

```
mov ah, 48h              ; allocation request
mov bx, paragraphs       ; number of paragraphs
int 21h                  ; call RxDOS
jnc _noerror             ; if no error —>
```

Allocation should not be made from just any available free block. If the default choice is always the first large enough memory block, a more suitable memory block may never be allocated and compromise a product's ability to allocate memory. For example, suppose there are two blocks of free memory, one with 10K and another with 5K. If the first memory allocation request is for 5K and the first block is always arbitrarily chosen, this leaves memory with two remaining 5K blocks. Though there remains 10K of total free memory, a subsequent request for 6K or more of memory would fail. Alternatively, if we followed the same allocation request example, but instead allocated on a best-fit basis, the second block would have clearly been the best first choice, and the remainder would have been one 10K memory block. The example is somewhat contrived, but any number of models can tell you that under tight memory conditions you'll want to really manage which block is allocated first.

DOS provides for allocation strategies, through DOS function 58h, by correctly letting the application choose between first-fit, best-fit, and last-fit strategies. Further, the DOS allocation strategy function doesn't just choose which strategy but where to make the allocation. The strategy function is the only way in which an application can choose to allocate blocks exclusively in upper memory.

One particular aspect of the strategy functions is that when the strategy is changed, it changes the way in which DOS allocates memory for your application and for all other applications that follow! Therefore, it is important to save the current strategy value and restore it after an allocation strategy change.

I believe that letting the allocation strategy remain changed after a program has terminated is an oversight somewhere with the DOS testers. A DOS application that sets the allocation strategy has no reason to know what applications will follow. Clearly, an application that sets the strategy but forgets to restore it is not well behaved, so one could argue that applications should clean up after themselves. DOS cleans up any memory allocated by the application, but it should also have had the foresight to clean up the strategy setting.

DOS defaults to the first-fit strategy, and the following game can be played to show that DOS itself doesn't clean up the allocation strategy in DOS 6. The program sethigh sets the allocation strategy to allocate only in high memory, and then exits. After you run sethigh, try running Windows. You'll get an error message not to run Windows high. That means both that the allocation strategy stays after program termination and that the strategy is not changed when loading programs. Without having to reboot your system, run setdef, which restores the default allocation strategy. You should not try this test in a DOS session under Windows but outside Windows; otherwise, you'll get other error messages, and the test will not perform correctly.

```
// sethigh.c
#include <string.h>
#include <stdio.h>
#include <dos.h>

// defines
#define MEM_BESTFIT_HIGH            0x0041

////////////////////////////////////////////////////////////////
main()
{
    union _REGS r;
    struct _SREGS s;

    // set high only allocation strategy
    r.x.ax = 0x5801;
    r.x.bx = MEM_BESTFIT_HIGH;
    _intdosx( &r, &r, &s );           // es contains seg address of DOS
}

// setdef.c
#include <string.h>
#include <stdio.h>
#include <dos.h>

// defines
#define MEM_FIRSTFIT_LOW            0x0000

////////////////////////////////////////////////////////////////
main()
{
    union _REGS r;
    struct _SREGS s;

    // set default low first allocation strategy
    r.x.ax = 0x5801;
    r.x.bx = MEM_FIRSTFIT_LOW;
    _intdosx( &r, &r, &s );               // es contains seg address of DOS
}
```

First-fit Strategy

The DOS default strategy is called first-fit. Under this strategy, DOS satisfies the allocation request when it finds the first block large enough from which to make the allocation. Once a block is found, the block is split into the allocation part and the free part, with the allocation part always occupying the lower memory address portion of the block. The remaining portion of the block is given its own memory control block and remains free (unallocated).

The first-fit allocation strategy is the fastest allocation algorithm because not all blocks are searched, and it has the advantage of allocating lower memory blocks before higher memory blocks. However, it also can lead to the greatest fragmentation. Memory fragmentation occurs eventually when small unallocated memory blocks are left over from allocations that by themselves are too small to be of any practical use to an application. Since DOS is so overwhelmingly a single-process system, fragmentation of this type is highly unlikely. That is because no matter how fragmented memory gets, all of it released when an application is terminated, resulting in the recovery of the fragmented memory blocks. However, holes are often left by TSRs, which free their environment space before going resident.

The differences in the effect of allocation strategies are shown in Figure 7-5.

Best-Fit Strategy

The best-fit strategy searches through all memory blocks and allocates memory from the block that will leave the least amount of unused memory. This strategy is particularly useful when lots of blocks are being allocated and released and has the benefit that memory fragmentation is kept to a minimum.

Last-Fit Strategy

The last-fit strategy would seem to allocate from the back first, and to all appearances, the blocks at the end of the available memory get allocated first. However, DOS has no mechanism for walking through memory blocks backward and does not even know where the last memory block is located. To locate the last block, DOS must actually look at each memory block from the beginning, as it does with all other strategies, but it allocates only the last block that can fit the allocation request. This strategy is useful where memory blocks at the end of memory are known to be available and would theoretically leave large spaces that may exist in the middle intact. Finally, the last-fit strategy does not allocate a block from the end of the block. Rather, like all other strategies, it allocates an available block of memory from the beginning of a block.

DOS allocation strategy not only describes how memory will be allocated and searched but where memory will be searched first. Allocation strategy can be set to permit and even demand that the memory will be searched exclusively in the upper memory blocks. The upper memory block allocation works as follows. The default is to allocate from just low, or conventional, memory. This strategy remains compatible with existing DOS products. Alternatively, the strategy may be set to search upper memory blocks first and then search lower memory blocks. Finally, a strategy option is to search upper memory exclusively. With any strategy, if a block is not found that satisfies the allocation request, the allocation function will fail but will return the largest available block size. When the strategy is set to search only the upper or only the lower memory blocks, the largest block value returned is the largest block for that region and not the largest block for all memory.

Figure 7-5. The difference in allocation strategies

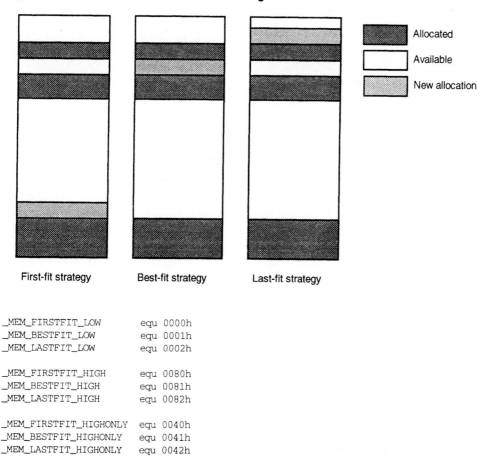

First-fit strategy   Best-fit strategy   Last-fit strategy

```
_MEM_FIRSTFIT_LOW           equ 0000h
_MEM_BESTFIT_LOW            equ 0001h
_MEM_LASTFIT_LOW            equ 0002h

_MEM_FIRSTFIT_HIGH          equ 0080h
_MEM_BESTFIT_HIGH           equ 0081h
_MEM_LASTFIT_HIGH           equ 0082h

_MEM_FIRSTFIT_HIGHONLY      equ 0040h
_MEM_BESTFIT_HIGHONLY       equ 0041h
_MEM_LASTFIT_HIGHONLY       equ 0042h
```

DOS Memory Allocation Is Not malloc( )

`malloc()` is a C function used extensively to allocate memory. Some users think that `malloc()` utilizes the DOS memory allocation functions and that all memory allocation has to somehow always go through a DOS function call. It doesn't. Applications, including the memory management provided automatically by the C function library, allocate a large block of memory from DOS. `malloc()` then suballocates space from this memory pool or heap.

There are several excellent reasons for doing this within an application. For example, you may be able to compact the freed space more readily, thus always maintaining greater efficiency than possible under DOS.

To allocate the largest possible memory block from DOS, first request an amount of memory that is expected to fail, such as a megabyte of memory. Although the request fails, DOS returns the size of the largest available block. This size can then be used in a subsequent allocation request that should succeed. The logic should follow this example.

```
mov ah, 48h
mov bx, 0ffffh        ; all of memory
int 21h               ; allocate
jnc _expectedtofail   ; if it didn't ->  (??)

mov ah, 48h           ; maximum already in bx
int 21h               ; allocate
jc _expectedtosucceed ; if allocated ->

; can't get a straight answer out of DOS ?
; display error.
```

Internally, malloc() essentially uses the same strategy to create a heap of allocatable space. When a C program starts up, and before it calls main(), a memory heap is allocated depending on the memory model. The heap space is allocated from DOS. malloc() then allocates space from this heap.

Allocate Memory

	On Entry	On Return
AX	AH = 48h	allocated segment, if no error
BX	size in paragraphs	maximum available mem block, if error
CX		
DX		
Flags		CY = set if error

Related Functions:
   49h Free Memory; 4Ah Resize Memory; 5800h Get Allocation Strategy;
   5801h Set Allocation Strategy.

The memory allocation function returns the segment address of an allocated block. The function must first scan for available memory blocks but only within the region permitted by the strategy flags. Within the designated region, the block selected must also meet the first-fit, last-fit, and best-fit strategy considerations. The function returns the segment address to the allocated data. A memory control block, as shown in Figure 7-6, precedes the block.

Figure 7-6. The caller to the DOS function gets back the segment address to data

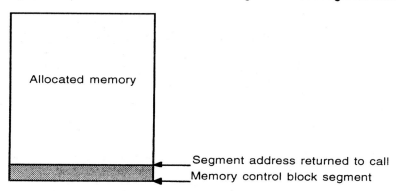

Once a block is selected, it must be divided into two parts. The unallocated portion of the memory block remains free and is given its own free memory control block. The allocated portion of the original block is updated to reflect the allocated size and the new owner. The code flow for allocation looks like the diagram in Figure 7-7.

Figure 7-7. Code flow for memory allocation.

```
_AllocateMemory
    _allocateUpperMB
        _localAreaAllocateMemory

    _allocateConvMB
        _localAreaAllocateMemory
```

The code for the DOS memory allocation function is split between _Allocate Memory (in rxdos.asm) and two functions located in rxdosmem.asm, _allocateUpperMB, and _allocateConvMB. _allocateUpperMB first tries to allocate memory blocks in the upper memory blocks if it's allowed to by the strategy flags. If it cannot allocate any blocks there, or if it is not allowed to allocate blocks in the upper memory area, it then calls _allocateConvMB, which tries to allocate memory in conventional memory. However, _localAreaAllocateMemory (in rxdosmem.asm) is the routine that actually does the scanning, fit analysis, and allocation work.

```
;'''''''''''''''''''''''''''''''''''''''''''''''''''''''''''''''';
;  48h Allocate Memory                                           ;
;- - - - - - - - - - - - - - - - - - - - - - - - - - - - - - - -;
;                                                                ;
;  bx    # paragraphs of memory requested                        ;
;                                                                ;
```

```
;   Returns:                                                        ;
;   ax    segment address of allocated memory block                ;
;   bx    size of largest block of memory available in             ;
;         paragraphs, if allocation fails.                          ;
;...............................................................;

_AllocateMemory:

        call _allocateUpperMB              ; allocate upper mem blocks
        jnc _AllocateMemory_12             ; if allocation made ->
        call _allocateConvMB               ; allocate lower mem blocks

_AllocateMemory_12:
        RetCallersStackFrame ds, si
        mov word ptr [ _AX ][ si ], ax     ; error or segment allocation
        jnc _AllocateMemory_16             ; if not error ->

        mov word ptr [ _BX ][ si ], dx     ; largest block

_AllocateMemory_16:
        ret
```

The routines _allocateUpperMB and _allocateConvMB return any allocated block in the AX register. The largest allocatable block is returned by these functions in the DX register, which is then returned to the user in the BX register.

The RetCallersStackFrame macro, which we described in "How to Read the Source Code" in Chapter 1, is used by the allocate memory service routine to return values to the caller. RxDOS retrieves a pointer back to the caller's stack and then changes the register values on the stack in order to return values.

Both _allocateUpperMB and _allocateConvMB functions have very similar logic and intentions. The only major difference between them is which region to start scanning (searching) for free memory blocks.

```
;'''''''''''''''''''''''''''''''''''''''''''''''''''''''''''''';
;   Allocate Upper Memory Blocks                                   ;
;- - - - - - - - - - - - - - - - - - - - - - - - - - - - - - - -;
;                                                                  ;
;   bx    # paragraphs of memory requested                        ;
;                                                                  ;
;   Returns:                                                        ;
;   ax    segment address of allocated memory block                ;
;   dx    size of largest block of memory available in             ;
;         paragraphs, if allocation fails.                          ;
;...............................................................;

_allocateUpperMB:
        test word ptr [ _RxDOS_AllocStrategy ],
                (_MEM_FIRSTFIT_HIGH + _MEM_FIRSTFIT_HIGHONLY )
        jnz _allocateUpperMB_14            ; if search upper memory blocks ->

_allocateUpperMB_12:
        xor dx, dx                         ; largest block available (none)
```

```
        SetError errNotEnoughMemory
        ret


_allocateUpperMB_14:
        mov ax, _RxDOS_HIGHMEMBLOCK
        call _localAreaAllocateMemory
        ret                             .
```

_allocateUpperMB first checks the strategy flags. The function must test for allocation in the upper memory blocks. If it can, the memory block search begins at _RxDOS_HIGHMEMBLOCK, the address of the memory block immediately below the start of upper memory. The high memory block address is set at startup by DOS when it determines that access to high memory can be enabled. The config file must have included a line that contains DOS=HIGH, and a high memory driver like emm386 should have also been loaded.

```
        ;'''''''''''''''''''''''''''''''''''''''''''''''''''''''''''''';
        ;  Allocate Conventional Memory Blocks                          ;
        ;- - - - - - - - - - - - - - - - - - - - - - - - - - - - - - - -;
        ;                                                               ;
        ;  bx    # paragraphs of memory requested                       ;
        ;                                                               ;
        ;  Returns:                                                     ;
        ;  ax    segment address of allocated memory block              ;
        ;  bx    size of largest block of memory available in           ;
        ;          paragraphs, if allocation fails.                     ;
        ;.............................................................;

_allocateConvMB:
        test word ptr [ _RxDOS_AllocStrategy ], (_MEM_FIRSTFIT_HIGHONLY )
        jz _allocateConvMB_14                   ; if search conv memory blocks -->

_allocateConvMB_12:
        xor dx, dx
        SetError errNotEnoughMemory
        ret

_allocateConvMB_14:
        mov ax, word ptr [ _RxDOS_pStartMemBlock ]
        call _localAreaAllocateMemory
        ret
```

_allocateConvMB also first checks the strategy flags but this time to make sure it's not excluded from searching the lower memory blocks. The search for memory control blocks must start at the beginning of conventional memory. Recall in our earlier description that the start of memory control blocks is stored by DOS at the label _RxDOS_pStartMemBlock. This is the segment address that is passed to the search routine.

Finally, and mercifully, we analyze the work horse of the memory allocation routine, _localAreaAllocateMemory. The search block size is the original search block size passed by the caller to DOS and is passed in the BX register. The setup routines set the starting segment of where to search in the AX register.

The routine makes use of the `Entry` macro (which must be followed by the proper `Return` macro at the end). To learn what `Entry` and `Return` actually do, see the section on "How to Read the Source Code" in Chapter 1. The `Entry` macro creates a stack work area. The work area will contain two temporary variables, `_bestFit` and `_lastFit`, which hold segment addresses for the best-fit and last-fit free memory arenas.

The routine checks each block first for a proper signature byte, which must be either an M or a Z, identified in the code as `_RxDOS_MEMSIGNATURE` or `_RxDOS_ ENDSIGNATURE`, respectively. Then it checks to make sure that the block is free and that it is at least large enough to satisfy the allocation request. The block is free if there is no assigned owner, that is, if the owner word contains zeros. The fitness of the block is determined by subtracting the allocation request size from the block size. The answer is left in the `SI` register. A negative number means the free block is too small, and the code processes the next block. If the block size is positive or zero, the code looks at the strategy considerations. For first fit, the code uses this block, the first encountered, and goes on to perform the allocation. Allocations are all performed at `_allocMem_30`. If the strategy is last fit, the segment address is saved in the temporary location `_lastFit`.

For best-fit strategy, the code has to maintain two values. The code must remember the address of the best-fit block, and it must remember the fitness of the block. How each available block fits is determined by the amount of space that goes unallocated for each block. For any previous block saved, we need to remember how well the previous block fit. That information is saved throughout the search in the CX register. For any new block, the fitness of this block must exceed the fitness of any previous block saved. The fitness of the current block, which we learned is in the `SI` register, is compared with the best fit from any previous block, kept in the CX register. If the current block wasted less space, the current block's segment value is saved in `_bestFit`, and the new fitness is saved in the CX register.

While all this searching is going on, there is the possibility that no block will satisfy the allocation request. The routine is required to return the size of the largest block encountered in the DX register, which eventually gets returned to the caller of DOS function 48h in the BX register. As each free block is encountered, the size of the block is compared with the previous large block, and if greater, the size of the new larger block is copied to the DX register.

```
;''''''''''''''''''''''''''''''''''''''''''''''''''''''''''''''''';
;  Local Zone Memory Allocation                                   ;
;- - - - - - - - - - - - - - - - - - - - - - - - - - - - - - - -;
;                                                                 ;
;  ax    paragraph to begin search                               ;
;  bx    # paragraphs of memory requested                        ;
;                                                                 ;
;  Returns:                                                       ;
;  ax    segment address of allocated memory block               ;
;  bx    size of largest block of memory available in            ;
;            paragraphs, if allocation fails.                     ;
;.................................................................;

_localAreaAllocateMemory:
        Entry
        def _bestFit, 0000              ; segment pointer to best fit
        def _lastFit, 0000              ; segment pointer to last fit
```

```
        push ds
        push es                             ; save segment registers

        or ax, ax                           ; zero if no mem allocated
        jnz _allocMem_10                    ; mem list available —>
        xor dx, dx                          ; no memory available
        SetError errNotEnoughMemory, _allocMem_44  ; error —>

;- - - - - - - - - - - - - - - - - - - - - - - - - - - - - - - - - - -
;  scan memory blocks
;- - - - - - - - - - - - - - - - - - - - - - - - - - - - - - - - - - -
_allocMem_10:
        cli                                 ; prevent interrupts
        xor dx, dx                          ; largest available
        mov cx, 0ffffh                      ; best fit

_allocMem_12:
        mov es, ax                          ; point to memory seg
        cmp byte ptr es:[ _memSignature ], _RxDOS_MEMSIGNATURE
        jz _allocMem_14                     ; if valid arena —>
        cmp byte ptr es:[ _memSignature ], _RxDOS_ENDSIGNATURE
        jz _allocMem_14                     ; if valid arena —>
        SetError errInvalidBlock, _allocMem_44  ; else, if error —>

_allocMem_14:
        cmp word ptr es:[ _memParent ], 0000  ; 0000 for parent means its free
        jnz _allocMem_20                    ; not a free block —>

        mov si, word ptr es:[ _memAlloc ]   ; get available space
        sub si, bx                          ; is block within allocation size ?
        jc _allocMem_16                     ; no —>

        storarg _lastFit, ax                ; seg address of last fit
        test word ptr [ _RxDOS_AllocStrategy ], _MEM_FIRSTFIT_STRATEGY
        jz _allocMem_30                     ; ok to allocate this block ->

        cmp cx, si                          ; is this block a better fit ?
        jc _allocMem_16                     ; not a better strategy —>
        mov cx, si                          ; else save fit
        storarg _bestFit, ax                ; seg address of best fit

_allocMem_16:
        cmp dx, word ptr es:[ _memAlloc ]   ; larger block ?
        jc _allocMem_20                     ; no —>
        mov dx, word ptr es:[ _memAlloc ]   ; get size

_allocMem_20:
        inc ax                              ; skip past arena header
        add ax, word ptr es:[ _memAlloc ]
        cmp byte ptr es:[ _memSignature ], _RxDOS_ENDSIGNATURE
        jnz _allocMem_12                    ; not at end yet —>

;- - - - - - - - - - - - - - - - - - - - - - - - - - - - - - - - - - -
;  available block not found or allocation deferred to here
;- - - - - - - - - - - - - - - - - - - - - - - - - - - - - - - - - - -
```

```
            getarg ax, _bestFit
            test word ptr [ _RxDOS_AllocStrategy ], _MEM_BESTFIT_STRATEGY
            jnz _allocMem_24                      ; if best fit ->

            getarg ax, _lastFit
            test word ptr [ _RxDOS_AllocStrategy ], _MEM_LASTFIT_STRATEGY
            jz _allocMem_26                       ; if not last fit ->

_allocMem_24:
            or ax, ax                             ; determine if no allocation
            jnz _allocMem_30                      ; if block available ->

_allocMem_26:
            SetError errNotEnoughMemory, _allocMem_44

;- - - - - - - - - - - - - - - - - - - - - - - - - - - - - - - - -
;   Allocate block.
;
;   assumes es: points to free block to allocate
;
;- - - - - - - - - - - - - - - - - - - - - - - - - - - - - - - - -
_allocMem_30:
            mov es, ax
            push es                               ; segment to return
            push bx                               ; size requested
            mov dl, byte ptr es:[ _memSignature ] ; current block signature

            mov ax, word ptr es:[ _memAlloc ]     ; get allocation
            sub ax, bx                            ; this is remaining alloc balance
            jz _allocMem_38                       ; if exact fit ->

            dec ax                                ; make room for second mem control block

            mov cx, es
            add cx, bx                            ; space we'll need
            inc cx                                ; where next block will be

            push dx
            mov es, cx                            ; create a block here
            xor bx, bx                            ; this block is free
            call _initializeMemoryBlock           ; initialize memory block
            pop dx
            mov byte ptr es:[ _memSignature ], dl ; signature from previous block
            mov dl, _RxDOS_MEMSIGNATURE

; update old mem control block

_allocMem_38:
            pop bx                                ; request size
            pop es                                ; seg address (es: )

            mov cx, word ptr [ _RxDOS_CurrentPSP ]
            mov word ptr es:[ _memParent ], cx    ; current owner
```

```
        mov word ptr es:[ _memAlloc ], bx        ; allocate what we need
        mov byte ptr es:[ _memSignature ], dl

        mov ax, es
        inc ax                                   ; seg address of data
        or ax,ax                                 ; no carry

_allocMem_44:
        pop es                                   ; restore segment registers
        pop ds

        sti
        Return
```

Eventually, the code finds the last of the memory blocks and must determine if any of the blocks scanned matches the fit strategy. If no block has been selected, both _bestFit and _lastFit will be zero, and error exit takes place. Otherwise, the block address in either of these temporary values is the block that will be allocated. For first-fit strategy, the code has already chosen the requisite block and has jumped to _allocMem_30, where the selected memory block will be allocated. The selected block segment address is passed in the AX register.

The selected block will be divided into two blocks, one for the allocated portion of the block and another for the unallocated (free) portion of the block. The signature of the current block must be carried over to the second or free remaining portion. This carries forward the end signature, the Z block to the last block.

The code does the following: It remembers the segment address passed in AX, the allocation request size passed in BX, and the current block's signature saved temporarily in the DL register. If the block is exactly the same size as the allocation request, then no block splitting is required, and the code jumps to _allocMem_38. Otherwise, the code continues with the block splitting. The size difference between the allocation request and the size of the block, now in the AX register, is passed to a memory initialize routine, _initializeMemoryBlock. The owner, passed in the BX register, is set to a free block (zeros). The old signature, in the DX register, is saved on the stack. The new segment block address is computed by taking the address of the existing block and adding the space we'll require. The size of the block is reduced by one paragraph for the control block. Once the second memory control block has been created, the original memory control block must be updated to reflect the new allocated size and owner. The owner field for the newly allocated block is the address of the current-running PSP, taken directly as

```
        mov cx, word ptr [ _RxDOS_CurrentPSP ]
        mov word ptr es:[ _memParent ], cx        ; current owner
```

The segment address returned to the caller is the segment address of the allocated data and not the address of the memory control block. Since these are segment addresses, and the memory control block occupies one paragraph, the segment address of the data is computed by taking the segment address of the memory control block plus 1.

Free Allocated Memory

	On Entry	On Return
AX	AH = 49h	AL = error, if carry set
BX	segment address of block	
CX		
DX		
Flags		CY = set if error

Related Functions:
   48h Allocate Memory; 4Ah Resize Memory; 5800h Get Allocation Strategy;
   5801h Set Allocation Strategy.

The free memory function expects the segment address of an allocated memory area. This is the same segment address that was returned as part of the allocate function. Within DOS, the block is first checked for validity before it is returned to a free block. In RxDOS, a check is made of the surrounding blocks to determine if the block should be combined to form a larger free block, thus avoiding fragmentation. MS-DOS frees the memory block but waits to reclaim adjacent free blocks during the allocate function.

One little known fact about the DOS free memory function is that it will not check to verify that the block being deleted actually belongs to the application requesting the block delete. An application can delete any valid memory block. The function checks only the signature byte of the memory control block and will return a memory corrupted error if it believes that the memory control block does not contain a valid signature byte. This can happen in one of two ways, either the segment address sent to the function is not the segment address returned from the allocate function call or the signature byte and possibly other parts of the memory control block have been corrupted.

_FreeAllocatedMemory function, in rxdos.asm, and _collectMemoryBlocks, in rxdosmem.asm, contain all the code to perform the free function. _FreeAllocatedMemory first determines if the memory control block for the referenced block is valid by checking its signature byte. Then, if this is a legitimate block, the parent field for the block is zeroed, which frees the block. This would be sufficient to merely free the block. To avoid needless fragmentation, all free blocks are collected together using _collectMemoryBlocks, listed in rxdosmem.asm.

Why have a separate function to collect empty blocks? When a program terminates and performs an exit (DOS function 4Dh), a routine, _releaseOwnerMemoryBlocks, is called to free all blocks allocated by the terminating program by marking them as free. The _collectMemoryBlocks function is then called to collect all freed blocks into individual large free blocks.

Conventional wisdom might make you believe that when a block is freed we should check the immediately preceding and following blocks. The code in _collectMemoryBlocks uses a different method, which we discuss next.

```
(in rxdos.asm)
        ;,,,,,,,,,,,,,,,,,,,,,,,,,,,,,,,,,,,,,,,,,,,,,,,,,,,,,,,,,,,,,,;
        ;   49h Free Allocated Memory                                 ;
        ;- - - - - - - - - - - - - - - - - - - - - - - - - - - - - - -;
```

```
        ;                                                    ;
        ;  es   paragraph to free                            ;
        ;.................................................;

_FreeAllocatedMemory:
        RetCallersStackFrame es, bx
        mov bx, word ptr es:[ _ExtraSegment ][ bx ]
        dec bx                                  ; preceding seg contains block

        mov es, bx                              ; is this a valid memory block ?
        cmp byte ptr es:[ _memSignature ], _RxDOS_MEMSIGNATURE
        jz _freeallocateMemory_12
        cmp byte ptr es:[ _memSignature ], _RxDOS_ENDSIGNATURE
        jz _freeallocateMemory_12

;- - - - - - - - - - - - - - - - - - - - - - - - - - - - - - -
;  invalid block.
;- - - - - - - - - - - - - - - - - - - - - - - - - - - - - - -

        RetCallersStackFrame es, bx
        mov word ptr es:[ _AX ][ bx ], errInvalidBlock
        stc
        ret

;- - - - - - - - - - - - - - - - - - - - - - - - - - - - - - -
;  block is valid.  free it.
;- - - - - - - - - - - - - - - - - - - - - - - - - - - - - - -

_freeallocateMemory_12:
        xor ax, ax
        mov word ptr es:[ _memParent ], ax     ; free memory block
        call _collectMemoryBlocks              ; save space
        or ax, ax                              ; no carry
        ret

(in rxdosmem.asm)
        ;'''''''''''''''''''''''''''''''''''''''''''''''''''''''''''';
        ;  Collect Memory Blocks                                    ;
        ;- - - - - - - - - - - - - - - - - - - - - - - - - - - - - -;
        ;                                                           ;
        ;  This routine will scan all memory blocks and merge all free  ;
        ;  memory blocks together.                                  ;
        ;.................................................;

_collectMemoryBlocks:
        push ds
        push es
        mov ax, word ptr [ _RxDOS_pStartMemBlock ]

;- - - - - - - - - - - - - - - - - - - - - - - - - - - - - - -
;  is block free ?
;- - - - - - - - - - - - - - - - - - - - - - - - - - - - - - -
_collectMemoryBlocks_08:
        mov ds, ax                              ; next in ax
```

```
_collectMemoryBlocks_12:
        cmp byte ptr ds:[ _memSignature ], _RxDOS_ENDSIGNATURE
        jz _collectMemoryBlocks_36             ; done ->

        cmp word ptr ds:[ _memParent ], 0000   ; is block free ?
        jnz _collectMemoryBlocks_26            ; no, go to next ->

;- - - - - - - - - - - - - - - - - - - - - - - - - - - - - - -
;  is next also free ?
;- - - - - - - - - - - - - - - - - - - - - - - - - - - - - - -
        mov ax, ds                             ; get current segment
        add ax, word ptr ds:[ _memAlloc ]      ; increment to next block
        inc ax
        mov es, ax
        cmp word ptr es:[ _memParent ], 0000   ; is next block free ?
        jnz _collectMemoryBlocks_08            ; no, go to next ->

        mov ax, word ptr es:[ _memAlloc ]      ; get next allocation
        inc ax                                 ; kill interim Mem block as well
        add word ptr ds:[ _memAlloc ], ax      ; add to current block

        mov al, byte ptr es:[ _memSignature ]  ; last signature passed to curr
        mov byte ptr ds:[ _memSignature ], al  ;
        jmp _collectMemoryBlocks_12

;- - - - - - - - - - - - - - - - - - - - - - - - - - - - - - -
;  go to next
;- - - - - - - - - - - - - - - - - - - - - - - - - - - - - - -
_collectMemoryBlocks_26:
        mov ax, ds                             ; get current segment
        add ax, word ptr ds:[ _memAlloc ]      ; increment to next block
        inc ax
        jmp _collectMemoryBlocks_08

;- - - - - - - - - - - - - - - - - - - - - - - - - - - - - - -
;  done
;- - - - - - - - - - - - - - - - - - - - - - - - - - - - - - -
_collectMemoryBlocks_36:
        pop es
        pop ds
        ret
```

_collectMemoryBlocks does not actually join all free blocks. It only joins free blocks that happen to lie next to each other, as shown in Figure 7-8. Several free blocks are grouped together into individual singular blocks, but all free blocks are not actually joined. The importance of this is that memory blocks remain where they are allocated and are not moved in order to reclaim fragmented free space.

To join all free blocks, which the routine does not actually do, would involve moving or relocating memory blocks, particularly allocated blocks. Moving a block would change its allocated segment address and invalidate any pointer that the application may have built for an allocated block.

_collectMemoryBlocks scans through all memory blocks, beginning at the memory segment value stored in _RxDOS_pStartMemBlock, the start of the memory list. Each memory block encountered is checked to see if it has a valid signature byte and whether the block is free. When a free block is located, the immediately following block is checked to determine if it also is free. If it is not, the search continues. Otherwise, the two adjoining blocks are both free and need to be combined. The size of the second block is added to the size of the current block, plus one for the space occupied by the second memory block, and the signature of the first block is replaced by the signature byte of the second block just in case the second block is the end or last block.

Once the two blocks are joined, the block immediately following the currently joined blocks is checked to determine if it too is free. If it is, these two blocks (the already joined block and the block that adjoins it) are joined in the same way as the previous two blocks. This process continues until all the free blocks are joined.

MS-DOS waits until a memory allocation request is made before it collects all the available free blocks. It would seem that this would have to be done in two places, once in allocate and once in reallocate, which we discuss next, and always as complete pass through all memory. At any rate, there is probably little marginal difference in performance either way.

Figure 7-8. Before and after collecting free blocks

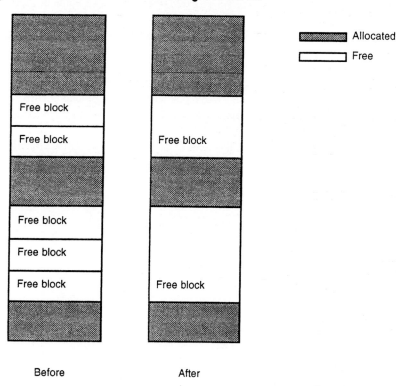

Before   After

Reallocate Memory

	On Entry	On Return
AX	AH = 4Ah	AL = error, if carry set
BX	new size in paragraphs	
CX		
DX		
ES	segment address of block	
Flags		CY = set if error

Related Functions:
   48h Allocate Memory; 49h Free Memory; 5800h Get Allocation Strategy;
   5801h Set Allocation Strategy.

The reallocate memory function is used primarily to release space that had been allocated but is no longer necessary, but it may also be used to expand the allocated size. What often happens is that a program is given or allocates to itself all memory when it begins to run. Eventually, it is necessary to leave as small a footprint as practical. For example, a TSR program gives back some of its initially allocated space.

When requesting additional space, as opposed to releasing space, the function is trickier and may fail if memory beyond the current block has already been allocated by another allocation request. The function fails and does not relocate an expansion request that it cannot satisfy.

To release allocated space, the function creates a free block immediately after the new size and then uses _collectMemoryBlocks to join this new free block with any free block that may follow. In MS-DOS, in contrast with RxDOS, this collection of free blocks is handled the next time that a memory block is allocated.

Like the free memory function, one little known fact about the DOS modify memory function is that it will not check owners when the block is modified. Any program can change the size of any memory block.

```
(in rxdos.asm)
        ;''''''''''''''''''''''''''''''''''''''''''''''''''''''''''';
        ;   4ah Modify Allocate Memory                              ;
        ;- - - - - - - - - - - - - - - - - - - - - - - - - - - - - -;
        ;                                                           ;
        ;   es   paragraph to free                                  ;
        ;   bx   new paragraph size                                 ;
        ;...........................................................;

_ModifyAllocatedMemory:
        RetCallersStackFrame es, si
        mov si, word ptr es:[ _ExtraSegment ][ si ]
        dec si                                  ; preceding seg contains block

; already have bx from call

        mov es, si                              ; is this a valid memory block ?
```

```
        cmp byte ptr es:[ _memSignature ], _RxDOS_MEMSIGNATURE
        jz _modifyallocateMemory_12
        cmp byte ptr es:[ _memSignature ], _RxDOS_ENDSIGNATURE
        jz _modifyallocateMemory_12

_modifyallocateMemory_10:
        SetError errInvalidBlock, _modifyallocateMemory_66


;- - - - - - - - - - - - - - - - - - - - - - - - - - - - - - - -
;  are we expanding allocation ?
;- - - - - - - - - - - - - - - - - - - - - - - - - - - - - - - -
_modifyallocateMemory_12:
        mov cx, word ptr es:[ _memAlloc ]
        cmp bx, cx                              ; current size in cx
        jz _modifyallocateMemory_66             ; same size as now, ignore ->
        jc _modifyallocateMemory_32             ; no, contracting allocation ->

        push es
        cmp byte ptr es:[ _memSignature ], _RxDOS_ENDSIGNATURE
        jz _modifyallocateMemory_14

        mov ax, es
        add ax, word ptr es:[ _memAlloc ]
        inc ax                                  ; point to next block
        mov es, ax
        mov dl, byte ptr es:[ _memSignature ]   ; existing signature
        cmp word ptr es:[ _memParent ], 0000    ; is next block free ?
        jz _modifyallocateMemory_16             ; yes, ok to try to expand ->

_modifyallocateMemory_14:
        pop es
        SetError errNotEnoughMemory, _modifyallocateMemory_66

_modifyallocateMemory_16:
        add cx, word ptr es:[ _memAlloc ]       ; add extra space
        cmp bx, cx                              ; is extra block enough to expand ?
        jz _modifyallocateMemory_18             ; yes, ok to try to expand ->
        jnc _modifyallocateMemory_14            ; yes, ok to try to expand ->

_modifyallocateMemory_18:
        pop es
        mov word ptr es:[ _memAlloc ], bx       ; expanded allocation

        mov ax, es                              ; current allocation
        add ax, word ptr es:[ _memAlloc ]       ; where next block will appear
        inc ax
        mov es, ax                              ; create a block here

        push dx
        mov ax, cx                              ; total size
        sub ax, bx                              ; part acquired by expansion
        xor bx, bx                              ; parent of new remainder is free
        call _initializeMemoryBlock             ; initialize memory block.
        pop dx
```

```
        mov byte ptr es:[ _memSignature ], dl      ; previous signature stays

        clc
        ret

;- - - - - - - - - - - - - - - - - - - - - - - - - - - - - - - - - -
;  collapse allocated space
;- - - - - - - - - - - - - - - - - - - - - - - - - - - - - - - - - -
_modifyallocateMemory_32:
        mov cx, es                           ; current segment
        add cx, bx
        inc cx                               ; where to create next mem seg

        mov ax, word ptr es:[ _memAlloc ]    ; existing space
        sub ax, bx                           ; size of remaining block
        dec ax                               ; make room for mem header
        jz _modifyallocateMemory_66          ; not enough room -->

        mov byte ptr es:[ _memSignature ], _RxDOS_MEMSIGNATURE
        mov word ptr es:[ _memAlloc ], bx    ; reallocate space

        mov es, cx
        xor bx, bx                           ; free block
        call _initializeMemoryBlock          ; initialize memory block
        call _collectMemoryBlocks            ; collect free blocks
        clc

;- - - - - - - - - - - - - - - - - - - - - - - - - - - - - - - - - -
;  return
;- - - - - - - - - - - - - - - - - - - - - - - - - - - - - - - - - -
_modifyallocateMemory_66:
        ret
```

_ModifyAllocatedMemory, listed in rxdos.asm, first loads the arguments passed by the caller to the DOS function by getting a pointer to the saved registers on the stack. The segment address of the memory block whose size is to be changed was passed in the ES register. After verifying that the block is valid by checking its signature, the routine branches into two parts; it will be either expanding or contracting the size of the block. The allocated size is compared to the requested size, and the code jumps to _modifyallocateMemory_32 to contract the block's size.

Block expansion is possible only when the block that follows the current block is free. If the block is available, the size of the free block is added to the size of the current block, and a check is made to determine if the size is sufficient. If it is, the allocation is made by changing the size of the current block, and the address of a new block is computed. Where does this new block come from? Actually, not all the space of the free block may actually be allocated, and the unused portion of the free block is left as a new free block.

Block contraction is easier. The new size of the block being contracted is updated, and a new free block is created at the end of the new smaller block. Using _collectMemoryBlocks, the new free block is collected with any free blocks that may follow.

Set Allocation Strategy

	On Entry	On Return
AX	AH = 58h, AL= get/set code	
BX	Allocation strategy code	
CX		
DX		
Flags		

Related Functions:
  48h Allocate Memory; 49h Free Memory; 4Ah Resize Memory.

Function 58h provides the only means to set or test the underlying memory allocation strategy. It is possible to set the strategy in such a way as to prevent DOS from ever being able to run any other programs. This is because, as implemented by MS-DOS, the strategy-setting logic is not automatically reset when an application terminates. I believe that this represents if not an outright bug than at least a major oversight in the design of DOS itself.

To create the bug within DOS, use the sethigh program provided with this book. This program forces all allocations to the upper memory blocks. You'll be able to run any program that can run high and that fits within whatever memory is available in the UMB. Some programs, as we noted earlier, like Windows, just don't want to run high. At this point, you are locked out of running almost all programs, maybe even our own setdef, which restores the memory to the default allocation strategy.

If DOS really intended for the strategy to be settable across applications, which is highly unlikely, then it should have made a different subfunction that sets the strategy permanently, as opposed to just while the current process is running.

```
(in rxdos.asm)
        ;'''''''''''''''''''''''''''''''''''''''''''''''''''''''''''''''';
        ;  5800h Get Allocation Strategy                                 ;
        ;  5801h Set Allocation Strategy                                 ;
        ;- - - - - - - - - - - - - - - - - - - - - - - - - - - - - - - -;
        ;                                                                ;
        ;  al = 00, get allocation strategy                              ;
        ;       01, set allocation strategy                              ;
        ;                                                                ;
        ;  bx   allocation strategy on set                               ;
        ;  ax   allocation strategy on get                               ;
        ;                                                                ;
        ;................................................................;

_GetAllocationStrategy:
        or al, al
        jnz _SetAllocationStrategy

        RetCallersStackFrame es, bx
        mov ax, word ptr [ _RxDOS_AllocStrategy ]
        mov word ptr es:[ _AX ][ bx ], ax
        ret
```

```
;- - - - - - - - - - - - - - - - - - - - - - - - - - - - - - - -
; set allocation strategy
;- - - - - - - - - - - - - - - - - - - - - - - - - - - - - - - -
_SetAllocationStrategy:
        mov word ptr [ _RxDOS_AllocStrategy ], bx
        ret
```

The following allocation strategies are valid:

```
_MEM_FIRSTFIT_STRATEGY   equ 0003h        ; masks for allocation test
_MEM_BESTFIT_STRATEGY    equ 0001h
_MEM_LASTFIT_STRATEGY    equ 0002h


_MEM_FIRSTFIT_LOW        equ 0000h                ; strategy requests
_MEM_BESTFIT_LOW         equ 0001h
_MEM_LASTFIT_LOW         equ 0002h


_MEM_FIRSTFIT_HIGH       equ 0080h
_MEM_BESTFIT_HIGH        equ 0081h
_MEM_LASTFIT_HIGH        equ 0082h


_MEM_FIRSTFIT_HIGHONLY   equ 0040h
_MEM_BESTFIT_HIGHONLY    equ 0041h
_MEM_LASTFIT_HIGHONLY    equ 0042h
```

CHAPTER 8

Command.Com

Parsing the Command Line—Loading and Executing Programs—
Executing Batch Files—Processing Commands—Conclusion

Almost everyone has used the command line paradigm on one computer or another. Even Windows and Macintosh users have used command lines. For them, the command line is a sort of confirmation of the superiority of graphical user interfaces (GUIs). The command line provides a way to manage, utilize, and organize the underlying file system, to set options, and to launch programs.

The command line interface survives today mostly because it is a part of DOS and because some things are just easier done with a command line. Batch files and device redirection are but some examples of how the command line interface sometimes works to the advantage of the user over graphical interfaces. That's not to say there aren't worthy and powerful contenders. There are batch and script languages for Windows, graphical DOS command shells like the one shipped with DOS itself, and other more powerful command shell replacements like 4DOS from J. P. Software. Of course, only command.com is guaranteed to be on everyone's machine and to work on everyone's system.

4DOS, for example, can completely replace command.com. So, just how is it possible that as central a part of DOS as command.com can be replaced? Won't DOS just crash into some kind of boot oblivion without it? The answer is not exactly. To be sure, when DOS boots, it expects to load at least one application; otherwise, there would be no way to launch any applications at all. Although it is possible to have DOS automatically start up any program, it should be an application that permits, at minimum, launching other applications, copying or transferring files, creating, removing, and listing directories, and setting environment variables. The keyword here is *should*, which doesn't mean "must" or "required."

MS-DOS by default automatically loads command.com, which it expects to find in the root directory, unless directed to do otherwise by the SHELL= line in config.sys. The command.com shell, in turn, automatically executes autoexec.bat, a batch file that then customizes the system to a specific user's requirements.

Command.com and the equivalent rxdoscmd.exe supplied by RxDOS are, in fact, just application programs. Features such as batch file execution, device redirection, and application program launching are all accomplished through DOS function calls available to any program. RxDOS utilizes only one undocumented DOS function. The filename passed as a parameter to some commands is expanded through DOS function 60h, the generally undocumented GetActualName function, which we described in Chapter 2.

4DOS is able to avoid the use of any undocumented functions by supplying the same logic within its code. One of the advantages of having knowledge of the development of both sides of an operating system is, of course, knowing about some of the hidden features, functions, and side effects. The point of this discussion is that a command shell doesn't make any special demands, nor does it enjoy a special relationship with DOS. It is just another program.

Parsing the Command Line

Commands are supplied to DOS for execution in a command line format, either entered at the now famous C> prompt or retrieved from a batch file. The first word encountered in the line is interpreted as a keyword or command that is looked up in an internal list of commands. Any command not understood is considered either a batch file or an executable program. The command shell searches the current directory and then all the directories named in the PATH= statement in the environment variables.

Although most users view the command line interface as limited to a single command per line, from the command parser's point of view, command lines may contain multiple commands, as in

```
c> dir *.exe | sort | more
```

This example comprises three separate commands. The directory command's output is piped to a temporary save file. The temporary file is then piped as the input to the sort program, whose output is piped to another temporary output file. Lastly, the more command reads the piped input from the previous command and displays it to the stdout device.

Execution of the command line begins by lexically scanning the line. This process builds an argument array where each entry contains a pointer to the first character of each argument, as shown in Figure 8-1. Each separator in the figure represents an entry in the argument array. The argument array is eventually used to identify and remove any device redirection statements.

Figure 8-1. Argument array examples

```
dir a:*.dat>\foo.txt
```

| dir | a:*.dat | > | \foo.txt | NULL | NULL | | | | |

```
dir a:*.dat | sort | more
```

| dir | a:*.dat | | | sort | | | more | NULL | NULL | | |

Regardless of where the command was retrieved, that is, whether or not it came from a batch file, the command is passed to the command parser as if it had been entered from the keyboard, as shown in Figure 8-2. The carriage return always follows the command but is never counted in the buffer count.

The maximum length of a DOS command is 126 characters, regardless of the source and of how many characters are entered in a batch file statement. This limit is imposed by the command processor on all input statements because this is the maximum number of characters that may be passed to an application program. It's unfortunate because it limits such truly useful commands as the PATH statement and other environment variables.

DOS copied the convention established by CP/M, which placed the tail part of the input command in the PSP, or Program Segment Prefix. This area is limited to 128 bytes. Of these, one byte is used to contain the length of the data in the buffer, and the other is used for the terminating carriage return. The remaining 126 characters became the defacto limit for DOS commands. No command line should be permitted, which cannot be transferred as a argument to a program.

By the way, even though we have accepted a command line, no mention was made of how it was input or how the prompt line was displayed. That subject will be partly glossed over in this chapter, mostly because it does not present any technical challenges. A loop exists to retrieve a command line. The command is read from the batch file or from the keyboard, depending on the current status of the batch mode switch. A keyboard line is input using DOS function 09h. The prompt is discussed under the section on the "Prompt" command.

Figure 8-2. Command line from read

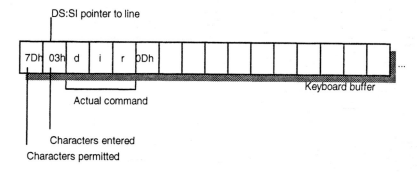

The Command Line Parser

The work flow logic of the command parser is shown in Figure 8-3. It begins at _CommandParser, located in rxdoscmd.asm. The function is misnamed. It does not simply parse the command line. It drives the execution of each command line from start to finish. It begins by building the argument array, already mentioned, and then calling the Arg Array execution routine. This routine executes all components of the command line even if there is more than one command.

Figure 8-3. Command line parse workflow

```
_CommandParser
  _BuildArgArray
  _executeCommandArray
    CmndLookup
      SplitArgs

  _executeProgram
```

Command parsing is called after a command line has been retrieved, either from a batch file or the command line. The pointer to the command line buffer is set in the DS:SI registers, as shown in Figure 8-2. Any resident program can format a command line and submit it for execution to the resident command processor using a special int 2Eh interface. Since a copy of the command processor remains in memory at all times, any valid command can be executed from an application at any time.

Another largely undocumented feature of the command processor enables expanding the set of available internal commands. When a command is parsed, the command name is extracted, and a int 2F, AH=AEh function is called. Any TSR designed to support an extended command may trap and execute the command. APPEND works in this way. Once loaded initially, it traps other calls to the APPEND program. The convention is generally useful and can be used to replace the functionality of existing internal DOS commands.

The command parser code called by the int 2Eh, which could have been called from anywhere with a command to parse, is shown next. It must switch to an internal command parser stack since it cannot safely assume that the caller's stack has sufficient space to parse the command. When it switches stacks, the first argument that it saves is a pointer to the caller's stack so that the stack pointer can be switched back. If the stack code appears in any way slightly complicated, it is because it is trying to affect no other registers. The code for the Int 2E intercept appears as follows:

```
(in rxdoscmd.asm)
        ;,,,,,,,,,,,,,,,,,,,,,,,,,,,,,,,,,,,,,,,,,,,,,,,,,,,,,,,,,,,,,,,,;
        ;   RxDOS Command Parser/ Execute                               ;
        ;- - - - - - - - - - - - - - - - - - - - - - - - - - - - - - - -;
        ;                                                               ;
        ;   Usage:                                                      ;
        ;     ds:si   command line beginning with a count               ;
        ;             (this fct does not rely on CR at end of buffer)   ;
        ;                                                               ;
        ;...............................................................;


_Int2E_CommandParser    PROC FAR

        push ds
        push si
        mov si, ss
        mov ds, si
        mov si, sp                              ; old stack to ds: si
```

```
        cld
        cli
        setSS cs
        mov sp, offset RxDOS_CmdParseStack          ; switch stacks
        sti

        saveRegisters ds, si                        ; save pointer to other stack
        lds si, dword ptr [ si ]                     ; restore old ds:si values.
        call _CommandParser                         ; call command parser

        cli
        pop si
        pop ss
        mov sp, si                                   ; back to old stack.
        sti

        pop si
        pop ds                                       ; restore ds: si values
        iret
_Int2E_CommandParser   ENDP
```

When the command is passed to the real internal command parser code, the routine copies the command line passed by the caller to an internal buffer. The buffer becomes NULL terminated. In addition, space is allocated to hold the all-important argument array. The command parser also fetches the switch character from DOS for future reference as an argument separator. The charac ter is set as the lead character in the table of other argument separators.

The argument array is then built by calling _BuildArgArray. Later, we list the routine with the command parser. The argument array produced by calling this function contains a list of point- ers to each argument in the command line. Arguments are identified by separator characters, which include the switch character, spaces, commas, quotes, and any of the redirection characters. Multiple spaces are treated as a single separator. The list of other argument separators is as follows:

```
        ;'''''''''''''''''''''''''''''''''''''''''''''''''''''''';
        ;   Special Command Separators                          ;
        ;........................................................;


_SwitchChar             db '/'                      ; switch character
_CmndParse_Separators   db ' <>|[],+=()%', doubleQuote, singleQuote, 0
```

The argument array builder simply scans the line for arguments and does not make any intelli- gent decisions about the validity of the command itself. It does, however, count the number of argu- ments stored in the Arg Array. If the command line contains no arguments, that is, the line was blank or contained only spaces, the routine exits without further action. None can be taken. The other fil- tering action is to determine if the command began with a colon character. The symbol is used in the batch file as a label and cannot be parsed further.

All commands, whether entered from a batch file or the command line, are parsed through this code. No distinction is made about whether the command is a batch file command. This philosophy extends to command execution. For example, the following commands, which are part of the DOS command language, may actually be entered at the keyboard and will work properly because DOS does not distinguish between batch file commands and other commands:

```
c> if exist \autoexec.bat dir
c> for %f in (*.doc *.txt) do dir %f
```

Once the argument array has been built, it is passed to an execute routine. It should be made clear that the command line itself contains all the valid data and is referenced by the pointers in the argument array. The command is executed by this function.

The command parser code appears as follows:

```
(in rxdoscmd.asm)
;'''''''''''''''''''''''''''''''''''''''''''''''''''''''''''''''''''''''';
;                                                                        ;
;   RxDOS Command Parser/ Execute                                        ;
;- - - - - - - - - - - - - - - - - - - - - - - - - - - - - - - - - - -  -;
;                                                                        ;
;   Usage:                                                               ;
;     ds:si   command line beginning with a count                        ;
;             (this fct does not rely on CR at end of buffer)            ;
;                                                                        ;
;     The command is executed, which may require loading another         ;
;     program.                                                           ;
;                                                                        ;
;........................................................................;


_CommandParser  PROC FAR

          Entry
          ddef _lpOriginalCmdLine, ds, si       ; argument is copied
          defbytes _commandLine, 128            ; argument is copied
          defwords __argarray, maxArgArray      ; argument array
                                                ; (last arg is null)

          SaveAllRegisters                      ; save all registers
          cld                                   ; and direction

;- - - - - - - - - - - - - - - - - - - - - - - - - - - - - - - - - - -
;  get switch character
;- - - - - - - - - - - - - - - - - - - - - - - - - - - - - - - - - - -
          Int21 GetSetSwitchChar, 00            ; get switch char
          mov byte ptr cs:[ _SwitchChar ], dl   ; save switch character


;- - - - - - - - - - - - - - - - - - - - - - - - - - - - - - - - - - -
;  copy command line
;- - - - - - - - - - - - - - - - - - - - - - - - - - - - - - - - - - -
          getdarg ds, si, _lpOriginalCmdLine

          lodsb
          mov cl, al                            ; length
          xor ch, ch
          or cx, cx                             ; any arguments ?
          jz _commandParser_36                  ; if no arguments —>

          setES ss
          lea di, offset [ _commandLine ][ bp ]
```

```
        rep movsb                                           ; copy command line

        xor ax, ax
        stosb                                               ; add a null terminator
;- - - - - - - - - - - - - - - - - - - - - - - - - - - - - - - - - - - -
;  parse
;- - - - - - - - - - - - - - - - - - - - - - - - - - - - - - - - - - - -
        mov cx, maxArgArray - 2                             ; # argument array entries
        lea si, offset [ _commandLine ][ bp ]
        lea di, offset [ __argarray    ][ bp ]
        call _BuildArgArray                                 ; break up into arg list
        jz _CommandParser_36                                ; if no arguments —>

        mov si, word ptr [ __argarray ][ bp ]               ; get lead argument
        cmp byte ptr [ si ], ':'                             ; label line ?
        jz _CommandParser_36                                ; ignore —>

        lea di, offset [ __argarray    ][ bp ]
        call _executeCommandArray

        cmp byte ptr [ _EchoStatus ], false                 ; echo ?
        jz _CommandParser_36                                ; if no echo —>
        call CRLF

;- - - - - - - - - - - - - - - - - - - - - - - - - - - - - - - - - - - -
;  command completed
;- - - - - - - - - - - - - - - - - - - - - - - - - - - - - - - - - - - -
_CommandParser_36:
        restoreAllRegisters
        Return

_CommandParser  ENDP
```

The routine needs some explanation because its logic isn't always obvious at first reading. The routine scans the command line, whose address is passed in the DS:SI register pair, from left to right. Every time it identifies the start of an argument, it records the address into the argument array. The routine tries to identify when a state change has occurred between arguments. It isn't always true, and this is what makes the code somewhat more complicated, that white space, that is, blanks or tabs, exists between arguments. The following is an example of a line with several run-on arguments, which the routine must properly handle:

```
dir/w filename.ext>file|copy filea+fileb/b foo
```

To detect state changes, the routine maintains the previous character in the CH register. It is initially set to a space since spaces are valid separators between arguments. This causes the start of the next argument—at the beginning, that would be the start of the first argument—to be saved in the argument array. This also causes the scan code to skip all leading spaces.

To understand how the routine works, it is better to understand its logic than a sequential rendition of the code itself. The start of words is identified when a letter or number, that is, any character that is not one of a few reserved special characters, is preceded by a space. This is trapped in the routine by the check for a space value in the CH register after all the special character checks. All the other argument terms are simply recorded when encountered in the command line so that when a redirection or switch character is encountered, its address is recorded in the argument array.

When the argument address is saved, the CH flag must be set to a space in order to record additional words. In the preceding example command line, the name that follows the redirection character must be saved as a separate argument. In order for the scanner to recognize that it is the beginning of a new term, the previous character flag is set to a space character. The space character is used as a universal new word flag. However, the space previous character is not set when a filename, pathname, or switch character was the start of the new argument. The difference between the start of a filename or a switch term and all other special characters is that special characters are automatically both the start and end of a term. The code knows that if there is more text, it must form another term when special characters are used.

Finally, the only other special code in the routine checks and skips quoted strings within a command line.

```
(in rxdoscmd.asm)
        ;'''''''''''''''''''''''''''''''''''''''''''''''''''''''';
        ;   Build Argument Array                                 ;
        ;- - - - - - - - - - - - - - - - - - - - - - - - - - - -;
        ;                                                        ;
        ;   Usage:                                               ;
        ;   ds:si   command line beginning with a count          ;
        ;           (this fct does not rely on CR at end of buffer) ;
        ;   ss:di   argument array                               ;
        ;           (returns a pointer into the command line at the ;
        ;            start of each argument.  Multiple switches are ;
        ;            detected by testing the get command switch char). ;
        ;   cx      max number of arguments allowed              ;
        ;                                                        ;
        ;   Returns:                                             ;
        ;   zr      if no arguments passed                       ;
        ;........................................................;

_BuildArgArray:
        Entry
        ddef _commandLine, ds, si
        ddef __argarray, ss, di                 ; (maxArgArray) arguments
        def _args, cx

        setES ss


;- - - - - - - - - - - - - - - - - - - - - - - - - - - - - - - -
;  scan argument
;- - - - - - - - - - - - - - - - - - - - - - - - - - - - - - - -
_buildArgArray_06:
        mov ch, ' '                             ; pretend previous char is a space

_buildArgArray_08:
        lodsb                                   ; get character
        or al, al                               ; end of line ?
```

```
        jz _buildArgArray_36                        ; yes, end of arg ->

        cmp al, ' '                                 ; space ?
        jz _buildArgArray_14                        ; yes, arg separator ->
        cmp al, byte ptr [ _SwitchChar ]            ; switch character ?
        jz _buildArgArray_18                        ; yes, record argument ->

        call _CmndParse_SeparatorCheck              ; parse break ?
        jz _buildArgArray_18                        ; yes ->

        cmp ch, ' '                                 ; previous also a space ?
        jz _buildArgArray_18                        ; yes, continue scanning ->

_buildArgArray_14:
        mov ch, al                                  ; save previous character
        jmp _buildArgArray_08                       ; continue scanning ->

;- - - - - - - - - - - - - - - - - - - - - - - - - - - - - - - - - - -
;  record argument
;- - - - - - - - - - - - - - - - - - - - - - - - - - - - - - - - - - -
_buildArgArray_18:
        mov ch, al                                  ; save possible string terminator

        mov ax, si
        dec ax
        stosw                                       ; store argument pointer
        dec word ptr [ _args ][ bp ]                ; more args allowed ?
        jle _buildArgArray_36                       ; no ->

        cmp ch, singleQuote
        jz _buildArgArray_30
        cmp ch, doubleQuote
        jz _buildArgArray_30

        cmp ch, '\'                                 ; path info ?
        jz _buildArgArray_24                        ; not a word breaker ->
        cmp ch, byte ptr [ _SwitchChar ]            ; switch character ?
        jz _buildArgArray_24                        ; yes, keep as part of word ->
        cmp ch, 'z'+1                               ; word break ?
        jge _buildArgArray_22                       ; if yes ->
        cmp ch, 'a'
        jge _buildArgArray_24

        cmp ch, 'Z'+1                               ; word break ?
        jge _buildArgArray_22                       ; if yes ->
        cmp ch, 'A'
        jge _buildArgArray_24

_buildArgArray_22:
        mov ch, ' '                                 ; indicate argument break

_buildArgArray_24:
        jmp _buildArgArray_08                       ; continue scanning ->
```

```
;- - - - - - - - - - - - - - - - - - - - - - - - - - - - - - - - - -
;   set inside string mode
;- - - - - - - - - - - - - - - - - - - - - - - - - - - - - - - - - -
_buildArgArray_30:
        lodsb                                     ; get character
        or al, al                                 ; end of line ?
        jz _buildArgArray_36                      ; yes, end of arg ->
        cmp al, ch                                ; string terminator ?
        jnz _buildArgArray_30                     ; no, continue saving ->
        jmp _buildArgArray_06


;- - - - - - - - - - - - - - - - - - - - - - - - - - - - - - - - - -
;   return
;- - - - - - - - - - - - - - - - - - - - - - - - - - - - - - - - - -
_buildArgArray_36:
        mov word ptr ss:[ di ], 0000              ; add null table terminator
        mov word ptr ss:[ di+2 ], 0000            ; two nulls is complete end

        mov di, word ptr [ __argarray. _pointer ][ bp ]
        cmp word ptr [ di ], 0000                 ; args passed ?
        Return
```

Executing a Command

Executing the contents of a command line is more complex than using the first keyword as a lookup in a table of internal commands. Among some of the complications, a single line, as we noted before, may contain multiple commands with each requiring its own device redirection. However, the general process remains easy to explain and visualize. Device redirection is removed from the line, and the command keyword is searched among the internal commands or among external files. When a match is located, the command is executed.

Device redirection is first removed from a command. The execute function builds an execution control block, known as an EXECCONTROL data structure. This control block is primarily used to track the device redirection used by a command, whether the command eventually will be executed as an internal command, a batch file, or a program. The control structure contains a pointer to the next argument in the argument array, the file handles for the redirected stdin and stdout files, the name of the temporary files it creates, and a load execution block required to launch programs.

```
;'''''''''''''''''''''''''''''''''''''''''''''''''''''''''''''''';
;   Execution Control                                            ;
;................................................................;


        EXECCONTROL struc
exCtrlArgArray              dd ?
exCtrlStdInHandle           dw ?
exCtrlStdOutHandle          dw ?

exCtrlFlags                 dw ?
exCtrlStdInFileName         db sizeEXPANDNAME dup(?)
exCtrlStdOutFileName        db sizeEXPANDNAME dup(?)
exCtrlLoadExecBlock         db sizeLOADEXEC dup(?)
        EXECCONTROL ends
```

The removal of the device direction arguments is handled by the assign redirected devices routine listed next. The argument array is scanned for arguments that contain any of the redirection characters. When they are located, a special handler removes the argument from the array.

A simple example of how redirection is removed from the command line can be seen by looking at the removal of the stdout redirection, beginning at the label _assignRedirect_StdOut, in the code that follows. The code prior to this label scanned the argument array for the redirection character. The DI register will point to the redirection argument in the argument array when the handler is called. The handler saves the value of the DI register and then deletes the redirection argument. The delete argument routine copies all subsequent arguments in the argument array up, in effect deleting the current argument by removing the pointer to it. The character is not actually removed from the command line itself.

Once the delete is accomplished, the argument pointed to by the DI register will point to the filename argument, if any was supplied. The filename is fetched and stored in the EXECCONTROL block. Since this is an output redirection request, the DOS create file function is used to create the output file. An error may occur if the filename is illegal, blank, or contains a reference to an illegal drive or directory. The error exit aborts the remainder of the command parsing. Because of the way in which the create file function works, the filename can actually be the name of any device, including the NUL, LPT, or CON devices.

If the create file function succeeds, it returns a file handle. The file handle is inserted at the stdout location in the Job Handle Table (located in the PSP). This sets up the device redirection. Any subsequent DOS function, whether from a command, batch file, or program, will be redirected to the file handle placed in the JHT.

The scan and assign device redirection code follows:

```
(in rxdoscmd.asm)
        ;'''''''''''''''''''''''''''''''''''''''''''''''''''''''''''''''';
        ;  Scan and Assign Redirection                                  ;
        ;- - - - - - - - - - - - - - - - - - - - - - - - - - - - - - - -;
        ;                                                               ;
        ;  Usage:                                                       ;
        ;   ss:di   argument array                                      ;
        ;   ss:bx   pointer to Execution Control Block                  ;
        ;...............................................................;

_assignRedirectedDevices:
        Entry
        def __argarray, di                      ; argument array
        def __contargarray, di                  ; continue argument array
        def __execCtrlBlock, bx                 ; execution control block


;- - - - - - - - - - - - - - - - - - - - - - - - - - - - - - - - - - -
;  scan remainder of command line for pipe, stdin and stdout args
;- - - - - - - - - - - - - - - - - - - - - - - - - - - - - - - - - - -
_assignRedirect_06:
        getarg di, __contargarray               ; continue argument array

_assignRedirect_08:
        mov si, word ptr [ di ]
        or si, si
        ifz _assignRedirect_36                  ; end of args ?
                                                ; yes ->
```

```
        mov ax, word ptr [ si ]                          ; get arg assignment
        cmp ax, '>>'                                     ; append to stdout ?
        ifz _assignRedirect_AppendStdOut                 ; yes —>
        cmp al, '>'                                      ; stdout ?
        jz _assignRedirect_StdOut                        ; yes —>
        cmp al, '<'                                      ; stdin ?
        jz _assignRedirect_StdIn                         ; yes —>
        cmp al, '|'                                      ; pipe ?
        jz _assignRedirect_Pipe                          ; yes —>

        inc di
        inc di
        jmp _assignRedirect_08                           ; go to next —>

;- - - - - - - - - - - - - - - - - - - - - - - - - - - - - - -
; stdout
;- - - - - - - - - - - - - - - - - - - - - - - - - - - - - - -
_assignRedirect_StdOut:
        storarg __contargarray, di                       ; continue argument array
        call deleteArg                                   ; kill '>' arg

        mov bx, word ptr [ __execCtrlBlock ][ bp ]       ; execution control block
        lea dx, offset [ exCtrlStdOutFileName ][ bx ]    ; offset to filename
        call _asgnGetFileName                            ; arg to [dx]

        xor cx, cx
        Int21 CreateFile                                 ; if not found, create
        ifc _assignRedirect_Error                        ; just display error —>

        push ax
        mov bx, ax
        mov cx, STDOUT
        call _assignGetCurrHandle
        getarg di, __execCtrlBlock
        mov word ptr [ exCtrlStdOutHandle ][ di ], ax    ; save old handle
        Int21 ForceFileHandle                            ; redirect stdout

        pop bx                                           ; frees file handle after
        Int21 CloseFile                                  ; force replicate handle
        jmp _assignRedirect_06

;- - - - - - - - - - - - - - - - - - - - - - - - - - - - - - -
; stdin
;- - - - - - - - - - - - - - - - - - - - - - - - - - - - - - -
_assignRedirect_StdIn:
        storarg __contargarray, di                       ; continue argument array
        call deleteArg                                   ; kill '<' arg

        mov bx, word ptr [ __execCtrlBlock ][ bp ]       ; execution control block
        lea dx, offset [ exCtrlStdInFileName ][ bx ]     ; offset to filename
        call _asgnGetFileName                            ; arg to [dx]
```

```
        Int21 OpenFile, OPEN_ACCESS_READONLY          ; try to open file
        ifc _assignRedirect_Error                     ; just display error ->

        mov bx, ax
        mov cx, STDIN
        call _assignGetCurrHandle
        getarg di, __execCtrlBlock
        mov word ptr [ exCtrlStdInHandle ][ di ], ax  ; save old handle
        Int21 ForceFileHandle                         ; redirect stdout
        jmp _assignRedirect_06

;- - - - - - - - - - - - - - - - - - - - - - - - - - - - - - -
;  pipe
;- - - - - - - - - - - - - - - - - - - - - - - - - - - - - - -
_assignRedirect_Pipe:
        storarg __contargarray, di                    ; continue argument array
        mov word ptr [ di ], 0000                      ; place an end marker in arg list

        mov bx, word ptr [ __execCtrlBlock ][ bp ]     ; execution control block
        lea bx, offset [ exCtrlStdOutFileName ][ bx ]  ; offset to filename
        mov byte ptr [ bx ], 0

        mov dx, bx
        mov cx, OPEN_ACCESS_READWRITE                 ; create read/write
        Int21 CreateUniqueFile                        ; if not found, create
        ifc _assignRedirect_Error                     ; just display error ->

        push ax
        mov bx, ax
        mov cx, STDOUT
        call _assignGetCurrHandle

        getarg di, __execCtrlBlock
        mov word ptr [ exCtrlStdOutHandle ][ di ], ax ; save old handle
        Int21 ForceFileHandle                         ; redirect stdout

        pop bx                                        ; free file handle after
        Int21 CloseFile                               ; force replicate handle

        getarg di, __contargarray                     ; continue argument array
        getarg bx, __execCtrlBlock                    ; execution control block
        mov word ptr [ exCtrlArgArray. _pointer ][ bx ], di
        or word ptr [ exCtrlFlags ][ bx ], exCtrlPiped ; say arg is piped.
        jmp _assignRedirect_36                        ; exit ->

;- - - - - - - - - - - - - - - - - - - - - - - - - - - - - - -
;  append stdout
;- - - - - - - - - - - - - - - - - - - - - - - - - - - - - - -
_assignRedirect_AppendStdOut:
        storarg __contargarray, di                    ; continue argument array
        call deleteArg                                ; kill '>' arg
        call deleteArg                                ; kill '>' arg
```

```
        mov bx, word ptr [ __execCtrlBlock ][ bp ]       ; execution control block
        lea dx, offset [ exCtrlStdOutFileName ][ bx ]    ; offset to filename
        call _asgnGetFileName                            ; arg to [dx]
        Int21 OpenFile, OPEN_ACCESS_READWRITE            ; try to open file
        jnc _assignRedirect_Append_08

        cmp ax, errFileNotFound                          ; if other than not found
        jnz _assignRedirect_Error                        ; just display error ->

        xor cx, cx
        mov bx, word ptr [ __execCtrlBlock ][ bp ]       ; execution control block
        lea dx, offset [ exCtrlStdOutFileName ][ bx ]    ; offset to filename
        Int21 CreateFile                                 ; if not found, create
        jc _assignRedirect_Error                         ; just display error ->

_assignRedirect_Append_08:
        push ax
        xor cx, cx
        xor dx, dx
        mov bx, ax
        Int21 MoveFilePointer, SEEK_END                  ; point to end of file

        mov cx, STDOUT
        call _assignGetCurrHandle
        getarg bx, __execCtrlBlock
        mov word ptr [ exCtrlStdOutHandle ][ bx ], ax    ; save old handle

        pop bx
        push bx
        Int21 ForceFileHandle                            ; redirect stdout

        pop bx
        Int21 CloseFile
        jmp _assignRedirect_06

;- - - - - - - - - - - - - - - - - - - - - - - - - - - - - - -
; redirection error
;- - - - - - - - - - - - - - - - - - - - - - - - - - - - - - -
_assignRedirect_Error:
        call DisplayError
        stc

;- - - - - - - - - - - - - - - - - - - - - - - - - - - - - - -
; return
;- - - - - - - - - - - - - - - - - - - - - - - - - - - - - - -
_assignRedirect_36:
        getarg di, __argarray                            ; argument array
        Return

        ;,,,,,,,,,,,,,,,,,,,,,,,,,,,,,,,,,,,,,,,,,,,,,,,,,,,,,,,,,,,,,';
        ; Assign Get Current Handle                                  ;
        ;- - - - - - - - - - - - - - - - - - - - - - - - - - - - - -;
        ;                                                            ;
```

```
        ;   Usage:                                                   ;
        ;      cx        handle whose value we want                  ;
        ;      ax        value of handle returned                    ;
        ;....................................................................;

_assignGetCurrHandle:
        push es
        push si
        push bx
        push cx
        Int21 GetPSPAddress

        pop si                                   ; restore handle offset
        mov es, bx                               ; set PSP address
        les bx, dword ptr es:[ pspFileHandlePtr ]   ; point to file handles
        mov al, byte ptr es:[ bx + si ]          ; recover existing handle
        xor ah, ah

        pop bx
        pop si
        pop es
        ret


        ;''''''''''''''''''''''''''''''''''''''''''''''''''''''''''';
        ;   Copy Arg                                                ;
        ;- - - - - - - - - - - - - - - - - - - - - - - - - - - - - -;
        ;                                                           ;
        ;   Usage:                                                  ;
        ;      si      pointer to argument                          ;
        ;      di      pointer to copy location                     ;
        ;                                                           ;
        ;   Returns:                                                ;
        ;      zr      no characters copies                         ;
        ;....................................................................;

_copyArg:
        or si, si
        jz _copyArg_36
        or cx, cx                                ; address of next arg zero ?
        sub cx, si                               ; real length

_copyArg_08:
        lodsb                                    ; get character
        stosb
        or al, al
        jz _copyArg_36
        loop _copyArg_08

_copyArg_36:
        ret
```

```
;//////////////////////////////////////////////////////////;
;  Get Filename From A Piped Or Redirected Argument        ;
;- - - - - - - - - - - - - - - - - - - - - - - - - - - - -;
;                                                          ;
;  Usage:                                                  ;
;    di      points to arg list                            ;
;    dx      destination where to copy arg                 ;
;                                                          ;
;  arg is removed from arg list (it is deleted) once copied;
;..........................................................;
_asgnGetFileName:
        push ax
        push dx
        push di
        mov cx, word ptr [ di + 2 ]          ; get arg that follows
        mov si, word ptr [ di ]              ; get current arg
        mov di, dx
        call _copyArg

        pop di
        call deleteArg                       ; kill arg

        pop dx
        pop ax
        ret
```

When the redirection request is to append to a file, the function must delete two arguments from the argument array, one for each of the > characters. They are each treated as an argument. The filename that follows is first opened, but if this fails, a file is created, and the position pointer is placed at the very end of the file.

Redirecting the stdin device assignment is very similar to redirecting the stdout, and so it shouldn't be covered extensively. Instead of a file create, the file is opened, and a failure to open the file results in the cancellation of the command line execution altogether.

Finally, the piping redirection involves creating a temporary file using the DOS unique file create function. By all appearances, piping looks very much like the redirection of the stdout device, for now. The piping flag is set in the EXECCONTROL flag word for future reference, and a NULL is placed where the piping argument address is located. Placing this NULL breaks up the command line arguments into two parts, in effect terminating the argument array for the command before the piping character.

The end result of this action is to edit both the argument array and the EXECCONTROL block to appear as shown in Figure 8-4. The EXECCONTROL block will contain the file handles in the JHT before the device redirection as well as other information, including the temporary assigned name of the piped file. The argument array is always terminated by two NULL arguments. A single NULL argument simply delineates one part of the command line arguments from another.

Figure 8-4. Argument array after device redirection

`dir a:*.dat>\foo.txt`

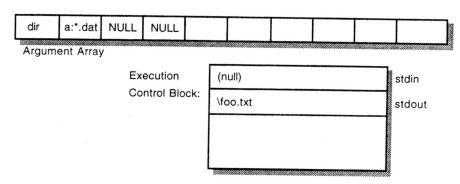

`dir a:*.dat | sort | more`

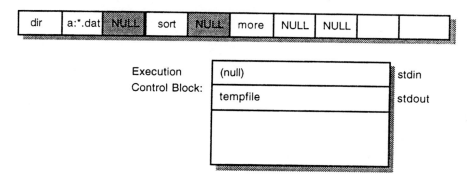

Piping and redirection involve more than just opening or creating files. The functionality described so far is only the first part during which any device redirection is extracted from the command line. The code for the command line execution routine, which we discuss in greater detail next, appears as follows:

```
(in rxdoscmd.asm)
        ;'''''''''''''''''''''''''''''''''''''''''''''''''''''''''''''''''''';
        ;  Execute Command Stored in Arg Array                               ;
        ;- - - - - - - - - - - - - - - - - - - - - - - - - - - - - - - - - -;
        ;                                                                    ;
        ;  Usage:                                                            ;
        ;    ss:di   argument array                                          ;
        ;....................................................................;

_executeCommandArray:
        Entry
        def __argarray, di                      ; argument array
        def __commandTail, si
        defbytes __commandName, 64              ; command name (max 64 bytes)
```

```
        defbytes __execCtrlBlock, sizeEXECCONTROL

;- - - - - - - - - - - - - - - - - - - - - - - - - - - - - - - - - -
;  scan remainder of command line for pipe, stdin and stdout args
;- - - - - - - - - - - - - - - - - - - - - - - - - - - - - - - - - -
        xor ax, ax
        lea bx, offset [ __execCtrlBlock ][ bp ]

        push di
        mov di, bx
        mov cx, sizeEXECCONTROL
        rep stosb                                    ; clear exec control block
        pop di

        mov dx, -1
        mov word ptr [ exCtrlStdOutHandle ][ bx ], dx   ; no stdout file
        mov word ptr [ exCtrlStdInHandle ][ bx ], dx    ; no stdin file

_executeArray_04:
        lea bx, offset [ __execCtrlBlock ][ bp ]
        call _assignRedirectedDevices                ; arg array in [di]

;- - - - - - - - - - - - - - - - - - - - - - - - - - - - - - - - - -
;  see if command is valid
;- - - - - - - - - - - - - - - - - - - - - - - - - - - - - - - - - -
        getarg di, __argarray                        ; restore pointer to arg array
        mov si, word ptr [ di ]                       ; get lead argument
        call _isolateCommandName            —         ; arg array in [di]
        mov word ptr [ __commandTail ][ bp ], si      ; ptr to command tail

        getarg di, __argarray                        ; restore pointer to arg array
        mov si, word ptr [ di ]                       ; get lead argument
        call checkInstallableCommandInterface         ; command executed ?
        jnz _executeArray_36                          ; yes —>

        getarg di, __argarray                        ; restore pointer to arg array
        mov si, word ptr [ di ]                       ; get lead argument
        mov di, offset RxDOS_InternalCommands
        call CmndLookup                              ; lookup command
        jnc _executeArray_26                          ; if command found —>

        call checkUnixStyleCommands                   ; Unix style commands ?
        jnz _executeArray_10                          ; if no unix cmds —>

        getarg di, __argarray                        ; restore pointer to arg array
        mov si, word ptr [ di ]                       ; get lead argument
        mov di, offset RxDOS_UNIXStyleCommands
        call CmndLookup                              ; lookup command
        jnc _executeArray_26                          ; if command found —>

;- - - - - - - - - - - - - - - - - - - - - - - - - - - - - - - - - -
;  see if valid drive letter
;- - - - - - - - - - - - - - - - - - - - - - - - - - - - - - - - - -
_executeArray_10:
```

```
        mov di, word ptr [ __argarray ][ bp ]              ; arguments pointer
        mov si, word ptr [ di ]                            ; get lead argument
        cmp word ptr ss:[ si+1 ], ':'                      ; disk select ?
        jnz _executeArray_12                               ; if unknown ->

        call CountArgs                                     ; count how many arguments
        call _DiskSelect                                   ; process disk select
        jmp _executeArray_36

;- - - - - - - - - - - - - - - - - - - - - - - - - - - - - - - - - -
;  see if .exe, .com, or .bat
;- - - - - - - - - - - - - - - - - - - - - - - - - - - - - - - - - -
_executeArray_12:
        lea dx, offset [ _pathArg ][ bp ]
        call _executeProgram                               ; try to execute program
        call _saveBatchArguments                           ; if batch file, save arguments
        jmp _executeArray_36


;- - - - - - - - - - - - - - - - - - - - - - - - - - - - - - - - - -
;  go process command
;- - - - - - - - - - - - - - - - - - - - - - - - - - - - - - - - - -
_executeArray_26:
        mov di, word ptr [ __argarray ][ bp ]              ; arguments pointer
        call SplitArgs                                     ; for cd.. cases

        inc di
        inc di                                             ; argument array past arg
        mov si, word ptr [ di ]                            ; get lead argument
        call CountArgs                                     ; count how many arguments
        call bx                                            ; go execute commands

;- - - - - - - - - - - - - - - - - - - - - - - - - - - - - - - - - -
;  done
;- - - - - - - - - - - - - - - - - - - - - - - - - - - - - - - - - -
_executeArray_36:
        mov byte ptr [ PageLines ], 00                     ; cancel page lines

        mov bx, STDIN
        mov ax, word ptr [ __execCtrlBlock. exCtrlStdInHandle ][ bp ]
        call _CloseRedirectedDevice

;- - - - - - - - - - - - - - - - - - - - - - - - - - - - - - - - - -
;  is arg piped ?
;- - - - - - - - - - - - - - - - - - - - - - - - - - - - - - - - - -
        getarg di, __argarray
        test word ptr [ __execCtrlBlock. exCtrlFlags ][ bp ], exCtrlPiped
        jnz _executeArray_38

        mov bx, STDOUT
        mov ax, word ptr [ __execCtrlBlock. exCtrlStdOutHandle ][ bp ]
        call _CloseRedirectedDevice
        Return


;- - - - - - - - - - - - - - - - - - - - - - - - - - - - - - - - - -
;  arg is piped
;- - - - - - - - - - - - - - - - - - - - - - - - - - - - - - - - - -
```

```
_executeArray_38:
        mov ax, word ptr [ di ]
        inc di
        inc di
        or ax, ax                                       ; at end of search ?
        jnz _executeArray_38                            ; keep loopking ->

_executeArray_42:
        and word ptr [ __execCtrlBlock. exCtrlFlags ][ bp ], NOT exCtrlPiped
        storarg __argarray, di                          ; next in arg array

    ; must reopen file given by temp...
    ; maybe should not have closed it.

        mov cx, STDOUT
        call _assignGetCurrHandle                       ; get current handle
        mov word ptr [ __execCtrlBlock. exCtrlStdInHandle ][ bp ], ax

        mov bx, STDOUT
        Int21 CommitFile                                ; close stdout

        xor cx, cx
        xor dx, dx
        mov bx, STDOUT
        Int21 MoveFilePointer, SEEK_BEG                 ; point to beg of file

        mov bx, STDOUT
        mov cx, STDIN
        Int21 ForceFileHandle                           ; redirect stdout -> stdin

        mov bx, STDOUT
        mov ax, word ptr [ __execCtrlBlock. exCtrlStdOutHandle ][ bp ]
        call _CloseRedirectedDevice

        getarg di, __argarray                           ; next in arg array
        jmp _executeArray_04
```

The routine is named _executeCommandArray because a command line may comprise
more than one command. The routine initializes the execution control block and uses the assign
redirection devices to remove the device redirection it locates up to and including the first piping
character. A NULL entry is inserted into the argument array to signify the end of the current command. What remains in the argument array are pointers to the arguments in the command to be executed.

To complete what happens to the device redirection, once the command completes, control
returns to this function, the execute command array function. The stdin and stdout devices are
closed if they were redirected. A test is then made to determine if piping was used. If it was, the
argument array pointer is advanced beyond the NULL terminator inserted by the piping command.
Essentially, this moves to the next command in the command line. Finally, the temporary file created by the piping command is reassigned to the stdin device. The execution of the remainder of
the command line begins by scanning what's left of the argument array for additional redirection
and other commands.

If no piping was used, the stdin/stdout handles are restored. In MS-DOS, the stderr handle is copied to the stdin/stdout handles. This is why `command.com` does not allow stderr to be redirected. In RxDOS, the current values of the stdin/stdout handles were saved in the EXECCONTROL block so that they can readily be restored from there.

To summarize, the execution of the command line is handled in a loop that begins by making the redirection assignments. When the command terminates, the redirection files are closed, and any piping is changed from output redirection to the input redirection. The code loops making this command line parsing until all the commands on the line have been executed or until an error is encountered.

Internal Commands

Inside the execution loop, that is, between the redirection code described, a dispatch is made to the required command service routine. A command service routine exists for each of the internal commands, and each expects a pointer to the lead argument in the argument array. A table relates a command name with its internal function through a command table such as this.

```
;'''''''''''''''''''''''''''''''''''''''''''''''''''''''''''''''''''''';
;  Internal Commands                                                   ;
;.....................................................................;

        Even

RxDOS_InternalCommands:
        Cmnd _ChangeDir,        'cd'                    ;
        Cmnd _ChangeDir,        'chdir'                 ;
        Cmnd _MakeDir,          'md'                    ;
        Cmnd _MakeDir,          'mkdir'                 ;
        Cmnd _RemDir,           'rd'                    ;
        Cmnd _RemDir,           'rmdir'                 ;

        Cmnd _Break,            'break'                 ;
        Cmnd _Call,             'call'                  ;
        Cmnd _Chcp,             'chcp'                  ;
        Cmnd _Cls,              'cls'                   ;
        Cmnd _Copy,             'copy'                  ;
        Cmnd _Ctty,             'ctty'                  ;
        Cmnd _Date,             'date'                  ;
        Cmnd _Delete,           'del'                   ;
        Cmnd _Dir,              'dir'                   ;
        Cmnd _Echo,             'echo'                  ;
        Cmnd _Delete,           'erase'                 ;
        Cmnd _EndCall,          'exit'                  ;
        Cmnd _For,              'for'                   ;
        Cmnd _Goto,             'goto'                  ;
        Cmnd _If,               'if'                    ;
        Cmnd _Loadhigh,         'lh'                    ;
        Cmnd _Loadhigh,         'loadhigh'              ;
        Cmnd _Path,             'path'                  ;
```

```
        Cmnd _Pause,              'pause'              ;
        Cmnd _Prompt,             'prompt'             ;
        Cmnd _Rem,                'rem'                ;
        Cmnd _Rename,             'rename'             ;
        Cmnd _Rename,             'ren'                ;
        Cmnd _Set,                'set'                ;
        Cmnd _Shift,              'shift'              ;
        Cmnd _Time,               'time'               ;
        Cmnd _Truename,           'truename'           ;
        Cmnd _Type,               'type'               ;
        Cmnd _Verify,             'verify'             ;
        Cmnd _Ver,                'ver'                ;
        Cmnd _Vol,                'vol'                ;
        dw -1
```

These are not the only set of internal commands supported by DOS. A disk change command, such as a: is also considered an internal command. When DOS recognizes this form of a command, it calls the _DiskSelect function.

The internal commands may be extended or replaced by use of the Installable Command Interface. Few applications use this largely undocumented DOS feature. The concept is that a TSR is given access to the DOS command line prior to any execution. APPEND is the only program to my knowledge that takes advantage of this interface.

The interface not only avoids disk search and access required of most programs, but it also avoids the interaction that a loaded program must undergo to locate previous copies of a specific TSR that may have been loaded. For example, PRINT is an example of a TSR that expects to be called repeatedly from the command line. It was implemented before the Installable Command Interface was made available. So, in order to affect the copy already loaded in memory, such as to update or display its print queue, it must locate the original loaded copy.

The order in which commands are processed is important. DOS first determines if the command is handled by any installable interfaces. This enables these functions to supersede, replace, or extend the available DOS functions. Next, DOS searches its known internal and disk change commands. Finally, it searches the disk for programs or batch files with the command name.

The Installable Command Interface, which we document here, utilizes int 2Fh, function AEh. Two sets of calls are defined: one to determine if a command is supported by any of the functions hooked to the interface, the other to execute the command. The first call is made with a 00h argument in the AL register. DOS expects a response of FFh in the register if the command is supported by an installable command function. The function is then recalled with an 01h argument in the AL register to execute the command. The command line address is passed in the DS:SI register pair.

The interface specifications are as follows:

Function AE00h: Is Command Supported ?

```
        mov dx, 0FFFFh              ; -1
        mov cx, 0FFFFh              ; -1
        mov bx, offset CommandLine  ; points to lead char count byte
        mov si, offset CommandName  ; name pulled out and capitalized
        mov ax, 0AE00h              ; is command supported ?
```

```
        int 2Fh
        cmp al, -1
        jnz _commandNotSupported
```

Function AE01h: Execute Command

```
        mov dx, 0FFFFh                    ; -1
        mov cx, 00FFh                     ; ch = 0
        mov bx, offset CommandLine        ; points to lead char count byte
        mov si, offset CommandName        ; name pulled out and capitalized
        mov ax, 0AE01h                    ; execute command
        int 2Fh
```

Both the command line and command name buffers begin with a lead count byte. They contain the number of valid characters in the line. The execute subfunction, that is, function code AE01h, must zero the command line buffer byte. Otherwise, the length byte identifies a command to execute. The Installable Command Interface is extremely careful about its interface. It presumes that the interfacing function has taken an active step to zero the buffer contents.

The installable commands are checked by the following function:

```
        checkInstallableCommandInterface            ; command executed ?
        jnz _executeArray_36                        ; yes ->
```

The remainder of the internal commands are searched by the CmndLookup function, which performs a fairly straightforward string compare function, as shown here.

```
(in rxdoscmd.asm)
        ;''''''''''''''''''''''''''''''''''''''''''''''''''''''''''''';
        ;   Lookup Argument                                           ;
        ;- - - - - - - - - - - - - - - - - - - - - - - - - - - - - - -;
        ;                                                             ;
        ;   Usage:                                                    ;
        ;   ds:si  pointer to command name (uppercase)                ;
        ;   cs:di  pointer to supported commands                      ;
        ;                                                             ;
        ;   Returns:                                                  ;
        ;   bx     pointer to command execution address               ;
        ;   cy     argument not supported internally                  ;
        ;.............................................................;

CmndLookup:
        push di
        push si

        inc di
        inc di                                      ; point to arg that follows

;- - - - - - - - - - - - - - - - - - - - - - - - - - - - - - - - -
;  compare argument against table
;- - - - - - - - - - - - - - - - - - - - - - - - - - - - - - - - -
cmndLookup_12:
        mov al, byte ptr [ si ]                     ; from command
```

```
        inc si
        or al, al                               ; end of command ?
        jc cmndLookup_18                        ; see if all chars match ->

        call _lowerCase                         ; lower case ...
        cmp al, byte ptr cs:[ di ]              ; compare
        jnz cmndLookup_18                       ; if not this command ->

        inc di                                  ; else keep looking
        jmp cmndLookup_12

;- - - - - - - - - - - - - - - - - - - - - - - - - - - - - - -
;  if end, see if end of both args
;- - - - - - - - - - - - - - - - - - - - - - - - - - - - - - -
cmndLookup_18:
        cmp byte ptr cs:[ di ], 0               ; end of command ?
        jnz cmndLookup_28                       ; not this command then ->

;- - - - - - - - - - - - - - - - - - - - - - - - - - - - - - -
;  return valid arg
;- - - - - - - - - - - - - - - - - - - - - - - - - - - - - - -
        pop ax                                  ; leave si pointing at end
        pop di
        mov bx, word ptr cs:[ di ]              ; where to execute
        clc                                     ; NoCarry
        jmp short cmndLookup_36

;- - - - - - - - - - - - - - - - - - - - - - - - - - - - - - -
;  find next entry in table
;- - - - - - - - - - - - - - - - - - - - - - - - - - - - - - -
cmndLookup_28:
        inc di
        cmp byte ptr cs:[ di ], 0               ; end of command ?
        jnz cmndLookup_28                       ; keep looking ->

        pop si
        pop bx                                  ; don't care about saved di
        inc di                                  ; get next word
        cmp word ptr cs:[ di ], -1              ; end of command table ?
        jnz cmndLookup                          ; no, lookup next ->

;- - - - - - - - - - - - - - - - - - - - - - - - - - - - - - -
;  return invalid arg
;- - - - - - - - - - - - - - - - - - - - - - - - - - - - - - -
cmndLookup_32:
        stc
        mov bx, offset _NotValidCommand         ; default not valid command

;- - - - - - - - - - - - - - - - - - - - - - - - - - - - - - -
;  return
;- - - - - - - - - - - - - - - - - - - - - - - - - - - - - - -
cmndLookup_36:
        ret
```

The command processor contains a bit of mischief. It supports a rudimentary set of Unix-style commands in addition to the normal DOS command set. Since command names conflict with programs names, the code enables the Unix-style command names only when the environment variable RXDOS=UNIX is set.

To be sure, this code does not support the command shell script that Unix supports. It essentially supports only aliases for equivalent DOS commands. This helps users who work on both systems work more effectively. Some very good programs are available that bring the power and flexibility of Unix commands to DOS. RxDOS provides a table of aliases for DOS functions. The `ls` command supported by RxDOS simply supports the DOS `dir` command. The Unix table is as follows:

```
;''''''''''''''''''''''''''''''''''''''''''''''''''''''''''';
;   Unix Style Commands                                      ;
;...........................................................;

        Even

RxDOS_UNIXStyleCommands:
        Cmnd _Type,         "cat"           ;
        Cmnd _Copy,         "cp"            ;
        Cmnd _Delete,       "rm"            ;
        Cmnd _Dir,          "ls"            ;
        Cmnd _Move,         "mv"            ; * future feature
        Cmnd _Set,          "setenv"        ;
        dw -1
```

Loading and Executing Programs

If the command is not an internal command, then it is searched on disk. The search logic utilized is known to virtually all DOS users. The search begins at the current directory and is then followed by each name in the PATH= environment variable. Somewhat less well known is that the search also involves specific file extensions. If the command name contains no explicit file extension, the command shell searches for com programs followed by exe programs and then bat files. This search order is repeated in every directory named in the path.

The execution order is determine by the contents of a table, as follows:

```
;''''''''''''''''''''''''''''''''''''''''''''''''''''''''''';
;   Execution Order                                         ;
;...........................................................;

RxDOS_ExecOrder:    asciz '.com'
                    asciz '.exe'
                    asciz '.bat'
                    dw -1
```

The entire searching process begins in a module called _executeProgram. The command name, that is, the first word in the command, is first searched for on disk using the _findProgram function. Whether a program or a batch file is located is determined by the file's extension. Batch files must have a .bat extension, and program files must have a .com or .exe extension. Programs are then loaded within the _loadProgram function, which utilizes DOS function 4B00h, the Exec function.

```
(in rxdoscmd.asm)
        ;'''''''''''''''''''''''''''''''''''''''''''''''''''''''''''''';
        ;                                                              ;
        ;   Execute Program or Batch File                              ;
        ;- - - - - - - - - - - - - - - - - - - - - - - - - - - - - -  -;
        ;                                                              ;
        ;                                                              ;
        ;   Usage:                                                     ;
        ;   ss:di  Arg Array                                           ;
        ;   ax     Number of arguments in array                        ;
        ;..............................................................;

_executeProgram:
        Entry
        def __argarray, di
        def __progname, si
        def _pathArg, dx
        def __type

;- - - - - - - - - - - - - - - - - - - - - - - - - - - - - - - - - -
;  find program
;- - - - - - - - - - - - - - - - - - - - - - - - - - - - - - - - - -
        getarg dx, _pathArg              ; fully qualified path name
        call _findProgram                ; locate program or bat file
        storarg __type, ax               ; arg type
        jc _executeprogram_Error         ; if program not found ->
        cmp ax, _BAT                     ; is it a bat program ?
        jz _executeprogram_12            ; yes ->

        getarg dx, _pathArg              ; fully qualified path name
        getarg di, __argarray
        call _loadProgram                ; else load and execute program

_executeprogram_12:
        clc

_executeprogram_Exit:
        getarg di, __argarray
        getarg si, __progname
        getarg dx, _pathArg
        getarg ax, __type
        Return                           ; return

_executeprogram_Error:
        call _NotValidCommand            ; not valid (not found )
        stc
        jmp _executeprogram_Exit
```

The _findProgram function, whose responsibility is to locate a program or batch file, first scans the filename passed for wild characters. If the name contains asterisks or question marks, the file is not searched, and an error return is made. The function also does not search names that contain any path or drive information. These references are treated as explicit references. Either the file is located as listed or an error return is made.

The search is performed by adding path information to the front of the command name, and filename extension information to the end of the name if no extension already exists. Otherwise, the filename extension is honored, and the search for different file types is limited to the single type passed by the extension. However, the file type must be a bat if the program is to recognize it as a batch file. All other extensions are treated as programs. To say that DOS automatically recognized the difference between an exe and a com file is to stretch the point a bit. DOS recognizes the exe file format and presumes anything else is com file format.

The code for the _findProgram function is as follows:

```
(in rxdoscmd.asm)
        ;'''''''''''''''''''''''''''''''''''''''''''''''''''''''''''';
        ;  Find Program or Bat File                                 ;
        ;- - - - - - - - - - - - - - - - - - - - - - - - - - - - - -;
        ;                                                           ;
        ;  Usage:                                                   ;
        ;  ss:si  pointer to file name.                             ;
        ;                                                           ;
        ;  Returns:                                                 ;
        ;  cy      not found anywhere in path                       ;
        ;  ax      contains type of program found                   ;
        ;          0000 - program is a batch file                   ;
        ;          0001 - program is a com or exe file              ;
        ;  bx      contains handle to file                          ;
        ;...........................................................;

_findProgram:
        Entry
        def _pathArg, dx                        ; where to store path
        def _pathpointer                        ; PATH=, if any
        def _endofname                          ; null this if extension
        def _endofpathname
        def _dontSearch, false
        def _extensioninname, false
        defbytes _execname, 128


;- - - - - - - - - - - - - - - - - - - - - - - - - - - - - - - - - -
;  isolate name from rest of command line
;- - - - - - - - - - - - - - - - - - - - - - - - - - - - - - - - - -
        lea di, offset [ _execname ][ bp ]       ; pointer to copy field

_findProgram_08:
        lodsb                                    ; get character
        stosb                                    ; copy it
        cmp al, ' '+1                            ; space or control character ?
        jc _findProgram_20                       ; yes ->
        cmp al, '|'                              ; pipe character ?
        jz _findProgram_20                       ; yes ->
        cmp al, '*'                              ; wild character ?
        ifz _findProgram_Error                   ; yes ->
```

```
        cmp al, '?'                              ; wild character ?
        ifz _findProgram_Error                   ; yes ->

        cmp al, byte ptr [ _SwitchChar ]         ; switch character ?
        jz _findProgram_20                       ; yes ->

        cmp al, '\'                              ; file name contains path info ?
        jz _findProgram_12                       ; don't search path= ->
        cmp al, '/'                              ; file name contains path info ?
        jnz _findProgram_14                      ; don't search path= ->

_findProgram_12:
        mov byte ptr [ _dontSearch ][ bp ], true

_findProgram_14:
        call _CmndParse_SeparatorCheck           ; separator character ?
        jnz _findProgram_08                      ; yes ->

;- - - - - - - - - - - - - - - - - - - - - - - - - - - - - - - - -
;   search through current directory first
;- - - - - - - - - - - - - - - - - - - - - - - - - - - - - - - - -
_findProgram_20:
        dec di
        mov byte ptr [ di ], 0                   ; place null terminator

;- - - - - - - - - - - - - - - - - - - - - - - - - - - - - - - - -
;   search through current directory first
;- - - - - - - - - - - - - - - - - - - - - - - - - - - - - - - - -
        lea ax, offset [ _execname ][ bp ]       ; pointer to copy field

_findProgram_22:
        cmp ax, di                               ; at beginning of field ?
        jz _findProgram_24                       ; yes, no extension ->

        dec di
        cmp byte ptr [ di ], '\'                 ; path character ?
        jz _findProgram_24                       ; yes, no extension ->
        cmp byte ptr [ di ], '/'                 ; path character ?
        jz _findProgram_24                       ; yes, no extension ->
        cmp byte ptr [ di ], '.'                 ; possible extension ?
        jnz _findProgram_22
        mov word ptr [ _extensioninname ][ bp ], true  ; disable

_findProgram_24:
        lea si, offset [ _execname ][ bp ]       ; pointer to copy field
        mov di, word ptr [ _pathArg ][ bp ]      ; pointer to path arg
        mov word ptr [ _endofpathname ][ bp ], di ; save end of path name pointer
        call _CopyString                         ; append filename

        mov dx, word ptr [ _pathArg ][ bp ]      ; pointer to path arg
        Int21 FindFirstFile                      ; locate file
        jnc _findProgram_50                      ; if located ->

        mov si, offset RxDOS_PathSpec
```

```
        call searchEnvVariable                      ; locate PATH=
        add di, dx                                  ; address after =
        storarg _pathpointer, di                    ; location of path statement

;- - - - - - - - - - - - - - - - - - - - - - - - - - - - - - - - - - - - -
;  search through search order (append extension)
;- - - - - - - - - - - - - - - - - - - - - - - - - - - - - - - - - - - - -
_findProgram_30:
        lea si, offset [ _execname ][ bp ]          ; pointer to copy field
        getarg di, _endofpathname                   ; where to copy name
        call _CopyString                            ; append filename

        dec di
        mov word ptr [ _endofname ][ bp ], di       ; save end name pointer
        mov si, offset RxDOS_ExecOrder              ; lookup names, current dir

_findProgram_32:
        cmp word ptr [ _extensioninname ][ bp ], true   ; is extension search disabled ?
        jz _findProgram_34

        getarg di, _endofname
        call _CopyString                            ; copy extension

_findProgram_34:
        push si                                     ; save pointer
        mov dx, word ptr [ _pathArg ][ bp ]         ; pointer to path arg
        Int21 FindFirstFile                         ; locate file
        pop si                                      ; restore si
        jnc _findProgram_50                         ; if located —>

        cmp word ptr [ _extensioninname ][ bp ], true   ; is extension search disabled ?
        jz _findProgram_38
        cmp byte ptr [ si ], -1                      ; end of search order list ?
        jnz _findProgram_32                         ; not yet —>

;- - - - - - - - - - - - - - - - - - - - - - - - - - - - - - - - - - - - -
;  locate next search path
;- - - - - - - - - - - - - - - - - - - - - - - - - - - - - - - - - - - - -
_findProgram_38:
        cmp byte ptr [ _dontSearch ][ bp ], true    ; search path ?
        jz _findProgram_CantFind                    ; no, can't find —>

        push ds
        mov ds, word ptr [ _EnvSegment ]
        mov si, word ptr [ _pathpointer ][ bp ]     ; path=
        mov di, word ptr [ _pathArg ][ bp ]         ; pointer to path arg

_findProgram_40:
        lodsb
        or al, al
        jz _findProgram_42
        cmp al, ';'
        jz _findProgram_44
```

```
        stosb
        jmp _findProgram_40

_findProgram_42:
        mov byte ptr [ _dontSearch ][ bp ], true       ; (end of path)

_findProgram_44:
        storarg _pathpointer, si                       ; save end of path search
        pop ds                                         ; restore ds

        mov al, '\'
        cmp al, byte ptr [ di - 1 ]                    ; pathname terminated by \ ?
        jz _findProgram_46                             ; yes ->
        stosb                                          ; add \ to pathname

_findProgram_46:
        storarg _endofpathname, di                     ; save path name
        jmp _findProgram_30

;- - - - - - - - - - - - - - - - - - - - - - - - - - - - - - - - - -
;  file found, determine if .exe or .com
;- - - - - - - - - - - - - - - - - - - - - - - - - - - - - - - - - -
_findProgram_50:
        mov si, offset [ RxDOS_DTA. findFileName ]

_findProgram_52:
        lodsb                                          ; get filename character
        or al, al                                      ; end of name ?
        jz _findProgram_58                             ; yes, assume .bat ->
        cmp al, '.'                                    ; extension located ?
        jnz _findProgram_52                            ; no, keep scanning ->

        or word ptr [ si ], ' '                        ; force lowercase
        or byte ptr [ si + 2 ], ' '                    ; force lowercase

        mov ax, _EXE                                   ; _exe
        cmp word ptr [ si ], 'xe'
        jnz _findProgram_54
        cmp byte ptr [ si + 2 ], 'e'
        jz _findProgram_62

_findProgram_54:
        mov ax, _COM                                   ; _com
        cmp word ptr [ si ], 'oc'
        jnz _findProgram_58
        cmp byte ptr [ si + 2 ], 'm'
        jz _findProgram_62

_findProgram_58:
        mov ax, _BAT                                   ; _bat
        cmp word ptr [ si ], 'ab'
        jnz _findProgram_Error
        cmp byte ptr [ si + 2 ], 't'
        jnz _findProgram_Error
```

```
_findProgram_62:
        or ax, ax                               ; no carry (no error)
        getarg si, _pathArg                     ; expanded argument name
        Return


;- - - - - - - - - - - - - - - - - - - - - - - - - - - - - - - - -
; error
;- - - - - - - - - - - - - - - - - - - - - - - - - - - - - - - - -
_findProgram_CantFind:
_findProgram_Error:
        stc
        Return
```

The _loadProgram function initializes two file control blocks by using DOS function 29h. The function converts a string into an FCB. It then utilizes an initialized EXEC block with pointers to the command tail, the environment block, and the initialized FCBs. DOS takes this block and launches the program. The launch function can fail, chiefly due to a lack of available memory.

```
(in rxdoscmd.asm)
        ;'''''''''''''''''''''''''''''''''''''''''''''''''''''''''''';
        ; Load Program                                               ;
        ;- - - - - - - - - - - - - - - - - - - - - - - - - - - - - -;
        ;                                                            ;
        ; Usage:                                                     ;
        ;   ss:si  program to load                                   ;
        ;   ss:di  argument array                                    ;
        ;............................................................;

_loadProgram:
        Entry
        ddef     _args, ss, di
        ddef     _progname, ss, si
        defbytes _ExecBlock, sizeEXEC
        defbytes _FCB1, sizeFCB
        defbytes _FCB2, sizeFCB

        push es
        push di
        setES ss

        lea di, offset _ExecBlock [ bp ]
        clearMemory sizeEXEC

        lea di, offset _FCB1 [ bp ]
        call _initFCB
        mov word ptr [ lexecFCB_1. _pointer ][ bx ], di
        mov word ptr [ lexecFCB_1. _segment ][ bx ], ss

        lea di, offset _FCB2 [ bp ]
        call _initFCB
        mov word ptr [ lexecFCB_2. _pointer ][ bx ], di
        mov word ptr [ lexecFCB_2. _segment ][ bx ], ss
```

```
        lea bx, offset _ExecBlock [ bp ]
        mov ax, word ptr [ _EnvSegment ]
        mov word ptr [ _ExecBlock. lexecEnvironment ][ bp ], ax

;- - - - - - - - - - - - - - - - - - - - - - - - - - - - - - - - - -
;  copy command tail.
;- - - - - - - - - - - - - - - - - - - - - - - - - - - - - - - - - -
        getdarg  es, si, _args
        add si, 2                               ; point to next entry
        cmp word ptr es:[ si ], 0000            ; any more arguments ?
        jz _loadProgram_20                      ; if no args ->

        mov si, word ptr es:[ si ]
        mov word ptr [ lexecCommandTail. _pointer  ][ bx ], si
        mov word ptr [ lexecCommandTail. _segment  ][ bx ], es

;- - - - - - - - - - - - - - - - - - - - - - - - - - - - - - - - - -
;  get FCB arguments
;- - - - - - - - - - - - - - - - - - - - - - - - - - - - - - - - - -
        mov ax, 2901h                           ; ok to skip leading sep
        lea di, offset _FCB1 [ bp ]
        int 21h

        mov ax, 2901h                           ; ok to skip leading sep
        lea di, offset _FCB2 [ bp ]
        int 21h

;- - - - - - - - - - - - - - - - - - - - - - - - - - - - - - - - - -
;  go run program
;- - - - - - - - - - - - - - - - - - - - - - - - - - - - - - - - - -
_loadProgram_20:
        setES ss
        lea bx, offset _ExecBlock [ bp ]
        getdarg ds, dx, _progname
        Int21 ExecuteProgram, 00

        pop di
        pop es
        Return
```

Executing Batch Files

Batch files represent a sort of programming language with loop, branch, test, and argument passing constructs. Within these programminglike statements, a batch file is a canned set of commands. Four areas must be explained about batch files: how the arguments are initialized, how variables are replaced in statements, how batch files call other batch files, and how batch files terminate.

Batch file processing begins when DOS recognizes a command as a batch file. _findProgram decides that a file is a batch file simply because it has a .bat extension. Control is passed to the _saveBatchArguments function, where the command line arguments are saved.

The arguments saved actually *replace* the current batch file arguments. To preserve the current batch arguments and the current position within the batch file, the `call` statement must be used, which we discuss further in this section.

RxDOS maintains all the arguments to a batch file in a BATCH_ARGS data structure. The data structure contains pointers to strings stored in the `batchArgStore` variable. This is a 128-byte area sufficiently large to contain all the arguments that can be passed since the total argument area can never exceed the length of a command line. The batch file argument area appears as follows:

```
;''''''''''''''''''''''''''''''''''''''''''''''''''''''''''''''''''''''''';
;   Batch Arguments                                                       ;
;.........................................................................;

        BATCH_ARGS struc
batchArgPtrs                    dw ?                    ; 0
                                dw ?                    ; 1  arg pointers
                                dw ?                    ; 2      .
                                dw ?                    ; 3      .
                                dw ?                    ; 4      .
                                dw ?                    ; 5      .
                                dw ?                    ; 6      .
                                dw ?                    ; 7      .
                                dw ?                    ; 8      .
                                dw ?                    ; 9      .

batchNumArgs                    dw ?                    ; number of batch arguments
batchFileHandle                 dw ?                    ; batch file handle
batchFilePosition               dd ?                    ; batch file position
batchArgStore                   db 128 dup(0)
        BATCH_ARGS ends
```

The save argument routine is called with an argument type, which must be _BAT, a pointer to the argument array, and the fully expanded filename of where the batch file was located. The argument array is built at the time the command was parsed. Each entry points to a command argument in the command line.

The save batch argument function closes the currently executing batch file, if any, and then checks to ensure that the new batch filename is accessible, that is, that the batch file can be opened and executed. A file may be inaccessible because of network or SHARE file locks. Next, each argument in the argument array is NULL terminated and the strings copied to the batch save area.

The save function code is as follows:

```
(in rxdoscmd.asm)
        ;''''''''''''''''''''''''''''''''''''''''''''''''''''''''''''''''''''''''';
        ;   Save Batch File Arguments                                             ;
        ;- - - - - - - - - - - - - - - - - - - - - - - - - - - - - - - - - - - - -;
        ;                                                                         ;
        ;   Usage:                                                                ;
        ;     ss:di   pointer to ArgArray                                         ;
        ;     ss:dx   pointer to fully expanded pathname                          ;
        ;     ax      type, which must be set to _BAT                             ;
        ;                                                                         ;
```

```
        ;  Returns:                                              ;
        ;  cx       length of new string                         ;
        ;..............................................................;

_saveBatchArguments:
        Entry
        def __argarray, di
        def __pathArg, dx
        def __type, ax
        def __tempargptr, di

;- - - - - - - - - - - - - - - - - - - - - - - - - - - - - - - - -
;  is type _BAT ?
;- - - - - - - - - - - - - - - - - - - - - - - - - - - - - - - - -
        cmp ax, _BAT
        jnz _saveBatchArguments_Error


;- - - - - - - - - - - - - - - - - - - - - - - - - - - - - - - - -
;  is file accessible ?
;- - - - - - - - - - - - - - - - - - - - - - - - - - - - - - - - -
_saveBatchArguments_08:
        mov bx, word ptr [ RxDOS_BatchFile. batchFileHandle ]
        or bx, bx                                       ; batch file in progress ?
        jz _saveBatchArguments_10                       ; no ->
        Int21 CloseFile                                 ; close current batch file
        mov word ptr [ RxDOS_BatchFile. batchFileHandle ], 0000

_saveBatchArguments_10:
        getarg dx, __pathArg
        mov al, ( OPEN_ACCESS_NOINHERIT + OPEN_ACCESS_READONLY )
        Int21 OpenFile
        jc _saveBatchArguments_Error                    ; quit batch file ->
        mov word ptr [ RxDOS_BatchFile. batchFileHandle ], ax

        getarg di, __argarray                           ; arguments pointer
        call nullTerminateArgs
        mov di, offset ( RxDOS_BatchFile. batchArgStore )
        mov word ptr [ RxDOS_BatchFile. batchNumArgs ], 0

_saveBatchArguments_32:
        getarg si, __tempargptr
        mov si, word ptr [ si ]                         ; arg
        or si, si                                       ; null terminator ?
        jz _saveBatchArguments_Exit                     ; then all done ->

        add word ptr [ __tempargptr ][ bp ], 2
        mov bx, word ptr [ RxDOS_BatchFile. batchNumArgs ]
        add bx, bx
        mov word ptr [ RxDOS_BatchFile. batchArgPtrs ][ bx ], di
        mov word ptr [ RxDOS_BatchFile. batchArgPtrs + 2 ][ bx ], 0000
        inc word ptr [ RxDOS_BatchFile. batchNumArgs ]

        call _CopyString
        jmp _saveBatchArguments_32
```

```
_saveBatchArguments_Error:
        stc

_saveBatchArguments_Exit:
        getarg  di, __argarray
        getarg  dx, __pathArg
        getarg  ax, __type
        Return
```

Argument Replacement in Batch Files

The preceding code subtly changes the way the command processor reads the next command line. The batch file handle argument saved when the batch file is opened serves as a switch. When the argument is nonzero, the code reads from the batch file instead of the command line. The difference is more than just the file handle passed to the read function; different read routines are used because the batch file code must perform additional processing.

When a command is passed to the command parser, the differences between whether they were entered on a command line or retrieved from a batch file have been removed. The remainder of the code in the command processor does not care, nor does it distinguish the source of the command. All batch file parameter replacement is taken care of by the batch file read routine, which is a part of the command line input code.

When a statement is retrieved from the batch file, it is automatically passed to the replace temporary variables function. The routine scans the line buffer passed to it, searching for arguments that begin with a % character. If the character that follows is a digit from 0 to 9, the argument is replaced by the corresponding string saved in the BATCH_ARGS structure described earlier. If the characters that follow contain letters, the name is searched in the environment variables list.

The replace argument routine utilizes functions such as DeleteString and InsertString to edit the line retrieved from the batch file. None of this name or argument replacement takes place when the command is entered from the command line, as opposed to from a batch file, because there are different command line input routines depending on the source.

The replace argument function follows, including code for the insert and delete strings:

(in rxdoscmd.asm)
```
        ;''''''''''''''''''''''''''''''''''''''''''''''''''''''''''';
        ;  Replace Temporary Variables                              ;
        ;- - - - - - - - - - - - - - - - - - - - - - - - - - - - - -;
        ;                                                           ;
        ;  Usage:                                                   ;
        ;    ss:si  points to null terminated string                ;
        ;                                                           ;
        ;  Returns:                                                 ;
        ;    cx      length of new string                           ;
        ;...........................................................;

ReplaceTempVariables:
        Entry
        def  _stringPointer, si
```

```
        def   _deleteFrom
        defbytes _tempVar, 128

        push di
        push si

;- - - - - - - - - - - - - - - - - - - - - - - - - - - - - - - - -
;  scan for % argument
;- - - - - - - - - - - - - - - - - - - - - - - - - - - - - - - - -
_replaceTempVar_08:
        lodsb                                   ; scan for % symbol
        or al, al                               ; null terminator ?
        ifz _replaceTempVar_36                  ; yes ->
        cmp al, '%'                             ; percent character ?
        jnz _replaceTempVar_08

        mov al, byte ptr [ si ]                 ; get character immed after
        or al, al                               ; null terminator ?
        ifz _replaceTempVar_36                  ; yes ->

        cmp al, '%'                             ; %% case ?
        jz _replaceTempVar_PercentPercent       ; yes ->

        dec si                                  ; backup over %
        cmp al, '9'+1                           ; outside arg values ?
        jnc _replaceTempVar_EnvVariable         ; yes ->
        sub al, '0'                             ; outside argument values ?
        jc _replaceTempVar_EnvVariable          ; yes ->

;- - - - - - - - - - - - - - - - - - - - - - - - - - - - - - - - -
;  numeric argument
;- - - - - - - - - - - - - - - - - - - - - - - - - - - - - - - - -
        mov cx, 2                               ; bytes to delete
        call deleteString                       ; delete cx bytes at si

        xor ah, ah
        cmp ax, word ptr [ RxDOS_BatchFile. batchNumArgs ]
        jge _replaceTempVar_16                  ; just delete arg ->

        add ax, ax                              ; index pointer
        mov di, ax
        mov di, word ptr [ RxDOS_BatchFile. batchArgPtrs ][ di ]
        or di, di
        jz _replaceTempVar_16                   ; if no arg value ->
        call insertString                       ; insert arg at [ di ]

_replaceTempVar_16:
        jmp _replaceTempVar_08

;- - - - - - - - - - - - - - - - - - - - - - - - - - - - - - - - -
;  %% case
;- - - - - - - - - - - - - - - - - - - - - - - - - - - - - - - - -
_replaceTempVar_PercentPercent:
        mov cx, 1
```

```
        call deleteString                       ; delete cx bytes at si
        jmp _replaceTempVar_08

;- - - - - - - - - - - - - - - - - - - - - - - - - - - - - - - - - - -
;  environment variable
;- - - - - - - - - - - - - - - - - - - - - - - - - - - - - - - - - - -
_replaceTempVar_EnvVariable:
        lea di, offset [ _tempVar ][ bp ]
        storarg _deleteFrom, si
        inc si                                   ; skip init %

_replaceEnvVariable08:
        lodsb                                    ; scan for next % symbol
        stosb                                    ; save at _tempvar
        or al, al                                ; null terminator ?
        jz _replaceTempVar_36                    ; yes ->
        cmp al, '%'                              ; percent character ?
        jnz _replaceEnvVariable08                ; keep searching ->

        mov word ptr [ di-1 ], '='               ; cancel trailing %

        mov cx, si
        sub cx, word ptr [ _deleteFrom ][ bp ]   ; delete from
        push si
        push cx                                   ; delete length

        lea si, offset [ _tempVar ][ bp ]
        call searchEnvVariable                    ; environment string found ?
        jnz _replaceEnvVariable36                 ; not found ->

        pop cx
        push cx                                    ; length to delete
        mov si, word ptr [ _deleteFrom ][ bp ]    ; delete from
        call deleteString                          ; delete cx bytes at si

        push ds
        mov si, di
        add si, dx                                 ; contents of variable
        mov ds, word ptr [ _EnvSegment ]           ; point to segment
        lea di, offset [ _tempVar ][ bp ]          ; where to copy
        call _CopyString                           ; copy null term string

        pop ds
        mov si, word ptr [ _deleteFrom ][ bp ]     ; delete from
        lea di, offset [ _tempVar ][ bp ]          ; where to copy
        call insertString                          ; insert
_replaceEnvVariable36:
        pop cx
        pop si
        jmp _replaceTempVar_08

;- - - - - - - - - - - - - - - - - - - - - - - - - - - - - - - - - - -
;  done
;- - - - - - - - - - - - - - - - - - - - - - - - - - - - - - - - - - -
_replaceTempVar_36:
```

```
        xor ax, ax
        mov cx, -1
        getarg di, _stringPointer
        repnz scasb
        neg cx
        sub cx, 2

        pop si
        pop di
        Return

        ;'''''''''''''''''''''''''''''''''''''''''''''''''''''''''';
        ;  Delete String                                          ;
        ;- - - - - - - - - - - - - - - - - - - - - - - - - - - - -;
        ;                                                         ;
        ;  Usage:                                                 ;
        ;    ss:si  points inside string                          ;
        ;    cx     bytes to delete                               ;
        ;.........................................................;

deleteString:
        push di
        push ax
        push si
        push cx
        or cx, cx                               ; if null call
        jz deleteString_36                      ; nothing to do ->

deleteString_08:
        lodsb                                   ; test for null term
        or al, al
        jz deleteString_32
        loop deleteString_08

        pop cx
        pop si
        push si
        push cx
        mov di, si
        add si, cx                              ; skip pointer

deleteString_12:
        lodsb                                   ; copy byte
        stosb
        or al, al
        jnz deleteString_12

        dec si                                  ; point to null byte

deleteString_32:
        mov byte ptr [ si ], 0

deleteString_36:
        pop cx
```

```
        pop si
        pop ax
        pop di
        ret

        ;''''''''''''''''''''''''''''''''''''''''''''''''''''''''''''''''';
        ;  Insert String                                                 ;
        ;- - - - - - - - - - - - - - - - - - - - - - - - - - - - - - - -;
        ;                                                                ;
        ;  Usage:                                                        ;
        ;   ss:si  points inside string                                  ;
        ;   ds:di  points to insert string (null term)                  ;
        ;                                                                ;
        ;  Returns:                                                      ;
        ;   ss:si  points to char past insert string                    ;
        ;................................................................;

insertString:
        push cx
        push ax
        push di

;- - - - - - - - - - - - - - - - - - - - - - - - - - - - - - - - - -
;  compute length of insert string
;- - - - - - - - - - - - - - - - - - - - - - - - - - - - - - - - - -
        xor ax, ax
        mov cx, -1
        repnz scasb                     ; search string for end

        neg cx                          ; make len-1 positive
        sub cx, 2                       ; kill null string arg
        sub di, 2                       ; point to byte before null
        push di                         ; end of arg pointer
        push cx                         ; length of insert string

;- - - - - - - - - - - - - - - - - - - - - - - - - - - - - - - - - -
;  compute length of master string
;- - - - - - - - - - - - - - - - - - - - - - - - - - - - - - - - - -
        xor ax, ax
        mov cx, -1
        mov di, si
        repnz scasb                     ; search length of insert string
        neg cx                          ; make len-1 positive
        dec cx                          ; kill null string arg
        dec di

;- - - - - - - - - - - - - - - - - - - - - - - - - - - - - - - - - -
;  open string
;- - - - - - - - - - - - - - - - - - - - - - - - - - - - - - - - - -
        std                             ; copy reverse direction
        pop ax
        push ax                         ; length of insert string
        mov si, di                      ;
        add di, ax                      ; where to copy to
```

```
        rep movsb

        pop cx
        pop si
        push di                                 ; save return pointer
        rep movsb                               ; insert string
        cld                                     ; restore direction

;- - - - - - - - - - - - - - - - - - - - - - - - - - - - - - -
;  done
;- - - - - - - - - - - - - - - - - - - - - - - - - - - - - - -
        pop si                                  ; return pointer - 1
        inc si

        pop di
        pop ax
        pop cx
        ret
```

Call Statement Processing

Unless the call statement is used, a batch file reference will abruptly terminate an executing batch file. The execute command logic, in launching the new batch file, will close the existing batch file and replace its arguments. The purpose of the call statement is to provide the capability for nested batch file calls.

The _call function saves the critically important BATCH_ARGS on the stack. At the very top of the stack created by the command shell, space is reserved for a single copy of the BATCH_ARGS data structure. When a call statement is executed, the arguments for the current batch file are copied to this save area. The stack reservation pointer is moved down, and the number of stack saved copies is incremented. This counter prevents restoring more copies of arguments than actually have been saved.

The stack reservation pointer sets the top of the stack for the next command. The call statement saves parameters and moves the stack reservation pointer down. This in no way affects the current contents of the stack. However, it does alter where the stack pointer is set for the next command.

As the current statement processing terminates, all functions called will return to the original caller, which is the code that reads the next command. The command read loop resets the stack pointer according to the stack reservation value. The next command will use a stack that is a little bit farther down, preserving the saved batch file arguments. As each batch file terminates, the arguments from the stack are restored, and the stack reservation pointer is moved back up.

After preserving the current batch arguments, it initializes the parameters for the called batch file by calling _saveBatchArguments. The code for the call processing function is shown here.

(in rxdoscmd.asm)

```
        ;''''''''''''''''''''''''''''''''''''''''''''''''''''''''''''';
        ;  Call batchfile arguments                                   ;
        ;- - - - - - - - - - - - - - - - - - - - - - - - - - - - - -;
        ;                                                             ;
        ;  Unlike most other commands, cd command will be processed if ;
        ;  part of the cd command, as in cd\...                        ;
        ;                                                             ;
        ;  Usage:                                                      ;
        ;   ss:di  Arg Array                                           ;
        ;   ax     Number of arguments in array                       ;
        ;.............................................................;

_Call:
        Entry
        def __argarray, di
        def __tempargptr
        defbytes _pathArg, 128

;- - - - - - - - - - - - - - - - - - - - - - - - - - - - - - - -
;  find and execute program (unless its a batch file)
;- - - - - - - - - - - - - - - - - - - - - - - - - - - - - - - -
        lea dx, offset [ _pathArg ][ bp ]
        call _executeProgram                      ; load and execute
        jc _call_22                               ; if some kind of error ->
        cmp ax, _BAT                              ; is it a bat program ?
        jz _call_12                               ; yes ->

        clc                                       ; clear error
        jmp short _call_22

;- - - - - - - - - - - - - - - - - - - - - - - - - - - - - - - -
;  execute (call) batch
;- - - - - - - - - - - - - - - - - - - - - - - - - - - - - - - -
_call_12:
        xor cx, cx
        xor dx, dx
        mov bx, word ptr [ RxDOS_BatchFile. batchFileHandle ]
        Int21 MoveFilePointer, SEEK_CUR          ; get current position
        mov word ptr [ RxDOS_BatchFile. batchFilePosition. _low ], ax
        mov word ptr [ RxDOS_BatchFile. batchFilePosition. _high ], dx

        mov si, offset RxDOS_BatchFile
        mov di, word ptr [ RxDOS_PrevStackFrame ]
        mov cx, sizeBATCH_ARGS
        rep movsb                                 ; copy current args to save area

        sub word ptr [ RxDOS_PrevStackFrame ], sizeBATCH_ARGS
        inc word ptr [ RxDOS_StackFrameNumEntries ]

;- - - - - - - - - - - - - - - - - - - - - - - - - - - - - - - -
;  setup batch file arguments
;- - - - - - - - - - - - - - - - - - - - - - - - - - - - - - - -
        mov ax, _BAT                              ; exit must contain _BAT type
```

```
        getarg di, __argarray
        add di, 2                                       ; skip 'call' argument
        lea dx, offset [ _pathArg ][ bp ]               ; pointer to file name
        call _saveBatchArguments                        ; if batch file, save arguments
        jnc _call_22                                    ; all done ->

        add word ptr [ RxDOS_PrevStackFrame ], sizeBATCH_ARGS
        dec word ptr [ RxDOS_StackFrameNumEntries ]     ; if error
        stc

_call_22:
        getarg di, __argarray
        Return
```

How Batch Files Terminate

Eventually, batch files terminate. When the batch file read function routine detects an end of file, it calls the _EndCall function. It closes the batch file, restores the saved parameters, and resets the stack reservation pointer. If there are no parameters to restore, it nulls out the batch file handle. This handle serves, as we noted earlier, as a switch between line and batch file processing.

The _EndCall function is shown here.

```
(in rxdoscmd.asm)
        ;'''''''''''''''''''''''''''''''''''''''''''''''''''''''''''''';
        ;                                                              ;
        ;  End Call                                                    ;
        ;- - - - - - - - - - - - - - - - - - - - - - - - - - - - - - -;
        ;                                                              ;
        ;  Usage:                                                      ;
        ;   ss:di  Arg Array                                           ;
        ;   ax     Number of arguments in array                       ;
        ;..............................................................;

_EndCall:
        mov bx, word ptr [ RxDOS_BatchFile. batchFileHandle ]
        Int21 CloseFile                                 ; close file
        mov word ptr [ RxDOS_BatchFile. batchFileHandle ], 0000

        cmp word ptr [ RxDOS_StackFrameNumEntries ], 0000
        jz _endcall_18                                  ; if no more files ->

        dec word ptr [ RxDOS_StackFrameNumEntries ]
        add word ptr [ RxDOS_PrevStackFrame ], sizeBATCH_ARGS

        mov si, word ptr [ RxDOS_PrevStackFrame ]
        mov di, offset RxDOS_BatchFile
        mov cx, sizeBATCH_ARGS
        rep movsb                                       ; restore args

        mov si, word ptr [ RxDOS_PrevStackFrame ]
        cmp word ptr [ RxDOS_StackFrameNumEntries ], 0000
        jnz _endcall_18                                 ; if more files to backup to ->
```

```
        mov byte ptr [ _EchoStatus ], Yes

_endcall_18:
        ret
```

Processing Commands

So far, we've dealt with only a few aspects of command processing, including command input and parsing and how batch files are processed. Our attention now shifts to how commands like `for`, `if`, and `goto` are handled. As we noted earlier, internal commands are identified by matching their names in a command table. The table also contains the address of a command service routine designed to further process the command.

The command service routines are passed the argument array created during parsing. The array pointers point to the command as input by the user in the command line. The service routines must verify that the correct number of arguments were entered, that the arguments are valid, and that command line switches, such as in the `dir/w`, are valid. It must then execute the command.

Some common helper routines help in the further processing of the command line. One function is `PreProcessCmndLine`, which identifies and removes valid command line switches. It then checks that the number of arguments passed is within acceptable ranges. An excellent example is the `dir` command, which may optionally have an argument. It also accepts switches like `/p` for pause and `/w` for wide.

The preprocess command line function begins by scanning and counting the arguments passed in the argument array. The number of arguments, excluding switches, must fall between the acceptable high and low ranges. The `dir` command passes the following parameters to the preprocess parser:

```
        mov cx, 0000                    ; min args
        mov dx, 0001                    ; max args
        getarg di, _args                ; ptr to arg array
        mov bx, offset _DirSwitches     ; dir switches
        call PreProcessCmndLine         ; process switches and args
        ifc _dir_86                     ; if error ->
```

The minimum number of arguments is passed in the CX register, the maximum in the BX register, the pointer to the command argument array is passed in the DI register, and the BX register points to a table of command line switches. No switches are expected or allowed if a NULL address is passed.

The allowable command line switches, of which the `dir` command probably has the richest set, are described by a table. Each entry contains three arguments. The table appears as follows:

```
        ;''''''''''''''''''''''''''''''''''''''''''''''''''''''''''';
        ;   Dir Switches                                           ;
        ;.........................................................;

_DirSwitches:
_DirPauseSwitch:                Switch 'p', 0
```

```
_DirWideSwitch:                    Switch 'w', 0
_DirAttribSwitch:                  Switch 'a', SW_LETTERCHOICE, SW_DIR_ATTRIB
_DirOrderSwitch:                   Switch 'o', SW_LETTERCHOICE, SW_DIR_ORDER
_DirSubDirSwitch:                  Switch 's', 0
_DirLowerCaseSwitch:               Switch 'l', 0
_DirBareSwitch:                    Switch 'b', 0
                                   db -1

SW_DIR_ATTRIB:                     db '-dnsra', 0
SW_DIR_ORDER:                      db '-negsd', 0
```

The first argument in a switch table entry identifies the switch. This can be any character, letter, or number. The second entry identifies the possible other argument syntax, followed by an optional third address argument. The second argument, which identifies the syntax of the command line switch, is meant to be general enough to support a wide range of switch options. For example, there is an option that reads the argument beyond the switch as a number.

For the `dir` command, the switches either have no optional format or the format shown is tagged as SW_LETTERCHOICE, meaning that switch may be followed by any one of the letters pointed to by the third argument. For example, `-oen` would be a valid argument because the `-o` argument can be followed by the letter e or n.

When switches are processed from the command line, they are identified and then removed from the command line. When a switch is identified, by the `_GetSwitch` function, it sets the SW_SWITCHSET flag next to the matched switches. That is, the arguments in the switch table are set with this flag when identified in the command line. This makes it extremely easy to check later if a switch was selected.

For example, if the `/w` switch was used in the `dir` command, it can later be checked by using the following simple line of code:

```
test word ptr [ _DirWideSwitch. _Flags ], SW_SWITCHSET
```

Several helper routines exist that check for no arguments, one argument, or an optional argument. The routines are shown here and proceed the command line argument preparser.

```
(in rxdoscmd.asm)
        ;'''''''''''''''''''''''''''''''''''''''''''''''''''''''''''''''''';
        ;  Check Number of Arguments                                       ;
        ;- - - - - - - - - - - - - - - - - - - - - - - - - - - - - - - - -;
        ;                                                                  ;
        ;  Usage:                                                          ;
        ;   bx/ dx are set with the number of expected arguments.          ;
        ;                                                                  ;
        ;  Returns:                                                        ;
        ;   cy      too many arguments message output                      ;
        ;..................................................................;

CheckNoArgs:
        xor dx, dx                              ; no args
        xor bx, bx                              ; no switches
        jmp short PreProcessCmndLine            ; check
```

```
CheckOneArg:
        mov cx, 0001                            ; must have one arg
        mov dx, 0001                            ; must have one arg
        xor bx, bx                              ; no switches
        jmp short PreProcessCmndLine            ; check

CheckOptOneArg:
        mov cx, 0000                            ; must have none,
        mov dx, 0001                            ;   or one arg
        xor bx, bx                              ; no switches

        ;''''''''''''''''''''''''''''''''''''''''''''''''''''''''''''';
        ;  Pre Process Command Line                                   ;
        ;- - - - - - - - - - - - - - - - - - - - - - - - - - - - - - -;
        ;                                                             ;
        ;  Usage:                                                     ;
        ;   ss:di  pointer to argument array                         ;
        ;   cx     acceptable min # args                             ;
        ;   dx     acceptable max # args                             ;
        ;   bx     pointer to switches                               ;
        ;                                                             ;
        ;  Returns:                                                   ;
        ;   cy     too many arguments message output                 ;
        ;.............................................................;

PreProcessCmndLine:
        push di
        push cx
        push dx

        call _GetSwitches                       ; switches ok ?
        jc _preProcessCmndLine_08               ; no —>

        pop dx
        pop cx
        push dx
        push cx
        call CountArgs                          ; see how many args remain
        call _TooManyArguments                  ; too many still left ?
        jc _preProcessCmndLine_08               ; yes —>

        call nullTerminateArgs                  ; null terminate args
        or ax, ax                               ; how many args passed

_preProcessCmndLine_08:
        pop dx
        pop cx
        pop di
        ret

        ;''''''''''''''''''''''''''''''''''''''''''''''''''''''''''''';
        ;  Tests for Too Many Arguments                               ;
        ;- - - - - - - - - - - - - - - - - - - - - - - - - - - - - - -;
        ;                                                             ;
```

```
        ;  Usage:                                                       ;
        ;    ss:di   pointer to argument array                          ;
        ;    ax      actual argument count                              ;
        ;    cx      acceptable min # args                              ;
        ;    dx      acceptable max # args                              ;
        ;                                                               ;
        ;  Returns:                                                     ;
        ;    cy      too many arguments message output                  ;
        ;...........................................................;

_TooManyArguments:
        push di
        push ax
        push cx

        cmp ax, dx                              ;
        jz _TooManyArguments_16                 ; if expected # args ->
        jg _TooManyArguments_06                 ; if greater than expected ->
        cmp ax, cx
        jge _TooManyArguments_16                ; if within min/max
        mov dx, offset CmndError_ParametersMissing
        jmp short _TooManyArguments_08

_TooManyArguments_06:
        mov dx, offset CmndError_TooManyParameters
        Call DisplayLine

        pop cx
        push cx
        add cx, cx
        add di, cx                              ; argument ptr that is extra
        mov dx, word ptr ss:[ di ]              ; get arg address

_TooManyArguments_08:
        call DisplayLine                        ; show arg
        stc

_TooManyArguments_16:
        pop cx
        pop ax
        pop di
        ret
```

The code shown next checks whether command line switches are valid. It is passed both a command line set of arguments in the form of the argument array and a table of allowable switches. A NULL pointer means that no switches are valid. This routine is called only when a known internal command is executed, so it never attempts to mediate command line switches for program calls.

The allowable switches are defined in a table. A bit flag is set within this table for every switch detected in the command line.

Each argument in the argument array is then checked. If it begins with the DOS-recognized switch character, the switch is matched by comparing it to the elements in the table. The SW_SWITCHSET flag is set, and the switch is removed as an argument from the argument array.

Throughout this code, there is a test to determine whether any switches are permitted. An error message is displayed if a switch is recognized but no switches are permitted, just as an illegal switch was used in the command line.

```
(in rxdoscmd.asm)
        ;''''''''''''''''''''''''''''''''''''''''''''''''''''''''''''''''''';
        ;   Test/ Process Switches                                         ;
        ;- - - - - - - - - - - - - - - - - - - - - - - - - - - - - - - - - -;
        ;                                                                   ;
        ;   Usage:                                                          ;
        ;   ss:di  pointer to argument array                               ;
        ;   bx     pointer to switches to process (or null)                ;
        ;                                                                   ;
        ;   Returns:                                                        ;
        ;   cy     if invalid use of switches                              ;
        ;                                                                   ;
        ;           Otherwise, switch array passed is filled with info.   ;
        ;- - - - - - - - - - - - - - - - - - - - - - - - - - - - - - - - - -;
        ;                                                                   ;
        ;   Switch array consists of a switch letter followed by:          ;
        ;                                                                   ;
        ;   'x'        switch letter                                        ;
        ;   flags      type of data value expected                         ;
        ;   min        min value expected                                  ;
        ;   max        max value expected                                  ;
        ;   actual     actual value passed in command                      ;
        ;                                                                   ;
        ;   a flag bit is set if the flag was encountered in cmnd.         ;
        ;...................................................................;

_GetSwitches:
        Entry
        def _switches, bx

        push di
        push si
        push cx

        or bx, bx                               ; switches expected ?
        jz _getSwitches_06                      ; no -->
        call _initSwitchTable                   ; init switches expected

;- - - - - - - - - - - - - - - - - - - - - - - - - - - - - - - - -
; walk through all args
;- - - - - - - - - - - - - - - - - - - - - - - - - - - - - - - - -
_getSwitches_06:
        mov si, word ptr ss:[ di ]              ; get arg
        or si, si                               ; is it a null arg ?
        jz _getSwitches_36                      ; yes, exit -->

        mov al, byte ptr ss:[ si ]              ; get value at arg
        cmp al, byte ptr [ _SwitchChar ]        ; switch arg ?
        jnz _getSwitches_12                     ; no -->
```

```
        getarg bx, _switches
        or bx, bx                               ; any switches allowed ?
        jz _getSwitches_24                      ; if not allowed, drop from list

        mov ax, word ptr ss:[ si + 1 ]          ; get switch characters
        call _matchSwitch                       ; is this switch valid ?
        jc _getSwitches_24                      ; not allowed ->

        or word ptr [ swFlags ][ bx ], SW_SWITCHSET   ; switch is set
        call deleteArg                          ; remove this argument
        jz _getSwitches_36                      ; if no more args ->

_getSwitches_12:
        inc di
        inc di
        jmp _getSwitches_06

;- - - - - - - - - - - - - - - - - - - - - - - - - - - - - - - -
;   switch is illegal
;- - - - - - - - - - - - - - - - - - - - - - - - - - - - - - - -
_getSwitches_24:
        push si                                 ; save argument ptr
        mov dx, offset CmndError_BadSwitch
        call DisplayLine                        ; error message

        pop dx
        call DisplayLine                        ; show arg
        stc

;- - - - - - - - - - - - - - - - - - - - - - - - - - - - - - - -
;   done
;- - - - - - - - - - - - - - - - - - - - - - - - - - - - - - - -
_getSwitches_36:
        pop cx
        pop si
        pop di
        Return

        ;,,,,,,,,,,,,,,,,,,,,,,,,,,,,,,,,,,,,,,,,,,,,,,,,,,,,,,,,,,,,,,,;
        ;   Match Switch                                               ;
        ;- - - - - - - - - - - - - - - - - - - - - - - - - - - - - - - -;
        ;                                                              ;
        ;   Usage:                                                     ;
        ;   al      character                                          ;
        ;   bx      switch table                                       ;
        ;                                                              ;
        ;   Returns:                                                   ;
        ;   bx      pointer to matching switch entry                   ;
        ;   cy      match not found                                    ;
        ;..............................................................;

_matchSwitch:
        call _lowerCase
```

```
_matchSwitch_04:
        cmp al, byte ptr cs:[ bx ]
        jz _matchSwitch_08

        add bx, sizeSWITCHENTRY                  ; next entry
        cmp byte ptr cs:[ bx ], -1              ; end of table ?
        jnz _matchSwitch_04                     ; not yet —>

        stc

_matchSwitch_08:
        ret

        ;'''''''''''''''''''''''''''''''''''''''''''''''''''''''''''''''';
        ;  Init Switch Table                                            ;
        ;- - - - - - - - - - - - - - - - - - - - - - - - - - - - - - -;
        ;                                                              ;
        ;  Usage:                                                      ;
        ;  bx      switch table                                        ;
        ;..............................................................;

_initSwitchTable:
        push bx

_initSwitchTable_04:
        cmp byte ptr cs:[ bx ], -1              ; end of table ?
        jz _initSwitchTable_08                  ; yes, all done —>
        and word ptr cs:[ swFlags ][ bx ], not SW_SWITCHSET
        add bx, sizeSWITCHENTRY                  ; next entry
        jmp _initSwitchTable_04

_initSwitchTable_08:
        pop bx
        ret
```

Break

The break command sets the DOS break value to either ON or OFF. If the command is entered without an argument, the current setting of the break value is displayed. The function first determines whether there is an optional argument. If there is more than one argument, an error message is displayed and the function ignored.

Next, the function determines if there were any arguments. If there were, the command lookup function is used, but the table passed to the function contains simply the ON and OFF arguments. If the lookup function cannot match these arguments, an error message is displayed. Otherwise, the value returned by the lookup function is passed to DOS to either set on or turn off Control-C and Control-Break testing.

If no arguments had been on the command line, the current setting of the Control-C checking is read from DOS and the appropriate message displayed.

(in rxdoscmd.asm)

```
        ;,,,,,,,,,,,,,,,,,,,,,,,,,,,,,,,,,,,,,,,,,,,,,,,,,,,,,,,,,,,,;
        ;   Break [ ON | OFF ]                                       ;
        ;- - - - - - - - - - - - - - - - - - - - - - - - - - - - - -;
        ;                                                            ;
        ;   Sets, clears or reports on RxDOS break option.           ;
        ;                                                            ;
        ;............................................................;

_Break:
        Entry
        ddef __argarray, ss, di
        def _args, ax

        call CheckOptOneArg                         ; see if 1 arg
        jc _BreakError                              ; if not on/off, print line ->

        or ax, ax                                   ; any arguments ?
        jz _BreakPrintcurrent                       ; none, print current status ->

;- - - - - - - - - - - - - - - - - - - - - - - - - - - - - - -
;  test for On/ Off
;- - - - - - - - - - - - - - - - - - - - - - - - - - - - - - -
        mov si, word ptr [ di ]                     ; get single argument
        mov di, offset RxDOS_OnOff
        call CmndLookup                             ; lookup command
        jc _BreakError                              ; if not on/off, print line ->

        mov dl, bl
        Int21 CtrlBreakCheck, setControlC           ; set/clear Ctrl Break check
        Return

;- - - - - - - - - - - - - - - - - - - - - - - - - - - - - - -
;  must specify on or off
;- - - - - - - - - - - - - - - - - - - - - - - - - - - - - - -
_BreakError:
        mov dx, offset CmndError_MustSpecifyOnOff
        call DisplayErrorMessage
        Return

;- - - - - - - - - - - - - - - - - - - - - - - - - - - - - - -
;  print verify on/off value
;- - - - - - - - - - - - - - - - - - - - - - - - - - - - - - -
_BreakPrintcurrent:
        Int21 CtrlBreakCheck, getControlC           ; get/clear Ctrl Break check

        mov bl, dl
        xor bh, bh
        add bx, bx
        mov dx, word ptr [ _BreakOptions ][ bx ]
        call DisplayLine
        Return
```

Change Directory

The change directory command performs two services. Without an argument, it displays the current directory. When an argument is passed, the function attempts to perform a directory change function. The command was recently changed to also permit a drive parameter, changing both the current drive and directory. No action is taken if the parameters passed are illegal.

The command first checks for an optional parameter. If none is provided, the command displays the current directory. It retrieves from DOS the current disk drive and converts it to an ASCII value. It then retrieves the current directory to a buffer immediately after the drive. The buffer is lowercased, and the resulting text is displayed.

If an argument was passed with the command, the argument is fully expanded using the little known Get Actual Filename function. This will expand the argument into a drive and path form, even if the argument passed was the parent or child subdirectory, that is, a . or .. directory. The drive letter is extracted from this expanded form and used to perform a drive select. The drive select will fail if it is illegal, and an error message will be displayed.

If the drive select is successful, a directory change is issued. If the command returns an error, the `DisplayError` function is called with the DOS error code. The code is looked up in a table, and the corresponding error message is displayed. Otherwise, the command succeeded.

```
(in rxdoscmd.asm)
        ;'''''''''''''''''''''''''''''''''''''''''''''''''''''''''''''''';
        ;  Change Directory                                              ;
        ;- - - - - - - - - - - - - - - - - - - - - - - - - - - - - - - -;
        ;                                                                ;
        ;  Changes the default directory for a drive.                    ;
        ;                                                                ;
        ;  Usage:                                                        ;
        ;    ss:di  Arg Array                                            ;
        ;    ax     Number of arguments in array                         ;
        ;................................................................;

_ChangeDir:
        Entry
        def  _disk
        ddef __argarray, ss, di
        defbytes _tempstring, 128

        call CheckOptOneArg                    ; see if 1 arg
        ifc  _changeDir_32                     ; if switch not expected —>
        jnz  _changeDir_18                     ; if argument passed —>

;- - - - - - - - - - - - - - - - - - - - - - - - - - - - - - - - - - - -
;  display current
;- - - - - - - - - - - - - - - - - - - - - - - - - - - - - - - - - - - -
        Int21 CurrentDisk                      ; get current disk

        mov  dl, al                            ; save drive letter
        or   al, 'a'                           ; drive
        lea  di, offset [ _tempstring + 3][ bp ]
```

```
        mov byte ptr [ di - 3 ], al
        mov byte ptr [ di - 2 ], ':'
        mov byte ptr [ di - 1 ], '\'

        inc dl
        mov si, di
        Int21 GetCurrentDirectory                   ; get current directory

        push ss
        push si                                      ; where string
        call _lowerCaseString

        lea dx, offset _tempstring [ bp ]
        call DisplayLine
        Return

;- - - - - - - - - - - - - - - - - - - - - - - - - - - - - - - - - -
;  change drive: directory
;- - - - - - - - - - - - - - - - - - - - - - - - - - - - - - - - - -
_changeDir_18:
        mov di, word ptr [ __argarray. _pointer ][ bp ]
        mov si, word ptr ss:[ di ]                   ; pointer to lead argument
        lea di, offset [ _tempstring ][ bp ]
        mov word ptr [ di ], '\'                     ; init area
        Int21 GetActualFileName                      ; expand name

        mov di, word ptr [ __argarray. _pointer ][ bp ]
        mov si, word ptr ss:[ di ]                   ; pointer to lead argument
        cmp byte ptr [ si+1 ], ':'                   ; drive ?
        jnz _changeDir_22                            ; no ->

        mov al, byte ptr [ si ]                      ; get drive letter
        call _lowerCase                              ; lowercase letter
        mov dl, al                                   ; to dl
        sub dl, 'a'                                  ; drive maps to 0, ...
        mov byte ptr [ _disk ][ bp ], dl             ; save disk

        Int21 SelectDisk                             ; can we select a drive ?
        Int21 CurrentDisk                            ; get current disk

        inc si
        inc si                                       ; point [si] past drive
        cmp al, byte ptr [ _disk ][ bp ]             ; disk changed ?
        jz _changeDir_22                             ; yes ->

        mov dx, offset CmndError_InvalidDrive
        call DisplayErrorMessage                     ; display message
        jmp short _changeDir_32

;- - - - - - - - - - - - - - - - - - - - - - - - - - - - - - - - - -
;  change directory
;- - - - - - - - - - - - - - - - - - - - - - - - - - - - - - - - - -
_changeDir_22:
        mov dx, si                                   ; points to change string
```

```
        Int21 ChangeSubdirectory                    ; try changing dir
        jnc _changeDir_32                           ; if invalid
        call DisplayError                           ; if error

_changeDir_32:
        Return
```

Cls (Clear Screen)

The clear screen function turns out to be slightly more involved than just clearing the screen. After all, the command's output could have been redirected to a file instead of the screen. The clear screen function uses the DOS IoControl function (DOS function 44h) to determine if stdout is redirected to a file. If it is, a control-L is output by the command.

Physical screen blanking is handled by PhysScreenClear, which first determines the total screen lines and then blanks them using the BIOS. The current screen lines are available as a value in the BIOS communications area at segment 0040h.

```
(in rxdoscmd.asm)
        ;''''''''''''''''''''''''''''''''''''''''''''''''''''''''''''''''''''';
        ;   Clear Screen                                                     ;
        ;....................................................................;

_Cls:
        mov bx, STDOUT
        Int21 IoControl, 00h                        ; is device piped to a file ?
        jc _clsScreen                               ; we'll assume it's to screen ->

        test dx, 80h                                ; if bit 7 = 0, handle is a file
        jnz _clsScreen                              ; its a physical device ->

        mov dl, 'L'-40h                             ; to a file we'll pipe ^L
        Int21 DisplayOutput
        jmp short _cls_36

;- - - - - - - - - - - - - - - - - - - - - - - - - - - - - - - - - - - -
;  see how many lines
;- - - - - - - - - - - - - - - - - - - - - - - - - - - - - - - - - - - -
_clsScreen:
        call PhysClearScreen

_cls_36:
        ret

        ;''''''''''''''''''''''''''''''''''''''''''''''''''''''''''''''''''''';
        ;   Physical Screen Clear                                            ;
        ;....................................................................;

PhysClearScreen:
        call GetScreenLines
        mov dh, al                                  ; max lines to dh
```

```
        mov dl, 80                          ; max width is 80 chars

        mov ax, 0600h                       ; entire screen
        mov bx, 7100h                       ; blue/white
        mov cx, 0000h                       ; from home row
        int 10h

        mov ax, 0F00h                       ; read current mode
        int 10h                             ; get page into BH

        mov ax, 0200h
        mov dx, 0100h
        int 10h                             ; position cursor
        ret
```

Copy

The copy command is used to copy files from one location to another, typically another disk or directory. It can also be used to combine files. Copy is generally straightforward. A buffer in memory is used to read then write the contents of a file. This buffer is used repeatedly until the entire file is copied.

Copy cannot overwrite a source file no matter how complex the path and filename. The source and destination files cannot reference the same file. The reason for this has more to do with the way the copy command works. To create the destination file, copy uses the DOS File Create function, which deletes the file if it already exists. If the source and destination file referenced the same file, the file create would inadvertently delete the source file.

To prevent this problem, the DOS Find First or Find Next function is used to locate both the source and destination files. A field within the FINDENTRY record returned by the functions contains the drive and starting cluster address. The copy is not performed if the drive and cluster addresses for both arguments are equal.

The copy command begins by ensuring that at least two arguments are on the command line. The last argument in the command line is removed, leaving the command line with only source filenames. The last argument is copied to a temporary area that will eventually be used to form the destination filename. The destination name is then checked to determine if it contains only a destination directory. The destination directory name is filled with question marks to create a universal destination template.

Next, the source arguments are scanned. If a plus symbol is encountered, the _AddMode flag is set. All the names in the command line are checked to be sure they exist and they don't conflict with the destination file. Once all the necessary checking is completed, the destination file is created followed by a read/write loop. Copying is performed by reading into an allocated buffer. The buffer is at maximum 64K it is smaller if less memory is available. As much of the buffer is filled as possible, before the file is written to disk.

Once the end of the source file is reached, the source file is closed. If the add mode flag is set, the destination file is not closed, and a jump is made to fetch the next source argument. When all the source files have been processed, and typically there is only one file, the destination file is closed.

Since the source filename may have contained wild characters, a search is made for the next file matching file. If one is found, the copy command continues.

```
(in rxdoscpy.asm)
        ;''''''''''''''''''''''''''''''''''''''''''''''''''''''''''''''''';
        ;   Copy filenameA+filenameB+filenameC filenameDest              ;
        ;- - - - - - - - - - - - - - - - - - - - - - - - - - - - - - - -;
        ;                                                                ;
        ;   Usage:                                                       ;
        ;    ss:di  Arg Array                                            ;
        ;    ax     Number of arguments in array                        ;
        ;................................................................;

_Copy:
        Entry
        def __argarray, di                      ; args array
        def __numArgs, ax                       ; # args
        def __Mode, 0000                        ; non-z if ascii/ z if binary
        def __AddMode                           ; 0000 not add mode
        def __NextAddMode                       ; 0000 next is add mode
        def _endoffile
        def _filesCopied, 0000
        def _srcHandle , 0000
        def _destHandle , 0000
        ddef _destCluster
        ddef _srcCluster

        defbytes _destFilename  , 130
        defbytes _createFilename, 130
        defbytes _copyFilename  , 130
        defbytes _buffer, 128

        _tempFilename = _copyFilename           ; equate temp filename

;- - - - - - - - - - - - - - - - - - - - - - - - - - - - - - - - - -
;   get/test destination filename
;- - - - - - - - - - - - - - - - - - - - - - - - - - - - - - - - - -
        cmp ax, 2                               ; must have at least two args
        ifc _copyError                          ; any less means error ->

        dec ax
        add ax, ax                              ; args offset in words
        add di, ax                              ; point to last arg
        push word ptr [ di ]                    ; get last arg address
        call deleteArg

        pop si
        lea di, offset [ _tempFilename ][ bp ]
        call _copyArgument                      ; copy argument

;- - - - - - - - - - - - - - - - - - - - - - - - - - - - - - - - - -
;   see if dest is just a directory name
;- - - - - - - - - - - - - - - - - - - - - - - - - - - - - - - - - -
        mov cx, ATTR_DIRECTORY
```

```
        lea dx, offset [ _tempFilename ][ bp ]
        Int21 FindFirstFile                             ; locate file with name
        jc _Copy_18                                     ; not a directory ->

    ; if . or .. handle special

_Copy_08:
        test byte ptr [ RxDOS_DTA. findFileAttribute ], ATTR_DIRECTORY
        jz _Copy_18                                     ; if not a dir entry ->

        cmp byte ptr [ RxDOS_DTA. findFileName ], '.'
        jnz _Copy_24                                    ; if dir and not . or .. ->

        Int21 FindNextFile                              ; locate next file
        jnc _Copy_08                                    ; see if also a dir ->

;- - - - - - - - - - - - - - - - - - - - - - - - - - - - - - - - -
; scan name for just directory
;- - - - - - - - - - - - - - - - - - - - - - - - - - - - - - - - -
_Copy_18:
        lea di, offset [ _tempFilename ][ bp ]

_Copy_20:
        cmp byte ptr [ di ], 00                         ; null ?
        jz _Copy_26                                     ; yes, done ->
        inc di
        cmp byte ptr [ di-1 ], ':'                      ; only drive /colon entered ?
        jnz _Copy_20                                    ; no ->
        cmp byte ptr [ di ], 00                         ;
        jnz _Copy_26

_Copy_24:
        mov si, offset RxDOS_AllFiles                   ; dummy path
        call _AppendPathName                            ; append all files

_Copy_26:
        lea si, offset [ _tempFilename ][ bp ]
        lea di, offset [ _destFilename ][ bp ]          ; expansion area
        mov byte ptr [ di ], '\'                        ; (in case no output generated)
        Int21 GetActualFileName                         ; expand name
        ifc _copyError                                  ; destination doesn't exist ->

        xor ax, ax
        mov cx, 4
        lea di, offset [ _destCluster ][ bp ]           ; clusters
        rep stosw                                       ; clear clusters

;- - - - - - - - - - - - - - - - - - - - - - - - - - - - - - - - -
; main loop through all args
;- - - - - - - - - - - - - - - - - - - - - - - - - - - - - - - - -
_Copy_30:
        mov word ptr [ __AddMode ][ bp ], 0000          ; not add mode
        mov word ptr [ __NextAddMode ][ bp ], 0000      ; next is not add mode
```

```
_Copy_32:
        mov di, word ptr [ __argarray ][ bp ]           ; get arg pointer to next arg
        mov si, word ptr [ di ]                          ; point to text
        or si, si                                        ; null entry ?
        ifz _Copy_Return                                 ; yes, return ->

        add word ptr [ __argarray ][ bp ], 2             ; skip this argument next time

        mov al, byte ptr [ si ]
        cmp al, byte ptr [ _SwitchChar ]                 ; switch ?
        ifz _Copy_TestSwitch                             ; yes, go test switch ->

        cmp al, '+'
        ifz _Copy_AddMode                                ; set add mode ->

        lea di, offset [ _copyFilename ][ bp ]
        call _copyArgument

        call _scanForwardArgArray                        ; see if followed by +
        mov word ptr [ __NextAddMode ][ bp ], ax         ; next add mode

        mov dx, di                                       ; copy filename
        mov cx, ATTR_NORMAL
        Int21 FindFirstFile                              ; locate file with name
        jnc _Copy_36                                     ; if file found ->

        mov dx, offset CmndError_FileNotFound
        call DisplayLine
        jmp _copyErrorCleanUp

;- - - - - - - - - - - - - - - - - - - - - - - - - - - - - - - - - - - -
;  open source file
;- - - - - - - - - - - - - - - - - - - - - - - - - - - - - - - - - - - -
_Copy_36:
        lea di, offset [ _copyFilename ][ bp ]
        call _replaceWithRealName

        Int21 OpenFile, OPEN_ACCESS_READONLY
        storarg _srcHandle, ax
        ifc _copyError

        mov bx, ax
        call GetClusterValue                             ; src cluster
        mov word ptr [ _srcCluster. _low  ][ bp ], ax    ; (cluster)
        mov word ptr [ _srcCluster. _high ][ bp ], dx    ; (drive )
        jz _Copy_44                                      ; if not a file ->

        call _compareClusters
        jnz _Copy_44                                     ; no ->

    ; error: file destroyed

        mov dx, offset CmndError_ContentsLostBeforeCopy
        call DisplayErrorMessage
```

```
        jmp _copyErrorCleanUp

;- - - - - - - - - - - - - - - - - - - - - - - - - - - - - - -
;  attempt create file
;- - - - - - - - - - - - - - - - - - - - - - - - - - - - - - -
_Copy_44:
        getarg bx, _destHandle
        or bx, bx                                   ; any dest file ?
        jz _Copy_48                                 ; no, MUST create ->
        cmp word ptr [ __AddMode ][ bp ], 0000      ; add mode ?
        jnz _Copy_56                                ; yes, append to existing file ->

_Copy_48:
        lea si, offset [ _destFilename ][ bp ]      ; destination filename
        lea di, offset [ _createFilename ][ bp ]    ; make destination name
        call _CopyString                            ; copy string

        lea di, offset [ _createFilename ][ bp ]    ; make destination name
        call _makeUniqueName                        ; make unique name

        lea dx, offset [ _createFilename ][ bp ]    ; destination filename
        Int21 OpenFile, OPEN_ACCESS_READONLY        ; we'll try open first
        jc _Copy_52                                 ; MUST create ->

        mov bx, ax
        call GetClusterValue                        ; cluster of dest
        mov word ptr [ _destCluster. _low ][ bp ], ax   ; (cluster)
        mov word ptr [ _destCluster. _high ][ bp ], dx  ; (drive )
        Int21 CloseFile                             ; release file

        call _compareClusters
        jnz _Copy_52                                ; if not same files ->

        mov dx, offset CmndError_CannotCopyUntoSelf
        call DisplayErrorMessage
        jmp _copyErrorCleanUp


;- - - - - - - - - - - - - - - - - - - - - - - - - - - - - - -
;  create file
;- - - - - - - - - - - - - - - - - - - - - - - - - - - - - - -
_Copy_52:
        mov cx, ATTR_NORMAL
        lea dx, offset [ _createFilename ][ bp ]    ; destination filename
        Int21 CreateFile                            ; create
        storarg _destHandle, ax                     ; save handle
        ifc _copyError                              ; if error ->

        mov bx, ax
        call GetClusterValue                        ; cluster of dest
        mov word ptr [ _destCluster. _low ][ bp ], ax   ; (cluster)
        mov word ptr [ _destCluster. _high ][ bp ], dx  ; (drive )
```

```
;- - - - - - - - - - - - - - - - - - - - - - - - - - - - - - - -
; display filename
;- - - - - - - - - - - - - - - - - - - - - - - - - - - - - - - -
_Copy_56:
        mov word ptr [ _endoffile ][ bp ], 0000

        getarg bx, _srcHandle
        Int21 IoControl, 0000                      ; is source a char device ?
        test dx, DEV_CHAR                          ; test device flag
        jz _Copy_62                                ; if file, display filename ->
        storarg __Mode, 01                         ; else switch to ascii mode
        jmp short _Copy_66

_Copy_62:
        mov dx, offset [ RxDOS_DTA. findFileName ]
        call DisplayLine                           ; display line
        call CRLF                                  ; cr/lf


;- - - - - - - - - - - - - - - - - - - - - - - - - - - - - - - -
; copy loop
;- - - - - - - - - - - - - - - - - - - - - - - - - - - - - - - -
_Copy_66:
        mov cx, 128
        getarg bx, _srcHandle
        lea dx, offset [ _buffer ][ bp ]
        Int21 ReadFile                             ; read
        ifc _copyDisplayError                      ; if error ->
        or ax, ax                                  ; end of file ?
        jz _Copy_78                                ; yes, all done ->

        mov cx, ax                                 ; how many bytes actually read
        cmp word ptr [ __Mode ][ bp ], 0000        ; ascii mode ?
        jz _Copy_70                                ; no ->

        push cx
        mov al, 'Z'-40h
        lea di, offset [ _buffer ][ bp ]
        repnz scasb                                ; scan buffer for ^Z
        pop cx
        jnz _Copy_70                               ; if ^z not located ->

        mov word ptr [ _endoffile ][ bp ], -1      ; set end of file mode
        dec cx                                     ; don't copy ^Z

_Copy_70:
        or cx, cx                                  ; any more to copy ?
        jz _Copy_78                                ; no more ->

        getarg bx, _destHandle
        lea dx, offset [ _buffer ][ bp ]
        Int21 WriteFile

        cmp word ptr [ _endoffile ][ bp ], 0000    ; end of file ?
        jz _Copy_66                                ; not end of file yet ->
```

```
;- - - - - - - - - - - - - - - - - - - - - - - - - - - - - -
;  close source file
;- - - - - - - - - - - - - - - - - - - - - - - - - - - - - -
_Copy_78:
        getarg bx, _srcHandle
        Int21 CloseFile
        storarg _srcHandle, 0000

        cmp word ptr [ __NextAddMode  ][ bp ], 0000    ; is next add mode ?
        jnz _Copy_82

        getarg bx, _destHandle
        Int21 CloseFile                                ; if no adds left ...
        storarg _destHandle, 0000
        inc word ptr [ _filesCopied ][ bp ]            ; # files copied.

        Int21 FindNextFile                             ; see if more files to copy
        ifnc _Copy_36                                  ; if file found ->

_Copy_82:
        jmp _Copy_30

;- - - - - - - - - - - - - - - - - - - - - - - - - - - - - -
;  return
;- - - - - - - - - - - - - - - - - - - - - - - - - - - - - -
_Copy_Return:
        getarg bx, _destHandle
        cmp bx, 5
        jle _Copy_ReturnClose_08
        Int21 CloseFile                                ; close last file
        inc word ptr [ _filesCopied ][ bp ]            ; # files copied.

_Copy_ReturnClose_08:
        lea di, offset [ _filesCopied ][ bp ]
        push di                                        ; first arg encountered

        mov di, offset _Copy_FilesCopied
        push di
        lea di, offset [ _buffer ][ bp ]
        push di
        call _sprintf
        add sp, ax                                     ; # args passed
        call DisplayLine

        Return

;- - - - - - - - - - - - - - - - - - - - - - - - - - - - - -
;  add mode
;- - - - - - - - - - - - - - - - - - - - - - - - - - - - - -
_Copy_AddMode:
        mov word ptr [ __AddMode  ][ bp ], -1          ; set add mode
        jmp _Copy_32

;- - - - - - - - - - - - - - - - - - - - - - - - - - - - - -
;  test switches
;- - - - - - - - - - - - - - - - - - - - - - - - - - - - - -
```

```
_Copy_TestSwitch:
        mov al, byte ptr [ si+1 ]
        call _lowerCase                             ; test switch option

        goto 'a', _copyAsciiSwitch
        goto 'b', _copyBinarySwitch

        push ax
        mov dx, offset CmndError_BadSwitch
        call DisplayLine                            ; show error message

        pop dx
        call DisplayLine                            ; show arg
        Return

;- - - - - - - - - - - - - - - - - - - - - - - - - - - - - - - - -
;  if ascii switch
;- - - - - - - - - - - - - - - - - - - - - - - - - - - - - - - - -
_copyAsciiSwitch:
        storarg __Mode, 01                          ; ascii mode
        jmp _Copy_32

;- - - - - - - - - - - - - - - - - - - - - - - - - - - - - - - - -
;  if binary switch
;- - - - - - - - - - - - - - - - - - - - - - - - - - - - - - - - -
_copyBinarySwitch:
        storarg __Mode, 00                          ; binary mode
        jmp _Copy_32

;- - - - - - - - - - - - - - - - - - - - - - - - - - - - - - - - -
;  error in rename command
;- - - - - - - - - - - - - - - - - - - - - - - - - - - - - - - - -
_copyDisplayError:
        call DisplayError
        jmp _copyErrorCleanUp

_copyError:
        mov dx, offset CmndError_CannotCreateFile
        call DisplayErrorMessage

_copyErrorCleanUp:
        getarg bx, _destHandle
        or bx, bx                                   ; if not assigned,
        jz _copyErrorCleanUp_08                      ; don't delete ->
        Int21 CloseFile                             ; close last file

_copyErrorCleanUp_08:
        Return

        ;''''''''''''''''''''''''''''''''''''''''''''''''''''''''';
        ;  Copy Argument                                          ;
        ;- - - - - - - - - - - - - - - - - - - - - - - - - - - - -;
        ;                                                         ;
        ;  Usage:                                                 ;
```

```
        ;   si      points to argument start              ;
        ;   di      points to destination                ;
        ;..............................................;


_copyArgument:
        push di

_copyArgument_06:
        lodsb                                       ; get character
        stosb
        cmp al, ' '+1                               ; space or control character ?
        jc _copyArgument_10                         ; yes ->

        cmp al, byte ptr [ _SwitchChar ]            ; switch character ?
        jz _copyArgument_10                         ; yes ->
        call _CmndParse_SeparatorCheck              ; parse break ?
        jnz _copyArgument_06                         ; no, go to next char ->

_copyArgument_10:
        mov byte ptr [ di-1 ], 0                     ; place null terminator
        pop di
        ret


        ;////////////////////////////////////////////////////;
        ;  LookAhead Add Mode                                 ;
        ;- - - - - - - - - - - - - - - - - - - - - - - - - - -;
        ;                                                     ;
        ;  Usage:                                             ;
        ;   si      points to argument start                 ;
        ;   di      points to destination                    ;
        ;..............................................;


_scanForwardArgArray:
        push di
        mov di, word ptr [ __argarray ][ bp ]       ; get arg pointer to next arg
        xor ax, ax                                  ; next is NOT add

_scanForwardArgArray_10:
        mov si, word ptr [ di ]                      ; point to text
        or si, si                                   ; null entry ?
        jz _scanForwardArgArray_12                   ; yes, return ->

        add di, 2
        cmp byte ptr [ si ], '/'
        jz _scanForwardArgArray_10
        cmp byte ptr [ si ], '+'
        jnz _scanForwardArgArray_12
        mov ax, -1                                  ; next IS add

_scanForwardArgArray_12:
        pop di
        ret


        ;////////////////////////////////////////////////////;
        ;  Get Starting Cluster Value for a given Handle      ;
        ;- - - - - - - - - - - - - - - - - - - - - - - - - - -;
```

```
;                                                         ;
; Input:                                                  ;
;    bx      file handle                                  ;
;                                                         ;
; Output:                                                 ;
;    ax      starting cluster value                       ;
;.........................................................;

GetClusterValue:
        push es
        push di
        push bx
        Int21 GetPSPAddress                    ; returns bx with segment
        mov es, bx                             ; set PSP address

        pop si                                 ; restore handle offset
        push si                                ; (save handle)
        les bx, dword ptr es:[ pspFileHandlePtr ]   ; point to file handles
        mov bl, byte ptr es:[ bx + si ]        ; get real sft offset
        xor bh, bh

        mov ax, 1216h
        int 2fh                                ; UNDOCUMENTED DOS CALL
        mov ax, word ptr es:[ sftBegCluster ][ di ]
        mov dx, word ptr es:[ sftDevInfo    ][ di ]
        and dx, sftDrivemask

        pop bx
        pop di
        pop es
        ret


        ;'''''''''''''''''''''''''''''''''''''''''''''''''''''''''''''';
        ; Compare Drive/Cluster Info                                   ;
        ;- - - - - - - - - - - - - - - - - - - - - - - - - - - - - - -;
        ;                                                             ;
        ; NZ if not equal                                             ;
        ;.............................................................;

_compareClusters:
        cmp word ptr [ _destCluster. _low  ][ bp ], 0000
        jnz _compareClusters_NotEqual
        cmp word ptr [ _srcCluster. _low  ][ bp ], 0000
        jnz _compareClusters_NotEqual

        mov ax, word ptr [ _destCluster. _low  ][ bp ]  ; (cluster)
        cmp ax, word ptr [ _srcCluster. _low ][ bp ]
        jnz _compareClusters_NotEqual

        mov ax, word ptr [ _destCluster. _high ][ bp ]  ; (drive )
        cmp ax, word ptr [ _srcCluster. _high ][ bp ]
        jnz _compareClusters_NotEqual
        ret
```

```
_compareClusters_NotEqual:
        mov ax, -1
        or ax, ax
        ret

        ;''''''''''''''''''''''''''''''''''''''''''''''''''''''''''''''';
        ;  Make Unique Name                                             ;
        ;- - - - - - - - - - - - - - - - - - - - - - - - - - - - - - - -;
        ;                                                               ;
        ;  Usage:                                                       ;
        ;  di      name expected with wild characters                   ;
        ;...............................................................;

_makeUniqueName:
        Entry
        def _name, di
        defbytes _expandedname, sizeExpandedName

        push di

        mov si, di
        lea di, offset [ _expandedname ][ bp ]
        call _splitpath

        mov cx, 8
        mov si, offset [ RxDOS_DTA. findFileName ]
        lea di, offset [ _expandedname. expFilename ][ bp ]
        call _makeReplacement

        inc si
        mov cx, 3
        lea di, offset [ _expandedname. expExtension + 1 ][ bp ]
        call _makeReplacement

        lea si, offset [ _expandedname ][ bp ]
        getarg di, _name
        call _makePath

        pop di
        mov dx, di
        Return

        ;''''''''''''''''''''''''''''''''''''''''''''''''''''''''''''''';
        ;  Make Replacement                                             ;
        ;...............................................................;

_makeReplacement:
        cmp byte ptr [ di ], '?'
        jnz _makeReplacement_08

        mov al, byte ptr [ si ]
        mov byte ptr [ di ], al

_makeReplacement_08:
```

```
        inc di
        inc si
        cmp byte ptr [ si ], '.'
        jz _makeReplacement_12
        cmp byte ptr [ si ], 00
        jz _makeReplacement_12
        loop _makeReplacement

_makeReplacement_12:
        mov byte ptr [ di ], 00
        ret

        ;'''''''''''''''''''''''''''''''''''''''''''''''''''''''''''''';
        ;  Replace with Real Name                                      ;
        ;- - - - - - - - - - - - - - - - - - - - - - - - - - - - - - --;
        ;                                                              ;
        ;  Usage:                                                      ;
        ;   di     full expanded name expected                         ;
        ;..............................................................;

_replaceWithRealName:
        push di
        mov dx, di

_replaceWithRealName_04:
        cmp byte ptr [ di ], 0                       ; find end of string
        jz _replaceWithRealName_08
        inc di
        jmp _replaceWithRealName_04

_replaceWithRealName_08:
        cmp dx, di
        jz _replaceWithRealName_12

        mov al, byte ptr [ di-1 ]
        cmp al, ':'
        jz _replaceWithRealName_12
        cmp al, '\'
        jz _replaceWithRealName_12

        dec di
        jmp _replaceWithRealName_08

_replaceWithRealName_12:
        mov si, offset [ RxDOS_DTA. findFileName ]    ; expanded name
        call _CopyString

        pop di
        mov dx, di
        ret
```

Date

The date command sets or reports the current date as maintained by DOS. DOS maintains the date and time through the CLOCK$ device driver. The driver typically reads and interprets the BIOS-reported date and time, which is updated by a BIOS-supported clock interface. The exact BIOS support mechanism doesn't need to be addressed here other than to state that, although it varies, most modern machines are capable of accurately reporting the date and time.

For the longest time a bug existed within DOS-based systems where the system lost one or more days when it was left turned on but unattended. The BIOS increments a counter at every clock tick. This counter is initially set to the ticks since the beginning of the day. When the counter exceeded 24 hours, it was reset, and a flag was set indicating that it had overflowed a day. When the system is left unattended for more than one day, the flag indicates only that the clock counter has overflowed but not by how many times.

Some more recent BIOS code maintains the clock independent of DOS and traps either the DOS Get Date/Time call or the CLOCK$ call. It then reports its own date and time, totally bypassing DOS. RxDOS traps the DOS idle (int 28h) interrupt. If it detects the time of day wraparound, it resets the flag and increments the date. This fix coexists with the BIOS fix.

The purpose of the date command is not to sort out this issue, but merely to display or change the DOS system date. If no arguments were passed with the command, the current date is displayed, and a prompt is made for a new date. Otherwise, the command sets the date passed as an argument if there were no errors. The date's format is based on the local country setting.

The command parser checks first to determine if an optional argument was passed. If it wasn't, the current date is formatted and displayed using _sprintf, an internal function minimally designed like the C library equivalent. It accepts a format string and parameters as a variable number of stack-passed arguments and formats an output string. This internal function conveniently returns the address of the format output buffer in the DX register, which is required by the display line function.

Once the current system date has been displayed, a prompt for a new date is displayed, and a line is read from the standard input device. The input buffer is checked to determine if any characters have been entered. If none have, the function simply returns. Otherwise, the input buffer should be no different in its format than if a value was passed with the command. The function uses the same code to parse either argument.

Unlike most other DOS functions, the date and time formats depend on the current country setting. Each country setting has a different date template, as shown in the following table. Each date is still made up of days, months, and years, even if in a different order and separated by different separator characters.

```
RxDOSIntl_DateTimeTable:        intldate 001,  "mm/dd/yyyy hh:mm:ss.00" ; USA
                                intldate 002,  "yyyy-mm-dd HH:mm:ss,00" ; Canada-French
                                intldate 003,  "dd/mm/yyyy hh:mm:ss.00" ; Latin America
                                intldate 031,  "dd-mm-yyyy HH:mm:ss,00" ; Netherlands
                                intldate 032,  "dd/mm/yyyy HH:mm:ss,00" ; Belgium
                                intldate 033,  "dd.mm.yyyy HH:mm:ss,00" ; France
                                intldate 034,  "dd/mm/yyyy HH:mm:ss,00" ; Spain
```

```
intldate 036, "yyyy-mm-dd HH:mm:ss,00" ; Hungary
intldate 038, "yyyy-mm-dd HH:mm:ss,00" ; Yugoslavia
intldate 039, "dd/mm/yyyy HH.mm.ss,00" ; Italy
intldate 041, "dd.mm.yyyy HH,mm,ss.00" ; Switzerland
intldate 042, "yyyy-mm-dd HH:mm:ss,00" ; Czechoslovakia
intldate 044, "dd/mm/yyyy HH:mm:ss.00" ; United Kingdom
intldate 045, "dd-mm-yyyy HH:mm:ss,00" ; Denmark
intldate 046, "yyyy-mm-dd HH.mm.ss,00" ; Sweden
intldate 047, "dd.mm.yyyy HH:mm:ss,00" ; Norway
intldate 048, "yyyy-mm-dd HH:mm:ss,00" ; Hungary
intldate 049, "dd.mm.yyyy HH:mm:ss,00" ; Germany
intldate 055, "dd/mm/yyyy HH:mm:ss,00" ; Brazil
intldate 061, "dd/mm/yyyy HH:mm:ss.00" ; Intl English
intldate 351, "dd-mm-yyyy HH:mm:ss,00" ; Portugal
intldate 358, "dd.mm.yyyy HH.mm.ss,00" ; Finland
dw -1
```

Date parsing works as follows. Internally to the date routine, the date is stored in day, month, year order regardless of the current country. The layout of the DATE structure is shown here. Regardless of the preference in order given by the local country, the values are mapped into this order.

```
;''''''''''''''''''''''''''''''''''''''''''''''''''''''''''''''''';
;  Date Control Block                                             ;
;................................................................;


        DATE struc
_DAY        dw ?
_MONTH      dw ?
_YEAR       dw ?
        DATE ends
```

The date parser locates the current country's format, also referred to as a date template. It builds an argument order array from this template. For example, if the local country preference is for year first, then month and year, the first entry in the argument order array will point to the year field of the DATE structure, the second argument will point to the month field, and the last argument will point to the day field.

The first set of digits is read from the date string entered by the user and is stored indirectly into the DATE structure using the arguments in the argument order array built. This continues through all three required fields for the date. The year value, now correctly stored at the DATE._YEAR offset, is checked to ensure that it is within the 80-plus range. The values of the date field are then passed to DOS, which will determine if they are valid. An invalid date will result in a reprompt for a correct date.

When the command parser displays the message to please enter a date, it uses a date prompt routine that also locates and extracts the date template from the template table based on local country preference. The template is displayed with the prompt.

The code for date and all its support routines follows:

```
(in rxdosprm.asm)
        ;''''''''''''''''''''''''''''''''''''''''''''''''''''''''''';
        ;  Date [ date ]                                           ;
        ;- - - - - - - - - - - - - - - - - - - - - - - - - - - - - ;
```

```
        ;                                                        ;
        ;  Usage:                                                ;
        ;   ss:di  Arg Array                                     ;
        ;   ax     Number of arguments in array                 ;
        ;.................................................................;

_Date:
        Entry
        def __argarray, di                      ; args array
        defwords _parsedDatePtrs, 3
        defbytes _parsedDate, sizeDATE
        defbytes _buffer, 128                   ; input buffer
        defbytes _printbuffer, 128

        call CheckOptOneArg                     ; see if 1 arg
        ifc _dateInvalid                        ; if error in args

        mov si, word ptr [ di ]                 ; get first arg
        or si, si                               ; if arg, go parse ->
        jnz _date_26

;- - - - - - - - - - - - - - - - - - - - - - - - - - - - - - - -
;  display current date
;- - - - - - - - - - - - - - - - - - - - - - - - - - - - - - - -
        lea di, offset [ _buffer ][ bp ]
        push di                                 ; address of
        call formatCurrentDate                  ; get current date

        mov di, offset _ShowCurrentDate
        push di
        lea di, offset [ _printbuffer ][ bp ]
        push di
        call _sprintf
        add sp, ax                              ; # args passed
        call DisplayLine

;- - - - - - - - - - - - - - - - - - - - - - - - - - - - - - - -
;  please enter date
;- - - - - - - - - - - - - - - - - - - - - - - - - - - - - - - -
_date_12:
        call DisplayPleaseEnterDate

        lea di, offset [ _buffer ][ bp ]
        mov byte ptr [ bufMaxLength ][ di ], 128
        mov word ptr [ bufActualLength ][ di ], 0

        mov dx, di                              ; where buffer
        call _getStdinLine                      ; read buffer

        call CRLF

        mov bl, byte ptr [ _buffer. bufActualLength ][ bp ]
        and bx, 255
        ifz _dateReturn
```

```
        add bx, bp
        mov byte ptr [ _buffer. bufData ][ bx ], 00      ; place a null terminator
        lea si, offset [ _buffer. bufData ][ bp ]        ; parse text

;- - - - - - - - - - - - - - - - - - - - - - - - - - - - - - - -
;  parse arg at [ si ]
;- - - - - - - - - - - - - - - - - - - - - - - - - - - - - - - -
_date_26:
        push si
        lea si, offset [ _parsedDate ][ bp ]             ; start of buffer
        lea di, offset [ _parsedDatePtrs ][ bp ]
        call _GetDateTemplate

        pop si
        call _GetNumber                                  ; get argument
        mov di, word ptr [ _parsedDatePtrs ][ bp ]
        mov word ptr ss:[ di ], dx                       ; store first argument

        cmp byte ptr [ si-1 ], '-'
        jz  _date_28
        cmp byte ptr [ si-1 ], '/'
        jz  _date_28
        cmp byte ptr [ si-1 ], '.'
        jnz _dateInvalid                                 ; else invalid ->

_date_28:
        call _GetNumber                                  ; get argument
        mov di, word ptr [ _parsedDatePtrs + 2 ][ bp ]
        mov word ptr ss:[ di ], dx                       ; store second argument

        cmp byte ptr [ si-1 ], '-'
        jz  _date_32
        cmp byte ptr [ si-1 ], '/'
        jz  _date_32
        cmp byte ptr [ si-1 ], '.'
        jnz _dateInvalid                                 ; else invalid ->

_date_32:
        call _GetNumber                                  ; get last argument
        mov di, word ptr [ _parsedDatePtrs + 4 ][ bp ]
        mov word ptr ss:[ di ], dx                       ; store third argument

;- - - - - - - - - - - - - - - - - - - - - - - - - - - - - - - -
;  parse Year
;- - - - - - - - - - - - - - - - - - - - - - - - - - - - - - - -
        mov ax, word ptr [ _parsedDate. _YEAR ][ bp ]    ; start of buffer
        cmp ax, 1980                                     ; greater than 1980 ?
        jnc _date_42                                     ; valid ->
        cmp ax, 80                                       ; less than 80 ?
        jnc _date_36                                     ;
        add ax, 2000                                     ; must be between 2000 - 2099

_date_36:
        cmp ax, 100                                      ; between 80 and 100 ?
```

```
        jnc _date_38                                    ; no ->
        add ax, 1900

_date_38:
        cmp ax, 1980
        jc _dateInvalid                                 ; if invalid ->
        cmp ax, 2100
        jnc _dateInvalid                                ; if invalid ->

_date_42:
        mov cx, ax                                      ; year
        mov dh, byte ptr [ _parsedDate. _MONTH ][ bp ]  ; month
        mov dl, byte ptr [ _parsedDate. _DAY   ][ bp ]  ; day
        Int21 SetDate
        or al, al                                       ; date valid ?
        jnz _dateInvalid                                ; no ->

;- - - - - - - - - - - - - - - - - - - - - - - - - - - - - - - - -
;  return
;- - - - - - - - - - - - - - - - - - - - - - - - - - - - - - - - -
_dateReturn:
        Return


;- - - - - - - - - - - - - - - - - - - - - - - - - - - - - - - - -
;  invalid date
;- - - - - - - - - - - - - - - - - - - - - - - - - - - - - - - - -
_dateInvalid:
        mov dx, offset CmndError_InvalidDate
        call DisplayLine
        jmp _date_12

        ;'''''''''''''''''''''''''''''''''''''''''''''''''''''''''';
        ;  Get International Date Template                        ;
        ;- - - - - - - - - - - - - - - - - - - - - - - - - - - - -;
        ;                                                        ;
        ;  Usage:                                                ;
        ;  si    pointer to DayMonthYear buffer                  ;
        ;  di    pointer to DayMonthYear array of pointers to be ;
        ;            returned.                                   ;
        ;........................................................;


_GetDateTemplate:
        Entry
        def _DayMonthYear, si
        def _DayMonthYearPtrs, di

        mov word ptr ss:[ di ], si
        mov word ptr ss:[ di + 2 ], si
        mov word ptr ss:[ di + 4 ], si                  ; initialize pointers to base

;- - - - - - - - - - - - - - - - - - - - - - - - - - - - - - - - -
;  scan date template
;- - - - - - - - - - - - - - - - - - - - - - - - - - - - - - - - -
        call returnDateTimeTemplate
```

```
        xor bx, bx                              ; argument order
        getarg di, _DayMonthYearPtrs            ; start with arg array

_GetDateTemplate_14:
        lodsw                                   ; get characters
        Goto 'd', _GetDateTemplate_Day          ; if day    ->
        Goto 'm', _GetDateTemplate_Month        ; if month  ->
        Goto 'y', _GetDateTemplate_Year         ; if year   ->
        jmp short _GetDateTemplate_Done

_GetDateTemplate_Day:
        add word ptr ss:[ di + bx ], _DAY
        jmp short _GetDateTemplate_SkipToSeparator

_GetDateTemplate_Month:
        add word ptr ss:[ di + bx ], _MONTH
        jmp short _GetDateTemplate_SkipToSeparator

_GetDateTemplate_Year:
        add word ptr ss:[ di + bx ], _YEAR
      ; jmp short _GetDateTemplate_SkipToSeparator

;- - - - - - - - - - - - - - - - - - - - - - - - - - - - - -
;  skip to next argument
;- - - - - - - - - - - - - - - - - - - - - - - - - - - - - -
_GetDateTemplate_SkipToSeparator:
        lodsb
        or al, al                               ; end of string ?
        jz _GetDateTemplate_Done                ; yes, done ->
        cmp al, 'a'                             ; none text ?
        jnc _GetDateTemplate_SkipToSeparator    ; still on text ->

        inc bx
        inc bx                                  ; advance reference pointer
        jmp _GetDateTemplate_14                 ; continue ->

;- - - - - - - - - - - - - - - - - - - - - - - - - - - - - -
; done
;- - - - - - - - - - - - - - - - - - - - - - - - - - - - - -
_GetDateTemplate_Done:

        Return

        ;'''''''''''''''''''''''''''''''''''''''''''''''''''''''''''';
        ;  Display Get Date Prompt                                  ;
        ;...........................................................;

DisplayPleaseEnterDate:
        mov dx, offset _PleaseEnterDate
        call DisplayLine

        mov dl, '('
        Int21 DisplayOutput
```

```
        call returnDateTimeTemplate
        mov cx, bx
        sub cx, si                                      ; length of string.
        dec cx

DisplayPleaseEnterDate_08:
        lodsb
        mov dl, al
        Int21 DisplayOutput
        loop DisplayPleaseEnterDate_08

        mov dl, ')'
        Int21 DisplayOutput
        mov dl, ':'
        Int21 DisplayOutput
        mov dl, ' '
        Int21 DisplayOutput

        ret

        ;''''''''''''''''''''''''''''''''''''''''''''''''''''''''''''';
        ;  Find International Date /Time Template                     ;
        ;- - - - - - - - - - - - - - - - - - - - - - - - - - - - - -;
        ;                                                            ;
        ;  Returns:                                                  ;
        ;  si      pointer to Date Template                          ;
        ;  bx      pointer to Time Template                          ;
        ;  ax      country code                                      ;
        ;............................................................;

returnDateTimeTemplate:
        Entry
        def _countryCode
        def _dateTemplate
        def _timeTemplate
        defbytes _countryInfo, sizeCOUNTRYINFO

        push di
        lea dx, offset [ _countryInfo ][ bp ]
        Int21 CountryDependentInfo, 00                  ; get country info
        mov word ptr [ _countryCode ][ bp ], bx         ; save value.

;- - - - - - - - - - - - - - - - - - - - - - - - - - - - - - - - -
;  locate international template
;- - - - - - - - - - - - - - - - - - - - - - - - - - - - - - - - -
        mov di, offset RxDOSIntl_DateTimeTable

returnTemplate_08:
        inc di
        inc di
        cmp bx, word ptr [ di - 2 ]                     ; is it current entry ?
        jz returnTemplate_12                            ; yes ->

        mov cx, -1
```

```
        xor ax, ax
        repnz scasb                                 ; scan for null terminator

        cmp word ptr [ di ], 0000                   ; end of table ?
        jnz returnTemplate_08                       ; no, continue looking ->

        mov di, offset RxDOSIntl_DateTimeTable      ; assume USA if no valid entry

;- - - - - - - - - - - - - - - - - - - - - - - - - - - - - - - - - -
; compute time template
;- - - - - - - - - - - - - - - - - - - - - - - - - - - - - - - - - -
returnTemplate_12:
        storarg _dateTemplate, di

        mov al, ' '
        mov cx, -1
        repnz scasb                                 ; search for space delimeter

        mov bx, di                                  ; time template address
        getarg si, _dateTemplate                    ; date template address
        getarg ax, _countrycode                     ; country code

        pop di
        Return
```

Delete

The delete command expects a single argument. If more or fewer arguments are passed to the function, an error message is displayed. The delete function utilizes DOS function 41h, the pathname DOS delete function. It, unfortunately, does not support wild characters in the filename, so the same support is provided by the Find First/Delete Loop within the command service routine.

The first part of the delete function uses the information supplied by the DOS Find First function to detect whether the argument passed with the command comprises entirely wild characters. The function fills the FIND data structure with a search mask in the FCB-style format. If these 11 characters are filled with question marks, the request is to delete all files. If this is the case, a message is displayed.

```
        All files in directory will be deleted!
        Are you sure (Y/N)?
```

The second part of the delete routine begins by using the Find First function to determine if a file exists that can be deleted. If it does, the pathname is expanded into a work area using the undocumented DOS function Get Actual File Name. Calling this function will not take the filename that was returned by the Find First function and create an expanded name. It will take the command argument and expand it, including all wild characters. The string produced by this expansion is scanned backward to the last directory name. The actual name of the file to be deleted is then appended to the expanded name. The resulting name can then be used with the DOS Delete file function. It contains a fully expanded filename and no wild characters.

The code loops through the directory locating the next available file to delete. When there are no additional files to delete, the code determines whether any files were deleted; if there weren't, it displays a message.

```
(in rxdoscmd.asm)
        ;'''''''''''''''''''''''''''''''''''''''''''''''''''''''''''''''';
        ;  Delete filename                                               ;
        ;- - - - - - - - - - - - - - - - - - - - - - - - - - - - - - - -;
        ;                                                                ;
        ;  Usage:                                                        ;
        ;    ss:di  Arg Array                                            ;
        ;    ax     Number of arguments in array                        ;
        ;................................................................;

_Delete:
        Entry
        def __argarray, di
        def _nfiles, 0000
        def _filename
        defbytes _expandedname, 128

        call CheckOneArg
        jnc _Delete_06                          ; arguments wrong ->

        mov dx, offset CmndError_FileNameMissing
        call DisplayErrorMessage
        Return


;- - - - - - - - - - - - - - - - - - - - - - - - - - - - - - - - -
;  delete all files ?
;- - - - - - - - - - - - - - - - - - - - - - - - - - - - - - - - -
_Delete_06:
        mov dx, word ptr [ di ]                 ; point to filename arg
        storarg _filename, dx                   ; save pointer

        xor cx, cx
        getarg dx, _filename                    ; get filename pointer
        Int21 FindFirstFile                     ; does file exist ?
        jc _Delete_36                           ; no more ->

        mov al, '?'
        mov cx, sizeFILENAME
        mov di, offset [ RxDOS_DTA. findSrchName ]  ; expanded fcb match name
        repz scasb                              ; *.* field ?
        jnz _Delete_16                          ; no, proceed ->

_Delete_08:
        mov dx, offset _DeleteAllFiles
        call DisplayLine                        ; display line

        Int21 ConsoleInputNoEcho                ; read keyboard
        call _upperCase

        push ax
```

```
        call CRLF
        pop ax
        cmp al, "Y"                              ; if Yes —>
        jz _Delete_16
        cmp al, "N"                              ; repeat if not right —>
        jnz _Delete_08
        jmp short _Delete_42                     ; else, its No —>

;- - - - - - - - - - - - - - - - - - - - - - - - - - - - - - - -
;  try to locate file (s)
;- - - - - - - - - - - - - - - - - - - - - - - - - - - - - - - -
_Delete_16:
        xor cx, cx                               ; files only
        getarg dx, _filename                     ; get filename pointer
        Int21 FindFirstFile                      ; does file exist ?
        jc _Delete_36                            ; no more —>

        getarg si, _filename                     ; get filename pointer
        lea di, offset [ _expandedname ][ bp ]
        Int21 GetActualFileName                  ; expand name
        jc _Delete_36                            ; can't resolve name —>

        lea di, offset [ _expandedname ][ bp ]
        push ss
        push di
        call _stringLength
        add di, cx

_Delete_20:
        cmp byte ptr ss:[ di - 1 ], '\'
        jz _Delete_22
        dec di
        loop _Delete_20

_Delete_22:
        mov si, offset [ RxDOS_DTA. findFileName ]   ; current name
        call _copyString                         ; append directory name

        lea dx, offset [ _expandedname ][ bp ]
        Int21 DeleteFile                         ; delete file
        inc word ptr [ _nfiles ][ bp ]
        jmp _Delete_16

;- - - - - - - - - - - - - - - - - - - - - - - - - - - - - - - -
;  try to locate file
;- - - - - - - - - - - - - - - - - - - - - - - - - - - - - - - -
_Delete_36:
        cmp word ptr [ _nfiles ][ bp ], 0000     ; any files deleted ?
        jnz _Delete_42                           ; yes —>

        mov dx, offset CmndError_NoFilesFound
        call DisplayErrorMessage

_Delete_42:
        Return
```

Dir

Recently in the history of DOS, the directory command underwent some radical improvements. The command can now perform subdirectory search for every occurrence of files (the /S switch), display files with selected attributes (the /A switch), order files for display purposes (the /O switch), and display files in lowercase mode (the /L switch). One additional feature of the directory command displays the compression ratios of files.

Interesting and useful as these features are, the directory command in RxDOS supports only the very basic directory display. The files in a directory are displayed in the traditional columnar sequence together with its size and date. It's the traditional directory display, as follows:

```
Volume in drive C is MIKEPAPI
Volume Serial Number is 1ACE-73BC
Directory of C:\RXDOS

RXDOSBIO ASM     55597 04-03-94    9:11p
RXDOSCCB ASM     21903 03-28-94   12:34a
RXDOSCPY ASM     29616 12-31-93   10:57p
RXDOSDEV ASM     75149 06-12-94    5:50p
        4 file(s)      182265 bytes
                     36519936 bytes free
```

To support some of the more elaborate directory features, a directory command function with a different design should be employed. To support sorting, for example, the directory entries must be read into memory from where they can be sorted. The directory can be displayed from the resulting sorted list. The list would have to be saved in additional memory that's allocated by DOS.

Whether or not the directory is to be sorted, the directory is read using the Find First and Find Next functions. These functions fill a FINDENTRY block in the current disk transfer address area for each file found. The attributes are examined, and the contents of the entry are displayed. To format each line, a local variation of the C function library function, sprintf, is used. This function accepts a line that contains embedded format parameters, such as %s and %d, to insert string and decimal values. As the directory is processed, the number of files, the amount of disk space used by these files, and the amount of disk free space are added and displayed at the end of the directory listing.

The command line argument for a directory command cannot, unfortunately, simply be used on an as-is basis. The argument may contain only the drive letter and colon or it may only contain the name of a subdirectory. In both of these cases and the case where no argument is supplied at all, the *.* term needs to be added to the argument. The code begins by trying to determine in which cases the argument needs to be altered. The logic is not straightforward or easily readable.

The code begins by first retrieving the get current and max available drive values. If the argument is missing altogether or contains only a drive, detected by the presence of a colon (:) in the argument, the *.* term is appended. The commands dir and dir c: become dir *.* and dir c:*.*, respectively. Next, the GetActualFileName function, the undocumented DOS function, is used to retrieve the fully expanded filename.

This expanded filename is a big help since it contains the full current directory path for the selected drive, including if the drive is the current drive. However, the last term of the expanded name may point to a file or a directory. The expanded filename is split between the drive term, the known directories in the pathname, and what it presumes to be a filename and extension, if any. The filename is tested in the current directory to determine if it is a directory name. The exact expanded filename is then constructed. If the last name pointed to a directory, the *.* term is added.

The directory command can now begin. Unless no header is desired, the volume label is read from disk. Depending on whether a volume label is found or not, the address of one of the following two messages is pushed on the stack, together with its requisite arguments. Notice the %s and %d arguments in the display messages.

```
_Dir_NoVolumeLabel:     asciz " Volume in drive %c has no label", 13, 10
_Dir_VolumeLabel:       asciz " Volume in drive %c is %s", 13, 10
```

The messages are formatted, not displayed, by the _sprintf function. It expects the number of arguments on the stack to correspond to the number of arguments it finds in the format string. It also expects a pointer to the format string and a pointer to an output buffer. The buffer must be large enough to support the resulting display line. No checks are made for buffer overflow. In addition, none of the arguments are removed from the stack. However, it does return the number of arguments it has processed in the AX register. The processed arguments can be removed from the stack, as in the example shown. The function also returns the address of the formatted display output in the ES:SI register pair.

```
    push                    ; argument n
    push                    ; argument n-1
    ...
    push                    ; argument 2
    push                    ; argument 1
    push                    ; format line address
    push                    ; print buffer address
    call _sprintf           ; format line
    add sp, ax              ; remove excess arguments from stack
```

Each file display line is formatted by one of the following two format lines, depending on whether the entry to be displayed is a file or a directory. However, unlike the equivalent C function, numbers are always right justified.

```
_Dir_FileEntry:     db "%8s %3s %9ld %s   %s", 13, 10, 0
_Dir_DirEntry:      db "%8s %3s <DIR>    %s   %s", 13, 10, 0
```

The general format of a replaceable argument is in the form %nlx, where n is an optional field size argument, l is used when a long argument is pushed on the stack, and x is an argument type. The only types supported are c, d, and s, for character, decimal value, and string. Numbers, displayed in decimal value fields, are always right-justified if there is a field size.

The remainder of the directory routine begins with a FindFirstFile DOS function call. This retrieves the first file to be displayed, if any. Its date and time fields are converted to strings, and the arguments are pushed on the stack and formatted for display. The arguments and format used depend on whether the entry is a file or a directory entry. The routine continues to search for additional directory entries using the FindNextFile function.

As the directory entries were displayed, the number of entries and their size have been summed and are finally displayed at the end of the command, together with the amount of free disk space.

```
(in rxdosdir.asm)
        ;''''''''''''''''''''''''''''''''''''''''''''''''''''''''''''''';
        ;  Directory                                                    ;
        ;- - - - - - - - - - - - - - - - - - - - - - - - - - - - - - -;
        ;                                                               ;
        ;  Usage:                                                       ;
        ;    ss:di  Arg Array                                           ;
        ;    ax     Number of arguments in array                        ;
        ;...............................................................;

_Dir:
        Entry
        def  _currdisk
        def  _maxdisk
        def  _filesread
        def _extensionFlag
        ddef _freespace
        ddef _totalfilespace
        def __argarray, di                            ; arg array

        defbytes _asciiFileTime, 20
        defbytes _asciiFileDate, 20
        defbytes _pathname, 128                        ; search pathname
        defbytes _filename, 128                        ; search filename
        defbytes _expandedname, sizeExpandedName
        defbytes _printbuffer, 128

        xor ax, ax
        mov word ptr [ _filesread ][ bp ], ax
        mov word ptr [ _totalfilespace. _low  ][ bp ], ax
        mov word ptr [ _totalfilespace. _high ][ bp ], ax

        mov cx, 0000                                   ; min args
        mov dx, 0001                                   ; max args
        mov bx, offset _DirSwitches                    ; dir switches
        call PreProcessCmndLine                        ; process switches and args
        ifc _dir_86                                    ; if error ->

        mov ax, word ptr [ _DirPauseSwitch. swFlags ]
        call setPagingMode

;- - - - - - - - - - - - - - - - - - - - - - - - - - - - - - - - - -
; get current, max disks
;- - - - - - - - - - - - - - - - - - - - - - - - - - - - - - - - - -
        Int21 CurrentDisk                              ; get current disk
        mov dl, al
        inc al                                         ; a=1, ...
        storarg _currdisk, ax                          ; save disk letter

        Int21 SelectDisk                               ; use select disk to get max
        storarg _maxdisk, ax                           ; save max disk letter
```

```
;- - - - - - - - - - - - - - - - - - - - - - - - - - - - - - - -
; if no args, create a *.* arg
;- - - - - - - - - - - - - - - - - - - - - - - - - - - - - - - -
        mov di, word ptr [ __argarray ][ bp ]
        mov si, word ptr [ di ]                    ; locate dir argument
        or si, si                                  ; no name provided ?
        jnz _dir_06                                ; name provided ->
        mov si, offset RxDOS_AllFiles              ; dummy path

_dir_06:
        lea di, offset [ _pathname ][ bp ]
        call _CopyString                           ; copy whatever was entered

_dir_08:
        dec di                                     ; back up over null
        cmp byte ptr [ di-1 ], ' '                 ; only entered drive and colon ?
        jz _dir_08                                 ; no ->
        cmp byte ptr [ di-1 ], ':'                 ; only entered drive and colon ?
        jnz _dir_10                                ; no ->

        mov si, offset RxDOS_AllFiles              ; dummy path
        call _CopyString                           ; append all files

;- - - - - - - - - - - - - - - - - - - - - - - - - - - - - - - -
; is name a directory ?
;- - - - - - - - - - - - - - - - - - - - - - - - - - - - - - - -
_dir_10:
        lea si, offset [ _pathname ][ bp ]
        lea di, offset [ _expandedname ][ bp ]
        call _splitpath

        mov al, byte ptr [ _expandedname. expExtension ][ bp ]
        mov byte ptr [ _extensionFlag ][ bp ], al  ; save extension present flag

        lea si, offset [ _pathname ][ bp ]
        lea di, offset [ _filename ][ bp ]
        mov word ptr [ di ], '\'                    ; init area
        Int21 GetActualFileName                    ; expand name
        jnc _dir_16                                ; if valid ->
        call _CopyString                           ; if error, use original

_dir_16:
        lea si, offset [ _filename ][ bp ]
        lea di, offset [ _expandedname ][ bp ]
        call _splitpath
        jnz _dir_28                                ; if wild characters found ->

        mov cx, ATTR_DIRECTORY
        lea dx, offset [ _filename ][ bp ]
        Int21 FindFirstFile                        ; locate file

;- - - - - - - - - - - - - - - - - - - - - - - - - - - - - - - -
; if . or .. handle special
;- - - - - - - - - - - - - - - - - - - - - - - - - - - - - - - -
```

```
_dir_20:
        jc _dir_28                                        ; not found, try expanding ->

        test byte ptr [ RxDOS_DTA. findFileAttribute ], ATTR_DIRECTORY
        jz _dir_28                                        ; if a directory, add \*.*  ->

        cmp byte ptr [ RxDOS_DTA. findFileName ], '.'
        jnz _dir_22

        Int21 FindNextFile                                ; locate next file
        jmp _dir_20                                       ; see if also a dir ->

;- - - - - - - - - - - - - - - - - - - - - - - - - - - - - - - - - - -
;  if a directory name, change to include *.* for all files
;- - - - - - - - - - - - - - - - - - - - - - - - - - - - - - - - - - -
_dir_22:
        lea si, offset [ _expandedname. expFilename ][ bp ]
        lea di, offset [ _expandedname. expPath     ][ bp ]
        call _AppendPathName                              ; append pathname

        lea si, offset [ _expandedname. expExtension ][ bp ]
        call _CopyString                                  ; append to pathname

        mov byte ptr [ _expandedname. expExtension ][ bp ], 00

        mov si, offset [ RxDOS_AllFiles ]
        lea di, offset [ _expandedname. expFilename ][ bp ]
        call _CopyString
        jmp _dir_36                                       ; if none, ok to make path

;- - - - - - - - - - - - - - - - - - - - - - - - - - - - - - - - - - -
;  is name is not a directory
;- - - - - - - - - - - - - - - - - - - - - - - - - - - - - - - - - - -
_dir_28:
        lea di, offset [ _expandedname. expFilename ][ bp ]
        cmp byte ptr [ di ], 00
        jnz _dir_32
        mov word ptr [ di ], '*'

_dir_32:
        lea di, offset [ _expandedname. expExtension ][ bp ]
        mov al, byte ptr [ _extensionFlag ][ bp ]         ; extension required
        or al, byte ptr [ di ]                            ; or extension provided
        jnz _dir_36                                       ; if either ->
        mov word ptr [ di ], '*.'
        mov byte ptr [ di+2 ], 0

;- - - - - - - - - - - - - - - - - - - - - - - - - - - - - - - - - - -
;  rebuild and edit name
;- - - - - - - - - - - - - - - - - - - - - - - - - - - - - - - - - - -
_dir_36:
        lea si, offset [ _expandedname ][ bp ]
        lea di, offset [ _pathname ][ bp ]
        call _makePath
```

```
        lea si, offset [ _pathname ][ bp ]
        lea di, offset [ _filename ][ bp ]
        mov word ptr [ di ], '\'                         ; init area
        Int21 GetActualFileName                          ; expand name
        jnc _dir_38                                      ; if ok ->

        lea si, offset [ _pathname ][ bp ]
        lea di, offset [ _filename ][ bp ]
        call _CopyString

;- - - - - - - - - - - - - - - - - - - - - - - - - - - - - - - - - - - -
; extract drive letter
;- - - - - - - - - - - - - - - - - - - - - - - - - - - - - - - - - - - -
_dir_38:
        lea di, offset [ _filename ][ bp ]
        cmp byte ptr [ di+1 ], ':'
        jnz _dir_42

        xor ah, ah
        mov al, byte ptr [ di ]
        mov word ptr [ _currdisk ][ bp ], ax             ; save current disk

;- - - - - - - - - - - - - - - - - - - - - - - - - - - - - - - - - - - -
; display header
;- - - - - - - - - - - - - - - - - - - - - - - - - - - - - - - - - - - -
_dir_42:
        test word ptr [ _DirBareSwitch. swFlags ], SW_SWITCHSET
        jnz _dir_52                                      ; skip header ->

        mov bx, offset _Dir_NoVolumeLabel                ; assume no volume label
        mov al, byte ptr [ _currdisk ][ bp ]             ; get current disk value
        call returnVolumeName                            ; get volume for drive
        ifc _dirError                                    ; cannot open drive ->
        jnz _dir_44                                      ; if no volume name ->

        push di                                          ; save vol label pointer
        mov bx, offset _Dir_VolumeLabel                  ; print statement format

_dir_44:
        lea di, offset [ _currdisk ][ bp ]               ; pointer to current disk
        push di                                          ; current disk
        push bx                                          ; format
        lea di, offset [ _printbuffer ][ bp ]
        push di
        call _sprintf
        add sp, ax                                       ; # args passed
        call DisplayLine

;- - - - - - - - - - - - - - - - - - - - - - - - - - - - - - - - - - - -
; display drive: path
;- - - - - - - - - - - - - - - - - - - - - - - - - - - - - - - - - - - -
        lea si, offset [ _filename ][ bp ]
        lea di, offset [ _pathname ][ bp ]
        call _copyString                                 ; copy to pathname
```

```
_dir_48:
        dec di
        cmp byte ptr [ di ], '\'                       ; isolate path
        jnz _dir_48

        mov byte ptr [ di ], 0

        lea di, offset [ _pathname ][ bp ]
        push di                                        ; first arg encountered

        mov di, offset _Dir_DirectoryOf
        push di
        lea di, offset [ _printbuffer ][ bp ]
        push di
        call _sprintf
        add sp, ax                                     ; # args passed
        call DisplayLine

;- - - - - - - - - - - - - - - - - - - - - - - - - - - - - - - - - -
;  scan through files
;- - - - - - - - - - - - - - - - - - - - - - - - - - - - - - - - - -
_dir_52:
        mov cx, ATTR_DIRECTORY
        lea dx, offset [ _filename ][ bp ]             ; pointer to search filename
        Int21 FindFirstFile                            ; locate file
        ifc _dir_72                                    ; if none located ->

_dir_54:
        inc word ptr [ _filesread ][ bp ]             ; files read

        mov ax, word ptr [ RxDOS_DTA. findFileTime ]
        lea di, offset [ _asciiFileTime ][ bp ]
        call _dirTimeToAscii
        push di

        mov ax, word ptr [ RxDOS_DTA. findFileDate ]
        lea di, offset [ _asciiFileDate ][ bp ]
        call _dirDateToAscii
        push di

        test byte ptr [ RxDOS_DTA. findFileAttribute ], ATTR_DIRECTORY
        ifnz _dir_60                                   ; if a directory ->

        mov di, offset [ RxDOS_DTA. findFileSize ]
        mov ax, word ptr [ _low  ][ di ]
        mov dx, word ptr [ _high ][ di ]
        add word ptr [ _totalfilespace. _low  ][ bp ], ax
        adc word ptr [ _totalfilespace. _high ][ bp ], dx

        push di                                        ; third arg: file size

_dir_60:
        mov di, offset [ RxDOS_DTA. findFileName ]     ; locate extension
        mov al, byte ptr [ di ]                        ; start of filename
```

```
        call _endofString                                 ; point to null terminator

        push di                                           ; terminator, in case no extension
        cmp al, '.'                                       ; filename either . or .. ?
        jz _dir_64                                        ; yes, no need for extension ->

        mov al, '.'
        mov cx, offset [ RxDOS_DTA. findFileName ]        ; search length
        xchg di, cx                                       ; determine search length
        sub cx, di                                        ; search length
        repnz scasb                                       ; else scan for extension
        jnz _dir_64                                       ; if found, di points to extension
        mov byte ptr [ di-1 ], 0                          ; else, di points to null
        pop ax
        push di                                           ; extension address, if found

_dir_64:
        mov di, offset [ RxDOS_DTA. findFileName ]
        push di                                           ; pointer to filename

        mov di, offset _Dir_FileEntry
        test byte ptr [ RxDOS_DTA. findFileAttribute ], ATTR_DIRECTORY
        ifz _dir_66                                       ; if not a directory ->

        mov di, offset _Dir_DirEntry

_dir_66:
        push di
        lea di, offset [ _printbuffer ][ bp ]
        push di
        call _sprintf
        add sp, ax                                        ; # args passed

        test word ptr [ _DirLowerCaseSwitch. swFlags ], SW_SWITCHSET
        jz _dir_68                                        ; not lowercase option ->
        push ss
        push si                                           ; where string
        call _lowerCaseString                             ; lowercase string

_dir_68:
        call DisplayLine                                  ; print line

        Int21 FindNextFile                                ; locate next file
        ifnc _dir_54                                      ; if none located ->

;- - - - - - - - - - - - - - - - - - - - - - - - - - - - - - - - - - -
;  print number of files
;- - - - - - - - - - - - - - - - - - - - - - - - - - - - - - - - - - -
_dir_72:
        cmp word ptr [ _filesread ][ bp ], 0000           ; any files read ?
        jnz _dir_76                                        ; yes ->
```

```
        mov dx, offset CmndError_NoFilesFound
        call DisplayLine                              ; file not found
        jmp short _dir_86

;- - - - - - - - - - - - - - - - - - - - - - - - - - - - - - - - - - - -
;  display files, space used, space free
;- - - - - - - - - - - - - - - - - - - - - - - - - - - - - - - - - - - -
_dir_76:
        mov dl, byte ptr [ _expandedName. expDrive ][ bp ]
        and dl, 15                                    ; drive
        Int21 GetFreeDiskSpace

        mul cx                                        ; total space
        mul bx
        stordarg _freespace, dx, ax

        lea di, offset [ _freespace ][ bp ]
        push di
        lea di, offset [ _totalfilespace ][ bp ]
        push di
        lea di, offset [ _filesread ][ bp ]
        push di

        mov di, offset _Dir_Files
        push di
        lea di, offset [ _printbuffer ][ bp ]
        push di     ___
        call _sprintf
        add sp, ax                                    ; # args passed
        call DisplayLine                              ; print line

;- - - - - - - - - - - - - - - - - - - - - - - - - - - - - - - - - - - -
;  done
;- - - - - - - - - - - - - - - - - - - - - - - - - - - - - - - - - - - -
_dir_86:
        Return

;- - - - - - - - - - - - - - - - - - - - - - - - - - - - - - - - - - - -
;  if error
;- - - - - - - - - - - - - - - - - - - - - - - - - - - - - - - - - - - -
_dirError:
        mov dx, offset CmndError_InvalidDrive
        call DisplayErrorMessage                      ; display message
        Return
```

The _sprintf function is listed next. It creates the formatted output statement by scanning and copying the contents of the input format string. When it encounters a control identifier, represented by the % symbol, it reads and processes through the arguments it may encounter. For example, a control identifier may be followed by a field length number, or the letter l, representing a long number. Once one of the format codes is reached, that is, another % or an s, d, x, or c, the code dispatches to handler code. That code fetches the next argument value or address from the stack and is formatted or copied to the output format.

To format and display a number, a field is initialized to blanks in the output string. The field size was defined by the format command. The decimal value is taken from the argument on the stack, converted to ascii, and right-justified within the blanked field.

For a string field, the field size is blanked, the address of the string is retrieved from the stack, and the string is copied to the output string.

The routine is listed here.

```
(in rxdosdir.asm)
        ;'''''''''''''''''''''''''''''''''''''''''''''''''''''''''''';
        ;  Scan Print Buffer                                         ;
        ;- - - - - - - - - - - - - - - - - - - - - - - - - - - - - -;
        ;                                                            ;
        ;  This routine accepts a variable number of arguments and for- ;
        ;  mats an output buffer.  It works very similar to C's sprintf ;
        ;  function.                                                 ;
        ;                                                            ;
        ;  The input buffer may contain embedded formatting codes:   ;
        ;                                                            ;
        ;  %c     insert character (pointer to character on stack)   ;
        ;  %s     insert string   (pointer to string on stack)       ;
        ;  %d     insert decimal  (pointer to decimal on stack)      ;
        ;  %ld    insert long     (pointer to long on stack)         ;
        ;                                                            ;
        ;  If a format command contains numbers, the number is inter- ;
        ;  preted as a field width.  The output value will be right- ;
        ;  aligned within the field width if the width is preceded   ;
        ;  with a negative sign.  Any character that exceeds the field ;
        ;  width is ignored.                                         ;
        ;                                                            ;
        ;  If a format command contains a comma, the number will be  ;
        ;  decimal edited.                                           ;
        ;- - - - - - - - - - - - - - - - - - - - - - - - - - - - - -;
        ;                                                            ;
        ;  Usage:                                                    ;
        ;    stack   argument                                        ;
        ;      .     argument                                        ;
        ;      .     argument                                        ;
        ;    stack   argument                                        ;
        ;    stack   format buffer                                   ;
        ;    stack   output buffer                                   ;
        ;                                                            ;
        ;  Returns:                                                  ;
        ;    dx      pointer to output buffer                        ;
        ;............................................................;

_sprintf:
        Entry 2
        arg _format
        arg _output
        def _args, 0000
        def _varg
        def _fieldwidth
        def _fieldflags
```

```
;- - - - - - - - - - - - - - - - - - - - - - - - - -
;   scan/copy buffer
;- - - - - - - - - - - - - - - - - - - - - - - - - -
        lea di, word ptr [ _format ][ bp ]
        add di, 2                           ; point to prev arg
        storarg _varg, di                   ; save var arg pointer

        mov si, word ptr [ _format ][ bp ]
        mov di, word ptr [ _output ][ bp ]

_sprintf_06:
        mov word ptr [ _fieldwidth ][ bp ], 0000    ; no width
        mov word ptr [ _fieldflags ][ bp ], 0000    ; no flags

_sprintf_08:
        lodsb                               ; get character
        stosb                               ; copy to output
        or al, al                           ; all done ?
        ifz _sprintf_86                     ; yes -->

        cmp al, '%'                         ; format code ?
        jnz _sprintf_08                     ; not yet -->


;- - - - - - - - - - - - - - - - - - - - - - - - - -
;   format code
;- - - - - - - - - - - - - - - - - - - - - - - - - -
        mov word ptr [ _fieldwidth ][ bp ], 0000    ; no width
        mov word ptr [ _fieldflags ][ bp ], 0000    ; no flags

        dec di                              ; kill format % in output
        mov byte ptr [ di ], 0              ; stick a null code there

_sprintf_12:
        lodsb                               ; get character that follows
        call _lowerCase                     ; make it lowercase

        or al, al                           ; all done ?
        ifz _sprintf_86                     ; yes -->

;- - - - - - - - - - - - - - - - - - - - - - - - - -
;   is it long ?
;- - - - - - - - - - - - - - - - - - - - - - - - - -
        cmp al, 'l'                         ; long flag ?
        jnz _sprintf_14                     ; no -->
        or word ptr [ _fieldflags ][ bp ], SPRINTF_LONGFLAG
        jmp _sprintf_12

;- - - - - - - - - - - - - - - - - - - - - - - - - -
;   is it a left-justify?
;- - - - - - - - - - - - - - - - - - - - - - - - - -
_sprintf_14:
        cmp al, '-'                         ; left-justify
        jnz _sprintf_16                     ; no -->
        or word ptr [ _fieldflags ][ bp ], SPRINTF_LEFTALIGN
```

```
            jmp _sprintf_12

;- - - - - - - - - - - - - - - - - - - - - - - - - - - - - - -
;  is it a comma (decimal) delimeter ?
;- - - - - - - - - - - - - - - - - - - - - - - - - - - - - - -
_sprintf_16:
            cmp al, ','                             ; decimal delimeter ?
            jnz _sprintf_18                         ; no —>
            or word ptr [ _fieldflags ][ bp ], SPRINTF_COMMADELIM
            jmp _sprintf_12

;- - - - - - - - - - - - - - - - - - - - - - - - - - - - - - -
;  is it a field width ?
;- - - - - - - - - - - - - - - - - - - - - - - - - - - - - - -
_sprintf_18:
            cmp al, '9'+1                           ; number ?
            jnc _sprintf_22                         ; no —>
            cmp al, '0'                             ; number ?
            jc _sprintf_22                          ; no —>

            and ax, 15                              ; get number
            mov dx, word ptr [ _fieldwidth ][ bp ]  ; get width
            add dx, dx                              ; x2
            add dx, dx                              ; x4
            add dx, word ptr [ _fieldwidth ][ bp ]  ; x5
            add dx, dx                              ; x10
            add dx, ax
            mov word ptr [ _fieldwidth ][ bp ], dx
            jmp _sprintf_12

;- - - - - - - - - - - - - - - - - - - - - - - - - - - - - - -
;  see if its a valid formatting code
;- - - - - - - - - - - - - - - - - - - - - - - - - - - - - - -
_sprintf_22:
            cmp al, 'd'                             ; decimal output ?
            jz _sprintf_26
            cmp al, 'x'                             ; hex output ?
            jz _sprintf_26
            cmp al, 'c'                             ; character ?
            jz _sprintf_32
            cmp al, 's'                             ; string ?
            jz _sprintf_36
            cmp al, '%'                             ; percent percent ?
            jz _sprintf_46

            jmp _sprintf_06

;- - - - - - - - - - - - - - - - - - - - - - - - - - - - - - -
;  decimal
;- - - - - - - - - - - - - - - - - - - - - - - - - - - - - - -
_sprintf_26:
            push si
            getarg si, _varg                        ; get variable arg ptr
            mov si, word ptr [ si ]                 ; get argument pointer
```

```
        add word ptr [ _varg ][ bp ], 2
        inc word ptr [ _args ][ bp ]

        xor dx, dx
        mov ax, word ptr [ si ]                    ; get number
        test word ptr [ _fieldflags ][ bp ], SPRINTF_LONGFLAG
        jz _sprintf_28
        mov dx, word ptr [ si+2 ]                         ; get long

_sprintf_28:
        mov bx, word ptr [ _fieldflags ][ bp ]     ; flags
        mov cx, word ptr [ _fieldwidth ][ bp ]     ; width
        call _sprintfNum                           ; convert numeric to ascii

        pop si
        jmp _sprintf_06

;- - - - - - - - - - - - - - - - - - - - - - - - - - - - - - - -
; character
;- - - - - - - - - - - - - - - - - - - - - - - - - - - - - - - -
_sprintf_32:
        push si
        getarg si, _varg                           ; get variable arg ptr
        mov si, word ptr [ si ]                     ; get argument pointer
        add word ptr [ _varg ][ bp ], 2
        inc word ptr [ _args ][ bp ]

        mov cx, word ptr [ _fieldwidth ][ bp ]     ; width
        call _sprintfInitField

        mov al, byte ptr [ si ]
        stosb                                      ; store character

        pop si

        mov cx, word ptr [ _fieldwidth ][ bp ]     ; width
        or cx, cx
        ifz _sprintf_06

        dec cx
        call _sprintfPadField
        jmp _sprintf_06

;- - - - - - - - - - - - - - - - - - - - - - - - - - - - - - - -
; string
;- - - - - - - - - - - - - - - - - - - - - - - - - - - - - - - -
_sprintf_36:
        push si
        getarg si, _varg                           ; get variable arg ptr
        mov si, word ptr [ si ]                     ; get argument pointer
        add word ptr [ _varg ][ bp ], 2
        inc word ptr [ _args ][ bp ]

        mov cx, word ptr [ _fieldwidth ][ bp ]     ; width
        call _sprintfInitField
```

```
_sprintf_38:
        lodsb
        or al, al                                       ; null terminator ?
        jz _sprintf_40                                  ; yes ->
        stosb
        or cx, cx                                       ; fixed count ?
        jz _sprintf_38
        loop _sprintf_38

_sprintf_40:
        or cx, cx                                       ; still more length to go ?
        jz _sprintf_42                                  ; no ->
        add di, cx                                      ; advance field length

_sprintf_42:
        pop si
        jmp _sprintf_06


;- - - - - - - - - - - - - - - - - - - - - - - - - - - - - - - - -
;  %
;- - - - - - - - - - - - - - - - - - - - - - - - - - - - - - - - -
_sprintf_46:
        stosb
        jmp _sprintf_06


;- - - - - - - - - - - - - - - - - - - - - - - - - - - - - - - - -
;  all done
;- - - - - - - - - - - - - - - - - - - - - - - - - - - - - - - - -
_sprintf_86:
        mov ax, word ptr [ _args   ][ bp ]
        add ax, ax                                      ; # words left on stack
        mov si, word ptr [ _output ][ bp ]
        mov dx, si
        Return


        ;'''''''''''''''''''''''''''''''''''''''''''''''''''''''''''';
        ; Convert Long (dx:ax) to Ascii                             ;
        ;- - - - - - - - - - - - - - - - - - - - - - - - - - - - - -;
        ;                                                           ;
        ; Usage:                                                    ;
        ;   dx:ax  long value                                       ;
        ;   cx     size of field to right justify                   ;
        ;   bx     display option flags:                            ;
        ;          8000  insert decimal commas                      ;
        ;                                                           ;
        ;...........................................................;

_sprintfNum:
        Entry
        defbytes _decDisplay, 16
        def _decimalflag, bx
        def _fieldwidth, cx
        def _spacing
```

```
            push si
            push di
            call _sprintfInitField                      ; init field to spaces
            mov byte ptr [ _spacing ][ bp ], 03         ; set spacing

            lea di, offset [ _decDisplay ][ bp ]
            push di

_sprintfNum_08:
            mov cx, 10
            call _div32                                 ; divide by 10
            or cl, '0'
            mov byte ptr [ di ], cl                     ; store character
            inc di

            mov cx, dx
            or cx, ax                                   ; more to go ?
            jz _sprintfNum_10                           ; no ->

            test word ptr [ _decimalflag ][ bp ], SPRINTF_COMMADELIM
            jz _sprintfNum_10                           ; no ->
            dec byte ptr [ _spacing ][ bp ]             ; spacing break ?
            jnz _sprintfNum_10                          ; not yet ->

            mov byte ptr [ _spacing ][ bp ], 03         ; set spacing
            mov byte ptr [ di ], ','                    ; store comma
            inc di

_sprintfNum_10:
            mov cx, dx
            or cx, ax                                   ; more to go ?
            jnz _sprintfNum_08                          ; yes ->

            pop cx
            sub di, cx                                  ; total # chars output
            mov cx, di                                  ; length to cx

            pop di
            push di                                     ; where to begin right justify
            lea si, offset [ _decDisplay ][ bp ]        ; where data stored
            cmp word ptr [ _fieldwidth ][ bp ], 0000    ; left-justified output ?
            jz _sprintfNum_20                           ; yes ->

;- - - - - - - - - - - - - - - - - - - - - - - - - - - - - - - - -
; right-justified
;- - - - - - - - - - - - - - - - - - - - - - - - - - - - - - - - -
            add di, word ptr [ _fieldwidth ][ bp ]      ;
            push di

_sprintfNum_16:
            lodsb                                       ; get character
            dec di
            mov byte ptr [ di ], al
            loop _sprintfNum_16
```

```
        pop di
        jmp short _sprintfNum_32

;- - - - - - - - - - - - - - - - - - - - - - - - - - - - - - - - - -
;  left-justified
;- - - - - - - - - - - - - - - - - - - - - - - - - - - - - - - - - -
_sprintfNum_20:
        lodsb                                   ; get character
        stosb
        loop _sprintfNum_20

;- - - - - - - - - - - - - - - - - - - - - - - - - - - - - - - - - -
;  done
;- - - - - - - - - - - - - - - - - - - - - - - - - - - - - - - - - -
_sprintfNum_32:
        pop si                                  ; drop saved di
        pop si
        Return

        ;'''''''''''''''''''''''''''''''''''''''''''''''''''''''''';
        ;  Init Field to Spaces                                   ;
        ;- - - - - - - - - - - - - - - - - - - - - - - - - - - - -;
        ;                                                         ;
        ;  Usage:                                                 ;
        ;   di     pointer to buffer                              ;
        ;   cx     width of field                                 ;
        ;   bx     8000 if right justified                        ;
        ;.........................................................;

_sprintfInitField:
        or cx, cx                               ; fixed count ?
        jz _sprintfInitField_08                 ; no ->

        push di
        push cx
        push ax
        mov al, ' '
        rep stosb

        pop ax
        pop cx
        pop di

_sprintfInitField_08:
        ret

        ;'''''''''''''''''''''''''''''''''''''''''''''''''''''''''';
        ;  Pad Field                                              ;
        ;.........................................................;

_sprintfPadField:
        or cx, cx                               ; still more length to go ?
        jz _sprintfPadField_08                  ; no ->
        add di, cx                              ; advance field length
```

```
_sprintfPadField_08:
        ret

        ;,,,,,,,,,,,,,,,,,,,,,,,,,,,,,,,,,,,,,,,,,,,,,,,,,,,,,,,,,,,,,;
        ;  32 Bit Divide                                             ;
        ;- - - - - - - - - - - - - - - - - - - - - - - - - - - - - -;
        ;                                                            ;
        ;  Input:                                                    ;
        ;    ax:dx   numerator                                       ;
        ;    cx      divisor                                         ;
        ;                                                            ;
        ;............................................................;

_div32: or cx, cx                           ; protect from zero divisor
        stc                                 ; in case of error
        jz _div32_return                    ; if so, just return with carry

        push bx
        mov bx, dx
        xchg ax, bx
        xor dx, dx
        div cx

        xchg ax, bx
        div cx                              ; remainder will be in dx
        mov cx, dx
        mov dx, bx
        pop bx

_div32_return:
        ret
```

Echo

The echo statement is used to turn ON or OFF batch file displaying. Disabling batch file echo is used to more carefully control what a user observes on the screen during batch file processing. The echo statement is used for two additional purposes. An echo statement with no parameters simply displays the current echo status. An echo statement with more than simply the on and off arguments is displayed on the screen.

The echo statement processing begins by checking whether arguments were passed. If they weren't, the status of the echo line is displayed. A check is then made for the presence of a single argument. If more arguments are passed, the entire line is displayed.

If a single argument is passed, it is tested to determine if it is either the ON or OFF. If it fails these tests, the entire line is printed. Otherwise, the status value is saved for future reference.

The command does not check or care whether it is executing in a batch file.

```
(in rxdoscmd.asm)
        ;,,,,,,,,,,,,,,,,,,,,,,,,,,,,,,,,,,,,,,,,,,,,,,,,,,,,,,,,,,,,,;
        ;  Echo                                                      ;
        ;- - - - - - - - - - - - - - - - - - - - - - - - - - - - - -;
        ;                                                            ;
```

```
        ; Usage:                                                       ;
        ; ss:di  Arg Array                                             ;
        ; ax     Number of arguments in array                         ;
        ;.............................................................;

  _Echo:
        Entry
        ddef __argarray, ss, di
        def _args, ax

        or ax, ax                             ; no arguments ?
        jz _echo_printcurrent                 ; none, print current status ->

        dec ax                                ; just one argument ?
        jnz _echo_printline                   ; no, print line ->

;- - - - - - - - - - - - - - - - - - - - - - - - - - - - - - - -
; test for On/ Off
;- - - - - - - - - - - - - - - - - - - - - - - - - - - - - - - -
        mov si, word ptr [ di ]               ; get single argument
        mov di, offset RxDOS_OnOff
        call CmndLookup                       ; lookup command
        jc _echo_printline                    ; if not on/off, print line ->

        mov byte ptr [ _EchoStatus ], bl      ; set echo status
        Return

;- - - - - - - - - - - - - - - - - - - - - - - - - - - - - - - -
;  print current line
;- - - - - - - - - - - - - - - - - - - - - - - - - - - - - - - -
_echo_printline:
        mov di, word ptr [ __argarray. _pointer ][ bp ]
        mov dx, word ptr [ di ]               ; get start of string
        call DisplayLine
        call CRLF
        Return

;- - - - - - - - - - - - - - - - - - - - - - - - - - - - - - - -
;  print on/off value
;- - - - - - - - - - - - - - - - - - - - - - - - - - - - - - - -
_echo_printcurrent:
        mov bl, byte ptr [ _EchoStatus ]
        xor bh, bh
        add bx, bx
        mov dx, word ptr [ _EchoOptions ][ bx ]
        call DisplayLine
        Return
```

Exit

The exit statement is used to terminate processing of a batch file before the actual end of file is reached. The exit statement calls the _EndCall function already listed in the section on "How Batch Files Terminate." The code should not be repeated here. To understand how batch files terminate, it is necessary to understand other related issues, such as how batch files call each other. We provided an explanation of the process in the section on "Call Statement Processing."

For

The for statement executes a command on each of a set of arguments. The command encloses a set of arguments within parentheses. The arguments are interpreted as files. The command that follows the arguments is applied to each argument. In the following example, the command after the DO clause is applied to each file in the current directory:

```
c> for %v IN ( *.txt ) DO type %v
```

The command searches for files in the current directory that contain a .txt extension. It replaces the variable name with each file located and executes the command. There is no restriction that the command be used in batch files.

The for statement handler parses through the command by checking and identifying each argument. A legal for statement must contain at least eight arguments. This includes the variable argument, the two parentheses, and each of the keywords, all of which are counted as arguments. Any statement with fewer arguments has at least one of its parameters missing and is obviously considered to be in error.

The first argument in the statement must contain the percent symbol. If it does, the letter immediately following it is retrieved, lowercased, and saved. The next two arguments are checked to be sure that they are the IN keyword and a parenthesis. The address to the argument following the parenthesis, that is, the first argument in the argument set, is saved for future reference. This is then followed by scanning the command line to the matching right parenthesis. The argument that follows is checked to be sure that it is the DO keyword.

The syntax checking is required to properly identify the three key elements of the for statement. These are the variable letter, the start of the argument set, and the command to execute. Once these elements have been located, the for statement execution can begin at the _ForNext label, which loops through each of the arguments in the argument set.

A check is made to determine whether the last of the arguments in the argument set has been reached. If the hasn't been reached, the argument pointer is retrieved. The argument's length is computed by scanning for a space or parenthesis terminator. Then the argument is checked to determine if it contains wild characters. If the argument does not contain any wild characters, the term is simply replaced in the command, and the command is executed.

When the argument contains a wild character like an asterisk or a question mark, the current directory is searched. The first matched filename is retrieved, and the command is executed. The command is repeated on every matching filename. This can be accomplished because the next filename is retrieved using the DOS Find Next file function, which utilizes the DTA, or Disk Transfer Area, to maintain its current position in the directory. Since it doesn't know the effects of the command that it will execute, the DTA is first switched to an internal DTA, the search is performed, and the DTA is restored before executing any command. This creates a protected DTA in order to search effectively through a directory.

Processing continues until the Find Next function fails. The command then advances the argument pointer to the next argument in the argument set and repeats the process described until all the arguments in the set have been processed.

```
(in rxdosfor.asm)
        ;'''''''''''''''''''''''''''''''''''''''''''''''''''''''''''''';
        ;   FOR %variable IN (set) DO command [command-parameters]     ;
        ;- - - - - - - - - - - - - - - - - - - - - - - - - - - - - -  -;
        ;                                                              ;
        ;   Replace %var in command.                                   ;
        ;                                                              ;
        ;..............................................................;

_For:
        Entry
        def __argarray, di
        def __arg
        def __cmdline
        def __endrepeatArg

        def _letter
        def _length
        def _WildChars
        ddef _CurrentDTA, 0000, 0000

        defbytes _DTA, 128
        defbytes _commandLine, 128
        defbytes _replacement, 128

;- - - - - - - - - - - - - - - - - - - - - - - - - - - - - - - -
;  get variable arg letter
;- - - - - - - - - - - - - - - - - - - - - - - - - - - - - - - -
        call CountArgs                          ; must have min of 8 args
        cmp ax, 8                               ; min args
        jge _For_08                             ; if at leats 8 ->
        jmp _ForError                           ; else if less, syntax error ->

_For_08:
        mov si, word ptr [ forVarIdent ][ di ]  ; point to arg
        cmp byte ptr [ si ], '%'                ; is arg a % variable ?
        ifnz _ForError                          ; if not, then syntax error ->

        mov al, byte ptr [ si + 1 ]             ; get letter
        call _lowerCase
        cbw
        storarg _letter, ax

;- - - - - - - - - - - - - - - - - - - - - - - - - - - - - - - -
;  check for 'in' argument
;- - - - - - - - - - - - - - - - - - - - - - - - - - - - - - - -
        mov si, word ptr [ forInArg ][ di ]     ; point to next arg
        mov di, offset RxDOS_ForArgs
        call CmndLookup                         ; lookup command
        ifc _ForError                           ; if not, then syntax error ->
```

```
        cmp bx, _IN                                 ; 'in' returns a zero
        ifnz _ForError                              ; if not 'in', then error ->

;- - - - - - - - - - - - - - - - - - - - - - - - - - - - - - -
;  check for ( argument
;- - - - - - - - - - - - - - - - - - - - - - - - - - - - - - -
        getarg di, __argarray
        add di, forInStartParen + 2
        mov si, word ptr [ di - 2 ]                 ; point to next arg
        cmp byte ptr [ si ], '('                    ; is arg a ( variable ?
        ifnz _ForError                              ; if not, then syntax error ->

        storarg __arg, di                           ; di points to an argument

;- - - - - - - - - - - - - - - - - - - - - - - - - - - - - - -
;  search for ) do ...
;- - - - - - - - - - - - - - - - - - - - - - - - - - - - - - -
        dec di
        dec di

_ForSearchForParen:
        inc di
        inc di
        mov si, word ptr [ di ]                     ; point to next arg
        or si, si                                   ; end of args ?
        ifz _ForError                               ; if not, then syntax error ->

        cmp byte ptr [ si ], ')'                    ; is arg a ) variable ?
        jnz _ForSearchForParen                      ; keep looking ->

;- - - - - - - - - - - - - - - - - - - - - - - - - - - - - - -
;  search for last ) in case ))) ...
;- - - - - - - - - - - - - - - - - - - - - - - - - - - - - - -
_ForSearchForDoLastParen:
        inc di
        inc di
        mov si, word ptr [ di ]                     ; point to next arg
        or si, si                                   ; end of args ?
        ifz _ForError                               ; if not, then syntax error ->

        cmp byte ptr [ si ], ')'                    ; is arg a ) variable ?
        jz _ForSearchForDoLastParen                 ; keep looking ->

;- - - - - - - - - - - - - - - - - - - - - - - - - - - - - - -
;  test for a 'do' argument
;- - - - - - - - - - - - - - - - - - - - - - - - - - - - - - -
_ForSearchForDo:
        push di
        mov di, offset RxDOS_ForArgs
        call CmndLookup                             ; lookup command
        pop di                                      ; restore arg pointer
        ifc _ForError                               ; if not legit, syntax error ->

        cmp bx, _DO                                 ; 'do' returns a 1
```

```
        ifnz _ForError                                  ; if not found ->

        inc di
        inc di
        storarg __cmdline, di                           ; where command line is

        sub di, 4
        storarg __endrepeatArg, di                      ; end repeat arg

;- - - - - - - - - - - - - - - - - - - - - - - - - - - - - - - - - - -
;  initialize DTA area
;- - - - - - - - - - - - - - - - - - - - - - - - - - - - - - - - - - -
        Int21 GetDTA
        stordarg _CurrentDTA, es, bx


;- - - - - - - - - - - - - - - - - - - - - - - - - - - - - - - - - - -
;  sequentially walk through each arg
;- - - - - - - - - - - - - - - - - - - - - - - - - - - - - - - - - - -
_ForNext:
        getarg bx, __arg                                ; point to arg list
        cmp bx, word ptr [ __endrepeatArg ][ bp ]       ; end repeat arg ?
        ifz _ForReturn                                  ; if at end, exit ->

        storarg _WildChars, 0000
        mov si, word ptr [ bx ]
        call _computeLength                             ; compute length
        storarg _length, cx                             ; save length

        call _Seeif_WildCharacter                       ; see if wild characters in name.
        jc _ForNext_30                                  ; if no ->

        lea di, offset _replacement [ bp ]              ; where to copy
        rep movsb                                       ; copy argument
        xor ax, ax                                      ; null terminate
        stosb                                           ; null terminate
        storarg _WildChars, -1                          ; wild characters used.

        lea dx, offset [ _DTA ][ bp ]
        Int21 SetDTA

        lea dx, offset _replacement [ bp ]              ; search for argument
        Int21 FindFirstFile                             ; any found ?
        jc _ForNext_36                                  ; if none ->

;- - - - - - - - - - - - - - - - - - - - - - - - - - - - - - - - - - -
;  create replacement variable
;- - - - - - - - - - - - - - - - - - - - - - - - - - - - - - - - - - -
_ForNext_14:
        lea si, offset [ _DTA. findFileName ][ bp ]
        lea di, offset _replacement [ bp ]              ; search for argument
        call _CopyString                                ; get command line

;- - - - - - - - - - - - - - - - - - - - - - - - - - - - - - - - - - -
;  build command line to execute
;- - - - - - - - - - - - - - - - - - - - - - - - - - - - - - - - - - -
```

```
_ForNext_30:
        getarg di, __cmdline                        ; ptr->arg array where command line
begins
        mov si, word ptr [ di ]                     ; ptr-> text
        lea di, offset [ _commandLine + 1 ][ bp ]
        call _CopyString                            ; get command line

        mov al, byte ptr [ _letter ][ bp ]
        lea bx, offset [ _replacement ][ bp ]
        lea si, offset [ _commandLine + 1 ][ bp ]
        call ReplaceForVariables                    ; replace variable letter

        call DisplayPrompt                          ; display prompt

        lea dx, offset [ _commandLine + 1 ][ bp ]
        call DisplayLine                            ; echo line
        call CRLF

        push ds
        getdarg ds, dx, _CurrentDTA
        Int21 SetDTA                                ; temp set DTA
        pop ds

        lea si, offset [ _commandLine ][ bp ]
        mov byte ptr [ si ], 128
        call _CommandParser                         ; reparse remainder of line

        cmp word ptr [ _WildChars ][ bp ], 0000     ; wild character search ?
        jz _ForNext_36                              ; no, skip to next arg in set ->

        lea dx, offset [ _DTA ][ bp ]
        Int21 SetDTA

        Int21 FindNextFile                          ; search for next matching file
        jnc _ForNext_14                             ; continue ->

;- - - - - - - - - - - - - - - - - - - - - - - - - - - - - - - -
;   get next argument
;- - - - - - - - - - - - - - - - - - - - - - - - - - - - - - - -
_ForNext_36:
        mov di, word ptr [ __arg ][ bp ]            ; get current pointer to arg array
        mov dx, word ptr [ di ]                     ; get current reference
        add dx, word ptr [ _length ][ bp ]          ; offset to past current arg
        sub di, 2

_ForNext_38:
        add di, 2
        mov si, word ptr [ di ]                     ; get current reference
        cmp si, dx                                  ; beyond or equal to current ?
        jc _ForNext_38                              ; not yet ->

        mov word ptr [ __arg ][ bp ], di            ; remember reference
        jmp _ForNext
```

```
;- - - - - - - - - - - - - - - - - - - - - - - - - - - - - - - -
;  error
;- - - - - - - - - - - - - - - - - - - - - - - - - - - - - - - -
_ForError:
        mov dx, offset CmndError_SyntaxError
        call DisplayErrorMessage


;- - - - - - - - - - - - - - - - - - - - - - - - - - - - - - - -
;  return
;- - - - - - - - - - - - - - - - - - - - - - - - - - - - - - - -
_ForReturn:
        cmp word ptr [ _CurrentDTA. _segment ][ bp ], 0000
        jz _ForReturn_08

        push ds
        getdarg ds, dx, _CurrentDTA
        Int21 SetDTA                                  ; temp set DTA
        pop ds

_ForReturn_08:
        Return

        ;''''''''''''''''''''''''''''''''''''''''''''''''''''''''''''''';
        ;  Compute Length                                              ;
        ;- - - - - - - - - - - - - - - - - - - - - - - - - - - - - - - -;
        ;                                                              ;
        ;  Usage:                                                      ;
        ;  cx    length of string                                      ;
        ;  si    starting address of string.                          ;
        ;..............................................................;

_computeLength:
        push si

_computeLength_06:
        cmp byte ptr [ si ], ' '+ 1
        jc _computeLength_08
        cmp byte ptr [ si ], ')'
        jz _computeLength_08
        cmp byte ptr [ si ], ','
        jz _computeLength_08
        cmp byte ptr [ si ], ';'
        jz _computeLength_08

        inc si
        jmp _computeLength_06

_computeLength_08:
        pop cx
        xchg cx, si
        sub cx, si
        ret

        ;''''''''''''''''''''''''''''''''''''''''''''''''''''''''''''''';
        ;  See if Wild Characters Are Used.                           ;
        ;- - - - - - - - - - - - - - - - - - - - - - - - - - - - - - - -;
```

```
        ;                                                          ;
        ;  Usage:                                                  ;
        ;  cx    length of string                                  ;
        ;  si    starting address of string.                       ;
        ;                                                          ;
        ;.............................................................;

_Seeif_WildCharacter:
        push si
        push cx

_WildCharacter_08:
        lodsb
        cmp al, '?'
        jz _WildCharacter_12
        cmp al, '*'
        jz _WildCharacter_12

        loop _WildCharacter_08
        stc

_WildCharacter_12:
        pop cx
        pop si
        ret
```

Goto

The goto statement is utilized only with batch files. It is used to locate and reposition the execution of a batch file at a text label position. Batch file processing depends on reading the next batch statement at the current position pointer. In other words, it presumes that processing is sequential through the file. The goto statement searches for the label in the batch file and sets the position pointer at the line immediately after the label. Normal batch processing then continues to read from this updated position.

The code begins by determining that there is one argument, that the argument does not begin with a colon character, and that batch file processing is in progress. It then retrieves the current file position, which it saves and repositions to the beginning of the file. The search always begins from the beginning of the file.

As each batch file line is read, any leading spaces are ignored and a test is done to ensure that it is a label reference. The first nonblank character must be a colon. If a label is located, the search string is compared to the label read. The search continues until a matching label is located or the end of file is reached.

If the label cannot be located, the file pointer is set back to its original position. The batch file's normal processing will be unaware that the search took place. If a match is located, the file's position pointer is already at the start of the next line, and the function simply returns.

(in rxdoscmd.asm)

```
        ;'''''''''''''''''''''''''''''''''''''''''''''''''''''''''''';
        ;  Goto Label                                                ;
        ;- - - - - - - - - - - - - - - - - - - - - - - - - - - - - - -;
        ;                                                            ;
        ;  if batch file, locate label                              ;
        ;............................................................;

_Goto:
        Entry
        def  _labelPtr, si
        ddef _filePosition
        defbytes _buffer, sizeCmdLineStruct

;- - - - - - - - - - - - - - - - - - - - - - - - - - - - - - - - -
;  prep argument
;- - - - - - - - - - - - - - - - - - - - - - - - - - - - - - - - -
        call CheckOneArg
        jc   _Goto_36                                  ; error ->

        getarg si, _labelPtr

_goto_06:
        cmp byte ptr [ si ], ':'
        jnz _goto_08
        inc si
        jmp _goto_06

_goto_08:
        storarg _labelPtr, si

;- - - - - - - - - - - - - - - - - - - - - - - - - - - - - - - - -
;  running batch file ?
;- - - - - - - - - - - - - - - - - - - - - - - - - - - - - - - - -
        cmp word ptr [ RxDOS_BatchFile. batchFileHandle ], 0000
        jz  _Goto_36                            ; if not running a batch file ->

        call getBatchPosition                   ; save current batch file position
        mov word ptr [ _filePosition. _low  ][ bp ], ax
        mov word ptr [ _filePosition. _high ][ bp ], dx

;- - - - - - - - - - - - - - - - - - - - - - - - - - - - - - - - -
;  read lines
;- - - - - - - - - - - - - - - - - - - - - - - - - - - - - - - - -
        xor cx, cx
        xor dx, dx
        mov bx, word ptr [ RxDOS_BatchFile. batchFileHandle ]
        Int21 MoveFilePointer, SEEK_BEG          ; start at beg of file

_goto_16:
        xor ax, ax                               ; no echo searching lines
        mov bx, word ptr [ RxDOS_BatchFile. batchFileHandle ]
        lea si, offset [ _buffer ][ bp ]
```

```
        mov byte ptr [ bufMaxLength ][ si ], sizeCmdLine
        call _ReadBatch                                     ; read batch line
        jz _goto_32                                         ; set position ->

;- - - - - - - - - - - - - - - - - - - - - - - - - - - - - - - - - - -
;  compare to search argument
;- - - - - - - - - - - - - - - - - - - - - - - - - - - - - - - - - - -
        xor bh, bh
        mov bl, byte ptr [ _buffer. bufActualLength ][ bp ]
        lea di, offset [ _buffer. bufData ][ bp ]
        mov byte ptr [ di + bx ], 00
        mov si, word ptr [ _labelPtr ][ bp ]

_goto_18:
        cmp byte ptr [ di ], ' '
        jz _goto_22
        cmp byte ptr [ di ], ':'
        jnz _goto_26

_goto_22:
        inc di
        jmp _goto_18

_goto_26:
        call _compareSubString                              ; label located ?
        jnz _goto_16                                        ; no ->
        jmp short _goto_36                                  ; line located !

;- - - - - - - - - - - - - - - - - - - - - - - - - - - - - - - - - - -
;  can't find, reset line location
;- - - - - - - - - - - - - - - - - - - - - - - - - - - - - - - - - - -
_goto_32:
        mov dx, word ptr [ _filePosition. _low  ][ bp ]
        mov cx, word ptr [ _filePosition. _high ][ bp ]
        mov bx, word ptr [ RxDOS_BatchFile. batchFileHandle ]
        Int21 MoveFilePointer, SEEK_BEG                     ; restore pointer

;- - - - - - - - - - - - - - - - - - - - - - - - - - - - - - - - - - -
;  return
;- - - - - - - - - - - - - - - - - - - - - - - - - - - - - - - - - - -
_goto_36:
        Return
```

If

The if statement is not limited to batch files. It is used as a conditional statement and is often used with a goto statement. The command may take one of three forms. It may be followed by a modifier clause containing an optional NOT clause and followed by one of the following: ERROR-LEVEL, EXIST, or string comparison. A valid DOS command must follow, which is then resubmitted for execution by calling the command parser. The essence of the command is to determine whether the condition expressed in the modifier clause is TRUE.

The code begins by attempting to identify the first five arguments in the argument array. Each argument that follows the if clause is looked up in a table of valid if-statement modifiers. The type is stored, together with a pointer to the text, in an alternate table. There is no need to also remember the text pointer since the alternate argument array entries parallel the pointers in the original argument array. This structure was created simply to ease pointer references.

Types are values assigned to each type of keyword expected, defined in the following table:

```
        ;''''''''''''''''''''''''''''''''''''''''''''''''''''''''''''''';
        ;  If Options                                                   ;
        ;...............................................................;

RxDOS_IfOptions:                Cmnd  IF_ERRORLEVEL,     "errorlevel"
                                Cmnd  IF_EXIST,          "exists"
                                Cmnd  IF_EXIST,          "exist"
                                Cmnd  IF_NOT,            "not"
                                dw  -1


        ;''''''''''''''''''''''''''''''''''''''''''''''''''''''''''''''';
        ;  If Special Values                                            ;
        ;...............................................................;

IF_NOT                          equ 01h
IF_ERRORLEVEL                   equ 02h
IF_EXIST                        equ 03h
```

Once the first five parameters are identified, the lead argument is checked to determine if it is a NOT argument. If it is, a flag is set, and the argument pointer is advanced. Next, the argument is checked to determine if it is either an ERRORLEVEL or an EXIST keyword. The code jumps to service these types of commands. If neither of these conditions is met, the code checks to determine whether an == argument appears between two text arguments. If none of these conditions are met, an error message is displayed, and the command terminates.

If the statement type was to compare string values, the code continues executing at _ifEquals. The addresses of the arguments before and after the == symbols are retrieved into the SI and DI registers. In the listing, the address of the argument after the equal signs is addressed as an offset of 12. This may be considered less than perfect programming practice. It was derived as follows. The BX register points to the first argument in the alternate argument array. This alternate array requires 4 bytes per entry. The next two entries are the address of two equal signs, respectively. The fourth entry points to the second string address. The offset of 12 represents the start of this fourth entry counting from a zero base.

If any of the strings are missing, denoted by a null string address, a syntax error message is displayed. The length of both strings is computed and compared. Strings of different lengths are considered to not match. Finally, a case-dependent string compare is performed. The strings are equal if the zero bit is set. The status byte is moved to the AH register and toggled if the NOT flag was set earlier. If the result of these logical operations sets the zero flag, the string comparisons are said to be equal. The command that follows is then executed; otherwise, it is ignored.

The command that follows the if statement is executed at _ifTrue by essentially passing the argument to a processed argument array to the execute command array function. This function doesn't care where the argument array resides or how it was created. In fact, it was created by the standard command processor when the if statement was first parsed.

Because of the variable number of arguments possible in the if statement, the compare strings portion of the code saved the argument pointer to the second of the two string pointers. This string pointer is saved as the last-used pointer. The logic at _ifTrue scans the original argument array for the argument whose pointer value matches the second string. It then skips to the next argument since this is where the command starts.

The other variations of the if statement, the ERRORLEVEL and EXIST, set the last-used argument array pointer as well. This enables any variation of the command to have a different number of arguments.

The ERRORLEVEL command fetches the return code returned by DOS, representing the error code returned by the last application. The argument that follows in the command line is returned as a number by the _GetNumber function and is then compared to the DOS-returned value. The conditions are true for executing the remainder of the command if the carry bit is set. The number retrieved from the command line is decremented by 1 in order to make an equal comparison set the carry flag. The flag is then toggled by the not status, if set. If the resulting carry bit flag is set, the command is executed.

The IF EXIST command searches the parameter that follows on disk using the find first file DOS command. The carry flag is set if the file was not found. So long as the flag is not set, the command is executed.

```
(in rxdoscmd.asm)
        ;,,,,,,,,,,,,,,,,,,,,,,,,,,,,,,,,,,,,,,,,,,,,,,,,,,,,,,,,,,,;
        ;  If [not] ERRORLEVEL number command                       ;
        ;  If [not] EXIST filename command                          ;
        ;  If [not] string1==string2 command                       ;
        ;..........................................................;


_If:
        Entry
        def __argarray, di
        defwords _argtypeArray, 20              ; 5 args (type and text pointers)
        def _notflag, 0000
        def _returnvalue
        def _usedportion, 0000


;- - - - - - - - - - - - - - - - - - - - - - - - - - - - - - -
;  type first few arguments
;- - - - - - - - - - - - - - - - - - - - - - - - - - - - - - -
        lea di, offset [ _argtypeArray ][ bp ]   ; pointer to arg store value
        push di

        xor ax, ax
        mov cx, 5 * 4                            ; words to clear
        rep stosw

        pop bx
        mov cx, 5                                ; # args to scan
        getarg di, __argarray
```

```
_If_08:
        mov si, word ptr [ di ]                       ; get argument passed
        or si, si                                     ; no more args ?
        jz _If_16                                     ; quit typing —>

        mov word ptr [ bx. _argtext ], si             ; pointer to text

        push di
        push bx
        push cx
        mov di, offset RxDOS_IfOptions
        call CmndLookup                               ; lookup command
        mov ax, bx                                    ; save type

        pop cx
        pop bx
        pop di
        jc _If_12
        mov word ptr [ bx. _argtype ], ax             ; value returned from lookup

_If_12:
        add bx, 4                                     ; lookup first three args
        add di, 2                                     ; lookup first three args
        loop _If_08

;- - - - - - - - - - - - - - - - - - - - - - - - - - - - - - - - - -
; see if == special case
;- - - - - - - - - - - - - - - - - - - - - - - - - - - - - - - - - -
_If_16:
        lea bx, offset [ _argtypeArray ][ bp ]        ; pointer to arg
        cmp word ptr [ bx. _argtype ], IF_NOT         ; not argument ?
        jnz _If_20                                    ; no —>
        add bx, 4                                     ; then we'll use next as base
        storarg _notflag, -1                          ; if not

_If_20:
        cmp word ptr [ bx. _argtype ], IF_ERRORLEVEL
        ifz _ifErrorLevel
        cmp word ptr [ bx. _argtype ], IF_EXIST
        ifz _ifExist

        mov si, word ptr [ bx + 4 ][ _argtext ]       ; next arg
        or si, si                                     ; no text ?
        jz _IfSyntaxError                             ; syntax error —>

        cmp word ptr [ si ], "=="                     ; equals case ?
        jz _ifEquals

;- - - - - - - - - - - - - - - - - - - - - - - - - - - - - - - - - -
; syntax error
;- - - - - - - - - - - - - - - - - - - - - - - - - - - - - - - - - -
_IfSyntaxError:
```

```
        mov dx, offset CmndError_SyntaxError
        call DisplayErrorMessage                        ; display message
        Return

;- - - - - - - - - - - - - - - - - - - - - - - - - - - - - - - -
;  if equals
;- - - - - - - - - - - - - - - - - - - - - - - - - - - - - - - -
_ifEquals:
        mov si, word ptr [ bx     ][ _argtext ]
        or si, si                                       ; arg before =='s
        jz _IfSyntaxError                               ; if syntax error ->

        mov di, word ptr [ bx + 12][ _argtext ]
        or di, di                                       ; arg after =='s
        jz _IfSyntaxError                               ; if syntax error ->

        storarg _usedportion, di

        push si
        call _ifStringlength                            ; get length of source string
        mov cx, ax

        push di
        call _ifStringlength                            ; get length of dest string
        cmp cx, ax                                      ; compare lengths
        jnz _IfSyntaxError                              ; if syntax error ->

        rep cmpsb                                       ; strings compare equal ?
        lahf                                            ; zer/not zero to ah
        xor ah, byte ptr [ _notflag ][ bp ]            ; toggle Not Equal Bit
        and ah, 01000000b                               ; not zero if logical continue
        jnz _ifTrue

        Return

;- - - - - - - - - - - - - - - - - - - - - - - - - - - - - - - -
;  if errorlevel
;- - - - - - - - - - - - - - - - - - - - - - - - - - - - - - - -
_ifErrorLevel:
        Int21 GetReturnCode                             ; get return value
        and ax, 255                                     ; get previous return value
        storarg _returnvalue, ax

        mov si, word ptr [ bx + 4 ][ _argtext ]        ; get text pointer to next arg
        storarg _usedportion, si
        or si, si
        jz _IfSyntaxError                               ; if syntax error ->

        call _GetNumber                                 ; get expected number
        jc _IfSyntaxError                               ; if syntax error ->
        dec ax                                          ; need to force carry
        cmp ax, word ptr [ _returnvalue ][ bp ]        ; current >= return value ?
        lahf                                            ; status to ah
        xor ah, byte ptr [ _notflag ][ bp ]            ; toggle Carry Bit
```

```
        and ah, 00000001b                           ; not zero if logical continue
        jnz _ifTrue                                 ; do rest of line ->

        Return


;- - - - - - - - - - - - - - - - - - - - - - - - - - - - - - - - -
;  if exist
;- - - - - - - - - - - - - - - - - - - - - - - - - - - - - - - - -
_ifExist:
        mov cx, ATTR_DIRECTORY
        mov dx, word ptr [ bx + 4 ][ _argtext ]     ; get text pointer to next arg
        storarg _usedportion, dx
        Int21 FindFirstFile                         ; does this file exist ?

        lahf                                        ; status to ah
        xor ah, byte ptr [ _notflag ][ bp ]         ; toggle Carry Bit
        and ah, 00000001b                           ; not zero means not True
        jz _ifTrue                                  ; do rest of line ->

        Return


;- - - - - - - - - - - - - - - - - - - - - - - - - - - - - - - - -
;  if cond is true. execute command that follows
;- - - - - - - - - - - - - - - - - - - - - - - - - - - - - - -
_ifTrue:
        getarg di, __argarray
        getarg dx, _usedportion                     ; used args
        sub di, 2

_ifTrue_08:
        inc di
        inc di
        cmp word ptr [ di ], 0000
        ifz _IfSyntaxError
        cmp word ptr [ di ], dx                      ; located used part of If ?
        jc _ifTrue_08                                ; not yet ->

        inc di
        inc di
        call _executeCommandArray
        Return


;- - - - - - - - - - - - - - - - - - - - - - - - - - - - - - - - -
;  compute string lengths
;- - - - - - - - - - - - - - - - - - - - - - - - - - - - - - - - -
_ifStringlength:
        Entry 1
        arg   _str

        push si
        push di
        getarg si, _str

_ifStringlength_08:
```

```
        cmp byte ptr [ si ], ' '
        jz _ifStringlength_12
        cmp byte ptr [ si ], '='
        jz _ifStringlength_12
        cmp byte ptr [ si ], 0
        jz _ifStringlength_12

        inc si
        jmp _ifStringlength_08

_ifStringlength_12:
        mov ax, si
        sub ax, word ptr _str [ bp ]

        pop di
        pop si
        Return
```

Loadhigh

The loadhigh command, either `loadhigh` or `lh`, is used to load programs into upper memory blocks. The command can be followed by the optional /L switch, which identifies the areas in high memory that can be accessed and allocated to and by the program. Although it is entirely possible that a program can fit into one or more upper memory blocks, the behavior of the loadhigh command is to restrict access to specific designated areas.

The parameters passed with the /L switch can be used to effectively squeeze the largest amount of utility out of the upper memory areas. DOS's best-fit strategy cannot always understand the requirements that may be made when loading programs. It determines the best fit only for the current program and does not have a complete picture of all programs destined for the upper memory blocks.

When the command processor loads for the first time, it builds an assessment of the upper memory areas available. This assessment is based on blocks of memory available before any programs are loaded high and is stored in `UMBAccessTable`. Up to nine areas may exist.

When a program is to be loaded high, the command line is tested for the /L and /S switches. Each area referenced by the /L switch is made accessible to the loading program as follows: The area id is saved in a table. When all the ids have been processed from the command line, the pointer to the remaining command line is saved. The areas referenced by the command remain available. The remainder are temporarily allocated to DOS. The memory strategy is set to first fit upper memory blocks while the current strategy is saved. The program is loaded as a normal program.

The strategy depends on the program loading high and returning to the command shell using the TSR exit. When the command shell is rerun, the blocks that were protected by the allocation scheme are freed.

Make Directory

The make directory command attempts to create a new directory on disk and is a straightforward command line interface for the DOS Create Subdirectory function. The command checks that it contains only a single argument. The pointer to the argument is then passed to the Create Subdirectory function. If the return value is an error, the error code is checked, and an error message is displayed.

If the DOS function call returned with no errors, the subdirectory was created on disk.

```
(in rxdoscmd.asm)
        ;'''''''''''''''''''''''''''''''''''''''''''''''''''''''''''''''';
        ;  Make Directory                                                ;
        ;- - - - - - - - - - - - - - - - - - - - - - - - - - - - - - - -;
        ;                                                                ;
        ;  Usage:                                                        ;
        ;   ss:di  Arg Array                                             ;
        ;   ax      Number of arguments in array                        ;
        ;................................................................;

_makeDir:

        call CheckOneArg                        ; see if 1 arg
        jc _makeDir_32                          ; if error ->

_makeDir_22:
        mov dx, word ptr [ di ]                 ; point to filename arg
        Int21 CreateSubdirectory                ; try changing dir
        jnc _makeDir_32                         ; if valid ->

        cmp ax, errAccessDenied                 ; access denined ?
        jnz _makeDir_26                         ; show other errors ->

        mov dx, offset CmndError_SubDirAlreadyExists
        call DisplayErrorMessage
        jmp short _makeDir_32

_makeDir_26:
        call DisplayError                       ; if error

_makeDir_32:
        ret
```

Path

The path command sets or displays the value of the PATH environment variable. The environment block variable defines the directories that can be searched when a program or batch file is to be executed. The path command cannot add new directory entries to an existing path variable. It is limited to replacing the entire path variable.

In what might appear as a strange constraint, the path command can add directories to an existing path environment variable only when used in a batch file. This is because of a somewhat unrelated feature of batch file processing. Within a batch file, a path command can be used to add new directories only when used in either of the following two forms:

```
path %path%;\newdir
path \newdir; %path%
```

These forms of the path command are expanded when the batch file line is first read. The %path% keyword is replaced with the contents of the path variable. The resulting command line is subject, unfortunately, to the 128-character limitation imposed by DOS.

The PATH command processing first locates the existing path variable in the environment block using the search environment block function, searchEnvVariable. If the variable is found, it returns with the zero status flag, and the argument's address is saved. Otherwise, the function returns with a pointer to the end of the environment block, and it is saved.

The command is then checked for arguments. If none were passed and the path environment variable was found, its contents are displayed. If an argument was passed, the environment variable is replaced by first deleting the environment variable and then inserting a new argument. The insert routine needs the environment block end pointer, which is provided as a result of one of two operations. Either it is provided as part of the delete argument routine or it was returned earlier by the environment block search routine.

```
(in rxdoscmd.asm)
        ;''''''''''''''''''''''''''''''''''''''''''''''''''''''''''''';
        ;  Path                                                       ;
        ;- - - - - - - - - - - - - - - - - - - - - - - - - - - - - -;
        ;                                                             ;
        ;  Usage:                                                     ;
        ;    ss:di  Arg Array                                         ;
        ;    ax     Number of arguments in array                     ;
        ;.............................................................;

_Path:
        Entry
        def __argarray, di
        def _pathArgBeg
        def _pathEndPtr, 0000


;- - - - - - - - - - - - - - - - - - - - - - - - - - - - - - -
;  locate current path arg, if any.
;- - - - - - - - - - - - - - - - - - - - - - - - - - - - - - -
        mov si, offset RxDOS_PathSpec       ; locate PATH=
        call searchEnvVariable              ; env variable located ?
        jz _Path_08                         ; if arg located ->
        storarg _pathEndPtr, di             ; else this points to end
        xor di, di                          ; say not found

_Path_08:
        storarg _pathArgBeg, di
```

```
;- - - - - - - - - - - - - - - - - - - - - - - - - - - - - - - - - - - -
;  if no command given, type out current path value
;- - - - - - - - - - - - - - - - - - - - - - - - - - - - - - - - - - - -
        getarg di, __argarray
        mov si, word ptr [ di ]
        or si, si                               ; any args passed ?
        jnz _Path_16                            ; yes, go update path ->

        getarg dx, _pathArgBeg
        or dx, dx                               ; if arg passed ,
        jz _Path_14                             ; else, display NoPath

        push es
        mov es, word ptr [ _EnvSegment ]
        call DisplayLine                        ; show current path
        call CRLF                               ; cr/lf
        pop es
        Return

_Path_14:
        mov dx, offset CmndError_NoPath
        call DisplayLine                        ; show current path
        Return

;- - - - - - - - - - - - - - - - - - - - - - - - - - - - - - - - - - - -
;  else, set path
;- - - - - - - - - - - - - - - - - - - - - - - - - - - - - - - - - - - -
_Path_16:
        push si                                 ; env string to add
        getarg di, _pathEndPtr                  ; get pointer to end
        getarg dx, _pathArgBeg                  ; restore arg to path
        or dx, dx                               ; was any found ?
        jz _Path_24                             ; no, no need to delete ->

        mov di, dx
        call deleteEnvVariable

_Path_24:
        mov si, offset RxDOS_PathSpec           ; locate PATH=
        call insertEnvVariable

        dec di
        pop si
        call insertEnvVariable
        Return
```

Pause

The pause command is utilized in batch files to stop the processing pending some user input. The only permissible response is the carriage return or a Control-C. Any other input is ignored. One service that the function correctly provides is to fully clear the keyboard buffer prior to pausing. This forces a user to be fully synchronized with the messages and actions displayed on the screen.

Like all other statement processing, pause does not care whether it is actually executed within a batch file. The pause code displays the press-any-key-to-continue message and then calls the DOS function to clear the keyboard buffer and wait for a line of text. When the user enters the return key, the pause statement processor positions at the beginning of a new line and returns to normal processing.

```
(in rxdoscmd.asm)
        ;///////////////////////////////////////////////////////////;
        ;  Pause                                                     ;
        ;- - - - - - - - - - - - - - - - - - - - - - - - - - - - - -;
        ;                                                            ;
        ;  Usage:                                                    ;
        ;    ss:di   Arg Array                                       ;
        ;    ax      Number of arguments in array                   ;
        ;...........................................................;

_Pause:
        mov dx, offset _PressAnyKeyToContinue
        Int21 DisplayString
        Int21 ClearBufferedKeyboardInput, KeyboardInput

        call CRLF
        ret
```

Prompt

The prompt command sets the prompt environment variable. The environment variable is used by the prompt display routine, `DisplayPrompt`, when a prompt is to be displayed. The prompt command itself is very easy to implement. The real work is in the prompt display routine. Since we have not discussed it in any detail before, we discuss it here.

The prompt command always replaces the existing prompt environment string variable. If no parameters were specified with the command, the default prompt consisting of the string dg is used. It causes the generation of the all-too-familiar and somewhat uninformative C> prompt. That prompt has become a sort of cultural icon.

If the prompt command cannot locate an argument, it uses the default prompt string. The prompt environment variable is searched and, if located, deleted. The prompt is then replaced by the insertion of the new prompt string. In MS-DOS, the prompt environment variable is deleted if no argument was passed in the command.

The code is listed here, but as we noted, the real work is in displaying the prompt.

```
        ;///////////////////////////////////////////////////////////;
        ;  Prompt                                                    ;
        ;- - - - - - - - - - - - - - - - - - - - - - - - - - - - - -;
        ;                                                            ;
        ;  Usage:                                                    ;
        ;    ss:di   Arg Array                                       ;
        ;    ax      Number of arguments in array                   ;
        ;...........................................................;
```

```
_Prompt:
        mov si, word ptr [ di ]                         ; get pointer to arg
        or si, si
        jnz _prompt_08
        mov si, offset RxDOS_DefaultPrompt

_prompt_08:
        mov di, offset RxDOS_Prompt
        call _CopyString

;- - - - - - - - - - - - - - - - - - - - - - - - - - - - - - - - - - - -
;  insert prompt=
;- - - - - - - - - - - - - - - - - - - - - - - - - - - - - - - - - - - -
        mov si, offset RxDOS_PromptSpec                 ; locate PROMPT=
        call searchEnvVariable                          ; env variable located ?
        jnz _prompt_12                                  ; if no arg located ->
        call deleteEnvVariable

_prompt_12:
        mov si, offset RxDOS_PromptSpec                 ; insert PROMPT=
        call insertEnvVariable

        dec di
        mov si, offset RxDOS_Prompt
        call insertEnvVariable
        ret
```

DisplayPrompt is called whenever the command processor wants to display a prompt. It needs to display the prompt only when it will be accepting a command line input and then only from _ReadLine. The purpose of the routine is to locate the prompt environment variable or use an internal default string. By interpreting the format codes in the string, a properly formatted output string can be produced.

The environment string is first searched and copied to a local buffer for easier access. The default string is copied if no environment string can be found. The local copy of the string is the scanned. Any character that is not a command identifier, that is, a dollar sign ($), is copied to an output prompt string. When a command identifier is detected, the character that follows is tested. The display copied to the output prompt depends on the command and could include any of the following: date, time, drive, pathname, DOS version id, carriage returns, line feeds, as well as a few other codes shown in the listing.

Once the line is completely formatted, it is displayed.

```
(in rxdosprm.asm)
        ;'''''''''''''''''''''''''''''''''''''''''''''''''''''''''''''';
        ;  Display Prompt                                              ;
        ;- - - - - - - - - - - - - - - - - - - - - - - - - - - - - - - -;
        ;                                                              ;
        ;  Usage:                                                      ;
        ;  $q       =                                                  ;
        ;  $$       $                                                  ;
        ;  $t       time                                               ;
        ;  $d       date                                               ;
```

```
        ;     $p        drive:path                                      ;
        ;     $v        current rxdos version                           ;
        ;     $n        drive                                           ;
        ;     $g        >                                               ;
        ;     $l        <                                               ;
        ;     $b        | (pipe)                                        ;
        ;     $_        cr lf                                           ;
        ;     $e        esc                                             ;
        ;     $h        backspace                                       ;
        ;............................................................;

DisplayPrompt:
        Entry
        defbytes _buffer, 128

;- - - - - - - - - - - - - - - - - - - - - - - - - - - - - - - - -
;   locate init (env) prompt string
;- - - - - - - - - - - - - - - - - - - - - - - - - - - - - - - - -
        push di

        mov si, offset RxDOS_PromptSpec
        call searchEnvVariable                      ; locate prompt= spec
        jnz DisplayPrompt_06                         ; if none —>

        push ds
        add di, dx                                   ; point to env string
        mov si, offset RxDOS_Prompt
        mov ds, word ptr [ _EnvSegment ]             ; seg of env strings
        xchg di, si
        call _CopyString
        pop ds

DisplayPrompt_06:
        mov si, offset RxDOS_Prompt
        lea di, offset [ _buffer ][ bp ]
        mov byte ptr [ di ], 00

;- - - - - - - - - - - - - - - - - - - - - - - - - - - - - - - - -
;   scan prompt
;- - - - - - - - - - - - - - - - - - - - - - - - - - - - - - - - -
DisplayPrompt_08:
        lodsb

DisplayPrompt_10:
        stosb
        or al, al
        ifz DisplayPrompt_48

        cmp al, '$'
        jnz DisplayPrompt_08

;- - - - - - - - - - - - - - - - - - - - - - - - - - - - - - - - -
;   special case
;- - - - - - - - - - - - - - - - - - - - - - - - - - - - - - - - -
```

```
        dec di
        lodsb
        or al, al
        ifz DisplayPrompt_48

        call _lowerCase
        Translate 'q', '=', DisplayPrompt_18
        Translate '$', '$', DisplayPrompt_18
        Translate 'g', '>', DisplayPrompt_18
        Translate 'l', '<', DisplayPrompt_18
        Translate 'b', '|', DisplayPrompt_18
        Translate 'e', '['-40h, DisplayPrompt_18

        cmp al, 't'
        ifz DisplayPrompt_Time                      ; $t time —>
        cmp al, 'd'
        ifz DisplayPrompt_Date                      ; $d date —>
        cmp al, 'p'
        ifz DisplayPrompt_Path                      ; $p path —>
        cmp al, 'v'
        ifz DisplayPrompt_Version                   ; $v version —>
        cmp al, 'n'
        ifz DisplayPrompt_Drive                     ; $d drive —>
        cmp al, '_'
        jz DisplayPrompt_CRLF                        ; $_ crlf —>
        cmp al, 'h'
        jz DisplayPrompt_Backspace                   ; $b backspace —>
        jmp DisplayPrompt_10

;- - - - - - - - - - - - - - - - - - - - - - - - - - - - - - - - - -
; translate
;- - - - - - - - - - - - - - - - - - - - - - - - - - - - - - - - - -
DisplayPrompt_18:
        mov al, ah
        stosb                                       ; translated value
        jmp DisplayPrompt_08

;- - - - - - - - - - - - - - - - - - - - - - - - - - - - - - - - - -
; backspace
;- - - - - - - - - - - - - - - - - - - - - - - - - - - - - - - - - -
DisplayPrompt_Backspace:
        dec di
        jmp DisplayPrompt_08

;- - - - - - - - - - - - - - - - - - - - - - - - - - - - - - - - - -
; cr lf
;- - - - - - - - - - - - - - - - - - - - - - - - - - - - - - - - - -
DisplayPrompt_CRLF:
        mov ax, 0a0dh
        stosw
        jmp DisplayPrompt_08

;- - - - - - - - - - - - - - - - - - - - - - - - - - - - - - - - - -
; time of day
;- - - - - - - - - - - - - - - - - - - - - - - - - - - - - - - - - -
```

```
DisplayPrompt_Time:
        call formatCurrentTime
        jmp DisplayPrompt_08


;- - - - - - - - - - - - - - - - - - - - - - - - - - - - - - -
;  date
;- - - - - - - - - - - - - - - - - - - - - - - - - - - - - - -
DisplayPrompt_Date:
        call formatCurrentDate
        jmp DisplayPrompt_08


;- - - - - - - - - - - - - - - - - - - - - - - - - - - - - - -
;  path
;- - - - - - - - - - - - - - - - - - - - - - - - - - - - - - -
DisplayPrompt_Path:
        push si

        Int21 CurrentDisk
        mov dl, al                              ; save drive letter
        add al, 'A'                             ; get drive
        stosb

        mov ax, '\:'
        stosw                                   ; d:\ ...

        inc dl
        mov si, di
        mov byte ptr [ si ], 0
        Int21 GetCurrentDirectory               ; get current directory

DisplayPrompt_Path_08:
        lodsb
        or al, al
        jnz DisplayPrompt_Path_08

        dec si
        mov di, si

        pop si
        jmp DisplayPrompt_08


;- - - - - - - - - - - - - - - - - - - - - - - - - - - - - - -
;  version
;- - - - - - - - - - - - - - - - - - - - - - - - - - - - - - -
DisplayPrompt_Version:
        push si
        mov si, offset RxDOS_Version
        call _CopyString
        dec di
        pop si
        jmp DisplayPrompt_08


;- - - - - - - - - - - - - - - - - - - - - - - - - - - - - - -
;  drive letter
;- - - - - - - - - - - - - - - - - - - - - - - - - - - - - - -
```

```
DisplayPrompt_Drive:
        Int21 CurrentDisk
        add al, 'A'                                            ; get drive
        stosb
        jmp DisplayPrompt_08

;- - - - - - - - - - - - - - - - - - - - - - - - - - - - - - - - - - - -
; display prompt
;- - - - - - - - - - - - - - - - - - - - - - - - - - - - - - - - - - - -
DisplayPrompt_48:
        lea dx, offset [ _buffer ][ bp ]
        call Displayline

        pop di
        Return

        ;'''''''''''''''''''''''''''''''''''''''''''''''''''''''''''''''';
        ;  Format Time String                                          ;
        ;.............................................................;

formatCurrentTime:
        Entry
        defbytes _countryInfo, 128

        push si
        push di
        mov si, offset RxDOSIntl_TimeTemplate
        call _CopyString

    ; eventually, make this international

        lea dx, offset [ _countryInfo ][ bp ]
        Int21 CountryDependentInfo                       ; get country info

        Int21 GetTime

        pop di
        mov al, ch                                       ; hours
        call ConvTo2CharDecimal

        inc di
        mov al, cl                                       ; minutes
        call ConvTo2CharDecimal

        inc di
        mov al, dh                                       ; seconds
        call ConvTo2CharDecimal

        inc di
        mov al, dh                                       ; hundreths
        call ConvTo2CharDecimal

        pop si
        Return
```

```
        ;/////////////////////////////////////////////////////////;
        ;  Format Date String                                     ;
        ;.........................................................;

formatCurrentDate:
        Entry
        defbytes _countryInfo, 128

        push si
        push di
        mov si, offset RxDOSIntl_DateTemplate
        call _CopyString

    ; eventually, make this international

        lea dx, offset [ _countryInfo ][ bp ]
        Int21 CountryDependentInfo                  ; get country info

        Int21 GetDate

        pop di
        xor ah, ah
        mov si, ax
        add si, si
        add si, ax                                  ; offset to day of week text
        add si, offset RxDOSIntl_DayOfWeek

        push cx
        mov cx, 3
        rep movsb                                   ; copy 3 bytes

        inc di
        mov al, dh                                  ; mon
        call ConvTo2CharDecimal

        inc di
        mov al, dl                                  ; day
        call ConvTo2CharDecimal

        inc di
        pop ax                                      ; year
        call ConvTo4CharDecimal

        pop si
        Return

        ;/////////////////////////////////////////////////////////;
        ;  Convert AL To 2 Char Decimal                           ;
        ;.........................................................;

ConvTo2CharDecimal:
        push cx
        xor ah, ah
        mov cl, 10
        div cl
        or ax, '00'
        stosw
```

```
        pop cx
        ret

        ;'''''''''''''''''''''''''''''''''''''''''''''''''''''''''''''';
        ;   Convert AX To 4 Char Decimal                              ;
        ;..............................................................;

ConvTo4CharDecimal:
        push cx
        add di, 4
        push di

__4CharDecimal_04:
        xor dx, dx
        mov cx, 10
        div cx

        dec di
        or dl, '0'
        mov byte ptr [ di ], dl

        or ax, ax
        jnz __4CharDecimal_04

        pop di
        pop cx
        ret
```

Rem

The simplest of all command service functions is the remark processor, which has absolutely nothing to do. The command parser interprets the remark statement as a command and calls this function, which ignores its contents altogether, thus making it a comment or remark.

(in rxdoscmd.asm)
```
        ;'''''''''''''''''''''''''''''''''''''''''''''''''''''''''''''';
        ;   Remark (Rem )                                             ;
        ;..............................................................;

_Rem:
        ret                                         ; do nothing
```

Remove Directory

The remove directory command attempts to remove an existing directory from disk. The command is a straightforward interface to the DOS Remove Subdirectory function. The command checks that it contains only a single argument. The pointer to the argument is then passed to the Remove Subdirectory function. If the return value is an error, an error message is displayed.

If the DOS function call returned with no errors, the subdirectory was removed from the disk.

```
(in rxdoscmd.asm)
        ;//////////////////////////////////////////////////////////;
        ;                                                          ;
        ;   Remove Directory                                       ;
        ;- - - - - - - - - - - - - - - - - - - - - - - - - - - - -;
        ;                                                          ;
        ;   Usage:                                                 ;
        ;    ss:di  Arg Array                                      ;
        ;    ax     Number of arguments in array                  ;
        ;..........................................................;

_RemDir:
        call CheckOneArg                        ; see if 1 arg
        jc _removeDir_32                        ; if error ->

        mov dx, word ptr [ di ]                 ; point to filename arg
        Int21 RemoveSubdirectory                ; try command
        jnc _removeDir_32                       ; if valid ->
        call DisplayError                       ; if error

_removeDir_32:
        ret
```

Rename

The rename command can be used not only to change the name of files but also to move files across directories within the same drive. That functionality is provided by DOS function 56h, the Rename function. Files can be moved across directories because they don't need to be reallocated or copied. Only their directory entries need to be moved from one directory to the next.

Although the DOS Rename function provides the aforementioned features, it does not provide basic wild-character-based renaming. That capability must be provided by code in the command processor. To support wild characters, the command processor builds individual complete source and destination names from parameters that may contain wild characters.

The code, shown next, begins by using the command line preprocessor function to count the number of arguments passed. Two arguments must have been provided. The second of the two arguments is then expanded using _splitpath. This function will split an argument into its components, isolating the drive, path, filename, and extension. The second argument cannot contain a drive letter, and an error is produced if one is located.

Next, the first and second arguments are checked for wild characters. If neither argument has them, the Rename function can be executed without any name changes. Otherwise, the command must walk through the source directory, that is, the directory named or implied by the first argument, locating files that match the argument name. This is, of course, accomplished by using the DOS FindFirst and FindNext functions.

Once a file is located using these functions, its name is mapped to a destination name. The wild characters in the destination name serve as a mask. Only the character positions that match the wild characters in the destination name are actually copied from the source name. This is the method used by DOS, but it can create some renaming problems. Consider, for example, the following ordinary rename command:

```
c> ren a*.* foo*.*
```

For this command to successfully work, all the original or source filenames must contain at least four characters, that is, one greater than the minimum length of the destination filename. Here's why: Assume that the filenames found were a1, a2, a3, and so on. Each of these filenames is converted to foo. Although the first file encountered is renamed successfully, an error message is produced when the second file is renamed.

At any rate, once the name is mapped to its destination name, the file is renamed. The process continues until no additional files can be found by the Find Next function.

```
(in rxdosren.asm)
        ;///////////////////////////////////////////////////////////;
        ;  Rename filenameA filenameB                                ;
        ;- - - - - - - - - - - - - - - - - - - - - - - - - - - - - - ;
        ;                                                            ;
        ;  Usage:                                                    ;
        ;  ss:di  Arg Array                                          ;
        ;  ax     Number of arguments in array                      ;
        ;............................................................;

_Rename:
        Entry
        def _filesRenamed                       ; how many renamed
        def __argarray, di                      ; args array
        defbytes _renamedFileName, 15
        defbytes _expandedname, sizeExpandedName

        mov cx, 2                               ; must have two arguments
        mov dx, cx                              ; must have two arguments
        xor bx, bx
        call PreProcessCmndLine                 ; make sure args are ok
        ifc _renameError                        ; if error —>

;- - - - - - - - - - - - - - - - - - - - - - - - - - - - - - - - - - -
;  make sure second arg contains no drive or path info
;- - - - - - - - - - - - - - - - - - - - - - - - - - - - - - - - - - -
        mov di, word ptr [ __argarray ][ bp ]
        mov si, word ptr [ di + 2 ]             ; second argument
        lea di, offset [ _expandedname ][ bp ]  ; test expansion
        call _splitpath                         ; expand name components

        cmp byte ptr [ _expandedname. expDrive ][ bp ], 0
        ifnz _renameError                       ; if error —>

;- - - - - - - - - - - - - - - - - - - - - - - - - - - - - - - - - - -
;  test for simple (no wildcard case)
;- - - - - - - - - - - - - - - - - - - - - - - - - - - - - - - - - - -
        mov di, word ptr [ __argarray ][ bp ]
```

```
        mov si, word ptr [ di ]                 ; first arg
        call _scanWildCharacters                ; first arg have wild chars ?
        jz _rename_12                           ; yes ->

        mov si, word ptr [ di + 2 ]             ; second arg
        call _scanWildCharacters                ; 2nd arg have wild chars ?
        jz _rename_12                           ; yes ->

        mov dx, word ptr [ di ]                 ; first arg
        mov di, word ptr [ di + 2 ]             ; second arg
        Int21 RenameFile                        ; rename file
        jc _renameError                         ; if error ->

        Return

;- - - - - - - - - - - - - - - - - - - - - - - - - - - - - - - -
;  split pathname into [drive:] [path] [filename]
;- - - - - - - - - - - - - - - - - - - - - - - - - - - - - - - -
_rename_12:
        mov cx, sizefnName
        lea si, offset [ _expandedname. expFilename ][ bp ]
        call _expandWildCharacters

        mov cx, sizefnExtension+1
        lea si, offset [ _expandedname. expExtension ][ bp ]
        call _expandWildCharacters

;- - - - - - - - - - - - - - - - - - - - - - - - - - - - - - - -
;  determine if files to rename
;- - - - - - - - - - - - - - - - - - - - - - - - - - - - - - - -
        storarg _filesRenamed, 0000             ; none renamed so far

        mov di, word ptr [ __argarray ][ bp ]
        mov dx, word ptr [ di ]                 ; first arg
        Int21 FindFirstFile                     ; locate file with name
        jc _rename_36                           ; if no more ->

_rename_18:
        mov si, offset [ RxDOS_DTA. findFileName ]
        lea bx, offset [ _expandedname. expFilename ][ bp ]
        lea di, offset [ _renamedFileName    ][ bp ]
        call _renameCopy

        lea bx, offset [ _expandedname. expExtension ][ bp ]
        cmp byte ptr [ bx ], 0
        jz _rename_22

        push di
        mov al, '.'
        mov cx, (sizefnName+1)
        mov di, offset [ RxDOS_DTA. findFileName ]
        repnz scasb                             ; locate '.'
        mov si, di
        pop di
```

```
        jnz _rename_22

        stosb                                           ; add period if one located
        inc bx                                          ; skip expansion period.
        call _renameCopy

_rename_22:
        mov dx, offset [ RxDOS_DTA. findFileName ]
        lea di, offset [ _renamedFileName    ][ bp ]
        Int21 RenameFile                                ; rename file
        jc _renameError                                 ; if error —>

        inc word ptr [ _filesRenamed ][ bp ]            ; number renamed
        Int21 FindNextFile                              ; more files to rename ?
        jnc _rename_18                                  ; if more —>

;- - - - - - - - - - - - - - - - - - - - - - - - - - - - - - - - -
;  return
;- - - - - - - - - - - - - - - - - - - - - - - - - - - - - - - - -
_rename_36:
        cmp word ptr [ _filesRenamed ][ bp ], 0000      ; any files renamed ?
        jz _renameError                                 ; if none —>
        Return

;- - - - - - - - - - - - - - - - - - - - - - - - - - - - - - - - -
;  error in rename command
;- - - - - - - - - - - - - - - - - - - - - - - - - - - - - - - - -
_renameError:
        mov dx, offset CmndError_FileAlreadyExists
        call DisplayErrorMessage
        Return

        ;''''''''''''''''''''''''''''''''''''''''''''''''''''''''''''''';
        ;  Scan For Wild Characters                                    ;
        ;- - - - - - - - - - - - - - - - - - - - - - - - - - - - - - - -;
        ;                                                              ;
        ;  Usage:                                                      ;
        ;    ss:si  pointer to null terminated name                    ;
        ;..............................................................;

_scanWildCharacters:
        push si

_scanWildCharacters_08:
        lodsb
        or al, al
        jz _scanWildCharacters_16

        cmp al, '?'
        jz _scanWildCharacters_18
        cmp al, '*'
        jz _scanWildCharacters_18
        jmp _scanWildCharacters_08
```

```
_scanWildCharacters_16:
        cmp al, '?'

_scanWildCharacters_18:
        pop si
        ret

        ;'''''''''''''''''''''''''''''''''''''''''''''''''''''''''';
        ;  Expand Wild Characters                                 ;
        ;- - - - - - - - - - - - - - - - - - - - - - - - - - - - -;
        ;                                                         ;
        ;  Usage:                                                 ;
        ;   ss:si  pointer to null terminated name                ;
        ;.........................................................;

_expandWildCharacters:
        lodsb
        or al, al
        jz _expandWildCharacters_10

        cmp al, '*'
        jz _expandWildCharacters_12
        loop _expandWildCharacters

_expandWildCharacters_10:
        ret

_expandWildCharacters_12:
        mov di, si
        dec di
        mov al, '?'
        rep stosb                               ; fill with ? ...

        xor ax, ax
        stosb                                   ; add null terminator
        ret

        ;'''''''''''''''''''''''''''''''''''''''''''''''''''''''''';
        ;  Create Renamed Name                                    ;
        ;- - - - - - - - - - - - - - - - - - - - - - - - - - - - -;
        ;                                                         ;
        ;  Usage:                                                 ;
        ;   ss:si  current name of file from find                 ;
        ;   ss:bx  wild character matching template               ;
        ;   ss:di  output name field                              ;
        ;.........................................................;

_renameCopy:
        mov al, byte ptr [ si ]
        or al, al
        jz _renameCopy_12
        cmp al, '.'
        jz _renameCopy_12
```

```
        mov al, byte ptr [ bx ]
        or al, al
        jz _renameCopy_12
        cmp al, '?'
        jnz _renameCopy_08

        mov al, byte ptr [ si ]

_renameCopy_08:
        mov byte ptr [ di ], al

        inc si
        inc di
        inc bx
        jmp _renameCopy

_renameCopy_12:
        mov byte ptr [ di ], 00
        ret
```

Set

The set command displays, sets, or removes environment string variables. The number of arguments passed are checked. If the command contains no arguments, the contents of all the environment variables are displayed. Otherwise, an individual environment variable is either set or cleared.

To display all the environment variables, the address of the environment block is fetched. Then the strings that follow are displayed. Each string in the environment block is a NULL terminated string and can be displayed by the DisplayLine function. The code loops through all the arguments.

If an argument was passed, the command either sets or clears an environment string. The command is scanned for an equal sign. The command sets a string if any characters follow the equal sign. The command may be setting a new value for an existing environment variable. The logic takes advantage of this fact by using the following algorithm. The environment variable is searched and deleted. If an insert string exists, it is then inserted. This logic performs inserts, deletes, and replacements based on whether it finds strings in the environment block or at the command line.

```
(in rxdoscmd.asm)
        ;'''''''''''''''''''''''''''''''''''''''''''''''''''''''''''''''''''''''''''';
        ;   SET                                                     ;
        ;   SET variable=                                           ;
        ;   SET variable=string                                     ;
        ;- - - - - - - - - - - - - - - - - - - - - - - - - - - - - -;
        ;                                                           ;
        ;   Display, set or remove environment variable.            ;
        ;...........................................................;

_Set:
        Entry
        def __argarray, di
```

```
        call CountArgs
        or ax, ax                                   ; if no args
        jnz _SetEnvVariable                         ; set/ clear env variable ->

;- - - - - - - - - - - - - - - - - - - - - - - - - - - - - - - - -
;  display environment variables
;- - - - - - - - - - - - - - - - - - - - - - - - - - - - - - - - -
_SetDisplay:
        xor si, si
        mov es, word ptr [ _EnvSegment ]

_SetDisplay_08:
        cmp byte ptr es:[ si ], 00
        jz _SetDisplayReturn
        cmp byte ptr es:[ si ], ';'                 ; if comment,
        jz _SetDisplay_12                           ; skip ->

        mov dx, si
        call DisplayLine
        call CRLF

_SetDisplay_12:
        inc si                                      ; scan to end of env string
        cmp byte ptr es:[ si - 1 ], 00
        jnz _SetDisplay_12
        jmp _SetDisplay_08

;- - - - - - - - - - - - - - - - - - - - - - - - - - - - - - - - -
;  set/clear environment variable
;- - - - - - - - - - - - - - - - - - - - - - - - - - - - - - - - -
_SetEnvVariable:
        mov di, word ptr [ __argarray ][ bp ]
        mov si, word ptr [ di ]                     ; get lead arg

_SetEnvVariable_08:
        inc si
        cmp byte ptr [ si-1 ], '='                  ; line contains a break ?
        jz _SetEnvVariable_12                        ; yes ->
        cmp byte ptr [ si-1 ], 00                    ; end of string ?
        jnz _SetEnvVariable_08                       ; not yet ->

        mov dx, offset CmndError_SyntaxError
        call DisplayErrorMessage                     ; display message
        Return

;- - - - - - - - - - - - - - - - - - - - - - - - - - - - - - - - -
;  uppercase up to '='
;- - - - - - - - - - - - - - - - - - - - - - - - - - - - - - - - -
_SetEnvVariable_12:
        mov si, word ptr [ di ]                     ; get lead arg

_SetEnvVariable_14:
        mov al, byte ptr [ si ]
        or al, al
```

```
              jz _SetEnvVariable_16
              cmp al, '='
              jz _SetEnvVariable_16

              call _upperCase
              mov byte ptr [ si ], al
              inc si
              jmp _SetEnvVariable_14

;- - - - - - - - - - - - - - - - - - - - - - - - - - - - - - -
;  search/ delete
;- - - - - - - - - - - - - - - - - - - - - - - - - - - - - - -
_SetEnvVariable_16:
              mov si, word ptr [ di ]                ; get lead arg
              call searchEnvVariable                 ; env variable located ?
              jnz _SetEnvVariable_18                 ; not found ->
              call deleteEnvVariable                 ; delete env variable

_SetEnvVariable_18:
              mov si, word ptr [ __argarray ][ bp ]
              mov si, word ptr [ si ]                ; get lead arg
              call insertEnvVariable                 ; insert at end

;- - - - - - - - - - - - - - - - - - - - - - - - - - - - - - -
;  return
;- - - - - - - - - - - - - - - - - - - - - - - - - - - - - - -
_SetDisplayReturn:
              Return
```

Shift

The shift command doesn't mean anything unless executed within a batch file. Its purpose is to shift the batch arguments once to the left. This command provides the support necessary to handle a variable number of batch file arguments and for the removal of optional parameters and switches. When a batch file begins, its arguments are stored in a batch file argument array. The shift command moves all the argument pointers up by one, removing the topmost argument.

The code that supports the shift command begins with a pointer to the first argument, that is, the pointer to the %0 argument in the batch file. It copies the argument that follows to this location. It then loops through the entire table moving all subsequent arguments up by one and places a null at the last argument position.

```
(in rxdoscmd.asm)
        ;'''''''''''''''''''''''''''''''''''''''''''''''''''''''''''''''''''''';
        ;  Shift                                                              ;
        ;- - - - - - - - - - - - - - - - - - - - - - - - - - - - - - - - - - -;
        ;                                                                     ;
        ;  No parameters expected                                             ;
        ;.....................................................................;

_Shift:
```

```
        mov si, offset ( RxDOS_BatchFile. batchArgPtrs ); copy args down
        mov cx, word ptr [ RxDOS_BatchFile. batchNumArgs ]
        or cx, cx
        jz _shift_32                                    ; if no arguments ->

_shift_08:
        mov ax, word ptr [ si + 2 ]
        mov word ptr [ si ], ax                         ; shift arg down
        add si, 2                                       ; point to next arg
        loop _shift_08                                  ; loop through all args

        dec word ptr [ RxDOS_BatchFile. batchNumArgs ]  ; decr # args

_shift_32:
        mov word ptr [ si ], 0000                       ; null out last arg
        ret
```

Time

The time command works in much the same way, and for many of the same reasons, as the date command. It sets or reports the current time maintained by DOS. That time is reported by the CLOCK$ device driver. The driver divides the clock ticks maintained by the BIOS into the hours, minutes, and seconds since the beginning of the day. The clock tick count is maintained in the BIOS communications area at segment 0040.

If the time command is passed with no arguments, the time is displayed, and a prompt will ask for a new time. Otherwise, the command sets the time passed as the argument if no errors were detected. The time's format is based on the local country setting. A template for the expected time format is maintained by the DOS command processor and is based on the local country value returned by DOS function 38h, the Get/Set Country Information function.

Whether the time was passed as an argument or prompted for within the command, the time must be parsed in order to be accepted. There are only minor variations in the way in which the time of day is expressed internationally. Although it is always in the hours, minutes, seconds order, there are variations in whether the hour is expressed in the 24-hour format, or in the 12-hour am/pm format. Additional minor variations exist in the separator character used between the terms.

The time command processor operates in many respects like the date command processing function. If no arguments were passed with the command, DOS displays the current system time and then prompts for a new time. Either the time entered by the user or the time passed as the command argument, whichever is available, is checked. The command shell is concerned only with identifying the values entered and does not attempt to verify the validity of the argument entered directly. It simply utilizes the DOS set system time function. The time is incorrectly input if the values fail in the DOS function.

```
(in rxdosprm.asm)
        ;'''''''''''''''''''''''''''''''''''''''''''''''''''''''''''''';
        ;  Time [ time ]                                               ;
        ;- - - - - - - - - - - - - - - - - - - - - - - - - - - - - - -;
```

```
        ;                                              ;
        ;  Usage:                                       ;
        ;  ss:di  Arg Array                             ;
        ;  ax     Number of arguments in array          ;
        ;...............................................;

_Time:
        Entry
        def _hours
        def _minutes
        def _seconds
        def _hundredths

        def __argarray, di                    ; args array
        defbytes _buffer, 128                 ; input buffer
        defbytes _printbuffer, 128

        call CheckOptOneArg                   ; see if 1 arg
        ifc _timeInvalid                      ; if error in args

        mov si, word ptr [ di ]               ; get first arg
        or si, si                             ; if arg, go parse —>
        jnz _time_26

;- - - - - - - - - - - - - - - - - - - - - - - - - - - - - - -
; display current time
;- - - - - - - - - - - - - - - - - - - - - - - - - - - - - - -
        lea di, offset [ _buffer ][ bp ]
        push di
        call formatCurrentTime                ; get current time

        mov di, offset _ShowCurrentTime
        push di
        lea di, offset [ _printbuffer ][ bp ]
        push di
        call _sprintf
        add sp, ax                            ; # args passed
        call DisplayLine

;- - - - - - - - - - - - - - - - - - - - - - - - - - - - - - -
; please enter time
;- - - - - - - - - - - - - - - - - - - - - - - - - - - - - - -
_time_12:
        mov dx, offset _PleaseEnterTime
        call DisplayLine

        lea di, offset [ _buffer ][ bp ]
        mov byte ptr [ bufMaxLength ][ di ], 128
        mov word ptr [ bufActualLength ][ di ], 0

        mov dx, di                            ; where buffer
        call _getStdinLine                    ; read buffer

        call CRLF
```

```
        mov bl, byte ptr [ _buffer. bufActualLength ][ bp ]
        and bx, 255
        ifz _timeReturn

        add bx, bp
        mov byte ptr [ _buffer. bufData ][ bx ], 00      ; place a null terminator
        lea si, offset [ _buffer. bufData ][ bp ]        ; parse text

;- - - - - - - - - - - - - - - - - - - - - - - - - - - - - - - -
;  parse arg at [ si ]       ** must internationalize by matching template **
;- - - - - - - - - - - - - - - - - - - - - - - - - - - - - - - -
_time_26:
        xor ax, ax
        storarg _hours, ax
        storarg _minutes, ax
        storarg _seconds, ax
        storarg _hundredths, ax

        call _GetNumber                                  ; get hours
        mov word ptr [ _hours ][ bp ], dx

        call _checkSeparator
        jc _timeInvalid
        jz _time_36
        call _GetNumber                                  ; get mins
        mov word ptr [ _minutes ][ bp ], dx

        call _checkSeparator
        jc _timeInvalid
        jz _time_36
        call _GetNumber                                  ; get seconds
        mov word ptr [ _seconds ][ bp ], dx

        call _checkSeparator
        jc _timeInvalid
        jz _time_36
        call _GetNumber                                  ; get hundreths of seconds
        mov word ptr [ _hundredths ][ bp ], dx

_time_36:
        mov dl, byte ptr [ _hundredths ][ bp ]
        mov dh, byte ptr [ _seconds    ][ bp ]
        mov ch, byte ptr [ _hours      ][ bp ]
        mov cl, byte ptr [ _minutes    ][ bp ]
        Int21 SetTime
        or al, al                                        ; date valid ?
        jnz _timeInvalid                                 ; no ->

;- - - - - - - - - - - - - - - - - - - - - - - - - - - - - - - -
;  return
;- - - - - - - - - - - - - - - - - - - - - - - - - - - - - - - -
_timeReturn:
        Return
```

```
;- - - - - - - - - - - - - - - - - - - - - - - - - - - - - - - - - - -
;   invalid time
;- - - - - - - - - - - - - - - - - - - - - - - - - - - - - - - - - - -
_timeInvalid:
        mov dx, offset CmndError_InvalidTime
        call DisplayLine
        jmp _time_12


        ;'''''''''''''''''''''''''''''''''''''''''''''''''''''''''''''';
        ;   Test Time Separator                                        ;
        ;.............................................................;

_checkSeparator:
        mov al, byte ptr [ si-1 ]                   ; get last character processed
        or al, al                                   ; if end of line –>
        jz _checkSeparator_24                       ; return end of line –>

        cmp al, ' '
        jnz _checkSeparator_06                      ; skip any spaces –>

        inc si
        jmp _checkSeparator

_checkSeparator_06:
        call _lowerCase

        cmp al, ':'
        jz _checkSeparator_24                       ; return end of line –>
        cmp al, '.'
        jz _checkSeparator_24                       ; return end of line –>

        cmp al, 'a'                                 ; am / pm ?
        jz _checkSeparator_12                       ; yes –>
        cmp al, 'p'                                 ; am / pm ?
        jz _checkSeparator_10                       ; yes –>

        stc                                         ; anything else is an error
        ret

_checkSeparator_10:
        cmp byte ptr [ _hours ][ bp ], 12
        jge _checkSeparator_12
        add byte ptr [ _hours ][ bp ], 12

_checkSeparator_12:
        xor ax, ax

_checkSeparator_24:
        or al, al
        ret
```

Truename

The truename command is an undocumented DOS command that utilizes the undocumented DOS Get Actual Name function. Its purpose is to lexically expand the pathname passed. The function essentially prepends the current drive and directory to the source text and removes any relative directory terms such as . and .. terms. The resulting name is not checked to be valid in any form.

Although there is no truly useful purpose for the truename command, there are many uses for the DOS Get Actual Name function. For one, it is used by the command shell to create the directory name that is displayed during a `dir` command.

The function checks to be sure that an argument was passed. The argument becomes the source argument to the DOS Get Actual Name function. The returned output is then displayed.

```
(in rxdoscmd.asm)
        ;''''''''''''''''''''''''''''''''''''''''''''''''''''''''''''';
        ;  Truename [ anypath ]                                       ;
        ;- - - - - - - - - - - - - - - - - - - - - - - - - - - - - -;
        ;                                                            ;
        ;  Displays the DOS expanded filename.                       ;
        ;                                                            ;
        ;............................................................;

_Truename:
        Entry
        defbytes _buffer, 128

        call CheckOptOneArg                        ; should have an arg
        jc _truename_36                            ; error -->

        mov si, word ptr [ di ]                    ; get argument passed
        lea di, offset [ _buffer ][ bp ]
        Int21 GetActualFileName

        lea dx, offset [ _buffer ][ bp ]
        call DisplayLine                           ; print line

_truename_36:
        Return
```

Type

The type command lists a file to the stdout device. The original plans for the implementation of this command in RxDOS were to permit multiple arguments, which could have included wild characters. The type command used the number of arguments check routine to process the pagination switch. Notice that because of the multiple possible arguments, the limit on the number of arguments is set to between 001 and 999, providing for a more than ample set of arguments.

The routine isolates the first argument and then determines whether this argument matches a valid DOS file. If it does not, it displays an error message, and the code moves on to the next argument. Otherwise, the file is opened, the filename is displayed, and the file is read and displayed on screen. The file is assumed to contain all the necessary carriage returns and line feeds. The routine checks throughout the read loop for a control break or control-C in order to provide the user with adequate command termination support.

When the end of the current file is reached, the command parser determines if additional files can be located by using the DOS Find Next Entry function. This trick prevents having to actually determine if the argument contained wild characters in the name. The process continues through each successive argument until all arguments have been processed.

```
(in rxdoscmd.asm)
        ;''''''''''''''''''''''''''''''''''''''''''''''''''''''''''''''';
        ;  Type filename                                                ;
        ;..............................................................;

_Type:
        Entry
        def __argarray, di
        def _handle
        defbytes _buffer, 130

        mov cx, 0001                            ; at least one arg
        mov dx, 099
                            ; unlimitd number of args
        mov bx, offset _TypeSwitches
        call PreProcessCmndLine                 ; process switches
        jc _TypeReturn                          ; if error ->

        mov ax, word ptr [ _TypePauseSwitch. swFlags ]
        call setPagingMode

;- - - - - - - - - - - - - - - - - - - - - - - - - - - - - - - - - -
;  get next argument
;- - - - - - - - - - - - - - - - - - - - - - - - - - - - - - - - - -
_TypeNext:
        mov di, word ptr [ __argarray ][ bp ]
        mov dx, word ptr [ di ]
        or dx, dx                               ; any more args ?
        jz _TypeReturn                          ; if no more ->

        xor cx, cx
        Int21 findFirstFile                     ; filename found for arg ?
        jnc _TypeOpenFile                       ; no, go to next ->

        push dx
        mov dx, offset _TypeCannotFind
        call DisplayLine

        pop dx
        call DisplayLine                        ; show arg
        jmp _TypeNext

;- - - - - - - - - - - - - - - - - - - - - - - - - - - - - - - - - -
;  open and print
;- - - - - - - - - - - - - - - - - - - - - - - - - - - - - - - - - -
```

```
_TypeOpenFile:
        mov di, word ptr [ __argarray ][ bp ]           ; arguments pointer
        call nullTerminateArgs                          ; null terminate args

        mov dx, word ptr [ di ]
      ; mov dx, offset [ RxDOS_DTA. findFileName ]
        Int21 OpenFile, 0000                            ; open
        storarg _handle, ax
        jc _TypeNext

        call CRLF

        mov dx, offset [ RxDOS_DTA. findFileName ]
        call DisplayLine                                ; show arg
        call CRLF

;- - - - - - - - - - - - - - - - - - - - - - - - - - - - - - -
;  read and list
;- - - - - - - - - - - - - - - - - - - - - - - - - - - - - - -
_TypeReadFile:
        mov cx, 128                                     ; how much to read
        getarg bx, _handle                             ; get handle
        lea dx, offset [ _buffer ][ bp ]               ; where to read
        Int21 ReadFile                                 ; read buffer
        jc _TypeCloseFile

        or ax, ax                                       ; at end of file ?
        jz _TypeCloseFile                               ; yes, go to next ->

        mov cx, ax                                      ; how much read
        lea dx, offset [ _buffer ][ bp ]               ; where to read
        call DisplayLineCount
        jmp _TypeReadFile

;- - - - - - - - - - - - - - - - - - - - - - - - - - - - - - -
;  close file
;- - - - - - - - - - - - - - - - - - - - - - - - - - - - - - -
_TypeCloseFile:
        getarg bx, _handle                             ; get handle
        Int21 CloseFile
        call CRLF

      ; Int21 findNextFile                             ; more files ?
      ; jnc _TypeOpenFile                              ; yes, open file ->
      ;
      ; add word ptr [ __argarray ][ bp ], 2
      ; jmp _TypeNext                                  ; else go to next ->

;- - - - - - - - - - - - - - - - - - - - - - - - - - - - - - -
;  return
;- - - - - - - - - - - - - - - - - - - - - - - - - - - - - - -
_TypeReturn:
        Return
```

Ver

The ver command prints the current DOS version and copyright statement. The command processing function checks to ensure that no arguments were passed. Usually, an argument may indicate that a redirection character was improperly entered. The code then displays the current version and copyright statements.

(in rxdoscmd.asm)

```
        ;//////////////////////////////////////////////////////////;
        ;  Version                                                 ;
        ;- - - - - - - - - - - - - - - - - - - - - - - - - - - - - -;
        ;                                                          ;
        ;  No parameters expected                                  ;
        ;..........................................................;

_Ver:
        call CheckNoArgs                        ; check for no arguments
        jc _ver_32                              ; if error ->

        call CRLF

        mov dx, offset RxDOS_Version
        call DisplayLine

        mov dx, offset RxDOS_VersionCopyright
        call DisplayLine

_ver_32:
        ret
```

Verify

The verify statement sets or displays the status of the DOS disk verify flag. If verify is set ON, disk writes are checked to ensure that they can be reread. The block is not physically reread, just the disk control and checksum logic, but the operation, though more secure, takes more time.

The verify statement first checks to determine if there is an optional argument. Any more than one argument is treated as an error. If there are no arguments with the command, the status of the DOS verify flag is read, and the appropriate message is displayed. Otherwise, the argument is looked up in a table. If the argument is valid, the verify flag is set in DOS.

(in rxdoscmd.asm)

```
        ;//////////////////////////////////////////////////////////;
        ;  Verify [ ON | OFF ]                                     ;
        ;- - - - - - - - - - - - - - - - - - - - - - - - - - - - - -;
        ;                                                          ;
        ;  Sets, clears or reports on RxDOS disk verify parameters. ;
        ;                                                          ;
        ;..........................................................;
```

```
_Verify:
        Entry
        ddef __argarray, ss, di
        def _args, ax

        call CheckOptOneArg                     ; see if 1 arg
        jc _VerifyExit                          ; if error ->

        or ax, ax                               ; any arguments ?
        jz _VerifyPrintcurrent                  ; none, print current status ->

;- - - - - - - - - - - - - - - - - - - - - - - - - - - - - - - -
; test for On/ Off
;- - - - - - - - - - - - - - - - - - - - - - - - - - - - - - - -
        mov si, word ptr [ di ]                 ; get single argument
        mov di, offset RxDOS_OnOff
        call CmndLookup                         ; lookup command
        jc _VerifyError                         ; if not on/off, print line ->

        mov al, bl
        Int21 SetVerifySwitch                   ; set or clear verify switch
        Return

;- - - - - - - - - - - - - - - - - - - - - - - - - - - - - - - -
; must specify on or off
;- - - - - - - - - - - - - - - - - - - - - - - - - - - - - - - -
_VerifyError:
        mov dx, offset CmndError_MustSpecifyOnOff
        call DisplayErrorMessage
        Return

;- - - - - - - - - - - - - - - - - - - - - - - - - - - - - - - -
; print verify on/off value
;- - - - - - - - - - - - - - - - - - - - - - - - - - - - - - - -
_VerifyPrintcurrent:
        Int21 GetVerify

        mov bl, al
        xor bh, bh
        add bx, bx
        mov dx, word ptr [ _VerifyOptions ][ bx ]
        call DisplayLine

_VerifyExit:
        Return
```

Vol

The volume statement displays the volume label of a given disk drive. If the argument is missing, the volume label for the current disk is displayed. The function checks for an argument, and if present, determines if it references a valid drive. Because the command relies on the DOS FindFirst function, which will detect missing or invalid drives, the only checking performed by the command processor is that the drive be a letter A and Z.

The volume label is read by searching in the root directory for a file with the Volume Label attribute. The command handler builds the search string shown here. The drive argument passed with the command replaces the drive parameter, and the DOS FindFirst function is called. If the volume label is not found, an error message is displayed; otherwise, the volume name is displayed.

```
                                db "c:"
RxDOS_RootDirectory             db "\*.*", 0            ; root directory

(in rxdoscmd.asm)
        ;'''''''''''''''''''''''''''''''''''''''''''''''''''''''''''''''';
        ;  Volume                                                        ;
        ;- - - - - - - - - - - - - - - - - - - - - - - - - - - - - - - -;
        ;                                                                ;
        ;  Displays Volume Information                                   ;
        ;                                                                ;
        ;................................................................;

_Vol:
        Entry
        def _currdisk, 0000
        defbytes _printbuffer, 128

        Int21 CurrentDisk
        add al, 'A'                             ; get drive
        mov byte ptr [ _currdisk ][ bp ], al    ; save current disk

        call checkOptOneArg
        jc _Vol_60                              ; parameter is wrong ->
        jz _Vol_30                              ; if no parameters ->

        mov si, word ptr [ di ]                 ; get pointer to first arg
        mov ax, word ptr [ si ]
        cmp ah, ':'                             ; not a drive specification ?
        jnz _Vol_62                             ; no ->

        call _lowerCase                         ; disk id
        and ax, not 20h                         ; uppercase

        cmp al, 'Z'+1
        jnc _Vol_62
        cmp al, 'A'
        jc _Vol_62

        storarg _currdisk, ax                   ; save disk

;- - - - - - - - - - - - - - - - - - - - - - - - - - - - - - - - - -
;  get disk volume
;- - - - - - - - - - - - - - - - - - - - - - - - - - - - - - - - - -
_Vol_30:
        mov bx, offset _Dir_NoVolumeLabel       ; assume no volume label
        call returnVolumeName
```

```
        jc _Vol_62                              ; cannot open drive ->
        jnz _Vol_34                             ; if no volume name ->

        push di                                 ; save vol label pointer
        mov bx, offset _Dir_VolumeLabel         ; print statement format

_Vol_34:
        lea di, offset [ _currdisk ][ bp ]      ; pointer to current disk
        push di                                 ; current disk
        push bx                                 ; format
        lea di, offset [ _printbuffer ][ bp ]
        push di
        call _sprintf
        add sp, ax                              ; # args passed
        call DisplayLine

;- - - - - - - - - - - - - - - - - - - - - - - - - - - - - - - - - -
;   return
;- - - - - - - - - - - - - - - - - - - - - - - - - - - - - - - - - -
_Vol_60:
        Return


;- - - - - - - - - - - - - - - - - - - - - - - - - - - - - - - - - -
;   drive specification error
;- - - - - - - - - - - - - - - - - - - - - - - - - - - - - - - - - -
_Vol_62:
        mov dx, offset CmndError_InvalidDrive
        call DisplayErrorMessage
        Return

        ;''''''''''''''''''''''''''''''''''''''''''''''''''''''''''''';
        ;   return volume name                                        ;
        ;- - - - - - - - - - - - - - - - - - - - - - - - - - - - - - -;
        ;                                                             ;
        ;   Usage:                                                    ;
        ;   al      is disk to read volume                            ;
        ;   di      pointer to volume name (in DTA)                   ;
        ;   cy      drive has no volume name                          ;
        ;.............................................................;

returnVolumeName:
        cmp al, 'Z'-40h
        jnc returnVolumeName_08

        or al, al                               ; default disk ?
        jnz returnVolumeName_06                 ; no ->

        Int21 CurrentDisk
        inc al                                  ; a=1, ...

returnVolumeName_06:
        add al, 'a'-1

returnVolumeName_08:
```

```
        mov  di, offset RxDOS_RootDirectory - 2
        mov  byte ptr [ di ], al

        mov  dx, di
        mov  cx, ATTR_VOLUME
        mov  di, offset [ RxDOS_DTA. findFileName ]
        mov  byte ptr [ di ], 0
        Int21 FindFirstFile                             ; find volume name

        mov  dx, 0                                      ; assume no error
        jnc  returnVolumeName_18                        ; return zero (found )

        mov  dx, 1                                      ; else assume not found error
        cmp  al, errPathNotFound                        ; if path not found,
        jnz  returnVolumeName_18                        ; then return NZ ->
        stc
        ret

returnVolumeName_18:
        or   dx, dx
        ret
```

Conclusion

The command processor is not just an interface to DOS functions. In several ways, the commands augment and extend the capabilities of DOS functions. For example, rename provides the much needed wild character support, and copy permits the concatenation of several files. The command shell is a replaceable component of DOS, and there are several worthy contenders. I urge you to try them all as they may be to your benefit.

INDEX